BLUE
THUNDER

BLUE
THUNDER

THE TRUTH ABOUT **CONSERVATIVES**
FROM **MACDONALD** TO **HARPER**

BOB PLAMONDON

KEY PORTER BOOKS

Library and Archives Canada Cataloguing in Publication

Plamondon, Robert E.
      Blue thunder / Bob Plamondon.

ISBN 978-1-55263-961-0

      1. Conservatism—Canada. 2. Canada—Politics and government—1867-2008. 3. Canada—Politics and government—1867-2008. 4. Canada—Politics and government—2008-. I. Title.

JC573.2.C3P528 2008   320.520971   C2008-902212-2

The publisher gratefully acknowledges the support of the Canada Council for the Arts and the Ontario Arts Council for its publishing program. We acknowledge the support of the Government of Ontario through the Ontario Media Development Corporation's Ontario Book Initiative.

We acknowledge the financial support of the Government of Canada through the Book Publishing Industry Development Program (BPIDP) for our publishing activities.

Key Porter Books Limited
Six Adelaide Street East, Tenth Floor
Toronto, Ontario
Canada M5C 1H6

www.keyporter.com

Text design: Martin Gould
Electronic formatting: Alison Carr

Printed and bound in Canada

09 10 11 12 13 5 4 3 2 1

To my father
Every day is Christmas

ACKNOWLEDGEMENTS

THE FOUNDATION for *Blue Thunder* is the seminal published works about Canadian Conservative leaders, a review of the extensive archive material available over the Internet and through the resources of the Ottawa Public Library, and personal interviews.

Among the authors to whom I am most indebted (in alphabetical order): Conrad Black, Robert Craig Brown, John C. Courtney, Donald Creighton, John Crosbie, John English, Tom Flanagan, Robert Fyfe, Larry Glassford, Jack Granatstein, Richard Gwyn, Trevor Harrison, George Hogan, J. Castell Hopkins, David Humphreys, William Johnson, John Kendle, L. Ian MacDonald, Peter C. Newman, George Perlin, Patricia Phenix, André Pratte, Kathleen Saunders, Jeffrey Simpson, Denis Smith, Geoffrey Stevens, Warner Troyer, Peter B. Waite, Paul Wells, and John L. Williams. I commend readers to delve more fully into any of the books by these authors.

In the course of speaking about my last book, I was introduced to students with a keen interest in Tory politics. At McGill University, before a dynamic class led by Tasha Kheiriddin, I met Dan King and Tim Mak. When I struggled to find material on George Drew, Tim Mak sifted through a wide range of sources to uncover content on a figure whose life has never been the subject of a biography. Dan King helped with background research on John Thomson, Robert Manion, and interim leader R.B. Hanson.

No one did more to help craft this book from cover-to-cover than Dany Horovitz. Dany has worked on Parliament Hill as an MP's assistant and is currently completing a combined LLB and MBA at Western. One day Dany will be a significant political figure in his own right, no doubt as a Conservative.

This is my second book with Key Porter. At the *Full Circle* book launch publisher Jordan Fenn insisted I pen another Tory tome and did not relent until *Blue Thunder* was under contract. My agent Rick Brodhead provided sound advice throughout, and promptly navigated every issue that arose from concept to completion. Jonathan Schmidt, my editor-in-chief, provided a constructive and critical eye as well as a firm grip on delivery dates. Gillian Scobie took the edges off my rough work. Martin Gould applied his creative skill to design the cover, easily proving that none of my ideas improved on his original concept.

Whenever I put my fingers on the keyboard Clare McKeon, editor of *Full Circle*, is never far away from my mind and soul. While she was not part of the Key Porter team on *Blue Thunder*, she is someone I regularly turn to for advice and encouragement.

It is difficult to have a conversation about politics, even among like-minded people, without getting a different point of view and often an argument. With *Blue Thunder* I needed many of these conversations, particularly among those familiar with Tory history. Tory stalwarts John Weissenberger, Harry Near, Lee Richardson, Senator Michael Meighen, Graham Fox and Bill Pristanski were among those who played a role in helping to draw out different perspectives. I am also grateful to Senator David Angus and his staff, Jim Williams and France Lépine, for their support and encouragement. Others who supported this project include Kurt Rufelds, John Usborne, Jim Lambe, Jane Holden, Bill McCloskey, Dan Dorion, and Doug Bertoia.

I am particularly indebted to Conrad Black for reviewing the manuscript and offering numerous helpful suggestions. He is making productive use of his time while incarcerated and I admire his forbearance in the face of injustice. His willingness to contribute to public debate enriches us all.

There is hardly a story in this book that at some time over the last two years I have not run by respected journalist, publisher, and radio talk-show host Mark Sutcliffe. As my running partner, Mark is the person I spend the most time with other than my wife. It's amazing how many three-hour runs that can be filled talking about Tory politics and the publishing business.

I have a passion for golf, which puts me in regular contact with journalist Lawrence Martin. He is not only one of Canada's most gifted writers; he provided me with ample and valuable advice on such practical matters as book title, cover design, and the writer-publisher relationship. Other journalists who offered insightful comments on my rough work included Keith Boag and Chris Hall from the CBC, and Tonda MacCharles from the *Toronto Star*.

Blue Thunder should be considered a family endeavour. When I met my wife while training for an endurance race in 2003, she assumed I had lots of free time on my hands. She did not expect that in addition to growing a public policy consulting business that over the ensuing five years I would write three books. She has learned, to her frustration, that when I'm in deep concentration I don't hear voices very well. My children—Nathaniel, Charlotte, Megan, and Michael—are all loving souls; each of which can keep me up at night, though usually for different reasons. Their grandparents, Jim and June Coke, do nothing but enrich the lives of those around them; mine especially. My mother remains my saint and guardian angel who, for all she has given, is entitled to enjoy every single moment of her life. My father, who passed away in 1997, was a man who constantly challenged his five children by asserting that whatever we accomplished could always be improved upon. I like to think with this book I might have met his highwater mark, at least for one moment.

CONTENTS

INTRODUCTION

BY CONRAD BLACK

THIS IS AN INVALUABLE ANALYSIS of the leaders and fluctuations of fortune of the Canadian federal Conservative Party (under different names) over 141 years, of what it needs to succeed, and why it has often failed.

The genius of Sir John A. Macdonald is generally conceded, but rarely laid out as clearly, and with such economy of words, as here. He won an astonishing six majority victories in general elections (after two in the pre-confederation, so-called United Province of Canada), and was only defeated once.

The largely forgotten Sir Robert L. Borden was tortoise to Sir Wilfrid Laurier's hare, and the two split four elections evenly.

In the eighty-five years from the retirement of Borden to the rise of Stephen Harper, Mr. Plamondon explains how two rather random events, and the generally high cunning of successive Liberal leaders, caused the Conservatives to lose eighteen of twenty-five general elections to the Liberals.

Borden, who was not at all anti-French, produced the first event when he imposed conscription for overseas service in 1917, out of his passionate loyalty to the Canadian army in France that was making such heroic sacrifices. This added only a few thousand reluctant warriors to the front lines, while the United States, which had just entered the war, was pouring over 100,000 soldiers a month into the Western Front, and steadily tilting the balance of forces in favour of the Allies. This enabled the supreme Allied commander, Marshal Foch, to launch his great offensive of August 8, 1918, which carried through to the German request for peace terms concluded on November 11.

For this gesture to the volunteer army, Borden, as he foresaw, destroyed the Conservative Party in Québec for two whole generations, as Liberal orators pilloried Tories as British colonialists happy to send French Canadians overseas to fight and die for Britain. In the twenty-five elections mentioned, the Conservatives won more MPs in Québec than the Liberals only three times, twice under Brian Mulroney, when the Conservatives finally elevated a Québec leader and ceased effectively to forfeit the significantly French-speaking third of the country's constituencies before the election campaigns started.

The other successful election for the Conservatives in Québec had almost nothing to do with the Conservatives themselves. In 1958, Maurice Duplessis, the five-term premier and almost omnipotent "chef" of Québec, delivered fifty MPs to John Diefenbaker, to settle scores with the federal Liberals from when they had intervened against him in the Québec election of 1939. Apart from this windfall for the Conservatives, Brian Mulroney remains the only Conservative leader to defeat the Liberals in Québec in a federal election since Macdonald in 1891.

The second random event that squandered Mulroney's party-building achievement and laid the federal Conservatives lower than they have ever been since Confederation, was the election of Kim Campbell as leader over Jean Charest, to succeed Mulroney. An attractive and capable woman, she had no idea how to lead a national party in an election and the Conservative caucus shrunk, in 1993, from 169 to two (not including the outgoing prime minister, whose next official position was consul general in Los Angeles).

The Reform Party took almost all Conservative support west of Ontario; the Bloc Québecois took all of what Mulroney had painstakingly built up in Québec; and the Liberals destroyed the Conservatives in Ontario and the Atlantic provinces. The Progressive Conservative Party was atomized and endured a futile decade of four more crushing electoral defeats while Jean Chrétien frolicked in the vacuum, until Stephen Harper and Peter MacKay reassembled the pieces yet again.

In this book, several obscure Conservative leaders, including John J. C. Abbott, J.S.D. Thompson, and the generally disparaged R. B. Bennett, emerge as having more merit and significance than is generally believed. And more familiar Conservative leaders, including Borden, Diefenbaker (whose strengths are indisputable but often hard to identify precisely), and Mulroney, are plausibly presented as more accomplished prime ministers than conventional opinion has generally held.

Robert Plamondon has performed an important service. He has shown that Canadian federal Conservatives are not just, as they have often appeared, a hodgepodge of disparate elements and political losers who don't happen to be Liberals, and who receive a chance, which they squander, one election in four. And he has shown how the Conservatives can win federally and can regain the status, lost for nearly a century, of a natural party of government.

PREFACE

ALTHOUGH THE TORY PARTY has produced some of this country's most colourful leaders and prime ministers, their contributions to Canada are rarely recognized, let alone understood. It's time Canadians learned the truth about its Conservative political history.

Blue Thunder explores 141 years of Canadian Conservative leadership revealing what has worked for Tories and what has not. Along the way it gets to the truth by correcting the distortions perpetuated by a cunning opponent, a willing media, and an academic community that is loath to embrace anything Conservative.

Of course, it's been tough being a Conservative in Canada. For every three years Liberals have been in power, Conservatives have held office for two. Not counting the Macdonald years, Liberals hold a two-to-one margin. If Conservatives have an inferiority complex, the same cannot be said for Liberals, the nation's so-called "natural governing party." Liberals tell us that Tory times are hard times and that Conservative leaders do not represent Canadian values. To the same end, historians have consistently underplayed the Tory contribution to the development of Canada. Books about Conservative political history, if you can find them, come with such catchy subtitles as "syndrome . . . renegade . . . rogue . . . blues . . . interlude . . . decline." Except for Macdonald, there is little praise for Tory leaders. Even then, the national poll for the CBC program *The Greatest Canadians* absurdly ranked both Pierre Trudeau and Lester B. Pearson ahead of Sir John A. Macdonald.

True, the Conservative electoral record is appalling. But more important than raw statistics, Conservatives have made fundamental and far-reaching contributions to Canada while in and out of office. Tories led the country through some of its more tumultuous times and initiated many of the transformative changes that define the nation today. Conservatives did much of the tough sledding by implementing necessary and often unpopular measures that improved our quality of life and enhanced our political and economic sovereignty, often to their short-term political detriment. They would do more for Canada, however, if they learned from their political blunders.

Blue Thunder chronicles Tory history by examining the careers of its nineteen leaders; from Sir John A Macdonald to Stephen Harper (in Harper's case to the beginning of 2009). Surprisingly, this is the first book that covers the life of the Tory party, or any Canadian political party for that matter.

Blue Thunder explores winning and losing strategies, the scandals, the best quotes, leadership transitions, and the stories that amuse and entertain. The story is not told with speculative psychological profile, but through the deeds and the words of the leaders themselves. Along the way myths are exposed, blame is assessed, and heroes are chosen.

What emerges from this longitudinal and critical assessment of 141 years of Tory politics are seven determinants of success and failure; a framework that helps us judge the careers of Conservative leaders past, present, and future.

1. Are they nation builders who are relevant in all parts of Canada?
2. Do they offer a vision that inspires the nation?
3. Is the party united behind them?
4. Do they build broad and sustainable coalitions?
5. Are they tough, but not authoritarian?
6. Do they divide and conquer their opponents?
7. Are they absolutely committed to winning?

Regardless of the leader or circumstances, Conservative leaders who have answered affirmatively to these questions have achieved electoral success. Those who have fallen short in several categories have undermined their ability to govern effectively or even govern at all.

Any assessment of political performance is bound to launch a vibrant dialogue and debate, one that I am pleased to host. I invite interested Canadians to share their perspectives about Tory success and failure (past and present) over the Internet at www.bluethundertalk.com. This site also provides the footnotes to *Blue Thunder*.

So, from the pre-confederation genius of Sir John A. Macdonald, to the narrow escape of Stephen Harper's minority government from a coalition of three opposition parties in December 2008, here is the bold, blue, thundering truth of Canadian Conservative leadership.

SECTION I

JOHN A. MACDONALD: THE CHIEFTAIN

CHAPTER 1

BIRTH OF A NATION

*Treat the French as a nation and they will act as a free people generally
do—generously. Call them a faction and they become factious.*

JOHN A. MACDONALD HAS NO EQUAL. His vision and guiding hand moulded
this nation. He led the party that founded Canada and he steered the country through a series of seemingly insurmountable obstacles over most of
the latter half of the nineteenth century.

His beginnings were modest. John Alexander Macdonald was one of
four children, born to Hugh and Helen Macdonald in Glasgow, Scotland, on
either January 10 or 11, 1815. John was five years old when his family emigrated to Canada. His father was a shopkeeper, and later ran a milling
business. John attended boarding school in Kingston, but his family could
not afford to send him to university. He entered the workforce at age fifteen
in the prestigious commercial law practice of George Mackenzie.

The hard working and ambitious Macdonald had opened his own law
office on Quarry Street in Kingston by the age of twenty and was admitted to
the bar a year later. By coincidence, his first articling student was Oliver
Mowat, a man who would later become premier of Ontario and a political foe
over much of Macdonald's career. Macdonald was successful in criminal law,
then switched to a more lucrative commercial practice. His major client was
the Commercial Bank of the Midland district, where he was also a member of
its board of directors.

Macdonald entered the workforce at a time of political tension and uncertainty. Fuelled by a weak economy and a desire for democratic reform, matters flared up on December 6, 1837 when a group of Reform radicals led by William Lyon Mackenzie gathered with 1,000 men at the Montgomery Inn in Toronto in an attempt to seize control of the government. Although Macdonald was not sympathetic to Mackenzie's cause, he legally defended eight of his supporters who had protested, with weapons in hand, on the streets of Kingston and secured an acquittal on technical grounds.

Macdonald was not a reformer: he was committed to British institutions. The primary cause for this loyalty is debatable: his high regard for British institutions, perhaps? His conservative nature that resisted change to established order? Or his fear that Canada would not survive annexation to the United States without the might of the British military by its side? Macdonald's ties to Great Britain included membership in the Celtic Society, for which he served as recording secretary. The Society had similarities to the Orange Order, an organization with anti-Catholic and anti-French views. Macdonald rejected these views, but joined the Society to expand his business contacts. Though not much of a military man, like every able-bodied male at the time, Macdonald served in the sedentary militia, a minimal commitment involving one day of annual training that coincided with the birthday of George III.

At the age of twenty-eight Macdonald entered the realm of politics. Like the Celtic Society, politics provided Macdonald with an opportunity to expand his community profile and fortify his law practice. He ran for Kingston town council without any grand vision: "[I ran] to fill a gap. There seemed to be no one else available, so I pitched in." But he remembered names and faces and made people laugh and feel good about themselves, developing the reputation for being something of a charmer. The local *Chronicle and Gazette* declared: "We are not aware that a more eligible person could offer. His experience in public business, his well-known talents and high character, render him peculiarly fit for the office, and we sincerely hope, for the sake of the town, that he will be elected." Financial gain may have inspired him to enter the political arena, but as his skills developed, Macdonald discovered a higher purpose: nation-building. Later in his career he remarked, "I don't care for office for the sake of money, but for the sake of power: for the sake of carrying out my own view of what's best for the country."

With an exuberant campaign that included print advertising, Macdonald won by a margin of 156 to 43. That same year, 1843, he married his cousin, Isabella Clark, six years his senior. It would be a sorrowful marriage, burdened by Isabella's poor health and the death of their first child at the age of one. The cause of death remains uncertain. Some biographers suggest it was the result of a fall; others that it was Sudden Infant Death Syndrome (SIDS). On March 13, 1850, another child, Hugh John, was born.

Isabella died when Hugh was seven. Thereafter, he was mostly raised by Margaret Williamson, Macdonald's sister. Macdonald, like most men of his stock and generation, was a hearty drinker, and it was during this time that he began to drink heavily, sometimes in binges. Following Isabella's death, and the decade after, Macdonald's drinking became most troublesome. Drinking helped him escape both the burden of responsibility and the heartache of personal tragedy. Henry Northcotte, governor of the Hudson's Bay Company, noted in his diary, "People do not attribute his drinking to vice, but to a state of physical exhaustion which renders him obliged sometimes to have recourse to a stimulant, and which gives the stimulant a very powerful effect. When he once begins to drink he becomes almost mad and there is no restraining him till the fit is over." Macdonald wanted to limit his drinking, and was, for a year, a member of the Sons of Temperance in Kingston.

JOHN A. MACDONALD was a man of vision and progress, not details and ideology. A moderate, he was more interested in accomplishment than in debate. He refused to be drawn into argument where a positive outcome was not possible, writing in 1844: "In a young country like Canada, I am of the opinion that it is of more consequence to endeavor to develop its resources and improve its physical advantages, than to waste the time of the legislature and the money of the people in fruitless discussions on abstract and theoretical questions of government."

More than 200 residents signed the petition that drafted Macdonald as a Conservative into the 1844 election for the Assembly of the Province of Canada. Accepting the nomination, Macdonald outlined the cornerstone of a vision that would endure throughout his political career: "I . . . scarcely need state my belief that the prosperity of Canada depends upon its permanent connection with the Mother country and that I shall resist to the utmost any attempt which may tend to weaken that union." Macdonald won the election by a margin of 275 votes to 42.

While Conservatives held the majority in the legislature, with almost exclusively English-speaking members, they were divided in state. The caucus could not reconcile the old-line right-wing Tories with the more moderate liberal–conservative group that Macdonald followed. Though Macdonald was a Tory, he was not kin to the Big Business establishment

Tories from Toronto. Instead, he admired William Henry Draper, the moderate Conservative leader who sought to strengthen the party by reaching out to elements of French Canada. It was Draper who established that the proceedings of Parliament be printed in French and English.

In Parliament, Macdonald fought extreme elements from both sides of the aisle. Opposing annexation by the United States, or countering Tory elements that sought to assimilate the French, Macdonald stood for tradition. He distinguished himself among his Conservative colleagues. Before Macdonald travelled to England in the summer of 1850, the Governor, Lord Elgin, supplied Macdonald with a letter of introduction to Earl Grey, the Colonial Secretary: "He is a respectable man, intolerably moderate in his views . . . who belongs to the section of the Conservatives who are becoming reasonable."

In 1847, Macdonald accepted the invitation to serve in Cabinet as Receiver General. Given Macdonald's general disregard for his personal finances, the appointment was an odd choice and the press panned it. The Montréal *Gazette* claimed, "The intrusion of a young lawyer into the situation of Receiver General appears to our eyes, and if we are not very much mistaken, will appear also to those of the public, a blunder of the most stupid kind." If establishing low expectations, then exceeding them, is a mark of good politics, Macdonald was off to a great start.

By the age of thirty-seven, Macdonald was sitting in his third Parliament. His legal career was a distraction while a promising political future beckoned. Macdonald was seen as heir apparent to Draper to lead the Conservatives.

Macdonald was leadership material, not because he had great oratorical skills or passion, but because of his inclusive and amicable approach to issues and people on all sides of the legislature. A conversationalist with an endearing capacity for flattery, he was an entertaining storyteller who often used wit to extract himself from a tough spot. To one supporter's demand for a specific patronage appointment, Macdonald countered, "Why on earth would a man like you want a paltry job like that? It's not good enough for you. Just you wait awhile, and we'll find you something much better." Another man pursued Macdonald at the funeral for a deceased senator, declaring, "Sir John, I would like to take that man's place." Macdonald replied, "I'm afraid it's too late. The coffin is nailed shut."

Macdonald saw his role as a centrist coalition builder. A leading political commentator of the day described Macdonald's unique skill: he could herd cats. Macdonald himself often used the term "catching loose fish," by which he meant bringing to his side members with no commitment to any particular party. Macdonald understood that to achieve power and accomplish what he wanted, he needed to be in government and used his various talents to that end. He was clever and mischievous, taking every opportunity imaginable to encourage divisions in the opposition parties.

Tolerant, and opposed to the rigid separation of church and state, Macdonald believed that government must recognize and respect religious diversity and the cultural divisions between English- and French-speaking Canada.

Though a man with grand designs, Macdonald opposed tinkering with the Constitution. He opposed the Representation Bill of 1853, which increased the number of members of each section of the province to 65. "If there is one thing to be avoided," Macdonald warned, "it is meddling with the Constitution of the country, which should not be altered till it is evident that people are suffering from the effects of that Constitution as it actually exists." It is a warning that most subsequent prime ministers refused to heed, particularly Trudeau, who spent decades wrangling with the Constitution before enacting changes that were vehemently opposed by the government of Québec.

In 1853, Canada East and Canada West had an equal number of seats in Parliament. When the Union was established in 1840, the population of Canada East was larger, but the 1851 census revealed that Canada West now had the greater number. George Brown, Reform politician, publisher of the Toronto *Globe*, and a frequent nemesis of Macdonald, advocated representation by population. He opposed any connection between church and state and was anti-Catholic and anti-French. Macdonald felt that representation by population would divide Canada and abrogate the deal that had been struck to form the Union in 1841. Maintaining that union, including its bilingual provisions and its connection with Great Britain, was essential to Macdonald.

Macdonald hoped to fashion a new coalition of Conservatives, combining moderate Reform elements with French-Canadian support. George Brown sought a Conservative coalition of his own that, in part, stood for the end of French-Canadian supremacy in the legislature. Macdonald was clear that his goal was to unite all the peoples of Canada, regardless of language or religion. In a letter to a colleague, he wrote: "Our aim should be to enlarge the bounds of our party so as to embrace every person desirous of being counted as a progressive Conservative, and who will join in a series of measures to put an end to the corruption which has ruined the present government and debauched all of its followers."

After failing to unite Conservative forces and win power in the election of 1854, Macdonald despondently told a colleague: "Party is nowhere—damned everlasting. I will go down and get the bank bill passed and retire. I am resolved upon it." There would be many such utterances by Macdonald over his career when faced with defeat or frustration. But he always came back.

Macdonald learned that the political landscape could quickly change. Not long after the 1854 election, a new coalition formed, with Macdonald as Attorney General of Canada West. Not an authoritarian by nature, Macdonald compassionately commuted the death sentences of eight railway workers who had plotted to kill their foreman; and reduced from life to five years the sentence of a man convicted of stealing $20. But he was not soft on criminals, noting, "The primary object of the penitentiary is punishment, and the incidental one, reformation."

On another issue of the day, the legislature and the population found itself strongly divided over reparations from the Clergy Reserves. Established in 1791, the Clergy Reserves originally made up one-seventh of the public lands of Upper and Lower Canada, and supported the maintenance of a "Protestant clergy." The Church of England began to sell the land in 1819, but this led to disputes over the sharing of proceeds among other Protestant churches. By the early 1850s, secularization of the reserves was widely demanded, along with provisions to pay life stipends to clerical incumbents. Many in the legislature opposed the Clergy Reserves Bill on principle. Macdonald took a more practical approach: "I believe it is a great mistake in politics and private life to resist when resistance is hopeless . . . there is no maxim which experience teaches more clearly than this, that you must yield to the times. Resistance may be protracted until it produces revolution. Resistance was protracted in this country until it produced rebellion."

When George Brown attacked the notion of religious schools, Macdonald defended the historical rights of French-Canadian Roman Catholics: "[H]e should be sorry if a legislature, the majority of whose members were Protestants professing to recognize the great Protestant principle of the right of private judgment, should yet seek to deprive Roman Catholics of the power to educate their children according to their own principles."

When the Separate School Bill passed in 1855, George Brown called it French-Canadian tyranny, and reaffirmed his commitment to representation by population. His goal was to diminish the influence of French-speaking legislators. However, it was not just the church and the language that Brown sought to control. He also wanted to make French culture extinct, just as Lord Durham had proposed in his 1839 *Report on the Affairs of British North America*, when he described "two nations warring at the bosom of a single state . . . a struggle not of principles, but of races."

Writing to a reporter for the Montréal *Gazette*, Macdonald lambasted the Anglophone attitude towards the French in Lower Canada: "The truth is that you British Lower Canadians never can forget that you were once supreme—that Jean Baptiste was your hewer of wood and drawer of water. You struggle, like the Protestant Irish in Ireland, like the Norman Invaders in England, not for equality, but ascendancy—the difference between you and those interesting and amiable people being that you have not the honesty to admit it."

Macdonald believed that any attempt to assimilate or dominate the French was pointless and ignored reality: "No man in his senses can suppose that this country can, for a century to come, be governed by a totally unfrenchified government. If a Lower Canadian Britisher desires to conquer he must 'stoop to conquer.'"

Macdonald's moderate and respectful views enabled him to build bridges with French Canadians. He understood that for the French these battles were a matter of survival. Far ahead of his time, he was perhaps the first English politician to recognize the French people of Québec as a nation: "(We) must make friends with the French, without sacrificing the status of his race or religion or language (we) must respect their nationality. Treat them as a nation and they will act as a free people generally do—generously. Call them a faction and they become factious."

Presciently, Macdonald foretold how French Canadians would react when threatened: "Supposing the numerical preponderance of British in Canada becomes much greater than it is, I think the French would give more trouble than they are said now to do. At present they divide as we do, they are split up into several sections, and they are governed by more or less defined principles of action. As they become smaller and feebler, so they will be more united; from a sense of self-preservation, they will act as one man and hold the balance of power . . . So long as the French have twenty votes they will be a power, and must be conciliated. I doubt very much however if the French will lose their numerical majority in Lower Canada in a hurry. . . . I am inclined to think they will hold their own for many a day yet."

These views were instinctive to Macdonald. His impulse was to look to the French to build a stronger coalition in the Union. He understood that whoever could forge and sustain a partnership with francophones would govern. The "representation by population" forces were motivated, not by pure democratic principles, but by a desire to diminish the French fact and French influence. By standing up to these forces, Macdonald solidified his coalition with the Bleue Canadien members. "Do not put yourself in opposition to the

French," Macdonald told a colleague. "The French are your sheet anchor."

To Brown and his ilk, Macdonald had sold his soul for the sake of power. Macdonald countered that his interest was not power, but simple fairness. His responsibility was to govern "for the good of the *whole* country and the equal interests of all."

In the century that followed Macdonald's death, some Conservative leaders treated Québec as a political wasteland and failed to embrace Macdonald's inclusive national views. Not until 1984 would Conservatives have a leader from Québec on the ballot, Brian Mulroney, who would put forward constitutional packages that recognized Québec as a distinct society. In 2006, Stephen Harper would place before Parliament a resolution recognizing the Québecois as a nation within a united Canada. In these instances, Mulroney and Harper followed Macdonald's pre-Confederation instincts. For all three, the consequence was a decline in support for Québec separation and a rise in the fortunes of the Conservative party.

Macdonald was one of the few English-speaking politicians to gain the respect of his French-speaking colleagues in the legislature. While leading his party in Canada West, Macdonald served as deputy to Étienne-Paschal Taché, the leader in Canada East and premier of the United Province of Canada. This partnership lasted eighteen months. In November of 1857, Macdonald became premier, with poet, corporate lawyer, and prominent French Canadian Georges-Étienne Cartier serving as his deputy from Canada East. Cartier was atypical: a French-speaking *monarchist* who had named one of his daughters Reine-Victoria and who called the French Revolution an episode of "misery and shame." The alliance between Macdonald and the bleue Canadien politicians loyal to Cartier was the foundation of Tory governments pre- and post-Confederation. Few if any Canadian political partnerships have been as close or productive as that of Macdonald and Cartier.

THE LOCATION OF THE CAPITAL of the United Province of Canada was a source of ongoing and acrimonious debate. After a brief time in Kingston, the capital was moved to Montréal where it stayed from 1843 to 1849. Following an outbreak of violence at the legislative buildings in Montréal the capital was moved again and alternated between Toronto and Québec city. In 1856, Québec City was given permanent status, but the assembly could not decide on funds for the construction of the legislature. Elected members were divided strictly on lines of geography and could reach no clever compromise or consensus. Macdonald decided to take the issue out of the hands of parochial politicians and asked Queen Victoria to choose. Though a politically wise strategem, this action nevertheless acknowledged that the elected assembly, which was hoping to be granted responsible government, was not yet mature enough to make its own decisions. In their wisdom, in 1857, the Colonial Office and the Queen, on advice if not direction from Macdonald, recommended the boisterous lumber town of Ottawa as capital of the Province of Canada (the union of Canada East and Canada West). It was the choice Macdonald had had in mind all along.

Given the difficulty the legislature had in choosing a capital, it must have seemed ridiculous to think its members could agree on expanding the boundaries of the Union. However, Alexander Tilloch Galt boldly proposed the idea of establishing a federation of British North American colonies to form one great nation. Macdonald was interested, but cautious. Confederation, as it would be called, may have seemed daunting to a man who was frustrated and fatigued: "We are having a hard fight in the house and shall beat them in the votes," Macdonald wrote to his sister in 1858. "But it will, I think, end in my retiring as soon as I can with honor. I find the work and annoyance too much for me."

Macdonald overcame his lethargy and showed examples of feistiness. He challenged Colonel Arthur Rankin to a duel after offensive remarks were made in the legislature. Rankin wisely retracted his remarks and the duel was averted. Macdonald eventually found the work of defining a nation intoxicating. Varying visions were debated. Some thought the problems of the Province of Canada made expanding the boundaries of the nation impracticable. Some thought contraction—dissolving the Union of Canada and restoring Canada East and Canada West as separate colonies—was a better option. Others proposed representation by population.

With Macdonald and Cartier in power just over eight months, Reform party leader George Brown seized upon what he thought an opportunity to divide the Tory caucus and defeat the government. It was over the pesky issue of relocating the capital. Macdonald placed the Queen's recommendation before the House with the resolution that, "Ottawa ought to be the permanent seat of government of this province." Brown joined with Conservatives from Canada East who did not want to lose the Quebec city as part-time capital and they defeated the motion on July 28, 1858, by a vote of 64 to 50. Anticipating the rocky road that lay ahead, Macdonald dutifully submitted the resignation of his government to Governor Head the following day.

After consulting with the governor, George Brown set about the task of establishing a government. At the time, any member entering Cabinet was legally required to resign his seat and face his constituents in a by-election. This was often, but not always, a formality because newly-minted Cabinet ministers typically ran unopposed. However, when Brown's Cabinet ministers resigned, the strength of his Reform caucus was reduced to minority status. Brown desperately needed the legislature to be dissolved to allow time for by-elections to be held so that his numbers could be restored. But the House had only recently been formed and several measures, including financial matters, needed attention. Governor Head declined to adjourn the House, a decision he forewarned to Brown both verbally and in writing.

Macdonald anticipated what would happen to Brown's government, and teased Brown in the House for his eagerness and inexperience in claiming power: "Some fish require to be toyed with. A prudent fish will play around with the bait sometime before he takes it, but in this instance the fish scarcely waited till the bait was let down. He jumped out of the water to catch it."

On August 2, the Brown-Dorion government was sworn into office and was immediately put to a test of no-confidence in the legislature. With his Cabinet ministers unable to vote, the government was defeated. Brown appealed to Governor Head to dissolve Parliament and call an election. The Governor refused. Brown's became the shortest government in Canadian history, lasting all of four days.

With Brown out, Governor Head invited Alexander Galt to form a government, but Galt declined. Next, Cartier was summoned and he accepted the invitation with Macdonald as his deputy premier. Cartier and Macdonald faced the same problem as Brown had: appointing ministers would weaken their numbers in the House. But Macdonald was familiar with the fine print of the seventh clause of the Independence of Parliament Act, which provided that an officeholder who accepted a different portfolio within a one-month period was not obligated to resign his seat. The provision was originally designed to allow a change in ministry within the same government, but it now proved useful to Macdonald for a different purpose. So on August 6, the ex-ministers from the last Macdonald-Cartier administration were brought back into the Cabinet, but in a different ministry from the one they previously held. Within hours the ministers resigned their new portfolios and took up the ones they had held in the previous administration. The reinstated government retained its strength with sufficient numbers to lead Parliament. In less than a week, the Macdonald-Cartier government had been defeated, replaced, and then returned to power. This episode was famously called the "double shuffle."

Brown and his Grit supporters were humiliated. They accused

Macdonald of fraud and his Cabinet ministers of perjury. Brown claimed the one-day ministries were a sham and offensive to parliamentary tradition. Macdonald replied just as vigorously: "It is a charge that I am a dishonorable man. . . . I say it is false as hell."

In executing the double shuffle, Macdonald showed himself to be a master of political strategy. Like a chess player, he anticipated many moves ahead to put himself in the best possible position. He was once accused in a campaign of being "the biggest liar in all of Canada." Macdonald replied, "I dare say it's true enough." What mattered was not how he played the game, but that, in the end, he won the game. While Brown bore the brunt of defeat within his party, subsequent Liberal leaders took note. Perhaps the best contemporary parallel is the defeat of Joe Clark's Tory government in 1979 mere months after an election that left the Conservatives a few seats shy of a majority. Clark naively assumed the Liberals would not defeat his government to reclaim the power they had held for the previous seventeen years. Like Macdonald, however, Trudeau, who had resigned his post, was wily and nervy. Clark was ousted while, brazenly, Trudeau was returned to office.

Had the mischievous Double Shuffle not played out as it did, Confederation might never have happened. With renewed confidence, the Cartier-Macdonald government made the most of its political victory. On August 7, 1858, Cartier boldly spoke in Parliament of a new arrangement for Canada that would unite the provinces of British North America.

A delegation not including Macdonald—consisting of Cartier, John Ross, and Alexander Galt—travelled to England to explore the case for a Canadian federation. The five colonies included in Canada's proposal were Nova Scotia, New Brunswick, Prince Edward Island, Newfoundland, and Canada. At the time, the Maritime provinces were considering a union among themselves and were opposed to joining with the Canadian provinces. The colonial office supported Confederation but it was looking for some indication that the venture would succeed before endorsing it.

Brown continued to articulate an alternate vision. He liked the design of the United States of America: representation by population, a written constitution, the separation of executive from the legislature, and restraints on federal powers. But above all, Brown wanted a rebalancing of the Union Parliament. He was inspired by the 1861 census that revealed that the population of Canada West had outstripped that of Canada East by approximately 285,000.

If the American model had any credibility, it vanished on April 12, 1861 when cannons were fired at Fort Sumter, South Carolina, starting the Civil

War. The American design, with its weak central government, now looked flawed. Macdonald, in fact, thought it so unstable that it would eventually divide America in two. With talk of a federal union of British colonies in North America, Macdonald feared that powerful provinces in a federated state of British colonies could also lead to conflict and war.

Unlike Brown, Macdonald wanted the federal government to have all the key powers of sovereignty. He wanted Canada to speak with one clear voice to avoid the risk of inter-provincial conflict. He envisioned, "an immense Confederation of free men, the greatest confederacy of civilized and intelligent men that ever had an existence on the face of the globe."

In the election campaign of 1861, Macdonald argued for his design of Confederation. Macdonald's remarks in that campaign indicate that, even 150 years ago, Canada learned from America's weaknesses. "We must take advantage of the faults and defects in their constitution [and] not run the risk in this country, which we see on the other side of the frontier, of one part of the country destroying the other part."

Macdonald used the American Civil War not only to argue for a strong central government but to make the case that Confederation itself would counter an American takeover. The American threat was evident from many sources. William Seward, Lincoln's Secretary of State, believed Canada was "ripe fruit" that would naturally fall into the hands of post–Civil War America. J.R. Potter, American consul general in Montréal, told a group of international businessmen that problems over trade and duties could easily be solved by the United States annexing Canada. Macdonald thought otherwise.

Not long before the critical debates on Confederation were held, the Macdonald-Cartier government resigned after a group of French-Canadian supporters sided with the opposition to defeat a bill to appropriate $500,000 for the militia in May 1862. The bill called for a military of 50,000 men, in large measure to protect Canada against an invasion from America (then in the middle of a civil war). The defeat met with annoyance in Great Britain as an editorial in the London *Spectator* noted in July 1862: "It is, perhaps, our duty to defend the empire at all hazards; it is not part of it to defend men who will not defend themselves."

Macdonald wrote to his sister to express, not disappointment, but relief, sensing he was free of the burden of politics. "You will have seen that I am out of office. I am at last free, thank God . . . and can now feel as a free man. I have longed for this hour and only a sense of honour has kept me chained to my post . . . I have now fulfilled my duty to my party and begin to think of myself."

Yet even in defeat, Macdonald was strategic and patient and his sense of relief was less than sincere. To Macdonald, there was a time to be in power and a time to consolidate a coalition, a political astuteness that led to his nickname of "Old Tomorrow." "We can put a Ministry out whenever we like, but the pear is not yet ripe . . . We have shown that we did not wish to cling to office for its own sake and we wish to show that we prefer the good of the country to mere party triumph. . . ."

His was right. The Liberal government of John Sandfield Macdonald was defeated, leaving John A. Macdonald and Étienne-Paschal Taché to form an administration under the banner of the Liberal-Conservative party on May 30, 1864. Macdonald appealed to his caucus to follow only one maxim: "Let there be no splits."

THE MACDONALD-TACHÉ GOVERNMENT did not take the lead on Confederation. It was Macdonald's long-time nemesis, George Brown, who introduced a resolution in the legislature asking that a committee examine alternative forms of federation. Most likely because it was a Brown initiative, Macdonald, Cartier, and Galt voted against the resolution. Nonetheless, it passed. The committee reported on June 14 that, "A strong feeling was found to exist among members of the committee in favour of changes in the direction of a federative system, applied either to Canada alone or to the whole British North American provinces." To Brown, a federation was a way to segregate Canada West and Canada East and achieve both representation by population and a diminished influence by the French over Canada West. It would provide a framework to consider the interests of both parts of the province and settle them. Including the Atlantic provinces in a federation was a possibility, but Brown would have been satisfied with a "mini-confederation" of Canada West and Canada East with some undefined political structure above them both. The fate of the English in Canada East was of no concern to him.

Macdonald disagreed with Brown's intent to isolate the French, but he agreed with the design. For Macdonald, keeping the British colonies strong both affirmed Canada's independence from America and assured its connection with Great Britain. As a result, his government was fully committed to a general federal union of British North America when, on August 29, 1864, he and some colleagues set sail aboard the Queen Victoria for Charlottetown, PEI, to drop in on a conference that was considering a possible union of the Maritime provinces. Unlike Brown, Macdonald was determined that the Atlantic provinces would join in Confederation.

Together with Galt and Cartier, Macdonald persuaded the Maritimes to set aside the idea of a Maritime-only union, not a difficult sell because the federated model would enable each Maritime province to retain its border (whereas the proposed Maritime union would have created a single entity). A second conference to consider the larger national union was scheduled for October at Québec City.

Cartier spoke there of the benefits for the French in Confederation: "Confederation is a tree whose branches extend in different directions, all of which are firmly attached to the trunk. We French Canadians are one of those branches. It is for us to understand this, and to work for the common good ... [T]olerance is indispensable ... it is on that condition only that we can always conserve the rights acquired by our distinct nationality. We shall enjoy these rights as long as we remain worthy of them."

The seventy-two resolutions passed at Québec City became the basis for the British North America Act. Canada would be a federal union, formed under its "mother country" Great Britain. There would be a general government charged with matters of common interest to the whole country and local governments charged with the control of local matters in their respective sections. (It is noteworthy that the term "general" was used rather than "federal"; "local" rather than "provincial.")

The Maritime provinces, fearful that their interests would be subservient to the larger populations of Canada East and Canada West, wanted equal representation in the Senate. However, the Senate was designed with regional, not provincial, equality in mind. There were to be 24 members each for Canada East and Canada West; and 24 for the Maritime provinces (Nova Scotia: 10, New Brunswick: 10, and Prince Edward Island: 4). Members of the Senate would be appointed by the Crown, after being nominated by local governments. Those nominated were to include those from opposition parties in each province so that all political parties would be fairly represented. Macdonald believed an appointed Senate composed of men of substance was necessary. "The rights of the minority must be protected, and the rich are always fewer in number than the poor."

With notable exceptions, the House of Commons was to be representation by population. The allocation at Confederation was: Canada West 82; Canada East 65; Nova Scotia 19; New Brunswick 15; Newfoundland 8 and PEI 5. Representation from each section was to be re-adjusted on the basis of population after every decennial census. One exception was that Canada East was permanently assigned sixty-five members; with each of the other sections entitled to representation on a proportionate basis. Another exception was that the numbers of federal representatives could not be reduced unless the population in a section decreased by five percent.

The general Parliament, which required elections at least every five years, had the power to make laws for peace, welfare, and good government in a broad range of categories. Critically, the Parliament would hold residual powers for all general matters that weren't reserved for the local governments and legislatures. Parliament also enjoyed the power to appoint the lieutenant governor of the provinces, a position Macdonald considered the equivalent of a chief executive officer. This power of appointment gave the general government something of an oversight role over the local governments.

The local legislatures had more limited responsibilities including direct taxation; agriculture; immigration; education (except any rights and privileges which the Protestant or Catholic minority might possess for denominational schools); sea coast; inland fisheries; the establishment, maintenance and management of hospitals, asylums, charities, and charitable institutions; municipal institutions; licensing for shop, saloon, tavern and auctioneers; incorporation of private companies; and property and civil rights. The provinces also enjoyed residual rights. These were limited to private or local matters not assigned to the general Parliament. To ensure the authority of the general government, its laws were to be supreme in any area of shared jurisdiction. Macdonald hoped that the provinces would, in effect, ultimately become municipalities.

Both English and French were to be used in the general Parliament and in the local legislature of Canada East, and also in the federal Courts and the courts of Canada East.

The weighting of powers and jurisdiction was, as Macdonald had sought in the negotiations, precisely toward a strong federal Parliament. "We . . . make the Confederation one people in one government, instead of five peoples and five governments, one united province, with the local governments and legislatures subordinate to the general government and legislature."

Macdonald's centrist orientation produced a division of responsibilities that was appropriate at the time. However, he did not anticipate the dramatically increased presence that governments would have in the lives of Canadians in the generations that followed. Had Macdonald foreseen state-controlled health care he would probably have placed it in the hands of the federal government. Macdonald would be astonished that today the collective revenues of provincial governments exceed those of the federal government. In contrast to Macdonald, most Conservatives since Bob Stanfield have generally been advocates of provincial rights, as they are set out in the Constitution of 1867. Indeed, the 2006 Constitution of the

Conservative Party of Canada states as a basic principle, "A belief in the federal system of government as the best expression of the diversity of our country, *and* in the desirability of *strong* provincial and territorial governments." This principle would have troubled Macdonald.

Among the more controversial provisions incorporated into Canada's governance at Confederation was the power of disallowance. In addition to the power of the Queen to disallow legislation of the general government, the governor general also had the right to disallow local government legislation within one year of its passing. The authority of the governor general to disallow generally fell upon the general government to exercise, and was consistent with the strong general government that Macdonald wanted. But this power proved problematic for him. Whenever a province passed legislation that upset either minorities in that province or the sensibilities of another province, pressure was placed on the prime minister to intervene. Macdonald did not fully appreciate the dilemma until certain provinces sought to squelch the right of the French-speaking minority to educate their children in their native tongue.

At Confederation, the general government took ownership of the assets and liabilities of the local governments. Annual grants, based on population at 80 cents per head, were to be given as an offset for the loss in authority and taxing power. Positive adjustments were made for provinces that brought proportionally less debt into Confederation. As today, Canada was then a financial bargain box filled with transfers, equalization payments, and promises to build infrastructure.

The resolutions adopted at the Québec Conference had no authority until sanctioned by the imperial and colonial Parliaments. But for Macdonald, the man who had authored a majority of the resolutions, it was an impressive start. Only a month after inviting himself to Charlottetown, he was leading the ambitious design for a new nation. Because none of the participants had experience in drafting constitutions, it is no surprise that the ensuing documents contained flaws—the more serious of which were the failure to consider an amending formula, the terms under which dissolution might be caused, and the status of Aboriginal people.

The next stage of the journey was passage through provincial legislatures and the imperial Parliament in London. Because the conferences in Prince Edward Island and Québec took place behind closed doors, public opinion would now have to be brought onside. However, Macdonald did not see this as a matter that needed to be brought before the public for approval: "It would be unconstitutional and anti-British to have a plebiscite. If by petitions

in public meetings Parliament is satisfied the country do not want the measure, they will refuse to adopt. If on the other hand Parliament sees that the
country is in favour of the Federation, there is no use in an appeal to it.
Submission of the complicated details to the country is an obvious absurdity."

WHENEVER CONFEDERATION was in political danger, Macdonald would
raise the spectre of problems south of the border. He had faced problems of
his own with the Americans when, on October 19, 1864, in the village of
St. Albans, Vermont, 13 Confederate agents, dressed in civilian clothes,
escaped to Canada after robbing three banks of $200,000. One American
pursuer was killed. The raiders were arrested in Canada East, but were later
released on a technicality by a Montréal police magistrate. There was pressure on President Lincoln to invade Canada and capture the raiders, but he
declined, fearing an international incident. Even though the raiders were
recaptured and returned to America, other retaliatory measures were contemplated, including the abrogation of the Reciprocity Treaty and an
executive order requiring passports from all persons entering the United
States from the provinces. (The next time Americans would invoke the passport provisions was in 2006 in response to fears that terrorists might enter
the U.S. via Canada.)

Macdonald thought complaining about retaliation over the proposed passport measure would only strengthen American resolve and make Canada look
weak. He was not prepared to give the Americans this satisfaction, since "it
would give [U.S. Secretary of State] Mr. Seward an exaggerated idea of the
inconvenience and the loss sustained by Canada and would be kept up as a
means of punishment or for purposes of coercion. The sure way to succeed is
for the Canadian government to assume an indifferent tone in the matter."

Macdonald took the Québec resolutions to the legislature in the Province
of Canada, where he made his belief in the principle of a monarch who was
beyond the reach of politics in the House. His case for a strong central government and subordinate local governments, with lieutenant governors
appointed by the general government, was central to this argument.

Meanwhile, all was not well in the Maritime provinces. Prince Edward
Island did not make it into the first phase of Confederation. In Nova Scotia,
Joseph Howe took up the struggle against the Québec plan and demanded
a referendum or election on the issue. He believed that Confederation
would weaken the bond with the British; that it would be used by the
British to justify withdrawing its troops from Nova Scotia, and thus weaken
commercial ties.

One particularly contentious element of the Québec plan was the construction of the inter-colonial railway. This key commitment promised to build an Intercolonial Railway from Rivière-du-Loup through New Brunswick to Truro in Nova Scotia. When pressed, Macdonald would not say whether this provision represented a constitutional guarantee. This caused concern in New Brunswick. "Now I can assure you," New Brunswick Premier Leonard Tilley wrote to Macdonald in 1865, "that no Delegate from this Province will consent to the Union unless we have this guarantee [of a railroad]." Macdonald, speaking without authorization, pledged that the guarantee would be inserted into an Imperial Act.

Both the Québec resolutions and Premier Tilley were defeated in the New Brunswick legislature. With an anti-confederation government in place in New Brunswick, expanding the union seemed doubtful. But, supported with ample secret donations arranged by Macdonald and railway supporters, Tilley was returned to power in short order and the Confederation resolution was adopted in 1866.

The Nova Scotia legislature approved the union in 1866, but its approval expired in the spring of 1867. Unless Confederation was a reality by that date, a new bill would have to be introduced. A provincial election was likely before then, providing another opportunity to derail Confederation in Nova Scotia.

Enter the Fenians. Irish immigrants to America, the Fenian Brotherhood was a radical group that sought independence for their home country from Great Britain. The Fenians' strategy was to take Canada hostage, then boldly negotiate Irish independence with England. In June 1866, the Fenians did defeat a small Canadian force along the Niagara frontier, but most Fenian attacks were haphazard and inconsequential. That same year, several hundred of the Brotherhood marched six miles into Canada to plant a green flag. They entered unopposed, then amused themselves by stealing food and liquor. Anticipating Canadian opposition, they bid a hasty retreat, only to have their guns confiscated upon re-entering American territory. The incident was ludicrous, but Macdonald used it to his advantage. What better way to protect British North America from American invasion, he suggested, than to bind the colonies together, backed by the full might of British military force? To reinforce the seriousness of the threat, Parliament was called into an emergency session to provide increased support for its military.

Within Canada West and Canada East, the Confederation debate drew generally positive conclusions, but for different reasons. In Canada East, George Brown triumphantly declared, ". . . constitution adopted—a most credible document—a complete reform of all the abuses and injustices we have complained of. Is it not wonderful? French-Canadianism is entirely extinguished." Brown's newspaper, the *Globe*, elaborated: "We desire local self-government in order that the separate nationalities of which the population is composed may not quarrel. We desire at the same time a strong central authority. Is there anything incompatible in these two things?" In Canada East, Québecers viewed Confederation as a framework that would allow them to control their own destiny. Editors at *La Minerve*, a newspaper closely aligned with the Tories, proclaimed, "As a distinct and separate nationality, we form a state within a state. We enjoy the full exercise of our rights, and the formal recognition of our national independence . . . In giving ourselves a complete government we affirm our existence as a separate nationality."

In Canada East, the threat of American domination came into play. Cartier observed, "The question is reduced to this: we must either have a British North America Federation or else be absorbed into the American Federation." Indeed, just as Confederation was becoming a reality, American expansionist designs included the purchase of Alaska from the Russians for US $7.2 million. American Senator Charles Sumner boasted that the purchase was "the visible step to the occupation of the whole North American continent." Perhaps Confederation had arrived in the nick of time.

The final battleground for Confederation was England, where the Imperial Parliament would be asked to pass the British North America Act. But first, the "London Conference" was convened on December 4, 1866 to hold hearings on the matter. Macdonald was chosen conference chair. Sir Frederick Rogers of the Colonial Office commented on Macdonald's mastery at nation-building. "Macdonald was the ruling genius and spokesman and I was very greatly struck by his power of management and adroitness. . . . the slightest divergence from the narrow line already agreed on in Canada was watched for—here by the French and there by the English—as eager dogs watch a rat hole; a snap on one side might have provoked a snap on the other; and put an end to the accord. He stated and argued the case with cool, ready fluency, while at the same time you saw that every word was measured, and that while he is making for a point ahead, he was never for a moment unconscious of any of the rocks among which he had to steer."

To secure agreement at the London Conference, a limited number of amendments to the Québec resolutions was required. Specifically, the Senate design was altered, enabling the Queen to appoint three or six additional senators, representing the three divisions of Canada. The central government was also given responsibility to protect the rights of minorities in education by invoking "remedial" legislation if required.

The style given to Canada was also debated. While Macdonald preferred the prefix of "Kingdom," British officials worried it would annoy American "Republican" sensibilities. The Colonial Office proposed the designation "Dominion": "And he shall have *dominion* also from sea to sea" from Psalm 72, verse 8—which was readily accepted.

Despite Joseph Howe's pleas to delay legislation until after the Nova Scotia election, the bill establishing Canada was first read in the British House of Lords on February 12, 1867 and passed four days later. Macdonald commented that the bill received the same consideration "as if it were a private Bill uniting two or three English parishes." Nonetheless, the Colonial Secretary, Lord Carnarvon, remarked, "We are laying the foundation of a great State, perhaps one which at a future date may overshadow this country."

In addition to being knighted, Macdonald was chosen by Queen Victoria, in advance of an election, to be Canada's first prime minister. He was, of course, the logical choice. He had carried the day on matters of vision with abundant political skill. And his peers had chosen him to chair the London Conference. This latter choice was the test the Queen used to identify the man who possessed the confidence of a Parliament that did not yet exist. Being chosen prime minister before Canada's first election gave Macdonald and his Liberal-Conservative colleagues an enormous advantage that they did not fail to exploit.

In pre-Confederation days, the Province of Canada had been governed by co-leaders, a premier from one part and a deputy from the other. In choosing Macdonald, however, Governor General Lord Monck set a different course: "In future, it shall be distinctly understood that the position of First Minister shall be held by one person, who shall be responsible to the Governor-General for the appointment of other ministers, and that the system of dual first ministers, which has hitherto prevailed, shall be put an end to."

When John A. Macdonald was sworn in as Canada's first prime minister on July 1, 1867, a national holiday was declared. But the slow and sometimes painful work of nation-building was only just beginning.

CHAPTER 2

FORGING A NATION

I am, as you may fancy, exceedingly desirous of carrying the elections
again; not for any personal object, because I'm weary of the whole
thing, but Confederation is only yet in the gristle, and it will require five
years more before it hardens into bone.

THE FIRST CANADIAN FEDERAL ELECTION took place between August 7 and September 20, 1867 with a respectable voter turnout of 73.1 percent. Macdonald and his Liberal-Conservative party took 100 of the 180 seats, winning majorities in Ontario and Québec, but taking only 4 of 34 seats in New Brunswick and Nova Scotia. New Brunswick went mostly Liberal, while Joseph Howe and his Anti-Confederate party won 18 of 19 seats in Nova Scotia. George Brown, unofficial leader of the Liberal party, lost in his constituency. The speech from the throne in Canada's first Parliament was read by Governor General Lord Monck on November 7, 1867.

Prime Minister Macdonald took his new responsibilities in stride. Along the road to Confederation he had acquired a new wife. At the London Conference, Macdonald had a chance encounter with Susan Agnes Bernard, the sister of Hewitt Bernard, Macdonald's deputy when he had been attorney general for Canada West. Agnes had been the object of Macdonald's affections for some time. First promising Hewitt that he would reform his drinking habits, John A. Macdonald, fifty-two, and Agnes Bernard, thirty-one, were wed at St. George's Church in London on February 16, 1867, just six months before the election. His wife commented in her diary on how well her husband dealt with the election stress: "He can throw off the weight of business in a wonderfully short time. He has a good heart and amiable temper which are the great secrets of the success."

Again in this election, Macdonald used his sense of humour to charm the voters and unsettle his opponents. He stood on a manure spreader to address a group of farmers and quipped, "This is the first time I've stood on a Liberal platform." Accused of being drunk at another public event, Macdonald made no effort to hide his lack of sobriety, and added, "The people would prefer to see John A. drunk than my opponent sober."

Macdonald's first major challenge was to win the support of skeptical Nova Scotians for their new country. In the Nova Scotia provincial election, anti-Confederates won 36 out of 38 seats. In the early days of Confederation, the Halifax Legislature passed a series of resolutions calling for Nova Scotia to leave the Union, appointing Joseph Howe its chief negotiator. The maneuver was designed to incite Nova Scotians and give them hope their crusade would be successful. But Macdonald steadfastly refused to discuss dissolution of the Union. "[Dissolution], it seems to me, would be giving up the whole question. . . . If the Duke of Buckingham says at once to Howe and his confrères that they have nothing to hope for from the British government, I think the matter will end there; but if he should be weak enough to say— 'you should give the system a fair trial for a year or two'—the consequence will be that the professional agitators will keep up the agitation for a year or two and then will return to the Colonial Office and plead their own factious course and its success as an evidence of the persistent refusal of the people to be incorporated in the Union."

Macdonald was not overly worried however, and to demonstrate his positive intent, he himself introduced the bill that provided for the construction of the intercolonial railway linking the Maritime provinces with Ontario and Québec.

When Nova Scotia pressed for a Royal Commission of Inquiry on Confederation, the British government, at Macdonald's request, rejected the idea. Eventually, Nova Scotia's government decided to pursue "pecuniary concessions," also known as "better terms." On this point Macdonald was ready to negotiate.

When Howe released a series of letters to the public outlining the need for "better terms," Macdonald wrote joyfully to Charles Tupper, "As you truly say, Howe has not only abandoned the ship repeal but has burnt the ship. Now everything depends upon the game being played properly."

Macdonald's game was to focus on Howe, rather than on the distant Nova Scotia government. He told Howe the glory was all his for negotiating a better deal for Nova Scotia: "This you will see is a bold game. But 'out of the nettle danger you will pluck the flower,' . . . there is a glorious and patriotic game before you; let me urge you to play it."

Negotiations with Howe began, not in Ottawa or Nova Scotia, but in Portland, Maine. The better terms for Nova Scotia provided that federal subsidies would be calculated on the same rate as New Brunswick's. Macdonald's strategy and patience worked brilliantly, punctuated by Howe joining his Cabinet in 1869. Howe relented after realizing that he could make no better deal with Canada and that the British government was indifferent to his pleas. Macdonald good-naturedly recalled that he had met Howe in the streets of London, England before Confederation, and joked, "Someday soon you will be one of us!" "Never! Never!" Howe replied, "You shall hang me first." Ultimately, Macdonald not only brought Nova Scotia onside, but used Howe to negotiate the entry of Manitoba into Confederation.

Thomas D'Arcy McGee, a parliamentary colleague and a close friend, was also persuasive in bringing Howe and Nova Scotia to embrace Canada. Though McGee was not included in Macdonald's Cabinet, there was a genuine fondness between the two, and Macdonald once joked with McGee that "This Government can't afford two drunkards—and you've got to stop." McGee had attended the Charlottetown and Québec City conferences and is one of the Fathers of Confederation. McGee's outspokenness against Irish Republicanism and the Fenians caused Macdonald to warn McGee that his personal safety was at risk. After delivering an impassioned speech on national unity in the House of Commons on April 6, 1868, McGee returned to his rooming house on Sparks Street where he was shot and killed. Macdonald, woken with the shocking news in the middle of the night, was devastated and immediately rushed to the scene to be at his friend's side. McGee was given a state funeral. Patrick James Whelan was convicted and hanged for the murder. He professed his innocence to the end, his final words being, "God save Ireland and God save my soul."

MACDONALD'S ALL-CONSUMING PASSION for politics overwhelmed both his law practice and his need for financial security. He relied on his partners to produce income and was often on the brink financially, and professionally. Unexpectedly, in 1869 Macdonald was informed by the president of the Merchants' Bank that his personal debt amounted to $79,500. A dollar then is the equivalent of about $30 today, which puts Macdonald's burden at over $2 million. His $5,000 annual salary as prime minister would not even cover the interest on such a debt. In fairness, the debt was partly the consequence of the sudden death of his law partner, A.J. Macdonnell. Bankruptcy could have meant the end of his political career, however, and all manner of methods were used to raise funds, including Agnes placing a mortgage on the family's house in Kingston. Macdonald's friends took up a private subscription to ensure his debts were discharged and his family supported.

Agnes gave birth to a daughter, Mary, on February 8, 1869. The child was hydrocephalic (an abnormal increase of cerebrospinal fluid around the brain resulting in an enlarged head; a lifetime disability). Macdonald was devoted to Mary, and had a special second-floor landing built in the family residence so Mary could hear the political discourse that took place in the dining room. In fact, Mary outlasted her parents, living into her sixties, but despair over Mary's disease was another key factor that stirred Macdonald to drink; sometimes in binges, to a degree that caused embarrassment to himself and the nation. Easily exaggerated by sensational storytellers, such incidents gave rise to Macdonald's reputation as a "falling-down-drunk." Certainly there were moments of great stress and despair in Macdonald's life, both political and personal, that led to notable incidents of excess. But these incidents have been persistently and unfairly overplayed in history books to the point where high school students are as likely to remember Macdonald's drinking prowess as his accomplishments as a politician. Macdonald's descendants express their frustration and anger over the characterization of Macdonald as a drunk. They state that at family gatherings there was no evidence of unrestrained consumption. Some suggest that Macdonald should not be remembered for his drinking any more than Winston Churchill is.

HAVING CONSOLIDATED four colonies of the British Empire within Confederation, Macdonald set his sights West and East. The grand design to include Newfoundland and Prince Edward Island was first articulated in the conferences at Charlottetown and Québec City. To the West, Canada wanted the territory held by the Hudson's Bay Company, but only if England provided financial and military support.

In April 1869, the Hudson's Bay Company accepted terms for the surrender of western Rupert's Land. This gave Canada all the land to the west excluding British Columbia. In early June, Newfoundland delegates in Ottawa agreed on terms to enter Confederation. With Nova Scotia pacified and Prince Edward Island poised to join, Macdonald wrote triumphantly to

Sir Hastings Doyle, the first lieutenant governor of Nova Scotia, "We have quietly and almost without observation, annexed all the country between here and the Rocky Mountains, as well as Newfoundland." It was inevitable that Macdonald would seek British Columbia's entry, to create a country that stretched from ocean to ocean. Most important to Macdonald was that British Columbia be kept out of the hands of the Americans.

William McDougall, a former George Brown colleague and member of Macdonald's Liberal-Conservative caucus, was the first governor of the newly acquired western territory. But the transfer of Rupert's Land into Canada, set for December 1, 1869, did not conclude as planned, mainly because of conflicts with the Métis, who had established a semi-military organization along the Red River. Macdonald realized the magnitude of the problems he faced, and was sensitive to the dilemma of the Métis: "No explanation has been made of the arrangement by which the country (Rupert's Land) is handed over to the Queen, and that it is her Majesty who transfers the country to Canada with the same rights to settlers as existed before. All these poor people know is that Canada has bought the country from the Hudson's Bay Company, and that they are handed over like a flock of sheep to us."

The situation was so precarious that Macdonald refused the territory when it came time to transfer the land into Canadian hands. Macdonald informed the Colonial Office: "Canada cannot accept North West until peaceable possession can be given. We advise Colonial Office to delay issue a proclamation."

Even if they were not directly involved in the Métis insurgency, Macdonald believed that the Americans relished Canada's inability to secure western territory and may have been involved in fomenting Métis dissent. Writing to John Rose, Canada's first minister of finance, Macdonald complained: "I cannot understand the desire of the Colonial Office, or of the Company, to saddle the responsibility of the government on Canada just now. It would so completely throw the game into the hands of the insurgents and the Yankee wire-pullers, who are to some extent influencing and directing the movement from St. Paul that we cannot foresee the consequences."

Confederation must have seemed easy to Macdonald compared with the obstacles he faced in 1869. His dream of extending Canada from coast to coast was suddenly very much in doubt. To the east, the pro-Confederate government in Newfoundland had been defeated with no real prospects of change. Looking West, though Canada was assured title to the territory, its forces faced a self-declared provisional government at Red River under Métis leader Louis Riel.

While Macdonald was inclined to seek a peaceful settlement of grievances in the West, a party of Canadians, led by McDougall and his surveyor
Colonel Stoughton Dennis, assembled an armed force to overtake the Riel-
led insurgents. In what Macdonald called a "series of inglorious intrigues,"
the Canadian forces were defeated by the much larger Métis forces.
Macdonald opposed the use of force and blamed much on McDougall and
Dennis: "The two together have done their utmost to destroy our chance of
an amicable settlement with these wild people, and now the probability is
that our commissioners will fail and that we must be left to the exhibition
of force next spring."

Macdonald's fears about absorbing the "wild west" had been realized.
And there had been no opportunity to use his political skills to achieve a harmonious union. Canada had neither the financial capacity nor the military
experience to conquer the inhospitable western territory. Macdonald feared
that American interests and the Fenians would fund and support the rebellion to forestall the British colony from extending its borders. In seeking
British military support, Macdonald put down the choices in very blunt
terms: "British North America must either belong to the Americans or
British system of government. It will be a century before we are strong
enough to walk alone." The prime minister was humble enough to admit that
Canada was not yet of age.

Early in 1870, the English- and French-speaking parishes of the Red
River settlements drew up a list of rights with a view to negotiating with the
Canadian government. Negotiating political settlements was Macdonald's
forte. But a party of Canadian forces pre-empted discussions and attacked
Riel's army. Once again, Riel was victorious. Macdonald was furious, not so
much at Riel, as with the Canadian military. "The foolish and criminal
attempt of Schultz and Captain Boulton to renew the fight had added greatly
to Riel's strength." In the aftermath, the Métis took Thomas Scott, an
Orangeman, prisoner. Scott's agitation in confinement was extreme and he
repeatedly offended the sensibilities of his captors. For his role in attacking
the provisional government, and other unspecified offences, Scott was tried
on March 2 before a Métis military tribunal and was then executed, all within
24 hours. This profoundly changed the political dynamic for Macdonald. Back
East, the Cabinet, and the country, split on linguistic lines: English-speaking
citizens demanded military action; the French supported negotiation.

A Fenian raid into Canadian territory was expected a little more than a
month after Scott's execution. Canada sought British military support, but
it was slow in coming. Macdonald complained to his friend Lord Carnarvon

about the lack of British support and American intervention: "At this moment we are in daily expectation of a formidable Fenian invasion, unrepressed by the United States government . . . And we are the same time called upon to send a military force to restore order in Rupert's Land. Her Majesty's Government have been kept fully informed of the constant threats from the Fenian body for the last five years, and they have been specially forewarned of the preparations for the present expected attack. And yet this is the time they choose to withdraw every soldier from us, and we're left to be the unaided victims of Irish discontent and American hostility. . . ."

On April 11, 1870, with Riel's blessing, representatives from the West (named Assiniboia) arrived in Ottawa to negotiate terms for entry into Canada. Father Noel-Joseph Ritchot and Alfred H. Scott were immediately arrested for aiding and abetting the murder of Thomas Scott the previous month. Both claimed "diplomatic immunity." A third western representative, Judge Black, arrived in Ottawa a few days later. Macdonald met him unofficially to discuss the list of rights and other terms for political compromise. Macdonald had been reluctant to attend such a meeting for a number of reasons: first, it might provide legitimacy to Riel and his provisional government; second, because of the negative political fallout in English-speaking Canada surrounding the trial and execution of Thomas Scott; and third, the possibility that Riel was acting in bad faith and had no intention of negotiating for a political settlement. In fact, Macdonald suspected an American conspiracy: "The unpleasant suspicion remains that he is only wasting time by sending this delegation, until the approach of the summer enable him to get material support from the United States."

Father Ritchot and Alfred Scott were released from jail, and the three western delegates met with Macdonald and Cartier. Assiniboia, later known as Manitoba, wanted to join Confederation, but under its own terms. The Métis feared the arrival of scores of English-speaking immigrants, mostly Protestant, and wanted assurances they would be able to sustain their language and culture. They also wanted provincial status, including guarantees for language and religion similar to those that existed in the Province of Québec. The Métis also sought land grants in settlement of their ancestral claims. Macdonald readily agreed to these terms, but refused one final request: amnesty in all matters arising out of the military conflict. Without the Scott execution, such a request might have been possible. Macdonald was personally inclined towards amnesty, but dared not risk the wrath of Ontario voters.

The negotiation concluded with Manitoba joining Confederation. Riel fled to America. While in exile he was elected on three occasions, twice by acclamation, to the House of Commons to represent the Manitoba riding of Provencher. The fugitive never took his seat.

Meanwhile, the strain of office and ongoing struggles in his family life contributed to Macdonald slipping into states of extreme intoxication. Sir Stafford Northcote, governor of the Hudson's Bay Company, reported to British Conservative leader Benjamin Disraeli that Macdonald had fallen into temporary drunkenness: "His habit is to retire to bed, to exclude everybody, and to drink bottle after bottle of port. All the papers are sent to him, and he reads them, but he is conscious of his inability to do any important business and he does not."

In the meantime, while progress was being made in the West, relations south of the border were deteriorating, with the issues of trade and fishing rights the most frequent irritants. International relations were not then a colonial purview, and Macdonald was frustrated that Canada was not properly represented in the British-led negotiations with the Americans. On the lack of representation for a dispute over the three-mile limit for the fishery, Macdonald remarked: "We must consider that if Canada allowed the matter to go by default, and left its interest to be adjudicated upon and settled by a commission composed exclusively of Americans having an adverse interest, and Englishman having little or no interest in Canada, the government here would be very much censured if the result were a sacrifice of the rights of the Dominion."

The Macdonald government was heavily criticized over the treaty that was eventually signed with the United States over the fishery. Great Britain had struggles of its own with the United States and was not about to consume political capital over what it considered a minor trade issue in one of its colonies. Macdonald understood—and reluctantly accepted—Canada's "inadequacies" when it came to self-representation. But he made certain his British masters understood the galling discomfort and humiliation Canadians felt at not having sovereignty over relations with their neighbours to the south. As he signed the treaty negotiated by England in 1871, Macdonald teased aloud so his British masters could hear, "Well, here go the fisheries . . . we give them away . . . here goes the signature . . . they are gone."

With Newfoundland and PEI showing little interest in a confederated Canada, Macdonald's attention again turned westward, this time to British Columbia, whose entry into Canada depended on commencing the construction of a railway across the continent within two years and finishing it within ten. The railway was to be built by the private sector, and paid for with subsidies from the government plus considerable grants of land. A condition imposed by Macdonald on the Pacific Railway was that, "Canadian interests are to be fully protected . . . no American ring will be allowed to get control over it." As Macdonald well knew, however, the operation could not be entirely Canadian: it required the financial support of loans and guarantees from England. And here Macdonald leveraged to his advantage the concessions England had made to the United States. He demanded compensation from the United States—through England—for the money Canada had spent to suppress the Fenian raids. But what he really wanted was financing for a transcontinental railroad.

Macdonald's uneasiness about the Americans was both sincere and strategic. He was eager to run for re-election on a theme of Canadian independence from America, to the point that he considered shedding the Conservative label. Writing to T.C. Patteson, editor of the *Mail*, Macdonald explored a new name for his party: "I think (the term Conservative) should be kept in the background as much as possible, and that our party should be called the 'Union party,' going in for union with England against all annexationist and independents and for the union of all the provinces of British North America . . . what think you of such a name as 'the Constitutional Union Party?'"

He then told Patteson his major policy plank: "The paper must go in for a National Policy in tariff matters, and while avoiding the word 'protection' must dedicate a readjustment of the tariff in such a manner as incidentally to aid our manufacturing and industrial interests."

The need for a National Policy fit well with Macdonald's view of the conspiracies that existed south of the border to undermine Canada. Asserting Canadian interests through trade restrictions may have been economically unwise, but it was politically saleable to a population wary of American influence. Macdonald's nationalistic fervour and instinctive distrust of the American neighbour would be matched in intensity by only one subsequent Conservative prime minister, John George Diefenbaker.

Meanwhile, the other great National Policy initiative, the transcontinental railroad, was beginning to take shape. The challenge was to assemble a Canadian-led team with the ingenuity, experience, and, most important, the financial capacity to do the job. No single company was capable of assuming so huge an undertaking, so Macdonald encouraged the creation of a public–private partnership on a scale not contemplated before or since.

The second Canadian federal election that took place in 1872, when the Macdonald government was in its fifth year, included British Columbia and

Manitoba. Macdonald's justification for seeking a second term was clear: the work of building the nation, he wrote to his minister of finance, was far from complete. "Confederation is only yet in the gristle, and it will require five years more before it hardens into bone."

But victory for Macdonald was far from certain. His Québec lieutenant, Georges-Étienne Cartier, was unwell and his popularity in his Montréal East riding was substantially diminished, partly due to a powerful consortium of railroad interests opposed to Macdonald's plans. Macdonald then sought support from the trade unions, a group he thought should be aligned with the Conservative cause. Macdonald believed in legislation to create better working conditions for workers and supported, with some humour, strengthening the role of trade unions: "I have a special interest in (unions) because I'm a working man myself. . . . If you look at the Confederation act, in the framing of which I had some hand, you will admit that I'm a pretty good joiner; and as for Cabinet making, I've had much experience."

Macdonald and Cartier were in a fight for their political lives. They feared the railroad project under the Liberals would flounder and with it, their vision for Canada. Sir Hugh Allan, who represented the Canadian Pacific Railway Company, was lobbying heavily to become president of a much larger railway consortium. In the heat of negotiations, Allan offered "financial assistance" to the Conservatives. Cartier initially set the "immediate requirements" as $60,000, to be split between Macdonald, Cartier, and Hector Langevin.

The sum of $25,000 was deposited into the Merchant Bank for Macdonald's use. None of it was used for his own election, instead being allocated to other Ontario constituencies. But it was not enough to meet Macdonald's campaign needs. In desperation, he pressed Allan's solicitor, John Abbott, for more. On August 26, Macdonald cabled Abbott: "I must have another $10,000. Will be the last time of calling. Do not fail me. Answer today."

Hugh Allan delivered. In the end, Macdonald accepted $45,000; Cartier and Langevin received $117,000, worth over $3 million in current value. But the donations came with strings attached, unspecified conditions that Allan and his company thought would be addressed over the course of negotiations concerning the railway. It also left Macdonald and his colleagues beholden to an unsavoury character with whom they would have substantial business dealings. It was a disaster in the making. Macdonald, however, arrogantly believed he could avoid scandal. Because the funds helped to advance the cause of Canada, he believed he was justified in accepting them.

Conservatives won the 1872 election, but just barely. The 99 Conservatives would need to rely on a few of the six independents to maintain power in the 200-seat legislature. The Tories won with substantial strength in the West, and took 37 of 65 seats in Quebec. They nearly swept Nova Scotia and New Brunswick. But the Liberals, with 95 seats, emerged a much stronger opposition force than in 1867. Ontario was solidly in Liberal hands. Unusual by today's standards, 52 of the 200 seats were won by acclamation, including 29 Conservative seats. Cartier was defeated, however, despite Allan's timely infusion of funds. It was no secret that Cartier was unwell, but it was still a shock when he died the following May. Distraught, Macdonald once again turned to drink for solace. Governor General Lord Dufferin wrote of Macdonald's heartache over Cartier's death: "It is really tragical to see so superior a man subject to such a purely physical infirmity, against which he struggles with desperate courage, until fairly prostrated and broken down."

Not long after the election results were confirmed, rumours began to swirl that huge cash contributions from the railways had found their way into Conservative Party coffers. On April 2, 1873, Lucius Seth Huntington, the Liberal member from Shefford Québec, rose in Parliament to demand an inquiry into the granting of the charter to the Canadian Pacific Railway Company. The mandate for the inquiry was twofold: explore possible American involvement and review financial contributions to the Conservative party from Sir Hugh Allan sourced in Canada and the United States. The Conservative forces defeated the Liberal motion, but proposed in its place a five-member committee of Parliament to look into the matter. With the government holding three positions on the committee, the outcome of a majority report was assured.

The press picked up the story, dubbing it the "Pacific Scandal." On July 18, the Toronto *Globe* and the Montréal *Herald* reported the contents of Macdonald's telegram to Abbott. Macdonald was dumbfounded: How did these telegrams find their way into the hands of the press? "It is one of those overwhelming misfortunes that they say every man must meet once in his life. At first it fairly staggered me," he said.

In fact, the telegrams had been stolen from Abbott's office, and sold to Montréal Liberals. The identity of the thief was not confirmed, but was believed to be a law clerk in Abbott's office named George Norris. As much as Macdonald wanted to draw attention to the skullduggery of the theft, such attention would only have heightened interest and given rise to accusations of a conspiracy. A depressed and despairing Macdonald once again

turned to the bottle and when he disappeared for a few days to collect himself, rumours again swirled, this time that he had committed suicide.
Macdonald reassured his friends in telegram messages that the rumours
were greatly exaggerated. "It is an infamous falsehood," he wrote. "I never
was better in my life."

Macdonald steadfastly maintained his innocence. Raising funds from
companies that conducted business with the government was nothing new.
The Canadian Pacific Railway had been promised nothing in the way of government contracts, he was certain, only that Sir Hugh Allan was slotted to
become company president. He told his friends not to worry too much
about Allan getting rich because, "where he is going his gold coins would
melt." Macdonald did not see the brewing scandal as a matter of concern to
the tax-paying public since they would not be paying Allan's salary. And, ultimately, the government quashed whatever plans it had in the works with
Canadian Pacific, including any financial links with the Americans. But to
Macdonald's horror, it turned out that American financiers had been the
supporters of Allan's scheme. The Opposition did not accept the government's diminishment of the scandal and it refused to attend the
Parliamentary committee.

Fearing the loss of a confidence vote, Macdonald secured a temporary
suspension of the House of Commons from Governor General Lord
Dufferin (a tactic Stephen Harper used in late 2008 to counter a coalition of
opposition parties intent on taking over the government). Months later, just
as Parliament was about to reconvene, Lord Dufferin wrote to Macdonald,
in tone and language the prime minister had not expected: "In acting as you
have, I am all convinced that you have only followed a traditional practice
and that probably your political opponents have resorted with equal freedom to the same expedients, but as Minister of Justice and the official
guardian and protector of the laws, your responsibilities are exceptional and
your personal connection with what has passed cannot but *fatally* affect your
position as minister."

Unclear whether the letter was a dismissal or a warning, Macdonald
was stunned by the tone. The word "fatal" leapt off the page. Macdonald met
Dufferin the following day, when it was made clear that the governor general was reserving for himself the ability to intervene ". . . to prevent the
conscience of Parliament and of the country from being forced by the mere
brute strength of party spirit."

The next day Macdonald met his Cabinet to discuss the controversy and
consider the question of resignation. Although some of his members were

wavering, Macdonald remained confident and thought he could defend the government in Parliament. At 2:30 a.m., the conclusion of a five-hour speech in the House of Commons, Macdonald made a plea for his government based on its past accomplishments:

> I have fought the Battle of Confederation, the battle of Union, the battle of the Dominion of Canada. I throw myself upon the House. I throw myself upon this country, I throw myself upon posterity, and I believe that, notwithstanding the many failings of my life, I shall have the voice of this country in this House rallying around me. . . . I can see past the decision of this House either for or against me; but whether it be for or against me, I know . . . that there does not exist in this country a man who has given more of his time, more of his heart, more of his wealth, or more of his intellect and power, such as they may be, for the good of this Dominion of Canada.

It was a rousing speech that brought most members on the government side to their feet. But not all, and the defections were enough to undo Macdonald's working majority. After meeting with the governor general, Macdonald resigned on November 5, 1873.

Alexander Mackenzie, the leader of the opposition Liberals, formed a government and seized the opportunity to capitalize on the Tory demise by going to the people on January 22, 1874. With the Pacific Scandal fresh in voter's minds, 129 Liberals were elected, compared with 65 Conservatives and 12 independents. In the first Canadian election to use a secret ballot, the Liberal sweep went right across the country.

In the aftermath, Macdonald resigned as party leader, saying, "My fighting days are over . . . I will never be a member of any administration again." His offer was refused by the Tory caucus. There was a dispute over the election results in his riding, however, and in the by-election held on December 29, 1874, Macdonald squeaked by with a 17-vote win. Had nine electors switched their votes, or had his caucus accepted his resignation, Macdonald might never have been a factor in Canadian politics again. But Macdonald knew that a life in politics comes with its ups and downs. "When fortune empties her chamberpot on your head, smile and say 'we are going to have a summer shower.'"

Not more than a year into the Liberal administration, Macdonald sensed opportunity. The Blake Liberals and Mackenzie Reformers—the forces that had combined to defeat the Tories in 1874—were coming unglued. Edward

Blake began to speak of narrow nationalist sentiments, such as diminishing ties to Great Britain, and opposed accommodations for British Columbia, saying he was "prepared to let them go." Concerned over finances, Mackenzie opposed proceeding with the transcontinental railroad. Macdonald thought if he was patient and didn't needlessly provoke unrest it was only a matter of time before the Liberal government would divide itself. "The great reason why I have always been able to beat (the opposition)," offered Macdonald, "is that I have been able to look a little ahead, while (they) could on no occasion forgo the temptation of a temporary triumph." Politics, he added, "is a game requiring great coolness and an utter abnegation of prejudice and personal feeling."

Macdonald distinguished his nation-building Conservatives from what he called "little Canadian Liberals." Macdonald raised the spectre of a growing American empire seeking to fulfill what some called its "manifest destiny." With British help, Macdonald believed, Canada would build a nation from "ocean to ocean." The Liberals, by contrast, were weak nation-builders because they were not prepared to invest in the infrastructure of a nation. Their focus on the "Pacific scandal" was so small-minded that it arrested progress on the railway itself. Macdonald said he could get the job done: "Until the road is built to British Columbia and the Pacific, this Dominion is a mere geographical expression. . . . until bound by the iron link, as we have bound Nova Scotia and New Brunswick by the Intercolonial Railway, we are not a Dominion in fact."

ASSERTING BRITISH TRADITION was fundamental to Macdonald's political mission. "The cardinal point in our policy is connection with Great Britain. I am a British subject, and British-born, and a British subject I hope to die. . . . Those who disliked the colonial connection spoke of it as a chain, but it was a golden chain, and he, for one, was proud to wear its fetters."

Macdonald saw the British connection with Canada as critical to its political independence from the United States. Independence from the Americans, connection with Great Britain, a nation from sea to sea, a national railway, and protection for Canadian industry were the cornerstones of Macdonald's national policies, and the guideposts that would sustain the remainder of his political life.

The Liberal leadership was proposing to remove trade barriers. Dissension in Liberal ranks was increasing, and Macdonald sensed it would take but a bit of wooing to cause the dissenters to switch sides. But Macdonald did not want to woo them at any cost. He wanted the rancorous division over trade policy to fester within Liberal ranks. If members of the Liberal caucus did jump ship, he wanted it to be on his terms, not theirs. Following the introduction of Mackenzie's budget in 1876, an entire delegation of Liberal members indicated they were ready to cross the floor of the House of Commons. In the House, Macdonald said: "I heard the threat—*the dire threat*—that the members from Montréal would go into opposition.... Well, Mr. Speaker, I have caught some queer fish in my time, but I'm afraid that my honorable friend—as during the previous session when he sat over in that corner—is too loose a fish for me ever to catch."

Loyalty to party—even above constituent needs—was sacred to Macdonald. Once elected, Macdonald believed, a parliamentarian was duty bound to complete the term with the party that he ran with. "A man's duty when he accepts a seat in Parliament is not to his constituents as a whole, but to the party that elected him ... unless they ask him to retire, he should remain."

To Macdonald the trade issue was neither ideological nor academic. The impact of a one-sided trade arrangement with the Americans, he thought, was causing real hardship to the Canadian economy. A depression had set in and Macdonald contended the Liberals were unwilling or unable to address the matter. "We are informed in the speech from the throne that there is a stagnation in trade.... and if it be true, I say that if there is ever a time when it is lawful, or allowable, or wise, or expedient for a government to interfere, now is the time."The campaign Macdonald wanted to fight was not for the odd Liberal defector, but for the hearts and minds of the Canadian people. The nation was suffering an economic depression, and Macdonald blamed it on American trade policy and the timidity of the Liberal government.

In the summer of 1876, Macdonald initiated a series of political picnics across the land, each attended by thousands of enthusiastic supporters. On July 27, over 5,000 people came to hear him at a picnic near Belleville, Ontario. Later that summer, Macdonald led a torch-light parade through the streets of Montréal, where 50,000 people gathered at Dominion Square to hear him speak. He labelled Liberal "laissez-faire" trade policy as gross neglect, and said he dreamed of a "Canada for the Canadians."

The Liberals sensed they were headed for defeat. Even the governor general, in a letter to the Colonial Secretary, remarked on their doomed prospects. "Blake is ill, thoroughly broken down with overwork and excitement and irritability of the brain ...As for Mackenzie he looks like a washed out rag and limp enough to hang up on a clothesline."

With renewed purpose and conviction, Macdonald was by all accounts drinking little, if any, alcohol during this critical period. Within the ranks of his party, he implored unity: "Let us not, like the hunters in the fable, quarrel about the skin before we kill the bear. It will take our united efforts to kill a bear."

On September 17, 1878, the voters punished the Liberals for the depression and for the free trade policies they saw as its cause. The indiscretion of the Pacific Scandal had, apparently, been forgiven. The business establishments in major eastern cities supported trade protection and went solidly for the Tories. The Liberals won only half the seats they had taken in 1872, leaving Conservatives with 134 MPs in the 206-seat legislature. Solid Tory majorities were secured in every province except New Brunswick.

A satisfied Macdonald reflected on his win: "I resolved to reverse the verdict of 1874 and have done so to my heart's content." The only blemish on election night was Macdonald's loss in his home riding of Kingston to Alexander Gunn. While the defeat was attributed to lingering distaste over the Pacific Scandal, the loss was a mere inconvenience, and easily fixed in a by-election.

CHAPTER 3

CEMENTING THE BOND

Every American statesman covets Canada. The greed for its acquisition is still on the increase, and God knows where it will all end. . . . We must face the fight at our next election, and it is only the conviction that the battle will be better fought under my guidance than under another that makes me undertake the task, handicapped as I am, with the infirmities of old age.

BACK IN THE PRIME MINISTER'S OFFICE, Macdonald breathed life into his national vision. True to his campaign promise, he increased tariffs on imported American goods, which risked retaliation in the form of a prohibitive duty on the export of Canadian lumber. But it was the building of the transcontinental railroad that occupied most of his attention: "Until this great work is completed . . . we have as much interest in British Columbia as in Australia, and no more. The railway once finished, we become one great united country with a large inter-provincial trade and a common interest."

The railway was critical to increasing Canada's population, strengthening its economy, and enhancing its ability to sustain itself against American incursions. Macdonald knew that Canada could not take on a project of such magnitude on its own and sought loan guarantees from the British government.

With the levers of power at his disposal, Macdonald put the might of patronage to work. He would not make appointments prior to an election, thus encouraging his campaign staff to "work harder for your return." When Toronto Tories grumbled about the lack of jobs coming their way,

Macdonald retorted "As soon as Toronto returns Conservative members, it will get Conservative appointments." Macdonald eagerly dished out patronage jobs, although he was frustrated that there were not enough to satisfy his party. "Five years' opposition have made our friends rather hungry and they are worrying me about office, but the departments have all been crammed by the Grits so that it will be sometime before there will be any vacancies."

Macdonald dreamed of a more independent and assertive Canada, but he remained committed to Great Britain. Macdonald was prepared for the time being to have the British Empire represent Canada to the world, hoping "to stave off for a very long time to come any wish on the part of Canada for a separate set of representatives in foreign countries." The prerequisite to an independent voice for Canada on the international stage was economic and military self-sufficiency. "The sooner the Dominion is treated as an auxiliary power rather than a dependency, the sooner will it assume all the responsibilities of the position including the settlement of its contribution to the defence of the Empire whenever and wherever assailed."

And Canada was coming of age. In 1879, Macdonald's former finance minister, Alexander Galt, persuasively argued the case for Canada to the Colonial office: "Canada has ceased to occupy the position of an ordinary possession of the Crown. She exists in the form of a powerful central government, having already no less than seven subordinate local executive and legislative systems, soon to be largely augmented by the development of vast regions lying between Lake Superior and the Rocky Mountains."

Macdonald succeeded in establishing semi-diplomatic standing between Canada and Great Britain, which bypassed, to a degree, the representatives of the Colonial Office stationed in Ottawa. However, the rank of Canada's emissary to Britain was to be a representative with limited authority. A British dispatch reported of the representative, "His position would necessarily be more analogous to that of an officer in the Home Service than to that of a minister at a foreign court." In the end, the title for Canada's representative to Great Britain was given the lofty and noble title "High Commissioner for Canada in London." Alexander Galt was its first holder.

Great Britain did not see Canada as an independent nation with the right to have its views represented directly on the world stage. It was understood that if Canada was threatened, Great Britain would come to its defence. Consequently, in the view of the British government, Great Britain should decide Canada's foreign policy. The foreign policy of Great Britain was the foreign policy of all of its colonies.

Besieged with pressing domestic and international issues, at age sixty-five Macdonald told his friends, "It is better to wear out than to rust out," but he urged his Cabinet to consider the issue of his succession on March 25, 1880. The Cabinet, however, would not let him go. Then again, Macdonald was not very serious about leaving. If he was addicted to anything, it was politics. He was passionate about the child he had created—Canada—and like an obsessed parent, he could not let go.

By 1879, due perhaps to Macdonald's protectionist policies, the economy had begun to strengthen. In the eyes of the nation, Macdonald's policies had been vindicated. Canada was growing again and was open for immigration. Macdonald's Conservatives believed in immigration and the railway was essential to Canada's growth and independence.

On October 21, 1880, the contract to build the Canadian Pacific Railroad was signed. It called for 1,900 miles of railroad between Callander, Ontario and Kamloops, B.C. Sir Hugh Allan was out and George Stephen was in as the railway's president. Businessman Donald Smith, whom Macdonald once called "the biggest liar I ever saw," was also involved. The railway was to be financed with British money, not American. Despite Macdonald's protectionist and nationalist policies, the terms of the contract stated that all materials used for the construction of the railway were to be imported duty-free. The consortium was exempt from taxes and could build whatever branches off the main rail line they chose. However, the railway contract, which included a subsidy of $26 million and a land grant of 25 million acres, would be profitable only if thousands of settlers took up the offers and purchased the land the railway had for sale.

While it made economic sense to divert the rail line south of the border, Macdonald would have none of it. Every single inch of the transcontinental railroad would have to go through Canada. To protect the economic viability of the all-Canadian routes, Canadian Pacific was given a monopoly over all rail traffic in Canada.

Liberals opposed the railway contract and its monopolistic provisions. Blake said it was irresponsible for the government to sanction a rail line through the scrub country north of Lake Superior, calling it a "criminal absurdity of nationalism." Common sense, the Liberal leader suggested, was to go west through American territory. Macdonald scoffed at the notion, suggesting that the Liberals had American money and American media on their side.

When a competing bid surfaced after the Canadian Pacific deal had been arranged, Macdonald saw it as a Liberal-concocted American-friendly sham.

"Mr. Speaker the whole thing is an attempt to destroy the Pacific Railway. I can trust to the intelligence of this House, and the patriotism of this country, I can trust not only to the patriotism but to the common sense of this country, to carry out an arrangement which will give us all we want, which will satisfy all the loyal, legitimate aspirations, which will give us a great, a united, a rich, an improving, a developing Canada, instead of making us tributary to American laws, to American railways, to American bondage, to American tools, to America's freights, to all the little tricks and big tricks that American railways are addicted to for the purpose of destroying our road."

When the bill to create the railway company passed in the House of Commons on February 1, 1881, Alexander Morris, one of the men who had conceived of Confederation, and who helped bring Macdonald and Brown together, wrote to Macdonald: "I write to congratulate you on the second crowning triumph of your more recent life, second only to that of Confederation. You have now created a link to bind the provinces indissolubly together, and to give us a future and a British nationality."

The election of 1882 on June 20 changed little in the composition of the House of Commons. Importantly, it confirmed the nation had indeed forgiven the Tories for the Pacific Scandal. Macdonald won support in all provinces, with a particularly strong showing in Québec, taking 52 of 65 seats. It was the first election for the new Liberal leader Edward Blake who, prior to Stéphane Dion, has the distinction of being the only official Liberal leader never to have served as prime minister.

It was inevitable that provincial governments seeking to assert their authority would clash with Macdonald's vision of a strong central government. With residual powers, Macdonald believed he held the upper hand, stating, "We are not half a dozen provinces. We are one great Dominion." He saw provincial lieutenant governors of the provinces as "officers of the Dominion." Nonetheless, he was not prepared to usurp the provinces in all respects. When Macdonald's French ministers wanted the Liberal-friendly lieutenant governor of Québec sacked, Macdonald resisted, telling the governor general that, "It was impossible to make Frenchmen understand constitutional government."

Macdonald feared Ontario was becoming too large and too powerful. The federal and Ontario governments clashed over a number of issues, notably Ontario's jurisdiction over liquor licenses. The federal government argued that its Temperance Act and residual powers trumped Ontario's attempts to regulate this field of activity. Ultimately, Ontario's legislation was upheld by the courts and other authorities.

The federal government's hand in sorting out jurisdictional matters was supported by its power of disallowance, a power that had proved problematic over the course of Macdonald's career as prime minister. Consistent with its monarchical beginnings, the British North America Act (section 55) requires royal Assent to any legislation passed by both houses of Parliament. (This "Imperial power of disallowance" has been used only once, in 1873. In 1930, it was agreed at an Imperial Conference that the power would never be used again.)

Another power of disallowance, articulated in section 90 of the British North America Act, gave the federal government the power to invalidate provincial legislation within one year of its enactment. As Father of Confederation and former prime minister Alexander Mackenzie noted, it was crucial that the federal government "have a control over the proceedings of the local legislatures to a certain extent . . . [as] the want of this power was a great source of weakness in the United States." This power was widely supported in pre-Confederation discussions by both the Colonial Office and Canadian politicians, although opponents such as member of Parliament Philip Moore, feared that "the veto power . . . if exercised frequently, would be almost certain to cause difficulty between the local and general governments."

Unlike the Imperial power of disallowance, the federal power of disallowance over the provinces has been used on more than 100 occasions. Macdonald used the power 29 times between 1867 and 1881, mostly to void provincial legislation that reached into areas of federal jurisdiction. When pressed to reject New Brunswick legislation on non-denominational and mandatory schooling, Macdonald refused, arguing that because the legislation did not violate the BNA Act he had no right to intervene; that it would be a ". . . violent wrench of the Constitution." During this time, Macdonald set himself up as a champion of provincial rights, but this would soon change.

In the 1880s, Macdonald set his principles aside and began to use disallowance power in an attempt to weaken the more powerful provinces, and as a partisan tool. When Ontario sought to expand its boundaries to the north and northwest, and then passed laws to regulate the use of rivers and streams, Macdonald was incensed at Ontario Premier Oliver Mowat, whom he once referred to as "a little tyrant."

Macdonald tired of the fight with provinces. The economy, which had been strong in 1881–82, weakened in 1883. Immigration slowed. The growing season for farmers was poor. The CPR had run out of money and needed government guarantees to survive. Some banks holding railway loans were on the edge of bankruptcy. Some provincial leaders were threatening suc-cession. The country was on the financial brink. In despair, Macdonald told a friend, "I have nearly made up my mind to get out of office. This is a good time for it and I'm breaking down. I can't conceal this for myself, perhaps not from my friends."

The Liberals opposed government support for the railway. Blake argued that the ill-conceived venture was underfinanced, monopolistic, and poorly designed. His arguments were not without foundation. Project management was indeed poor and the final price tag came in at double the original budget. Macdonald had difficulty keeping his own caucus together on the railway, with Québec MPs demanding support for their province in exchange for their votes on the railway. In frustration, Macdonald mused whether the French in Canada could ever be satisfied: "I had to circumvent a rather ignoble plot to cause a stampede of my French friends, by offering them, for their semi-insolvent province, large pecuniary aid. The plot failed, but this combination of the French to force the hand of the government of the day is a standing menace to Confederation."

As if Macdonald needed more trouble, in early July 1884 Louis Riel slipped back into Canada from the United States. Macdonald issued orders to keep Riel under close observation: "I don't attach much importance to these plots but my experience of the Fenian business has taught me that one should never disbelieve the evidence of plots or intended raids merely because they are foolish and certain to fail . . . One cannot foresee what they . . . under Riel's advice, may do."

Nevertheless, Macdonald wanted to address the legitimate needs of the Métis in a responsible manner. The Manitoba Act (1870) set aside 1.4 mil-lion acres of land for the Métis. That worked out to 240 acres of land for each child, and 160 acres of negotiable scrip to the head of each Métis fam-ily. Macdonald knew the dangers of passing out scrip: "The scrip is sold for a song to the sharks and spent in whiskey and this we desire above all things to avoid."

But political agitation from the Métis was enormous and Macdonald relented in an uncharacteristic moment of weakness. In the House of Commons, Macdonald outlined his fear: "I do not hesitate to say that I did it with the greatest reluctance. I do not easily yield if there is a better course open; but at the last moment I yielded and I said: well for God's sake, let them have the scrip; they will either drink it or waste it or sell it; but let us have peace."

Macdonald was prepared to be open minded and even generous with

Riel. He wrote to the governor general. "There is, I think, nothing to be feared from Riel. In his answer to the invitation sent to him, which was a temperate and unobjectionable paper, he spoke of some claims he had against the government. I presume these refer to his land claims which he forfeited on conviction and banishment. I think we shall deal liberally with him and make him a good subject again."

As expected, Riel made demands for his people to the Canadian government, amounting to some two million acres of land. But Riel also demanded benefits for himself: $100,000 and a job, and offered to end the turmoil if his personal demands were met. Macdonald reported to the House of Commons that Riel, "...came in for the purpose of attempting to extract money from the public purse. Of course, that could not be entertained for a moment."

Whatever settlement might have been negotiated with Riel ended on March 26, 1885, when forces clashed at Duck Lake. Macdonald's first response was all business. "This insurrection is a bad business but we must face it as best we may.... the first thing to be done is to localize the insurrection." Macdonald sent in the military. Transporting the troops gave the cash-strapped railway its first real test.

Riel and his followers were defeated at Batouche in what could hardly rank as a significant military accomplishment because the outcome was never in doubt. But Riel's surrender on May 15, 1885 was cause for celebration in Ottawa. Macdonald wrote to Tupper, "Canada as you will see is delirious with enthusiasm on the return of our volunteers. This has done more to weld the provinces into one nation than anything else could have done."

The trial of Louis Riel on six counts of treason began on July 20, 1885. Riel's counsel presented an insanity defence, which lasted all of one day, and which Riel himself rejected. The Chief Justice said, "he seems to have had in view, while professing to champion the interests of the Métis, the securing of pecuniary advantage for himself." Six jurors of English and Protestant stock convicted him of treason and Judge Hugh Richardson handed down the sentence of death by hanging. One of the jurors later remarked that the conviction might easily have been connected with the murder of Thomas Scott.

Macdonald was unmoved by pleas for clemency for Riel from French Canada, writing to the governor general: "I don't think that we should by a respite anticipate—and as it were court—the interference of the Judicial Committee." In other words, Macdonald did not want his government to intervene in a judicial matter, hardly a surprising statement for an elected official.

However, just as the last spike was about to be driven on the national railway, a solitary moment of great triumph, Macdonald's government was besieged by division in his party and in the country over the fate of Riel. In response, Macdonald launched an inquiry into the state of Riel's mental condition. A commission of three doctors, two English and one French, was asked to report on Riel's current mental state. In issuing instructions to the commission, Macdonald was very precise: "Remember that the jury have decided that he was sane when his treasons were committed, and at the time of his trial. . . . I need scarcely point out to you that the inquiry is not as to whether Riel is subject to illusions or delusions but whether he is so bereft of reason as not to know right from wrong and is not to be an accountable being."

The report of the commission concluded that Riel was accountable for his actions. In a letter to Macdonald, one commissioner, Dr. Jukes, added that Riel was "a vain ambitious man, crafty and cunning, with powers in a marked degree to incite weak men to desperate deeds. He seeks his own aggrandizement, and in my opinion, if he can attain his own ends, will care little for his followers." Dr. Lavell was of the same opinion. The French commissioner, Dr. F.X. Valade, disagreed: "I have come to the conclusions that he is not an accountable being, that he is unable to distinguish between wrong and right on political and religious subjects, which I consider well-marked typical forms of insanity under which he undoubtedly suffers, but on other points I believe him to be sensible and can distinguish right from wrong."

At its meeting on Wednesday November 11, the Cabinet confirmed that it would allow the verdict of the court to stand and would not pardon Riel or commute the sentence. In response, 19 Québec MPs telegraphed Macdonald to express their disapproval and disappointment.

In one of the more monumental underestimations in Canadian political history, Macdonald thought that the aftermath to the Riel execution would be short-lived: "He shall hang though every dog in Québec will bark in his favour." Macdonald tried to reassure his French-Canadian supporters: "Keep calm resolute attitude—all will come right. . . . we are in for lively times in Québec, but I feel pretty confident that the excitement will die out." Macdonald's assessment was that a megalomaniac seeking financial gain for himself could hardly command a sustained following. Riel was hanged on November 16, 1885.

The reaction astonished Macdonald. As if he himself had convicted, sen-

tenced, and pulled the lever of the gallows, Macdonald was referred to, particularly in Québec, as the prime minister of a "hangman's government."
Riel was cast as a Christian martyr, sacrificed to Orange fanaticism. Liberal
leader Wilfrid Laurier inflamed the bitter feelings by claiming that had he
lived on the banks of the Saskatchewan River, he would have taken up a rifle
against the Canadian government. However, Laurier's siding with Riel
revealed a rift among Liberals, particularly between Laurier and his Ontario
colleagues, who had no common ground with Riel. The Liberal predicament
was similar to the one Macdonald faced: commute Riel's sentence and face
outrage in Ontario; allow the execution and face fury in Québec.

The Québec legislature took Riel's side when the question of his execution came up for debate in May of 1886. The challenge of being both a
French Canadian and a Conservative was overwhelming to most Québecers.
Giving expression to Québec resentment was a new political party, "le parti
national." Called by the *Mail* newspaper "the party of race and revenge," it
was the first political party formed along the lines of race. French Québec
was distressed not just with the Conservatives, but also by being in Canada.

Macdonald's trouble with national unity went further than Québec.
Because of a weak economy, declining federal subsidies, and cutbacks in
shipbuilding, the popular view among Nova Scotians was that they had made
a mistake in joining Canada. On May 7, 1886, W.S. Fielding, the Liberal
leader, proposed a resolution in the Nova Scotia legislature for the repeal of
the Union and a referendum on the matter. The resolution passed with a
clear majority. Macdonald interpreted Nova Scotia's dissatisfaction as, once
again, a plea for "better terms," what he called blackmail.

Despite the distress in Nova Scotia and Québec, however, Macdonald
once again set his sights on expansion. He now had his intercontinental railway, but Canada, in his view, was not whole. "The Dominion cannot be
considered complete without Newfoundland. It has the key to our front
door." This lock, however, he was unable to open.

A DISPUTE WITH THE UNITED STATES over trade and fishing erupted in
1886 with the seizure of an American fishing schooner, the *David J. Adams*,
from Digby Harbour in Nova Scotia. The boat entered Canadian waters to
buy ice and bait. A recent federal law permitted entry only for the purpose
of acquiring wood, water, shelter, and repairs, and "for no other purposes
whatever." It seems peculiar and excessively nationalistic to deny a foreigner
the opportunity to give Canadians money for what they regularly sold, but
such was the sentiment of the day.

The Americans were understandably outraged. The Colonial Office initially sided with the Americans and set aside the Canadian law, which represented a humiliating setback for the Canadian government in its quest for independence. However, not long after, Macdonald persuaded the Imperial Government to consent to the Canadian bill and commit the Royal Navy to protect the Canadian fisheries.

A Québec provincial election was scheduled for October 14, 1886, the first time since Riel's execution that French-speaking voters would go to the polls. The provincial Conservatives lost the election—but barely—taking 29 of 65 seats. Macdonald realized that his ability to sustain a national coalition depended on keeping Conservative forces alive and vibrant in Québec. "The triumph of the Rouges over the corpse of Riel changes the aspect of affairs ... of the Dominion government completely. It will encourage the Grits and opposition generally; will dispirit our friends, and will, I fear, carry the country against us at the general election."

This gloomy prediction was partly influenced by the strong hand that Liberal Premier Oliver Mowat had in Ontario. But if there was any consolation in Québec, it was that Conservatives remained numerous in the legislature. It was far from a rout.

In Manitoba, the provincial government opposed the railway monopoly given to Canadian Pacific. Macdonald held firm. He was not about to allow his rail line to bleed into the United States. When the Manitoba government rebelled and passed legislation in 1887 creating its own competing Red River Valley Railway, an incensed Macdonald thundered to its Lieutenant Governor Atkins: "Your bankrupt population at Winnipeg must be taught a lesson, even if some of them are brought down to trial at Toronto for sedition." He elaborated on his frustration to his colleagues: "When you reflect on the legislature of 35 members, with a population of 110,000, coolly devoting a million of dollars to build a railway from Winnipeg to the frontier, between two lines owned by the CPR, running in the same direction, one on the east and the other on the west side of the Red River, when there is not enough business for one of the two existing lines, you can understand the recklessness of that body."

Within two weeks of the bill being passed by the Manitoba Legislature, it was "disallowed" by the federal government.

By 1887, more than four years had passed since the last federal election. Macdonald was biding his time, waiting for both the reaction to Riel's hanging and general provincial discontent to dissipate. But he could not avoid the inevitable forever, and the election was called for February 22, 1887.

Despite Macdonald's early predictions of defeat, his party won 122 of 215 seats, earning support from all parts of the country. The Liberals picked up only eight seats nationwide over their tally in 1872. Surprisingly, Macdonald outpolled the Liberals in Québec. Québecers, it seemed, expressed their disapproval in the provincial election, but spared Macdonald when the federal vote was taken. For generations to come, Macdonald would be blamed for the poor showing of Conservatives in Québec, yet his supposed affront to French Canada did not undermine his political career. Nonetheless, the Riel incident was something Liberals would exploit for political advantage for the next century.

Despite Macdonald's and his government's longevity, the situation in Canada looked gloomy. The editorial in the *Mail* newspaper on October 27, 1887 raised serious doubt about the future of Canada.

> Our enormous debt, the determination of the people of the Northwest to break loose from trade and transportation restrictions in defiance of the federal authority; the exodus of population from the North-west and the far larger stream pouring out of the older provinces; and threats of secession heard in the three Maritime provinces; the decline in our exports which are less today by five dollars per head of population than they were in 1873, although since then we have spent no less than $120 million of borrowed money in developing our resources; the gathering of the local premiers at Québec to devise ways and means of allaying provincial discontent and averting provincial bankruptcy—these, to go no further, are phenomena, which, if they presented themselves in any other country, young or old, we should regard as the forerunners of dissolution.

The basic question was whether Macdonald's vision of the confederation of British colonies, designed in large measure to resist an enormous pull of the United States, could be sustained. Would Canada succeed as an independent nation? Was Canada a mistake?

Despite a desire by Macdonald and the colonial office for a strong central government, the provinces had been winning more battles than they lost with the federal government. And citizen allegiance was proving to be more provincial than federal. The size of the provinces, particularly after expansion in Québec and Ontario, added to their power.

Macdonald envisioned provinces of roughly equal population, but seemed helpless when confronted with boundary changes. If he could not stop Ontario from growing, he had to let Québec acquire new lands to maintain balance. Macdonald feared more from provincial boundary readjustment than the other threats to nationhood. "I have little doubt that a great portion of the vast region asked for by the two provinces will be capable of receiving and will receive a large population . . . I look to the future in this matter . . . farther ahead perhaps than I should. But are we not founding a nation? Now just consider for yourself—what a country of millions lying between English Canada and the Atlantic will be."

Macdonald's battles with the provinces continued. In the fall of 1887 the new Québec premier Honoré Mercier announced his intention to call a conference of the provinces to consider "their financial and other relations" with the federal government. The provinces urged revocation of the federal power of disallowance and sought more money from the federal government. Macdonald scoffed at the conference. There was nothing in the Constitution that contemplated such an arrangement and he was not about to give it legitimacy. He would negotiate grievances only with individual provinces. Harper appears to be following Macdonald's lead, and did not hold a full-scale first minister's conference over his first term as prime minister.

Macdonald wanted to retire, however, and was constantly surveying his Cabinet for a successor. He also wanted his Cabinet take more of the load of governance. But whenever Macdonald challenged the Cabinet to develop policy and offer opinions it simply deferred to his judgment. In frustration, he remarked "now this acquiescence is flattering enough, but it does not help me."

Nevertheless, Macdonald opposed what he saw as a North America-centric vision for Canada. Liberals called for a commercial union and unrestricted reciprocity with the United States. To Macdonald, this was an unacceptable first step towards political integration. "It looks like sheer insanity (for Liberals) to propose practically to limit our foreign trade to the United States when there is such an immense opening for the development of our commerce with the rest of the world."

A larger threat to Canada than a debate over foreign trade policy, however, was the cultural divisions within its own borders. Agitator D'Alton McCarthy, a former Tory MP, had been fomenting discord over the use of the French language in Ontario and the West. He wanted Canada to pursue a vision and policies that supported a single national identity: an English one. He helped persuade the government of Manitoba to abolish the French language in public schools. Not long after, the North-West Territories followed suit. But the use of the French language in schools was a right guaranteed by the articles under which these provinces and territories joined Confederation, a right that had been fought for and won by Louis Riel and his followers at a time when the decline of French in the West seemed inevitable.

Macdonald foresaw the inevitable concentration of the French language in Québec and its gradual disappearance elsewhere in Canada. "The people of Québec . . . wisely, I think, desire to settle the lands as yet unoccupied in their province and to add to their influence in eastern Ontario. The consequence is that Manitoba and the North-West Territories are becoming what British Columbia now is, wholly English—with English laws, English, or rather British, immigration, and, I may add, English prejudices."

Macdonald's French-speaking colleagues wanted him to fight for the hard-earned rights of their brethren living outside Québec. But his English-speaking colleagues disagreed. With a divided caucus, Macdonald had to walk a fine line, opting for local self-determination and mutual respect on issues of language. "There is no paramount race in this country; there is no conquered race in this country; we are all British subjects, and those who are not English are nonetheless British subjects on that account . . . we must take great care, Mr. Speaker, that while we are calming the agitation and soothing the agitated feelings of the people of Québec, we are not arousing the feelings of the free men of the north-west by passing a resolution which postpones for an indefinite time, it may be a long period, a question which we can see, from the resolution they have adopted, that they are greatly interested."

When a Liberal member from Québec moved an amendment that abolition of language rights in the North-West Territories was inappropriate, he was supported by every French-speaking member of Parliament and opposed by almost every English-speaking member. Parliament was divided not along the lines of party, but along the lines of race, English and French.

Macdonald offered an unconvincing pretense of national unity after the federal government allowed the North-West Territories more autonomy on language laws. Macdonald had deluded himself into thinking that issues respecting the French language would go away: "Let us forget this cry, and we shall have our reward in seeing this unfortunate fire, which has been kindled from so small a spark, extinguished forever, and we shall go on, as we have been going on since 1867, as one people."

Having responded to problems in the North-West Territories, Macdonald was confronted with new challenges in Manitoba. In 1890, the

Manitoba Legislature unilaterally abolished legal guarantees for the use of the French language in the public school system. The federal government was called upon to disallow the legislation. As in the North-West, Macdonald was opposed to political intervention by the federal government, favouring a local resolution to the issue. Macdonald washed his hands of the matter in this letter to a French language resident of Manitoba: "I am strongly of [the] opinion that the only mode by which the separate school question can be satisfactorily settled in your province is by an open appeal to the courts." The will of the majority, the letter suggests, was stronger than the provisions of the Constitution of the land.

As Macdonald faced domestic challenges, he still sought a better deal for Canada abroad. Increasingly, Canada was frustrated at being represented in the United States by a diplomat from Great Britain. Charles Tupper wrote to Macdonald urging him to take a stand on the matter.

In 1890, Macdonald was 75 and not up for many more battles with Britain or the United States. But despite his age, he did indeed have one more election to fight. He would die in office, he reasoned, fighting for his vision of strong and independent Canada, inextricably linked with Great Britain and firmly independent from the Americans. In a speech he could just as easily have delivered 30 years previously, Macdonald told the nation that he was in a fight to save it from the vultures in the United States who wanted Canada to fail. "Every American statesman covets Canada. The greed for its acquisition is still on the increase, and God knows where it will all end. . . . We must face the fight at our next election, and it is only the conviction that the battle will be better fought under my guidance than under another that makes me undertake the task, handicapped as I am, with the infirmities of old age."

Parliament was dissolved on February 2, 1891 and Macdonald went to the people with the same national policies and ballot questions that had defined his career. "The question which you will shortly be called upon to determine resolves itself into this: shall we endanger our possession of the great heritage bequeathed to us by our fathers, and submit ourselves to direct taxation for the privilege of having our tariff fixed at Washington, with the prospect of ultimately becoming a portion of the American Union? . . . As for myself, the course is clear. A British subject I was born, a British subject I will die."

On March 5, 1891, Macdonald won his sixth election, besting his Liberal opponent, Québec native son Wilfrid Laurier, 117 to 90. The Liberals won Québec by the narrow margin of 33 to 27. Once again, the shadow of Riel affected Macdonald, even if minimally.

But Macdonald's electoral win was soon eclipsed by his rapidly declining health. A few short months after his election victory, on Friday, May 29, 1891, a sombre Sir Hector Langevin addressed the House of Commons. "I have the painful duty to announce to the house that the news from Earnscliffe just received is that the First Minister has had a relapse, and that he is in a most critical condition. We have reports from the medical men in attendance on the right honorable gentleman, and they do not seem to believe that he can live many hours longer."

The legislature was adjourned. A hush fell over the nation. Macdonald died at 10:15 p.m. on Saturday, June 6, 1891.

The passing was difficult for friend and foe alike. Sir Wilfrid Laurier responded for the Liberal party. "Mr. Speaker, I would have wished to continue to speak of our dear departed friend, and spoken to you about the goodness of his heart, the witness of which I have been so often, but I feel that I must stop; my heart is full of tears. I cannot proceed further."

Macdonald's testament declared, "I desire that I shall be buried in the Kingston cemetery near the grave of my mother, as I promised her that I should be there buried."

Since its founding, Canada had been guided by only one man. His vision, his determination, and his skill forged a nation and sustained its unity. Had the gristle of Canada, as he once called it, hardened into bone? Had Macdonald created a country that could survive his passing?

SECTION II

THE FOLLOWERS

CHAPTER 4

JOHN ABBOTT:
THE RELUCTANT LEADER

I hate politics, and what are considered their appropriate methods. I
hate notoriety, public meetings, public speeches, caucuses, and everything that
I know of that is apparently the necessary incident of politics—
except doing public work to the best of my ability.

MACDONALD COULD NOT BE REPLACED. Indeed, the Tory party would go through its second, third, fourth and be on its fifth leader before the next election was held. Dwarfed by Macdonald or burdened by ill health, none of these men made much of an imprint on the Tory party, although three sat in Macdonald's chair as prime minister of Canada. They are best known as the followers to Macdonald.

The unenviable task of following Sir John A. was given to John Abbott. He accepted this duty reluctantly. However, ill health and a brief tenure prevented him from making much of a mark as prime minister.

John Joseph Caldwell Abbott was born on March 12, 1821 in St. Andrew's, Lower Canada, moving to the Montréal area in 1843, where Abbott's father, once an Anglican missionary, became secretary of McGill College.

John Abbott was a brilliant student with a prodigious work ethic. He was admitted to the Québec bar in 1847 and made dean of the McGill Law faculty in 1855 where he served until 1880. One of Abbott's more notable students was a future Liberal prime minister, Wilfrid Laurier.

In addition to a career in academia, Abbott was one of the highest paid lawyers in the province, a help in raising four daughters and four sons with his wife Mary. His business success included leading and building the Canada Central Railway, a key link in the trans-continental line. From 1885–1891, largely while sitting as a senator and Cabinet minister, Abbott served on the board of directors of the Canadian Pacific Railway. He was a rich man who collected rare books and cultivated orchids.

When Abbott attended the first ever meeting of the Law Society of Lower Canada on July 24, 1849, he signed the "Annexation Manifesto," a document that promoted a political union between Canada and the U.S. Abbott eventually changed his mind on annexation and was occasionally asked to explain what he called his "outburst of petulance." Later in life he vehemently opposed trade reciprocity with the Americans because he feared it might lead to annexation. He further demonstrated his loyalty to the Empire during the Trent Affair of 1861, a conflict between Great Britain and the United States that barely avoided open war, by personally financing 300 recruits for the British.

Abbott first ran for office in 1857 as a candidate for Canada East's Legislative Assembly in the riding of Argenteuil, Québec. He lost the election, but contested the results on the basis that "men without property qualifications and from outside the constituency had been enticed to vote for his opponent." Abbott was awarded the seat after a lengthy trial. Over the next three years he served as Canada East's solicitor general.

Initially hesitant about Confederation over fears the English-speaking minority in Lower Canada would lose political power to the French-speaking majority, he successfully petitioned the Fathers of Confederation to protect the electoral borders of twelve English constituencies in Québec. However, Abbott thought enough of his French countrymen to learn their language, which he used to his advantage in both politics and business.

In 1864, Abbott defended the Confederate agents who raided three banks at St. Albans, Vermont before escaping to Canada. Abbott persuaded the court that it lacked jurisdiction and the prisoners were set free. After their re-arrest, Abbott convinced the judge that the raiders were belligerents in a Civil War and not criminals.

Abbott was elected to the House of Commons in 1867 to represent his home riding of Argenteuil. He won re-election or was acclaimed as the MP for Argenteuil on five subsequent occasions. In addition to serving as an MP in Macdonald's first government, Abbott was legal advisor for Sir Hugh Allan, president of the Canadian Pacific Railway. Abbott drafted the CPR charter and the monumental contract to construct Canada's national railway. As Allan's solicitor, Abbott had in the safe of his legal office the telegram from Prime Minister Macdonald to Sir High Allan pleading for funds for the election campaign. Abbott reportedly tried to minimize the impact of the Pacific scandal by tampering with evidence and attempting to influence the testimony of a potential witness.

On May 12, 1887, Abbott was summoned to the Senate, where he was made House Leader and a Cabinet member without portfolio. Later that year he was elected mayor of Montréal, where he was praised by his colleagues on city council for his tireless work. He ran unopposed for his second term as mayor, but declined to run for a third despite a petition, signed by most of the City Council and some five hundred prominent citizens, urging him to run. Abbott was actively engaged in good community works, was a founder of the Art Association of Montréal, helped to establish the Protestant Institution for Deaf-Mutes and for the Blind, and was a supporter of public libraries.

In 1891, Macdonald appointed Abbott president of the Privy Council. At the time, Macdonald told Sir John Thompson, "When I am gone, you will have to rally around Abbott; he is your only man." Powerful words, especially since they were uttered to Thompson, a leading contender to succeed Macdonald. Hours before his death, however, Macdonald is reported to have had a change of heart and to have told Thompson that Abbott could not be the prime minister because he was "too damned selfish."

Had the Liberal-Conservative party been in opposition, the caucus would likely have determined who was best qualified to succeed Macdonald. But because the party held power, it was the constitutional prerogative of the governor general to invite a member from the Conservative benches to become prime minister. The governor general could consider the views of the past leader and senior Cabinet ministers, but he was not beyond using his own judgment. Indeed, until the mid-1920s, Governors General enjoyed a remarkable degree of latitude in choosing the prime minister.

The governor general considered Sir Hector Langevin, Macdonald's French-Canadian deputy, but rejected him because of a scandal in his ministry. Sir Charles Tupper, then the Canadian High Commissioner to London, was offered the position, but declined. Sir John Thompson was next in line, but he also declined because he did not believe the country was ready for a Catholic prime minister. In fact, Thompson had converted from Methodism, making him even more controversial. Thompson recommended Senator John C. Abbott.

Although Abbott had been elected mayor of Montréal, he was not popular among French Canadians. He understood the party was divided and that the issues of the day would challenge him. Abbott was ready to exit political life, and twelve days before Macdonald's death he explained why. "I hate politics and what are considered its appropriate methods. I hate notoriety, public meetings, public speeches, caucuses. Why should I go where doing honest work will only make me hated and my ministry unpopular, and where I can only gain reputation and credit by practicing arts that I detest, to acquire popularity?"

Eventually Abbott relented, musing that the reason he was chosen to take over the prime ministership was because he was "not particularly obnoxious to anybody." He saw himself as the candidate who would least divide the party, taking office in ill health at the age of seventy. He was the first Canadian prime minister born in British North America, and one of only two to lead from the Senate. Other than Brian Mulroney, Abbott is the only Québecer to lead the Conservative party. Unlike Mulroney, however, Abbott could make no claim to affinity with French Canadians. His initial political assignment was to protect the rights of the English in Québec.

With Abbott leading from the Senate, Thompson held the fort for the government in the House of Commons. In fact, many observers saw Thompson as the de facto prime minister, biding his time to earn the confidence of his countrymen until they could overlook his religious conversion. Leading from the Senate amplified Abbott's challenge. He was detached from the cut and thrust of the elected House of Commons and too old to invigorate a factionalized party. The caucus—divided on lines of religion, ethnicity, and personal loyalties—could not be bridled by a mere mortal.

In the one year, five months, and ten days he held office, Abbott dealt with much of the government business left over from Macdonald's tenure. Abbott had no grand vision, but responsibly advanced government business in areas of civil service reform, criminal code amendments, and trade relations with the Americans. He also pressed for an attaché to the British mission in Washington who would be responsible for Canada's affairs. In short, Abbott was a caretaker prime minister who took on the difficult task of providing stability at the outset of the post-Macdonald era.

Abbott's most impressive accomplishment in office was the record number of Conservative wins during his time in office. He increased the party's majority by 13 seats, winning 42 of 52 by-elections. That record of by-election success remains unmatched in Canadian political history. But he was not much of a retail politician. Dignified yet grim, he never made a speech in public while holding office and preferred to play a quiet game of chess rather than attend caucus meetings.

After one year as prime minister, Abbott attempted to hand the reins over to Thompson, but the anti-Catholic faction of the party resisted. The issue of succession became imperative when Abbott fell severely ill with stomach cancer in August 1892, and was told by his doctors that he would die without rest. Abbott went to England to seek medical treatment, then resigned in December, without ever facing the country in a general election. He returned to Canada and died the following year.

Abbott is unknown to most Canadians and is rarely mentioned in the history books. His successor, John Thompson, explained why. "Sir John Abbott's great qualities of brain and heart, his great qualities of statesmanship, his great abilities and his great desire to serve this country will never be fully understood by the Canadian people because his career as first minister was too short to have made much of a mark on Canadian history. Perhaps Abbott will best be known simply as the prime minister who took on the impossible task of succeeding the Old Chieftain Macdonald."

CHAPTER 5

SIR JOHN THOMPSON: THE CATHOLIC

We look forward to (women's suffrage) as one of the aims which are to be accomplished in the public life of Canada, because the Conservative party believes that the influence of women in the politics of the country is always for good.

WHILE SIR JOHN ABBOTT GOVERNED from the Senate, Macdonald's true successor led the government in the House of Commons. John Sparrow David Thompson was the first of a long string of national politicians to come from Nova Scotia. Like Abbott before him, his time in office was cut short, abruptly so.

Born in Halifax in 1845, Thompson initially shadowed his father's career, working as a trial reporter before pursuing a career in law. Politics beckoned in 1878, and he won a provincial by-election in the riding of Antigonish. Thompson's reputation as a hard-working, honest, and fair-minded lawyer earned him a place in the Cabinet of Premier Holmes as attorney general. He had a reputation of being straight with electors and acted responsibly with provincial finances. He was also a loving and dedicated family man who heaped affection on his nine children.

In Ottawa, Thompson made a positive impression on Prime Minister Macdonald because he resisted blaming the federal government for provincial ills. Macdonald appreciated his responsible tone. Then as now in Atlantic Canada, it was difficult to find provincial politicians who would take responsibility for economic malaise rather than blame the federal government.

Premier Holmes was widely regarded as a bully. Thompson wanted out of his Cabinet, and the vacancies in Nova Scotia's Supreme Court caught his eye. But in 1891, fellow Nova Scotian and Macdonald loyalist Charles Tupper begged Thompson to lead the Nova Scotia Conservatives into the next provincial election. When Holmes resigned, Thompson agreed to assume the provincial leadership on the condition that he be handed the judgeship afterwards.

Macdonald was desperate to keep Nova Scotia's Conservative government afloat and suggested that he and Thompson go to the polls at the same time to confuse voters into thinking they were supporting the more popular federal Conservatives. The strategy didn't work. Thompson failed to win a majority of the seats and happily left politics to take up his seat on the Supreme Court of Nova Scotia's bench. Though not elected premier by the people of Nova Scotia, he briefly held the title after Holmes resigned.

Thompson was more comfortable in law than politics, an environment he called "slime." The perks and privileges of office were of no appeal to Thompson and unlike many of his colleagues sought no personal enrichment from politics. "I detest the idea of being beastly rich." He was happy sitting on the bench, and repeatedly refused Macdonald's invitations to enter his Cabinet as minister of justice. However, public encouragement proved overwhelming and on October 16, 1885, Thompson won the federal riding of Antigonish in a by-election.

Even the Liberal-friendly newspaper, the *Windsor Nova Scotia Courier*, applauded Thompson's win, commenting, "We congratulate the people of Nova Scotia upon having in the Dominion Cabinet a gentleman of Mr. Thompson's ability and untiring energy. He is an excellent speaker, a clear-headed lawyer, and will undoubtedly fill the office to the satisfaction of the country." In his welcoming address, even federal Liberal leader Edward Blake was reluctant to criticize Thompson: "I congratulate the honourable incumbent . . . he begins his Federal career at once as a Minister . . . No greater compliment could be paid a public man." In response, Prime Minister Macdonald would prophetically note that "even the honourable gentlemen opposite will admit before the session closes the correctness of my selection and choice."

It didn't take Thompson long to have a significant impact on parliamentary debate. In his maiden speech in the House, he rose on the matter of the execution of Louis Riel, asserting that Riel's treasonous behaviour deserved the death penalty. Instead of allowing passion and emotion to dominate his speech, as some members opposite had done, Thompson systematically picked apart his opponents' logic. He quoted the English Commission on Capital Punishment, arguing that "in cases of treason accompanied by overt acts of rebellion, assassination or other violence, the extreme penalty must be maintained." The speech, though a lengthy two hours, maintained the keen interest of every member of the House. After the speech, a Liberal motion to condemn the government's decision failed by a landslide, and Thompson was praised for his keen understanding of the issues and his persuasiveness in debate.

As minister of justice, Thompson revolutionized the law of the Dominion in two areas: the Criminal Code and copyright law. After consulting with legal scholars and responding effectively to the criticisms of other parliamentarians, he compiled the first Canadian Criminal Code, some 350 pages long. Working one hundred hours a week, he shepherded this legislative behemoth through Parliament, a substantial accomplishment because the new code replaced a disorganized series of enactments by various Parliaments. This Criminal Code was innovative. For instance, it allowed a suspect to testify on his or her own behalf and it gave juveniles special treatment under the law. It also represented a major achievement in nation-building because it further distinguished Canadian law from British law. Perhaps with the Riel incident in mind, Thompson's Criminal Code prevented judges from punishing those who committed crimes as a result of insanity. In summarizing the code, Thompson said: "It will deal with offences against public order, internal and external; offences affecting the administration of the law and of justice; offences against religion, morals and public convenience; offences against the person and reputation; offences against the rights of property and rights arising out of contracts, and offences connected with trade."

Thompson's second major area of interest as minister of justice was copyright law. He was troubled by the Imperial Copyright Act of 1842, which permitted copyright throughout the empire to any book published in the United Kingdom. Since it was more convenient for British publishing houses to supply copyrights to American publishers than to their Canadian counterparts, the Canadian market was flooded with American and British publications. This crippling of the nascent Canadian publishing industry worried Thompson, who argued that only books published in Canada should have copyright in Canada. His essentially protectionist and nationalist legislation, though praised by Parliament, was rejected by the British Commons.

Thompson did not seek to lead the Conservative party after Abbott's resignation, fearing his religious conversion was politically fatal. True, the
conversion which followed his marriage to Annie Affleck on July 5, 1870, was
initially an affront to many Tories. But following Abbott's resignation,
Thompson's colleagues believed that his even-handed approach would overcome any hesitation voters might have and Thompson was sworn in as prime
minister on December 5, 1892. Thompson—and later Charles Tupper—are
the only prime ministers in Canadian history to have also held the position of
provincial premier.

Thompson did not take his government in any dramatic new directions.
He was an advocate of the monarchy and sustained trade policies that
favoured Britain and her colonies and discriminated against the Americans.
He took this position when, as prime minister, he hosted the first intercolonial conference held outside of the United Kingdom.

Thompson was a Canadian nationalist, but agreed with Macdonald that
total independence from Britain would make Canada vulnerable to annexation by the United States. America's aggressive interventions in Hawaii
troubled him. There was a small faction within the Liberal party, known as
the Continental Union Association, that enthusiastically promoted political
ties to America. But Thompson thought that Canada should not consider
separating from the monarchy until the country was stronger and its population reached 50 million. Thompson also took the lead on the issue of
women's suffrage. "We look forward to it as one of the aims which are to be
accomplished in the public life of Canada, because the Conservative party
believes that the influence of women in the politics of the country is always
for good. I think, therefore, that there is a probability of the franchise being
extended to the women on the same property qualifications as men." This
contrasted with the view of Macdonald. When confronted by an angry
woman who thought the system unfair. Macdonald replied: "You cannot vote
and I cannot conceive."

Thompson was unable to resolve the dispute over the use of the French
language in the schools of Manitoba, where Roman Catholics wanted to
retain a separate school board, as Québec did. Western Protestants were
opposed. This issue would haunt subsequent Conservative prime ministers,
none of whom had Macdonald's deft touch for dealing with matters of cultural, ethnic, and linguistic sensitivity.

In late 1894, Thompson took a tour of Europe. Early in the trip the five
foot seven, 225-pound prime minister famously climbed the equivalent of 40
storeys to the top of the Dome of St. Peter's Basilica in Rome. His doctors

ordered rest. But only days later, Thompson died of a heart attack during lunch at Windsor Castle, where he was being sworn into the Imperial Privy Council. His term as prime minister had lasted only two years and six days.

He was the third Conservative prime minister to die in or be driven from office by poor health since the election of 1891. Like Abbott, Thompson never fought an election as leader. Queen Victoria returned Thompson to Halifax with full honours aboard the battleship HMS *Blenheim* and he was buried at Holy Cross Cemetery in Halifax.

CHAPTER 6

MACKENZIE BOWELL:
THE ORANGEMAN

*It is such a comfort to shake hands with honest men, after having
been in company with traitors for months.*

MACKENZIE BOWELL RANKS as one of Canada's least-respected prime ministers. When Sir John Thompson died suddenly in 1894, the leadership of the Conservative party was thrust upon Bowell by a meddlesome governor general. Prime minister for less than sixteen months, and one of only two to lead from the Senate, Bowell is known chiefly for inspiring a revolt in his caucus and for fumbling the Manitoba School crisis.

Mackenzie Bowell was born in Rickinghall, England on December 27, 1823. When he was nine, his family moved to Canada to join relatives in Belleville, Ontario. As a young man, Mackenzie Bowell worked for the *Intelligencer*, Belleville's local newspaper, and later became owner and editor. In 1847 he married Harriett Louisa Moore with whom he had four sons and five daughters. Bowell was a military man whose active duty included responding to Fenian disturbances. He retired from service in 1874 with the rank of lieutenant-colonel.

Bowell was also a proud member of the Orange Order, founded in 1795 in Ireland to commemorate William of Orange's victory at the Battle of the Boyne in 1690. In 1870, Bowell rose to the top rank of Grand Master. While the Order was widely subscribed outside Québec, it was not a unifying force in the nation—its members were not sympathetic to either Catholics or French Canadians. Macdonald was once a member of a similar order, although Orangemen took a dim view of his alliances with politicians from Québec. Likewise, Bowell found that his personal views were sometimes in conflict with those of the larger membership. While seeking election to the Upper Canada legislature in 1863, Bowell spoke out against allowing Catholics their own school boards. But once the law was passed he did not speak out or resist its implementation, despite requests from the more outspoken ranks of Orangemen for continued resistance. As far as Bowell was concerned, the bill had passed fairly and he refused further struggle. Dissatisfied, his fellow Orangemen arranged for his defeat at the polls.

Bowell accepted the Conservative nomination again in 1867. His opponent had voted against legislation to connect Belleville with Marmora by rail, causing Belleville Mayor Billa Flint to endorse Bowell. Keeping an eye on local issues helped Bowell to win seven consecutive general elections in Hastings North from 1867 through to 1891.

Bowell was a staunch Conservative, but by no means a blind partisan supporter of Macdonald. In his early days as a parliamentarian, Bowell often voted against government legislation. But Bowell's habit of speaking out only when voting against the government gave him the reputation of being a grumbler.

In 1874, Bowell was openly critical of his government after Thomas Scott, an Ontario Orangeman, was executed by a Métis firing squad under the leadership of Louis Riel. Bowell petitioned for Riel's expulsion from Canada and called it a "disgrace" that Macdonald thereafter consulted with Riel's representatives. Though strongly opposed to Macdonald's handling of Riel, and disdainful of Catholicism, Bowell was still an essential ally to Macdonald. With one in five voters from Ontario belonging to the Orange Order, Macdonald could not sustain his political coalition and ignore the group Bowell represented. Bowell served in Macdonald's Cabinet, holding portfolios for railways and canals, and later for trade and commerce.

After Macdonald's death in 1891, Bowell considered retiring, saying, "I do not care how soon I am relieved of the cares of official life of which I am getting tired." But he continued in Abbott's Cabinet, and when Thompson succeeded Abbott, he appointed Bowell government leader in the Senate as a reward for defending Thompson against religious attacks. Such a defence was unexpected from an Orangeman.

As Thompson's minister of trade and commerce, Bowell travelled to Australia to discuss trade between Canada and the colonies. During the visit,

Bowell secured host status for Canada for the next colonial conference.

While Thompson was on his fateful trip to Europe in 1894, the 71-year-old Bowell was the acting prime minister. Tories debated among themselves who should succeed Thompson. Sir Charles Tupper, the high commissioner to England, was their initial choice, but the governor general, Lord Aberdeen, held Tupper in low regard and rejected him. Lady Aberdeen especially disliked Tupper. She felt he was far too conservative, and disapproved of his reputation as a philanderer. Other potential candidates were also rejected. Then there was Bowell. He had served as acting prime minister, although, by convention, this fact often precludes consideration. His reputation as a fierce Protestant and ardent anti-Roman Catholic made him popular within certain segments of party ranks, particularly in Anglo-Québec. Officially, Bowell claimed no interest in the leadership, but the events that unfolded indicate otherwise. Lord Aberdeen met with him to discuss the future of the country. Bowell withheld information about the poor regard in which he was held by caucus. Lord Aberdeen then consulted with Sir Frank Smith, a Roman Catholic senator, about Bowell's capability. Sir Frank approved the choice, and Lord Aberdeen used his constitutional authority to ask Bowell to form a Cabinet.

Though much of the caucus did not want Bowell as leader, Lord Aberdeen made his own decision. By contemporary standards, the authority the governor general had in political affairs seems scandalous. Not so then, given the governor general's constitutional responsibility to ensure a stable and responsible government. And Lord Aberdeen clearly relied on his wife for advice, if not direction.

Bowell's appointment met with lukewarm reviews in the press. The Toronto *Globe* said: "The criticisms upon him must simply be that he is not a broad enough or a strong enough man for the position . . . He has the views and habits of thought of the average party man. Nobody need fear that as Premier he will be the author of any great political crime."

Bowell attempted to emulate the Old Chieftain. But Bowell was no Macdonald. He lacked Macdonald's intelligence, insight, wit, charm, and patience. More important, he lacked leadership skills and the respect of his caucus. His term as prime minister was doomed from the beginning.

The Manitoba Schools Question colours Bowell's entire term as prime minister. The Manitoba Act, passed in 1870, granted equal rights to French Catholic and English Protestant schools. Within a decade, however, the makeup of the province had changed dramatically. Many Métis had left and immigrants from Québec were far outnumbered by English-speaking

Protestants from Ontario. In 1890, Manitoba Premier Thomas Greenway passed the controversial Manitoba Schools Act, which eliminated public funding for Catholic schools, effectively ending French as an official language in the province. Catholics wanted the federal government to pass remedial legislation to restore the public funding that Greenway's government abolished. The Supreme Court of Canada ruled that the Manitoba Schools Act violated the earlier Manitoba Act. But in January 1895, a Judicial Committee of the Privy Council in Britain overruled that decision. At this point, Bowell still had the prerogative to intervene, as provided in the British North America Act.

This political landmine challenged Bowell beyond his ability. Québec strongly supported entrenched Roman Catholic rights. Protestant Ontario supported Manitoba. From the Senate, Bowell could not control the debate in the House of Commons, and the business of the nation ground to a halt. Bowell decided to restore the abridged language rights through remedial legislation, but to delay action for six months, hoping the English-French divisions within his own Cabinet could be overcome. But that delay only inflamed the debate.

Bowell's minister of justice, H.C. Tupper, insisted that Manitoba pass new legislation restoring language rights and that Parliament should then be dissolved and go to the people over the issue. Bowell hesitated. Tupper resigned. In a stinging resignation letter, he cited Bowell's poor leadership and cowardice in the face of an election: "I cannot be a party to a course dictated by the dread of the people. . . . We can . . . do nothing effectively or properly without a direct mandate from the people."

Eventually, Tupper would be brought back into the fold on the condition that if negotiations with Manitoba failed, federal legislation would be introduced.

Anglo-Québec journalist and author Robert Sellar fiercely opposed giving public funds to French Catholic schools, and inflamed French-speaking Canadians with his writing: "Force upon the Northwest separate schools, and the point of the wedge is entered which will involve the West in the troubles and difficulties that perplex Québec. The granting of separate schools concedes the principles that those to whom they are granted are entitled to special legislation apart from their fellow subject, and that dangerous principle once conceded, it logically requires that the legislature also provide for them, separate institutions for deaf mutes, for the blind, the poor, the sick, the insane, for dealing with the criminal call, all to be controlled not by the State, but by the hierarchy—the State merely providing the funds."

The issue was so divisive that a general election was widely anticipated. Bowell hesitated and stalled, however, and by the end of the year had still given no clear indication that he intended to dissolve Parliament.

Clinging to hopes of a negotiated agreement with Manitoba, Bowell allowed political tensions in his caucus to explode. Minister of Agriculture Auguste-Réal Angers resigned in July 1895. The Tories were defeated in two crucial by-elections in Québec. Increasingly, Québecers viewed the Tory party—now led by an Orangeman—as insensitive to their needs and aspirations. First Louis Riel and now the Manitoba Schools crisis. The mistakes made by Bowell over language rights were part of a series of missteps by Conservative leaders that condemned the party to weak or non-existent support in the province of Québec for generations to come.

On January 2, 1896, Parliament re-opened. On January 4, seven ministers resigned. Bowell famously labelled this group of mutineers "a nest of traitors." On January 7, one of the seven, George Eulas Foster, rose in the Commons and requested the prime minister's retirement. Bowell, who was watching from the wings, went into the Opposition benches and shook hands with the members there, saying loudly, "It is such a comfort to shake hands with honest men, after having been in company with traitors for months."

Bowell told the governor general that the seven men opposed remedial legislation and that their opposition to party policy could be resolved. But the so-called "traitors" despised Bowell. This crisis of confidence could not be resolved.

The constitutional limit on the life of the government was at its end and a general election had to be called by April 26, 1896. But if Bowell couldn't organize a Cabinet, the governor general would be forced to call an election before then. When Bowell failed to unite his caucus, he offered his resignation to Lord Aberdeen.

Lord Aberdeen refused the resignation, in the hopes that the remedial legislation issue could be worked out. When the seven members found out what Bowell had said to Lord Aberdeen, they explained they were not anti-remedialists. Fearful that the governor general would call upon the Liberals to form a government, the seven returned to Bowell's government. The Tories remained in power. But H.C. Tupper expressed his disappointment over their lack of political integrity: "We all turned in like sheep into the fold, at the very rumour of Liberals being asked to form government."

Six of the seven were brought back into Cabinet; H.C. Tupper was left out in the shuffle, replaced by his father, Sir Charles Tupper. Bowell continued to work with Manitoba, but it was clear that no remedial bill would pass before the April 26 deadline.

On April 27, Bowell's resignation was accepted and he returned to his duties in the Senate where he remained leader until 1906. He also returned to the *Intelligencer*, after having given up its control in 1878. Bowell continued to work well into the twilight of his life, until his death from pneumonia in 1917 at the age of ninety-three.

Conservatives often blame Lord Aberdeen for the disunity that followed the death of Sir John Thompson. Indeed, history would have been entirely different had Aberdeen's distaste for Charles Tupper not affected his judgment, or had he consulted with members of the Cabinet before selecting Bowell to succeed Thompson. Aberdeen made a difficult situation far worse by foisting Bowell upon the Conservatives.

But it is Bowell who is to blame for the fiascos of his administration. Lacking vision and leadership skills, he was unable to make important decisions in a timely manner. And he never gained the confidence of his caucus. When political capital was needed during the Manitoba Schools crisis, he had none to spend.

Bowell left his party in tatters. The Tories had gone through three leaders since the death of Macdonald without once facing the voters in an election. Now they needed a fourth. The Tory government was at the end of its constitutional mandate. And there was no reason for optimism with an election required within months.

CHAPTER 7

CHARLES TUPPER: THE LAST VETERAN OF CONFEDERATION

For the honour of having one single representative in the British Parliament, the three hundred and fifty thousand inhabitants of Nova Scotia would not only be called upon to suffer an enormous amount of taxation, but the person of every man in the Colony would be liable to be drafted at an hour's notice to fight the battles of Great Britain in India, or any other part of the world.

A FOUNDING FATHER OF CONFEDERATION with one of the most illustrious careers in Canadian politics, a notorious rake known to many as "The Ram of Cumberland," Sir Charles Tupper is a great character in Conservative history. His reign, however, was surprisingly short. The oldest prime minister, at seventy-four, ever to assume office, Tupper was never prime minister to a sitting Parliament and held onto the job for a mere sixty-nine days, the shortest term of any Canadian leader.

Charles Tupper was born on July 2, 1821, near Amherst, Nova Scotia. His father, when not tending the family farm, served as a Baptist pastor. Charles studied medicine at the University of Edinburgh, where he met and married Frances Morse. Though he would later be known as a womanizer, the marriage produced six children and spanned sixty-six years. The Tuppers established their home in Halifax, where Charles was an affluent and prominent doctor, presiding as president over the Medical Society of Nova Scotia from 1867–1870.

Tupper ran for election in 1855 for the Nova Scotia Parliament in Cumberland County, defeating Liberal Joseph Howe, who would later be best known as the chief opponent of Confederation. Tupper's defeat of Howe was exceptional in an election where the Liberals won a tremendous majority.

Once in office, Tupper wanted to eliminate all religious prejudice and decreed that the Conservative party "must reverse its hostile attitude towards the Roman Catholics; that the true policy was equal rights to all, with regard to race or creed." Tupper was a great believer that citizens of the new world should cast aside any religious or ethnic differences and work together with the resources available. After the Conservatives lost the 1859 election, largely because of sectarian divisions, F.C. O'Brien, Archbishop for Halifax, wrote to Tupper, calling him "the champion of equal rights for Catholics . . . Defeat with honour unstained is more glorious than victory purchased by the sacrifice of principle." The Conservative party returned to power in 1863. When Premier Johnstone resigned the following year, he was succeeded by Tupper.

Tupper was a visionary who in these pre-Confederation days shared Macdonald's passion for connecting and strengthening the British North American colonies. He initiated talks with New Brunswick and Canada to create an inter-colonial railway. Although these talks ultimately failed, Tupper later became a major player in the construction of the Canadian Pacific Railway. As premier, he championed railroads within Nova Scotia, from Truro to Pictou Landing, from Annapolis Royal to Windsor. He also made great strides in public education. In 1864, he helped pass the Free Schools Act to subsidize public education. The following year an amendment was introduced to allow funding for separate schools that conducted after-hours religious studies. This allowed the Catholic school boards to receive funding.

In 1866, Tupper engaged his former political foe in a battle over Confederation. Joseph Howe had published an article entitled *Confederation Considered in Relation to the Empire*, where he argued against a union with Canada.

> [The Maritime Provinces] owe no allegiance to Canada . . . they naturally desire to preserve the great privileges they enjoy, and to develop their resources without being involved in entanglements difficult to unravel, and from which, once enthralled, there may be no escape . . . [Canada's] proper mission would seem to be to cultivate amicable relations with her neighbours—to fill up her sparsely populated territory—to eliminate from her political system the anachronisms of dual leadership and double majorities, to control her Irish and Orange

factions, and to fuse into one race by patient tact and mutual forbearance, her Saxon, Celtic, and Norman elements.

Howe believed that through confederation, the Maritime provinces would be sucked into Canada's ethnic and linguistic problems with little to no financial benefit. At the time, the Maritimes were confident in their abundant natural resources. Howe had no objections to the current representational system for the colonies in the British Parliament and considered debating Confederation to be "wasting precious time with schemes to dismember the Empire."

Tupper quickly responded to Howe's article and took his case directly to the people of Nova Scotia:

> Mr. Howe proposes to reduce the British Colonists to the position of a Russian 'serf.' It would be impossible to conceive of a scheme more oppressive or unjust. For the honour of having one single representative in the British Parliament, the 350,000 inhabitants of Nova Scotia would not only be called upon to suffer an enormous amount of taxation, but the person of every man in the Colony would be liable to be drafted at an hour's notice to fight the battles of Great Britain in India, or any other part of the world.

The Maritime conference that ultimately became the meeting place for Confederation was a Tupper inspiration. He saw strengthening and unifying the Maritimes as a prerequisite to negotiations on a larger union.

Tupper was one of only eleven Fathers of Confederation to attend all three conferences in Charlottetown, Québec City, and London. Future Liberal leader Wilfrid Laurier described Tupper's contribution to Confederation: "I believe I speak my mind and speak the fair judgment of my countrymen when I say that, next to Macdonald, the man who did most to bring Canada into Confederation was Sir Charles Tupper."

Tupper had no fear of engaging Howe in debate. In the winter of 1864, delegates from the Maritime provinces were to meet in Charlottetown to discuss the possibility of a union of the Maritime colonies. Tupper wanted Joseph Howe present: "The first man I invited to attend, as I valued the strength of his influence." Howe, unable to participate, was enthusiastic about the project, and assured Tupper that he "would do everything in his power to carry out any policy [the delegates] adopted at Charlottetown." But when discussions about a Maritime union expanded to include

Confederation, Howe led the formidable forces of opposition.

Although few contributed more to Confederation than Tupper, he graciously set aside personal honour and status to ensure the success of the Dominion. As Tupper told the story, Macdonald was in a difficult position during the formation of the first government. He had asked Tupper to join his Cabinet, but this would have upset the religious and regional balance necessary for harmony in Macdonald's first government. "I went to [Thomas D'Arcy] McGee and said: 'The union of the Provinces is going to end in a fiasco unless we give way. We are the only two men who can avert that calamity.' I then proposed that he should stand aside in favour of Sir Edward Kenny, of Halifax, as the representative of Irish Catholics, and that I should likewise surrender my claims to a portfolio."

McGee agreed to this proposal and Macdonald offered Tupper a governorship, which he declined. "I would not take all the governorships rolled into one. I intend to run for a seat in the Dominion Parliament."

In the first Canadian federal election, Howe's anti-Confederation party won every seat in Nova Scotia, except for one—the seat won by Conservative Sir Charles Tupper. Howe sailed to England to request that Nova Scotia be removed from Confederation. He insisted he had the backing of "eight hundred men in each county of Nova Scotia who will take an oath that they will never pay a cent of taxation to the Dominion." Tupper—in bold response—made the same trip to offer the opposing view.

Tupper was determined to make Confederation work. He rebuked Howe's inflammatory claims by arguing that without taxes there would be no funds for necessary public services like roads and schools. Eventually, however, Tupper seduced Howe with a more pragmatic quid pro quo: "If you will enter the Cabinet and assist in carrying out the work of Confederation you will control all the provincial patronage and you will find me as strong a supporter as I have been opponent." Having secured an agreement, Tupper was able to send word to Macdonald that Howe was ready to abandon his anti-Confederate stance.

Tupper joined Macdonald's Cabinet on June 21, 1870, as president of the Privy Council. Two years later he became the minister of inland revenue. During the federal election that year, Tupper bragged of "not a single anti-confederate being elected." Following the Pacific Scandal, Tupper was one of only two Conservatives elected to the House from Nova Scotia in 1874.

His attacks on the Liberals were not all partisan bluster. Tupper genuinely opposed Prime Minister Mackenzie's tepid railway policies, in particular the unwillingness of the Liberal government to make the investments necessary to connect the country by rail. Tupper was also upset that Mackenzie was contracting the project out to non-Maritimers, which ran counter to the economic benefits that Confederation had promised.

Tupper made the railway an issue in the 1878 election, where Conservatives won government and took 14 out of 21 seats in Nova Scotia. When Tupper was made minister of public works, completing the railway was his top priority. But when he pressured a contractor on cost, and the quality of the work declined, a displeased Macdonald signalled to his inner circle that Tupper should not be seen as his successor.

In 1882, Tupper was made high commissioner to London. Four years later, Macdonald wanted Tupper to return to Canada to become finance minister and assist in the coming election. Macdonald was gloomy about the prospects and wrote to Tupper on June 21: "We are not in a flourishing state in the present state of public opinion . . . We have rocks ahead, and great skill must be exercised in steering the ship." Tupper wrote back that he heard positive reports from Nova Scotia and was of the opinion that he was not needed there. On January 11, 1887, Tupper received an insistent cablegram from Macdonald: "Come out. I sent message before. Must have miscarried.—Macdonald." Tupper dutifully responded on January 25, telling Macdonald he was at his disposal and would do whatever he thought would best serve the interests of the country.

Macdonald appointed Tupper finance minister on his return and Tupper once again helped to carry Nova Scotia in the 1887 election, with the Tories winning 14 of 21 seats. In 1888, Tupper resigned from cabinet and once again returned to his post in London.

Though a proud member of the British Empire, and a founding member of the Imperial Federation League in 1884, Tupper opposed colonies contributing money to the empire without receiving anything in return. He pushed instead for "a policy of mutual preferential trade between Great Britain and her colonies [that] would provide the tie of mutual self-interest in addition to the purely sentimental bond which now exists."

On Macdonald's death, Tupper paid tribute to the Old Chieftain in a letter to his son, Sir Charles Hibbert Tupper: "It is a source of great satisfaction to me in this sad hour to feel that through good and evil report I have stood at his side, and in sunshine and in storm have done all in my power to sustain and aid him in the great work to which he has, since we first met, devoted so successfully all his great powers. He has left a bright example for us to follow; let us endeavour to emulate him as far as we can, and we will deserve well of our country."

Tupper was overlooked as a candidate for prime minister by the governor general, who nominated Abbott, Thompson, and Bowell in succession. But as many in Cabinet long expected, the torch was ultimately, if belatedly, passed to Tupper, who had long had the support of Agnes Macdonald to succeed her late husband. Tupper recalled the short period that led to his taking over the government: "Asked by the recalcitrant members of the [Bowell's] Cabinet to assume leadership, I refused, declaring that I would not do so except at the request of the [Prime Minister] Mackenzie Bowell. It was not until all efforts on his part at reconstruction had failed that he requested me to become leader of the party."

After winning a seat in the House of Commons through a by-election in Cape Breton in February 1896, Tupper became the leader of the government in the House of Commons. He believed that the promise made to Catholic minorities had to be honoured and introduced a remedial bill to resolve the Manitoba Schools crisis. But it was too little too late. Parliament was dissolved, Bowell resigned and Tupper reluctantly became prime minister of Canada on May 1. Tupper, along with Kim Campbell (1993) and John Turner (1984), are the only prime ministers ever to hold the position without Parliament being in session.

The election, which finally came on June 23, 1896, was fought over one issue: the Manitoba Schools question, which divided the Tories and hurt them in French Québec. Liberal leader Sir Wilfrid Laurier, whose approach to national politics closely emulated Macdonald's, conveniently suspended his views on free trade and adopted Tory "national policies" of protection for Canadian industry. Laurier proposed dealing with the Manitoba schools crisis with reasonable accommodation and compromise; the so-called "sunny way." What this ultimately meant was striking a deal with Premier Greenway that allowed some religious instruction within the public schools but did not restore separate schools.

The Liberals won 117 seats, the Tories 86, in the 213-seat legislature. A strong Conservative showing in the Maritimes was more than offset by a drubbing in Québec, where the Liberal native son won 49 of 65 seats. It mattered little to Québecers that Tupper led the charge for remedial legislation to protect minority language rights, saying bravely in Toronto, "We must do right even if it means the downfall of the Conservative party." Tupper actually won the popular vote, but Lord Aberdeen refused to confirm his ministerial appointments because of the seat totals and the Conservatives were out.

During Tupper's term as leader of the Opposition a key issue was Canada's support for Britain's war in South Africa: "I pressed [Prime Minister

CHARLES TUPPER: THE LAST VETERAN OF CONFEDERATION   99

Laurier] in the strongest manner, and pledged him the support of my party to the policy of sending a Canadian contingent, and was fortunately able to induce him to change his attitude in regard to that important question."

Tupper did not fare much better in his last election than he had in his first. In 1900, the Liberals gained several seats despite Tory gains in Ontario. Tupper explained the losing strategy that meant the end of his leadership. "In Ontario, where Sir Wilfrid at the opening of the poll in 1900 had a majority of twelve, I reversed that, and at the close had a majority of eighteen seats, but it was not enough to counteract the Liberal landslide in the Province of Québec. In that election, I sustained my first personal defeat, as I devoted practically nearly all my time to the campaign in Ontario."

Tupper moved to Bexleyheath in England to live with his daughter Emma, and remained there for the rest of his days, though he returned to Canada numerous times to visit his sons. He was appointed to the British Privy Council in 1907, where he was an advocate of closer economic ties between the two nations. He died on October 30, 1915, at the age of ninety-four. He was eulogized the following day in the Toronto *Globe*: "It goes without saying that he was endowed with a more than ordinary equipment of physical vigour, corresponding to his intense intellectuality and his exceptional willpower. He was always a strenuous antagonist in a political contest, giving no quarter and expecting none . . . there will endure in the general memory only the inherent greatness of the man and the undoubted value of the services he rendered to his country during a long, strenuous, and story career."

Tupper's successor, Sir Robert Borden, remarked: "In Sir Charles Tupper passed away the greatest living Canadian . . . Premier of his native Province, Minister of Finance, Minister of Railways and Canals, High Commissioner of Canada in London, Prime Minister of Canada, no Canadian has had a more distinguished public career."

SECTION III

ROBERT BORDEN

CHAPTER 8

BACK IN GOVERNMENT

*I accepted the leadership with the stipulation that in the meantime
a committee should be appointed to select a permanent leader of
greater ability, experience and aptitude, one who would, perhaps, desire
the position from which I shrank.*

QUIET AND SERIOUS, a scholar and a lawyer, Robert Borden entered
politics on the condition that he would serve one, and only one,
term in Parliament. No one could have foreseen then that Borden
would become the second longest-serving Tory leader in Canadian history
and the third longest-serving Conservative prime minister. He led Canada
through the World War I and substantially advanced Canada's standing as an
independent nation.

Robert Laird Borden was born on June 26, 1854 in Grand Pré, Nova
Scotia. His father Andrew was a farmer and the local stationmaster. The
young Borden was more adept at his studies than farm chores. Largely self-
taught and proficient at Latin, he became assistant master at his school at the
age of fourteen. After a one-year stint at a New Jersey school board, he
returned to Nova Scotia and settled in Halifax, a bustling city of 30,000.

Ambition took Borden from teaching to the practice of law, then a profession pursued through apprenticeship. He was admitted to the bar in 1878
at the age of twenty-four. Borden stood at the top of his class for the Nova
Scotia bar exams, a notch ahead of Charles Hibbert Tupper, son of Nova

Scotia's most influential Father of Confederation. Borden was impatient with life. During his legal apprenticeship, he recalled: "I determined to accomplish much before the time came around for I did not wish to be two and twenty and an ignoramus. Well the time has come and gone, and how little has been accomplished. The chariot wheels of time have rolled all too swiftly for my tardy efforts."

Success came early to the highly-motivated Borden. As a partner in the well-known firm of Graham and Tupper, he argued important cases before the Supreme Court of Canada. He earned as much as $30,000 per year practising law, about one hundred times the average wage of the day. Borden became president of the Nova Scotia Barristers' Society and had a hand in establishing the Canadian Bar Association.

His was not an easy and carefree life. Borden's prodigious work effort and accomplishments were fuelled by a disposition to anxiety and nervousness. "During a week, sometimes ten days, of continuous counsel work I would be in a condition of such extreme nervous tension that I can hardly act for sleep. Curiously enough, this condition did not in the least manifest itself while I was in court."

Though there were Liberals in the family tree, Borden became a Conservative in 1886 after W.S. Fielding, a Liberal, was elected premier of Nova Scotia, promising secession from Canada. Borden believed in Confederation.

When Borden was asked by Sir Charles Tupper in 1896 to run for the federal Conservatives in Halifax, his initial response was negative. He reluctantly agreed on the condition that he would serve only one term in Parliament. Borden won his seat, in the first election with Tupper at the helm of the party, but the Conservative party found itself on the opposition benches for the first time in eighteen years. Since Confederation, the Tories had grown accustomed to governing, holding power for 24 of 29 years. Adjusting to Opposition was not easy.

What Borden lacked in charisma, style, and eloquence he compensated for with seriousness, and diligence. He immediately found himself on the front bench of the Conservative opposition, arguing against the perils of patronage and for a professional civil service.

Borden had married Laura Bond in 1889. They had no children. Borden wrote to his wife, who had remained home in Nova Scotia, to reassure her that his time in Ottawa would be short-lived: "This political life seems to me most stale and flat and unprofitable. I am convinced that it is absolutely unsuited to a man of my temperament and the sooner I get out of it the better. It is a miserable irregular life that one has to lead and I am more than sick of it. Unless I alter my mind greatly, nothing will induce me to again become a candidate."

Despite his complaints, Borden was once again a candidate in the election of November 7, 1900. He won, but Tupper, his seventy-nine-year-old leader, did not. Tupper lost not only the general election, but placed third in his Cape Breton riding. Tupper wanted the leadership to go to one of his supporters. Since the party was not in power, and a new leader would not automatically become prime minister, the governor general would not be called on to choose the Conservative leader. This gave Tupper significant latitude in choosing his replacement.

Charles Hibbert Tupper boldly wrote to Borden on his father's behalf to offer him the position. Borden declined saying, "It would be an absurdity for the party and madness for me." Undeterred, in February 1901 the younger Tupper nominated Borden at a caucus meeting, which came as a surprise to the seventy-nine caucus members. Sensing this was the direction the retiring leader wanted to go, the caucus quickly fell into line. Borden initially declined, but after a unanimous vote in caucus he agreed to accept the position of leader for a period of one year, with, as Borden put it: ". . . the stipulation that in the meantime a committee should be appointed to select a permanent leader of greater ability, experience and aptitude, one who would, perhaps, desire the position from which I shrank." The stipulation was not widely advertised because, Borden said, some of the older members thought doing so might diminish his authority.

Initially, Borden was not optimistic about what he could accomplish as leader. "The Conservative party was at the nadir of its fortunes and Sir Wilfrid Laurier was then approaching the zenith of his power and influence."

Borden was not a well-known figure in politics or elsewhere. He was steady and quiet, not a performer or entertainer in the style of Macdonald or Laurier. However, he was a man of well-considered policies and had the strengths of thoroughness and intelligence. He saw his role more as teacher and educator than political combatant.

During the second Boer War (1899–1902), Canadians were divided: most English Canadians supported Great Britain, while a majority of French Canadians wanted no part of any Imperial war. From the opposition benches, Borden said little, but it was clear from his statements that he did not believe Canada should blindly accept a call from Great Britain to take up arms. Borden advocated a strong and independent voice for Canada in international affairs. He was not satisfied with Canada merely being consulted on such matters by Her Majesty's Government. On this issue, he was ahead of most members of his party.

On matters of immigration, Borden was cautious. In his early days as Opposition leader Borden said, "Canada should look to quality rather than quantity ... [new citizens] should be of the same or similar race to those which now inhabit the country, and should be at least of a strain which will readily assimilate with our own people." Quietly, he agreed with the prevailing sentiment that the ethnic mix of French and English founders should not be diluted, adding that Canada should not become "a land of refuge for the scum of all nations."

In the general election of 1904, the Liberals increased their majority by 9 seats. Borden was able to win a bare majority of seats in Ontario, but the party was clobbered elsewhere. The significant Tory weakness was Québec, where the Liberals took 53 of 65 seats. Another embarrassing blow was being shut out in Borden's home province of Nova Scotia. Having lost his Halifax seat, Borden offered his resignation as leader, which was rejected by the Tory caucus. He returned to Parliament after being acclaimed in a by-election in the Ottawa riding of Carleton.

THE DEFEAT STUNG, and Borden took a new and more vigorous approach to politics. He severed his ties with his Nova Scotia law firm, moved to Ottawa and built a new team of Conservatives by enticing talented business leaders into the world of politics. Despite the renewal, however, few thought the plodding and serious Borden could overtake the popular and charismatic Laurier. Borden hammered away at the prime minister over Liberal corruption and indecisiveness, but hardly made a dent in Liberal fortunes. In any event, overtaking Laurier in Québec was unlikely. Borden realized that he could not win a contest based on leadership or personality. He needed an issue.

Meanwhile, Borden took aim at corruption in politics. In 1907, he proposed a 16-point platform focused largely on cleaning up the dishonest practices of government. This plan included a prohibition on corporate political donations and appointment by merit in the public service. Senate reform included a revamped appointment process. Borden also called for the nationalization of telegraphs and telephones and proposed free rural mail delivery, a bold move that had many free-enterprising Conservatives scratching their heads. Laurier thought enough of the platform that he adopted most of Borden's policies as his own.

The Conservatives tasted their third successive defeat, and Borden's second, in the 1908 election. The Tories gained ten seats nationwide over 1904, but won only 12 of 65 seats in Québec. That gave the Liberals, with no Bloc Québécois to sweep up nationalist Québec ridings, an insurmountable and seemingly impenetrable advantage.

Despite winning a majority of seats outside of Québec, the knives in caucus were being sharpened. Few leaders can survive successive political defeats. Many saw Borden as better suited to a courtroom than the jousting ring of politics. But as he repelled attacks from within, Borden's determination and confidence grew. He realized if he could mend internal party divisions, in part by building bridges with Conservative leaders from the provinces, then he had a shot at beating Laurier. He was—albeit belatedly—developing the toughness he needed to win government.

Laurier and Borden clashed in the House over Britain's request for financial support from Canada to bolster the Royal Navy. Imperialists, who tended to be Conservative, wanted the government to heed the request. Others, particularly from Québec, urged the government to reject Her Majesty's demands. In search of a compromise, Laurier proposed the Naval Service Bill in 1910 to create the Royal Canadian Navy, which would be placed at the disposal of Great Britain in times of war. The compromise satisfied few and created opponents to Laurier on many fronts. Nor was there any strategic military advantage to creating what came to be known as Canada's "tin pot navy."

Nationalist politicians from Québec, such as Henri Bourassa, opposed the policy and became fierce foes of Laurier. Borden jumped at the chance to build alliances in Québec, even if it was with nationalists. It was something Macdonald would have done—and Brian Mulroney and Stephen Harper. As a portent, Conservatives won a stunning victory in a Québec by-election in November 1910.

The more significant policy divide between Liberals and Conservatives, however, was over reciprocity in trade with the United States. Western farmers, tired of paying duties to protect manufacturing interests in Eastern Canada, demanded duty-free trade. After visiting the West on a cross-country tour, Laurier responded by endorsing free trade. It was a vision for Canada that was decidedly different from the more nationalistic approach Macdonald had advocated.

The mood in the Tory caucus was dejected. Borden wrote in his memoirs: "Many of our members were confident that the government's proposals would appeal to the country and would give it another term of office. . . . The Western members were emphatic in their statements that not one of them would be elected in opposition to reciprocity. One of them declared that he did not vote against the government's proposals."

The 1911 election became a virtual referendum on free trade. Borden needed an issue to overcome Laurier's charm and charisma, and now he had it. "No Truck nor Trade with the Yankees" was the Tory rallying cry. Borden upped the ante, arguing that reciprocity was about far more than trade policy: it undermined Canada's relationship with Great Britain, substituting in its place a political union with United States: "We are standing today at the parting of the ways . . . we must decide whether the spirit of Canadianism or Continentalism shall prevail on the northern half of this continent . . . with Canada's youthful vitality, her rapidly increasing population, her marvellous material resources, her spirit of hopefulness and energy, she can place herself within a comparatively brief period in the highest position within this mighty Empire. This is the path upon which we have proceeded—this is the path from which we are asked to depart."

Going into the campaign, Laurier was confident. He mistakenly assumed the Conservatives would divide themselves over free trade. He even called the election within three years of the previous campaign, far earlier than required.

Laurier wanted to debate the merits of free trade on economic terms, but he was overwhelmed by Canadian nationalists who saw the agreement as the beginning of the end of Canada. The emotional side of the debate was sparked by the American Speaker of the House of Representatives Champ Clark, when he explained his reasons for supporting a trade agreement with Canada: "I hope to see the day when the American flag will float over every square foot of the British North American possessions."

For the first time, Borden had Conservative provincial premiers on his side. His alliance with Henri Bourassa in Québec, who thought Laurier an imperialist, proved decisive. It mattered little to Bourassa that Borden and the Tories were arguably closer to the Empire than Laurier.

Eastern business interests and disgruntled Québecers turned against Laurier, as Conservatives took 132 seats to the Liberals' 85. Free trade gave Liberals a sweep of seat-poor Alberta and Saskatchewan. They also did well in the Maritimes. But the Liberal stranglehold on Québec ended as Borden won 28 seats. And the Tories won 71 of 86 seats in Ontario. The last time the Tories had won an election was in 1891, twenty years before. Robert Borden reclaimed the mantle long held by Macdonald.

UNFORTUNATELY FOR BORDEN, it was not a good time to be in government. The boom of the previous decade was replaced by recession. Poverty and unemployment were pervasive. Canada's confident and welcoming immigration policy, which brought 400,000 immigrants to the country in 1913, met with unrest and public opposition. The railways that relied on immigrants for revenue began to bleed red ink, bringing government loan guarantees into play. As governments are apt to do, Borden blamed his predecessors for the mess.

Borden also had an inherently difficult coalition to hold together. Keeping Québec nationalists aligned with imperialist Conservatives was something only Macdonald had mastered. Laurier was annoyed that the Conservatives had made an alliance with the nationalists in Québec and did whatever he could to disrupt the unity of the government.

Borden recognized the contradictions in his naval policy and he chose to deal with them while his government was still new. There was no clear way to unite the various factions that existed in caucus over the issue. Borden gathered evidence when he travelled to Britain in 1912 where he visited Winston Churchill, the First Lord of the Admiralty, and, at that time, a member of England's Liberal party.

On his return, Borden reported to the House of Commons that, because of trouble brewing in Europe, the need for military support was urgent. Many members of Borden's Cabinet rejected this idea, as did virtually all Liberals. On December 5, 1912, Borden's government introduced the Naval Aid Bill, which called for a contribution of $35 million to the British Navy. The debate in the House went around the clock with no end in sight. In a fit of frustration, Borden introduced a motion for closure, limiting the duration of the debate, and the bill passed. But the Liberal Senate refused to pass the bill, challenging Borden to call an election on the issue. Besides dealing with a weak economy, Borden was also apprehensive about his government's paltry support in Québec, and party members elsewhere were upset over Borden's reluctance to use his powers of patronage. It was not the time to call an election.

In June 1914, Borden was knighted, the last prime minister to be so honoured. (In 1919 the non-binding Nickel Resolution was passed asking that British honours not be given to Canadian-resident citizens. The motion was introduced by William Foger Nickle, a Conservative, ironically while Borden was still prime minister.) In 1914, that honour was one of the few bright spots on Borden's political horizon.

CHAPTER 9

WORLD WAR I

*More than 30,000 (soldiers) are under the sod, having died that we may live
and that our inheritance may be preserved. To desert them now on the ground of
quibble that they were merely volunteers would be as ignoble an evasion of moral
responsibility as any country in all history was guilty of.*

THE MOST EMPHATIC CASE for increased military support for the
empire was made on June 28, 1914 when Archduke Franz Ferdinand,
heir to the Austro-Hungarian throne, was assassinated. This quickly
set in motion the events that led to the outbreak of World War I.

On July 31, just days before Great Britain declared war, Borden assured
the British government that "Canada would put forth every effort and . . .
make every sacrifice to ensure the integrity and maintain the honour of our
empire." This was a promise of mobilization only because the regular
Canadian army of about 3,000 men had little to offer in defence of the realm.

When Britain declared war in early August, spontaneous parades
erupted across Canada. Canadians yet to enlist marched in their street
clothes, signifying their readiness to serve king and country. Young men in a
fit of rampant patriotism saw glory in war and were convinced they would
fight for the winning side. Those who cheered these young volunteers
thought a swift victory was inevitable.

Borden quickly put Canada on a war footing. Cabinet ministers, who
had been dispersed across the land to gain insight into the prospects for

110

a fall election, hurried back to Ottawa, where a decision was made to place two Canadian ships immediately at the disposal of the Admiralty and to reconvene Parliament for August 18. Canada would also place its forces under the strategic command of the king, while the Canadian government remained responsible for financing its contribution to the war effort. Cabinet moved quickly on communication and banking measures. All this was on an emergency basis without legislative support. The British government insisted that German Canadians serving in the army reserve be arrested and detained. Borden was hesitant to do this: "Having invited them to become citizens of this country, we owe to them, in the trying circumstances in which they are placed, the duty of fairness and consideration ... We have absolutely no quarrel with the German people, but with the military and the Kaiser."

Borden assured Canadians of German descent that they would not be targeted, believing they would be ". . . absolutely true to the country of their adoption." "Enemy aliens" would be protected in Canada, as long as they quietly went about their lives.

The government needed powers to respond with speed and flexibility to the inevitable crises. Cabinet approved the Emergency War Measures Bill on August 17, the day before Parliament was set to resume, giving the government the power to do whatever it needed to do in the event of war, invasion, or insurrection for the defence and welfare of Canada.

The governor general, the Duke of Connaught, was King George the Fifth's uncle and, unlike the members of Borden's Cabinet, an experienced soldier. Though his title of commander-in-chief was only ceremonial, the governor general presumptuously assumed powers beyond that. Rankled, Borden promptly informed the governor general's military secretary that, "The Duke takes up too much of our time and he has a false impression as to his status and powers as Commander-in-Chief."

Liberal leader Wilfrid Laurier pledged to assist the government in every way possible. "I have but one declaration to make: to aid these measures we are prepared to give immediate assent . . . if England were ever in danger, it would be the duty of Canada to assist the motherland to the utmost of Canada's ability ... it goes in the classical language of the British answer to the call to duty: 'Ready, aye ready.'" Borden, however, realized that the fever pitch of patriotism would not be sustained. Burdened by thoughts of the supreme sacrifices that lay ahead, he remarked: "Days may come when our patience, our endurance and our fortitude will be tried to the utmost ... let us see that no heart grow faint and that no courage be found wanting."

But there was no mistaking the prime minister's commitment to the task at hand. Borden said it was a moral and just war and Canada was duty bound to shoulder her share of the burden: "We stand shoulder to shoulder with Britain and the other British dominions . . . We do not shrink from the sacrifices . . . But with firm hearts we abide the event."

To finance the war effort, tariffs and duties were increased on coffee, sugar, spirits, and tobacco. Some Liberals thought these measures unfairly burdened the poor and argued that taxing incomes directly should be instituted. Liberal MP Michael Clark made the case in Parliament: "Instead of increasing the duties which bear upon the poor, the government would have the support of the great mass of the people of this country behind them if they had put a good fat tax upon incomes."

Income tax aside, there was not much debate or dissension on what Canada should do. By August 22, four days after the war Parliament first met, the legislation Canada needed to be at war cleared the House of Commons. The Senate passed the bills the day they were received and Royal assent was immediate.

Much of the logistics and planning for the war effort was placed in the hands of the minister of the militia and defence, Sam Hughes. In his teens, Hughes had received a medal for his role in defending Canada during the second Fenian Raid. He was elected member of Parliament for Victoria North in 1892 and held the seat in seven subsequent elections, during which he served in the Boer War in South Africa. Hughes could be difficult: he was dismissed from the army as a discipline problem for exposing what he saw as the incompetence of military command. Brash and brimming with confidence, Sam Hughes did things his way. He was under the illusion that enemies from within his government were working against him. Borden agreed, but told Hughes his two big enemies were his tongue and pen.

Rather than expand existing facilities, Hughes began the mobilization and training campaign by establishing a new army base at Valcartier, Québec, a bold new venture that created confusion and inefficiency. Hughes enjoyed the limelight and claimed that he was loved by millions and despised by only a few. But the few included those around the Cabinet table. Borden realized early on that Hughes would be a problem, but chose to protect his friend and supporter, fearing that a dismissal or reprimand would undermine confidence in the government. Borden would regret that decision.

A burst of patriotism, new government contracts, and increased activity in the economy invariably help a sitting government. Some ministers thought the early days of the war constituted an ideal time for a general election.

Others thought an election would be opportunistic and dangerous, and Laurier's complete support of government policy certainly took some urgency away from an election call. On October 14, Borden discussed an election with his Cabinet. Three members were opposed, including future party leader Arthur Meighen. There was concern that the lesser support in Québec for the war would be exposed, causing a rift in national unity. When some Cabinet ministers threatened resignation if an election was called, Borden listened.

Borden began to tour the country to bolster support for the war effort. In the early days there was a sense in the country that the war would be short-lived and Canadian boys would soon return victorious. Borden warned otherwise. He refused to speculate on when the war might end and what the final complement of troops would be. "I prefer to name no figure. If the preservation of our Empire demands twice or thrice that number (100,000) we shall ask for them. Canada will answer the call as readily and as freely as its men had volunteered since August . . . The cause for which we have drawn the sword shall be maintained to an honourable and triumphant issue."

Because the war was not popular in Québec, Borden brought more French Canadians into the inner circle of his Cabinet to help carry the message. He also emphasized the volunteer aspect of Canada's contribution at the outset of the war, adding that, "There has not been, there will not be, compulsion or conscription."

In Canada's willing and meaningful contribution to the British Empire, Borden saw an opportunity to assert independence. "There is only one respect in which we in Canada have not yet attained our full share of self-government, and that is with regard to foreign relations . . . I may see the day, and you young men will certainly see it, men of Canada, Australia, South Africa and the other Dominions will have the same just voice in these questions as those who live within the British Isles."

Canadian soldiers were ready to fight in spirit, but were poorly equipped, with substandard and defective rifles and boots ill-designed for war conditions. Often, Canadian-made equipment was discarded at tremendous waste, replaced by military goods used by British forces. When the Germans began to attack with chlorine gas, there was no immediate or effective response. Battle lines were drawn by yards and casualties mounted by the thousands. Intelligence was inadequate. Borden lamented that, "The continued long list of casualties is very depressing."

Borden did what he could to focus his public disgust at the German leadership. On the German sinking of the passenger ship Lusitania on May 7, 1915, which resulted in 1,198 civilian casualties, an inflamed Borden charged, "The whole incident is so horrible and brutal that the world cannot fail to realize the fiendish degradation of the German mind."

The number of men in the military increased from 50,000 to 100,000 and then to 150,000. Qualifications to join the forces were lowered. Married men no longer had to prove the consent of their wives to join.

Despite Borden's hopes, in the early period of the war there was limited communication between the Canadian and British governments. Borden was determined to represent Canadian interests directly to the British government and he secured an invitation to attend a British Cabinet meeting, the first time anyone not a British minister had taken part on the same footing as one of its members. Borden claimed new ground for Canada: "The old order has in some measure passed away. Once and for all it has been borne in upon the hearts and souls of all of us that the great policies which touch and control the issues of peace and war concern more than the people of these islands."

But the most lasting impression from his trip was not meeting the powerful in London. It was his visit to the frontline troops, where he attempted the impossible: to see every wounded soldier. "The courage and patience of the wounded are most pathetic. This war is most horrible. Occasionally I have come upon operations in the hospitals which almost unnerved me . . . It was difficult to restrain my tears when I knew that some poor boy, brave to the very last, could not recover."

By October 1915, Canadian forces numbered 250,000 men. In December, Borden suggested increasing the force again, this time to a staggering 500,000, a number designed to impress and to inspire victory. Borden suggested the number in a blind act of faith, without regard to military planning or the realities of recruitment. His parliamentary secretary, R.B. Bennett, was astonished. "I am afraid that we cannot possibly look at 500,000."

Despite his earlier progress, Borden remained troubled over Canada's limited opportunity to influence Britain's war plans. "If there is no available method and if we are expected to continue in the role of automata, the whole situation must be reconsidered. Procrastination, indecision, inertia, doubt, hesitation, and many other undesirable qualities have made themselves entirely too conspicuous in this war . . . Another very able Cabinet minister spoke of the shortage of guns, rifles, munitions, etc., but declared that the chief shortage was of brains."

Borden lost confidence in the British to formulate a meaningful plan for consultation. He saw it as his duty to impose Canada's will through his leadership.

The early years of the war saw little political controversy and continued cooperation with Laurier and the Liberals. They agreed that for six by-elections the incumbent party would run unopposed, although this was hardly a concession on Borden's part as it returned five Conservatives and only one Liberal. The budget in 1915 included a host of measures to increase revenues, but once again rejected the notion of an income tax.

When allegations of patronage and contract abuses were launched against the government, Borden threw two members of his government out of the party. Borden was serious about ethical contracting practices and established the War Purchasing Commission to support the commitment.

When the time for an election drew near, the government raised the issue of a soldier's right to vote. Borden believed that if someone was old enough to fight for his country he should also be able to vote. Laurier objected. "The soldier, in our economy, is no more entitled to favour than any other class of the community. The man who digs in the trenches of the sub-way is just as much entitled to favour as the man who takes to the trenches in France." In the end, the Military Voters Act, passed in 1917, permitted every soldier, male and female, to cast a ballot.

INEVITABLY, THE TRUCE between Liberals and Conservatives came to an end. Borden thought it fair game for the Opposition to criticize domestic policy, even war contracting abuses, but that it damaged morale and sustained the enemy when political disagreements over the war made headlines. A disgusted Borden wrote to the governor general: "Has your attention been directed to the attacks upon the personal honour, motives, sincerity, honesty and loyalty of members of the government which have appeared during the past three months in the Liberal press throughout Canada?"

As 1915 drew to a close, the governor general suggested amending the British North America Act to extend the term of the government until the end of the war. Borden rejected the suggestion, offering instead an extension of the interval between elections. It was a clever move. If the offer was rejected, Laurier, not Borden, would be blamed for an election during a time of war. Laurier's Liberals went on the offensive, taking aim at government mismanagement, profiteering, and patronage.

On the night of February 13, 1916, a fire engulfed the Parliament buildings, killing eight people, including a Liberal member of Parliament. Borden was in his office late that night and was led to safety. Determined to continue in the aftermath of the tragedy, he announced that the House of Commons would meet the next day at the Victoria Memorial Museum, where it was business as usual, except that Laurier agreed to amend the British North America act to enable Parliament to sit for one more year. In the process, Borden gave evidence he was a determined leader who would not be shaken by setbacks and tragic events.

The Business War Profits Tax was introduced as a financial measure, but also to counter growing public resentment over some companies gaining advantage from the war while others were suffering. On the domestic front, the perennial problems of the railways demanded attention, and here Borden had more trouble dealing with his own Cabinet than he did with Laurier. A royal commission had been struck, but in the meantime the government offered a bailout of some $18 million to the railways. Borden appointed three directors to the boards of the recipient companies to keep a watchful eye.

Another domestic issue was prohibition. The Woman's Christian Temperance Union had been lobbying government officials with varying degrees of success for decades. Rather than argue prohibition on moral grounds, they now claimed patriotism as the basis for a ban on alcohol, that all of the nation's resources be dedicated to supporting the troops. Borden's Cabinet was reluctant to legislate, preferring to leave the matter to the provinces. However, the government responded to the prohibitionist forces by making it illegal to transport liquor across provincial boundaries into a prohibitionist province.

Like every previous administration, Borden's government had to deal with the issue of French-language education. This time the battleground was Ontario where Regulation 17 decreed that provincial funding would only be available to schools that taught in English. The Ottawa Separate School Board refused to follow the policy and some schools were closed. By order of the Ontario Supreme Court in April 1915, the schools reopened under the administration of a government-appointed commission. There was intense pressure on Borden from Franco-Ontario and Québec backbenchers to intervene and disallow Regulation 17. Borden recognized the injustice, but noted his French Canadian ministers, who offered no advice or alternatives, were not helpful in finding a solution.

Fortunately for Borden, the Liberals were also divided on the question. A motion was placed before Parliament, "[T]hat this house, especially at this time of universal sacrifice and anxiety, when all energy should be concentrated on winning the war, while fully recognizing the principle of provincial rights and necessity of every child being given a thorough English education, respectfully suggest of the legislative assembly of Ontario the wisdom of making it clear that the privilege of the children of French parentage being taught in their mother tongue be not interfered with."

Borden worried the resolution, "could do no good, and might do much harm." Laurier took a more principled position. He wanted the issue brought out in the open and wanted Parliament to assemble "some sheet anchor with which to fight the nationalists." Laurier wanted to make a strong statement and encourage the Government of Ontario to restore the historical rights of French-speaking Ontarians. Borden meekly replied that it was a matter for provincial jurisdiction, worrying such a statement would only inflame relations between English and French.

The resolution was defeated. Borden won the day with 11 English-speaking Liberals supporting his laissez-faire stand, while five French-speaking Conservatives voted with Laurier. Although his position was sustained in the House, Borden was dejected by the debate. He saw war as a time to unite the country; not a time to highlight divisions: "In the fierce flame of this war, in the ordeal of sacrifice which it entailed, the strong elements of the Canadian nation will learn the better to understand each other, and through that understanding will be welded into a more perfect and splendid unity than ever before."

A hopeful sentiment, but not one Borden could carry in French-speaking Canada where his French-speaking colleagues thought it inconsistent that Borden would act on prohibition, but not on language. The French press wondered why French-Canadians should fight a war overseas when their real battles were in Canada, more specifically Ontario. Once more, Québec was slipping away from the Conservatives.

Accusations of contracting abuses in military purchasing were directed at Sam Hughes. Borden agreed to launch an inquiry into the matter and it turned out that large commissions were indeed received on some contracts, but not by Hughes. Nonetheless, Borden admonished Hughes and called him, "Wrong-headed and as stupid as ever."

Hughes sent an impertinent letter to Borden. This was the final straw for Borden. His reply was direct and cutting, accusing Hughes of disrespect and disregard for authority: "(Your attitude is) . . . wholly inconsistent with and subversive of the principle of joint responsibility upon which constitutional government is based . . . I regret that you have thus imposed upon me the disagreeable duty of requesting your resignation as Minister of Militia and Defence."

In the time it took for Borden to jettison Hughes, the Toronto *News* offered that Borden "suffers fools too gladly."

Meanwhile, war casualties were outstripping enlistments. Reaching a troop level of 500,000 was questionable. The recruiting effort, largely in the hands of volunteers, was decentralized, inefficient, and unprofessional. Many openly speculated that Borden's promise of "no conscription" would have to be reviewed. With the exception of Québec, recruiters across Canada were calling for a draft and recommending the first step in this process, a *registration* of qualified men. Borden was concerned and cautioned a colleague with this sober warning: "Registration means in the end conscription. And that might mean civil war in Québec."

Registration proceeded under the watchful eye of R.B. Bennett. The National Service Board met in Ottawa between October 9–12, 1916. Within a short period, an inventory was established and registration cards were sent to every male citizen of Canada. For those who wanted conscription, registration was not enough. For those who feared it, it was too much. Borden tried unsuccessfully to walk a fine line: "The idea was to make an appeal for voluntary National Service which would render unnecessary any resort to compulsion . . . I hope that conscription may not be necessary, but if it should prove the only effective method to preserve the existence of the state and of the institutions and liberties which we enjoy, I should consider it necessary to act accordingly."

Borden was convinced he could persuade French Québec of the need for a total dedication to the war effort. "There is not now, nor will there ever be in the future, any issue between the two races in Canada which cannot, and of right, should not be amicably and equitably settled." But such grand public statements were not supported by private words and deeds. Indeed, Borden told Sir Charles Hibbert Tupper that he was determined to follow the course he deemed necessary: "The vision of the French-Canadian is very limited. He is not well informed and he is in a condition of extreme exasperation by reason of fancied wrongs supposed to be inflicted upon his compatriots in other provinces, especially Ontario. It may be necessary to resort to compulsion."

As casualties mounted, however, the recruiting drive stalled. Registration had little impact on volunteerism. As it was, the size of the Canadian military was putting pressure on the Canadian labour force at home, with farmers and business leaders complaining about a lack of workers. This complaint had little impact on Borden, although he understood that he was losing the support of farmers who depended on their sons to run family farms.

The country had divided along lines of policy and principle more than of party. Joseph Flavelle, a successful businessman who became chief executive of the Imperial Munitions Board, first raised the idea of a coalition government in a speech to the Ottawa Canadian Club in December 1916. He argued that a coalition government would bring new efficiency to decision-making and a tighter focus on winning the war. Borden was not initially attracted to the idea. "So far as the war is concerned I believe the present government can carry it on more effectively than would be possible under the administration of a coalition government . . . The attitude of Laurier on bilingualism made coalition with him almost impossible. . . . (But a coalition) was hardly ever possible, until it was inevitable."

A continuing frustration was Canada's lack of involvement in military planning, strategy, and execution. Borden learned about the progress of the war the same way other Canadians did, from the press. In 1916, British Prime Minister Lloyd George told his House of Commons that Canada deserved a place at the decision-making table: "We must have even more substantial support from (Canada) before we can hope to pull through. It is important that they should feel that they have a share in our councils as well as our burdens." In February 1917, Borden attended "special and continuous meetings of the War Cabinet."

Canada had earned its seat at the table. By January 1917, there were 70,000 casualties, almost 11,000 dead after heroic battles at Vimy Ridge, Hill 70, Bourlon Wood, Passchendaele, and Ypres. Borden made the point directly to Lloyd George. "The Dominions have fought in the war upon the principle of equal nationhood . . . consecrated by the efforts and sacrifices of the Dominions' soldiers."

When the Governor General's term was set to expire, Borden asserted that the next appointment should not be done "without full consultation with us." He went further: "I am inclined to think the time has come, or at least is fast approaching, when a Canadian might with advantage be selected for such a position." Borden had thought of Laurier for the position. The British government thought otherwise and appointed the Duke of Devonshire.

But, expecting to be received as a partner in the War Cabinet, Borden was jarred by his experience. Some of Lloyd George's ministers were heard to say dismissively of colonial representatives, "When they are here, you will wish to goodness you could get rid of them." Lloyd George himself briefed the leaders of the Commonwealth countries and said, "Now what is it necessary for us to do? The first thing is this: we must get more men." This blunt assessment showed Borden why he was invited.

Borden's mature reaction to disrespect at the Imperial War Cabinet earned him the admiration of Lloyd George: "(Borden is) statesmanlike . . . the very quintessence of common sense. Always calm, well balanced, a man of cooperating temper, invariably subordinating self to the common cause, he was a sagacious and helpful councillor, never forgetting that his first duty was to the people of the great Dominion he represented, but also realizing that they were engaged in an Imperial enterprise and that an insistent and obstructive particularism would destroy any hope of achieving success in the common task."

Borden carried with him a number of positions that influenced the War Cabinet. While some at the table sought a limited and negotiated peace with Germany, both Lloyd George and Borden advocated total military victory over Germany. Borden supported a post-war "League of Peace" and thought a key aim of the League should be the overt cooperation of Great Britain and the United States. His view was that if these two powerful nations had been united in common cause, the war would never have started because no country would have dared challenge such an alliance.

The consultation ultimately achieved between Britain and Canada during the war was the model Borden wanted to follow for Canadian government involvement in international relations. Indeed, Resolution ix of the Imperial War Conference affirmed the "recognition of the Dominions as autonomous nations of an Imperial Commonwealth . . . (with an) adequate voice in foreign policy and in foreign relations, and should provide effective arrangements for continuous consultation in all important matters of common Imperial concern." The conference was a major step in changing the relationship between Britain and Canada—and between Canada and the rest of the world.

In Europe, Borden again spent as much time as possible visiting the front and consoling wounded soldiers: he called them "boys" and described the battlefields as "simply the abomination of desolation." He was often brought to tears. "I met many of our boys. One, Major Edwards, had lost both hands, another both legs. They were all very brave and cheerful."

In the month of April 1917, Canada suffered 24,000 casualties, whereas only 11,290 men had volunteered to serve resulting in a net loss in the number of troops. Then the United States officially joined the allied effort, some three years after Canadian soldiers had eagerly signed up to fight. Despite substantial American contributions to the war effort, however, Borden's Cabinet concluded in May that conscription was necessary. Even the Québec Cabinet ministers reluctantly agreed, which Borden viewed as a selfless political act. Presciently, Borden said conscription would "kill Québec ministers and the party for twenty-five years." But he was resolute. To Borden, conscription was necessary to win the war, but he knew it would be a death blow to the party as a national institution.

The other item on the agenda at the May meeting was coalition government. Borden wanted the strongest government possible to support the troops, implement conscription, and win the war. On May 18, 1917, he took his conscription plan to the House of Commons. To a hushed Parliament and a full gallery, Borden said he was responding to the call coming from wounded Canadian soldiers. "(In honour of) the men in the trenches and those who have fallen, (there would be) compulsory military enlistment on a selective basis of such reinforcements as may be necessary to maintain the Canadian army in the field as one of the finest fighting units of the empire."

Tory members cheered enthusiastically. So did many Liberals. On May 20, Cabinet approved an Order in Council that restricted potential conscripts from leaving Canada. Protests began to break out in Québec.

Borden wanted all MPs in the House, be they Liberal or Conservative, to join in this crusade. He discussed a coalition government with Cabinet, but not with his caucus. To entice Liberals to join his government, Borden initially proposed that there be an equal number of Cabinet representatives from the ranks of the Liberal and Conservative parties. Cabinet debated the merits of a coalition government without reaching a conclusion. Borden called off the discussions and said he would come to his own decision.

Laurier came to Borden's residence May 25 to discuss the possibility of forming a coalition government under Borden's leadership with an equal number of Cabinet members from each party, other than the prime minister. Borden told Laurier a wartime election would divert the nation's energy and attentions and cause disunity. Laurier favoured holding an election, even though he acknowledged the present government was likely to be returned. While Laurier opposed conscription, he believed the law would pass and would be obeyed. He left the issue of a coalition government open for discussion, saying he needed time for thought and consultation.

Given the core Liberal strength in Québec, Laurier correctly surmised he could not unite his party on any one side of the conscription debate. Conversely, Borden had sufficient strength outside Québec to believe he could fashion a campaign around conscription and retain government even if he was wiped out in Québec. Of course, that meant bringing Liberals who believed in conscription into his grand political tent. However, this strategy was not a means to retain power for power's sake. The goal was to support the troops and win the war.

Borden noted in his diary that some Cabinet ministers feared that even under a coalition they might be "beaten by French, foreigners and slackers."

Laurier was under enormous pressure and worried that if he supported conscription the flames of Québec separation would be ignited: "I would simply hand over the province to the nationalists, and the consequences might be very serious."

Borden offered Laurier an alternative. Join a coalition, pass the conscription bill, dissolve Parliament, then hold an election. Conscription would come into force only after the election.

In early June it looked as if Laurier was ready to join Borden. Laurier would be given veto power over both Conservative and Liberal members placed in Cabinet. Borden "felt sure that he would come into the coalition." But when the leaders met at noon on June 6, Borden was told there would be no coalition. Borden noted in his diary: "(Laurier) told me that he would not join a coalition government as he is opposed to conscription. Fears Bourassa's influence etc. Says he will endeavour to have the law observed." Laurier also opposed any extension of the government's term of office. With conscription as the only election issue, Laurier knew he would carry Québec and lose everywhere else.

Borden made preparations for a government composed of Liberals and Conservatives who supported conscription. He informed his caucus of his plans on June 7, and then requested that his entire Cabinet resign.

The Military Service Bill imposing conscription was introduced on June 11, causing some Québec Conservatives to leave the government. Borden forged ahead, arguing that conscription was a military imperative. "To prevent attacks at home it is necessary to strike abroad."

Borden saw it as his duty to support those who had volunteered for Canada. He would not let them languish simply because they were volunteers, believing "it is idle and shameless hypocrisy to pretend . . . that because these men went voluntarily, we at home have no obligation to support them. We encouraged them to go and we organized, trained and equipped them. They have offered themselves for the supreme sacrifice on our behalf. More than 30,000 of them are under the sod, having died that we may live and that our inheritance may be preserved. To desert them now on the ground of quibble, that they were merely volunteers would be as ignoble an evasion of moral responsibility as any country in all history was guilty of."

The Military Service Bill replaced the Militia Act and conscripted men between the ages of twenty and twenty-five, with unmarried men at the top of the list. There were numerous exemptions, including conscientious objectors and clergy, and a broad category of "serious hardship." A justice of the Supreme Court would hear individual appeals to the draft.

To demonstrate he had the support of the country, Borden was prepared to implement the bill only after a general election. But he would not yield on its passage. "If we do not pass this measure, if we do not provide reinforcements, if we do not keep our plighted faith, with what countenance shall we meet them on their return?" Laurier proposed an amendment: that enactment of the bill be put to a referendum. This was pure political theatre. Laurier knew his amendment would be defeated and that a referendum, if held, would pass easily in every province except Québec. The amendment *was* defeated, by a vote of 111 to 62.

The conscription bill passed the House of Commons in late July and became law on August 28. As promised, Laurier ceased his opposition once the bill passed through Parliament.

Soon after, the government adopted, as a temporary measure, a tax on income: 4 percent on corporate profits and a tax on personal incomes over $6,000. The tax was linked directly to financing the Canadian military in the post-conscription period, and ensured that those not serving in the military would contribute to the cause. The tax would be subject to review, "a year or two after the war is over."

Despite Laurier's prediction, Borden did not foresee certain re-election. Québec was lost, he knew, as was the farm vote because of distress over the shortage of family labour. A determined Borden sought to enhance his chances in the election by changing the voting franchise. The Military Voters Act and the Wartime Elections Act, both passed in 1917, extended the franchise to those most directly connected to the war effort. The underlying assumption was that most soldiers and their kin would vote for Borden. The vote was given to all British subjects serving in Canadian forces, including British subjects who came from the United States to join the Canadian military. Soldiers who could not specify their electoral district prior to enlistment were given the freedom to cast their ballot wherever they chose, which meant it could be cast in a riding where it could make a difference to an outcome. The Act boldly extended the vote to immediate female relatives of military personnel, providing the first opportunity for women to vote in a federal campaign. Macdonald had proposed extending the vote to "qualified unmarried women" in 1884, but the House of Commons had defeated the proposal.

Borden's legislation removed the franchise from certain people unlikely to vote in favour of conscription candidates. Those who came to Canada after 1902 from specified countries were denied the right to vote as were people convicted of an offence under the Military Service Act.

The Wartime Election Act was passed on September 20. The president of the Canadian suffragettes contended, "It would have been more direct and at the same time more honest if the Bill simply stated that all who did not pledge themselves to vote Conservative would be disenfranchised."

Despite these blatant measures to expand the Conservative vote, Borden still believed a coalition government was necessary. "Political partisanship is closely allied with absolute stupidity," he wrote in his memoirs. He was prepared to resign his leadership, if that was deemed the impediment to a union government. But Conservative MPs would not have it, leaving Borden speechless and near tears by the overwhelming support he received at a caucus meeting. Caucus members rose to their feet and sang a rousing rendition of "For he's a jolly good fellow." Borden declared his resolve: think first of what's best for the country, not the party. "I mean to keep my pledge to our soldiers; if dissident Liberals would come in I would give them equal representation in government."

Bringing Conservative and Liberal MPs into the same caucus, however, proved more difficult than Borden imagined. Some Conservatives, like future Tory leaders Arthur Meighen and Richard Bennett, objected to Liberal MPs joining the Cabinet. Borden was frustrated at the failure of unity and purpose: "They lack the spirit which prompted our young men to cross the sea and to go over the parapet. All of them are backward and cowardly." It was only Borden's threat to resign that brought the recalcitrant MPs into line. Invited Liberals were given little time to make the leap of faith: join the Union government or run the risk of becoming outsiders.

Forming a Union Cabinet proved a monumental challenge. Borden needed room to introduce a healthy sprinkling of Liberals into the mix. In each region, a political boss would have to be selected, meaning one Liberal or one Conservative would have to yield.

By October the new Cabinet was in place, with twelve Conservatives, eight Liberals, and one Labour, but only because of Borden's dogged persistence. He had faced powerful opposition. Laurier had toyed with the idea of joining, then backed off. Borden thought it was not only the right thing to do for the country, but the only way to assure victory in the next election. "Our first duty is to win at any cost the coming election in order that we may continue to do our part in winning this war and that Canada be not disgraced."

Borden's vision of a unity government was designed to attract as many Canadians and members of Parliament as possible to conscription and he brought into one party those who were prepared to make an all-out commitment to win the war. He did not distinguish between regions, races, cultures, or geography. Despite the inherent flaw, that he had no hope of winning the hearts and minds of Québecers, Borden called for national calm and reconciliation. "Inflammatory or abusive language towards those who may think differently . . . sectional, racial or religious appeals is what harms Canada." Formed of English-speaking Canadians who favoured conscription, however, the Union party could never claim to be a truly national government. The opposition would be largely anti-conscription French Canadians.

Although an attempt was made to assemble a platform, the election was about one issue only: whether Canada should continue or withdraw from the war.

The Union government had no cohesive and coordinated political machine. The new party also had to overcome the problem of nominating candidates between what had previously been rival factions. Preference was given to those "who had given consistent support to all war measures and particularly to compulsory service and for Union government."

Laurier did not campaign *against* conscription, but *for* a referendum on the question. He pledged to follow the wishes of the nation, although this would inevitably have left him with Québec voting in isolation. In some Québec constituencies, Liberal candidates ran unopposed.

Borden and Laurier were circumspect in their language. Not so their supporters. Rumours surfaced that blanket exemptions were being given to Québec conscripts, leading Winnipeg's Thomas Crerar poisonously to call French Canadians "damned traitors." Henri Bourassa suggested that Great Britain was responsible for the war and that its motives were based on commercial greed. It was a bitterly contested and divisive campaign. As Borden observed, "No more severe trial of the self-endurance of a democracy was ever made."

Borden blamed Laurier for the election call, arguing that the nation should not have been diverted from its mission to win the war. "It is not a two-party government; it is a no party government, and we are sitting around the council board, not as Liberals and Conservatives, but as Canadians. (The Union government) will keep faith with their fallen comrades . . . keep faith with those who have fallen with those who still live."

Outside of Québec, Borden faced opposition in farming communities, especially around Kitchener, Ontario with its large German-Canadian population. Borden reassured the farmers by promising that "sons who are honestly engaged in the production of food will be exempt from military service."

Eleven days before the election, on December 6, a Norwegian freighter, the *Imo*, and a French munitions ship, the *Mont Blanc*, collided in Halifax harbour. The explosion devastated the city, killing 1,900 and leaving 20,000 homeless. Borden arrived in Halifax the next day, pledging immediate emergency relief. He also arranged to postpone the polling in Halifax. So close to the election, the Halifax explosion was a stark reminder of the ravages of war.

On December 17, 1917, six years and three months since the election that made Borden prime minister, he was returned to office. Québec strongly supported Laurier with 62 of 65 seats. The three Unionist Québec seats came from largely anglophone ridings. Of the 173 seats outside of Québec, the Liberals won only 20. Borden's party received 56.9 percent of the national vote, the highest recorded in Canada. Of the 152 Union MPs, 113 were from the Conservative party while 39 came from Liberal ranks. Predictably, the Union government won 92 percent of the military vote, although that vote affected the outcomes of only 14 Union ridings across the country.

At times, Borden had done whatever he thought it would take to win and strengthen the hand of his government. Yet Borden had no illusions about the difficulties that lay ahead. On January 17, a resolution was placed before the Québec legislature that read: "This House is of the opinion that the province of Québec would be disposed to accept the breaking of the Confederation pact of 1867 if, in the other provinces, it is believed that she is an obstacle to the Union, progress and development of Canada."

This carefully worded statement was another way of saying Québecers were different from the rest of Canada; some would say distinct. It was an invitation to the rest of Canada to go their way without rancour or discord. Borden wisely decided not to intervene. Québec Premier Gouin opposed the resolution and it was withdrawn.

When the Military Service Act was first enforced, riots broke out in Québec City, and four civilians died. An additional 1,000 soldiers were ordered into the Québec garrison to quell the unrest. Borden was firm. "Persons who engage in active or forcible resistance to the enforcement of the act shall be forthwith enrolled in the military forces of Canada." He went further and threatened martial law to prohibit Québec newspapers from making utterances of a seditious nature. Premier Gouin pledged to control the forces of violence that emerged.

Although the Military Service Act was now in force, few conscripts were making it into service. Almost 90 percent of conscripted men sought exemptions, deeply complicating the military's manpower crisis. Urgent telegrams from David Lloyd George beseeched Borden and his government to "refit and maintain our armies in time." Borden summoned an unprecedented *secret* session of the House of Commons to deliver a full military briefing. His message was blunt and unequivocal: send more troops into battle *now*. He stunned the ministers when he announced that *all* exemptions granted under the Military Service Act were cancelled. The motion passed on Friday, April 19. Farmers who had been assured by Borden that their sons would not be sent overseas were outraged. Borden was decisive. "I regard as the supreme duty of the government to see to it that these men are sustained by such reinforcements as will enable them to hold the line." The official statistics indicate that 24,132 conscripted soldiers were sent to fight on the front lines in Europe. However, historian Michael Gravel recently revealed that about half this number included British-born Americans who had *volunteered* for service. Given the strain on national unity caused by conscription, and the relatively small number of troops it produced, we can seriously question whether Borden's policy was in the national interest.

On the home front, the government implemented daylight saving time to reduce energy consumption—some called it "Borden time"—and increased the income tax rate. The Canadian National Railway, which had been established as a Crown corporation, was to be overseen by a board of directors, without interference from government. The government also eliminated the use of hereditary titles, noting that such matters should be settled in Canada, not by some foreign power. Notably, Borden fulfilled an election promise and extended the federal franchise to all women, something nearly every Liberal member from Québec opposed.

Borden travelled to London in June 1918 to attend the Imperial War Cabinet. In making his case for a stronger voice for Canada on the world stage, Borden said: "I conceive that the battle for Canadian liberty and autonomy is being fought today on the plains of France and of Belgium. The nation is clothed with new dignity."

Sir Arthur Currie, commander of the Canadian Corps, briefed Borden on the military situation. Borden was shocked by reports of British High Command causing horrific Canadian casualties in circumstances that offered no meaningful impact to the outcome of the war. Lives were being wasted. Borden took his concerns directly to the War Cabinet and to Lloyd George. He was direct and forceful, claiming that there had been "conspicuous failure to remove incompetent officers," and continuing: "Canada will fight it out to the end. But earnestness must be expressed in organization, foresight and preparation. Let the past bury its dead, but for God's sake let's get down to earnest endeavours and hold this line until the Americans can come in and help sustain it till the end."

In private meetings, Lloyd George admitted he had been slow to remove incompetent leadership, largely because he could not carry Cabinet. To Borden that was no excuse: "Mr. Prime Minister, I want to tell you that, if ever there is a repetition of the Battle of Passchendaele, not a Canadian soldier will leave the shores of Canada as long as the Canadian people entrust the government of their country to my hands."

Lloyd George welcomed the intervention. He wanted Borden at the Cabinet table to help him emasculate the military bureaucracy. The next day the composition of the War Cabinet was changed so that the Dominions "should have a direct voice in the conduct of the war, and in the plans of campaign, so far as the War Cabinet had power to determine them."

The relationship between Canada and Great Britain continued to evolve. Rather than communication going through the Colonial Office, there was now direct contact at the level of prime ministers. On the issue of whether to accept a stalemate of sorts with the German military, or to continue to pursue absolute conquest, Borden urged total victory, saying that "a Germany half defeated was a Germany victorious . . . we should reckon our sacrifice and sorrow and burden as having been suffered and endured in vain unless we fought this war out to the finish." Borden's voice at the Imperial War Cabinet was clear and persuasive. The workings of the Cabinet, explained Borden, "fully exemplifies the principle of complete economy and equal status for which I had so earnestly striven."

The war turned favourably for the Allied Forces in the fall of 1918. Lloyd George summoned Borden to London. "It was very important that you should be here in order to participate in the deliberations which will determine the line to be taken at these conferences by the British Delegates." Thus was Canada invited to be a nation of influence in the affairs of the world. Robert Borden would be Canada's voice.

CHAPTER 10

INDEPENDENCE
FOR CANADA

Canada led the democracies of both the American continents. Her resolve had given inspiration, her sacrifices had been conspicuous, her effort unabated to the end. The same indomitable spirit which made her capable of that effort and sacrifice made her equally incapable of accepting at the Peace Conference, in the League of Nations, or elsewhere, a status inferior to that accorded to nations less advanced in their development, less amply endowed in wealth, resources and population, no more complete in their sovereignty and far less conspicuous in their sacrifice.

BORDEN WAS NOT INTERESTED in being an influence on British efforts in the post-war remake of Europe. Borden wanted a seat at the table for Canada *in its own right*. "The press and the people of this country take it for granted that Canada will be represented at the Peace Conference," Borden insisted in a cable to Lloyd George. "A very unfortunate impression would be created, and possibly a dangerous feeling might be aroused, if these differences are not overcome by some solution which will meet the national spirit of the Canadian people. New conditions must be met by new precedents."

Some Cabinet voices cried out Borden that had gone too far. But Lloyd George urged him to come at once: "I should value your presence greatly." Borden had already been at sea one day on his voyage to London aboard the Mauretania when the armistice was declared.

Borden recognized that in the aftermath of the war the reorganization of boundaries would be "the sternest, the most momentous, and the most difficult problem of all." A new world order was being determined, and Borden came to the conference advocating a number of fundamental principles, including Canada's position that "it did not go into war in order to add territory to the British Empire." More important, however, was the accord between Great Britain and America to prevent another war. "If the future policy of the British Empire meant working in cooperation with some European nation as against the United States, that policy could not reckon on the approval or support of Canada. Canada's view was that as an Empire we should keep clear, as far as possible, of European complications and alliances."

As the debate over Canada's standing in the conference continued, Borden became all the more convinced that Canada should have full sovereignty in international affairs. Lloyd George agreed, and offered Canada a seat at the negotiating table as the member of the British delegation to represent all the Dominions. Borden rejected the offer. He was not there to represent other Dominions; he was there to represent Canada. "The British ministers are perhaps doing their best, but their best is not good enough. . . . Canada got nothing out of the war except recognition." Borden reminded the conference that Canada lost more men in France than Portugal had troops during the war, and that as a proportion of its population Canada lost seven times as many troops as the Americans. Lloyd George eventually agreed to argue for direct representation for Canada at the conference. Ultimately the plenary conference would receive delegates from Canada, as well as Australia, South Africa, India, and New Zealand. Newfoundland was part of the British delegation.

The price of admission to the world of international affairs had been high, but nationhood is often forged out of battle. Those who say that Canada is different from the United States because its independence was not won on the battlefield are wrong. Canada's independence was gained on the battlefields of Europe between 1914 and 1918.

On another issue, the proposed League of Nations, Borden was cautious. "I am convinced, that unless public opinion becomes sufficiently advanced to establish such an organization and to enforce its decisions by an adequate sanction, the existing social order cannot and will not continue." Borden was also concerned that the early designs of the League of Nations excluded Canada, which would otherwise be represented by Great Britain. The British, however, raised no objection to Canada representing itself in the League.

The strong bond between Lloyd George and Borden helped Canada's cause. Borden led the British delegation at the conference with the Russians. He was the chief delegate of the British delegation that defined the boundaries between Greece and Albania. Yet Canada's role at the peace conference did not fully satisfy Borden.

Borden left the peace conference before the Treaty of Versailles was signed. He was compelled to return to Canada to quell the predictable conflict arising from the various factions that had been assembled to form his Union government. Tariff laws, inflation, labour shortages, and labour unrest threatened the economy and Borden's coalition. The governor general tactfully suggested in a telegram that Borden ought to return to steady the ship of state.

Borden insisted that Parliament debate the treaty before ratifying it. The overarching question was whether Canada would be regarded as an independent nation. Some, including members of his government, believed that Britain's signature on the treaty should suffice. Again, Borden stood firm: in a war that determined the destiny of the world, Canada's sacrifices were too great to accept a status inferior to less advanced nations.

Earlier in the year, Wilfrid Laurier had died. The Liberals had chosen William Lyon Mackenzie King as successor, but King had yet to enter the House of Commons. Liberal House leader D.D. McKenzie voiced his party's opposition to joining the League of Nations: "We are not a nation in the true sense of the term. We are part of the great Empire of which we are proud, and nothing else." Liberal MP W.S. Fielding took the view that Canada was not a nation in terms of international law. What would Canada do, asked the Liberals, if it opposed a resolution supported by Great Britain? Borden, of course, was prepared to stake out an independent voice for Canada even if that meant standing on the other side of an issue to the British government.

WITH PEACE IN EUROPE, unrest was brewing in Canada. In response to rising prices and lower wages, the number of workers represented by unions had risen dramatically. So too had the number of strikes and lockouts. The government, however, was determined not to lose production because of labour stoppages. In April 1918 it passed an Order-in-Council known as the "anti-loafing law." The law required all males between the ages of 16 and 60 to be employed. Municipalities were given funds to hire those unemployed. The government then passed an Order-in-Council in 1918 prohibiting both strikes and lockouts.

In theory, the government supported the rights of workers to organize and join unions, but it concluded that there was a growing Bolshevist sentiment in Canada and responded by banning group meetings where "enemy languages" were used. Anyone breaking this law was automatically forced to join the military.

Borden, who had just returned home from the peace conference, assured Canadians that law and order would be maintained. The government, which had employed a heavy hand during the war, maintained an authoritarian stance in the post-war period. This failure to adjust to the new post-war reality placed the government at odds with large groups of citizens including, to the shock and dismay of the Cabinet, returning soldiers.

On May 15, 1919, Winnipeg metal-trade workers walked off the job. This action expanded into a larger strike sanctioned by the Winnipeg Trades and Labour Council. Winnipeg postal workers refused to work and were fired. Except for essential workers, most of Winnipeg was on strike. On June 6, the House of Commons passed a resolution calling for the deportation, without right of appeal, of those advocating the use of force to change society. The government was attempting to thwart a possible "Bolshevik revolution" which might result in a "Soviet government," although the evidence of such a threat was minimal at best.

Parades and demonstrations were banned in Winnipeg by municipal officials, but in a stunning turn of events on June 7, returning veterans marched in the streets in support of the striking workers. The protesters were met by a brigade of the Royal North-West Mounted Police. Shots were fired and one man was killed. On June 21, which came to be known as "Bloody Saturday," strike leaders were arrested.

Six days later, Borden's interior minister, Arthur Meighen, introduced amendments to the Criminal Code that outlawed any organization advocating change by force. In the absence of proof to the contrary, those associated with these organizations would be presumed "guilty." As much as Borden supported the right of workers to organize into unions, he and his Cabinet did not tolerate violence and intimidation. Having guided the country through war, Borden was not about to let Canadian society degenerate into lawlessness.

But the war was over. Libertarian conservatives, who were inherently wary of the oppressive tendencies of government, recoiled from the strong-arm tactics being employed. Western members, mostly representing the farming community, wanted concessions on tariffs and freight rates. Borden worried that, "unless something material is done, we may have difficulty in holding the followers." Western "free trade sentiments" ran against the views of eastern Conservatives, who were more inclined to trade protection.

Many ministers threatened to resign. It became clear that with the war over and conscription no longer an issue, the Tory-dominated coalition would disintegrate. A host of Cabinet ministers did resign. The Union government was imploding.

Thinking ahead to the next election, Arthur Meighen wanted to establish the Union party as a permanent political institution, rather than a collection of MPs that assembled to support conscription. Borden was not convinced. "If Parliament reaches the conclusion that Union Government has served its purpose and should no longer be continued I do not know that any of us would have any right to complain." Borden had achieved his aims and, admittedly, had not clearly thought through the political reality he would face after the war was won.

Borden reached out to Québec voters, including a brave campaign-style swing through the province in the summer of 1919. The Québec premier asked Borden to intervene in the Ontario election by speaking out against the repressive Regulation 17 which squashed the rights of the French. But Borden was hesitant to get involved. "Premier Gouin thinks that the Dominion Prime Minister can exercise much influence on the Government of Ontario. In this he is mistaken."

In the fall of 1919, Borden proposed to Parliament enhanced status for Canada's representative in Washington, who was still attached to the British Embassy. The British foreign office worried that "this [enhanced status] was going a long way toward establishing the virtual independence of Canada." Indeed, the outcome Britain feared was precisely the one Borden desired.

But Borden was exhausted and appeared ready to step down. "I have no further political ambitions," he privately declared. His health was failing and his doctors urged him to retire. On December 16, Borden announced his retirement to his Cabinet, then immediately left the room, presumably to allow the Cabinet to ponder its—and the country's—future. In fact, Cabinet urged Borden to stay on. He retained the leadership but was advised to embark on a year-long vacation. To Borden, this was a clear indication the party lacked strength and permanence. But the man of duty agreed to stay on, and a carefully worded announcement outlined his "capacity for work." He would take a holiday to allow him "to resume the discharge" of his public duties. It fooled no one. Said Sir George Foster, who acted as prime minister during Borden's leave, "So now we are launched on the troubled sea without chart, compass or Captain." The government floundered without clear leadership and Borden's attempt at rest was routinely interrupted by his colleagues seeking advice and counsel.

By June 20, Borden unequivocally confirmed his retirement. Borden was offered the position of minister without portfolio, which he refused. Borden also refused a seat in the Senate, believing it should be an elected rather than an appointed body.

His enthusiasm for politics as a noble calling waned in retirement. When his nephew Henry was urged to enter politics, Borden replied: "I'm quite convinced that with a double burden of professional and political duties your health would collapse. You have not the physical stamina for running with such wild horses. Do not entertain the idea for a moment. Put it behind you forthwith."

In 1928, at age seventy-four, Borden became president of the Crown Life Insurance Company. From then on, his relations with subsequent Conservative leaders, especially R.B. Bennett, were contentious. Borden felt slighted that he had not received the enduring respect and recognition that he deserved after his retirement from public life.

"Mackenzie King never fails in courtesy or in the observance of social convention," noted Borden. "Unfortunately, Bennett usually fails in both these respects. Like Meighen, he lacks that indefinable but very distinctive quality called breeding."

Nevertheless, Borden routinely contributed to political discourse after returning to private life. He opposed Bennett's "new deal" approach to dealing with the Depression in 1932 by asserting conservative principles: "It would be unfortunate if the temporary necessities of the present should lead us to constant or general dependence on governmental intervention. Future prosperity will depend upon the people themselves, upon individual industry, energy, foresight, and resourcefulness rather than upon governmental activities. We have passed through more searching trials than the present. Let's face the future with high hope and undaunted courage."

Showing himself to be a fiscal Conservative, he opposed Alberta high school teacher William Aberhart's proposal for a $25 per month income for each person, something Borden called "a very handsome annuity for a family of six or eight." He was distraught when in 1934 Ontario Premier Mitchell Hepburn considered repudiating contracts with Ontario Hydro to purchase power from private producers in Québec: "Hepburn's conduct is so maladroit and eccentric, so characterized by vindictive and indecent truculence, so lacking in even a semblance of dignity, so devoid of any sense of responsibility, that grave doubts are entertained as to his mental balance."

Borden declared the Co-operative Commonwealth Federation was filled with "our young professors who, wholly out of touch with the realities of life, indulge in comfortable pipedreams." With the CCF on the scene, Borden longed for the two-party system with a working majority for the ruling party. He thought that Mackenzie King had "occupied the conservative seat, while Mr. Bennett has conducted the Conservative party into extreme, even radical paths." Mackenzie King took no quarrel with Borden's outspokenness and seconded the otherwise-retired former PM to represent Canada at international missions and at the League of Nations.

Reflecting on his career in 1933, Borden said, "Perhaps as much as any living man, I have striven for the right of full nationhood which the Dominions now enjoy." Borden was frustrated that his successors did not extend his reach.

In April 1937, Robert and Laura Borden were greatly fatigued when they returned home from a southern holiday. In one of his final letters, Borden wrote to his nephew, "Should it come to that, none of this Sir stuff at the cemetery, just plain Robert Laird Borden, born Grand Pré, Nova Scotia—1854; died Ottawa Ontario, 1937."

Borden died on June 10, 1937 and was laid to rest in Beechwood Cemetery in Ottawa. The funeral procession was replete with a thousand veterans of the Great War wearing their medals and saluting their commander-in-chief, arguably the best that Canada has ever known.

SECTION IV

HARD TIMES

CHAPTER 11

ARTHUR MEIGHEN: THE GREAT ORATOR

I stand for unity in Canada, for solidarity of conditions and freedom of enterprise within our own borders. The lesson for Canada and the free peoples of the British Empire is to avoid the pitfalls of all the nations which have preceded it and sunk into oblivion, and of those as well that are writhing in chaos and suffering. I shall strive with all my power for national unity, embracing all races, languages and creeds.

PERHAPS IT WAS HIS LOVE OF DRAMA that gave Arthur Meighen such presence in the House of Commons and earned him a reputation as the greatest political orator in Canadian history. Extraordinarily well-read, he could quote pages of Shakespeare from memory and was able to recall arcane facts and figures to the astonishment of his colleagues. His oratorical gifts, however, were not matched by other necessary and more pragmatic skills that make for success in politics.

Arthur Meighen was the first prime minister born after Confederation, in 1874, at his family's farm in Anderson, Ontario. He graduated with a bachelor's degree in mathematics from the University of Toronto in 1896, and tried his hand at various careers, notably in sales and as a teacher. His teaching career ended prematurely, however, when the school board reprimanded him for the excessively strict disciplining of his students. Meighen moved west in 1902, to Portage la Prairie, where he took over an established law practice. He then earned his law degree and was called to the Manitoba bar.

In 1904 Meighen campaigned on behalf of the unsuccessful local

Conservative nominee, Nathaniel Boyd, in the newly-created riding of Portage la Prairie. Meighen won the riding for the Tories in 1908. For Conservatives, these were lean years. At the time, the party had lost four consecutive elections to Sir Wilfrid Laurier.

When Laurier's government was finally brought down in 1911, Meighen became a key figure in Borden's Cabinet. It was Meighen's idea to introduce closure as a means to end the Liberal filibuster, when Liberals railed at Borden's Naval Aid Bill, which invested $35 million in Britain's Royal Navy. This was a clever maneuver that secured timely passage of the bill, but it also took away an important tool of the Opposition. Ironically, closure is a tool that Liberals used against the Tories, who occupied the Opposition bench for much of the twentieth century.

Meighen's resourcefulness earned him the position of solicitor general in 1913. Four years later, he was made secretary of state, where he was responsible for drafting the controversial Military Service Act. His convictions were always clearly expressed. "Whatever means are necessary to procure these men, they must be sent; and whatever action is necessary on our part to support our army at present in France, we must take . . . Surely, surely, an obligation of honour is upon us, and fortifying that obligation of honour is the primal, instinctive, eternal urge of every nation to protect its own security."

The Military Service Act provided that soldiers be drawn from across the country. Meighen felt that an equal number of soldiers should come from each province, and that therefore most of the soldiers to be drafted should come from Québec, where, before the election, the fewest number of soldiers had enlisted. In the House, Meighen provocatively argued: "How are we going to get an equality in the country unless in addition to the 8,000 of French-Canadian extraction already enlisted, we take 100,000 more?"

Québecers were inflamed, riots broke out, and four people were killed. The case for conscription was overstated, based more on emotion than on facts. But its impact on Conservative party fortunes in Québec was felt for generations to come. When Meighen later sought the votes of Québecers as party leader, they certainly remembered his role in conscription and in shepherding the controversial Wartime Elections Bill through the House of Commons. Meighen may have been motivated during the war by a duty to serve the prime minister, but a stain remained that he would never remove as leader.

After the 1917 election, Meighen was promoted to minister of the interior, responsible for legislation to nationalize the railways. Meighen wanted

Canada to capitalize on its resources, mostly its coal and water, adding that "if there is one possession more than another the value of which we have failed to realize ourselves, it is our forest wealth." Meighen wanted the private sector and international investors to take the lead in developing natural resources, boasting to the Royal Geographical Society in 1918 that, "Capital is as safe in Canada as in any country on Earth."

Meighen was the acting minister of Justice on May 15, 1919, when much of the working population of Winnipeg walked off the job. In response to the Winnipeg General Strike, the "Citizens' Committee of One Thousand" was formed among community business leaders. The Committee met with Meighen and the minister of Labour, Gideon Decker Robertson, both of whom had travelled west to quell the unrest, restore postal service, and seek ways to end the general strike. Meighen was not interested in compromise. He amended the Immigration Act so that strikers not born in Canada could be deported, and revised the Criminal Code to broaden the definition of "sedition" so that strike leaders could be imprisoned. Striking postal workers who did not return to their jobs were to be dismissed. Meighen would later comment in his first address as prime minister, that "the Bolshevism of Russia is the worst dictatorship . . . that ever disfigured humanity."

Meighen's reputation for toughness, bordering on nastiness during the war, grew. His handling of the Naval Aid Bill, conscription, and the Winnipeg strike established him as single-minded and disciplined. He was Borden's "fixer": someone with a sense of duty who tackled whatever nasty problems plagued the government.

When Borden informed his party of his pending resignation, there was no early or clear indication of who should be the next leader. Borden's personal choice was Sir Thomas White, a former finance minister. Meighen was the other main contender, but many in Cabinet worried about his standing in Québec. The caucus decided that Borden would choose the leader after giving due regard to their preferences, expressed individually in writing. Borden was to review the results, then ascertain which man carried the most confidence and support of his colleagues.

Borden regarded the letters from caucus members as "ballots," but he understood his role to be far more than that of an electoral officer. Arthur Meighen was the first choice with 65 out of 103 votes.

Meighen was reluctant to accept the position unless he could secure the confidence of Cabinet. Cabinet ministers indicated they were prepared to provide him that confidence *only if* White declined to form a government. At Borden's request, the governor general summoned White to ask him to form a government on July 7. White promptly declined, citing health and business reasons.

Meighen was furious that he had not been Borden's first choice, but Borden defended his actions: "(Meighen) apparently did not realize that this course was absolutely necessary in his own interests, because unless White had been sent for, the ministers would not support Meighen. I attended his Excellency again and asked him to receive Mr. Meighen and myself this evening."

Meighen, 46, was sworn in as prime minister on July 10, 1920, Canada's ninth and youngest prime minister. But his was not an auspicious debut. The press knew White had been the Cabinet's preference. Meighen saw the episode between White, Borden, and the governor general as a charade and a personal humiliation. To his mind, he had only been confirmed as "second-best."

He was widely regarded for his intelligence and polished oratory, but reservations remained over his ability to lead. He could appear cold, aloof, even uncaring and austere. Though his friends saw a robust sense of humour, few in government—and none of the Canadian public—ever saw this side of him.

Like his Conservative predecessors, Meighen was a nationalist who believed in protectionist trade policies. "The moment you adopt a policy which puts your industry at a disadvantage compared with a bigger industry that competes beside it . . . the first man that suffers is the labouring man of this country . . . The policy of the Government is to make goods here and keep people here with plenty of work for every class of men. The policy of the Government is to give Canadian industries of every kind just enough advantage in the Canadian market as to make it pay them better to stay here and expand."

Meighen's trade policy infuriated free-trade Unionists opposed to high tariffs. Some split from the Union ranks to rejoin the Liberals, while others gravitated toward a new western-based political party: the Progressives, led by Thomas Alexander Crerar, agriculture minister in Borden's Union government. Like Meighen, Crerar had been born in Ontario and represented Manitoba in the House of Commons.

Borden's coalition was falling apart. Meighen could find no compelling reason to keep it together and could fashion no new theme or issue to build nationwide support. He attempted to realign the coalition by changing the party name from Union to the National Liberal and Conservative party. The new party, Meighen declared, "stands for the best interpretation and the best meaning of both words. It is national because its care is the nation; its scope, its field is nation-wide and nation-big."The party harkened back to the early days of Macdonald and his coalition of Tories and reform-minded Liberals. However, Meighen's window-dressing was a flop, particularly after he failed in his earnest attempt to recruit Esioff-Léon Patenaude, a Cabinet minister in the Borden government, as his Québec lieutenant.

On December 6, 1921, voters had an unprecedented level of choice, with a large number of parties on the ballot—Liberal, Conservative, Progressive, Labour. The Conservative coalition had splintered, which enabled Liberals to win seats with only modest levels of support. Meighen spent most of the campaign on the defensive. To his detriment, he justified his government's record with complicated and unappealing statistics rather than the inspirational oratory for which he was famous. A weak economy compounded his electoral challenge.

Out in Winnipeg, J.S. Wordsworth, a clergyman opposed to conscription, and one of the ten strike leaders imprisoned during the Winnipeg General Strike, led a new Manitoba Independent Labour party, which would become the Co-operative Commonwealth Federation (CCF), and eventually the New Democratic Party (NDP). Labour won three seats in Western Canada, including two in Alberta.

Québec was a Conservative wasteland. In this election, the first after conscription was invoked and where Meighen played the heavy, the Tory party was wiped off the Québec electoral map, with a popular vote of 18.5 percent to the Liberals' 70.2 percent. All 65 seats went to Mackenzie King's Liberals. But it was the upstart Progressive party led by former Unionist Thomas Crerar that put the nail in the Tory coffin. It won 58 seats in the Conservative prairie heartland. The Progressive party was a 1920s version of the more recent Reform party, which took the Progressive Conservative party down to two seats in the 1993 election.

The Liberals won a majority, largely due to the Liberal sweep in Québec and Nova Scotia. Outside these two provinces, the Liberal showing was weak, taking only 37 of the remaining 154 seats across Canada. The government was elected with only 41.2 percent of the popular vote. King had a majority of one.

Meighen lost his seat in Portage La Prairie to Progressive Harry Leader by 177 votes, but later entered the House through a by-election in the eastern Ontario riding of Grenville. There is no clear and satisfactory explanation why Meighen fared poorly in his home constituency. Even his grandson, Senator Michael Meighen, was unable to offer an explanation when asked in 2008.

Although the Progressives won the second highest number of seats in the House, including one for Canada's first female MP, schoolteacher Agnes Macphail, Crerar declined to form the official Opposition. Crerar did not want to impose party discipline. He wanted, rather, to allow his MPs to vote according to the particular preferences of their constituents, a clear indication that the Progressives were a transient protest party with no intention of ever forming government. The role of Opposition fell to the Tories, then named Liberal-Conservatives, under Meighen and his 48 member caucus.

As Opposition leader Meighen retained his tough-minded approach to national security and defence. When British troops stationed at Chanak, a small seaport on the Dardanelles, were pinned down by Turkish forces in 1922, Britain looked for a show of support, asking Canada and other Dominions to contribute soldiers. King insisted that Parliament should decide the response. Meighen opposed King's lack of leadership and quoted former Liberal prime minister, Sir Wilfrid Laurier: "When Britain's message came then Canada should have said: 'Ready, aye ready; we stand by you.'"

Meighen's hawkish position met opposition in much of the country, but especially in Québec. In the Montréal newspaper, *Le Devoir*, Henri Bourassa wrote: "Mr. Meighen represents, in person and temperament, in his attitudes and his past declarations, the utmost that Anglo-Saxon jingoism has to offer that is most brutal, most exclusive, most anti-Canadian." The Chanak Crisis was short-lived, but Meighen's response to it further tainted his reputation in Québec. When the Tories could not capture a single seat in one of Québec's by-elections, even in former Tory strongholds like St. Antoine, Meighen was blamed.

Meighen's fortunes turned in the October 29, 1925 general election. The Conservatives won a plurality of seats, eight seats short of a majority. Normally, that would have resulted in a Tory minority government. The final tally was 115 Tories, 100 Liberals and 22 Progressives. Conservatives swept much of Ontario and the Atlantic. The Liberals picked up 67 of their 82 seats in Québec, where the Tories managed to win only four, despite doubling their popular vote. Meighen won 46.1 percent of the popular vote, about five percentage points higher than the popular vote that had given King a majority four years earlier. But Mackenzie King, even though he lost his own York North seat by almost 500 votes, defiantly refused to resign and struck a deal with the Progressives to cling to power.

Meighen had made some inroads in Québec, and was determined to take a risk to win seats in French ridings in a subsequent election. To that end, he pledged in a Québec by-election shortly afterward not to send troops overseas without a clear mandate from the people. This pledge was not enough to win the by-election, although it did offend many Tory Imperial loyalists.

A weakened and desperate Liberal party was unable to hold its coalition together for very long. A scandal arose when it was discovered that Jacques Bureau, a known bootlegger and King's minister of customs, had accepted bribes. King swiftly fired Bureau, but soon after excused his bad behaviour by appointing him to the Senate, leaving the impression that King himself had been corrupted. Having lost the support of the Progressives, and not wanting to lose a vote of confidence and surrender the government to Meighen, King requested that Lord Byng, the governor general, dissolve Parliament and call an election. Lord Byng used his reserve powers to refuse this request, leaving King no choice but to resign.

King feigned outrage that the foreign-appointed head of state had denied the request of a sitting prime minister. The tempest that ensured is known in Canadian history as the King-Byng affair. King argued that no prime minister in the last hundred years had been refused dissolution. Meighen, thirsting for the prime minister's chair, countered that in 1910, British prime minister Herbert Asquith, had asked for dissolution of Parliament, and when refused by the king, appealed his case. Five days later dissolution was granted. Meighen, demonstrating his eagerness, contended that a precedent for delay was a precedent to refuse.

Meighen believed he could form "a strong Government" with support from the Progressives. Because the Conservatives held the most seats, Lord Byng did invite Meighen to form a government. He accepted the invitation and was sworn in as prime minister on June 29, 1926.

Meighen did not swear any of his Cabinet ministers into the Privy Council, choosing instead to make them acting ministers only. The duties of an acting minister, Meighen maintained, "carried the same responsibility in every way . . . as ministers appointed with portfolio, but those accepting draw no salary and, therefore, do not vacate their seats and, of course, need not be re-elected." Had Meighen's ministers been formally appointed they would have been forced to run in by-elections. Meighen was not about to make the same mistake George Brown had made back in 1858 when he was "double shuffled" out of government by Sir John A. Macdonald. Meighen himself was forced to resign his seat in order to be sworn in as prime minister. Unlike Macdonald's graceful maneuvering, however, Meighen's appeared contrived and heavy-handed, born of his ambition to become prime minister. As Macdonald might have said, "the pear was not yet ripe for picking." Without securing the support of the Progressives, Meighen's government lasted only a few days. The Opposition introduced a motion declaring Meighen's acting ministry unconstitutional. The motion to bring down the government declared that the acting ministers had no legal right to sit in the House of Commons and so had no business controlling the business of government.

Meighen pointed out the various flaws contained in the motion, based mostly on false assumptions about acting ministers, but did so in an uncharacteristically awkward performance. He believed he had been absolutely correct in appointing his acting ministry. The Liberals were determined to prove otherwise. For support, King approached the Progressives, who only days earlier had abandoned his government. Not all the Progressives were convinced, but King was able to garner enough support for a confidence motion that was passed by a single vote. Meighen was left with no choice but to ask the governor general to dissolve Parliament. Seeing no other party able to regain the confidence of the House, Lord Byng issued the writ for an election date of September 14, 1926, less than a year after the last contest.

King can easily be taken to task for clinging to power and for putting the governor general in a tough spot by calling for an election without giving the Tories an opportunity to govern. But King declared that the 1926 election was about a desperate and power-hungry Arthur Meighen. The Tory prime minister was left to defend Byng, leaving the impression he thought it acceptable for the British-appointed governor general to intervene as he did. It was a stretch for King to sustain his position because in the previous election his party had received fewer seats and fewer votes than the Tories did, yet he clung to power through a backroom deal with the Progressives. And King's claim of collusion and unfair treatment was audacious: it was a Liberal scandal that had brought down his government in the first place.

Meighen's strategy of accepting Byng's offer to form a government had been flawed. He would have been better off refusing the lure of the prime minister's chair then go directly to an election against the tarnished Liberal government. Meighen had simply been too eager, or too naive.

In the election campaign, King forged an agreement with both the Progressive and Progressive-Liberal parties not to run candidates against one another in individual ridings. The Liberals ran 202 candidates, compared with 28 Progressives and 12 Progressive-Liberals. This agreement ensured the Liberal vote would not split. In Manitoba, Conservatives captured 40 percent of the vote but not one single seat. (This example is often used in arguments against the first-past-the-post system and in favour of proportional representation.)

In the campaign, Meighen accused King of fearmongering, especially in Québec. "While [King] was talking unity in English Canada, and presenting himself as its only true guardian and apostle, his lieutenants were adopting every means known . . . to stir up old war animosities and to conjure new fears and new hostilities in the minds of the good people of Québec." But Meighen was unable to improve on the four Québec seats he had captured in the previous campaign.

King won 116 seats in the 245 seat legislature; another minority. But again he struck a deal, this time with the Liberal-Progressives, who won 8 seats. He was back in charge with a working majority. The Tories, who had received the most votes in the country, returned to the Opposition benches with just 91 seats, 14 less than they had had in 1925. Meighen once again lost his own seat in Portage la Prairie and resigned as party leader.

Meighen's political involvement in the period after the election was minimal. The new Tory leader, Richard Bennett, did not ask for Meighen's help during the 1930 election, but in 1932, he appointed Meighen to the Senate, making him government leader in the upper chamber. Meighen had long been an advocate of a useful Senate that distinguished itself from the more partisan House of Commons: "It is well to recall that for eleven years prior to Confederation the nominative system had been abolished and the elective system adopted in the Legislative Council of Upper Canada; therefore, it was after eleven years' experience that the latter was chosen by the great men of that time . . . The Senate is worthless if it becomes merely another Commons divided upon party lines and indulging in party debates such as are familiar in the Lower Chamber session after session. . . . Members of the Second Chamber must get away, lift their minds far from those hard-drawn lines of party, or they cannot serve their country. . . ."

Everyone expected that Meighen would drift into the realm of elder statesman. However, the Senate turned out to be anything but a step towards retirement. About Meighen's position as party leader, there was another chapter yet to be written.

CHAPTER 12

RICHARD BEDFORD BENNETT: THE EARLY YEARS

*If you believe that in big business, that in capitalism, there are abuses
which work hardship upon the people of this country, if you believe that the faults
of capitalism have brought about injustices in her social state, if
you believe that these injustices manifest themselves in lower wages and too high
cost of living and unemployment, then support my party.*

SIR JOHN A. MACDONALD was well into his first term as prime minister when Richard Bedford Bennett was born in Hopewell, New Brunswick on July 3, 1870. Hope was in short supply during Bennett's tenure as prime minister as he took the reins of the nation at the outset of the deepest depression in Canadian history.

The eldest of five children, Bennett grew up in a family that knew economic success and failure. R.B. was determined to experience more of the former than the latter. Focused and determined, he usually reached his objectives. His high school yearbook notes that Bennett possessed the harsh qualities of conceit and impatience, made all the more potent by a quick tongue. In short, he had all the makings of a future prime minister.

The ever-ambitious Bennett began an unlikely career as a schoolteacher and rose to the position of principal. He supplemented his earnings by joining the militia and also worked part-time as a clerk in the law office of Lemuel J. Tweedie, a distinguished barrister who would later become leader of the provincial Conservative party in New Brunswick. The clerkship turned into a junior partnership, allowing Bennett to enter Dalhousie University to prepare for a career in law. He helped pay his tuition by working in the university library.

Bennett never married, though he came close. An offer of marriage to Elma Russell was refused because, apparently, the object of Bennett's desire worried she would play perpetual second-fiddle to Bennett's true mistress: ambition and hard work. Bennett's bachelorhood caused some consternation, and once a national newspaper commented: "Mr. Bennett is a bachelor, which no member of Parliament ought to be. A single state he attributes to his having been too busy to talk to the ladies. But you can never accept the explanations of a bachelor of 45." One explanation that might be acceptable involved a health problem. Bennett was reported to have phimosis, a disease involving an abnormally tight foreskin that could make for excruciatingly painful erections. Nevertheless, questions about Bennett's personal life persist.

Something of an eccentric, he never owned a house in Canada, and following one accident in his youth, he never drove a car. He ate voraciously, determined to remain overweight, but not obese, an appearance he believed indicated status and wealth. One friend recalled that Bennett's daily breakfast was a plate of porridge, bacon and two eggs, and plenty of toast with honey or marmalade. Unlike his father, he consumed neither tobacco nor alcohol.

In 1897, Senator James Lougheed, a wealthy Conservative lawyer from Calgary, asked the dean of Dalhousie Law School to identify his "best and brightest." R.B. Bennett was given the nod and went West. It was not too long before Lougheed pegged Bennett as a man destined for greatness: "Bennett can solve any problem he puts his mind to. No man is quicker to strip a problem of unnecessary verbiage and translate it into a simple and understandable language. Some day Bennett will be called upon to solve the greatest problems in Canada. Some day Canada will turn to him to get the country out of its difficulties."

A quick study and a master of detail, Bennett prospered early and often. He secured the very best clients, such as the Canadian Pacific Railway and the Hudson's Bay Company, and invested wisely. By the time Bennett turned 40, he was a millionaire many times over.

The wealthy Bennett was not inclined to pursue travel, leisure, or sports. But after business, his passion was politics. He was not an ideologue, and could best be described as a monarchist, a protectionist, and a nationalist (in the sense of remaining independent of the United States).

Once Bennett found a home in the Conservative party he became a fierce partisan.

In 1898, Bennett was elected as a Conservative to the Assembly of the North-West Territories. In 1900 he won the Conservative nomination for the Calgary seat in the Alberta Provisional District, but was defeated by Liberal Oliver Frank. He returned to the Territorial Assembly in 1901.

At about the time Alberta joined Confederation in 1905, Bennett became the first leader of the Alberta Provincial Conservative party. Success was elusive and his party won only two seats with Bennett at the helm. The leader's was not one of them. In the next provincial election of 1909, Bennett was one of only two Conservative members elected.

When Conservatives banded together in 1911 to defeat Prime Minister Laurier and his Reciprocity Treaty on free trade with the United States, Bennett was once again called to federal politics. He won his Calgary seat, and Robert Borden won the country.

Not initially chosen for Cabinet, Bennett was given the honour of moving the address in reply to the speech from the throne. Demonstrating a vision beyond protecting the interests of the privileged and wealthy with which he was associated, Bennett remarked: "In my judgment, in this complex civilization of ours, the great struggle of the future will be between human rights and property interests and it is the duty and function of government to provide that there shall be no undue regard for the latter that limits or lessens the other."

Bennett soon tired of life as a backbench MP, and lamented to a friend, "I am sick of it here. There is little or nothing to do and what there is to do is that of a party hack or department clerk or messenger. I will probably leave here."

Bennett had done well by the free enterprise system and was a voice in caucus that did not condone government handouts or loans to the private sector. He opposed government support for the railways, an issue that created tension between he and future party leader Arthur Meighen. Over time, Bennett proved himself reliable, and Borden gave him the responsibility of mobilizing labour for both industry and military service. Bennett was such a fervent supporter of Borden's military policies that he earned the nickname "Bonfire" Bennett after an antiwar group burned him in effigy.

A determined partisan, Bennett did not support Borden's attempts to build a coalition with Liberals under a Union government. His dissatisfaction was so great he was unwilling to run in the 1917 election. Bennett thought he had a deal with Borden and would be appointed to the Senate.

But Borden appointed a Liberal instead, to satisfy the demands of his coalition. An angry Bennett sent the prime minister a 20-page letter to which he never received a reply.

With Arthur Meighen leading the Tories in 1921, Bennett was recruited just prior to the general election to serve as minister of Justice. It was a brief interlude: in Alberta, the 11 Conservatives and lone Liberal elected in 1917 were replaced with eight Progressives, two Labour, and two United Farmers of Alberta. Bennett lost his Calgary West seat by 16 votes. (Had the elections officer accepted checkmarks on marked ballots, in addition to the traditional x, Bennett would have won.)

In the 1925 election, Bennett took the Calgary West seat by a margin of 4,216 over Joseph Shaw of the Labour party. This was the election where Liberal Mackenzie King brazenly held power with the tenuous support of the Progressives.

When the Liberal government fell on a vote of confidence, and Arthur Meighen briefly regained the position of prime minister, Bennett served as minister of finance. After the Tories lost the 1926 election, and Meighen lost his seat in the House of Commons, the leadership of the Conservative Party was up for grabs. In the interregnum, which lasted one year and one day, Hugh Guthrie served as interim leader. A native of Guelph, Ontario, Guthrie, a lawyer, sat in the Liberal caucus for 17 years under Sir Wilfrid Laurier. After siding with Borden over the conscription issue, Guthrie joined the Union government in 1917 where he served as solicitor general and then minister of Defence. In Meighen's short-lived government of 1926, Guthrie held two portfolios, justice and defence.

To replace Meighen, Conservatives opted, for the first time, to hold an open leadership convention, rather than the traditional method where elected MPs chose from among their caucus. The federal Liberals had set the precedent for a national delegated convention when they chose Mackenzie King to succeed Laurier in 1920. The Conservative convention successfully represented the country as a whole. Of the 1,586 delegates attending the October 1927 convention in Winnipeg, 1,230 came from constituencies, 243 came from the party "at large," and 113 were *ex officio*.

Party delegates also used this rare national gathering to debate policy. However, they were warned by former leader Robert Borden against developing a platform by committee. "You must not forestall too much a leader who will be responsible to you, to Parliament and to the country, for the policy which is put before the people."

Consequently, the resolutions that passed were general, committing the party to vague aims: "promoting industrial peace and human welfare is the duty of the state . . . so far as is practicable, and to support social legislation designed to conserve human life, health and temperance, to relieve the stress during periods of unemployment, sickness and in old age." Federal interventions on social programs advocated by Tories at this convention represent, arguably, a first cut at "equalization," since the program, as proposed, would be disproportionately funded from federal tax revenues generated by the well-off provinces.

The party used the convention to demonstrate its capacity for openness and change. Not only was it the first convention where delegates would select their leader, but all proceedings of the convention were translated. Delegates were free to address the convention in either English or French. Youth and women delegates were also given special attention. There remained, however, a divide at the convention between established eastern business interests and the more reform-oriented delegates from rural Canada. And despite the bilingual nature of the convention, Québec Conservatives felt that their presence was only tolerated rather than embraced.

This was an era when overt ambition was considered unseemly and a detriment to leadership, and prospective candidates, particularly the front-runners, took pains to profess their lack of interest. Coming into the convention, Ontario Premier Howard Ferguson was considered the favourite to win. He had the double distinction of being the Ontario premier and being popular in Québec, an unusual and potent combination. Ferguson was respected in Québec because his Ontario government had repealed legislation passed in 1912 that had limited French language instruction in Ontario schools. In May 1927, Ferguson professed to a friend he was not interested in leading the federal Tories: "Because I made two or three patriotic addresses, everybody apparently jumped to the conclusion that I was angling for the Dominion leadership, so I stopped talking." Despite reports in the *Globe* that Ferguson need only throw his hat into the ring and the contest was his to win, Ferguson remained aloof, even days before the leadership convention. Some Conservatives thought Arthur Meighen should succeed himself, but, though no one in the party disputed his intelligence and oratory abilities, losing three elections was a record not easily dismissed. Meighen conceded: "It has never been my thought to become my own successor; and in any event I have not seen throughout this country any general desire that this should take place."

At the convention, Meighen delivered an address to defend a policy he had articulated a year ago in a speech in Québec. He explained that "in the event of an outbreak of war, the government would come to its decision; act upon its decision in the way of mobilization and organization; and obtain the verdict of the people."This meant Canada would not go to war without having the support of the people as expressed in a referendum or general election. There had been widespread opposition to this policy, particularly among Tories outside Québec, but by the close of his address, a conciliatory Meighen appeared to have won the hearts and minds of the delegates.

That is, until Ferguson, the front runner, took the microphone. "I never could see the wisdom of digging up a corpse that had been buried for two years for the purpose of raising a smell."To a chorus of boos from delegates, Ferguson continued. "If Mr. Meighen adheres to that view, I want you to understand that I, as a Liberal-Conservative, entirely disagree with him and repudiate that view; and if this convention chooses to endorse him, I will disassociate myself from the activity of the convention."The party was split, Meighen on one side and Ferguson on the other. The party knew that, divided, it could not win the country. Ferguson was suddenly out of consideration.

The first leadership ballot included former minister Robert Rogers of Manitoba and five members of caucus: Hugh Guthrie, the interim leader, Sir Henry Drayton, C.H. Cahan, R.J. Manion, and R.B. Bennett.

At fifty-seven, Richard Bedford Bennett was the second youngest of the six candidates. It seemed of little consequence to delegates that Bennett had chosen not to run for re-election in 1917 (because of Borden's decision to include a Bennett rival, Liberal Arthur Sifton, in Cabinet). Bennett had the support of the convention's most influential delegates. Ferguson worked the convention floor for Bennett, as did H.H. Stevens. His support was of such value that Bennett told Stevens: "Henry, I owe this entirely to you.You are the one that put me here."

The unilingual Bennett did not have support from Québec, and spoke not a single word of French at the convention. But Hugh Guthrie, his closest rival, had even greater problems in Québec after declaring at the convention that a united Canada should, "obliterate class distinctions . . . race distinctions . . . geographical distinctions." In Guthrie's Canada, French Canadians were in the melting pot. Guthrie's momentum was also limited because, of his twenty-seven years as a parliamentarian, seventeen were as a Liberal. Whatever suspicions lingered within the party over Guthrie's long Liberal past were heightened when he addressed Tory delegates by welcoming them to the "greatest National *Liberal* convention in history."

The other strong contenders were Charles H. Cahan and Robert J. Manion. Cahan was a hardline Conservative who advocated a pure form of free enterprise combined with rugged individualism. Manion, another for-mer Liberal, came in a respectable fourth place on the first ballot and was well-placed for a run at the leadership when it next came available.

It took only two ballots to determine the outcome. But for three votes, there would have been a third ballot. Bennett won on the second ballot with 50.2 percent support.

Bennett committed all his energy, and much of his personal wealth, to his party. In thanking delegates for their confidence, he said: "You have determined for me that henceforth so long as I have health and strength I must dedicate my time, my talents, such qualities as I may have and the for-tune that God has been good enough to give me, to the interests of my country, to the great party that I'm privileged to lead."

Bennett's public acknowledgement of his personal wealth and his prom-ise to make it available to the party may seem peculiar in today's process-driven climate of strict controls over political finances. And for Bennett this was no an idle boast. In short order, the Conservative party would receive hundreds of thousands of dollars from his personal bank account.

At the leadership convention, the party committed itself to greater openness and a new process of consultation with members. Bennett did not like this, but he agreed to support it: "You understand that if I were doing this myself I would not have this (consultation) meeting . . . but the meeting was provided for in Winnipeg and I'm bound to carry out the terms of the reso-lution . . . I have chosen the path of least resistance."

Bennett then resigned his corporate directorships, stating: "No man may serve you as he should if he has over his shoulder always the shadow of pecuniary obligations." He staked his policy ground on the tried and true Conservative themes established by Macdonald: protectionism and national-ism, telling Conservatives in 1928: "Whenever you send raw materials from this country and bring back the manufactured product you are depriving men and women of this country an opportunity for work." He declined to say that whenever Canada exported its goods in an environment of open trade, it created lasting jobs for Canadians.

Bennett entered Parliament as Conservative leader with a caucus of 91 MPs, a substantial number, but not representative of the nation. There were no members in Québec, nor from Manitoba and Saskatchewan, and Bennett was the lone MP from Alberta.

Bennett tended to a party that was both disorganized and in poor financial condition. And he strengthened the party in every necessary dimension. Before Bennett, the party ran its own business out of the back of MPs' offices. This did not meet Bennett's business standards for efficiency and effectiveness, or his desire for control and in short order he hired a national director for the party. He then established a new national headquarters in the Victoria Building across from Parliament Hill, which housed up to thirty full-time staff working in research, publicity, and administration. Satellite offices were located in major centres across the country and Bennett travelled widely to build national support for the Tory party. He also effectively used the depth and breadth of his caucus by assigning them portfolios, which were designed to hold the government accountable in critical or sensitive areas.

Despite being a political nationalist, Bennett was not beyond using the latest in political technology from south of the border. The latest marvel was an "addressograph," a tool that enabled Tory headquarters to produce targeted and personalized letters from the leader or party headquarters to thousands of Canadians across the land. With the addressograph, combined with MPS' free mailing privileges, the party was soon sending out personalized letters to 200,000 voters at a time.

Bennett had few newspapers he could count on to spread his Conservative perspective. In response, the Tories established the seemingly legitimate Standard News Service, which produced and distributed news stories favourable to Tory fortunes to hundreds of weekly newspapers. All efforts were made to camouflage the party connection so as to enhance the credibility and acceptance of the manufactured news stories.

Normally, political organization and success in fundraising are linked. Not so with Bennett. He coughed up the money himself. Despite the stock market crash of 1929, Bennett had contributed some $600,000 before the writ was dropped for the 1930 election. The Liberals had no such individual benefactor, although they were supported by the Beauharnois Power Company to the tune of some $700,000. The Tories had declined a similar contribution.

Going into the election, bad news for the economy was good news for Bennett. The economy had unravelled and was entering the longest and most severe depression ever recorded. A bad economy effectively guaranteed the defeat of the incumbent Liberal government. But the bad news for Bennett was that he would have to govern during impossible times. In the period leading up to the election, the faces of millions of Canadians were etched in heartbreak, desperation, and deprivation.

Prime Minister Mackenzie King was slow to recognize the suffering in the nation and was ill-suited to respond. When pressed to help unemployed Canadians, King retorted that he "would not give 'a five cent piece' in federal assistance to any (provincial) Tory government in this country for these alleged unemployment purposes." Liberal arrogance and disdain were on full display.

Faced with Liberal inaction, voters looked for a plan. At the time, the Conservative policy of tariffs to protect Canadian industry made sense. Indeed, Liberal Finance minister Charles Denning had liked the Tory proposals so much he had included them in his earlier budget. Bennett gleefully accepted this endorsement: "It is always a matter of satisfaction," he said in the House of Commons, "to see sinners turn from their sins." Bennett claimed the only reason the Liberals were raising protective tariffs was to retaliate against protectionist measures adopted by the United States. "A countervailing duty that is now to prevail in the Dominion of Canada is a policy made in Washington," Bennett charged and suggested the Liberal conversion was nothing more than a sign of weakness. Bennett was following traditional Tory trade policy, only this time he was able to claim he was protecting Canadian jobs. In the past, Tory trade policy was often seen as a sop to eastern business interests.

Bennett effectively managed his transition to leadership and had his party firing on all cylinders in every province but one. Québec had been something of an enigma to Bennett. Québec voters believed Tories were too closely tied to the British. Bennett assured Québecers that his party was "Canada first, then the empire." Appointing a Québec lieutenant to tend to political matters in the province was an obvious course to follow, but the factions of Conservatism in Québec were unreconciled at the time. "Until these factions are united," said a frustrated Bennett, "we cannot hope for support (in Québec). And they cannot be united if I select any person as chief lieutenant in Québec."

A Conservative conference was held in Montréal on May 15, 1929. There, Bennett chose Joseph Rainville, a Montréal lawyer and businessman, as his organizer for Montréal and surrounding area and Thomas Maher his Québec city lead. Maher proceeded to launch a pro-Conservative Québec city weekly newspaper, *Le Journal*, in December of 1929.

With a strengthened and more innovative organization, the party was better prepared to face a national election than at any time since Borden's victory some nineteen years earlier.

On May 6, 1930, Bennett introduced a motion of non-confidence in the House of Commons. After two weeks of debate, Parliament was dissolved and an election set for July 28, 1930. Bennett's platform had three main themes. First was trade policy, which featured the odd mixture of protectionist measures combined with increased trade within the British Empire. "I will use (tariffs) to blast away into the markets that have been closed to you," he told voters. Second were improvements in the Canadian transportation system, including a national highway, new rail lines, and the opening of the St. Lawrence waterway to the Great Lakes. Third was old-age pension reform, pledging that a Bennett government would pay 100 percent of old-age pensions, relieving the provinces of their 50 percent share. The old-age pension pledge was designed to dispel the Tory image of a bunch of penny-pinching bankers who cared more for the balance sheet than human need.

During the campaign, Bennett comforted Canadians with his confidence and his conviction that the economy would rebound under his leadership: "I propose that any government of which I am the head will, at the first session of Parliament, initiate whatever action is necessary to that end, or *perish* in the attempt." Mackenzie King completely misunderstood the nation's anxiety about the economy, writing in his diary: "The men who are working are not going to worry particularly over some of those who are not." King pledged to confer with expert advisors to consider the problem of unemployment, whereas Bennett offered leadership and action.

Tory protectionism was an easy sell to Canadian farmers, especially after what had happened to the butter market. Following a change in government policy in 1925, imports of butter from New Zealand increased from 162,000 pounds to 39 million pounds by 1930 and the price of butter plummeted. Canadian dairy farmers received little more than half of what the tariff-protected American dairy farmers did. That was all Canadian farmers needed to know about the benefits of protectionism in trade policy.

Bennett learned the art of campaigning after becoming leader. According to journalist Bruce Hutchison: "His manner was at once lofty and sympathetic. His radiant smile encouraged the weak and humble. Before a vast audience or a small group he struck a pose of natural sublimity. No more than King could he ever be one of the boys, but he seemed to symbolize and promised the age of abundance which, briefly lost, but quickly returned under his guidance."

The five Conservative premiers at Bennett's disposal were a vital instrument of the campaign. The Liberals could not match the Tory organizational strength. "Really we have no organization," lamented Mackenzie King. "Candidates have gotten into the field here and there, but many constituents are still without anyone, literature is not reaching the candidates, speakers are not arranged for as they should be. Our opponents on the other hand have a splendid organization, own their own printing press, (and) have been getting at literature right along. At every turn the Conservatives are getting ahead of us."

Tories, in fact, established the first political "war room" in Canada, in 1930. Conservatives had copies of Liberal pamphlets and literature the day they were off the presses, facilities for reviewing Liberal constituency advertising before it was published, and Conservative candidates were briefed on Liberal propaganda before it hit the streets.

The outcome was never in doubt, although the result was closer than expected. Conservatives took 134 seats in the 245-seat legislature while the Liberals held 90. Bennett earned a solid majority, but the popular vote was tight, with Tories at 47.8 percent support to the Liberals' 45.5 percent. Atlantic Canada elected 23 Conservatives to 6 Liberals. In Québec, the Tories had a breakthrough, going from four to 24 seats. Ontario changed little, remaining a Conservative stronghold with 59 Conservatives and 22 Liberals. Because the United Farmers of Alberta won nine seats, holding a majority in their home province, the West was more competitive. There, Conservatives took 27 seats to the Liberals' 22. The only provinces with core Liberal support were Québec and Saskatchewan.

Despite the hard times, in 1930 Canadians believed the Depression would be short-lived. Since the Great War, North America had been giddy over a boom that no one thought would end. Although shaken by the Crash of 1929, everyone was hopeful that good times would soon return. However, a newly-elected Bennett realized the grip of the Depression was tight and unyielding at the same time that, because of the hope he offered during the campaign, expectations for his government were high.

Bennett did not know the full extent of the challenges that lay ahead. He blindly assured the nation that the solution to its problems was a Conservative government. "After I am Prime Minister on July 28," he said, "I will see that my promises are carried out or the government will go out of power trying to do so." Bennett was sworn in as prime minister on August 7, 1930. But the economy was yet to reach its nadir.

GETTING ELECTED IS ONE THING; keeping a government together is another. Bennett's strengths—quickness, decisiveness, and intelligence—were highly valued in the law and in business, but those strengths created a prime minister who seemed aloof, uncaring, and something of a loner. Bennett was not a team builder. He was a man of action more than words, of decision, not emotion. Indeed, Bennett believed in himself more than in the people he represented. He once remarked, "Universal franchise without educational test of any kind is a very great danger." "He was not a consensus man," said journalist Grattan O'Leary. "He was not above asking the opinions of others, he was only above accepting them."

Bennett would use business metaphors to describe political realities. He occasionally called himself chair of a board of directors rather than prime minister; and he referred to citizens as shareholders. "We asked between now and the expiration of the next fiscal year that the Board of Directors of this country . . . shall discharge its duties from a financial standpoint as it best can and take the chances that are incident to so doing by submitting an account of its stewardship." To this Mackenzie King, correctly, replied, "It is not the Cabinet of which he is Prime Minister that is the Board of Directors; it is this House of Commons. The Cabinet is a committee of the House of Commons."

Bennett's opponents derisively referred to him as the nation's chief workaholic in a leader-centric government: "Bennett manages to get things done, whether for the best or not. He has a great driving power," said Mackenzie King. To this Bennett replied, "It may be a one-man government, but certainly it has more than one-man support." He was ready to act immediately after being sworn in as prime minister, appointing 19 ministers to his Cabinet, seven from Ontario and five from Québec, three of the five being francophones. Bennett also reserved for himself the ministry of finance in addition to external affairs, a portfolio then traditionally held by the prime minister. Cabinet meetings were frequent, initially almost daily, and long. Bennett suspended meetings whenever he suspected information was leaking to the press.

The first post-election speech from the throne on September 8, 1930 contained only twenty-one lines, and just one paragraph of noteworthy content: "The necessity for dealing with exceptional economic conditions and the resultant unemployment has induced me to summon you at an earlier date than would otherwise be necessary. Measures will be submitted for your consideration, including amendments to the Customs Act and the Customs Tariff, which it is anticipated will do much to meet the unusual conditions which now prevail."

One of Bennett's first acts of Parliament was to provide $20 million for public works, largely under the administration of provincial and municipal governments. These infrastructure programs, funded on a 50–50 basis with the provinces, were of little use in the Prairies where local governments could not come up with their share. Here the rules were changed and the federal government provided half the funding in grants and half in loans. Canadians who wonder why deeply impoverished and heavily indebted foreign nations continue to borrow money, and why stronger countries continue to lend it to them, need only look at the Canadian experience in the early 1930s. Distressed provincial and municipal governments could not refuse help regardless of the terms.

Bennett then moved swiftly to protect Canadian industry by increasing tariffs, a measure that was as unsuccessful then as it would be later whenever Conservative and Liberal governments tried to counter the realities and benefits of trade with protectionist measures.

With legislation on its key campaign planks in place, Bennett's government looked to other solutions. The next speech from the throne, on March 12, 1931, was longer, two and a half pages in Hansard. It granted that the Depression was a worldwide phenomenon, but Bennett was not about to let his predecessors off the hook. "My government has explored the origins of our difficulties and is firmly of the belief that many of our problems do not arise out of a worldwide depression, but are antecedent to it; and that domestic factors have also largely determined the degree of economic distress from which this country is suffering." The last part of the sentence was a veiled reference to the Liberals' slow conversion to protectionist trade policies.

Bennett represented Canada at the 1931 Imperial Conference of Dominion and colonial prime ministers, which passed the Statute of Westminster, giving Canada, Newfoundland, Australia, New Zealand, the Irish Free State, and South Africa the full power to make laws having "extraterritorial operation." It further specified that no Act of the British Parliament would extend to any of the Dominions. While the Statute had been in the works for years, its passage was a banner day for Canadian independence. Some provinces were concerned that the British North America Act (BNA) remain in force, however, to ensure their constitutional rights were not abridged, particularly in the area of constitutional amendment. As a result, Bennett secured an exemption, thereby keeping the BNA intact for generations to come.

As important as this coming of age was to Canada, however, Bennett's main preoccupation at the conference was trade: "I offer to the mother country and to all other parts of the empire, preference in the Canadian market in exchange for a like preference in theirs, based upon the addition of a 10 percent increase in preventing prevailing general tariffs." The policy was one-part free trade with the British empire and one-part economic nationalism with the United States. (For instance, it would soon be a crime to import used cars from the United States.)

Before the dustbowls hit the prairies in the early thirties, Canada had had a surplus of wheat. With depressed prices for wheat, farmers now needed bank loans to survive. The Dominion Agricultural Credit Co. Ltd. was established to guarantee bank loans to farmers, conditional on a central selling agency being put in place. The government was involved in this venture to the extent that its nominee would be appointed general manager of the wheat pools.

In order to shore up wheat prices, Canada, along with other nations, agreed to a system of supply management. This included the creation of an emergency Wheat Control Board. To objections of economic interference from his own caucus and Cabinet, Bennett replied, "The purpose of the agreement is to raise the price of wheat, which can only be done when the surplus carryovers have been removed from the market." Later, the Bennett government introduced the Natural Products Marketing Act. The Liberals opposed the measures, claiming they diminished the rights of the individual and contravened the sharing of powers in the Constitution.

As the Depression deepened, it caused unbearable hardship. Governments all over the world were expected to act. The free enterprise system, as it was imperfectly configured in the late twenties and early thirties, had failed the people. Unemployment reached highs of 27 percent. With no end in sight, Canada was coming unglued. R.J. Manion, who had been on the leadership ballot with Bennett, worried that the government was slow to pursue remedial policies, other than trade measures, to respond to the suffering, saying "My great fear is that we may hesitate too long and have serious riots verging on a revolution in which life may be taken which would be . . . a terrible catastrophe . . . hungry men can hardly be blamed for refusing to starve quietly."

Bennett was prepared to consider unprecedented measures to help the unemployed, but he was a law and order man and he had no tolerance for social unrest: "If the government is given reason to believe that there is a subtle purpose in the minds of a considerable number of people . . . to take actions against the maintenance of law and order . . . then we will take such action . . . (and) free this country from those who have proven themselves unworthy of our Canadian citizenship."

The government's remedy for the hungry was relief camps, also known as work camps. Established in 1932, the camps provided a place to work, sleep and eat for single, unemployed men, giving the government cheap labour to construct, for example, new roads in remote areas. Though saved from starvation, the men in the camps nevertheless grumbled that they were housed in conditions somewhere between slavery and prison.

Other major government infrastructure projects were in the works. With the United States, the federal government began construction on a deep waterway system for shipping along the St. Lawrence River and into the Great Lakes. Québec was opposed, fearing its ports would lose an advantage.

Bennett took centre stage when he brought the 1932 British Empire Economic Conference to Canada, and used his position as host to bring a new vision to the table: "With the adoption of the Statute of Westminster, the old political empire disappears . . . I found the people looking forward to the conference in the belief that we would lay down at Ottawa the foundations of a new economic empire in which Canada is destined to play a part of ever increasing importance."

Bennett proposed "Imperial Free-Trade." But his proposals for boosting trade among Commonwealth countries were not supported by the British government. The ideas gaining favour at the conference were largely those of British economist John Maynard Keynes, notably lower interest rates and more government spending to stimulate a lagging economy.

On the non-economic front, the government responded to the 1929 Aird Royal Commission and its recommendations for public broadcasting for Canada. As expected, private broadcasters were opposed. So was Québec, which launched a losing court case over broadcasting jurisdiction. When it was clear in 1932 that the federal government had the authority to act, Bennett was ready. He saw public broadcasting as a national asset that should work in the country's interest. "Properly employed, the radio can be a most effective instrument in nation building, with an educational value difficult to estimate." A parliamentary committee was formed to study the issue. Its report served as the basis for the Canadian Radio Broadcasting Act.

Bennett shed his conservative instincts and wanted this new nation-building tool in public hands: "This country must be assured of complete control of broadcasting from Canadian sources, free from foreign interference or influence . . . public ownership can ensure to the people of this country, without regard to class replace, equal enjoyment of the benefits and pleasures of radio broadcasting."

The business community began to look at the Bennett government with added suspicion when the Canadian Radio Broadcasting Commission, the predecessor to the CBC, began operating at public expense.

Bennett might well have intervened more in economic matters if he had had the authority to do so. In April 1931, he had pledged to introduce a system of mandatory unemployment insurance. Following objections from the provinces, the matter was placed before a Dominion-Provincial conference in January 1933, but the first ministers could not agree on how to enable federal interference in areas of provincial jurisdiction.

Every economic instrument came under scrutiny during the Depression as the government continually sought new levers and powers to show that it was acting in the interests of its citizens. Canadian banking and monetary policy was certainly not spared. At the time, Canada did not have a central bank. Each bank issued its own currency, although to the consternation of other chartered banks, the Bank of Montréal was the government's banker. Farmers were particularly angry about bank foreclosures and high interest rates during a period of deflation. In the area of monetary policy, even industry was willing to give the government more control. On July 31, 1933, Bennett appointed the Royal Commission on Banking and Currency to consider the establishment of a central bank.

Headed by Britain's Lord Macmillan, the commission recommended in favour of a central bank by a vote of three to two. The two opposed were representatives of the banking industry. The commission submitted its report on September 27, and it was endorsed by Bennett less than two months later. The banks were then required to transfer their gold reserves to the Bank of Canada, which they vehemently opposed. A determined Bennett declared, "We are going to get that gold and it is just about time for us to find out whether the banks or this government is running this country." The Bank of Canada went into operation on March 11, 1935.

While prime minister, Bennett gave all his time and energy to governing and, unwisely given his leadership responsibilities, very little to the interests of the Conservative party. Ending the Depression and lifting the hearts and minds of Canadians was what mattered most to him. The Conservative political machine, in which he had previously invested his time, money, and technology, was left to languish. Conservative party offices were shut down virtually the day after the 1930 election. The publicity machine, with its pamphlets, letters, and newsletters ceased to function. "We have no organization," Bennett admitted in 1932.

Political donations had dried up for all parties. And patronage, always a powerful government currency, was seldom used to stir the troops. Québec Conservative organizer Thomas Maher said, "Our people fail to grasp how and why their cherished ideal of responsible government fails to work adequately with our party in office. To put it grossly, they asked us everywhere that same question . . . why do we elect members to Parliament? Is it only to make speeches?" Bennett did reward Premier Baxter of New Brunswick with an appointment to the bench, and Premier Ferguson of Ontario was appointed High Commissioner to Britain. However, these two allies were then sorely missed on the ground during the next election.

The political antenna that had served Bennett so well in opposition failed to operate while he was governing. In particular, he failed to perceive the political nuances in Québec. French-speaking MPs, some of whom could not speak English, had no voice in caucus. Québec MP J.A. Barrett complained openly in a letter to Le Devoir that the needs of Québecers were being ignored by the Bennett government. One point of conflict was the presence in caucus of Saskatchewan MP, Dr. W.D. Cowan. Cowan was the treasurer of the Canadian Ku Klux Klan, an organization well-known for its virulent racial discrimination, and its anti-Catholic and anti-French views.

It was clear to Liberals that Conservative unity was on shaky ground in Québec. To expose and exploit the divide, a Liberal backbencher put a motion before the House of Commons calling for paper bank notes to be bilingual. Some bigoted and outspoken Conservative MPs denounced the initiative. Later, when Bennett government tried to cut costs by centralizing translation services in one department, Québec MPs protested the loss of jobs for the mostly francophone translators.

With the Depression unremitting, by 1933, Bennett finally prepared to change course. He concluded that better economic relations and trade with the United States might be in Canada's best interests. After visiting Washington, Bennett agreed to a joint communiqué: "We have agreed to begin a search for means to increase the exchange of commodities between our two countries."

Everything Bennett had turned his hand to before becoming prime minister had been a roaring success. But his prodigious skill and titanic determination were no match for the Depression, and the times took their toll. He wrote to a friend, "The truth is I'm very tired. I would really like to be relieved of this job." His health declined throughout his time as prime minister, but he never looked like a man who had been defeated. Customarily dressed in top hat and cutaway coat and comfortably ensconced in a lavish suite at the fashionable Château Laurier hotel, Bennett presented to Canadians a prime minister in the pink of health and good fortune. And a captain of industry utterly indifferent to their suffering.

At one point, Bennett became determined to change that impression. In a radio broadcast in 1935, he attempted to demonstrate his conversion from raw unfeeling capitalism to populism. "If you believe that in capitalism, there are abuses which work hardship upon the people of this country ... then support my party. For my party has already undertaken and will pursue to the end, a program of reform which will rid the system of these disabilities ... My party stands ... for the greatest good of the greatest number of the people."

But it was too little too late. Facing what appeared to be the inevitable loss of government, Bennett delayed calling an election until deep into the government's fifth year. But while the Depression eased a bit, the promised "better times" never materialized. On March 7, 1935 Bennett suffered a heart attack and was confined to bedrest for four weeks.

As much as Bennett wanted to lead a compassionate and interventionist government, he did not want to do it on borrowed money. Bennett feared that if he did so, Canada would lose its ability to borrow money in international and domestic markets. He needed a currency that investors could reply on, something that runaway and unending deficits would place in jeopardy. The government was disinclined to lower rates artificially, fearing a run on the dollar that would unsettle Canada's credit. "The preservation of our national credit is an indispensable prerequisite to the return of prosperity," said Finance Minister E.N. Rhodes in his 1933 budget speech. To the suggestion that lower interest rates by themselves were a possible economic remedy Bennett scoffed, saying that such a proposition was "a lot a damn communism."

Rather than ease interest rates, the government gave those facing bankruptcy access to more debt. The Farmer's Creditors Arrangement Act provided more flexible payment terms, and amendments were made to the Canadian Farm Loan Act to improve credit access. The Companies' Creditors Arrangement Act was passed in 1933 to help non-farmers deal with their credit problems.

The government strategy on finances was to put as much money as possible into employment and public works programs, while simultaneously reducing the cost of government and its administration. In the 1931 budget, $37 million of $241 million was cut in controllable spending. In 1932, public service salaries were slashed by 10 percent. Bennett established the Office of the Comptroller of the Treasury to review all public spending. Ultimately, even large-scale public works projects were set aside, in favour of programs targeted to the needy.

To avoid government debt and make more funds available to reduce poverty, the government substantially increased taxes. In 1931, sales tax increased four-fold, from one to four percent. Corporate income tax rates increased from eight to ten percent. All imports were subject to a 1 percent excise tax. In 1932, sales tax was raised again, to 6 percent, corporate tax to 11 percent, and the excise tax to 3 percent. A special surtax was added on incomes over $5,000. In 1933, the corporate tax was raised to 12.5 percent. Despite these increases, the deficit ballooned: to $114 million in 1931–32; $221 million in 1932–33; and $134 million in 1933–34.

Bennett's government could claim action, but few results. It provided emergency relief funds at unprecedented levels; haphazardly intervened in trade policy; organized and financed the trade in wheat; nationalized radio broadcasting; began construction of the St. Lawrence Deepwater Way in coordination with the United States; increased the federal contribution to old-age pension and raised all taxes; and directed government spending away from administration and towards Canadians in need. But inevitably Mackenzie King posed the devastating question, "Were Canadians better off in 1935 than they were in 1930?" The indisputable answer was no. Indeed, King lamented, Tory times were hard times, and Bennett was identified as the chief cause. Automobile owners, who could not afford gas, had horses pull their vehicles and named them Bennett Buggies.

The high expectations Bennett had set for himself—and the nation— had not been realized. By the time Bennett finally changed course, it was too late: especially with forces from within who were conspiring against him.

CHAPTER 13

BENNETT: THE DEMISE

This party is an instrument for the good of Canada; that purpose is
to use the collective power for the general good.

IN JANUARY 1934, Henry Stevens, Bennett's minister of industry and
commerce, was asked to fulfill a speaking engagement for the prime minister at a convention of the boot and shoe industry. Stevens took the
opportunity to denigrate the large department stores for squeezing small
business in the retail trade and for abusing small manufacturers in a quest for
perpetually lower prices. He suggested that large Canadian retailers were
exploiting the Depression to commercial advantage. The T. Eaton Co. took
offence and demanded he either prove wrongdoing or retract his statements.
Bennett publicly reprimanded Stevens for "going further in formulating policy, without reference to the head of the government or his colleagues than
the minister should go under sound constitutional practice."

Stevens responded by submitting his resignation, which Bennett refused.

Despite the audacity of his freewheeling Cabinet minister, Bennett challenged Stevens to chair a parliamentary committee to explore issues facing
the retail trade. It was not the commission Stevens wanted, but he accepted.
His mandate would be to investigate the so-called large "price spreads," mass
buying, and their impact on labour conditions. Future Liberal prime minister Lester B. Pearson served as the committee's secretary, and coordinated
research and analysis.

Insiders believed the prime minister had been pushed into launching the committee, and outsiders perceived that a rift was appearing in Tory ranks over economic policy. Bennett claimed otherwise. To outsiders, the potential for split was real and the question remained: who was the true reformer, R.B. Bennett or Henry Stevens?

From the outset, Stevens' work betrayed a clear prejudice. He was a populist Conservative who acted as prosecutor rather than judge and was determined to portray retailers as shameless, heartless profiteers. Responding to one submission to his committee, Stevens remarked, "Thank you very much for the illustrations attached to show the evil influence of the department and chain-store system. We are now continuing the investigation and hope to build up a pretty strong case." Stevens revered small-business capitalism. He had nothing but contempt for "the unscrupulous and cold-blooded . . . little coterie at the top" who were not playing by the rules.

Whereas some Conservatives liked the attention the committee received, the business community felt it was being unfairly and unjustly attacked in a circus-like atmosphere. When the parliamentary session ended in July 1935, the committee was transformed into a more serious royal commission, once again chaired by Stevens. The commission painted capitalism in the most negative light. "The evidence before us . . . has shown that a few great corporations are predominant in the industries that have been investigated; also that this power, all the more dangerous because it is impersonal, can be ruled in such a way that competition within the industry is blocked, the welfare of the producer disregarded, and the interests of the investor ignored. . . ."

Stevens enjoyed the attention, so much so that he exaggerated for effect. A highly inflammatory speech he gave on June 26, 1935, which his office circulated widely to the press, caused a furious C.L. Burton of Simpson's department store to fire off a letter to the prime minister threatening a lawsuit. Bennett attempted to halt distribution of any more copies of the speech, and fumed: "The difficulty is that the statements in the document are incorrect, and when they are corrected it places the minister in a very difficult position and the government in a worse one."

Bennett admonished Stevens in a Cabinet meeting. When news of the reprimand was leaked to the press, Stevens resigned. This time the prime minister accepted. Their spat became open warfare in Conservative ranks. Bennett's comment to Stevens was made public. "I cannot but think it is the duty of any member of a government who is responsible for the publication and circulation of the pamphlet containing inaccurate statements, to take the earliest opportunity to correct or withdraw such statements, with an appropriate expression of regret."

Stevens' reply was swift and direct: "I deeply resent your thinly veiled insinuation that I have been deliberately untruthful.... I cannot but bring to my mind the countless thousands of citizens of Canada who are patiently suffering while others, whom you champion in such eloquent terms, have been reaping rewards far beyond that which any citizen might reasonably expect to win."

To the public, Stevens appeared to be on the side of long-suffering Canadians, and he was certainly winning the publicity battle in this Conservative party civil war. The impression of Bennett as cold-hearted and aloof was reinforced.

Many recommendations made by Stevens' committee were ignored, and he was ultimately barred from the Tory caucus. Bennett unwisely took the rhetoric against Stevens to another level: "The first step towards dictatorship in Europe was . . . a prejudicial appeal to the little man . . . then followed the inevitable utter disregard of constitutional limitations." In thus defending the status quo, Bennett left Stevens ground to be the voice of reform.

The political disease of division and disunity had taken hold of the party before it had even completed one full term in office. Populists and traditional free-enterprising, capitalist, laissez-faire Conservatives were in open revolt. Bennett endeavoured to lead this divided and undisciplined group. Some in Cabinet wanted to apologize to business leaders for Stevens' bombastic attacks; others defended him as a hero to the little man for standing up to the elite and wealthy.

South of the border, Franklin Delano Roosevelt, sworn into office on March 4, 1933, was selling his New Deal to a grateful population. Bennett wanted a made in Canada deal of his own. In 1935, very late in his mandate, he slipped into the cloak of "reformer" by accepting with enthusiasm and conviction a new program of government intervention. There would be even stronger support for farmers and the unemployed, more emphasis on international trade, and direct relief for those facing bankruptcy.

Bennett wanted to reform the federation to address the nation's social and economic ills. Since social policy was primarily in provincial jurisdiction, Bennett needed constitutional change to undertake his preferred initiatives. Ontario and Québec were unwilling. Even though the Unemployment Insurance Act was ruled unconstitutional, the government's willingness to forge ahead with such reforms paved the way for subsequent cooperation with provincial governments.

Bennett took his line of attack directly to the people in speeches delivered in Brockville, Halifax, Toronto, Montréal, and Ottawa. In a radio address on January 2, 1935, he said: "The old order is gone. If you believe that things should be left as they are, you and I hold contrary and irreconcilable views. I am for reform. And, in my mind, reform means government intervention. It means government control and regulation. It means the end of laissez-faire."

He promised to implement many of the recommendations of the Price Spreads Commission and to introduce unemployment insurance. To many economic Conservatives in his party, Bennett was speaking a foreign tongue and living on a different planet. The government was prepared to regulate the economy, introduce unemployment insurance, set labour standards, protect consumers and small investors against the forces of the powerful and mighty, and establish an economic council to gather and interpret data paving the way for even greater government involvement in the operation of the economy. Bennett spoke like a true believer but neither Canadians nor Conservatives could decide if his new deal was sincere.

Even pledging reform, however, the Conservative government could not calm the brewing social unrest. Fifteen hundred men trekked from Vancouver to Ottawa protesting conditions in the relief camps. The government was determined to end the march. When the protestors arrived in Regina, a riot erupted. One police officer was killed; scores of police, rioters, and citizens were injured, and more than 100 protesters found themselves in prison. Like the riots in Winnipeg near the end of the Borden government, the Regina riot left a stain on Bennett that he was hard pressed to remove.

Bennett counted on Mackenzie King to oppose his reforms, thus forcing King to become the defender of the status quo. The Liberals, however, refused to take the bait. Wisely, they supported the notion of reform, but attacked the particulars. The Bennett government, King argued, was inept and insincere. When the Liberals urged Conservatives to bring forward the reform measures, Bennett and his government were not ready. The Liberals cried foul, pouncing on the appearance of Conservative insincerity. When the government finally did present reform-minded bills in the House, they passed with near-unanimous consent.

With Bennett's health failing, the Liberals were now content to let the government defeat itself. Mackenzie King, confident of victory in the next election, decided to play it safe. "I stressed the importance of the Liberal party not making a target for its enemies to fire at . . . the main thing from now on is to realize that the people vote against, rather than for something, and to keep their mind focused on Bennett and his mismanagement of things."

Signs such as increased investment and employment gave the appearance that the end of the Depression was in sight. Even though one million Canadians were dependent on government for relief, and personal income had declined in real terms by about one-quarter during Bennett's administration, the wisdom of waiting until the fifth year of Parliament before calling an election looked like it might pay off. The Liberals were discomfited at Bennett's move to the centre-left, even if there remained a rift in the Tory coalition.

BENNETT HAD CONSIDERED retiring in the spring of 1935. But he could not stomach the thought of Stevens assuming the Tory leadership. The two crossed swords in Parliament on June 19, 1935. Stevens severely rebuked the prime minister for inaction. The prime minister parried: "If the people of the country have been led into the belief that this Parliament can pass any kind of legislation it likes regardless of the Constitution, the age of lawlessness is upon us."

Just as the Tories saw a glimmer of hope, however, Henry Herbert Stevens made his move, on July 7, 1935 and announced he had received a petition asking him to lead a new party dedicated to reconstruction and reform.

A split had been brewing for months, and the gloves—finally—were off. In a letter to Stevens, Bennett declared that he was prepared to fight Stevens on the hustings, John L. Sullivan-style, a reference to the former world heavyweight boxing champion.

The election was called for October 14, 1935, stretching the government's term to five years, two and a half months.

In the campaign, Stevens' Reconstruction party relied on the magnetism of its self-appointed leader, but also sought support from the Retail Merchants Association. The Reconstruction platform called for a more equitable distribution of wealth and the elimination of unemployment. Policy measures included increased taxes on the wealthy, easier credit, profit restrictions, and increased public works. But the real platform was Henry Stevens himself, who during the campaign remarked, "As I address the meetings I found that my very clearest and best arguments, based on statistics, were usually received with respect, but with little understanding. . . . the moment I touch the human side of the story, such as economic slavery, sweatshops etc. or condemn the banks I would get the audience on their toes at once." Some Conservatives, such as R.J. Manion, deluded themselves into thinking Stevens would attract anti-government votes that otherwise would go Liberal.

The Conservative platform continued Bennett's new deal and included easier credit, credit relief, earlier retirement, national broadcasting, neutrality in foreign wars, freer trade with the United States, and constitutional reform to strengthen the federal government in economic matters. Bennett's policy of neutrality on foreign wars was an attempt to gain support in Québec, an important signal because the Italian army had invaded Ethiopia and fears were mounting over war in Europe. As Stephen Harper would much later maintain regarding Canada's military involvement in Afghanistan, Bennett said military policy was an issue for Parliament to decide.

Bennett had the courage to run on his record, which he claimed was "a proud one." In particular, he noted the improvements since 1933, and the many reforms his government had undertaken to relieve the despair of the unemployed. Mackenzie King countered that the government had done enough to defeat itself. "You've had five years of the Bennett government," King reminded voters. "I wonder if any of you are as well off now as when it started." The Liberals portrayed Bennett as an autocrat. Mackenzie King, they promised, would unite Canadians and work cooperatively and in a conciliatory fashion. Mackenzie King shared the platform with many provincial leaders, including Premier John Bracken of Manitoba (who would later became Conservative leader).

The ballot was crowded. In addition to the Liberal and Conservative parties—who together had taken 93.3 percent of the vote in the previous election—there were the CCF, Social Credit, and Reconstruction parties. The many choices and the resulting worry about minority government were issues Mackenzie King exploited. Minority parties, he warned, might be in a position to extract unhealthy concessions from the governing party. "Stability and an unmistakable majority are more essential than ever," explained King. Liberal campaign posters boldly carried the arrogant slogans: "King or chaos!" and "Only King can win: give them a working majority!" In the end, a minority Parliament was avoided, but the two main political parties ended up with only 74.5 percent of the vote in 1935, a decline of 18.8 percentage points.

Bennett did not go down without a fight. He filled the Montréal Forum and Toronto's Maple Leaf Gardens with rousing rallies. But like a weary boxer, down he went. The Conservative drubbing was both dramatic and inevitable; the party was reduced to a mere 39 seats. Mackenzie King now commanded a majority government caucus of 178 members. The Reconstruction party won only one seat, its leader's. Social Credit picked up 17 seats, including 15 of 17 in Alberta. The lone Alberta seat that went Tory was Bennett's.

But the seat tally wasn't the whole story. In fact, compared with the 1930 election, the Liberal share of the popular vote decreased, from 45.5 percent to 44.7 percent. Conservative support declined more dramatically; from 47.8 percent to 29.8 percent—the party was reduced to one seat in Atlantic Canada, five in Québec (none French speaking), 25 in Ontario, and nine in Western Canada.

The Reconstruction party earned an impressive 8.8 percent of the vote, most of it drawn from the Conservatives. Blame this Conservative defeat, or at least its magnitude, on divisions within Conservative ranks. The rift between Bennett and Stevens, and Bennett's inability to keep Stevens within the Conservative tent, proved fatal. Combining Reconstruction and Conservative votes would have yielded an additional 42 seats, a substantial number but still not enough to form a Conservative government.

The prolonged misery of the Depression, combined with the widespread impression of Tories as cold-hearted and indifferent to the working class, was enough to defeat the government. Poor organizational depth and its lack of discipline was enough to defeat the party. The magnitude of the defeat could probably have been reduced with a more politically astute leader at the controls, a leader who could demand—and get—unity in Cabinet and caucus.

WHEN PARLIAMENT RESUMED and Conservative forces found themselves once again on the Opposition benches, a bitter Bennett began to sound more like a traditional conservative. Gone suddenly was the rhetoric of a new-deal reformer. He thundered against the rise of dictatorships around the world, such as Germany, and for greater investment in national defence. He warned of the dangers of protectionism and advocated freer trade.

Bennett led the minority Conservative party through 1936, though he was never able to reconcile the two bickering factions in caucus: the right-wing capitalist bloc and the more populist reform-oriented wing. The Conservative cause, federal and provincial, had been weakened across the country. In 1931 Conservatives had held power in Ottawa and in five of nine provinces. By the end of the Depression it held none, although a Tory friendly government held power in Québec. The federal Conservative party was a shadow of its former self. Its caucus no longer represented the country. Half its members hailed from southern Ontario and most of its stalwarts in the front benches were toothless relics.

Still, Bennett took his responsibilities to hold the new Liberal government to account seriously. In the House, he was a one-man show, just as he had been as prime minister. When Mackenzie King proposed a "made in Canada" defence policy, Bennett reverted to traditional Tory policy: "When Britain goes we go." This did not build new bridges into Québec. It was clear that the Tory party needed to be rebuilt. The convention to choose Bennett's successor was set for Ottawa on July 5, 1938. It was here that the party changed its name from Liberal Conservative party to the less confusing National Conservative party. Bennett addressed the convention and, once again, revealed that he did not understand Québec. "My friends from Québec, you and I are British subjects together, not English or French, but British subjects, and in that proud name I ask you to join with other British subjects not only in Canada but in every part of this great world, to ensure the prosperity of Canada and the safety of the Commonwealth."

Delegates from Québec had come to the convention seeking a national referendum before Canadian troops could be sent overseas. Liberals, who had set up a debate in the House of Commons on defence policy in the days before the Conservative convention, could only smile at Bennett's convention message.

Bennett was willing to entertain a movement at the convention for him to remain party leader. But the policy resolutions placed before the convention favoured traditional conservative ideology and took the party away from where Bennett had been leading it. With Bennett waiting in the wings, his brother-in-law, advisor, and confidant, William D. "Wild Bill" Herridge, addressed the convention and introduced a motion to assert Bennett's interventionist approach: ". . . be it therefore resolved that the new Liberal Conservative party pledge itself to undertake whatever economic and monetary reforms may be required to stabilize production upon its *maximum* level, and to raise purchasing power to that level, recognizing that such reforms will involve a measure of *government planning and control of the economic and monetary systems.*"

A seconder to the motion could not be found.

Bennett wanted all the other leadership candidates to withdraw to support him enthusiastically. But Robert J. Manion was unwilling to do so. With less than an hour to go before voting began, Bennett signalled that he was not in the race. Herridge realized Bennett's day was done and fumed: "Ladies and gentlemen . . . I tell you this Conservative party will disappear, and history will record this as the day of its funeral service. Ladies and gentlemen, you stand either for reaction or for reform."

Herridge was correct on one point: the Conservative party would not know power for another two decades.

As Bennett faced retirement, veteran journalist Grattan O'Leary painted a picture of the former prime minister as a talented man fundamentally disconnected from the heart of the nation: "Between 1930 and 1935 the Conservative party . . . was out of touch with its leader, and its leader out of touch with the people. Mr. Bennett, living between his office in the Parliament buildings and in his rooms in the Château Laurier was remote from realities. He could be magnificent in Parliament. He could know what to do when England went off the gold standard . . . he did not know what the people were saying, what they were thinking, what many of them were enduring. It was not that he was indifferent or callous. He was simply without facilities for knowing. Yet no leader of a national party in our day may live the life of a monastic, no matter what his integrity or his talents."

At Bennett's retirement dinner at Toronto's Royal York Hotel on January 16, 1939, former prime minister Arthur Meighen paid tribute to Bennett's strength and vision. In words that would comfort any unpopular leader, Meighen contended that it is the duty of a prime minister to sacrifice political popularity in order to do what is right for the nation: ". . . in our Dominion where sections abound, a dominion of races, of classes and of creeds, of many languages and many origins, there are times when no prime minister can be true to the nation he is sworn to serve. . . . the guest of tonight must not leave our shores with any consciousness in his heart of failure as directing head of this country. There was no failure in that capacity."

Robert Borden gave a more balanced review of Bennett's record in 1935: "His splendid ability, his keen grasp of general conditions, both national and international, his complete devotion to public duty in the welfare of our country, the admirable resourcefulness and courage with which he faced the overwhelming difficulties of the past five years, entitle him to the respect, admiration and gratitude of all right-thinking Canadians."

Some criticized Bennett's mercurial leadership style. Said Bennett's long-time Cabinet colleague C.H. Cahan, "The sun never sets on the day on which the Prime Minister has insulted some good and loyal conservative."

Bennett was not one to admit to error. In his farewell as party leader in 1938 he proclaimed: "I have nothing to regret and nothing to retract—not a thing." Indeed, many of his reforms have stood the test of time. The institutions and programs he created—the CBC, the Bank of Canada, farm credit agencies and agricultural marketing boards, unemployment insurance—remain in place to this day. Bennett said, "This party is an instrument for the good of Canada; that purpose is to use the collective power for the general good." Bennett used the power of the state to correct the perceived inadequacies of the capitalist system. The suffering during the Depression was all the evidence he needed to justify deep government intervention.

In the summer before his defeat, Bennett had written, "I believe there is written a record of which no one need be ashamed, although it is quite probable that we have made mistakes as all poor human creatures must." Bennett concluded that the Depression, though not of his making, was the cause of his defeat. But he also blamed Stevens. "As a result of Mr. Stevens's treachery, the Liberals are in power."

In his brilliant book portraying Bennett and his government, *Reaction and Reform*, Larry Glassford offered this insight: "Perhaps the greatest need was for a leader able to harmonize the divergent strands of opinion within Canadian conservatism, and then inspire its followers to battle Grits and socialists, rather than each other."

Bennett was unforgiving in the face of rejection and peevishly chose to retire in England. He disposed of all his Canadian assets, and left endowment funds to Dalhousie and Mount Allison Universities.

When the future mayor of Ottawa, Charlotte Whitton, asked him in 1939 to return to Canada, Bennett bitterly replied, "Don't you think I was given a furlough by the Canadian people in 1935? They rejected me and all my plans and ideas and hopes ...As for wanting me back that is sheer nonsense, Charlotte, and you must know it. They gave me a great sendoff for many reasons. Some for conscience sake; some for real regard; some glad to be rid of me. But it just became a bit of mob manifestation; hosanna in the highest and crucify him a week later." Bennett was not entirely unoccupied. In 1940, British Prime Minister Winston Churchill commanded Bennett to review the national security implications of employing alien engineers and aircraft workers during the war. Bennett recommended against their employment. He entered the House of Lords on July 23, 1941.

Bennett died peacefully on June 26, 1947 and was buried in England.

CHAPTER 14

ROBERT J. MANION: DEFEATED BY LEGACY

King has the luck of the very devil—just as he was on the verge of going out,
this crisis comes along and allows people to forget his past sins.

ROBERT MANION ENTERED the world of politics as a Liberal. Later, his centrist approach to policy and a unique relationship with Québecers looked like a winning combination as he led Tories into the 1940 election. But Canadians thought otherwise after the outbreak of World War II fearing how the Tories might govern.

Dr. Robert James Manion, born November 19, 1881 in Pembroke, Ontario, was a resident of Fort William, Ontario for most of his life. A graduate of Queen's University, Manion served with the Canadian Army Medical Corps where he was awarded the Military Cross for heroism at the battle of Vimy Ridge. Manion was asked to run for Parliament by his friend, Wilfrid Laurier, and was a member of the Liberal party before the Great War. But his patriotic instincts led him away from the Liberal party because he supported conscription. Manion explained his conversion this way: "I, as a young man, inherited the Liberal tradition and followed it rather actively.... However, there existed the one justification for a party man leaving his party—difference of opinion on a great principle."

Manion was elected as the Liberal-Unionist MP for Fort William in the conscription election of 1917 and served Robert Borden as minister of soldiers' civil re-establishment. Unlike most Conservatives from Ontario,

Manion was a Catholic. More unusual, he was married to a French Canadian, Yvonne Desaulniers, and his children were bilingual. He was a fascinating figure in Conservative circles, particularly in Québec where most thought Ontario Tories were anti-French and anti-Catholic Orangemen. Manion offered an opening in Québec that few other Conservatives could.

Manion won the leadership on July 7, 1938 in an unpredictable convention where the field of candidates was unknown beforehand. It was not even clear a leadership vote would occur until the final moment, when R.B. Bennett was unable to achieve unanimous support to continue his leadership. Manion won the leadership on the second ballot with 53 percent of the vote, compared with 41.4 percent for Murdoch Alexander MacPherson, who had no campaign material and was utterly unprepared to run, and whose wife did not even bother to attend.

Manion had built an improbable coalition of Orange Order supporters from Ontario and delegates from Québec. On the night Manion was elected, Mackenzie King confidently wrote in his diary, "Liberalism should be able to retain power in Canada for some years to come." Manion, 56, entered the House of Commons following a November 1938 by-election in London, Ontario.

An advocate of social policy reform, Manion was a new breed of Tory. He rankled the right-wing editorialists at the Montréal *Gazette*, who warned: "If the new leader has any inclination to move to the left he can of course indulge it, but he cannot take the Conservative party with him. In his own interest he should be warned against a false step which may lead him away from the great political element in this country upon whose support he must rely, a step which may conceivably compel that element to seek a new allegiance."

Manion was a compassionate Conservative: "I believe that action is necessary at the present time to cure the block of unemployment and to bring a greater measure of social justice to all our citizens." To many in the party, this sounded like socialism. Manion confided to his son that his "terrible crime" was his willingness to give opportunities to those who wanted to work and earn wages.

Manion did not get along with Arthur Meighen, who was then leading the party in the Senate. They clashed over railway policy: Manion opposed consolidation and Meighen favoured unification. Meighen cast doubt on Manion's ability as leader. "(There) are very serious questions whether he can win, and still graver questions as to how he could handle the job after he did win."

But Manion was convinced Mackenzie King's popularity was in decline and that the government would defeat itself. "If we can only avoid some big issue coming up that may completely befuddle the minds of the electorate, I feel convinced that King is on his way out."

With the threat of war again looming over Europe, Canada was preparing for its role in the conflict. Once again, the issue was conscription. Would Manion follow the policies established by Borden or set a new course? He well knew what was in the hearts and minds of Québecers on this issue, and he did not want the party to be seen as an English-only enterprise. In a speech on March 27, 1939, Manion boldly climbed off the fence. "I do not believe Canadian youth should be conscripted to fight outside the borders of Canada . . . Canada can play her part in the Empire and in support of our democratic institutions by full cooperation with Great Britain through volunteer units, through supplying munitions, foods and other necessities to our allies, and by fully protecting Canada's own territory."

Manion thus outraged many Conservatives who believed he was turning his back both on the empire and on traditional Tory policies. Grumblings about Manion's Liberal past, his religion, and his pandering to Québec rolled through the backrooms of the party. Staunch imperialists bitterly complained that Manion's position was no different from Mackenzie King's. Manion—a decorated war hero—countered that he had taken the position he thought was right for Canada *and* his party.

Determined to curry political favour in Québec, Manion brokered an agreement with Québec Premier Maurice Duplessis. For Québec, Manion promised federal funds. From Québec, Manion would get votes. Said Duplessis: . . . "We are prepared to do the following just as soon as the date of the federal election is finally announced. Without advertising it in any way each Québec member of the Union National will be requested and instructed to cooperate only with the Conservative candidate in his county. . . . in return . . . the Conservative party promises to cooperate fully with the Québec provincial government in starting, immediately after the election, extensive unemployment relief works in all the counties of the province of Québec, where help is needed."

Manion replied confidently that "[The Duplessis] government can count on 100 percent cooperation from me when the time comes." The Tories had not been in such a strong position in Québec since the days of Macdonald.

Then, on September 1, 1939, the Nazis invaded Poland. This was the "big issue" that Manion feared might rescue King. "King has the luck of the very devil," said Manion. "Just as he was on the verge of going out, this crisis comes along and allows people to forget his past sins . . . of course it all depends on how he carries on; and I cannot imagine that he will do very well."

King did not take a strong leadership position at the outset of the war, declaring that war policy was a matter for Parliament to decide. The House was brought into session on September 7 to gain support "for the defence of Canada." "There can be no neutrality for Canada," Manion declared, "while Britain is engaged in a war of life and death." By September 10, Canada was at war. King never dealt with the issue of "When Britain is at war, Canada is at war," because Canada had passed its own resolution to enter the war without regard to any request from the British. The imperialist purists were annoyed at the lack of "ready-aye-ready," but there were no objections from the governor general, Lord Tweedsmuir: "The prime minister has succeeded very skillfully in aligning Canada alongside Britain with a minimum of disturbance. He, of course, is being criticized for not declaring himself roundly and clearly, but in my view his policy has been the right one."

A political truce was declared so that by-elections would go to the party currently holding the seat and the by-election would be deferred until after the next session of Parliament. But the political truce quickly ended when in late September, Québec Premier Duplessis called an election. Duplessis claimed Mackenzie King was finagling to centralize power in Ottawa and assimilate Québec. Federal Liberals wanted to stop Duplessis at all costs and undermine or negate his pledge to Manion. If Duplessis won, they warned Québecers ominously, it would be a first step towards conscription and a "war happy" Conservative government in Ottawa. Despite Manion's declaration that he opposed conscription, Liberals asserted that "everyone knew, in their hearts, that Tories wanted conscription." Three senior Québec Cabinet ministers in the King government threatened to resign if Duplessis won. Manion replied, "Why should they resign because of a provincial result no one knows; but, of course, their purpose was to try and frighten the French Canadians into voting against Duplessis and give (Liberals) a chance to get their filthy machine back in power down there, then perhaps pull an election up here in the hope of sweeping the country."

During the Québec election, on the advice of his Québec lieutenants, Manion stayed out of Quebec. Duplessis was trounced by Liberal leader Joseph-Adélard Godbout, 70 seats to 15. His cooperation agreement with the federal Conservatives was now moot. Manion was dismayed that Duplessis had gone to the polls and stunned that Liberals could have cast the re-election of the Union Nationale as a vote for conscription. Conservatives, who had not won a majority of seats in Québec since 1882, were once again outfoxed and dead in French Canada.

Conservatives began to wonder if they had made a mistake choosing Manion, and their attention was drawn to Ontario Conservative leader George Drew who was attacking King in public for ". . . so little effort to prosecute Canada's duty in the war in the vigorous manner the people of Canada desire to see." This was a throwback to Tory policy in World War I: stand with the empire whatever the cost.

Sensing Conservative weakness, and fearing bad news on the war front, King repudiated a commitment at the outset of the war not to call an election. His own notes reveal his thinking: "The greatest relief of all is the probability of having the election over before the worst of the fighting begins in Europe. I have dreaded having to choose the moment for the campaign and specifically to choose a time when human lives are being slaughtered by hundreds of thousands, if not by millions. In this way, we can probably have the election over before the spring campaign in Europe begins."

A federal election was called for March 26, 1940. King contended that for reasons of unity he needed a mandate. Referring to provincial Tory George Drew's slogan, "King must go," King asserted: "How can I be expected to do what is expected of me by this country . . . if all of my time and thought is to be surrounded by the animosities of political opponents seeking to undermine every effort . . ." Manion was shocked at King's reversal and his naked ploy for power. In moving forward with the election, King had broken his word. The Conservative party, having, unwisely, trusted the Liberal prime minister, was not ready for the election. "The understanding was that the House of Commons would be called in regular session and that we would discuss the activities of the government. . . ."

Manion learned a lesson, one that all subsequent Conservative leaders would need to take to heart: when it comes to acquiring or maintaining power, Liberal leaders will do whatever it takes, commitments and promises be damned. It was a lesson that good-natured future Tory leaders Stanfield and Clark ought to have learned, but did not. Both would fail to exploit their advantage because they believed what they were told by Liberals.

On January 26, the Conservative caucus met to plan election strategy. It unanimously endorsed Manion's policy against conscription and, reaching back to the success the party had enjoyed in 1917, proposed "a national government . . . in the sense that the very best brains obtainable among our people are drafted to serve in the Cabinet." This represented a reversal of position for Manion. Less than a year earlier he had rejected this notion, arguing that, "Under our system, there must be a government and opposition."

This change in course threw the Conservative party into disarray. It was awkward and confusing for party workers to pitch a new non-political institution in the middle of an election campaign. Non-Conservatives were encouraged to seek the party's nomination in local constituencies if they believed "they were the best for the times." Chaos ensued.

For a coalition to work, the Conservatives had to attract Liberal or CCF supporters to their side. This did not happen. There was no contentious single issue like conscription to draw them in. All Manion had to sell was the idea that he would be open to inviting the best and the brightest among those elected to join in his government. However, Mackenzie King and CCF leader J.S. Wordsworth said they would have nothing to do with a Manion government. Furthermore, despite Manion's position against conscription, there was a lingering fear among the electorate that, of all the political parties, Conservatives were the ones most likely to change their minds on the issue.

Norman Rogers, King's minister of defence, clearly stated that the election was a question of trust: "There is only one outstanding issue. It is the choice of those to whom you are prepared to commit the direction of the Canadian war effort during the critical years that lie ahead of us."

Manion was frustrated and became short-tempered over his inability to gain support for his plans for a national government. He accused Rogers of being ". . . an irresponsible little falsifier . . . an unscrupulous little man . . . with a contempt for the truth." Manion appeared desperate. Donors stayed away in droves as Liberals out-fundraised the Tories by a margin of two-to-one.

The result was a Liberal landslide. Mackenzie King's Liberals took 184 seats. Only forty Tory/National government candidates were elected. Conservatives had done no better than when they were defeated after the Depression. The country endorsed King's cautious response to the war and, out of fear, rejected the imperial-loving Conservatives. King's sneak attack in calling the election was rewarded with an overwhelming victory. Manion lost his seat and, for obvious reasons, wanted to resign, but hinted he would follow the will of caucus. He was prepared, in fact eager, to carry on the fight if the party was willing. "If you accept my resignation I shall be quite content, for my personal wish is to retire. I realize that my first obligation is to the party, as is yours. Therefore, if you decide that in the best interests of the party, you cannot accept my resignation; my duty will be to return to the House of Commons as soon as it is possible to render the highest possible public service of which I am capable."

After some back-and-forth discussion with Manion, his resignation was accepted by a vote of twenty-six to five. Even though he had offered his resignation, Manion nonetheless expected more: "It was damned rotten of them to do it and the insulting manner in which they got it. Seemed almost indecent haste. As usual, I find that some who owed me much and other supposed friends were the men who hurried acceptance of my resignation." The caucus then elected R.B. Hanson to lead the party in Parliament.

Manion was thoroughly disillusioned by politics. His instinctively moderate positions did not reconcile with the Tory image that lingered after Borden, Meighen, and Bennett. If only Duplessis had not lost in 1939; if only the Liberals had not been so effective in distorting Manion's positions; if only the Liberals did not fearmonger; if only the Liberals were not so effective in keeping power for themselves. If only Tories knew how to win.

Manion died three years after resigning the leadership.

CHAPTER 15

THE WAR YEARS:
HANSON AND MEIGHEN

Who will dare to say that Canada is even in sight of a total war? I shall,
therefore, urge with all the power I can bring to bear compulsory selective
service over the whole field of war.

AFTER MANION, the man the Tories selected to lead their party in
Parliament was a lawyer and twice mayor of Fredericton. R.B.
Hanson had served in the House of Commons from 1921 to 1935,
including one year as minister of trade and commerce in the Bennett government. He was one of the few Tories to win a seat in 1940. Hanson
wanted Meighen to leave the Senate and return as leader. Meighen declined.
Hanson had no leadership aspirations, which is perhaps why he was chosen
by caucus to lead the party in the House of Commons on an interim basis.
Hanson's interregnum lasted longer than anyone would have predicted,
however, and he ably led a party struggling for an identity over a period that
covered much of World War II.

A year into the war, the country grew impatient over its lack of
progress, and public opinion mounted on Prime Minister Mackenzie King
to change his view on conscription. King noted in his diary, "It would create a worse situation in Canada than it would remedy." To ensure national
unity, the Conservatives under Hanson were prepared to form a national
government with the Liberals. King laughed off the suggestion. "[A] party
which represents in this Parliament some 183 members of a total membership

of 245 may pretty well claim to be a national government in the true sense of the word."

Nonetheless, King was prepared to invite opposition MPs into a war committee of the Cabinet. But Hanson correctly interpreted the offer as meaningless and declined. The Tories provided a more important service to the country by holding the government accountable for its performance. Though small in number, King wrote that Conservatives deserved credit for their responsible and effective conduct in the House: "The opposition has been helpful in causing the government to perhaps determine more quickly and definitely what was to be done in some matters that might otherwise have been the case. On the whole, their attitude has been constructively helpful, although there has been more party politics than one would have liked to see at a time like this."

Parliament was non-partisan in the early years of the war. The Conservative party lacked purpose and fundraising was so abysmal that to meet its payroll a hat was passed among MPs and senators and each member contributed 50 dollars.

Conservative strategists such as J.M. Macdonnell, president of the National Trust Company, worried the party might not survive. The chief concern was not Liberal hegemony, but the CCF, which was emerging as a force and a compelling alternative government in the eyes of the public. "The lower we fall, the more I feel [the Tories] are needed. The opposition should not be allowed to get into the hands of the CCF. Only a handful of people in this country want socialism." An unofficial "invitation-only" conference of Conservative supporters was held in Montréal on January 11 and 12, 1941, "... for the purpose of considering what they could do to assist the party to resume the important part it has played in the maintenance of constitutional government in Canada." Hanson and future leaders George Drew and John Diefenbaker also attended. Despite high hopes, the conference accomplished little. That's because the ingredient necessary to reinvigorate the Conservative party was new leadership. As an unelected, interim leader, Hanson properly declined to set any new policies for the party.

The National Resources Mobilization Act passed in June of 1940 required a national registration and compulsory military training for single men between the ages of twenty-one and twenty-four. In April of 1941, the conscripted soldiers would be assigned permanently to coastal defence units, thereby resulting in two armies: conscripts for home defence and the regular army for overseas service. Hanson favoured conscription. But sensing that the Liberal government would be forced to lead on conscription,

Hanson waited on the sidelines for the government to admit its miscalculation. This apparent lack of leadership did not go over well with many Conservatives. Tory MP Dr. Herbert Bruce spoke out in favour of full conscription, adding he "didn't care a damn about the fortunes of the Conservative party."

By 1941, 300,000 men out of a total population of 11.5 million had volunteered for service. The military was absorbing volunteers as fast as they could be processed. Meanwhile, recruitment in Québec was weak. The military itself was not well equipped to integrate French-speaking soldiers. Its equipment, manuals, and other supporting material were often available only in English. And the ability of French-speaking soldiers to rise in the ranks was limited. There was no Québec military college and no French brigade.

When Hanson toured Europe in 1941, he met with Churchill who said that conscription was not a pressing concern for Canada *at the moment*. Later that fall, Hanson addressed the Tory elite at Toronto's Albany Club, saying, "Conscription is bound to come to the front more insistently; but it must come from the people themselves. To make a political move would defeat the very purpose of those who have it in view." Arthur Meighen, who observed Hanson from his perch in the Senate, expressed dismay. "If the people have to be enlightened on the subject have we not a duty to enlighten them?"

Hanson agreed to lead the party into the parliamentary session until the end of 1942, but added, "Beyond this I will not go." The executive and the party met on November 7, 1941 to discuss the time and place for a national leadership convention.

Editorials in the *Globe* called for renewal in the Conservative party, to "keep the faint spark of democracy from being stamped out." What were characterized as the dictatorial practices of Mackenzie King—such as incarceration without trial—were cited as reasons why the country needed a strong opposition. The *Globe* called for a new but not unfamiliar leader. "A leader of experience in war administration who is at the same time skilled in parliamentary debate, equipped with a keen intellect and fortified by moral courage . . . Arthur Meighen."

Meighen had been publicly critical of both Hanson and Manion for not leading the charge in favour of conscription. When war broke out, Meighen was angry over King's lack of preparedness. He felt that the Liberals had sent too few men to Europe, with not nearly enough support. He chastised the government from the floor of the Senate: "Do not be always looking years ahead. Try to get the utmost done in the next month, still more in the second, still more in the third." Meighen later spoke against the National Resources Mobilization Act; he agreed with the general principle of enhancing Canada's war effort, but felt that the bill was a shabby attempt at the job. "It confines [the mobilization of solders] to a home area where there can be no fighting—none, at least, until by defeat on decisive theatres the war has already been lost."

His opponents remembered Meighen as the driving force behind conscription in the last war and the resulting alienation of French Canada, for his heavy-handed response to the Winnipeg strike, and for alienating immigrants with restrictive voting and civil-liberty measures. Anticipating a bloody debate in the party on conscription, the sole Québec Conservative MP left the caucus to sit as an independent. Joseph Sasseville Roy, the MP from Gaspé, went further in condemning his former party: "(A Québec Conservative) is at best a tolerated stranger; accepted from necessity and looked at with a certain degree of curiosity . . . he is and always will be a poor relation . . . Conservatives are firm in the opinion that we French-Canadians are a source of trouble in their endeavours to make Canada an American England."

Meighen realized he was in a no-win situation. "They are determined to name a leader and to come out for a total war, national government and conscription. . . . I'm in a terrible position." He travelled to Manitoba to visit Premier John Bracken. Though Bracken led the Liberal-Progressive Party, the Liberal moniker was of no consequence because Bracken had run Manitoba like a conservative over the previous 20 years. Meighen may have planted a seed, but he was unable to persuade Bracken to seek national leadership.

The party held a meeting on November 7, 1941 to discuss leadership. Many thought the party should dispense with a convention and move immediately to name Meighen as leader. A 54-member committee was given the task of choosing the best course to follow. Its choice was less than unanimous, 37 to 13, but Meighen was nonetheless asked to take over the party's top job. He refused, saying he would not accept the position without a unanimous vote.

After many attempts to sort through the chaos, the delegates as a whole voted 129 to 4 in favour of Meighen. A motion to make the vote unanimous was declared, though Meighen had already left the meeting by that time. He was told of the unanimous resolution at the train station. He declined, but then reconsidered. Meighen may have been swayed by the fact that his sons, Ted and Max, were serving in the Canadian military. Just a few months before he had written, "I never knew what human longing was until separated by war from the sons I love so much . . . I sit in my office just gazing on the folder with its two photos."

King was not thrilled to face his old political rival in the House again: "I am getting past the time when I can fight in public with a man of Meighen's type who is sarcastic, vitriolic and the meanest type of politician." But he need not have worried. The country had previously rejected Meighen and the likelihood of a former leader successfully reclaiming high office was not strong.

Back in the saddle as Conservative leader, Meighen challenged King to form a coalition government, invoke conscription and dramatically intensify Canada's war effort. Meighen wanted to form a government out of the Conservative caucus and conscription-minded Liberals, just as Borden had done in World War II, but first he needed a seat in the House of Commons. He chose perhaps the safest Conservative seat in the country: York South. The riding had elected only Conservatives; it was even won by 2,482 votes during the Liberal sweep of 1940.

The Liberal party did not field a candidate against Meighen. This was not a Liberal act of courtesy, rather, according to Meighen, "(King) did so, so the vote opposing me would not be divided. He wanted it entirely concentrated and did not care much under what office it was concentrated." And so the anti-Meighen forces lined up behind CCF candidate Joseph Noseworthy.

Meighen's advisors recommended he downplay conscription and national government. However, a campaign had already begun across Ontario called "Total War Now." In the meantime, Mackenzie King began to discuss a plebiscite—rather than an election—on the issue of conscription. The speech from the throne, delivered on January 22, 1942, said: "My ministers . . . will seek, from the people, by means of a plebiscite, release from any obligation arising out of any past commitments restricting the methods of raising men for military service."

It was an unexpectedly difficult by-election for Meighen. When asked if he was prepared to conscript capital as well as men for the war effort, he replied: "If we have to conscript wealth to win the war, we will, but people of common sense don't advocate that until the last gasp." People wondered if Meighen was more interested protecting the wealthy than in saving Canadian soldiers' lives. Exploiting Meighen's stumble, the Liberal party gleefully contributed $1,000 to the CCF campaign.

In the end, Meighen was clobbered, losing 16,408 to 11,952, a humiliating defeat that he did not take well: "The result, I must admit, was much worse than I thought possible."

Meighen claimed that he had been denied entry into the House of Commons by the resolve of the leaders of three parties—Liberal, CCF, and Communist. This left the Conservative party in chaos, and Meighen sent a cautionary letter to caucus on February 26, 1942: ". . . you have expressed your unanimous wish . . . that I should not now retire from leadership. I am prepared to cede to this desire and to wait for a reasonable time the development of events."

King's promised plebiscite on conscription took place on April 27, 1942, and passed in every province except Québec, where it received only 27.1 percent support. On June 10, King famously interpreted the results: "Not necessarily conscription, but conscription if necessary." Clever politics. Voting for conscription liberated the government from its past policies and supported the direction the government wanted to take. Voting against conscription affirmed a long-held government policy. King could not lose. Most Conservatives favoured conscription and voted yes in the referendum, effectively condoning King's actions.

After Meighen's by-election disaster, the Tories were a spent force. Hanson remained leader in the Commons, but mostly declined to attack the government on its war policies when instructed by Meighen. Hanson wanted to prepare for post-war elections and thought renewal on leadership and policy were the priorities. This process of renewal began at a non-sanctioned conference held on August 4, 1942, in Port Hope, Ontario to "discuss Canada's war and postwar problems." The invitation-only "Roundtable on Canadian policy" was the brainchild of J.M. Macdonnell.

The conference was about policy and strategy, not leadership. Anyone who might seek to lead the party was not invited. One conference organizer remarked, "It is true that we cannot speak of the party or its leaders . . . but what we decide here will inevitably have an effect on their conduct and on the attitude of the Canadian people to the Conservative party." Nor did the conference speak for French Canada. Only ten of the 159 who attended represented Québec.

The point was to urge Conservatives to think "progressively," particularly in the area of social policy. The conference debated a new "national policy," not based on protection and railways, but in favour of social security, "to see that every citizen is provided with employment and wage which will enable him to live with decency." Fear of the CCF motivated party members to take this more humanistic approach. As one delegate put it, "Would you rather adopt a policy which will retain to the largest amount possible a free enterprise system or hand government over to the CCF? In plain words I would say, half a loaf is better than no bread at all."

While every conference delegate supported the free enterprise system, most advocated a shift to a "middle way."

Arthur Meighen greeted the delegates by letter. It was clear that the former leader, who wanted to talk about the war rather than social policy, was fatally out of sync with the conference objectives. "(We must sustain) our British inheritance of free institutions . . . to become at whatever cost to itself the instrument of a great all-Canadian league for war . . . whose mission is to forge into one irresistible force with a single thought of victory those who are really resolved to win this war, to live and not to die."

Delegates were encouraged to consider how to turn around Conservative fortunes in Québec. They offered inclusion and understanding: "Through a fruitful partnership between two great races, French and English . . . the two cultures are part and parcel of our future development and Canada's true greatness depends on sympathy and understanding between these two original races."

The delegates called for strengthening Canada's relationships with the Commonwealth and the United States. They also discussed support for farmers struggling with debt. The conference was union-friendly, supporting "full freedom of association, self organization and designation of representatives of their own choosing" in labour negotiations.

However, the main bank of resolutions was in the area of social policy. The final manifesto could just as easily have been endorsed by a political party with socialist roots.

> Full employment with sufficient income to enable him to maintain a home in a family . . . a national long-range low-cost housing plan underwritten by the government . . . increased immigration . . . social security . . . including unemployment insurance . . . pensions . . . disability pensions . . . a national system of medicine . . . full employment at fair wages and under proper and progressively improving standards is the fundamental objective of the state . . . a program of medical service because we recognize the obligation of government to make available to every citizen adequate mental, dental, nursing, hospital and prenatal care so that health may be safeguarded and preserved.

These utopian resolutions of the Port Hope conference won the delegates the dubious moniker of "Port Hopefuls." Their program, though predicated on the preservation of the free enterprise system, afforded ample room for government intervention in the social and economic matters of the nation to benefit hard-working Canadians. If there were another depression, the Tory party would not be accused of sitting on its hands until it was too late. Hanson liked what the conference proposed, but worried that the resolutions were too radical.

A report from the conference in *Saturday Night* magazine concluded that delegates had moved to the political centre-left. "It will not, after Port Hope, be possible for the Conservative party to attempt to insinuate itself to the right of the Liberals. . . . [it is] a party somewhere further left of the Liberals but not so disturbingly left as the CCF." Owing to the party's support of conscription the French newspaper *Le Devoir* wrote, "chez nous, le parti conservateur est mort."

Meighen drew the same conclusion as *Le Devoir*, but for different reasons: "Flagrant and mischievous dishonesty. Plainly, it is an attempt to outbid the CCF and out King King." But Grant Dexter of the *Winnipeg Free Press* saw a rebirth of the Tory party. "The ruins of the present Conservative party were dynamited, the ground cleared and the foundation laid for a new party. In the cleanup, scarcely a vestige remained of the grand old party. At the lowest estimate, the conference recorded the first definite signs of health, of lusty life, in the Conservative party since the disaster of 1935."

While a report in the *Montréal Star* suggested the Tory party had lost its sense of history, if not its bearings: "The program it drafts would make Sir John A. Macdonald's bones rattle in their coffin . . . It does not make a move to the left. It takes a leap, and a long leap in that direction. Some of its policies are apparently intended to demonstrate that it could be far more extreme than anything the CCF has suggested to date."

In any case, the battle to rebrand the Canadian Conservative party mattered little to Canadians, because the country was at war. Meighen tried to lead the party with Hanson as House leader. Meighen focused on the war effort and Hanson on social and economic reform, but the arrangement did not work. Meighen therefore called for a leadership convention for the following December. At the convention, he reflected on his years of public service: "It has fallen to me to lead this party through three general elections . . . Fortune came and fortune fled; but believe in my sincerity when I say that this is no reason for sympathy. . . . As a matter of truth, health and happiness are better in adversity, and no man need feel that he has failed unless, in looking back, the retrospect is blank, or unless time and events have proved that he was wrong. . . . The future can assess it or forget it, and it will be all right with me."

Meighen's public life came to an end. Despite his intellect and overpowering oratorical skills, he was no match for Mackenzie King, the wily politician. Known for "black and white" positions on issues, Meighen changed little over his 30 years in politics. He fought campaigns during the second war as if it were the first. What worked for Borden did not work for Meighen. And unlike Macdonald, Meighen failed to understand the needs and aspirations of Québec, and so effectively surrendered one-quarter of the House of Commons to the Liberal party. In three elections Meighen won only 4.1 percent of the seats available in Québec. But he was not anti-French. In fact, he insisted his son enroll at Laval Law School to learn French. Meighen just lacked the cleverness, wit, and political skill of Macdonald. Unfortunately for the party, these faults do not distinguish Meighen from most Conservative leaders, before or since.

CHAPTER 16

JOHN BRACKEN:
THE PROGRESSIVE

*If, therefore, the convention were prepared to give visible evidence of
its progressive content by association of these two names, progressive and
conservative, I would be willing to become a candidate for the leadership.*

NO ELECTED PROVINCIAL PREMIER had ever been elected prime
minister of Canada. Tories hoped to make history when they chose
Manitoban John Bracken as leader in 1942.

The outbreak of World War II left the Conservative party floundering,
without vision and purpose. Such times require a caucus to be patriotic and
united. But the party was not united: one faction wanted a return to protectionist and nationalist roots, with deep commitments to the monarchy
and an intense war policy. Another, with an eye to the post-war period,
wanted to outflank the CCF by presenting a new vision of conservatism mod-
elled after the recommendations of the Port Hope conference. In Québec,
Tories were neither seen nor heard.

Prime Minister Mackenzie King was not worried.

Clearly, the Conservative party needed new leadership. The clarion call
was made by Arthur Meighen in a September 23, 1942 press release, where
he made one last attempt to urge the party toward conscription. The leadership convention was slated for Winnipeg on December 9, 1942.

The contenders lined up just prior to the convention. On December 2,
John Diefenbaker threw his hat into the ring, saying he had made up his

mind when he heard that the convention "was going to be a cut and dried affair." Fellow caucus member Howard Green followed suit. Henry Herbert Stevens, the architect of disunity in 1935, boldly offered his candidacy. Murdoch McPherson, a favourite of the Port Hope delegates, was considered a strong candidate. Arthur Meighen strongly endorsed Manitoba premier John Bracken.

Bracken had served as premier of Manitoba for twenty years. He was a reformer and a progressive with impeccable credentials among farmers, and such broad appeal that he had been considered as a possible candidate by the CCF. Meighen saw Bracken as the populist antidote to a rising CCF and its socialist manifesto.

Meighen also liked Bracken because he had called King's plebiscite a "crowning indignity." Meighen thought of Bracken as a national figure rather than a partisan politician, with the potential to lead a national government. It was rare for Meighen and Hanson to agree, but they both thought Bracken was the right man for the job.

John Bracken was born in 1883. His career began as a bureaucrat in the department of agriculture. In 1920 he became president of the Manitoba Agricultural College. When the United Farmers of Manitoba found themselves leaderless, they turned to Bracken, who became leader in 1922. He merged his party with the Liberals in 1932 and became leader of the Liberal-Progressive party. In 1940, he formed a provincial government from among what he thought were the best representatives in the legislature.

Meighen met Bracken on November 24, 1942 to finalize his entry into the leadership race. Bracken made three demands. First, he wanted the leadership without a convention fight. Second, he wanted the name of the party to be changed to "Progressive Conservative." Third, he wanted the resolutions from the Port Hope conference to be adopted as party policy. Even though Meighen was no fan of the Port Hopefuls, he was encouraged that Bracken was considering the leadership.

By Wednesday evening of convention week, the delegates had largely confirmed the policy resolutions from Port Hope. Bracken then challenged the convention to change the party name. If they did so by Thursday evening, he informed delegates, he would enter the race. Bracken saw the name change as a way for the party to demonstrate it was sincere about reform and to indicate that someone from outside the party hierarchy could win its leadership.

This demand from Bracken, who up until then had worked outside Tory circles, struck delegates as audacious and it caused resentment on the convention floor. Some worried it meant the end of the Conservative party and its legacy to Macdonald, Borden, Bennett, and even Meighen. The formal resolution, introduced Thursday morning, was met by a chorus of boos so loud they drowned out anyone who might have attempted to second the motion.

In fact, approving Bracken's request was the equivalent of choosing the party leader. Change the name and Bracken was in. Don't change it and the contest was wide open. To ensure that the naming issue was considered on its own merits, and to quell delegate unrest, J.M. Macdonnell proposed that the vote on the name change take place after the leader had been selected, which delegates readily accepted. That meant that if Bracken wanted to be leader he had to compromise on his demands.

The deadline for nominations was 8 p.m. By 7:30, there was no indication from Bracken that he would enter the contest. Mrs. Bracken wrote about these final frantic moments in a letter to her sons, who were serving in the armed forces.

> At four minutes to eight Mr. Smith of Calgary called and wanted to know where Jack was . . . Mr. Smith asked frantically . . . 'Mrs. Bracken, do you know what your husband is going to do? There are only four minutes to go and if he is not here soon it will be too late.' . . . I told them that dad had gone to the auditorium to speak and be a candidate for the leadership . . . (but) every traffic signal was against them, they got into a traffic jam, and arrived at one of the doors at five minutes to eight, but it was not the right entrance and had a reporter that knew Jack not been there it is doubtful if the committee would have gotten him in time to sign his nomination papers. As it was, [there was] just one minute to spare when the signatures were attached.

In his speech to the delegates Bracken claimed that he "spoke the language of the common man . . . if you take me you take my views too." Delegates understood that in choosing Bracken the party would be charting a new political course.

Bracken came within 16 votes of winning on the first ballot (Bracken 420, McPherson 222, Diefenbaker 120, Green 80, Stevens 20). Stevens and Green dropped off and Bracken won easily on the second ballot with 62 percent support. In the glow of victory, the resolution to change the party name passed without debate. But few thought the new Progressive Conservative party was ready to take on the Liberals. The target for Tories was not government as much as it was to thwart the hopes and aspirations of the CCF.

Bracken did not immediately contest a seat in the House of Commons because he thought his time was better spent travelling and learning about the country. He was also insecure about his performance in debates and wanted time to hone his skills. Mackenzie King thought Bracken was unwise not to face him: "He is making a fatal mistake in staying out of the House and going to curling matches. . . . Is he afraid to face the government?"

When Hanson stepped down as parliamentary leader, Bracken suggested that caucus should replace him from among its own members. This was a stunning abdication of his leadership. Better to put his own man on the job, someone who was loyal and would defer to him in every instance. The caucus chose Gordon Graydon. Caucus member Rodney Adamson wrote of the selection in his diary: "Caucus reconvenes and Gordon is chosen leader by one vote over John Diefenbaker. John voted for Gordon and Gordon voted for himself. This is a swell set."

It remained to be seen whether the old guard of the party would make way for Bracken and a new set of policies. Bracken supporter and party organizer James Macdonnell wrote; "If we are not very quickly able to make it apparent that there is a new crowd taking hold, there will be widespread disappointment." Richard Bell, 29, who had been working on Conservative political causes since the age of 21, was brought in for advice. He advocated a transformation of the party structure with a full-time director, organizers, and bureaus for publicity and research. Bell pointed out that in the past the party had hoped the leaders would do all the work. His approach was to build a strong, professional, and sustainable organization that would support and complement the leader's efforts. It was something Bennett had done while in Opposition, but ignored once in power. On April 19, 1943, Bracken chose Bell as national director for the party. Bell hired a publicity director and established a new Conservative monthly newspaper, *Public Opinion*.

Bell coordinated his work with provincial Conservative parties, but often found that they were largely, if not exclusively, focused on their own success, making a partnership difficult to sustain. On August 4, 1943, George Drew narrowly became Tory premier of Ontario winning a minority government. Opposing the 38 Tory MPPs were 34 CCFers and 15 Liberals. Federal Tories were deeply involved in Drew's campaign, even stalling their own organizational efforts to work on the provincial campaign.

The success of the CCF in Ontario worried Conservatives. More surprising was the fact that the CCF was the choice of Canadian soldiers. The CCF argued that since controls imposed on the economy during the war led to greater output, why not retain these controls after the war? In other words, why retain capitalism when extensive government intervention is more efficient? Under a CCF government, it further maintained, everyone would get a fair deal, and the ravages of a depression would never again impinge upon the common man more severely than upon the powerful and wealthy. The CCF led nationally in a September 1943 public opinion poll, registering its strongest support in the West. Both the Liberals and Tories shifted policies to the left and Social Security was now front and centre.

Old-line Tories, particularly the blue-suited banker types from Toronto, were reluctant to see their party move left. They proposed that Toronto be made the centre of the party's organization and that a committee of successful business executives should lead the development of the Tory platform. Richard Bell saw this as a threat to Bracken's leadership and told him so: "The interest of these men is based not on the belief that the Progressive Conservative party, under your leadership, can build a greater Canada but only upon fear of the CCF and the bulldog determination to retain, at any cost, their favoured position in society. . . ."

Meanwhile, Bracken was having a hard time keeping his party in the centre of the political spectrum, real estate that Mackenzie King wanted to occupy as well. The bona fides of each party were tested over proposals to implement a "baby bonus." John Diefenbaker and Howard Green supported the measure. But Dr. Herbert Bruce, who would later be elected to the House of Commons, referring to the relatively high birthrate in the province of Québec, called it "a bribe of the most brazen character, made chiefly to one province and paid for by the taxes of the rest." Punctuating his remark, Dr. Bruce exclaimed that it would "bonus families who've been unwilling to defend their country." In the end, the baby bonus passed unanimously, but there was a lingering sense that Tory support for it was insincere.

The socialist tide swelled again on June 15, 1944, when the CCF won 47 of the 55 seats in the Saskatchewan legislature. Conservatives won none, ran third in every constituency, and failed to recover a single deposit.

The year 1944 was dominated by debate over whether to send conscripted forces overseas. There was a fundamental question whether these troops—the so-called "zombies" who were protecting the home front—were actually needed overseas, or whether the debate was simply a demonstration of patriotism and support for the troops abroad. The government was advised by the military that these troops were needed at the battlefront. This seemed to meet the test offered in the plebiscite, that the troops would be sent overseas "if necessary." But the Liberal Cabinet split over the issue. King responded by agreeing to send only a portion of the conscripts overseas. Compromise was always his operating principle: "If there's anything to which I have devoted my political life, it is to try to promote unity, harmony and amity between the diverse elements of this country. My friends can desert, they can remove their confidence from me, they can withdraw the trust they have placed in my hands, but never shall I deviate from that line of policy."

There were riots in Québec, as well as condemnations from the Québec legislature. Bracken was unmoved: "I call upon the government to fulfill its duty to our men overseas and to carry out the will of the people as expressed in the plebiscite by passing the necessary order in Council and sending the available men in the home army as reinforcements forthwith." Bracken had been leader two years, but still spoke from outside the House of Commons. Even though there had been by-elections that Conservatives had won, he was still disinclined to run.

He was trying to make inroads in the province of Québec and spoke in measured terms on the conscription issue, but he could not hide his personal views or shed Borden's legacy. The best hope for Tories in Québec was to build an alliance with the Union Nationale, but, according to Richard Bell, little could be done at the moment. "It is the belief of Duplessis and his group that these men should not compromise themselves in federal affairs until after the provincial election is over. It is their belief that association with the Bracken cause federally would do injury to their provincial chances."

On August 8, 1944, Duplessis was returned to power in Québec. There was now a good chance that Bracken could tap into the political organization of the provincial government. But an allegiance with the government in Québec posed problems for Bracken in the rest of the country. The *Winnipeg Free Press* offered an account of negotiations between the federal Tories and provincial Union Nationale in 1944: "And so the traditional strategy of the Conservatives begins to take on form. The chief ingredients of success are that the Conservatives run no candidates in Québec—except in English speaking seats—but back the nationalists with hard cash and promissory notes. In the past the notes have always been paid. In English speaking Canada, the strategy calls for attacks on the Liberals for pandering to Québec."

Conservatives were optimistic about their chances heading into the 1945 election. The Liberal government was generally unpopular and the CCF had strength in the West and was likely to take Liberal held seats. Hanson predicted the CCF would win 60 seats, the Liberals around 50, with about 60 seats in Québec going to a string of nationalist candidates running as a bloc. This would leave the Tories with a minority government, provided the war was not yet over. "If the election is held before the German collapse, Bracken might win," Hanson maintained.

Before the election was called, Bracken had emphasized the compassionate and progressive side of Conservatism, displayed in his speech at the party's annual meeting on March 3, 1944: "The job of the Progressive Conservative party is to make good on the word 'progressive'—It means . . . providing for one major change in the attitude of the state towards its economy and its human resources—human welfare must be made the primary function of the state and not just one which is incidental or secondary or a by-product of some system."

In April, Mackenzie King called the election for June 11. He chose not to run on his record during the war, but focused instead on a program of social reforms, including full employment. His slogans left no doubt where Mackenzie King wanted to take the country: "Build a new social order— vote Liberal" and, "Liberal family allowances provide food, education, health, security." In a radio broadcast, King added: "The Liberal party has never accepted extreme positions. We do not believe that more employment and prosperity will be created by the mere fact of changing the ownership of property from individuals or corporations to the state. . . . For the Liberal party, the test is what will best serve the general interest, rather than special interests, whether those special interests be the interests of a financial oligarchy or a particular class."

King was staking out the political centre, putting the Tories on the far right and the CCF on the far left. This is what the 1945 handbook of the National Liberal Committee said about Conservatives: "The Tory tradition is to follow the British way of life. The Tory is British first, and secondly Canadian. The Liberal is Canadian first and a British subject afterwards— sometimes a long way afterwards . . . the Tories put money and property first. The Liberals place humanity and equality of opportunity first . . . the Tories are anti-Catholic—intolerant—and hate Québec. The Liberals believe in freedom of worship, tolerance—and love Canada . . . Toryism means reaction. Liberalism means progress."

It was typical arrogance for a party that at the time was flush with cash from a long list of grateful war contractors who feared CCF influence.

Abandoning the Port Hope declarations, the Tory campaign retreated to familiar ground. "Bracken or socialism" was the theme. The leader was the message: Bracken was a farmer, a worker, and a progressive. He was any-thing but the eastern businessman or banker with which the party had come to be associated.

For the first time in many elections, Conservatives had money to spend. They even sent cigarettes along with campaign literature to troops in the field. Candidates were trained and a speaker's bureau established. More than half the Tory candidates were veterans. Québec, however, remained a weak spot and fielded only 29 Tory candidates in 65 ridings.

As the campaign progressed, Bracken spoke less about social policy and more about conscription, but his message was more theoretical than inspi-rational: "The Progressive Conservative party sets opportunity and prosperity as the goal which the nation should attain, rather than the rationed scarcity of the socialist state, or the elaborate and burdensome sys-tem of Social Security which the Liberal party is seeking to create."

On May 16, 1945, Bracken proposed a "Charter for a Better Canada." Inexplicably abandoning the policies and program that had been developed in Port Hope, the platform called for Canada to assume a "fair share of respon-sibility" in the Pacific campaign, including using the draft to send troops overseas. All the Québec politicians, including the nationalists Bracken hoped to co-opt, spoke out against the Tory leader. And Bracken broke any pretense of leading a national party as he demeaned and discarded Québecers: "The patriotic among Canada's sons will again be asked to die for Canada, while others will stay at home to populate the land their brothers saved."

Bracken had clearly written off Québec and was prepared to lead a party that divided the country—not what is expected of national leaders.

There was confusion about whether independents running in Québec were aligned with the Conservative party. Bracken sought to clarify the issue by saying that it had made no deals with any other political group but that if independents happened to support Conservative positions, so much the bet-ter. This was ammunition for Mackenzie King to say that any vote in Québec not for a Liberal was a vote for the conscriptionist Tories.

A week before the federal election, George Drew swept Ontario, and proclaimed "A federal issue is exactly the same as was decided in Ontario. The issue is the same because the Dominion Liberal party through its open accept-ance of support of the Communists has got itself to the socialist doctrines which are opposed to the principles of the Progressive Conservative party."

The Liberals won 127 seats, reduced from the 182 from the previous elec-tion, but still a majority. The CCF won 28 seats, while the Conservatives took 68, a gain of 28. Forty-eight were from Ontario and two were from Québec.

The biggest disappointment for Conservatives was the West. They won only two of 17 seats in Bracken's home province of Manitoba, one of them Bracken's, one seat in Saskatchewan and two in Alberta. And they lost the military vote, running third: 118,537 Liberal, 109,679 CCF, and 87,530 Tory.

The Tories lost because they were dominated by Toronto-based business interests, they were insensitive to Québec, and they campaigned for an aggressive war policy that Canadians opposed. The long shadow Arthur Meighen and Robert Borden cast over the party dimmed the goal of electoral success. The country wanted social reform, something the Liberals delivered with the baby bonus.

Not seeking a seat in the House was fatal to Bracken's hold over caucus and the party and allowed forces within caucus to undermine the direction in which he had intended to take the party when he first won the leadership. The party went back to its instincts—and lost, again.

CHAPTER 17

GEORGE DREW: PATRICIAN

Make no mistake about it; we are fighting for personal and economic freedom here in Canada today. We are in a very real danger of losing that fight to the bureaucrats who accept the basic philosophy of Karl Marx no matter what political name they adopt.

GIVEN HIS FIVE YEARS as Ontario premier and eight years as leader of the federal PC party, it is odd that George Drew remains one of the least understood politicians in Canadian history. There has been no biography or serious study of his career. Historian Jack Granatstein was scheduled to write a biography of Drew, but the project was cancelled due to a lack of access to original and private documents. What is clear is that though Drew was a powerful orator, he lacked the cunning and tactical skills required of a politician. He was not a nation-builder and insulted French Canadians. Like many Tories of his day, he strongly opposed communism and sought to maintain a strong Imperial and Commonwealth bond. He is noteworthy for launching a Tory dynasty in Ontario that lasted forty-two years. But he joins the ranks of every elected provincial premier who has gone on to lead a federal political party without achieving the office of prime minister. Among Tory leaders who fought two or more federal elections, Drew has the worst record of them all.

George Drew was born into a political family on May 7, 1894 in Guelph, Ontario. His grandfather sat behind John A. Macdonald as a Conservative in Canada's first Parliament.

Tall, handsome, and patrician, with an engaging personality, he attended Upper Canada College, the University of Toronto, and Osgoode Hall Law School. He married Fiorenza Johnson, a "lady of queenly distinction," the daughter of the general manager for the Metropolitan Opera.

Drew enlisted in the army during World War I and served as an artillery officer. He was wounded in battle, returned from overseas in 1917, and spent two years recovering. During peacetime he rose to the rank of Lieutenant-Colonel of the 64th Battery—Canadian Field Artillery. For much of the rest of his life, close friends would refer to him as Colonel Drew. The military was never far from Drew's life or heart. He wrote a moderately successful book on Canada's role in World War I and his favourite article of clothing was his red and blue artillery tie.

Drew entered municipal politics in his late twenties in his hometown of Guelph, first as alderman, then mayor. He was appointed master of the Supreme Court of Ontario in 1929 and became the first chairman of the Ontario Securities Commission in 1931. Despite the turmoil of the Depression market, his performance over five years earned him the reputation of a man with integrity who cleared out many of the "shysters, phony promoters and swindle sheet publishers" who then infested Bay Street.

When Liberal Mitchell Hepburn was elected Ontario Premier in 1934, he promised to clean up waste and mismanagement at Queen's Park. George Drew, along with many other senior civil servants, was dismissed. This so angered Drew that he defiantly sought the leadership of the Ontario Conservative party when it came open in 1936. Running on his military accomplishments and experience in municipal politics, he lost, but remained involved with the party as an organizer for the next few years.

Drew was dismayed that Tories were not taking a hard line against labour unions and ran as an independent candidate for the Ontario legislature, an action that confirmed him as a stubborn and politically divisive figure. By not working with the Tories, Drew contributed to the election of his nemesis, Liberal Mitch Hepburn. The Ontario Conservative party, however, did not bear a grudge and elected Drew leader in 1938 on the first ballot. He won a by-election in Simcoe East and entered the provincial Legislature.

But Drew had his eye on the national stage. After the capture of Hong Kong by Japanese troops in 1941, he levelled allegations of mismanagement against Prime Minister Mackenzie King, chiding him for sending improperly trained Canadian troops to fight with inferior equipment. Mackenzie King responded by calling a royal commission to investigate. Unsatisfied, Drew claimed the commission was biased, which caused Justice Minister Louis St. Laurent to launch a prosecution against Drew under the Defence of Canada regulations. Drew added St. Laurent to the list of Liberals with whom he had a score to settle.

Drew entered the 1943 Ontario election with a 22-point program for social and economic development. His optimistic vision of a bright future for Ontario resonated with those across the province expecting a prosperous period of reconstruction after World War II. His platform was progressive, calling for increased spending in education, universal medical and dental care, and old age pensions. It also went against market forces to propose establishing marketing boards for farmers, nationalizing stockyards, and a plan for timber management and reforestation. Drew set aside his anti-union beliefs and promised that a Tory government would pass the "fairest and most advanced laws governing labour relations in the country." Drew's performance and his plan ended a decade of Liberal rule and earned the Tories a minority government, with 38 of 90 seats in the legislature.

Once in office, Drew paid little heed to the opposition and governed as if he held a majority. As Ontario leader he displayed intolerance and prejudice toward Québec. In 1944, he attacked the federal government's plans for a family allowance, saying he would not support legislation that brought about any more of those "French Canadian bastards." Mitchell Hepburn attacked Drew's opposition to family allowance legislation and voted no-confidence in the Drew government in March 1945 on its Throne speech. Drew eagerly accepted the challenge.

A week and a half before Election Day, in what became known as the "Gestapo affair," CCF leader Ted Jolliffe went on air to allege that Drew was maintaining a government spy organization to keep himself in power. Drew denied the charges and within days ordered a public inquiry. Drew's command of the situation and of his government met with voter approval and he won 66 seats in the 90-seat legislature. Jolliffe was defeated and his CCF party was reduced to eight seats from 34.

When the promised inquiry began, Jolliffe produced evidence that a provincial police captain had been operating a secret spy group. He claimed this group spied on CCF members in order to link as many of them as possible to the Communist party. Evidence emerged that the police captain prepared at least 41 reports which included lists of thousands of leftist Ontarians. But the inquiry found no evidence that Drew had ordered this secret police force to carry out their actions. However, the inquiry also concluded that Drew's attorney-general, Leslie Blackwell, should have stopped the police captain when he started receiving activity reports. Nevertheless, Drew emerged from this event largely unscathed.

At the helm of a majority government in the robust post-war period, Drew invested heavily to upgrade the province's electrical system and highways. Drew reformed the penal system to emphasize rehabilitative rather than punitive approaches. He also led a campaign that brought 10,000 skilled British immigrants to Ontario. Not one for study or procedure, Drew made arrangements to fly British immigrants to Canada on the spur of the moment after meeting an airline executive at a social function in Britain. Despite protests that immigrants were taking jobs away from Ontarians, Drew convinced his province that skilled immigrants were crucial to economic development.

Ontario's restrictive liquor laws were a boon for bootleggers. Drew's response was to permit lounges in the province to sell liquor. Those opposed to the consumption of alcohol reacted aggressively and swiftly. The "drys," as they were known, were well-organized and committed to their principles. In the ensuing election the Tories retained a diminished majority government, but Drew lost his seat. Despite having won power, Drew never returned to Queen's Park as premier.

A MONTH AFTER THE ONTARIO ELECTION, federal Conservative Party leader John Bracken resigned and Drew entered the race against John Diefenbaker and Donald Fleming. Drew was an attractive candidate: experienced in government; well-known nationally; and with politically useful ties to Québec Premier Duplessis. But in Québec, Drew's support for conscription and his tirade against family allowance were obstacles that not even Duplessis could overcome. Despite his weakness in Québec, however, Drew won the federal leadership on the first ballot with 67 percent delegate support. Twelve years younger than Prime Minister Louis St. Laurent, Drew gave the Tories hope.

In December 1948, Drew won a seat in the House of Commons representing the riding of Carleton near Ottawa. In an all-candidates meeting during the campaign, candidates were to be introduced by a notable person of the candidate's choosing. The CCF candidate, Eugene Forsey, chose William Temple, the MPP who had beaten George Drew in the Ontario election. Temple accused Drew of being a "tool of the liquor interests," which whipped Drew into a fury. The confrontation escalated and both men had to be restrained. After this, questions about Drew's temperament were raised in the media.

Foregoing the usual first-day formalities, Drew's first speech in the House of Commons began with a flurry. Drew had not forgiven St. Laurent for prosecuting him in 1942 and made no effort to engage in friendly dialogue. His two-hour speech was a blistering attack on the Liberal government, which, he charged, had failed to respect provincial rights.

Drew's attack awakened the Liberal front bench. So did reports from the Canadian Institute for Public Opinion which revealed a substantial increase in the Tory polling numbers. But Drew could not maintain this momentum. He had always been hostile towards communism and in a speech at McGill University he made sweeping and ill-advised allegations about the political allegiances of Canada's public servants, allegations he could not substantiate: "Make no mistake about it; we are fighting for personal and economic freedom here in Canada today. We are in a very real danger of losing that fight to the bureaucrats who accept the basic philosophy of Karl Marx no matter what political name they adopt."

St. Laurent sprang to his feet to defend the civil service in the House of Commons and challenged Drew to substantiate his allegations with evidence. With no proof to connect civil servants to Marxism, Drew's charges fell flat.

Drew's first national election came on June 27, 1949. His cold stare, old money looks, and stern policies stood in sharp contrast to the comfort and kindness of a prime minister Canadians affectionately called "Uncle Louis." Drew was simply not a "man of the people." One writer remarked that Drew was a "big, handsome aristocrat, the least common man [I had ever] come across." Drew was seen as a man of privilege, disconnected from the stress and worry of everyday Canadian life. During the course of the election the press nicknamed him "Gorgeous George." Attempts to shake Drew's image as a member of the elite turned laughable when one of his supporters remarked, "Why just last week, George and I were sitting around the swimming pool on my estate . . ." The press repeated this story often.

The Toronto *Star* attacked Drew mercilessly for his links to Maurice Duplessis and Montréal Mayor Camillien Houde. The *Star* suggested that electing Drew would lead to the disintegration of Canada. Days before the election, The *Star*'s front page warned, "Keep Canada British/Destroy Drew's Houde/God Save the King." The headline would have been offensive to anyone like Drew with a deep loyalty to the Crown.

As the campaign drew to a close, it was clear to everyone except Drew that he was going to lose. Close friend and future Tory senator Grattan O'Leary visited his apartment the night before the election and managed to convince Drew he was going to be beaten.

That night O'Leary also noticed the Drews' rather modest living conditions. Believing that the leader of the Opposition should live in a much nicer dwelling, O'Leary later convinced the publisher of the *Montréal Star* to put $10,000 toward the purchase of a house named Stornoway in Rockcliffe Park. This became the residence of the leader of the Opposition, and was occupied by many Tories in the 50 years that followed.

O'Leary was right. The Liberals took 49.1 percent of the vote and 191 of 262 seats. The Tories, with 29.6 percent held 41 seats. But the extent of the drubbing surprised everyone—Drew, the party, and even the media. Québec remained a sore spot, and the Tories won only 2 seats to the Liberal's 68. Drew got crushed even in his home province of Ontario, taking only 25 seats to the Liberal's 55. He not only lost the province but, for reasons still unknown, he had divided the federal party from the provincial organization led by Leslie Frost. According to Dalton Camp, a Tory organizer from New Brunswick who once worked for the Liberal Party of Canada, "The Ontario Tory bonne entente all had hoped for under Drew's leadership had become, instead, a deep, unfathomable estrangement. No one understood it, and no one could repair it either. Without it, Drew's authority in his own party was tenuous and limited. You could not organize the Progressive Conservative Party of Canada in the name of George Drew."

Following the 1949 debacle, Drew gained new respect for St. Laurent's skills as a politician and for his personal qualities. Drew may have held a grudge against St. Laurent, but respected him enough to say in 1951 that he had "no reservations whatever about . . . his personal courage and in his willingness to accept the full responsibility of the high office which he holds." Later that year, at a party marking St. Laurent's ten years in public life, Drew offered the following remarks: "Whether it may be in public or private life, I trust and am confident that the Prime Minister will at all times have in his heart a feeling of satisfaction in knowing that, whatever our political opinions may be, we all respect him for the public services he has rendered."

Perhaps one reason Drew warmed towards St. Laurent was the latter's surprising decision in 1953 to appoint Drew to the Privy Council, but their improved relations were likely due more to St. Laurent's affability and desire to "reduce partisan feeling" than to Drew's willingness to forgive and forget.

Meanwhile, Drew's second term as leader of the Opposition happened to coincide with Joseph McCarthy's campaign against communists in the United States. Like McCarthy, Drew made unsubstantiated allegations about the existence of Marxists in the government bureaucracy. With the

McCarthy furor raging in the United States, Drew turned his sights on attacking communism as a means of gaining political support.

At the opening of the parliamentary session of 1950, Drew accused the St. Laurent government of failing to take appropriate measures to prevent Canadian institutions from being infiltrated by communists. In May 1950, Drew proposed legislation that would make communist activities in Canada an offence punishable under the Criminal Code. However, Drew's anti-communist sentiments garnered little attention from the Canadian public.

The next Tory campaign platform, in 1953, featured a 16-point agenda, including a promise to reduce taxes by $500 million. The Liberals immediately put Drew on the defensive by asking where he would get that money. Would pensions be cut? Would social services be watered down? Because the source of the money was not explicitly outlined in the platform document, the Liberals were able to control the issue. Drew was not prepared to respond.

Dalton Camp called the campaign and the $500 million promise an exercise in futility. He claimed the Tory party lost all its flexibility and manoeuvrability on a single issue. Because of tax cuts there would be no money for have-not provinces, no increases in welfare and pension payments, no salary increases for the Armed Forces and the public service, and no new public works.

The August 10 election delivered another easy Liberal victory, although the Tories and the CCF each picked up ten new seats. The Tories doubled their seat total in Québec: but going from two to four was meaningless. Without support in Québec, Drew had no chance of winning the country and there was no Tory beachhead anywhere in Canada on which to build.

Drew may have been ready to continue, but his party was broke, morale was low, and his political capital was spent. He had thrown every accusation he could at the Liberals in the election without results. The only good news for the Tories was that with five successive majority governments they had given Liberals' a sense of invincibility and arrogance that reached new heights. Indeed, the resounding 1953 Liberal victory led to a sense of Liberal entitlement and overconfidence that would later become their undoing.

Dalton Camp, who went on to serve as the party's director of publicity, offered a critical assessment of the Tory brain trust under Drew's direction: "The party's hierarchy seems to have evolved principally on the basis of survival, so that the elite were essentially made up of amiable and elderly mediocrities. I'd come to realize how few men, a very few at the center, determine party policy and strategy, and how few of those had any genuine gift of political judgment."

The Tories had no great plan for the parliamentary session that began in January 1956, but the session included a debate that would contain "the most serious parliamentary upheaval since the conscription crisis in 1944." When the Liberal government sought rapid construction of a natural gas pipeline from Alberta to Eastern Canada, C.D. Howe, the man known as the "minister of everything," led the government charge. American-owned Transcanada Pipelines would construct and own the pipeline, but it would require a government loan of $80 million to get started. Although the bill was delayed in Cabinet, Howe gave Parliament little time for debate. So tight was the deadline, the bill to finance the pipeline was introduced on May 8, 1956, with construction to begin in July. Before the bill was even introduced, the government announced it would use closure to severely limit debate, which it did on four occasions.

This was contempt for Parliament beyond anything the Liberals had attempted in the past. Tories were outraged, less by the content of the bill— although they were uncomfortable with the extent of American influence—than by the manner in which their duties as parliamentarians were nullified. In opposition, the Conservatives and CCFers used every delaying mechanism and obstructive tactic left to them to prevent the legislation from passing through the various stages of debate.

When Donald Fleming was denied his right to introduce a point of order, the Speaker expelled him from the House. His colleague, Ellen Fairclough, draped the Union Jack flag over his desk in his absence. George Drew charged bias on the part of the Speaker of the House and asked for his resignation.

The Liberals got their pipeline, but the Tories won the public to their side. The Liberal government displayed hubris and arrogance that debunked the myth that the Liberal government could do no wrong, that it was "untouchable." Rising Tory fortunes were the result of Liberal arrogance rather than the Tory leader's cunning political wizardry. Nonetheless, Drew sensed that his time in the sun was near.

Just as Drew's political prospects shone brighter, however, tragedy struck. The fatigue of nearly twenty years in politics had taken its toll. Not long after the pipeline debate, Drew was sidelined with a viral infection. His doctors told him he would not recover unless he relinquished the leadership. Drew initially ignored the warnings. His wife couldn't bear to tell him the hard truth—that his doctors predicted he would be dead in six months if he didn't retire. When his friend Grattan O'Leary finally confronted him with the facts, Drew reluctantly resigned.

Drew recovered, but never re-entered formal politics. In 1957, the newly elected Tory government appointed Drew high commissioner to the United Kingdom. He returned to Canada in 1964. After his wife died the next year, he served as a member of the board of governors at the University of Toronto and chancellor at the University of Guelph. George Drew died on January 4, 1973, at the age of seventy-nine.

The transition from provincial government into federal politics is thorny, especially for a premier who believes strongly in provincial rights. George Drew became well-known in Ontario and then the rest of Canada when he teamed up with Québec Premier Maurice Duplessis during provincial-federal conferences to take on the federal government. This made for good provincial politics, but voters were uneasy placing a man with these views at the head of the federal government.

And despite the efforts of his predecessors to overcome decades-old resentment against Tories in Québec, Drew went in the opposite direction. He described the French as "a defeated race" and said "any rights they had were only theirs because of the tolerance and generosity of English Canadians." Such statements extinguished any chance of winning votes in French Canada.

Drew did not lack perseverance, but there was nothing particularly impressive about spending nearly ten years in opposition. There is no single initiative that he championed or won in federal politics, and his real shot at becoming prime minister was deflected by illness.

Despite his many years in politics, Drew did not make much of an impression on the Conservative party or on Canadian society. He possessed none of the nation-building skills of Macdonald or Borden. He spoke well, but his rhetoric was hollow, especially to Québecers. He attracted the loyalty of those he knew and he did not lack personal charm. His colleague Donald Fleming noted in his memoirs that Drew always wrote him a personal letter at the close of each session to thank him for his hard work. But he could also be stubborn, destructively independent, and blinded by spite over his opponents when he should have been focused on winning power. It felt good to lash out against the communists, but it mattered little to Canadians, who saw Colonel Drew as the wrong man in the wrong place at the wrong time.

SECTION V

DIEFENBAKER: THE CHIEF

CHAPTER 18

MAN OF DESTINY

This is the vision: One Canada. One Canada, where Canadians will
have preserved to them the control of their own economic and political
destiny. Sir John A. Macdonald saw Canada from east to west: I see a new
Canada—Canada of the North . . . this is the vision.

PRAIRIE LEGEND JOHN GEORGE DIEFENBAKER was born on
September 18, 1895 in Neustadt, a small Ontario village about 170 kilometres northwest of Toronto. In the summer of 1903, the family moved
west and, after living in a number of remote communities, settled in Saskatoon.

Diefenbaker's father, William, was a teacher. The original family name
was Diefenbacker, but was shortened by William to sound less German.
Nonetheless John Diefenbaker wore his heritage on his heart and sleeve, taking pride that he was (and remains) the only prime minister to have a
surname of neither English nor French origin. He colourfully described his
ancestors as an odd-lot of "dispossessed Scottish Highlanders and discontented Palatine Germans."

Diefenbaker's childhood heroes were Sir John A. Macdonald and Sir
Wilfrid Laurier. He was eight or nine years old when he told his mother that
he was going to be prime minister. A bright and curious student, he blamed
his less-than-stellar academic standing on his reluctance to accept unchallenged the views of his teachers and those in authority. Little would change
over his lifetime.

Diefenbaker was fifteen years old when he first encountered a federal politician. He describes in his memoirs selling newspapers at the Saskatoon train station when Prime Minister Sir Wilfrid Laurier happened to breeze through: "I sold him a newspaper. He gave me a quarter—no better way to establish an instant rapport with a newsboy. We chatted about Canada. I had the odd feeling that I was in the presence of greatness. That afternoon, when he laid the cornerstone, he included in his remarks a reference to his conversation with a Saskatoon newsboy which, he observed, had ended with my saying, 'sorry Prime Minister, I can't waste any more time on you. I've got work to do.'"

In 1912, Diefenbaker participated in a mock Parliament at university. Cited in the debates for zealousness, he boldly predicted that he would be leader of Her Majesty's Loyal Opposition by 1955. His prediction was off by only one year. However, his sense of destiny was tested with many early setbacks.

His passion for politics meshed well with an interest in the law. "[I was] impressed by the lives of those who, in the practice of law, stood for the liberties of the individual and the assurance that no one, however poor, should be denied justice." Diefenbaker consistently identified with the underdog in legal matters. Not particularly motivated by money, he had no blue chip clients in his roster.

In his early teens, he was prone to nervousness and was a reluctant public speaker, something he overcame with training, practice, and persistence. He learned the art of salesmanship in the summer of 1915, setting records selling a series of Christian books under the title *The Chosen Word* in small towns across Saskatchewan. The ambitious Diefenbaker travelled the province by bicycle.

In March 1916, before finishing his academic studies, Diefenbaker enrolled in the military, receiving a commission on May 16 as a lieutenant in the Infantry of the Active Militia. Later that summer he completed his studies and began his law articles in the Saskatoon office of Russell Hartney.

He resumed his military career, but after five months of training in Europe, he was declared medically unfit for overseas service and returned to Canada in February 1917. Diefenbaker and his biographers are at odds over the nature and extent of the medical condition that ended his military service, and it remains unclear whether it was gastric or psychosomatic. Diefenbaker offered only the more socially acceptable physical diagnosis as the reason.

In 1919, Diefenbaker opened a law practice in Wakaw, Saskatchewan and the next year he took a seat at village council. He developed a flair for the dramatic, which was put to good use in Council chambers and the court-room. He was persuasive, believable, and confident, and showed conviction with penetrating eyes and a flair for his robes. With wildly gesticulating arms and hands, he was a showman with a commanding presence.

With his Germanic surname, Diefenbaker identified with the discrimi-nation faced by many minorities in Canada. When school board trustees Rémi Éthier and Léger Boutin were found guilty of violating the law pro-hibiting French instruction in public schools, Diefenbaker took the high-profile case on appeal. He won, albeit on a technicality. Diefenbaker instinctively dismissed warnings that taking on such cases would harm what-ever political career might lie ahead. If he later succeeded in politics, it was not because he had courted the powerful or wealthy. He sometimes went against his natural instincts to act as crown prosecutor when requested to do so, but thought he did a "lousy job at it" owing to the large number of con-victions he secured.

Despite his father's Liberal inclinations and admiration of Sir Wilfrid Laurier, Diefenbaker was only sixteen years old when he first identified with Conservatives. "The [1911] election had a profound influence on me, and perhaps more than anything else made me a Conservative. I attended all the meetings in Saskatoon. . . . we cleaved to our British heritage in defiance of American manifest destiny and Grit continentalism. The result was a tremendous revelation of Canadian determination to be Canadian. This impressed me greatly." Later in life Diefenbaker reflected on the choice he had made at such a young age: "I chose it because of certain basic princi-ples and these . . . were the Empire relationship of the time, the monarchy and the preservation of an independent Canada. None of these things I thought the Liberal party could support."

He opposed Borden's war policy which disenfranchised naturalized Canadians who came from enemy countries after 1902, but he eagerly cam-paigned for the Union cause in 1917. For decades Saskatchewan had had a deep attachment to the Liberal party, federally and provincially. In choosing the Conservative party, Diefenbaker followed his beliefs as well as his instincts to align with the underdog.

In 1925, Diefenbaker ran for the Tories in Prince Albert, Saskatchewan. He finished third with fewer than half the votes of the Liberal candidate. The Tory party won the most seats, but was prevented from forming a government because of a fleeting coalition between Mackenzie King's Liberals and Thomas Crerar's Progressive party. When the coalition collapsed, and after an ill-fated attempt by Arthur Meighen to form a government, the country returned to the polls.

In the 1926 campaign, Diefenbaker was again a candidate in the riding of Prince Albert. But this time his opponent was Liberal leader Mackenzie King. One eastern Tory supporter inflamed Diefenbaker by claiming King had gone to Prince Albert because "he doesn't like the smell of native-born Canadians. He prefers the stench of garlic stinking continentals, Eskimos, bohunks, and Indians." A Tory candidate from Ontario sneered, "King is running in a riding among the Doukhobors, up near the North Pole where they don't know how to mark their ballots." The racist taunts of eastern Tories savagely insulted Prince Albert electors. Diefenbaker instinctively distrusted Tories from Ontario, and the shameless conduct of his eastern colleagues in the 1926 campaign cemented this view. Mackenzie King received 8,933 votes to Diefenbaker's 4,838.

Diefenbaker supported Hugh Guthrie in the 1927 leadership contest. But soon after, Diefenbaker's attention was diverted to provincial politics and an ambitious attempt to revive the fledgling Tory cause in Saskatchewan. Though the Conservative party gained ground in popular support in the provincial election of 1929, it won no seats.

Failing to win in three elections only intensified Diefenbaker's ambition. Becoming prime minister, he informed his future wife, was more than his goal, it was his destiny. Married life softened his disposition and enhanced his social skills. His law practice thrived and Diefenbaker found himself in the middle of numerous high-profile murder cases, many unwinnable, which only enhanced his reputation as someone who was not afraid to take on a challenge or the establishment. In 1933, when the mayoralty contest in Prince Albert was headed for acclamation, Diefenbaker entered the race at the last possible moment. With only one week to campaign, he came within 48 votes of victory.

NOT INITIALLY A SUPPORTER of R.B. Bennett, Diefenbaker came to admire the Tory leader's willingness to represent the common man over the moneyed establishment. Bennett's independent streak and willingness to defy "the self-appointed eastern bosses of the party" while leading a government that did not "sit on its hands" earned Diefenbaker's respect.

Just before the leadership convention that replaced R.B. Bennett in 1938, Diefenbaker implored convention delegates, saying, "Unless the party is united in the leader ... the Conservative party will pass out of existence." Diefenbaker noted remarks made by Bennett in his closing address and kept a copy of the speech in his papers for future reference: "Every time you publicly criticize anyone in your party you do a great harm to your party and every time you publicly criticize the leader of your party you add fuel to the fires of opposition that must always burn against him . . . I ask you—why assist the enemy?"

Diefenbaker seemed to understand the need for loyalty and duty when he was approached to stand for the leadership of the Saskatchewan Conservative party. Party unity and support for its leadership was a pre-condition Diefenbaker put on the table, "I would sooner stay at my profession as I know what a sacrifice it will be on my part, . . . I'm prepared to take a try at it, but only if the party would unite behind me."

On October 28, 1936, a string of men were nominated for the party's leadership from the convention floor, but only one rose to accept—John Diefenbaker. Of the new leader, the Regina *Leader Post* remarked, "He carries his 40 years lightly, is dark, slim and erect, and thunders forth his convictions and ideas in resonant tones of purposeful youth."

Diefenbaker was determined to bring his provincial party closer to the middle of the political spectrum. In so doing, he advocated policies that were no more radical than those advocated by R.B. Bennett during the Great Depression. But he inherited a Saskatchewan Conservative party with limited depth, a shambles of an organization, and no money. For the 1938 election, he made a personal loan to the party to cover election deposits for 22 Tory candidates. He was distressed to encounter Alberta-born Ernest Manning in the campaign, the Social Credit party's chief organizer and prime architect of conservative vote-splitting. Social Credit's role in the campaign contributed to the Tory party being shut out on election night, where Diefenbaker was perceived as a strong leader of a weak cause. His offer to resign was refused.

Between his federal, municipal, and provincial campaigns the chief was now zero for five. Defeat led to dejection, stress, insomnia, and even medication. He would return to politics, but was no longer prepared to serve as the patron saint for lost causes. He wanted the federal nomination in the riding of Lake Centre, but only if it was given to him with the unanimous support of constituency members and pledges of financial support.

The 1940 war-time campaign was difficult for Tories. They were disorganized, unprepared, and unwilling to deal harshly with the Liberal government of Mackenzie King. Diefenbaker fought his campaign in Lake Centre on the basis of his personal attributes and beliefs. He was one of only three Conservatives elected on the Prairies, and won by the narrow margin of 280 votes. His losing streak ended and he went on to win 11 successive elections.

In a letter of congratulations, his mother reminded him of his childhood ambition: "I can see by your letter that the aim of your ambition is to fill King's chair . . . well I think you will get there someday, if you work hard enough." She was right.

In Ottawa, Diefenbaker camped out at the Château Laurier. Wife Edna became his personal parliamentary assistant and head cheerleader. She was known to brag brashly about her husband's skills and inevitable rise to leadership. Fellow MP and friend Paul Martin remarked: "I have my ambitions too, but I have my wife better trained."

Obsessed with politics, short-tempered, and moody, John Diefenbaker was not the ideal husband. Naturally flirtatious, Edna was rumoured to be in the company of other men. She became depressed, and put herself in the care of a Toronto psychiatrist who encouraged John to be more attentive. Edna was given electric shock therapy and pleaded with her husband to take her away from her nightmare. Diefenbaker was attentive, but less sympathetic or compassionate than his wife required. Not long after the 1949 election, Edna was diagnosed with leukemia. Paul Martin, then minister of health, arranged for experimental drugs from the United States. Edna died in early February 1951.

DIEFENBAKER LAID THE FOUNDATION of his beliefs in his maiden speech in the House of Commons on June 13, 1940. Delivered in a time of war, his "One Canada" speech was understandably patriotic: "Let us build up in this country an unhyphenated Canadianism that is dominant, proud and strong." He affirmed that Canadians of German origin were indisputably loyal to their adopted home, and condemned the practice of the Census Bureau tracking country of origin. Diefenbaker opposed the plebiscite to release the Liberal government from its pledge not to invoke conscription. He suggested conscription be decided in the House of Commons, leaving political considerations out of it.

When Diefenbaker considered running for the leadership in 1942, a Toronto friend advised against it. Lawyer David Walker had canvassed the party establishment and reported a grim assessment to Diefenbaker: "Most people that knew you conceded that you were one of the most brilliant debaters in the House of Commons with one of the keenest minds and a tremendous fighter. Admitting all your qualities, the people I talked with, for one reason or another, including such silly reasons as your name and physique, refuse to consider you seriously as their choice as leader of the party. Every one of them conceded that you would be and should be a member of the cabinet. Since our friendship would not be worthwhile unless we were frank with one another, I know that you will accept this letter in the spirit in which it is written."

DIEFENBAKER MADE FEW PREPARATIONS prior to the convention. There was no campaign team or written material in support of his candidacy. However, he was encouraged by convention sentiment that the party was ready for a leader from the West. The front runner was Manitoba premier John Bracken, the choice of retiring leader Arthur Meighen.

Diefenbaker's strengths—his theatrical manner and oratorical gifts— were not in evidence when he delivered his convention speech. Reading from a text, he stiffly reiterated the themes that had characterized his political life: the security of the common man, a fight for the return of democratic institutions, a fair deal under a system of private initiative, Canadian unity based on a Canadianism with no racial basis, concluding, "I believe that Canadian unity must be assured; that it must be built on the basis of a Canadianism that knows no racial origin; that of the various races and creeds of this Dominion must evolve a united Canada."

Finishing third in a field of five gave Diefenbaker a respectable position on the first ballot, enough to assure him a position of prominence on the front benches of the party, now the *Progressive* Conservative party under the leadership of John Bracken.

When Bracken declined to enter the House of Commons through a by-election, the position of house leader was up for grabs. Bracken decreed the leader would be selected by a vote of caucus members. Diefenbaker honourably voted for his opponent. He lost the position by one vote.

During war, Diefenbaker believed, the party in Opposition had a responsibility to be patriotic. The House of Commons, he said, should not be "a cockpit of contending factions, each desirous of preparing for the hustings ... (Parliament should) strengthen the resolution of the people to carry on to the end." His partisanship was for Canada.

In the 1945 election, Diefenbaker characteristically set a course distinct from his leader and party. On his own initiative, he pledged support for the South Saskatchewan River dam and opposed sending Canadian troops to Japan. This was likely a wise move on his part because Diefenbaker was the only Tory to win in Saskatchewan. He was dismayed that out of the 66-member Tory caucus elected in 1945, 48 came from Ontario and only 10 from Canada's four western provinces. The heavy influence of central Canada in caucus frustrated Diefenbaker.

Increasingly, he became less of a team player and drew the limelight to himself. It helped his cause that the press could always count on Diefenbaker for a pithy quote. This, combined with a short temper and unwillingness to do committee work, left him isolated from the Tory caucus. He was beginning to exhibit the traits that would have him labelled a renegade much later in his career. According to party worker Dalton Camp: "John Diefenbaker was an enigma. Popular with the press, presumably admired by Liberals, greatly in demand as a platform orator, Diefenbaker maintained a distance from his Parliamentary colleagues. He rarely attended caucus, was not usually available to the Whip's office when it was attempting to organize the schedule of opposition speakers, and beyond the call of the duty roster for attendance in the house."

It is surprising that a man with leadership ambitions had such little concern with impressing his parliamentary colleagues. But his constituency was the common man, the disadvantaged, the dispossessed, and the persecuted. Standing up for minorities through a bill of rights became Diefenbaker's political mantra.

While a member of Parliament, Diefenbaker continued to practice law, notably selecting cases where he could represent the "little man" against powerful interests. After hearing of the case of Jack Atherton in 1950, a railway telegraph operator charged with manslaughter following a fatal train crash owing to alleged negligence, Edna Diefenbaker urged her husband to represent the 22-year-old Atherton regardless of cost or consequence. The railway union similarly pleaded with Diefenbaker to get involved. Diefenbaker paid $1,500 to join the BC Bar to gain standing in the court. Leaving nothing to chance, Diefenbaker obtained a psychological profile of the prosecutor. The case was national news and Atherton's acquittal enhanced Diefenbaker's reputation as a man of the people.

DIEFENBAKER HAD THE FIRST of many confrontations with Dalton Camp after a dinner in Winnipeg to honour Sir John A. Macdonald. George Drew was the keynote speaker and Diefenbaker and his wife were guests. The Chief was displeased over the treatment given his second wife, Olive whom he had married in 1953. Camp described the incident in his autobiography.

> *Diefenbaker:*   Sit down. I want to tell you something. I don't want my wife to be insulted again, you understand?

Camp:	I don't understand.
Diefenbaker:	I don't blame you. I know how they do these things, but I want you to know. I want to know that wherever I go, my wife goes. If I'm asked to sit at the head table, my wife sits with me. You see that's the way it is with me. My wife does not sit below the salt.
Camp:	There were too many people for the head table. We had to ask all the wives to sit together at another table.
Diefenbaker:	I believe Mrs. Drew was at the head table.
Camp:	She was the only exception, except the mayor's wife.
Olive Diefenbaker:	Camp explained it couldn't be helped. Let's not talk about it.
Diefenbaker:	Just a minute. I know how these things happen. But I want you to know, you see, there will never be a next time. That's all. If my wife can't be there, then I won't be there. Is that clear?

After this incident, Camp concluded Diefenbaker was a spent force in the twilight of his career. Camp believed Diefenbaker's chance at winning leadership had come and gone, and that now was the time for new blood.

EMERGENCY POWERS used by the Liberal Cabinet to override minority and individual rights were the springboard for Diefenbaker's attack on the government in 1946.

> Mr. Speaker . . . I do not believe the minds of liberty-loving Canadians, however much they hate communism, have become so apathetic in six years of domination by a state in a period when the political doctrines of regimentation . . . have been in effect. I believe the time has come for a declaration of liberties to be made by this Parliament. Magna Charta is part of our birthright. Habeas corpus, the Bill of Rights, the petition of right, are all part of our tradition. . . . I think out of the events of the last few years a responsibility falls upon Parliament to assure that Canadians . . . should have established by their legislature a Bill of Rights under which freedom of religion, of speech, of association . . . freedom from capricious arrests and freedom under the rule of law, should be made part and parcel of the law of the country.

Consistent with a bill of rights, Diefenbaker proposed the repeal of the War Measures Act. Passed by Parliament during the emotional outset of World War 1, the Act was a danger to society, Diefenbaker argued, "It constitutes an invitation to any government in the future . . . to declare an emergency to the detriment of the rights of our people. . . . (necessary in war), but in the days of peace, with the challenge that the state is making to the rights of the individual . . . the act should be repealed." The powers in the Act were so broad that it was like your grandmother's nightie: it covered everything.

When Diefenbaker issued his warning, he foretold the Act would be used in times other than war. Diefenbaker was correct. The "invitation" to invoke the War Measures Act would be issued by a handful of ragtag terrorists in October of 1970 in what became know as the "October Crisis." The temptation to unleash the power of the War Measures Act was so irresistible that peacenik Liberal Prime Minister Pierre Trudeau led the charge. Almost 500 Québec citizens were arrested and detained; the overwhelming majority never charged with a crime. If Diefenbaker had had his way in 1946, a fearful federal government would not have been able to invoke the draconian measures that unleashed the might of the military and an unencumbered police force on the civilian population of Québec that year. The unfortunate but predictable long-term consequence of this overreaction would be to diminish the attachment of the people of Québec to Canada. Diefenbaker did not speak out in 1970 when the War Measure Act was invoked, possibly because his name appeared on the assassination list of the Front de libération du Québec, the group that terrorized the nation. Diefenbaker was amused at the hundred or so soldiers assigned to guard him during the crisis and remarked that he had enough troops to conquer Cuba or arrest his political enemies.

AFTER BRACKEN RESIGNED IN 1948, Diefenbaker was the first to enter the race because, "I have something to contribute to Canada in the Crusade to mobilize Canadians everywhere for Canada. . . . To restore Parliamentary authority, the protection of provincial legislative powers, the promotion of free enterprise, the preservation of liberty under a national bill of rights, and generally fair and just treatment for all Canadians."

He told his mother he had no hope of winning. But to the press, Diefenbaker demonstrated his capacity for political spin. "Of course I will win. I mean that seriously." Noting the importance of momentum, he added, ". . . although I would not have said it two weeks ago."

Diefenbaker was once again a long-shot to win the leadership. But he had new supporters, including feminist Nellie McClung, who wrote to Diefenbaker, "I have admired your courage, and clear thinking, for a long time and hope you will be the new leader. You are young, modest, straight-forward, and have an open mind." It is difficult to imagine anyone, at any time, accusing Diefenbaker of modesty.

The Diefenbaker team was better organized for this contest than for the last. Buttons, pamphlets, posters, ribbons filled the noisy and boisterous Ottawa Coliseum. Diefenbaker's campaign speech maintained the themes of his address to the previous convention. "Canadians are asking for a party that will honestly try to end class warfare and hatred: that will regulate injustice and exploitation in enterprise while retaining an expanding free initiative; accept social security as a means not an end . . . while continuing to provide adequately for the aged and afflicted . . . protect our people against unfairness." This time Diefenbaker improved his standing from the last leadership convention by one spot, finishing second to George Drew, who won easily on the first ballot.

There was tension between Drew and Diefenbaker. Much of the animus Diefenbaker may have concocted himself to maintain a distance from Drew, but he pointed to an incident where he felt shabbily treated. "On the night after his victory, I was an intruder. I went to congratulate him. I walked into that gathering and it was as if an animal not customarily admitted to homes had suddenly come into the place."

In the 1949 election, Diefenbaker once again pursued a path independent of his party. When campaign material arrived from national headquarters he loaded it into a boat and defiantly threw it overboard. His main challenger came from the CCF, the party Diefenbaker penetratingly said would be the choice of most communist sympathizers. Diefenbaker retained his seat, but it was one of only seven for the Tories in western Canada. Drew could not win Ontario, let alone the nation, and the Tories were reduced to 41 seats.

While the Tories floundered again in the 1953 election, Diefenbaker's status in the party was on the rise. Local Conservative constituency associations sought Diefenbaker as the party's star attraction for fundraisers. Diefenbaker could cut through Liberal hypocrisy with lines delivered like lightning bolts. He made no friends on Bay Street when he told a Toronto audience that business executives convicted of anti-competitive conduct should be thrown in the slammer rather than slapped on the wrist with a mere fine. But some members of the parliamentary caucus resented

Diefenbaker's lack of team play. Donald Fleming observed, "To deserve loy- alty on the part of others a leader must have proven themselves loyal as a follower. . . ."

A feeling of inevitability surrounded Diefenbaker's rise to the leader- ship. "Stop Diefenbaker" campaigns were launched but quickly failed. Word around the circles close to Drew was, "If Diefenbaker wants it, let the crazy son of a bitch have it. People want John Diefenbaker and there is no use kicking against the pricks." Dalton Camp, who earlier predicted the demise of Diefenbaker, remained skeptical and decidedly negative towards his future leader, writing "Even though [his win was] certain, the achievement will not be graceful or painless. . . . (Diefenbaker) will be constantly reminded of the perils outside his door, where wicked forces combine to thwart his victory, even though the Conservative party has no other choice or purpose than to elect him and is, in fact, eager and anxious to do so."

Diefenbaker showed uncharacteristic humility as he announced his can- didacy. "[I]f Canadians generally believe that I have a contribution to make, if it is their wish that I let my name stand at the leadership convention, I am willing." Willing indeed—for the third time. And this time he had the sup- port of his much beloved Olive.

When the convention gathered on December 10, 1956, Diefenbaker was 61. "I have one love . . . Canada; one purpose . . . Canada's greatness; one aim . . . Canadian unity from the Atlantic to the Pacific." Sounding like a win- ner, Diefenbaker boasted there was no need for patience: he would win the next election.

Victory came on the first ballot, although not without controversy. Diefenbaker chose a proposer from the Atlantic and a seconder from the Pacific, foregoing the tradition of an English and French introduction. Many Québec delegates walked out of the convention when the outcome became apparent. In his acceptance speech, Diefenbaker pleaded for unity and com- mitment with a story from World War 1: "I know some of you have a defeatist attitude. I leave you with a message that raised the spirits of Canadians in the first Great War. The officers were asked to do a formidable task and each one in turn was fearful of the result and said it could not be done. Finally, the officer commanding said: 'Now, gentlemen, you have given me every reason why it cannot be done. Now go and do it.' My friends let us unite and go and do it."

After the convention Diefenbaker gave Camp a mission at party head- quarters. "I just want to know what's going on down there, you see. Will you do that?" the Chief asked. The relationship between the two steadily deteri- orated thereafter.

The press loved Diefenbaker for his crisp and colourful quotes. Thinking him something of a buffoon, the establishment Tories from Toronto waited for Diefenbaker to fall flat on his face. But the firebrand politician was exactly what Canadians needed after several successive plodding, uninspired, and arrogant Liberal administrations. When C.D. Howe was questioned in the House of Commons about the establishment of Transcanada Pipeline as socialism personified, the minister replied, "That's not public enterprise; that's my enterprise." When questioned about reneging on government commitments, the same minister replied, "Who would stop us? If we wanted to get away with it—who would stop us?" Confident of victory in the coming election, the Liberals went into the campaign with 16 vacancies in the Senate.

"It's time for a Diefenbaker government" was the Tory campaign slogan in 1957. The Chief brought the evangelical zeal of a preacher to campaign events, mesmerizing and energizing party supporters. Diefenbaker spoke in grand terms, much the way he had to his mother when he was a boy. "I'm one of those who believe that this party has a sacred trust, trust in accordance with the traditions of Macdonald. It has an appointment with destiny . . . one Canada, with equality of opportunity for every citizen."

Diefenbaker knew that to win he needed more than the natural Tory supporters in the country. In the previous five federal elections the best the party had mustered in the popular vote was 30.3 percent. The Tories needed a way to attract and motivate the undecided, the apathetic, and the disenchanted to the Tory side. The key was the populist Diefenbaker. He appealed to the average Canadian: "My abiding interest is your interest; my guiding principle is the welfare of the average Canadian." Whenever local Tory organizers tried to impress their leader by arranging transportation in a shiny new Cadillac or limousine, he declined, preferring to ride with campaign workers in a nondescript Chevrolet.

On his own, however, Diefenbaker was not enough to excite voters. He needed a vision for the country. Building on Macdonald's legacy of a national vision, Diefenbaker formulated a "New Frontier Policy" that would open up the vast resources of Canada's North and benefit all of Canada.

Canadian ownership of industry was an objective; so too was an increase in immigration, enhancing old-age pensions, and reducing taxes to eliminate surplus budgets.

Tories had had enough of losing. They were determined to win. Candidate and party president George Hees remarked to his candidates across the land, "I don't care if they like acrobats or cream cheese. If they like it; give it to them. It's about time we realized that people would rather be entertained than educated." Once described by C.D. Howe as a man with "the build of Adonis and the brains of a gnat," Hees told his party's candidates, "Whenever I see a hand sticking out of a sleeve, I shake it."

Audiences across the country responded enthusiastically to Diefenbaker's optimism and hope, although the Liberals, encouraged by favourable polls, dismissed evidence of Diefenbaker's rising popularity. When Diefenbaker predicted his party would win 97 seats, a member of the press gallery declared it wishful thinking. A poll taken June 8, two days prior to Election Day, had the Liberals ahead by five percentage points. *Maclean's* magazine went to press just as the votes were being counted and declared: "For better or for worse, we Canadians have *once again* elected one of the most powerful governments ever created by the free will of a free electorate. . . ." Liberals took the popular vote over the Tories by almost two percentage points. But because of huge Liberal pluralities were registered in Quebec seats, the larger popular vote total did not translate into a greater number of seats.

In perhaps the last Canadian election where the outcome surprised the nation, the final tally was 111 seats for the Conservatives, 104 for the Liberals, 25 for CCF, and 19 for Social Credit. The increase from 4 to 8 seats in Québec made the difference between Tory victory and defeat. The same sort of modest breakthrough in Québec, from zero seats in 2004 to 10 seats in 2006, would later propel Conservative leader Stephen Harper to 24 Sussex.

The contest was close enough that Prime Minister St. Laurent did not concede until the military vote was counted. Even after the final vote was tallied, Liberal ministers urged their leader to form a government and face the minority Parliament. Liberals had played this card once before, in 1925, when they were 15 seats short of the Tories but clung to power for a short period with the help of the 22 Progressive MPs. St. Laurent wisely rejected the advice: not only on account of his lower seat total but because of the lack of Liberal seats he held outside the Québec. Liberals had won 82 percent of the seats in Québec but only 22 percent of the seats in the rest of Canada.

The day after the election, Diefenbaker went fishing with a few friends and some reporters at Saskatchewan's Lac La Ronge. A friend said, "Not much of a fish you got there, eh?" to which Diefenbaker replied, "I caught the big one yesterday."

Diefenbaker's Cabinet did not differ in structure or number from its predecessor, but it did break barriers. Ellen Fairclough became Canada's first female minister. Michael Starr, of Ukrainian Orthodox descent, was the first MP of neither British nor French origin to enter Cabinet. Surprisingly, only one of the eight Tory MPs from Québec made it into the Cabinet of 16. Some ministers filled multiple roles. In addition to being first minister, Diefenbaker was also president of the Privy Council and secretary of state for external affairs, albeit for a brief period. A few months after the election, Diefenbaker recruited University of Toronto president Sidney Smith to the position.

Governing was an enormous challenge for Diefenbaker, whose experience in running an organization was limited to a small Saskatchewan law office and, for a brief period, a political party. His party had not held power since 1935 so his Cabinet ministers had limited experience in government. He wisely relied on the clerk of the Privy Council, Robert Bryce, for sound advice. For a man known to be vindictive, he made surprisingly few changes in the public service and even retained some ministerial assistants who were Liberal partisans.

He established strict rules for ministers and enacted a code of conduct to limit or eliminate conflict of interest. Cabinet deliberations were kept secret, with communications strictly controlled by the prime minister. Ministers were threatened with termination should they break these rules.

Diefenbaker could hardly believe he had reached the pinnacle of political success. Reality sank in when, a few months after being sworn in, he met Winston Churchill and the Queen at his first Commonwealth meeting. He often recounted in speeches a conversation he had with Churchill when Diefenbaker declined an offer to join the recently retired British PM for a drink.

Churchill:	Are you a prohibitionist or a teetotaler?
Diefenbaker:	A teetotaler.
Churchill:	Good. You will hurt no one but yourself.

Diefenbaker pressed for increased trade with Britain to diminish Canada's reliance on trade with the United States. A goal of diverting 15 percent of imports from the United States to the United Kingdom was established, a target Diefenbaker described as "reasonable, equitable and obtainable." He went further, suggesting that a free trade agreement with Britain be explored. But his proposals lacked any form of realism, insight, or meaningful analysis. Discriminating against the Americans in trade would run Canada afoul of the General Agreement on Tariffs and Trade (GATT), not to mention the plain economic common sense of trading with your next-door neighbour. Within a few months, the idea of trade diversion was dropped because no sensible means of achieving the target could be established.

Diefenbaker's trade and commerce minister, George Hees, was less concerned with whom Canada traded with as long as it traded. His tie clip was emblazoned with the letters *Y.C.D.B.S.O.Y.A.* In meetings he would fiddle with the clip until, invariably, someone would ask what the letters stood for. "What's it mean, you ask? Well, you can't do business sitting on your ass."

When the prime minister travelled to the United States in September 1957, he remarked that issues and problems were best solved in an atmosphere of unity and friendship. Diefenbaker wanted Canada to be less of an exporter of raw materials and more an exporter of finished goods. He also wanted greater Canadian ownership and control of industries. But the larger issue that would dominate Canadian–American relations during Diefenbaker's term as prime minister was defence.

The previous Liberal government had left many defence matters with the United States unresolved, largely to deflect discussion during the 1957 election campaign. Canadian and American military leaders had agreed upon a United Operational Command, which had been submitted to Cabinet on March 15, 1957. The matter was deferred and came before Diefenbaker in July. He approved the military agreement without much thought or any input from Cabinet. That would change in time.

It was Diefenbaker's good fortune that the former Liberal government had invited Queen Elizabeth to open the post-election session of Parliament. Diefenbaker sat next to Her Majesty when she read the speech from the throne on October 14, 1957, the first such Canadian speech she had ever read. The Diefenbaker government was in a generous mood and made commitments to increase pensions, enhance old age security, and provide additional support for farmers. It also pledged to eliminate discrimination against married women in unemployment insurance while extending unemployment insurance benefits from sixteen to twenty-four weeks. Reductions in corporate tax rates for small business and support for major infrastructure projects constituted major investments in Canada's future.

Though happy to govern, Diefenbaker wanted to convert his minority in Parliament into a majority as soon as possible. To ensure broad Tory appeal, he positioned his government firmly in the political centre. Diefenbaker's energy remained high and he continued to campaign as if an election was imminent. With the polls heavily in the Tories' favour and the Opposition in disarray, talk of an election buzzed around Parliament Hill. In January 1958, the Liberal party chose Lester B. "Mike" Pearson over Paul Martin as leader. Diefenbaker watched the convention on television and confidently remarked, "I saw one of the banners that the Young Liberals carried which was entitled, 'Diefenbaker—raw deal.' Even so, advertising, wherever it comes from, is always acceptable so long as one doesn't have to pay for it."

When the former diplomat and Nobel Prize winner stood as opposition leader in the House of Commons, he went on the offensive and challenged the Diefenbaker government to resign. But Pearson was not throwing down the election gauntlet and putting the seats of his Liberal caucus members on the line. He wanted his chance to be prime minister in a minority Parliament. "I would be prepared, if called upon, to form . . . a government to tackle immediately the formidable problem of ending the Tory pause and getting this country back on the Liberal highway of progress from which we have been temporarily diverted." His motion read in part, ". . . in view of the desirability, at this time, of having a government pledged to implement Liberal policies, His Excellency's advisors should . . . submit their resignations." Liberal arrogance in full flight.

Diefenbaker sensed a golden opportunity to belittle his unworthy opponent. "On Thursday there was shrieking defiance; on the following Monday there is shrinking indecision . . . the only reason that this motion is worded as it is is that my honorable friends opposite quake when they think of what will happen if an election comes . . . It is the resignation from responsibility of a great party."

Diefenbaker could use Pearson's motion to turn over the government as justification for the election he wanted. There was another reason why Diefenbaker wanted to go to the polls. Government revenues were falling because of a weakening economy, and some economists were predicting a recession. Diefenbaker wanted to act fast so he could blame the economic downturn on the Liberals for having failed to disclose and respond to a pending crisis. Diefenbaker laid his hands on a report, prepared by the former associate deputy minister of trade and commerce, Mitchell Sharp, that contained damaging evidence. Diefenbaker made his case in the House of Commons: "I intend to establish as clearly as the printed word will make possible that my honorable friend concealed from the Canadian people the facts. You [Mr. Pearson] secured the advice of the economists in your own departments and were advised as to what the situation was in March 1957. . . . They had a warning . . . did they tell us that? . . . Why did they not act when the House was sitting in January, February, March and April? . . . You [Pearson] concealed the facts, that is what you did. . . ."

Diefenbaker went to Québec City to meet Governor General Vincent Massey and claimed obstruction in Parliament by the Liberal party. The reality was that the Liberal party was weak and Diefenbaker wanted to take advantage of this opportunity. Parliament was dissolved and the election was scheduled for March 31, 1958, nine months and three weeks since the last campaign, not much longer than the period that Joe Clark would hold a Tory government in 1979–80, but with a far different outcome.

In the 1958 campaign, Diefenbaker's "northern vision" took shape. He promised "Roads to Resources" and respect for Northern Native communities. Voters could hear the echo of the great national vision of Sir John A. Macdonald in Diefenbaker's remarks: "This is the vision: One Canada. One Canada, where Canadians will have preserved to them the control of their own economic and political destiny. Sir John A. Macdonald saw Canada from east to west: I see a new Canada—Canada of the North . . . this is the vision!"

Diefenbaker captured the imaginations of Canadians from coast to coast to coast, an emotional experience inspired by the grand hope of a Prairie populist. He was a man of the people who campaigned under the slogan "Follow John." He followed Napoleon's maxim: a leader is one who peddles hope. "Instead of [the] helplessness and fear the Liberals generate," said Diefenbaker, "we have given faith; instead of desperation we offer inspiration."

As the northern vision took hold, Diefenbaker added other elements: "We'll build a nation of 50 million people within the lifetime of many of you here. I'm asking you to catch the Vision of the greatness and the potential of this nation." He gave life and credibility to the slogan offered by Liberal Sir Wilfrid Laurier, "The twentieth century belongs to Canada." With Diefenbaker at the helm, Canadians thought that just maybe it did. With Diefenbaker, Canada had a leader who stood up to the establishment and believed in the power of the common man. The Tory party had redefined itself in one quick and easy step: the stiff-shirted Bay-street banker was out; Canada's new folk hero was in.

After Diefenbaker cemented a relationship with Maurice Duplessis of the Union Nationale in Québec, the cradle and nexus of Liberal support, Pearson was dead in the water. It was Duplessis's opportunity to return the favour the Liberals had done him when they intervened in the Quebec campaign in 1939. In doing his research on Duplessis, Conrad Black was told the story of Yvon Tassé, a school architect, who was awakened by Duplessis shortly before eleven one evening, and told to get dressed and get into the premier's car, which was awaiting him at his front door, and come to accept a draft as the Tory candidate. Tassé said he didn't want the nomination. Duplessis told him that was irrelevant and he should do as asked if he wanted to go on designing schools in Québec.

On election night, Québecers jumped on the Tory bandwagon full force, giving Diefenbaker a majority of the popular vote and 50 of 75 seats in la belle province. Tory candidates swept Prince Edward Island, Nova Scotia, Manitoba, and Alberta. The CCF was reduced to eight seats and the once mighty Liberal party became a rump of 48 members. The Tories took their Social Credit cousins from nineteen seats to zero. Diefenbaker's caucus of 208 (out of a total of 265) was unprecedented. With 78.5 percent of total seats, no Canadian government of any stripe, before or since, has ever held such command of the House of Commons.

CHAPTER 19

MAN OF THE PEOPLE

*There are powerful interests working against us, national and
international. Everyone is against me, but the people.*

SIR JOHN A. MACDONALD ONCE SAID, "Given a government with a
big surplus, a big majority and a weak opposition, you could debauch
a committee of archangels." Now, with an overwhelming and unprecedented majority, the Chief was burdened by high expectations and a caucus
too large to be manageable. Politically, he had only one way to go, and that
was down.

Diefenbaker claimed his government was truly national: that it represented all people and race, that it was the manifestation of his concept of
One Canada. "This is a victory . . . not for any one person or party, but rather
a victory for the kind of Canadianism in which we all believe." This may have
been what Diefenbaker believed. More likely, Canadians had simply
responded to the charisma, conviction and charm of an enigmatic leader.

Richard Nixon, then vice president of the United States, wrote to
Diefenbaker to congratulate him on his overwhelming victory, saying that,
"history will record that you are one of the truly great political campaigners
of our time. The fact that within the space of just a few months you were
able to do what you did against what appeared to be insurmountable odds is
an achievement which has seldom been equaled in history."

Despite the trappings of office and the strict protocol attached to being prime minister, Diefenbaker did not lose touch. He asked each member of his caucus for their views on how he should approach important national issues. He was equally determined to maintain a dialogue with ordinary Canadians: "One thing which must be guarded against is complacency and its twin, arrogance, which are often the aftermath of great political victory. . . . I intend to maintain as close a relationship with the people as is possible and to ask various outstanding Canadians to give me the benefit of their views from time to time." He is the last prime minister who would see ordinary Canadians in his office without an appointment.

It was difficult, however, for the unilingual Diefenbaker to connect with Québecers. Diefenbaker didn't mind poking fun at himself on the subject. "Apparently I just can't pronounce French well while talking. An English-speaking friend joked to me, 'I love to hear you talk French on television. When you do, every English-speaking person in the audience, who doesn't know a word of French, can understand every word you say.'" It was inevitable that Diefenbaker's vision of One Canada would clash with the nationalist aspirations that would soon be expressed in Québec's Quiet Revolution. Despite having won a majority of its seats, Diefenbaker did not have political antennae on the ground in Québec. On a more practical level, he failed to give adequate weight to the French-speaking MPs in his caucus. Grumbling soon followed.

Diefenbaker believed his position within the party and as prime minister was unassailable. And he revelled in that adulation to the point of addiction. He was not the leader of a team or a party; he led a *movement* that was transfixed on the personal qualities and charisma of one man. Despite the responsibilities of office and a huge Parliamentary majority, Diefenbaker continued to travel the country and make speeches as if locked in campaign mode.

Parliament opened on May 12, 1958. The government put forward a set of policies designed to add to the social welfare of the nation, with new support for seniors, the unemployed, and farmers. Among other priorities, Diefenbaker's government would establish a regulatory agency for radio and television, respond to an economy in decline, curtail inflation, and minimize a projected deficit. Proceedings of the House of Commons were to be translated. But the crowning jewel of his administration's throne speech was a bill of rights.

In 1958, Diefenbaker went on an international tour. He clearly enjoyed being among world leaders and showed no signs of intimidation. When meeting his Holiness Pope John XXIII, he casually asked "How does it feel to be Pope anyhow?" The pontiff took it in stride: "Well, here I am near the end of the road and on top of the heap." Those who travelled with Diefenbaker said that he did not hesitate to take instinctive positions on issues about which his knowledge was limited. For example, he did not consult his advisors before declaring Canadian support to admit communist China to the United Nations, a policy that particularly annoyed the Americans. Most of his instincts, however, were ultimately proven correct and he can only be criticized for being ahead of his time.

The government soon encountered difficulties with the Bank of Canada and its governor, James Coyne, over the conversion and refinancing of wartime victory bonds. The ensuing controversy created friction between Diefenbaker and his finance minister, Donald Fleming. Tensions were exacerbated when Diefenbaker's instincts for the expansion of social spending clashed with Fleming's conservative-minded preference for restraint. However, compared with matters of national defence, disagreements over economic policy were small potatoes.

The integration of Canadian and American defence forces under NORAD had been an initiative of the previous administration, an arrangement Diefenbaker approved. Therefore, on defence issues, at the very least, Diefenbaker expected little opposition from the Liberal front bench. Indeed, Pearson did not dispute the need for cooperation with the United States in matters of national defence. However, he took the government to task for not bringing the international defence agreement to Cabinet for review and approval. Pearson accused Diefenbaker of entering into the agreement too hastily, without adequate review, consultation, or debate. In other words, he accused Diefenbaker of being an incompetent administrator of important matters of national security.

Few defence issues were thornier than the Avro Arrow, a prototype of a fighter plane designed to replace the CF-100. The Arrow had been on the books since 1953, but overwhelming technical difficulties were revealed as early as 1955 that caused the Liberal minister, C.D. Howe, distress: "I can say that now we have started on a program of development that gives me the shudders." The Liberals had decided to cancel the Arrow, but did not want to deal with the political fallout on the cusp of an election. The dislocation of thousands of aircraft workers and engineers was something best handled early in a mandate.

The economic viability of the Avro Arrow was contingent upon large-scale orders of the aircraft from the United States. Because of political considerations, the Cabinet was initially divided over how best to approach the future of the Arrow. Diefenbaker moved cautiously. Furthermore, the Arrow was not designed to deal with emerging military threats and in 1958, it was more important to develop technology to counter a Russian build up of intercontinental ballistic missiles, which was not within the capacity of fighter jets.

A briefing to Cabinet delivered by Defence Minister George Pearkes indicated the changing nature of a required military response: "The assessment of the threat to North America changed. In the 1960s, the main threat would probably be from ballistic missiles, with the manned bomber decreasing in importance after 1962–63. . . . The original requirements in 1953 for between 500 and 600 aircraft of the CF-105 fighter had been drastically reduced. Finally, the cost of the CF-105 program as a whole was now of such a magnitude that the chiefs of staff felt that, to meet the modest requirement of manned aircraft presently considered advisable, it would be more economical to procure a fully developed interceptor of comparable performance in the United States."

The recommendation made to Cabinet was to cancel further development of the Arrow and negotiate with the United States for the sharing of two Canadian Bomarc missile bases. According to Pearkes, the Bomarc was cheaper than the CF-105 and just as effective. The missiles could be fitted with an atomic warhead and the U.S. would probably supply the warheads. The military and financial implications pointed unequivocally to termination of the Arrow. However, with 25,000 jobs at stake, as well as potential technology transfers, it was as much a political as a military decision.

The country's top public servant, Robert Bryce, recommended cancellation and worked with the executive team at A.V. Roe, the designer of the Arrow, to minimize the economic and political implications of cancellation. Diefenbaker did not want to act abruptly and gave the company time to reorganize and redeploy its manpower. In the meantime, taxpayers' money continued to flow into the ill-fated Arrow.

In September 1958, Diefenbaker made an announcement that indicated the days of the Arrow were numbered. "In view of the introduction of missiles into the Canadian air defence system and the reduction in the expected need for manned, supersonic, interceptor aircraft, the government has decided that it would not be advisable at this time to put the CF-105 into production . . . the government has decided that the development program for the Arrow aircraft and the Iroquois engine should be continued until next March, when the situation will be reviewed again in light of all the existing circumstances at that time. . . . Although both the Arrow aircraft and the Iroquois engine appear now to be better than any alternatives expected to be ready by 1961, it is questionable whether . . . their margin of superiority is worth a very high cost of producing them."

The announcement was the equivalent of a severance package with six months notice. Diefenbaker thought continuing with the investment beyond that point was wasteful and unjustifiable. The press was largely supportive. Pundits were impressed by Diefenbaker's decisiveness in the face of negative political fallout. A *Globe and Mail* editorial called the decision, "not only wise and courageous, but one which will save the taxpayers a good deal of money." Editorials aside, the A.V. Roe Company did not surrender and launched a powerful lobby in support of its cause.

It is often said that Diefenbaker ran a one-man government. According to his ministers, however, he was slow to make decisions and routinely—even painstakingly—sought unanimity from his Cabinet. According to advisor Roy Faibish, Diefenbaker would keep trying to bring hold-outs around to reach a consensus. He didn't want to proceed otherwise.

For the Arrow, however, there was no delay, no lack of leadership, and no absence of consensus. On February 20, 1959, Diefenbaker told the House of Commons, "We must not abdicate our responsibility to assure that the huge sums which it is our duty to ask Parliament to provide for defence are being expended in the most effective way to achieve that purpose." Diefenbaker reminded the company that he had the interests of 18 million shareholders to protect.

The company immediately laid off all staff working on the project and was not prepared to follow an orderly six-month shutdown as the contract with the government provided. It wanted to make noise, lots of noise. Diefenbaker fought back. "Letting out thousands of workers . . . on Friday, was so cavalier, so unreasonable, that the only conclusion any fair-minded person can come to is that it was done for the purpose of embarrassing the government." The government was indeed embarrassed. Caught off guard, it had no plan to keep the skilled workers and technology in Canada. Indeed, many laid-off workers ultimately emigrated to the United States. The Diefenbaker government had lost its first major public relations battle.

Some speculate that the fallout over the cancellation of the Arrow paralyzed Diefenbaker's ability to make decisions, particularly on defence issues. Unpopularity is a risk with every decision, but Diefenbaker had grown fond of the adulation and political capital was not something he was inclined to squander. In a time of rapid economic growth and burgeoning surpluses, Diefenbaker would have been content eradicating social injustices while raising the plight of the weak and disadvantaged. But the economy was weak and a series of world crises would soon be upon him. It was not a time for indecision or inaction. The Cabinet became fractious and dysfunctional. And Diefenbaker was slow to react, even when the will of a majority of Cabinet was evident.

DIEFENBAKER WAS FRIENDLY with a select few reporters, offering them privileged access as long as the ensuing stories were supportive and flattering. Asked by a reporter for the name of his new minister for external affairs, Diefenbaker coyly replied, "Oh, I can't do that. Everyone in the press gallery would he mad at me. But who do you think it is?"When the reporter replied "Howard Green," Diefenbaker slowly walked over to the window and said with a smile, "Those lawns. They sure are nice and *green* aren't they?"

Diefenbaker was a libertarian by nature, unwilling to use the heavy hand of his government against its citizens. He recalled the episodes when Conservative prime ministers had reacted swiftly and aggressively to acts of protest—Meighen's response to the 1919 strike in Winnipeg or Bennett's determination to quell a protest march. Such incidents created the appearance that Tory leaders were disconnected from the plight of ordinary citizens and more responsive to established sources of power and money. This was not Diefenbaker's way.

His mettle was tested when the Newfoundland government requested the RCMP's help in dealing with a strike by the International Woodworkers of America in Grand Falls. Despite the obligation to supply RCMP forces when requested by a province, Diefenbaker refused: "It would be provocative and likely to cause further outbreaks of violence . . .Would Canada have been well served had every working man and woman come to regard the Royal Canadian Mounted Police as a strike-breaking force?" The pressing need for federal help was made clear when St. John's Constable William Moss was hit over the head with a pulpwood club and killed. Diefenbaker's failure to heed Newfoundland's requests for reinforcements led to the resignation of the commissioner of the RCMP.

More problems with Newfoundland surfaced after Joey Smallwood, its Liberal premier, requested $17 million in federal subsidies. Such a request, the federal government responded, was beyond its contractual obligations within the agreement signed in 1949. In protest, Smallwood ordered that public buildings be clad in black bunting to mark the tenth anniversary of provincehood. The gesture would inspire future Newfoundland premiers. In

2004, over a dispute concerning offshore royalties, Danny Williams issued an order to lower the Canadian flag from all provincial buildings.

Diefenbaker was capable of symbolic acts of his own. Although accused of being insensitive to the cultural and political aspirations of Québecers, his decision to replace Governor General Vincent Massey with Georges Vanier, a decorated military officer and former Canadian ambassador to France, was warmly received in French Canada. Simultaneous translation was introduced into the House of Commons under Diefenbaker's watch and government cheques started being printed in both English and French. He also earned the admiration of Aboriginal Canadians by appointing James Gladstone of Cardston, Alberta, to the Senate. Known as Akay-na-muka (Many Guns) in the Blood Tribe of the Blackfoot Nation, Gladstone was the first Aboriginal Canadian summoned to the red chamber.

Diefenbaker viewed the Canadian Bill of Rights as his government's most important piece of legislation. When he introduced the bill on September 5, 1958, Diefenbaker encouraged extensive discussion, review, and amendment. He knew that failing to put the bill of rights in a constitutional amendment severely limited its application. One critic called the narrow applicability of the bill a "timid and tepid affirmation of a political and social tradition." The Canadian Bar Association called it "window dressing." An unattributed quote is frequently used to describe the bill's limitation: "It provides protection to all Canadians, just so long as they don't live in any of the provinces."

Nevertheless, the bill was proclaimed law on August 10, 1960. Some 20,000 copies of key portions of the bill were printed on high-quality parchment and distributed to classrooms across the nation, with the prime minister's signature prominently affixed. One provision of the bill not included in the parchment version was a so-called "notwithstanding clause" that limited the application of the bill in certain circumstances. A variant of this clause would become a prominent feature of Pierre Trudeau's 1982 constitutional initiative, largely to ensure the ultimate power rested with elected politicians rather than appointed and unaccountable judges.

Diefenbaker saw the bill as an expression of Canadian values, rather than a raw legal instrument. Years later, he reflected on the meaning of the bill of rights. "Those law professors and politicians who condemned it had closed their eyes to what was happening. All the laws of this Dominion were made to conform to it. It became the standard and the pattern for those Canadian provinces that wished to enact their own provincial Bill of Rights."

The Conservative Cabinet was thought to be a straitlaced and uptight bunch. Diefenbaker was understandably surprised then, in December 1960, by a sex scandal involving his associate minister of defence, Pierre Sévigny, and German playgirl and alleged security risk, Gerda Munsinger. Diefenbaker summoned his associate minister and demanded answers, as well as a commitment that the affair be terminated. Munsinger had left Canada, but not before she was arrested for passing a cheque with insufficient funds. Satisfied that his minister had not revealed state secrets, Diefenbaker kept Sévigny in his Cabinet, thus avoiding embarrassment on many fronts. Diefenbaker was not judgmental towards his minister's sexual conduct, except to the extent it represented a risk to Canada's national security interests. He was sensitive to the personal upheaval that would follow the revelation of the affair, and he did not overreact. The Munsinger affair was not made public until 1966 when Liberal Justice Minister Lucien Cardin, provoked by Conservative questioning, disclosed one of Canada's first political-sexual scandals.

Diefenbaker was a strong believer in the British Commonwealth and was loath to see it weakened, but, unlike Great Britain, he was also deeply troubled by the presence of the apartheid regime of South Africa in the Commonwealth family. At Commonwealth meetings he sought "uncompromising denunciations of apartheid" that ultimately led to South Africa's withdrawal from membership. Britain wanted South Africa to remain in the Commonwealth, but Diefenbaker aligned with the non-white nations. Diefenbaker told the House of Commons, "We tried to do whatever was humanly possible to avoid a break without making a sacrifice of basic principles." Brian Mulroney would use this same model when, in opposition to Ronald Reagan and Margaret Thatcher, he pressed the Commonwealth in meetings throughout his term as prime minister to impose sanctions against South Africa, to remain in force until apartheid was dismantled. For his part Mulroney is often credited as the international leader who was most persuasive in securing Nelson Mandela's release from prison.

Tension in the Commonwealth, however, was overshadowed by anxiety over Soviet strength in intercontinental ballistic nuclear missiles, and the government had to decide how best to protect its population. Specifically, would it accept American nuclear warheads on Canadian soil? Diefenbaker announced that the use of these weapons from Canadian soil would be subject to the approval of both governments. Lester Pearson did not object to nuclear warheads in Canada, but believed they should be completely within Canadian control.

In matters of defence, Diefenbaker affirmed Canada's close relationship with its natural allies, the United States and Great Britain. "This is not the time to enter into criticisms or recriminations of our friends," Diefenbaker told reporters. With Dwight Eisenhower in the White House, Diefenbaker strongly supported building closer ties with NATO allies. "We must maintain our unity and strengthen it, and while striving for peace must maintain our defences against the propaganda of delusive ideas and the dangers of accurate missiles."

In July 1960, the Soviet military shot down an American reconnaissance plane. As tensions escalated between the two countries, British Prime Minister Harold Macmillan encouraged Diefenbaker to attend the United Nations General Assembly in a show of unity. Diefenbaker was in the assembly when Nikita Khrushchev delivered a provocative speech on September 23, and was the first Western leader to follow Khrushchev to the podium. Ignoring the advice of bureaucrats at external affairs to take a cautious diplomatic tone, Diefenbaker spoke boldly, provocatively, and instinctively:

> As one coming from Canada, I say that the United Nations constitutes the greatest hope for the middle and small powers, for the new and weaker states, indeed, for all the nations of mankind of every social and political system. . . . I came here prepared to accept, to adopt and to agree with any good suggestion Khrushchev might offer, for I am of those who believe that his suggestions must not be rejected out of hand. I have been disappointed. Mr. Khrushchev, in a gigantic propaganda drama of destructive misrepresentation, launched a major offensive in the Cold War. . . . We do not always agree with the United States, but our very existence—with one-tenth of the population of the United States and possessing the resources that we do—is an effective answer to the propaganda that the United States has aggressive designs. . . . President Eisenhower made a restrained, a wise and a conciliatory speech. . . . he opened the door to international conciliation and world Fellowship. I am sorry to say that Mr. Khrushchev tried to shut that door . . .

Responding to Khrushchev's comments about the end of colonial regimes, obliquely aimed at the British Commonwealth, Diefenbaker took the offensive.

> Indeed in this assembly the membership is composed in a very considerable measure of the graduates of empires, mandates and trusteeships

of the United Kingdom, the Commonwealth and other nations. *I ask this question: how many human beings have been liberated by the USSR?* Do we forget how one of the postwar colonies of the USSR sought to liberate itself four years ago and with what results? What of Lithuania, Estonia, Latvia? What of the freedom loving Ukrainians and many other Eastern European peoples which I shall not name for fear of omitting some of them? . . . I ask the chairman of the Council of ministers of the USSR to give those nations under his domination the right of free elections—to give them the opportunity to determine the kind of government they want under genuinely free conditions.

The speech was applauded at home and abroad in all democratic nations. Diefenbaker had courageously confronted the Russian bear and had triumphed on the world stage by standing up for the rights of all people to freedom and democracy.

While Diefenbaker was friendly with Eisenhower, he had little in common with incoming president John F. Kennedy. In fact, their relationship got off to a bad start after Kennedy took two weeks to return Diefenbaker's congratulatory Election Day phone call.

In preparations for a presidential visit to Ottawa in February 1961, Diefenbaker recoiled at the proposed security arrangements. "They want to put men with guns all over the place. They are not going to push me around." But the only injury on this trip came when President Kennedy attempted to plant a tree and reinjured his back. After Kennedy had teased Diefenbaker about his poor French, the president's injury was unlikely to invoke much sympathy from the prime minister.

After he met with Kennedy, Diefenbaker discovered a briefing note that was left behind titled, "What we want from the Ottawa trip." It contained four points:

- To push the Canadians towards an increased role in Latin America,
- To push the Canadians towards membership in the Organization of American States
- To push Canadians towards one percent foreign aid budget
- Canadian help for better monitoring of the Laotian–Vietnamese borders

All four points had been amicably discussed between the two leaders. When he read the briefing note, however, Diefenbaker was incensed. No one, not even the president of the United States, was going to *push* him or Canada around. Of course, the proper response would have been to return the briefing note to the American embassy. But Diefenbaker was reluctant to give up any evidence that proved American aggression. As dangerous as it was, he kept the note for use should the need arise in the future.

After Kennedy's visit, Diefenbaker told the House of Commons that in their meeting, "The president . . . leaves upon one the impression of a person dedicated to peace, to the raising of economic standards not only in his country but in all countries, and to the achievement in his day of disarmament among all the nations of the world." But privately Kennedy characterized the meeting very differently. He told his advisers that Diefenbaker was disingenuous and untrustworthy. Robert Kennedy was reported to have said, "I don't want to see that boring son of a bitch again." But according to Lee Richardson, Diefenbaker's executive assistant during his latter years in Parliament, Diefenbaker had no personal dislike of Kennedy and enjoyed being mentioned in the same breath. He simply wanted to be treated as an equal and not a weak sister of a much larger neighbour.

Tension between the young American Democratic president and the old Canadian Conservative prime minister was understandable. However, it came as a surprise when Diefenbaker took on Great Britain over its plans to join the European Economic Community. He feared the move would diminish the relationship between Canada and Great Britain and spin Canada further into the grasp of the United States. He went so far as to suggest the Americans were pushing Great Britain into closer ties with its European neighbours. Diefenbaker bellowed, "We have spent a hundred years resisting the magnetic pull of the United States. Now, this British application will put us in danger of being sucked into their orbit." Diefenbaker took some measure of satisfaction when Charles de Gaulle vetoed the British EEC application in January 1963.

Diefenbaker came to government without a clear vision of where he wanted to take the economy. When the economy slowed, he was determined to respond more rapidly and compassionately than R.B. Bennett had in the early 1930s. Unlike Bennett, Diefenbaker signalled his intention early on that a recession would not be a burden to the disadvantaged and that the unemployed would not suffer. However, in the midst of the economic downturn, the Bank of Canada aggressively flexed its muscles in an effort to reduce inflation. Diefenbaker was hearing credible criticisms that the governor of the bank, James Coyne, was not only indifferent to the plight of individual Canadians but was also wrong-headed on the fundamentals of monetary policy. In frustration, the premier of Ontario, Leslie Frost, wrote to Diefenbaker: "Should the whole economy of this country be dependent upon the unrestricted and uncontrolled decision of one man?" More persuasive was a December 1960 report sent to Diefenbaker by 29 university economists that they had "lost confidence in the ability of the Bank of Canada under its present management to play its proper role in ameliorating and resolving these (economic) difficulties."

Coyne was undeterred. He spoke out on matters of fiscal policy that were outside his area of responsibility and came perilously close to the realm of politics. His interventions increasingly embarrassed the government. The minister of finance privately admonished the governor after he called for a national highway system, the abolition of Canadian tourist tariff exemptions, and the establishment of a National Development Corporation. In meetings at the department of finance, Coyne got into a shouting match with Assistant Deputy Minister Simon Riesman (the man Brian Mulroney would later task in 1986 to negotiate the free trade agreement with the United States).

The government told Coyne his appointment would not be renewed and suggested that he take immediate leave with full pension. However, it came as a surprise to many in Cabinet to learn that the board of governors of the bank had recently and substantially increased the pension benefits for the governor, which was not publicized in the Canada *Gazette*, as the law required.

Coyne believed his integrity was under attack, and he refused to depart his post while under a cloud of suspicion regarding his pension. He promised the government that he would make no public statements if allowed to complete his term. The government, supported by the bank's board of governors, pressed for Coyne's immediate resignation. Much was invested in the battle over his termination, far more than was warranted.

Coyne issued a statement to the press, criticizing the government:

> On Tuesday, May 30 the minister of finance, on behalf of the government, requested that I resign at once as governor of the Bank of Canada without waiting for the end of my present seven year term of office which expires December 31 this year. To aid me in my consideration of this matter he said the cabinet were upset by the fact that the Bank's board of directors had taken action in February 1960 to improve the conditions of the pension, which according to the rules of the bank's pension fund had always been provided immediately on the termination of service of a governor or deputy governor. . . . The cabinet were

of the view that I had failed to discharge the responsibilities of my office in allowing the board of directors to take the action they did take unanimously and after a thorough consideration in amending the pension fund rules, an action which the Department of Justice had said was entirely within the powers of the board. The slander upon my integrity I cannot ignore or accept. It appears to be another element in the general campaign of injury and defamation directed against crown corporations, their chief executive officers and other public servants. I cannot and will not resign quietly under such circumstances."

Later, Coyne added the following point of principle: "The governor should not, however, resign merely because he is asked to do so."

In reply, the minister of finance attempted to demonstrate that the governor had lost the confidence of the government by taking public positions at odds with the government that far exceeded his role as central banker and would be terminated.

The government, however, did not have the authority to fire Coyne. That authority lay with Parliament. A simple one-sentence bill was introduced on June 20: "The office of Governor of the Bank of Canada shall be deemed to have become vacant immediately upon the coming into force of this act."

Pearson did not want to be seen defending the policies of the unpopular governor, but was quick to disparage the government for mismanaging the dismissal. Specifically, he criticized the lack of due process in which Coyne was given no official opportunity to defend himself. However, the Liberal-controlled Senate was only too happy to allow Coyne to offer up a defence in a public venue. All the while, Diefenbaker and Coyne engaged in a personal and vindictive public dialogue. Said Coyne, "Mr. Diefenbaker has been the evil genius behind this whole matter. It was his unbridled malice and vindictiveness which seized on the Bank of Canada's pension fund provisions . . . as a clever stick with which to beat me, and intimidate me." Diefenbaker countered that correspondence from Coyne confirmed he was unfit to run the Bank. "These letters reveal an attitude which, if accepted by the government, would result in two sovereignties in Canada, the Government of Canada and the Governor of the Bank of Canada; but not in that order."

When Pearson questioned Diefenbaker in the House of Commons, Diefenbaker replied: "Does the honourable member think $25,000 a year is a fair pension?" The amount, Diefenbaker pointed out, was greater than that due a retiring prime minister.

A committee of the Liberal-dominated Senate rejected the Bill calling for Coyne's dismissal. This enabled Coyne to control his destiny. He resigned on July 14, preserving his full pension. Louis Rasminsky was appointed governor, but with provisions for a reduced pension. He insisted on running the bank without government interference and cautioned he would resign should there be a persistent conflict between the government and the bank over monetary policy.

Diefenbaker spent a huge chunk of political capital in the Coyne affair, which left a sour impression of general incompetence over his tactics. Any gains were negligible—reducing by only a few months the term of an unpopular governor who had already agreed to sit quietly on the sidelines for the remainder of his term. Diefenbaker turned an unpopular purveyor of high interest rates into a hero who would be forever remembered for his bold and principled position to protect the independence and integrity of the Bank of Canada.

It was the beginning of the end for Diefenbaker.

THE DIEFENBAKER GOVERNMENT continued its reform agenda. It narrowed the list of crimes subject to the death penalty; established the National Parole Board and the Farm Credit Corporation; extended the vote to Native Canadians; provided greater flexibility for provinces in tax collections; and promised to build a causeway to Prince Edward Island. While the list of reforms was long and impressive, the great "northern vision" promised in 1958 had turned into something of a mirage. Mining in the Far North began to decline and only a handful of gas discoveries were made. New roads to the North were built, but only 4,000 of the 6,800 miles promised. Notably, however, the Diefenbaker government completed the historic Trans-Canada Highway.

Politically, the landscape in Québec had become much riskier for Diefenbaker. In the provincial election of 1960, the Tory-friendly Union Nationale, a shadow of its former self after the death of Duplessis, was defeated by Liberal Jean Lesage, a man Diefenbaker thought so pompous he "could strut sitting down." Without the levers of power and patronage that had worked for Diefenbaker in Québec, and without a political machine, a large block of his 1958 winnings were at risk. Outside Québec, the Tories took some comfort in winning three of four by-elections spread across four provinces in May of 1961. But as the traditional four-year term of government drew to a close, it was clear the Tories would lose a great many seats.

Diefenbaker went into the June 1962 election campaign behind in the public opinion polls. The magic spell he had cast over the nation four years before had been broken by a performance that fell short of expectations. Diefenbaker tried to turn the election into a referendum on the question of free enterprise versus socialism. However, this was not a battle over economic policy. To Diefenbaker, socialism was a euphemism for communism, and communism posed a grave threat to Canada's security. Diefenbaker would remind voters that under his leadership Canada had stood tough against Nikita Khrushchev at the United Nations.

Diefenbaker was convinced that the Kennedy administration was plotting to oust his Conservative government in favour of Pearson's Liberals. It distressed Diefenbaker no end that the president had hosted Nobel Prize winners, including Liberal leader Lester B. Pearson, at the White House just prior to the election. This, and a private meeting between Kennedy and Pearson, was labelled by Diefenbaker as "an intervention by the president in the Canadian election." Saying that Canada–U.S. relations would be a critical issue in the election, Diefenbaker considered revealing the contents of the president's confidential briefing memorandum that had accidentally been left in his office. However, disclosure came with serious risks. Diplomatic protocol called for a return of the note, and the likely consequence of such a breach of protocol was a serious split in relations with our most trusted ally.

Diefenbaker advised the American ambassador to Canada, Livingston Merchant, that he was in possession of the president's briefing memo. Diplomatic niceties aside, the prime minister told the ambassador he intended to use the note in the election to demonstrate that he "was the only leader capable of preventing United States domination of Canada." Merchant told Diefenbaker he had not yet informed the President of the prime minister's intent saying that the consequences would be "catastrophic" for Canada–U.S. relations and urged him to abandon the idea.

In the end, Diefenbaker backed down. Inevitably, however, the ambassador's memo reached Kennedy's desk. It was rumoured that Kennedy had written the letters SOB on the briefing note, referring to his opinion of Diefenbaker's character, but Theodore C. Sorenson, in his biography of Kennedy, said this was impossible since Kennedy had not yet drawn the conclusion. "I didn't know he was an s.o.b.—*at that time*," remarked Kennedy. Even though Diefenbaker retreated, his failure to return the memo promptly and courteously damaged his relations with the American president, and tainted Canadian–American relations. The best that could be said is that America knew it did not have Canada in its back pocket.

During Diefenbaker's administration, the Canadian dollar had declined in value against its American counterpart. A weakened Canadian economy and persistent budget deficits were cited as the key reasons for the dollar's decline. With the support of the International Monetary Fund, in early May, just six weeks before the election, the government determined to peg the dollar at 92.5 cents US, whereas it had traded above par the year previous. The Liberals, the press, and ordinary Canadians began to refer to the cheaper dollar as the "Diefendollar" or "Diefenbuck." Diefenbaker responded to the jabs alternately with humour and accusations of intolerance. "If I didn't have the name I have I don't know what the Liberal party would do . . . The playing with my name indicates what they think of those of non-French and non-English origin."

Pearson ridiculed the government for its economic mismanagement, saying it would inevitably lead to higher prices and a lower standard of living. Diefenbaker went on the offensive. Throwing aside his mantra of free enterprise, Diefenbaker promised he would defend the consumer at all costs: "I don't want any group or Corporation in this country, no matter how successful they may be, to take advantage of this situation. I serve notice here and now that if, in the next few days, (price gouging) is going on there will be action as effective as it is drastic."

Working against Diefenbaker in the campaign was a weak economy, high unemployment, a diminished Canadian dollar, administrative incompetence, and the Avro Arrow. In Québec, the Social Credit party was overtaking the Tories. But Diefenbaker gamely fought back. He effectively cast the Liberals as a contradiction—communist-loving friends of big business—and warned they would make Canada beholden to American interests. The Liberals campaigned under the slogan "Take a stand for tomorrow," but Pearson ran a poor campaign and appeared meek next to Diefenbaker. The disdain Diefenbaker held for Pearson was palpable; a man the Chief thought was a weak leader and a communist sympathizer who got too much credit for his diplomatic initiatives.

The Tory government was returned with a minority government. The Tory caucus was almost halved: from 208 to 116 seats. While the Liberal share of the popular vote increased by only 3.6 percentage points, the party doubled its seat total to 99. Social Credit, which had been shut out in 1958, picked up an astonishing 30 seats, 26 of which had been held by Tories. Given his position in the polls before the writ was dropped, the result was good news for the Chief: the Tories had just won their third successive victory. And they were only 17 seats short of a majority in a Parliament few expected would last very long.

The election did not end the crisis for the Canadian dollar. In the weeks following the campaign, the Bank of Canada was forced to deplete its reserves to dangerously low levels to stop a run on the dollar. To end the crisis, the government had to persuade financial markets that it would do what was necessary to manage the economy and reduce the deficit. Diefenbaker had no choice but to put the brakes on his plans for investments in social and infrastructure developments. Instead, his new policies were an increase in tariffs and duties and across-the-board cuts in government spending. The crisis was quickly, but painfully, resolved.

The speech from the throne was far-reaching, calling for, among other things, patriation of the constitution from Great Britain, a new flag, a Native land claims commission, division of the North West Territories into two territories; an independent election commission; an economic advisory board; the Medical Research Council; and, an old age pension program. These transformative initiatives would all become reality, but not under a Diefenbaker government.

Despite his victory at the polls, Diefenbaker's Cabinet was uneasy and some ministers were openly plotting for succession. Cabinet solidarity is essential in good times, but critical in a crisis. On October 14, 1962, U.S. reconnaissance planes took photographs of what appeared to be missile bases being built in Cuba. Through various indirect channels, Diefenbaker was made aware of the threat posed by Russian nuclear weapons ninety miles from American territory. Given the defence agreements between Canada and the USA, however, the prime minister was displeased not to have been briefed directly by the president or his ambassador.

Canada's department of external affairs suggested to Diefenbaker that Canada could play a neutral peacemaking role at the United Nations, rather than stand foursquare behind its American ally. When Diefenbaker suggested that a UN delegation go to Cuba to ascertain the nature and extent of the weapons installation, he indirectly undermined the Americans, who had already drawn their conclusions and issued an ultimatum to the Soviets. Diefenbaker took a cautious "wait and see" approach. This annoyed President Kennedy. It was not what he expected from America's closest ally. Thirty years later, Brian Mulroney would react differently when USSR President Gorbachev was removed from office in a military coup. Mulroney received the same sort of cautious advice from external affairs and its minister, Barbara McDougal: "Let the issue play out . . . don't take a strong position . . . don't take sides . . . keep your options open." But he rejected it and took a firm stand: the safety of Gorbachev and his family was of paramount importance and he should be returned to office forthwith. Unfortunately for Diefenbaker, the combination of weak advice from external affairs and his instinctive distrust of Kennedy left Canada isolated from our American neighbour and most important ally in a time of need.

As Diefenbaker hesitated, his minister of defence urged him to place Canadian forces on high alert. In a delaying tactic, Diefenbaker said he wanted to discuss the matter with his Cabinet. When Cabinet met, Diefenbaker argued for further delay and recommended moving to a higher state of alert only "if the situation deteriorated."

Kennedy and Diefenbaker discussed the crisis over the phone. Kennedy pressed the prime minister to increase the readiness level of Canadian forces. Diefenbaker complained: "When were we consulted?" Kennedy tersely replied: "You weren't."

Diefenbaker ultimately agreed to put Canadian forces on high alert, but only after he let it be known he didn't like being pushed around by America. After the crisis was resolved, and the Soviet missiles were removed from Cuba, Diefenbaker boasted that Canada "was the first nation to stop overflights of Soviet aircraft so as to prevent war material being carried to Cuba." The Cabinet knew differently. Even Diefenbaker's most loyal ministers questioned his leadership. Gordon Churchill remarked, "The country just could not afford to have the prime minister in that position at a time of crisis—he refused to act when action was absolutely necessary."

In the aftermath, Canada needed to repair relations with the United States. But the next flashpoint, accepting American nuclear warheads on Canadian soil, deeply divided Cabinet and the Tory party, and brought the Diefenbaker government to the brink of implosion. Diefenbaker's hesitation over accepting the missiles stirred PC party vice president George Hogan to condemn his leader in a speech, copies of which were circulated to the press: "He has done, and is still doing, more damage than any other single thing that has happened since we came into power. I gather from the press that the Cabinet is not solidly behind this policy. I profoundly hope so, because I believe we are in real trouble unless it is changed." Some in Cabinet threatened to resign if Diefenbaker did not clearly and decisively accept American weaponry. In contrast, Pearson was hawkish, and said Canada should be "ashamed if we accept commitments and then refuse to discharge them."

At the annual meeting of the PC party, a resolution was put forward on nuclear warheads despite Diefenbaker's attempt to remove it from the agenda, an indication Diefenbaker had lost control over the party apparatus.

Diefenbaker pleaded with delegates, "Do not tie my hands in the quest for peace." In the end, delegates approved a motion that urged the government to simply make a decision.

At this point, Cabinet became preoccupied less with nuclear warheads than with how to get rid of Diefenbaker. In some of the more confrontational Cabinet meetings Diefenbaker stared down his opponents, threatening an election or resignation. Other times, Diefenbaker would mollify them and pledge support for their views on the nuclear warhead issue, only to change his mind later. Defence Minister Douglas Harkness seized on one of Diefenbaker's pledges of support and issued a press release stating the government had chosen "a definite policy for the acquisition of nuclear arms." When Diefenbaker rebuked his minister, Harkness offered to resign, a safe move because Harkness knew that Diefenbaker wanted to suppress any talk of Cabinet divisions. Harkness also had little to fear because he was determined not to remain defence minister in a government that did not follow a course he deemed fundamental to national security.

The American government, meanwhile, grew weary of Canadian dithering, and took especial exception whenever Diefenbaker's remarks contradicted its version of the facts. The Canadian ambassador was occasionally summoned to the State Department for a dressing down. On one occasion, the American government issued a formal press release to clarify remarks made by Diefenbaker. The prime minister countered by recalling his ambassador "for consultation," then addressed the House of Commons and called the American statement an "unprecedented and unwarranted intrusion in Canadian affairs . . . Canada will not be pushed around or accept external domination or interference in the making of its decisions. Canada is determined to remain a firm ally, but that does not mean she should be a satellite."

George Hees, a high-profile minister who would subsequently serve in Brian Mulroney's Cabinet, said he would resign if the prime minister would not do so.

Diefenbaker replied, "I did not ask for this job; I don't want it, and if I'm not wanted, I'll go."

The defence minister offered a blunt assessment: "You might as well know that the people of Canada have lost confidence in you, the party has lost confidence in you, and the Cabinet has lost confidence in you. It is time you went." Diefenbaker fumed. He rose to challenge his Cabinet colleagues. "Those who are with me stand up, those against remained seated." The tally was eleven to nine against the prime minister. He immediately offered his resignation. "I propose that Donald Fleming be named prime minister. I will leave you to discuss the proposal. I will be in the library."

It was a case of "be careful what you ask for." The Cabinet was incapable of handling the crisis. Ministers supporting Diefenbaker called the dissidents a "nest of traitors," the same phrase Tory leader Mackenzie Bowell had used for dissident ministers in 1896. Alvin Hamilton took the lead: "You treacherous bastards. No Prime Minister has ever had to deal with so many sons of bitches." The Cabinet also feared that replacing the prime minister would cause the minority government to fall, and knew that an election would be disastrous for the party. With one exception, the call for Diefenbaker's resignation was abandoned. Instead, the Cabinet passed a resolution of support: "The Cabinet expresses its loyalty to the Prime Minister and its willingness to continue to give him full support."

Defence Minister Harkness, the lone holdout, resigned on February 4, 1963, in a letter to the prime minister: "It has become quite obvious during the last few days that your views and mine as to the course we should pursue for the acquisition of nuclear weapons for our armed forces are not capable of reconciliation." Addressing the House of Commons, Harkness said he "resigned on a matter of principle. The point was finally reached when I considered that my honor and integrity required that I take this step."

Pearson pounced on the divisions within the government and introduced a motion of non-confidence: "This government, because of lack of leadership, the breakdown of unity in the Cabinet, and confusion and indecision in dealing with national and international problems, does not have the confidence of the Canadian people."

While not revealed then or since, in the years before his death Dalton Camp told CBC reporter Keith Boag that the Diefenbaker government was kept alive by Social Credit because it was receiving regular cheques out of Tory coffers. Camp put and end to the payments, which contributed greatly, he observed, to the defeat of the government. Camp told Boag that he intended to reveal the tawdry dealings in his memoirs, but his passing prevented the story from coming to light.

But Diefenbaker needed the support of Social Credit to continue governing. Its leader, Robert Thompson, wanted to avoid an election and offered to support the government if it agreed to four conditions. Diefenbaker would have none of it. Rebuffing the Social Credit leader, Diefenbaker stated, "Thompson never loses a chance to humiliate me ... let Thompson know I will not be kicked around."

Thompson, under pressure from Alberta Premier Ernest Manning to bring Diefenbaker down, told a few Tory Cabinet ministers that he would back away from his four conditions and would oppose the motion of no-confidence if the prime minister resigned. Thus, just two days after Cabinet had pledged its loyalty and support to Diefenbaker, a group of ministers led by George Hees told Diefenbaker they would resign en masse if he did not do so. Hees suggested Diefenbaker could be appointed Chief Justice of the Supreme Court. Diefenbaker told Hees to "go to hell."

Diefenbaker took his case to the House of Commons. Turning to the 30 Social Credit MPs, and without referring to any offer they had made, he indicated he was prepared to respond to three of their four conditions. He ridiculed a possible alliance between Social Credit and the Liberals, claiming, "Pearson loves thee, but he loved you not until yesterday." But it was too little and too late for Social Credit to back Diefenbaker. Only his resignation would have prevented his government's defeat in the House. The motion of no-confidence passed along party lines by a vote of 142 to 111. An election was called for April 4, 1963.

But who would lead the Progressive Conservative party in the campaign? Was Diefenbaker still in charge? The editorial in the *Globe and Mail* made a clear case: "If Mr. Diefenbaker continues in the leadership he will do the party irreparable harm and perhaps destroy it as a national force." In a strident caucus meeting, Diefenbaker said he would stay only if he had its unanimous support. Diefenbaker was feisty, and caucus members began to think the Chief had one more good fight left in him yet. Caucus roared approval and gave the prime minister a standing ovation. The few ministers left seated were barely noticed. Diefenbaker turned to Hees: "George, we've got this election, and you and I are going to fight it together. I've got to have you beside me. I'll change the defence policy to better suit your fellows' views." Hees was overcome by the moment and later said, "I was so excited I jumped up on my feet, and I was crying; there were tears in my eyes. I figured here we were at last, in with the defence policy that meant something."

Despite caucus support, Diefenbaker was savaged in the press, ridiculed over his unwillingness to step aside, his indecisiveness as prime minister, and for dividing his party. The *Globe and Mail* took to task those Cabinet ministers who had threatened to resign but ultimately got cold feet. "Today the Prime Minister is still in office and the rebels, having deserted their cause, are still in Cabinet. They purchased their jobs, for a few weeks . . . these men lead a tattered party into the election with lies on their lips and a dual standard of morality in their hearts . . . They have abandoned the one among them who had the courage to resign, defence minister Douglas Harkness."

But it was all too much for George Hees and fellow Cabinet minister Pierre Sévigny. They met the prime minister at 24 Sussex Drive in the first week of the campaign and resigned. Diefenbaker claimed he was shocked by the resignations, and put on a brave face: "Elections are not won except in the last week. I am the underdog now and that means the fight must be strongly waged."

When Allister Grossart resigned as national director of the party, Diefenbaker made Dalton Camp the national campaign chairman. Camp proved immediately effective, taking the offence when, in an article titled "Canada's Diefenbaker: Decline and Fall," *Newsweek* magazine ridiculed Diefenbaker's facial features and gestures: "The India-rubber features twist and contort in grotesque and gargoyle-like grimaces . . . the eyebrows beat up and down like bats' wings; his agate-blue eyes blaze forth cold fire; . . . his enemies insist that it is sufficient grounds for barring Tory rallies to children under sixteen."

Newsweek was an American publication, completely outside the influence of the opposition parties, yet Camp, who made his living in advertising, was able to use the article and its inflammatory cover photo to advantage. Camp contended the magazine was friendly to the American administration, which wanted Diefenbaker out of office because he stood up for Canada. A bemused Diefenbaker remarked, "Satan saw my picture in *Newsweek*, and said he never knew he had such opposition in Canada." Then he turned it into an issue of discrimination: "How much easier it would have been to climb to be prime minister, if my name had been Campbell-Bannerman." Jean Chrétien would handle a similar situation to great effect in the 1993 election when he responded to Conservative party ads that belittled his facial features.

And then Diefenbaker proceeded to do what he did best: he campaigned, in an old fashioned whistle-stop adventure that connected him with ordinary rural Canadians. He boiled the controversy over national defence down to a message Canadians could understand: "Insofar as Canadian soil is concerned . . . we shall place ourselves in the position, by agreement with the United States, so that if war does come, or emergency takes place, we shall have available to us readily accessible nuclear weapons. *But in the meantime we shall not have Canada used as a storage dump for nuclear weapons.*"

In 2004, Liberal Prime Minister Paul Martin would claim that Stephen Harper was in George Bush's hip pocket. In 1963, Diefenbaker took a similar tack: "The Liberal high command seemed to mistake our country for the United States." Diefenbaker's passion and evangelical zeal stood in sharp contrast to the mild-mannered and intellectual Lester Pearson. Despite negative polls, Diefenbaker was making headway—his magic was not to be dismissed.

He would often remark, "There are powerful interests working against us, national and international. Everyone is against me, *but* the people." Those "powerful interests" included the establishment, the press, and the American president, among others. Critics scoffed that Diefenbaker was just being paranoid. But he backed up his charge with evidence. Reporter Val Sears of the Toronto *Star*, on boarding the Tory plane, was overheard saying to his fellow reporters: "To work, gentleman. We have a government to overthrow." When the *Globe and Mail* ran a front-page editorial that declared Diefenbaker unfit to lead, Diefenbaker responded, "The eastern magnates ran an editorial on the front page in Toronto Saturday, saying they wouldn't support us. The only reason they put it on the front page was because nobody would read it on the editorial page!"

Towards the end of the campaign, American Defence Secretary Robert McNamara unwittingly lent proof to Diefenbaker's allegations that Canada would be in harm's way if it accepted, without conditions, American nuclear weapons on its soil. McNamara appeared before the House Appropriations Subcommittee and, in response to a question, said: "At the very least [Bomarc missile sites] could cause the Soviets to target missiles against them and thereby increase their missile requirements or draw missiles onto these Bomarc targets that would otherwise be available for other targets."

Despite an attempt at clarification by the White House, Diefenbaker was able to launch a missile of his own. "The Liberal party would have us put nuclear warheads on something that's hardly worth scrapping. What's it for? To attract the fire of the intercontinental missiles. North Bay—knocked out. La Macaza—knocked out. Never, never, never, never has there been a revelation equal to this. The whole bottom fell out of the Liberal program today. *The Liberal policy is to make Canada a decoy for intercontinental missiles.*"

Diefenbaker had not lost his touch.

What Diefenbaker did not know was that in the midst of the campaign President Kennedy had offered advice to Pearson, through an intermediary. Pearson feared that the revelation of this fact could sink the Liberal campaign, but Kennedy's assistance never came to light. The president's national security adviser took the unprecedented step of sending a memorandum to the secretary of defence and the secretary of state outlining the president's wishes to avoid any appearance of interference in the Canadian election.

Diefenbaker accused Pearson of being a weak leader who was soft on communism. This sentiment was bolstered by a response Pearson made to a question from journalist Pierre Berton about what he would rather face: life under the communist Khrushchev or nuclear war. "I'd rather be red than dead," was Pearson's reply.

Momentum was building for Diefenbaker. But he would need a big push in the final week of the campaign. That's when news reports of the wayward presidential briefing memorandum appeared in the *Ottawa Citizen*. While Diefenbaker denied it, he was later reported to have been the source. In the end, the story did not gain much traction in the press and had little bearing in the outcome of the election. But there was little doubt who President Kennedy was cheering for on election night.

Despite a weak economy, the recent resignation of his defence minister, and a divided Cabinet, Diefenbaker surrendered only 21 seats. He swept Saskatchewan, took 14 of 17 seats in Alberta, 10 of 14 in Manitoba, and seven of 12 in Nova Scotia. However, losses in Ontario and Québec were sufficient to give the Liberals a minority government. The Tories went down in the popular vote by 4.5 percentage points; the Liberals went up by the same margin. With the Liberals only five seats short of a majority government, there was no realistic prospect of Diefenbaker testing his confidence in the House of Commons. Lester Pearson was sworn in as prime minister on April 22, 1963.

THE OBITUARIES ON THE Diefenbaker era began to pour in, none lengthier than the book released the October following the election by Peter C. Newman titled *Renegade in Power: The Diefenbaker Years*, which laid bare the story of an erratic Diefenbaker and a dysfunctional Cabinet. Diefenbaker called it "a terrible piece of muckraking and slander." Newman sent a copy of the book to Diefenbaker, inscribed "With deepest respect." Diefenbaker looked at Newman's inscription and said, "That, is the worst of all." Forty years later Newman would send a copy of his scandalous book *The Secret Mulroney Tapes* to Brian Mulroney with a similar tender inscription: "For Brian—At last Canadians will see you for the warm, funny and human person that you are."

With no provision in the constitution of the PC party requiring a leadership review—even after an election defeat—and with Diefenbaker showing no signs of retirement, those who wanted a change in leadership had a fight on their hands. At the February 4, 1964 party convention, Diefenbaker called for a vote of confidence in his leadership. A motion to make the confidence vote a secret ballot was defeated by a margin of three to one. With no opportunity for private dissent, support for Diefenbaker at the convention was nearly unanimous. The convention also elected Dalton

Camp party president. Eventually, under Camp's direction, the party executive and membership would assert authority over the issue of the retention of the leader. Like the change in 1927 that gave party members a vote in selecting the leader, a change was in the works that would give party members a vote in whether they wanted to retain the leader after an election in which government was not held or won. Call it improved accountability.

Taking an idea from the most recent Tory throne speech, Pearson brought forth his plan for a new and distinctive Canadian flag, designed around a maple leaf. Diefenbaker thought the matter should be decided in a national referendum. When the "three maple leaf design" was rejected in place of a single red maple leaf, Diefenbaker scoffed, saying it was a flag Peruvians would salute.

Diefenbaker led the attack against the government. Pearson, tired of being on the defensive, wrote a chilling letter to Diefenbaker, inquiring about the steps the former prime minister had taken to protect Canada's national security when he was made aware that one of his Cabinet ministers was associated with Gerda Munsinger. "I have been greatly disturbed by the lack of attention which, in so far as the file indicates, this matter received. This minister was left in a position of trust." The letter was little more than a threat. Keep up the attacks on Liberal ministers and the Munsinger affair would be brought out into the open. But Pearson seriously underestimated Diefenbaker's angry reaction to being blackmailed. Pearson sought to calm the matter. "We should not talk to each other like this, John. You know I am not a politician. I am a diplomat." Diefenbaker retorted, "A diplomat is someone who lies away from home."

Party president Dalton Camp, meanwhile, proceeded to conduct party business independent of the wishes or concerns of his leader. The day before a national executive meeting in February 1965 where the question of leadership would be discussed, Diefenbaker felt the need to reassert his leadership: "I am not leading the Conservative party into the wilderness. I intend to lead this party to another task ordered by Canada's destiny. I am reminded of the motto of Count Frontenac: 'I will answer the enemy from the mouths of my cannon.' Ferment inside a party is a sign of life. But ferment carried on when the time comes for political battle is something else. It is treachery. I have always given the leader under whom I have served my complete loyalty and support. I expect no less today as leader."

The next day, the national executive—an odd term, considering 116 people were in attendance—met to discuss the future of the party and its leadership and debated these four questions:

1. Should there be a leadership convention?
2. Should the leader resign?
3. Should there be a policy advisory committee?
4. Should the party fully accept the new Canadian flag?

Diefenbaker claimed the executive had neither authority nor mandate in regard to question two, and the delegates removed it, albeit narrowly, by a vote of 55 to 52. The results of other votes were confidential, but Dalton Camp advised the press the next day that there would be no leadership convention.

It was clear that Diefenbaker was not prepared in any way to submit to the will of the party's executive. He believed his mandate came from the Canadian people. In a television interview, Diefenbaker remarked: "I have been maligned. I have been condemned. No one since the days of Macdonald has gone through the like . . . My friends, they believe they will succeed in this way. I will follow the will of the People. Will it be the will of the People or those that are all powerful?"

Diefenbaker often invoked Macdonald. In fact, Diefenbaker used the same inkwell as Macdonald, placed a life-sized sculpture of Macdonald in his office, hung a portrait of Macdonald above his desk, slept in Macdonald's bed (an extended version) and sat in Macdonald's chair. Every January 11, Diefenbaker led a procession of Conservative MPs to lay a wreath at the foot of the statue of Macdonald on Parliament Hill. When troubled, Diefenbaker would read from Donald Creighton's compelling biography of Macdonald. It was the company Diefenbaker most wanted to keep.

Rather than deal with Tory party hierarchy, Diefenbaker preferred to connect with individual Canadians. He kept very close tabs on his mail, and spent much of his day reading letters and dictating replies to Canadians from all walks of life and all regions. However, to writers who took a moral tone of indignation against Diefenbaker and his government, he often sent the same short reply.

> Dear Sir:
> This is to inform you that some crackpot is using your name and has recently written to me over your signature putting forward views so eccentric in nature and so much at variance with your usual logical style that the letter could not possibly be from you. I felt I owed it to you to bring this to your attention.

Monitoring the missteps of the Pearson government kept Diefenbaker alive and vibrant. The Liberal government was embroiled in a series of scandals, one involving union leader Hal Banks, who was up on criminal charges and who had been allowed to secretly leave the country. Banks had been a notable financial contributor to the Liberal party. Early in 1965, a Québec Cabinet minister was charged with accepting a bribe. In another scandal, a senior ministerial staff member was implicated in a bribe related to a Montréal drug dealer, Lucien Rivard. When Rivard escaped from the Bordeaux jail, Diefenbaker hinted at a conspiracy. Rivard had climbed over the prison walls with the aid of a garden hose, which he had requested from prison authorities to water the ice rink on a warm spring evening. Diefenbaker made deft use of the embarrassing incident in his speeches. When, in a hot and steamy community centre, he would say, "It was on the night such as this that Rivard went to water the rink." The line, always anticipated, never failed to bring the crowd to its feet.

The Liberal brain trust concluded that the odds of securing a majority government would be highest while the Tory party was divided over Diefenbaker's leadership, and called an election for November 8, 1965, giving Diefenbaker another kick at the can. He went into the campaign with little, if any, organizational support. Communication between headquarters and the leader was otherwise non-existent, and tension within the party generally ran high.

Under the slogan *Maîtres chez nous*, Québec's quiet revolution was gaining momentum. Diefenbaker's call for "One Canada" was countered by the concept of "two nations." Diefenbaker campaigned on his vision: "The dismantling, piece by piece, of our country must stop. Canada cannot exist without Québec, nor can we visualize Québec without Canada." While he did not specifically support the aspirations of Québecers, he saw Québec as fundamental to the existence of the country. Diefenbaker did not explain how his vision would be acceptable to Québecers. It didn't help Diefenbaker's cause in Québec that the message he delivered to the rest of Canada was of a scandalously corrupt Liberal party, most of whom were Québec Cabinet ministers.

Diefenbaker tried to make Liberal wrongdoing and Pearson's weak leadership the defining issues in the campaign. "The Prime Minister talks of a majority and I believe in majorities, but if the present government had a majority, would the truth ever come out? Instead of condemning wrongdoing, they will not talk about it. . . . the Prime Minister's attitude is that of the three monkeys, see no evil, speak no evil and if you hear any evil, forget it . . ."

The election was a stalemate. The Liberals picked up three seats, lost 1.3 percentage points of the popular vote, and returned with a minority government. The Tories gained four seats over the 1963 election. The big loser was the Social Credit party, which had split into two factions, English and French, and which surrendered ten seats. The regional breakdown of Tory support remain largely unchanged: they swept the Prairies but won only 8 of 75 seats in Québec. Both Diefenbaker and Pearson were damaged by their inability to move their parties forward. Among the new faces in the Liberal caucus was Pierre Elliott Trudeau.

THE NEW PARLIAMENT WAS GREETED with new allegations of breaches of national security. Justice Minister Lucien Cardin announced that a postal worker had been accused of spying for the Russians and had been dismissed. Although charges were never laid, the postal worker's pension was forfeited. Diefenbaker demanded an inquiry. When Diefenbaker asserted ministerial incompetence in handling national security files, Cardin replied, "He is the very last person in the House who can afford to give advice on handling of security cases in Canada . . . and I'm not kidding . . . I want the right honorable gentleman to tell the house about his participation in the Monseignor (sic) case, when he was prime minister of this country." Later, after Pearson agreed to an inquiry, Diefenbaker belittled Cardin's threat. "Commonsense has now taken the place of stubbornness and absolute stupidity. There he stands, naked and unashamed, deprived of every argument he brought before this house."

The House of Commons degenerated into a circus. Cardin went public with specific accusations related to Diefenbaker's handling of the *Munsinger* affair. The *Globe and Mail* labelled the ensuing public inquiry headed by Supreme Court Justice Wishart Spence an unprecedented "witch-hunt" into the conduct of a previous government. However, the inquiry, headed by Mr. Justice Spence, drew damning conclusions about the conduct of Diefenbaker and his ministers in the Munsinger affair. What was under-played at the time was the involvement of George Hees with Munsinger. Conversations recorded by the RCMP reveal a boastful Hees in some stage of undress asking Munsinger, "Have you ever seen such a body?" RCMP offi-cers listening to wiretaps always found humorous the noise made when Sevigny's wooden leg hit the floor at some inevitable point during his encounters with Munsinger.

Diefenbaker steeled himself against the inevitable campaign to separate him from the leadership of the party. Dalton Camp, who had run for parliament in a Toronto riding in 1965 and lost, had proposed changing party rules to give members an automatic vote on holding a leadership contest following an election in which the party did not win or hold government. At the next general meeting of the party, Diefenbaker sought to oust Camp from the presidency. Camp retained his presidency by a vote of 564 to 502. Flora MacDonald, whom Diefenbaker had fired from national party headquarters because of her allegiance to Camp, was elected national secretary. The meeting then passed a resolution calling for a leadership convention to be held some time before January 1, 1968.

Though Camp's resolution offered "full hearted appreciation of his universally recognized services to the party," the preamble made it clear that Diefenbaker had no future as party leader. The party decided that a full-fledged leadership convention would be held. An emboldened Camp took his campaign for renewed leadership to a more personal level in his speeches as party president. "Leaders are fond of reminding followers of their responsibilities and duties to leadership. . . . What is seldom heard, however, is a statement on the responsibilities of the leader to those he leads. . . . The leader should give at least as much loyalty to his followers as he demands from them. This is not personal loyalty, but rather loyalty to the party, to its continuing strength, best interests, and well-being. Where the leader does not know the limits of his power, he must be taught, and when he is indifferent to the interest of his party, he must be reminded." Detecting his grip on power had been weakened, on the hustings Diefenbaker frequently quoted from the Ballad of Sir Andrew Barton, "I'll lay me down and bleed awhile. And then I'll rise again and fight again. Fight on, my men, I am hurt but I am not slain."

Diefenbaker did not leave gracefully. He had scores to settle against those who had undermined him. And at the top of the list was Dalton Camp. To unsettle the party hierarchy, Diefenbaker did not reveal his intention to contest the leadership of the party at the upcoming convention. Diefenbaker preferred to keep the party guessing, but those closest to the Chief thought it unlikely that he would enter the contest.

About a month before the convention, a Tory policy workshop at Montmorency, Québec raised the issue of recognizing Canada as "deux nations." Diefenbaker was outraged. "When you talk about special status and Two Nations, that proposition will place all Canadians who are of other racial origins than English and French in a secondary position. All through my life, one of the things I've tried to do is to bring about in this nation citizenship not dependent on race or color, blood counts or origin."

Thus did Diefenbaker have both renewed purpose and a cause to take to the September 1967 convention. He triumphantly entered Toronto's Maple Leaf Gardens surrounded by a band of pipers. On the opening night of the convention, the Chief unleashed a blistering attack on the "two nations" theory as foolhardy and divisive, and pointedly reminded his audience that he had fought it all his life. The next morning, at the last possible moment under the rules, he declared himself a candidate for leader.

Largely to avoid embarrassing the former prime minister, 271 delegates supported Diefenbaker on the first ballot. He came in fifth out of eleven candidates, with less than half the total votes of front-runner Robert Stanfield. Diefenbaker stubbornly remained on two more ballots, falling to 114 votes, before he finally bowed out. After Stanfield was declared the winner, Diefenbaker appeared onstage calling for unity and offered some final words. "My course has come to an end. I fought your battles, and you have given that loyalty that led us to victory more often than the party has ever had since the days of Sir John A. Macdonald. In my retiring, I have nothing to withdraw in my desire to see Canada, my country in your country, one nation."

In Stanfield's concluding remarks, he quipped, "Personally, I'm determined to get along with that fellow Camp." Diefenbaker was incensed. Stanfield later apologized and subsequently ensured that Camp was not visible when Diefenbaker was around. But Camp was once again a Tory candidate in the coming election in Don Valley. He lost.

DESPITE HIS PLEDGE OF LOYALTY to the new leader, Diefenbaker took private and public pleasure at the demise of those who followed him. He retained his vantage point in the House of Commons by winning four more elections in his Prince Albert riding. And he never gave up hope that the party would turn to him once again to lead. He quipped in his speeches, "You know, Gladstone was British prime minister at the age of 84." To the cheers in response Diefenbaker would pause: "Ah. You see, it's everywhere." He often arrived or left the podium to the stirring theme song "The Impossible Dream."

In the 1968 election he refused to campaign with Stanfield. Even though Stanfield and the party had disavowed the "two nations" concept, Diefenbaker continued to speak out against it. After Trudeau took the Tories down to 72 seats in 1968, 25 seats lower than Diefenbaker won in 1965, the Chief gloated: "The Conservative party has suffered a calamitous disaster."

In the House, Diefenbaker split with both his party and his leader over the Liberal bill on official bilingualism. He and 16 other Tories insisted on a recorded vote on the bill, causing Stanfield to remark, "Their stupidity was exceeded only by their malice. There are some things in a political party one simply does not do to one's colleagues."

Because of Diefenbaker's stature in the House of Commons, he would invariably be recognized by the Speaker during Question Period whenever he arose. To the consternation of Stanfield this could occur at heated moments when a Liberal minister was on the ropes. Diefenbaker would alter the rhythm of questioning by asking a question about something obscure such as the loss of the coat of arms from government letterhead. On some occasions the leader's office would ask Diefenbaker's staff to arrange for him an extended lunch to ensure there would not be a distraction during Question Period.

The feud with Dalton Camp never ended. Asked how he felt seeing Camp in a position of power, Diefenbaker proved he had not lost his touch for a pithy quote: "Psychologists have long since determined that nothing is more disturbing for the human mind than for a person to have his victim still around after an assassination." When chided loudly from government benches, Diefenbaker remarked, "The hon. member for Halifax [Gerald Regan] does nothing but engage in occasional desk tapping. It shows his intelligence that he makes that his major contribution."

On the occasion of Lester Pearson's funeral, a reporter asked for Diefenbaker's reflections. He briefly paused, then offered this: "He shouldn't have won the Nobel Prize." Lavishly praised in a *Globe and Mail* editorial for his support of the Gardiner Dam in Saskatchewan, adjacent to Lake Diefenbaker, the Chief, who was getting his hair cut while reading the editorial, turned to his barber and said, "They're trying to destroy me." A few days later his office photocopied and distributed the editorial.

Diefenbaker had once remarked during the 1963 campaign, "Where's Olive? If I lose her, I'll lose everything." His beloved wife died on December 22, 1976. He was devastated by Olive's death and became a lost and lonely soul.

After the leadership battle was over Diefenbaker spent his time embellishing his reputation and settling old scores. After days of planning to get Diefenbaker to a campaign event in 1972, his executive assistant Lee Richardson recalled that seconds prior to arrival the Chief inquired who had previously held the riding in the prior election? Upon hearing it was Douglas Harkness, the chief curtly commanded for the vehicle to "drive on" in full view of those who had waited hours for his arrival.

Over time, his disdain of Trudeau and admiration for Stanfield had him wishing once again for Tory success. He was no great fan of Joe Clark, whom he remembered as one of the "Campers" who sought to remove him from the leadership. With the Tories back in power under Clark, Diefenbaker found himself seated next to External Affairs Minister Flora MacDonald in the House of Commons. She reached out to Diefenbaker, the man who had ceremoniously fired her from party headquarters some fifteen years earlier. "You! You! He should never have made you Foreign Minister!" he replied. "Minister of Health, perhaps, or Postmaster General; but never Foreign Minister!" So much for reconciliation.

Diefenbaker died alone at his home on August 16, 1979. He had made plans for his own state funeral under the title "Operation Hope Not." His coffin was draped by the Canadian flag and the Red Ensign. He was taken by train from Ottawa to Prince Albert, with frequent stops at small towns along the way where huge crowds gathered to salute a great leader. The Liberals rejected his offer to donate his Ottawa home in the posh area of Rockcliffe Park as a museum.

DIEFENBAKER WAS A CHARISMATIC MAN with a strong connection to ordinary Canadians. A man of strong personal convictions and contradictions, he stood up to the most powerful forces and nations on earth in support of the country he loved. He held the highest office in the land, yet he instinctively mistrusted authority and the powerful. He wanted nothing of the elite or intellectuals; he was a populist. That's why, even though he had the largest majority in Canadian history, he did not proceed with unpopular measures. His mandate was less about policy than it was about hope and a grand vision. But on specific policy issues, his indecisiveness split his Cabinet.

His fundamental political weakness was that he didn't understand French Canada. His egalitarian vision of One Canada made him deaf to the cultural and linguistic aspirations of many Québecers. But even Québecers understood that he was a folk hero who cared for the common people.

Like Harper, he was not motivated by money. He refused gifts and wanted to be obliged to no one. After his death it was revealed that a trust fund, established in 1960, had been established in his name to ensure he could pursue a career in politics without having to worry about finances. The trust fund was never touched.

Some of Diefenbaker's biographers accentuated Diefenbaker's erratic behaviour, creating the impression of something of a madman. But what was so irrational about asserting Canadian sovereignty over American intrusions? Why does the idea of keeping nuclear weapons off Canadian soil unless absolutely necessary for national security seem crazy? And why should the governor of the Bank of Canada go unchallenged when many credible experts thought his monetary policies were damaging the economy?

At a speech to Toronto's Albany Club in January 2007, Prime Minister Stephen Harper observed: "If ever there was a Conservative prime minister whose reputation needs to be reclaimed from Liberal slander, it is the Chief, 'Honest John.' No other prime minister of any stripe did more for the cause of fairness and equality and inclusion. His Bill of Rights, for example, preceded the Liberal Charter of Rights by over two decades. . . . Moreover, like Macdonald and Borden, he was a vigorous defender of Canadian sovereignty."

It is understandable that Harper would come to Diefenbaker's defence. They are both Ontario-born, evangelical-Christian, western-based, non-elitist politicians with a modest inclination towards libertarian views. Though Harper is known to be more decisive than Diefenbaker, they share a reluctance to spend political capital or take positions that would be unpopular. It is difficult to imagine either of them implementing the GST or free trade.

Diefenbaker challenged discrimination of any form both in Canada and abroad. He showed new levels of respect for Native Canadians and created important national institutions that survive to this day. He raised the level of social justice with old age security, programs for the disabled, support for family farmers, and the unemployed. He enthralled the nation and gave it hope. The greatest tribute he can receive is to be forever known as a man of the people.

SECTION VI

OPPORTUNITIES LOST

CHAPTER 20

THE GENTLEMAN
FROM NOVA SCOTIA

*I never thought of it as a lifetime career. I didn't think I could take
the party very far. I thought we could get some people in the house in
opposition, and somebody else could take over.*

THE STANFIELD FAMILY were either the original Canadian environmentalists or fundamentally cheap. When Charles Stanfield noticed
that large quantities of steam were being exhausted from a nearby
laundry, he rigged up an underground pipeline to capture the heat for his
home. But the Stanfield's were not selfish money grubbers. Decency, not
short-term profit, was the essence of the Stanfield family business. When the
depression hit, the Stanfield family business suffered, but they took great
pains to help their employees stay afloat. Layoffs were shared to enable
workers to support their families. The values of decency, modesty, and moderation were abundant in Bob Stanfield. While appreciated by Nova Scotians,
Stanfield failed to translate his admirable qualities into success on the
national political stage.

The family business was underwear, making them the butt of many jokes.
Founded in 1856, much of its success was due to innovations in processing
and product, including the much-appreciated shrinkproof underwear. When
Maritimers ventured West to make money off the Klondike Gold Rush of
1897 and 1898, they brought their prized underwear with them. Over time,
the Stanfield name became known in all parts of Canada.

Politics was a Stanfield family passion. Politics was engrained in Robert Lorne Stanfield from the day of his birth on April 11, 1914. He was named after Sir Robert Borden, then prime minister of Canada, and Lord Lorne, the 9th Duke of Argyle, governor general of Canada from 1878 to 1883. It was natural for the Stanfields to align with the Conservatives: they were manufacturers and Conservatives supported protective trade policies.

Bob Stanfield inherited $350,000 on his twenty-fifth birthday and invested all of it in blue chip stocks. While Stanfield could afford a lifestyle of comfort and grace, he lived modestly. For a Stanfield, being discreetly charitable and civic-minded was a way of life. The Stanfields were so admired throughout the community that no family member was ever personally defeated in a Nova Scotia election.

Bob Stanfield graduated from Dalhousie University in 1936 with a Bachelor of Arts. When he was awarded the Governor General's gold-medal for the highest academic standing, he donated the cash award to a fellow student in need. After graduation, he pursued a law degree at Harvard. Naturally curious, he studied socialism, but around the family dinner table the initials CCF, Canada's socialist political party, stood for "Cancel Canada's Freedom." Nonetheless, Stanfield was initially drawn to new theories of economic management; such as those of John Maynard Keynes. The active role of government in stabilizing the economy and employment during cycles of recession and rampant growth made intuitive sense to many, even if never proven in practice.

Stanfield married Joyce Frazee on June 5, 1940 with whom he had four children.

After being admitted to the Nova Scotia bar, he went to work for the Acadia Trust Company, an enterprise established by his father. "It was not a very exacting job and would give me enough leisure to do the things in economic theory I wanted to do," said Stanfield. Spending leisure time on economic theory placed Stanfield in rare company. His intellectual interests did not mark him for a career in politics, and his university friends pegged him for academia. His friend Philip Elman said, "It was a great surprise to me when I learned that Bob was going into politics, because he was so much the ivory tower type. He had none of the politician's arts. He was not a flatterer."

Denied the opportunity to serve his country in war because of a curvature of the spine, he joined the Halifax office of the Wartime Prices and Trade Board in 1942, where he served for the rest of the war. This assignment joined economic theory with the real world. The board was organized to control the cycles of wartime inflation. On a day to day level, Stanfield found himself dealing one-on-one with, for example, landlords accused of charging exorbitant rents. It was a useful vantage point from which to observe first-hand how government intentions and policy do not square with reality. "It probably had a fair effect on my attitude toward price controls and regulations ever since," Stanfield said later in his life. "I came away from the Wartime Prices and Trade Board experience with a strong feeling that regulations have quite a limited role to play except in case of emergency. It is extremely difficult to keep them in touch with reality." Following the war, Stanfield practised law and dreamt about a career in politics.

By the mid-1940s, Conservatives in Nova Scotia had held power for only twelve years since Confederation. They failed to win a single seat in the 1945 provincial election and managed only 33.5 percent of the popular vote. Liberal leader and Premier, Angus L. McDonald, was widely admired and respected, "All is well with Angus L.," the Liberals would say. He was even liked in Ottawa, where he served as minister of defence for naval services in the wartime Cabinet of Mackenzie King.

Stanfield wanted to restore meaningful democracy to Nova Scotia so he became active in Conservative politics. But at first he wasn't thinking that he would be a candidate or the leader. "I told [the party] I was interested in seeing a more aggressive attitude develop toward the problems of the province. . . . I said I was prepared to spend a certain amount of time doing some organizing with a view to getting the party to a position where it could attract a leader. That's really what I set out to do in that period."

It is worth delving into Stanfield's record as provincial politician and premier, not only to better understand the man, but also to reveal the sort of prime minister he might have been.

IN 1947, BOB STANFIELD was acclaimed president of the Progressive Conservative party of Nova Scotia. Recognizing his own lack of charisma, Stanfield wanted to test his performance on the public stage before "taking the plunge" into an election. Party members didn't know if Stanfield was being overly modest or realistic when he said in his early days, "I just haven't got what it takes [to be a candidate]."

Stanfield became a virtual full-time unpaid political organizer. Party members were thrilled to have a Dalhousie gold-medal winner and Harvard Law graduate doing its unglamorous field work. Intellectuals typically restrict their activities to writing op-ed pieces and formulating policy, but this policy wonk and political nerd was cajoling at the local riding level, and in the process getting a political education he could never get as a member of a debating team or representative in a mock Parliament.

His province-wide spade work left Stanfield as the obvious choice to lead the party. He was thirty-four when elected leader in November 1948. Stanfield's modesty seemed excessive: "I never thought of it as a lifetime career. I didn't think I could take the party very far. I thought we could get some people in the house in opposition, and somebody else could take over." Stanfield's inner circle, sometimes called the Nova Scotia mafia, included Dalton Camp, Finlay Macdonald, and Flora MacDonald, people who became key federal Tory operatives over the next 40 years.

Stanfield offered hope to his party and to Nova Scotia. He believed that the province had languished under successive Liberal administrations. Worse, Nova Scotians had stopped believing in themselves, and thought that their greatest days were behind them; that their lot was to be economically and socially deprived. "We do our province a disservice," said Stanfield, "if we create the impression abroad and in the rest of Canada that we are a depressed area. We do ourselves a disservice if we convince ourselves that our province is poor and downtrodden . . . Are we too ready to assume that something cannot be done here?"

Stanfield preached old-fashioned optimism and traditional Conservative views on responsibility and hard work. Nova Scotia *could* compete and attract world-class industry, he believed. He wanted to give Nova Scotian youth a reason to stay in the province rather than move to central and western Canada. His supporters were convinced he could lead Nova Scotia to better days, but the problem with "Honest Bob" was getting him elected. Dick Donahoe, the man who nominated Stanfield for leader, was optimistic: "We have chosen the man to lead our party who will be the hardest possible man to defeat." Another supporter, Ralph Shaw, was the realist: "He's going to be hard to elect, but if we ever get him elected, they'll never get him out."

Stanfield took on a party with no seats in the legislature. Achieving power was out of the question, but being effective in opposition was a reasonable goal. In the 1949 election, Stanfield won eight seats with 39.2 percent of the popular vote; an increase of six percentage points over the previous campaign. In 1953 the party surged to 13 seats and 43.6 percent of the vote. Normally, a leader with two consecutive election losses would be in a precarious position, but going from zero to 13 and holding the Liberals to less than a majority of the popular vote were monumental accomplishments. The Conservatives had not won an election since 1928, but both the party and its leader were prepared to be patient. Friend and advisor Finlay Macdonald, however, felt more urgency. "[Stanfield] was a lousy leader of the opposition. He'd support the damn government whenever it had a policy he thought was worth supporting. He wouldn't say anything for political advantage when he thought it would hurt someone personally. For God's sake, what sort of leader of the opposition was that?"

Stanfield's relationship with the Liberal Premier Angus L. McDonald was surprisingly open, collegial, and respectful. Perhaps the decision a premier holds most secret is the timing of an election. Yet just before the writ was dropped in 1953, McDonald chided Stanfield, "Bob, I don't think I would [go on vacation]. But you and I are the only ones who know that."

Tragically, Joyce Stanfield died in 1954 in a car accident as she and her three oldest children were returning home from a day at the beach. Stanfield's grief was intense, but—characteristically—was borne in private. The youngest of his four children, Mimi, was less than a year old. Burdened by his grief and the heavy weight of responsibility for his children, he considered leaving politics. His extended family and friends pitched in, and a full-time nurse enabled Stanfield to maintain focus on his work.

His party had been gaining seats slowly and steadily. Stanfield was now ready for power. He formulated a bold nine-point program for the industrial development of Nova Scotia, which included creation of the "Nova Scotia Industrial Development Corporation." Operated by prominent Nova Scotia business leaders, the corporation would make strategic investments to encourage industry to locate in the province.

Angus L. McDonald died in 1954, giving Stanfield his first realistic chance of winning government. Stanfield ended twenty-three years of Liberal rule in October 1956, winning 24 seats to the Liberals' 18, with one seat going to the CCF.

A month later, as the keynote speaker at the federal Conservative leadership convention that elected John Diefenbaker, Stanfield spoke about that victory: "Elections are not settled by public opinion polls, by prophecy or by political pundits. The Canadian people are, I believe, neither influenced nor moved much by any of these. Those who have studied the Canadian political scene for the past quarter of a century are impressed by the increasing number of independent voters. These are the voters who create majorities in elections."

It may seem odd by today's standards that Stanfield served not only as premier, but also as provincial treasurer for six years and minister of education for his entire 11-year term and governed with a staff of three. Patient and disciplined, Stanfield gave his staff the target of answering all mail within 24 hours. He rejected almost every perk that came with the office and preferred to walk to work rather than use a government limousine. He and his ministers travelled economy class. A citizen who wanted to contact Stanfield had only to look in the phone book for his home number. To the chagrin of some of his colleagues, Stanfield abolished the plush pension scheme adopted by his Liberal predecessor.

In 1957, Bob Stanfield married Mary Hall, daughter of Mr. Justice Hall of the Supreme Court of Nova Scotia. One of Joyce Stanfield's best friends, she had been a great help to the children in the aftermath of their mother's death.

IN A PROVINCE where political allegiances were well-known and nearly every public service position is reserved for political patronage—right down to road maintenance crews—Bob Stanfield was a maverick reformer. He did not hesitate to disappoint provincial Tories who assumed that, having been frozen out of government jobs for more than a generation—it was now their turn at the trough. Speaking to delegates at a party convention Stanfield stood their expectations upside down: "I do not intend to allow the claims of any individual seeking reward to jeopardize the future of the Conservative government or the Conservative party of Nova Scotia." He delivered the same message when addressing Conservatives at a national convention, explaining, "Some may say to me the important thing is to keep Conservatives happy, so that we will have an energetic party when the next election comes . . . (however) we will not retain the support (of the independent voter) if we are vindictive or self-seeking."

For loyal Conservatives, Stanfield gave tough love. Yet Stanfield himself was prone to acts of political loyalty. When his campaign manager's imprudent advice to campaign workers about using alcohol to buy votes became public ("Don't buy those knickers too soon or they won't stay bought,") Stanfield refused his offer of resignation. Although Stanfield was known to be straitlaced, he was also prepared to stand by his friends, even in their moments of weakness.

Stanfield was determined to revitalize Nova Scotia's economy. His government created Industrial Estates Ltd. with $12 million in taxpayer funds to invest in job-creating enterprises. While he was prepared to use public money to bolster private initiative, he knew government bureaucrats were not equipped to lead this venture. He recruited Frank Sobey, the man who transformed a Stellarton, Nova Scotia grocery store into a mammoth retail operation. Stanfield ensured that neither he nor his Cabinet ministers were involved in any of IEL's decisions.

IEL made loans, not grants, with rates of interest that were supposed to make IEL profitable and self-sustaining. It enjoyed initial success, attracting

THE GENTLEMAN FROM NOVA SCOTIA

two automobile manufacturers and Michelin, the French tire maker, which employed 1,500 workers at its plant in New Glasgow. Stanfield crowed to investors that Nova Scotia was open for business.

In Stanfield, voters saw a calm, measured, ruthlessly honest, and scrupulous premier. He was nicknamed "Honest" Bob, and the sobriquet stuck. Conservatives increased their margins of victory in successive elections: 26 seats and 49.3 percent of the vote in 1960, 41 of 44 seats and 56.2 percent in 1963, and 40 of 46 seats with 52.8 percent in 1967. Stanfield's level of popularity and electoral success now exceeded that of the revered Angus L. McDonald.

In a 1965 speech to the Halifax Board of Trade, Stanfield challenged the entire province to do better, saying it was up to Nova Scotians to determine their own destiny. "Is someone else really responsible for our incomes being about 25 percent below the Canadian average? Or are we partly responsible ourselves? Have we made the most of our opportunities? How many of our communities are hoping that some outside person or corporation will solve their problems by locating there? Are our business people perhaps too comfortable and complacent? Do too many of us sell out when the going gets rough and live on our investments instead of fighting on and perhaps doing the swallowing instead of being swallowed? Are we in Nova Scotia sometimes the prisoners of our past?"

As Stephen Harper would later learn, however, it one thing for a Nova Scotian to be critical of the province, it is quite another for someone on the national stage to take such liberties. In May 2002, seeking support in Atlantic Canada, Harper claimed there was: ". . . a culture of defeat in Atlantic Canada that had to be overcome . . . that there's a view of too many people in Atlantic Canada that it's only through government favours that there's going to be economic progress . . . that kind of can't do attitude is a problem." The message was little different from the one Stanfield had delivered nearly four decades earlier. But Harper, who has family in New Brunswick, was rebuked in a unanimous resolution of the Nova Scotia legislature which urged him to reflect on the successes of Nova Scotia and his own electoral failure in that province.

Stanfield's challenge to Nova Scotians was grounded by optimism. Said Cabinet minister Dick Donahoe, "We used to simply be a place where you raise two children for export to the rest of Canada and the United States. Today in this province there is a feeling that, properly handled and properly promoted, the province has a future. I think that is Stanfield's gift to the people of this province."

But belief is one thing and results are another. "Small c" Conservatives were hardly surprised when Industrial Estates Ltd. ran into difficulties after making two colossal blunders.

Clairtone Sound Corporation produced space-age stereo cabinets. The brainchild of future mining magnate Peter Munk and wealthy Torontonian David Gilmour, the company's founders were excellent promoters. They had cleverly managed lucrative product placement in hit movies like *The Graduate*, Clairtone stereos could be seen in the home of Playboy founder Hugh Hefner, and Frank Sinatra was brought in as pitch man. With support from IEL, Clairtone pursued a rapid plan of expansion in a swiftly changing and techno-logically advanced industry. At first it looked like the IEL loans—plus municipal tax concessions, a 30 percent subsidy on shipping rates, and a three-year holi-day from federal income tax—would pay off. Clairtone was flying so high that Munk and Gilmour invested in a private executive aircraft. When competition intensified, Clairtone embarked on an ambitious expansion plan, extremely expensive and ill-advised; as it turned out. Company shares, which at one point had traded at $15.25 on the Toronto Stock Exchange, plummeted. Munk and Gilmour sold 29,000 shares at $9.00 per share the day before a bad annual report drove the stock down to $1.00. There were calls in the Ontario legisla-ture for an investigation, but none was pursued. Soon company doors were closed. Munk paid off disgruntled shareholders who launched an action over insider trading. Nova Scotia taxpayers were left on the hook for defaulted loans.

Another blunder was a loan to bring a heavy water plant to Nova Scotia to supply nuclear power facilities. With Lester Pearson's federal Liberal gov-ernment on board, and a strong technical team, Stanfield thought he had another sure winner. But construction problems, labour strife, and techni-cal difficulties ground the project to a halt. When Premier Stanfield declared the unfinished plant open for business, the province's investment, initially pegged at $12 million, had grown to $83 million. In a calamitous string of errors, plant operators introduced salt water into the system, rather than freshwater, which caused the pipes to corrode, and introduced deadly hydrogen sulfide into the atmosphere.

In federal politics, meanwhile, John Diefenbaker was struggling to keep his party united after two successive defeats in the 1963 and 1965 federal elections. His time had passed. Even though an elected provincial premier had never gone on to be prime minister, the four-time Nova Scotia premier was considered a leading candidate. Stanfield had been an exuberant Tory at both the federal and provincial level, and dutifully attended the federal con-ventions, but initially rebuffed suggestions he consider himself a contender for the federal leadership: "I didn't see any role for myself at all at that time. . . . To some extent my attitude was based on the fact that I was running my own show in Nova Scotia . . . I wasn't tempted by any other role."

Claiming he wanted to remain in Nova Scotia politics, Stanfield nonetheless showed himself to be a nation-builder. In a speech before the Canadian Club in Montréal in April 1964, Stanfield spoke of the importance of having two cultures and two languages side by side: "Surely we can readily ease the fears of the French-speaking Canadians regarding their language and culture . . . English-speaking Canadians should accept and welcome the French language and culture in Canada as a continuing fact. This involves no more than the acceptance of reality and the recognition that the French tradition is a great tradition that has contributed and will contribute much to our national life. English Canadians ought to be prepared to accept measures that the federal government considers necessary to assure equality of opportunity for French Canadians in the Federal service." As premier, Stanfield extended French language education from grade eight through to grade twelve.

Stanfield's views were in sharp contrast to the "one Canada" position taken by John Diefenbaker. Yet, as a party man, Stanfield was loyal to Diefenbaker. Stanfield ensured that Nova Scotia delegates stood for Diefenbaker at the party's 1965 national convention but eventually, he also realized that Diefenbaker had to go. But the Nova Scotian couldn't have been terribly interested in the succeeding him: he had called a provincial election for May 30, 1967, some three months before the federal leadership convention. Once it was determined there would be no Ontario heavyweight in the running for the leadership, Stanfield and Manitoba Premier Duff Roblin received the most attention. When it appeared that neither would respond to the call, Dalton Camp contemplated his own candidacy. But it would have been difficult for the man most thought responsible for orchestrating Diefenbaker's demise to seek the top job himself. Camp still had Diefenbaker to reckon with as a possible candidate, and Camp was worried about party unity, knowing that anyone who ran against the Chief and won would take on a badly divided party.

Stanfield relented and announced his candidacy in the Red Room of Nova Scotia House on July 19, 1967. He began the campaign with his customary modesty: "I never thought I would reach this decision, but in my heart I feel it is what I should do."

Asked about his basis of support, Stanfield quipped, "I don't propose to know who will be supporting me." Asked how a man of such limited charisma could become prime minister, he responded, "Mackenzie King was a little dull." Stanfield was modest, but he was also Nova Scotia's most successful politician.

CHAPTER 21

STANFIELD:
THE GREATEST PRIME
MINISTER WE NEVER HAD

Some Progressive Conservatives would rather fight than win.

S TANFIELD'S QUICK EXIT following the Nova Scotia provincial election drew predictable howls of shame. James Aitchison, leader of the provincial New Democrats, said, "With his move in to federal politics, the people of Nova Scotia find that they bought a ten dollar suit of Stanfield underwear in the May election and are left with only the label."

Moving to the national stage did not affect Stanfield's modest and sometimes uninspiring demeanour. When asked why he was entering the race to become PC national leader, he understated the significance of his candidacy: "I had some concerns about the party and the country from the point of national unity and over some of the economic directions of the [federal] government, and I decided in the end to let the party decide whether it wanted me."

Future Conservative heavyweights lined up behind their favoured candidates. Norman Atkins, Dalton Camp's brother-in-law, took the lead in managing the convention for Stanfield. Nova Scotian Lowell Murray went with Davie Fulton, a British Columbian and former Diefenbaker Cabinet minister. Also working for Fulton was Brian Mulroney, then a twenty-eight-year-old Montréal lawyer, and Joe Clark, who later became a speech writer for Stanfield. Michael Meighen, grandson of former leader Arthur Meighen, supported Duff Roblin.

Stanfield had solid support from the federal caucus and dominated the Atlantic Canada delegate count. While the other candidates fought it out in the rest of Canada, Stanfield was positioned for strong second ballot support. He had no detractors and was a proven winner. His hands were clean from the Diefenbaker downfall, yet he appealed to those in the party who felt Diefenbaker was not modern or progressive on social issues. He appeared to be the delegates' safest choice.

One month before the convention, at a Tory "Thinker's Conference" in Québec, party gurus debated resolutions to liven up the convention and shake up the party's staid image as a bunch of blue-suited bankers. A resolution was proposed: "That Canada is and should be a federal state. That Canada is composed of two founding peoples (deux nations) with historic rights who have been joined by people from many lands. That the Constitution should be such as to permit and encourage their full and harmonious growth and development in equality throughout Canada."

The problem was all in the translation. When "two founding peoples" became "deux nations," an uproar ensued. In appealing to delegates from Québec, Stanfield said that "Québecers felt that they had to be given more authority over their economic and social affairs to achieve their aims."

The convention began on September 4, 1967 at Maple Leaf Gardens. Going into the convention, pundits thought Stanfield was in fourth place. After the initial round of speeches, he vaulted to frontrunner status. Stanfield won over delegates with his dignity and by articulating a new form of conservatism: "It is our purpose, in my opinion, to hasten the day when more and more of our fellow citizens may enjoy a more satisfactory personal sense of participation in the economic growth and development of this country; in the social, cultural, and political processes of our country; and can give fuller expression to their own distinctive and unique personality . . . The Progressive Conservative accepts the role of government in economic development . . . [and] the fact that there are no nice ideological solutions to economic problems, nor is there any original sin in economic planning."

Stanfield was moving the party decidedly to the left, a place most delegates wanted to go. He pledged that under his leadership the party "will be recognized not merely for its affluence, for its comfort, for its power, but for its humanity, for its compassion, and for its decency."

Said Claude Ryan, editor of Le Devoir: "The simple, sparse, and effective style of the man appears to us to correspond to an indistinct but real expectation of the Canadian people. The election of Mr. Stanfield would be the logical continuation of the spirit of renovation."

The day before the vote, John Diefenbaker entered the race to save the party from the "two nations" disaster. While it made for a messy convention, Dalton Camp said he was glad that Diefenbaker was on the ballot. "It was good for the party, for Stanfield, that Diefenbaker ran. If he hadn't run, the new leader would have suffered from the hypothesis that he was still wanting in proof, that he couldn't have beaten Diefenbaker."

Stanfield led after the first ballot with 519 votes. Duff Roblin, temporarily weakened by Diefenbaker's last-minute entry, was in second place with 347 votes. Davie Fulton tallied 342, and George Hees was in fourth place with 295 votes. Diefenbaker received 271 votes, sufficient delegate support to retain his dignity. He tested their resolve by staying on for two successive ballots before officially bowing out of the race.

Stanfield's support rose on the three subsequent ballots, but so did Roblin's. After the fourth ballot, Stanfield was still in the lead, but by only 94 votes—865 to 771. The kingmakers on the ballot were Davie Fulton with 357 votes, and Alvin Hamilton, who was forced out at 167 votes. At the urging of Lowell Murray and Brian Mulroney, Fulton withdrew from the contest and indicated he would vote for Bob Stanfield.

Stanfield took the final ballot with 54 percent of the votes. In his brief acceptance speech, Stanfield turned to Diefenbaker and said, "I appreciate very much the size of the shoes I am now trying to fill."

TO THE NATION, BOB STANFIELD came across as a serious fellow, somewhat dour, introspective, and not too exciting. It helped that Stanfield was not above poking fun at himself, but moments of self-parody were rare. What people knew most about Bob Stanfield was that his family was in the underwear business, he had been premier of Nova Scotia, he was wealthy, and he was considered to be progressive on social policy.

Stanfield's French was weak. But, more important, he believed in respecting and supporting French-speaking Canadians in their struggle to preserve and advance their language and culture. This was more than a political strategy: he believed it was right for Quebec and Canadian unity.

One area in which Stanfield distinguished his party from the Liberals was provincial rights and in the methods of addressing regional disparity. The federal government should help, he believed, but not impose its solutions on provincial problems. "While I think there is a role for the federal government in, for example, the field of health, I would say that if the federal government is not prepared to be an equal partner in the cost, it makes much more sense to let the provinces out (of shared cost programs) and turn over tax points with full equalization. . . . There doesn't seem to me to be an excuse for the federal government to try to maintain this degree of centralization, particularly when the provinces want to get out of it . . . I would exercise much more restraint in the use of constitutional powers and would not be quite so hyped on centralization."

Stanfield entered the House of Commons taking the seat of Colchester-Hants, Nova Scotia, in a by-election. He kept many of the people that had served Diefenbaker, but brought in Lowell Murray to lead his staff.

In his maiden speech in Parliament, Stanfield boldly moved a non-confidence motion in the government. Prime Minister Lester Pearson could not attend the scheduled vote and asked Stanfield to "pair" with him, a long-standing practice to nullify votes. Foolishly, Stanfield agreed—a rookie mistake—making him unable to vote on his own initiative. The motion was defeated 119 to 105.

Caucus members, who for years had affectionately called their leader "Chief," sought a nickname for their new leader. Tellingly, they settled on "Mr. Stanfield." He was capable of being both boring and bored. He wasted countless hours sitting in the nearly deserted House of Commons listening to inconsequential debates. Stanfield thought the place for a parliamentarian was in the House, failing to recognize there were no votes to be won there.

To the frustration of his caucus, Stanfield was not one to go for the jugular. In February 1968, a few months away from the scheduled Liberal leadership convention, the Tories orchestrated a snap vote on the third reading of a tax bill. When the effectively leaderless Liberal government lost the vote 84 to 82, the outcome should have been the dissolution of Parliament, forcing the Liberals to conduct a leadership contest in the midst of an election campaign. However, the ever-gracious Stanfield let the Liberals, whose numbers were down because they were too busy campaigning to replace Pearson, off the hook. The Liberals, for their part, used every tool at their disposal to hang on to power.

Pearson told Stanfield the defeat of the government would cause calamitous damage to the Canadian economy and a run on our dollar. He enlisted Louis Rasminsky, the governor of the Bank of Canada, to persuade Stanfield of the severity of the situation and the dire consequences if the government's tax measure was not passed. It was highly unusual for the non-partisan governor to intervene in a political crisis, but it worked just as Pearson had intended. Many Conservative MPs were furious and declared Stanfield "gutless" and a "jellyfish" for not bringing the government down. Stanfield gave Pearson twenty-four hours to regroup and, with the support of the

Ralliement des Créditistes, a motion was passed that declared the lost vote not a matter of confidence.

Letting the government off the hook was a mistake neither Diefenbaker nor Macdonald would have made. Such good-natured displays of integrity and statesmanship are reasons why Stanfield never became prime minister. Had Stanfield decided to play political hardball just this one time, the outcome of the Liberal leadership race, let alone the direction of the country, might well have changed.

On April 6, 1968, a regrouped Liberal party elected Pierre Trudeau leader. Three days after he was sworn in as prime minister, Parliament was dissolved and a general election called for June 25. The early polls gave Liberals a 22-point lead over the Tories. Dalton Camp knew it was not Stanfield's campaign to win: "It was because a few people in the media, making [Trudeau] into a god.... And everybody was having orgasms every time he opened his mouth."

In the midst of Trudeaumania, Stanfield managed a surprisingly strong campaign. He attracted star candidates, including defeated leadership candidate Duff Roblin, who resigned as premier of Manitoba to run. Stanfield did what he could to make the campaign about issues rather than personality. He talked about dramatic changes in social policy, such as a "guaranteed annual income."

Stanfield was so anxious to talk policy he made it up on the fly. He mused about building a tunnel to Newfoundland (perhaps a precursor to a great eastern vision), protectionist tariffs and quotas to protect fruit and vegetable growers, and partial deductions of mortgage interest. But he strenuously resisted well-defined, costed proposals. Trudeau ridiculed Stanfield for this: "I would not buy a set of long underwear if I didn't know how much it cost."

Predictably, the "deux nations" resolution from the Montmorency Conference came back to haunt the Conservatives. Even though the resolution had never passed—nor was even fully considered by the party—it painted Conservatives into an uncomfortable corner. Leading Québec Conservative Marcel Faribault explained that the question of two nations was no longer debatable in Québec: "...you must put, at the preamble of a new constitution, something that will be the recognition that there are in this country two founding peoples."

While "deux nations" was not in Stanfield's campaign platform, Diefenbaker mischievously used every opportunity possible on the campaign trail to denounce the concept, thereby permitting Liberals to exploit the confusion. They took out full page ads in Calgary newspapers claiming, "The Honorable Robert Stanfield says two nations—special status," forcing Stanfield on the defensive, "This is a deliberate lie. I have never advocated two nations. I believe in one Canada. I have never advanced special status. No province should be offered authority that is not offered to all the provinces. . . ." Trudeau apologized for overreaching, but the damage had been done. The division and dissension in Tory ranks caused by its former leader gave Liberals an edge.

Even though the Liberals had won the previous two elections, it was Trudeau—not Stanfield—whom voters thought represented meaningful change. As Stanfield biographer Geoffrey Stevens noted, the contrast between the two was dramatic: "Trudeau seemed to be the incarnation of the second century Canadian. . . . He was brilliant, perfectly bilingual, master of the media, unfettered by convention, and unsullied by old politics. A judo brown belt around his waist, flower behind his ear, a beautiful girl by his side—what more could the Canadian hope to have? By comparison, Stanfield was a man from a prehistoric age; a parochial provincial politician who had not yet learned how to play to a national audience. How could a tired, stooped, droopy-eyed middle-aged man from Truro, Nova Scotia hope to understand the Canadian dream?"

The Tories managed to narrow the Liberal lead during the course of the campaign, from 22 to 14 points, but Stanfield could not be mollified. On the final trip of the campaign he let down his guard to express his frustration to the media. "Trudeau's 'one Canada policy' is simplistic, unrealistic, and dangerously inflexible. For Christ's sake, doesn't he know that Québec isn't going to let the federal government get into education? God damn it, doesn't he know that Ontario has carried on relations for years with London? You know what he's done in this campaign? He's legitimized prejudice. Québec is too dangerous a matter to fool with. By playing it the way he did, he inflamed prejudice in such places as Calgary."

The night before the vote, a large gathering of dignitaries assembled to view the St. Jean Baptiste parade in Montréal. At one point their box was pelted with debris and security forces rushed in to shield the VIPs. Most ducked for cover. Trudeau, however, always game to engage anti-federalist forces, with a well-rehearsed shrug defiantly stood his ground. Euphoric Liberal strategists could not believe their luck; CBC replayed the scene endlessly nationwide, even though it was policy not to provide such political coverage so near the election. Trudeau's theatrical toughness wowed voters. It was one more nail in the Tory coffin.

Stanfield won 72 seats, a loss of 25. The popular vote, at 33.4 percent, was 1.1 percentage points below the 1965 election. Trudeau, with 45.3 percent of the vote, won 154 seats, 58.7 percent of those available. There were 22 New Democrats, and 14 Ralliement Créditistes (the Québec wing that had split from the Social Credit party). Social Credit, under the leadership of Robert Thompson, was shut out. Strong support for the Tories was recorded in Atlantic Canada, 25 of 32 seats, and the prairies, 25 of 45 seats. But Stanfield managed to win only four of 74 seats in Québec, 17 of 88 in Ontario, and none in B.C. Urban areas were a Tory wasteland: one seat out of 26 in Montréal; and no seats in Toronto, Vancouver, Winnipeg, Ottawa, or Québec City. The party had become the domain for predominantly older, less-educated rural Canadians.

Stanfield's post-election caucus was a disparate lot. Most from the West remained loyal to Diefenbaker and thought Stanfield was too placid to ever become prime minister. Said a gleeful Diefenbaker, "The Conservative party has suffered a calamitous disaster."

IN 1969, STANFIELD SUPPORTED Trudeau's Official Languages Act. In the Tory Western heartland, 70 percent were opposed. Alberta MP Jack Horner thought it would be Stanfield's demise and said, "Well, this fellow Stanfield is finished anyway and a little push won't do him any harm. We might as well give him one push." Nova Scotia MP Bob Coates agreed. "We accomplish nothing by trying to impose the French language upon Canadians by compulsion. It is my belief that the schism in evidence today in this nation between the two major groups could become an unbridgeable gap if we continue the debate on this bill." On second reading, 17 Conservatives voted against the bill; 41 supported it. Liberals were delighted by the division within Tory ranks, which was only evident because five Tory members forced a recorded vote when the bill could have passed second reading with no vote count being taken. "It was not so much that people had voted against the bill," said Lowell Murray, "but that they have embarrassed [Stanfield] and the party by standing and forcing a recorded vote. There were a lot of other guys with constituencies where the bill was very unpopular, but who voted for the bill because of the leader."

A furious Stanfield told his caucus that, though there may be disagreement on matters of principle, forcing a recorded vote in this instance was political stupidity. He said he was leading a national party that had to win seats in Québec if it hoped to become government. Since he intended to remain leader into the next election, any member who fell out of line would face the consequences. In other words, no more Mr. Nice Guy. He had, at last, taken control of his caucus. Fallout from the episode included the loss of Roch LaSalle from caucus, one of four Québec Tory MPs. (LaSalle ran as an independent in the 1972 campaign, but returned to the Tory fold in early 1974.)

Stanfield's harshest critics were impressed by his newfound toughness. He'd been tested by his caucus and had come out on top. He had a new edge. Stanfield was determined to lead a national political party and not a group of small-minded, disgruntled reactionaries. "We've got to have positions that suit the country—on constitutional matters, on measures such as the languages bill—ones that are compatible with us remaining a national party. This inevitably means having some strength in Québec as well as in other parts of the country.... We have to risk a certain amount of dissension in the party to move. To put it quite bluntly, I'd sooner run the risk of a certain amount of splintering, than see the simple disintegration of the party over a period of time because we maintained antediluvian positions for fear of causing a little splintering. If we had opposed the languages bill as a party we would have run the grave risk of being reduced to just a regional group. I think it would have been very doubtful whether we could have remained a national party."

Stanfield was tested once more by Prairie MPs dissatisfied with his leadership and progressive policies. In August 1970, maverick Alberta MP Jack Horner assembled the Prairie caucus. Not unlike what Preston Manning would say of Brian Mulroney in 1986, Horner thought that western attitudes were not being properly represented in the Tory party and in Parliament. Horner thought Stanfield was a socialist. "Stanfield is a nice man," Horner claimed "but he's not a leader of men. I can get along with the Red Tories. I like strong opinion. Stanfield never argues back. Trudeau makes decisions. He exercises power well. Everybody must know the limits. Stanfield isn't a leader . . . the leader should be a gigantic figure." Beyond a change in leadership, Horner wanted policies that spoke of less government, more free enterprise, and less Québec.

When Stanfield heard about the meeting, he reacted decisively and admonished the dissidents. In a four-hour caucus meeting, Stanfield exclaimed, "For God's sake, don't blow it." Thereafter, all regional meetings had to be approved by party headquarters and by the leader's office.

It was inevitable that the almost adolescent love affair Canadians had with Trudeau would end. Stanfield preached patience. "If we lash out incoherently and in obvious frustration because they are doing well in the first few months," said Stanfield, "we will make fools of ourselves." His experience in Nova Scotia had taught him that the path to power was long and stepped. He was prepared to let the Trudeau government falter and then defeat itself. "This attack has to be built brick by brick, not in one massive assault, or it will not be credible. It must be based on fact."

Stanfield wanted to reach beyond the traditional Tory base and connect with "independent voters", just as he had done in Nova Scotia. He abandoned the populism and nationalism that were central to the Diefenbaker government. His support of the Official Languages Act was an important marker to building support in Québec. However, in moving the party firmly to the centre, and being progressive and urban on every issue, he alienated many of his elected members and a wide swath of the party's natural supporters. In other words, he failed to keep the factions of his coalition content.

As far as the nation was concerned the contrast between Pierre Trudeau and Bob Stanfield could not have been more stark.

The country could not envision Bob Stanfield sliding down banisters or performing well-rehearsed pirouettes behind the Queen's back. Stanfield would not have called MPs "nobodys" fifty yards off Parliament Hill, or told opposition MPs in the House of Commons to "fuck off." No one believed Trudeau when he said the words he had used were actually "fuddle-duddle." Stanfield would not have asked Prairie grain farmers, "Why should I sell your wheat?" which was Trudeau's refrain when confronted by protesters in 1970.

Stanfield was more serious. His approach to policy development was—perhaps naively—apolitical, and was often led by academics, such as Thomas Simons, president of Trent University.

JUST AS STANFIELD WAS MAKING headway, the October crisis of 1970 dramatically changed the political landscape. But before the Front de libération du Québec (FLQ) kidnapped British diplomat James Cross and abducted and murdered Québec Cabinet minister Pierre Laporte, the Tories were 12 percentage points behind the Liberals in the polls. When the October crisis concluded, they were down 20 points.

The October crisis gave Trudeau an opportunity to talk tough and act tough against terrorists and separatists. Trudeau abandoned whatever idealism had existed in his mind about a "just society," or even basic individual rights and freedoms, when he invoked the War Measures Act in response to what was determined to be an "apprehended insurrection." Stanfield was in a difficult position when the War Measures Act was invoked. He had no way of assessing the full extent of the crisis, yet he risked accusations of disloyalty to the country should he not support the prime minister during a national emergency. Stanfield considered Trudeau's decision excessive. He urged the government to adopt new legislation that would give authorities the power needed in a crisis without resorting to a wholesale suspension of civil rights. A reasonable suggestion, perhaps. But under the circumstances, Stanfield pleased no one with what appeared to many as qualified support. According to one senior Tory, "The civil liberties people denounced us for not endorsing their cause and the rest denounced us for being weak-kneed on law and order."

The news from the polls would get far worse for Stanfield before it would get better. So bleak were Conservative prospects that leading Québec Conservative Brian Mulroney urged Stanfield not to contest by-elections scheduled for Québec. A determined Stanfield barked: "The hell you're not. You are going to run candidates."

Stanfield campaigned. He met one-on-one with the world's leaders, and flipped hamburgers across Canada at small-town BBQs. He was slowly and steadily regaining respect, but he was still no match for Trudeau's charisma. Said B.C. talk radio host Jack Webster: "He's one of the nicest, dullest subjects in the country. It's impossible to be rude to him."

Meanwhile, the more the world got to know of Pierre Trudeau, the less respect it had for Canada. Like many of his Liberal successors—Chrétien in particular—Trudeau went out of his way to annoy Americans. Trudeau enjoyed snubbing his nose at President Nixon by brazenly launching diplomatic initiatives with communist countries. In August 1971, as part of an economic recovery package, the United States imposed a 10 percent surcharge on a wide range of imports. No exemption was offered for Canada. Stanfield took Trudeau to task for recklessly and needlessly endangering the Canadian economy, saying, "[I]t is one thing to negotiate firmly with the United States about matters of substance in which our interests may diverge from theirs. It is quite another thing for Canada to give the impression that it is going out of its way to insult a good friend and neighbour. . . . we can and we must develop policies that are pro-Canadian without being anti-American."

On September 1, 1972, Trudeau called on the governor general to dissolve the twenty-eighth Parliament and call an election for Monday, October 30. Trudeau muddled his way through the opening of the campaign. "The challenge is nothing less than the integrity of Canada, the homeland of persons so dedicated to the social advantages of tolerance and moderation, so convinced of the value of a single, strong economic unit, so proud of our competence and our image that we are committed to Canada." Canadians were confused by the convoluted message. "The challenge to Canada, the challenge of this election," Trudeau continued, "is to ensure that Canadians continue to exhibit the self-confidence and the assurance that will permit Canada to pursue its own policies and demonstrate the advantages of its value system." Say again?

Liberal party arrogance was prominently displayed. "The traditional way is to view elections as a competition between parties," said Torrance Wylie, the Liberal party's national organizer. "I don't see it that way. I see an election as an opportunity to establish a relationship with a voter. That's what we will try to do. We will tell him what we have done, why we have done it, but we are planning for the future, and invite him to share it. I hate to admit it, but I spend no time thinking about the opposition parties, because I don't believe in elections as competitions."

The Liberal campaign lacked a strategy, a focus, a vision, or a plan. Its campaign slogan, "The Land is Strong," seemed oddly out of place and unconnected to voter beliefs and concerns. The Liberals, however, charmed by their belief in their own superiority and invincibility, utterly failed to consider defeat a possibility. They sailed into the election with what they assumed was a comfortable lead of ten percentage points (42 to 32) that would grow the instant Trudeau turned on the charm.

Despite receiving a strong majority in 1968, however, many of Trudeau's legislative initiatives had failed miserably. He had tried and failed to pass a bill to restrict foreign takeovers. He had proposed changes to the Social Security system that never passed. He had to withdraw a proposal for a new competition act. Initiatives for Canada's Native peoples were dropped. And the Liberal record on government finances was atrocious. Over four years, program spending increased 68.5 percent, from $11.5 billion in 1968–69 to $19.4 billion in 1972–73. The annual deficit nearly *tripled*. Unemployment was up sharply over 1968. None of this seemed to matter to Liberal strategists as long as they had the urbane and sexy Pierre Trudeau and the Tories had the plodding and unexciting Bob Stanfield.

Hours before the election was called, Stanfield mused about the Trudeau "mystique."

> In 1968, Mr. Trudeau was accepted as the new spirit, above politics in the ordinary sense of the term. . . . A great many doubt whether there is any warmth in his concern . . . I think he has difficulties in listening to people, difficulty in spending enough time with his caucus, keeping in touch with them and, through them, with the people of the country.

> I've always believed the party leader has to spend a lot of time with people. He has to spend a lot of time with members of his caucus and listen to things, listen to their arguments, some of which he frequently may not think much of. . . . I have the impression Mr. Trudeau is pretty largely making the main decisions himself and relying mainly for advice on people he chooses.

While the bloom was coming off Trudeau's rose, voters still had to come to grips with Bob Stanfield as a potential prime minister. He was perceived as intelligent and incorrigibly honest. These were positive—not sexy—attributes that ensured Stanfield would not be a negative to the Tory campaign. The one area where voters gave Conservatives a definite edge over Liberals was economic management. While Trudeau charmed his way to election day, Stanfield hammered away at bedrock issues he believed working Canadians truly cared about: taxes, unemployment, government spending, and inflation.

Québec, however, once again loomed as *the* Tory problem. They needed star candidates. Claude Wagner, a Québec judge and a former provincial Liberal justice minister, was chosen as Stanfield's Québec lieutenant. Brian Mulroney was dispatched to bring Wagner to the team.

Wagner liked Stanfield's more flexible approach to Québec and signed on to run. Wagner was given one of the safest seats in the province, although no Tory seat in Québec could ever be truly safe. The party invested huge sums in Québec, certainly disproportionate to the number of seats that might be earned. Even though Conservatives had no campaign on the ground in Québec, with Wagner as a candidate they created the impression across the country that they had a fighting chance in what would otherwise have been a political wasteland.

Not surprisingly, the Liberal platform was thin on content. It included measures to increase bilingualism in the public service, make-work programs to stimulate local economies, and incentives to reduce pollution. With Tory support on the rise, Trudeau reached into the "cookie jar" of the public treasury to win votes. As *Time* magazine reported, "goodies" for Atlantic Canada had been so blatantly distributed that, "they raised the possibility of Canada's first pork barrel backlash."

Stanfield gained ground whenever the media focused on economic issues. Under the colourless motto, "A Progressive Conservative government will do better," Stanfield promised lower income taxes to stimulate employment, indexation of the tax system, indexation of old age security, capital gains tax exemption for family farms, and the imposition of temporary wage and price controls, if necessary, to curb inflation. He also proposed a "constant dollar" tax scheme under which a worker would be taxed only on the real increase in income, not on the portion attributed to inflation. And he promised a "Canadian Investment Credit Incentive" to stimulate small businesses and a ministry to coordinate economic planning of government departments. Provinces would also receive 100 percent of the proceeds of offshore mineral rights. On accountability issues, Stanfield proposed increased powers for the auditor general and the disclosure of ministers' personal holdings. The Toronto *Star* was so impressed with the Tory platform that for the first time in its history it endorsed the Conservatives.

Stanfield clearly had the edge over Trudeau on the issue of economic management, but he needed to connect with Canadians on a more personal level. With rising unemployment and more people on welfare, the country was beginning to worry about its future. Stanfield had the vision that Trudeau lacked: "Let me tell you something about the kind of Canada I would like to live in, the kind of Canada I would like to see my children inherit, and their children after them.... It will be a country in which freedom of thought, freedom of expression, freedom of movement, freedom of determination will be available to all our citizens.... a country whose people are governed responsibly and gently by men and women who truly wish to serve the common good, a country in which to fill man's most profound aspirations and to live his finest dreams."

With one week until the election, the gap between the Liberals and Conservatives—ten points at the outset of the campaign—had shrunk to just four points. Because of the concentration of Liberal votes in Québec, it was conceivable Conservatives could lose the popular vote and still win a plurality of seats. Suddenly there was buzz and excitement in the Conservative campaign. They had captured the political elixir called momentum.

The election turned out to be the closet race in Canadian history. Not until the morning after the vote count was a winner determined. Conservatives held the Atlantic Provinces, although they dropped two seats in Newfoundland and one in PEI. They had hoped for 10 seats in Québec, but won only two. They narrowly won Ontario by four seats. The West had had enough of Pierre Trudeau, who captured only 7 of 68 seats; the Tories dominated with 42. Outside Québec, Liberals had 53 seats to the Conservatives' 105. The national tally gave the Liberals a microscopic edge of two seats (109 to 107) and a 3.4 percentage point advantage in popular vote. The NDP held the balance of power.

Stanfield contended the government had lost the confidence of the people and declared he was ready to form a government if the governor general gave him the opportunity. The NDP, however, chose to sustain the Liberals, and leader David Lewis would help Trudeau spend taxpayer dollars for the next few years.

Stanfield accepted the results philosophically, without bluster or recrimination.

> My priorities are basically the same as they were when I came up here in 1967. There is a problem of national unity and strengthening the country and making progress toward just living together a little more satisfactorily. When I first came to Ottawa, I thought of it mainly in terms of a French speaking—English speaking problem, but obviously regional differences are important. The West, as I discovered, has its own ax to grind; as I had one to grind when I came here from Nova Scotia. Cutting down at least on regional disparity was an important consideration with me then, and still is. I think I would put national unity and regional disparity at the top of my list, plus the general matter of getting rid of poverty so that people have something like equality of opportunity. This may sound corny, but I want to encourage people to sort of fulfill themselves; in other words, we not only need to have a country that is diverse in terms of space and regions and also cultures, but we need also to have more tolerance and respect for people who are different.

TRUDEAU HAD MADE A DEAL with Lewis to keep his government in power. Lewis was the socialist who had called Canadian corporations "corporate welfare bums." The quid pro quo for NDP support was the creation of a new Crown corporation: Petro-Canada. The informal Liberal-NDP alliance required that every proposal and piece of legislation be discussed and agreed upon between the parties. The minority Trudeau government lost eight recorded votes but only requested dissolution when it lost on budget legislation. The country paid dearly for this marriage of convenience. Government-financed programs, which had cost $16.8 billion in 1971–72, rose to $29 billion in 1974–75—a stunning 72.7 percent.

Though Stanfield was unlikely to make inroads in Québec, he steadfastly supported the Liberal policy of official bilingualism. Before the 1974 election, Stanfield refused to sign the nomination papers for Leonard Jones, the mayor of Moncton, after Jones refused to support the PC party policy on the issue. Jones ran and won as an independent; despite the fact that 30 percent of Moncton's population was francophone.

The common-law Liberal-NDP marriage lasted twenty painful months before an election was called for July 8, 1974. The defining policy issue of that campaign was inflation, with Stanfield calling for a ninety-day wage and price freeze. Trudeau, hardly the laissez-faire free enterpriser, called this a gross intrusion into matters of business and employment. He ridiculed Stanfield's hard-to-understand policy by saying you can't shut down an economy with the quip, "Zap, you're frozen." A year later, Trudeau would just shrug when he introduced the same wage and price controls he had ridiculed a year earlier.

The key image from this campaign was a photograph of Stanfield catching a football on an airport tarmac in North Bay. A photographer caught Stanfield grimacing as he fumbled the ball. That photograph became a metaphor for the campaign as a Trudeau-friendly press plastered the image on the front pages of newspapers across the country. No one in the press was interested in the photos of Stanfield throwing one of his many perfect spirals. Stanfield quipped that if he walked on water, the next day's headline would be "Stanfield can't swim."

The NDP was not rewarded for helping Trudeau. Its seat total was nearly halved. Stanfield's Tories lost only 0.44 percentage points of the popular vote from 1972, but it cost them 11 seats. They swept Alberta and took a majority of seats in all Western provinces, but their anemic showing in Québec continued. Ontario, where the Tories slipped from 40 to 25 seats, made the biggest difference. The Liberal government came back with a majority government, winning 141 seats in the 264-seat Parliament.

In 1976, after three election defeats and criticism from within, Stanfield resigned. In his farewell address at the convention that chose his successor, Stanfield bluntly told Conservatives they had been their own worst enemy and need look no further than the mirror to explain their electoral failure: "Some Progressive Conservatives would rather fight than win. Some of us wish to elevate a legitimate concern for individual self-reliance and individual enterprise into the central and dominating dogma and theme of our party. Why do we spoil a good case by exaggeration? Why do we try to polarize a society that is already taut with tension and confrontation?"

Afterwards, Stanfield occasionally weighed in on important issues, notably on the importance of free trade to the Canadian economy in the 1988 election, and later on the Meech Lake Accord. He died on December

16, 2003, only eight days after the Progressive Conservative party merged with the Canadian Alliance to form the new Conservative Party of Canada. He was buried in Camp Hill Cemetery, Halifax, Nova Scotia, next to his first wife Joyce.

In 2007, Prime Minister Stephen Harper spoke at the ceremony to rename the Halifax Airport the Robert L. Stanfield International Airport. The prime minister remarked: "Robert Stanfield . . . inspired people, not with grand schemes or fiery rhetoric, but with his practical ideas and fundamental decency. He connected best with people up close, in one-on-one situations, where they could fully appreciate the sincerity and the strength of his convictions. . . . In addition to setting the standard for dignity and civility in Parliament, he made tremendous contributions to national unity."

Throughout his tenure as leader, Bob Stanfield had the bad luck of facing the most charismatic Liberal prime minister since Sir Wilfrid Laurier. Stanfield was as reserved as Trudeau was flamboyant. Trudeau's ego and arrogance contrasted with Stanfield's humility and deference. In his youth Trudeau, perhaps wisely, used his family's wealth to travel the world and indulge his passions, while Stanfield invested in blue chip stocks and prudently watched his nest egg grow over time. Trudeau the impulsive, Stanfield the responsible. History will remember these two combatants: Trudeau as the four-time prime minister of Canada, Stanfield the best prime minister Canada never had.

CHAPTER 22

JOE WHO?

*I rise on a point of order. The government has lost the vote on a
matter which we have no alternative but to regard as a question of
confidence. I simply want to advise the House that I will be seeing his
Excellency the Governor General tomorrow morning.*

HIGH RIVER IS a small Alberta town about 40 kilometres south of
Calgary. Its independent weekly newspaper, *The Times*, was founded
by Charles Clark Sr., and handed down to his son Charles Clark Jr.
The paper left family hands with the next batch of sons, Peter and Joe. Said
Joe, "It became clear that neither my brother Peter, nor I, had the talent or the
temperament to carry it on." Lack of ambition was not the reason. Clark's passion in life was not journalism but politics. Despite rising to the highest office
in the land before reaching the age of forty, Clark remains a tragic figure in
Conservative party history.

Joe Clark was born in High River on June 5, 1939. Not much for the
outdoors, he was more inclined to read about sports than to play them.
Clark was a serious student and drawn to history. He was editor of the student newspaper and participated in public speaking contests. Clark's natural
curiosity was stimulated by exposure to luminaries, such as Arthur
Meighen, who dropped by the Clark family dinner table to talk politics.

Clark's prize for winning a public speaking contest in Grade 11 was a
trip to Ottawa. His visit to Parliament coincided with the famous pipeline

debate. Returning to High River, the serious-minded son did not tell his mother about the splendour of Parliament Hill or the people he met on his journey. Rather, his first comment was, "We don't have democracy in Canada." Clark was disgusted that the Liberals had stifled debate.

When John Diefenbaker visited High River in 1957, Clark's attachment to the Progressive Conservative party was cemented. So was his fervour for politics.

At the University of Alberta, Clark attended a national Progressive Conservative convention where he became president of its Student Federation. In a CBC radio interview stern and ambitious Clark told a national audience that the "Prime Minister and the Liberal backroom boys are trying to sneak this election past the Canadian people. They called an election when it was neither needed nor wanted . . . The Liberals are trying to sneak back into office."

Clark had no illusions about a career in politics. In his student days he commented on the difficulties of his chosen profession: "Public service, on any level, is a bed of thorns, not of roses. The glory in it, if there be any at all, is small return to the constant responsibility, the exhausting work, the lost sleep, and ever present complaints, for the public seldom show gratitude to its leaders."

While travelling in Europe, after completing his undergraduate degree, Clark received a telegram offering him a job writing pamphlets for Diefenbaker. It was a temporary assignment, but Clark welcomed the opportunity to eat and breathe politics.

In 1962 he entered Dalhousie Law School. At the end of his first year he went to British Columbia to help Davie Fulton in the 1963 provincial election. Clark ended up spending more time on politics that on his second year law studies. Unprepared for a property law exam, Clark attempted to obfuscate his lack of knowledge and intentionally wrote an illegible paper. He was commanded to appear for an oral exam, which he failed, losing the year.

Clark made his way back to the University of Alberta and completed a Masters degree in political science. Under the aegis of Peter Lougheed he became part of an inner circle of strategists and helped form the Alberta Progressive Conservative Party to take on the Social Credit dynasty, then led by Ernest Manning. Clark became vice president of the provincial party at the annual meeting of 1966 and, at twenty-seven, ran in the riding of Calgary South in the 1967 provincial election. He impressed and came in second, just 462 votes behind in an election where his party won only six seats.

Clark supported Davie Fulton in the 1967 federal leadership campaign.

So did two other well-known young Conservatives, Lowell Murray and Brian Mulroney. After Bob Stanfield won the leadership, he offered Clark a job as a speechwriter. Clark then helped to recruit Lowell Murray as chief of staff.

Stanfield thought Clark was unsuited to elected office: "I consider him too highly strung and nervous to be a practicing politician." To relax and improve himself, Clark read novels at night in French. He was not active on the dating scene, although Judith Maxwell, future head of the Economic Council of Canada, was once in his sights. Working in the leader's office was a good training ground for Clark, whose ambition was to win election to Parliament. His home constituency of High River was held by Conservative Jack Horner, so Clark chose to contest the nearby riding of Rocky Mountain, where he was a virtual unknown. Clark's tenacity won him a contested nomination on the second ballot. He handily beat the Liberal incumbent Alan Sulatycky in the 1972 election.

Clark hired Maureen McTeer as one of his Ottawa-based Parliamentary assistants. She had been fired from her research job with the PC party because she had a habit of working on causes and campaigns to the neglect of the responsibilities for which she was being paid. In the job interview, McTeer deadpanned, "I can't type, but I can think." McTeer did not complain about harassment when flowers arrived from a "secret admirer" on Valentine's Day; or when two weeks later, on her twenty-first birthday, she received a bouquet of twenty-one yellow roses from her thirty-three-year-old boss. Hardly before McTeer even realized Clark had romantic intentions, he proposed marriage. She was flabbergasted, but ultimately accepted the offer.

Clark won re-election in 1974 with an increased majority. But the Conservatives lost badly and Stanfield indicated he would resign. Clark was prepared to support Peter Lougheed, who declined to run because he did not speak French. Most people thought Clark was too young to contest the leadership, but they did not dismiss his candidacy out of hand. When Clark assembled a group of friends to discuss his ambition, ten were opposed and four were in favour. Clark would face such long odds throughout his career.

With few party heavyweights on his campaign team, he insisted on running, not for the experience or future considerations, but to win.

Clark worried about his lack of preparedness to deal with policy questions at the convention and invested considerable time studying approaches to economic management. His inclination to serious study and hard work impressed the delegates. Because he did not have any high profile supporters, he had rank-and-file delegates introduce him at the convention "to demonstrate his connection with the grassroots."

On the first ballot Clark had 277 votes, well short of expectations but a respectable third place behind Québec heavyweights Claude Wagner and Brian Mulroney. But he had only 12 percent delegate support, and his campaign team thought his day was done.

The big surprise on the first ballot was that Clark was ahead of Flora MacDonald by 21 votes. Some 250 delegates who had indicated support for MacDonald voted for someone else. (This phantom support, where delegates publicly support a candidate but vote for someone else, came to be known as "the Flora syndrome.")

The lower-ranked candidates and their delegates refused to consider either of the Québec candidates, who between them had 37.6 percent of the first ballot votes. With MacDonald faltering, Clark was best placed to scoop up votes. Mulroney called the assault on Québec Tories "the great political gang-bang." When the *Blue Tory* Sinclair Stevens gave his support to the *Red Tory* Joe Clark it was stark confirmation that the party was not prepared to be led by a Québecer.

On the second ballot Clark almost doubled his vote and was within striking distance of Mulroney. But Mulroney and Wagner still carried 46.4 percent of the delegates, enough that one or the other should have won. The four lower-ranked candidates dropped out and all went over to Clark, which vaulted him ahead of a stalled Mulroney on the third ballot and set up a final ballot showdown between Wagner and Clark.

To win, Wagner only needed to bring 41 percent of Mulroney's delegates to his side. But Mulroney sat on his hands: "I wanted to avoid the appearance of screwing anybody. If I supported Clark openly it would've looked like a conspiracy against a French Canadian." When Québecer Roch LaSalle approached Mulroney about voting for Wagner on the final ballot, he replied angrily, "You fellows made sure I haven't got (a vote)," Indeed, Mulroney could not vote because the Wagner team swept all the delegate spots in his home riding. Mulroney's bitterness towards Wagner's strong-arm tactics in Québec left the impression that he preferred Clark. Mulroney may also have been looking ahead to the next leadership convention, thinking that after Wagner the party would be hard-pressed to elect another Québecer.

Clark narrowly won the final ballot: 1,187 to 1,122. It was an outcome few had predicted. The next day the Toronto *Star* ran the front page headline, "Joe Who?" The phrase would reverberate throughout Clark's career. It implied that Clark was ahead of himself in seeking the leadership, let alone the job of prime minister. Because Clark's team did not respond to the "Joe

Who?" jab, the moniker stuck and will no doubt be mentioned in his obituary. When it was reported that Clark's wife Maureen had kept her maiden name, critics announced they finally had the answer to the question "Joe Who?" He was Maureen's husband.

Years later Mulroney would claim he was lucky to have lost to Clark since it was too soon for him to lead the party. This implied that it was bad luck for Clark, that the burden of his youth and inexperience was too much to overcome.

What underscored the scorching Toronto *Star* headline was that outside of politics Clark had accomplished little, and as a politician he was just a two-term opposition MP from Rocky Mountain Alberta. Now, as leader of Her Majesty's Loyal Opposition, Clark was the only person in Canada in a position to replace Pierre Trudeau as prime minister. Clark's determination, ambition, and capacity for hard work were important, but he lacked experience and vision. And Clark was reluctant to admit faults. Whenever he was accused of being weak and inexperienced, Clark proved his critics correct by taking unwise and uncalculated risks simply to demonstrate his manliness.

Clark's early days as leader were positive. In the afterglow of the convention, the Tory polling numbers rose to about 10 percentage points above the Liberals.' In early 1976, television came to the House of Commons. Everyone expected Pierre Trudeau would shine on the medium. But the ever-serious Clark had the advantage of low expectations, which he readily and impressively exceeded. The momentum, however, was short-lived.

WITH THE ELECTION OF RENÉ LÉVESQUE as sovereignist premier of Québec in 1976, Trudeau looked like a safer bet to voters and the federal Tories fell back into their customary second-place position. Conservative momentum was delivered a body blow when the party lost all five by-elections held May 24, 1977, including a seat in PEI they had held for two decades. It is unusual for a governing party to do well in by-elections, which are often used to send a message of disappointment without actually having to replace the government. Defections from the Tory caucus ensued, which reflected badly on Clark's leadership. Jack Horner joined Trudeau's Cabinet, saying Clark had made the move an easy one. Hochelaga MP Jacques Lavoie also went to the Grits. He had run on four occasions for the Tories in Québec before he finally won a by-election in 1975. He lasted less than two years in the Tory caucus. Then Stan Schumacher, in a gesture of disrespect, initially refused to step aside to allow Clark to run in his home constituency.

The Tories were at an anemic 32 percent in the polls when their 1977 convention was held in Québec City. Clark chose Québec City to demonstrate his commitment to winning seats in French Canada. Organizers were disappointed, however, that only 166 delegates from the host province showed up, far short of the 350 anticipated. The convention location stirred up old battles in the party over Québec's place in Canada. Clark argued that Canada needed a new federal voice. Not the federal-centric vision of Pierre Trudeau, but one where provinces received greater control over matters of education, language, and culture. Acknowledging the challenge of dealing with divergent Conservative views, Clark remarked, "Anyone who can bring the Conservative party together can bring the country together." Delegates seemed pleased with Clark and gave him 93.1 percent support for his leadership. It was his party to win or lose in the coming campaign.

What Clark lacked in charisma he made up in hard work. And Canadians were getting fed up with Pierre Trudeau. The country was ready for change, evidenced by two Tory by-election wins in 1978, in Toronto and Ottawa. Tory numbers were rising, not because Canadians were warming to Clark, but because they were moving away from Trudeau.

The Liberal government knew its prospects were bleak, and extended its mandate beyond the traditional four-year term by an additional ten months. All the while, Liberal arrogance, high inflation, and unprecedented government deficits ate away at Trudeau's chances of re-election.

The Tory campaign spoke to Liberal weakness with the slogans "Let's get Canada working again," and "It's time for a change—give the future a chance." Trudeau countered that a steady hand was required to govern Canada, especially with a referendum on sovereignty looming in Québec. "This is no time for on-the-job training," Trudeau warned.

The NDP played its customary minor role. Social Credit was no longer a national political force, but its Créditiste rump in Québec under leader Fabien Roy enjoyed the quiet support of the PQ sovereignist government. Officially, the party stood for the right of a province "to choose its own destiny within Canada."

Trudeau won the popular vote, 4.6 million to Clark's 4.1 million. But a seat-by-seat basis, Clark's Tories came out ahead: 136, to 114 for the Liberals. That left Clark six seats short of a majority government; precisely the number won by the Créditiste. The NDP under Ed Broadbent increased its seat total from 16 to 26.

Despite a Québec friendly platform, Clark won only two seats in Québec. Trudeau took 90 percent of the seats in Québec, but only 23 percent of the seats elsewhere. Pierre Trudeau had been defeated. After being out of office for 16 years, the Conservatives were finally back in power.

THE PRIME MINISTER-DESIGNATE was determined to do things differently. Clark stayed in Alberta during the transition period. His first trip to Ottawa was on a commercial plane. He followed his own timetable and delayed meeting Parliament longer than any previous prime minister. The size of his Cabinet, at twenty-nine, was smaller than Trudeau's. And there would be no Parliamentary secretaries. The prime minister's limousine was mothballed and replaced with a Chevy.

Clark was sworn in as prime minister on June 4, 1979, the day before he turned 40. He remains the youngest prime minister in Canadian history. When Clark arrived at the prime minister's Langevin Block office he was met by a sign posted by a Trudeau staffer that read: "We'll be back."

"That's what the Shah said," a confident Tory staffer quipped, referring to the recently-deposed Shah of Iran who had just been replaced as national leader by the Ayatollah Khomeini.

Despite the new blood and common touches, Tory pollster Allan Gregg wrote in an internal briefing memo that Clark came to office with virtually "no image" among Canadian voters. "It may not be an exaggeration to suggest that a national leader has rarely, if ever, assumed office with lower expectations concerning his ability to govern."

Ignoring the reality of the election results, Clark was determined to command Parliament as though he had a majority. But his math was faulty: he was six seats short. To carry out his legislative agenda he needed the support or acquiescence of at least one of the three other parties in the House.

After Trudeau announced his resignation on November 21, Clark believed the Tories had carte blanche to govern. Even arrogant Liberals, Clark thought, would not trigger an election while leaderless. One Tory MP exclaimed, "we're home free . . . until after their leadership convention in March we've got a blank check. We can do any god damn thing we like." A Liberal strategist responded, "Better a lame-duck leader than a turkey for a Prime Minister." The executive of the Liberal party called for a leadership convention for Winnipeg on March 28–30, 1980.

Clark was prone to clumsiness and error, and every journalist had a catalogue of Joe Clark jokes. The first time he was in the prime minister's limousine he missed the bench and ended up on the floor. He hesitated before signing a guestbook in Kenya, and Maureen McTeer quipped within earshot of reporters, "What have you done? Forgotten your name?" A little while later, as government leaders were posing for photographs, Maureen took charge: "Well, this is enough of the standing around and smiling. Let's go and eat." Clark was right on her heels. In the summer of 1979, John Diefenbaker remarked, "Canada celebrated the year of the child by electing Joe Clark as Prime Minister." Privately Diefenbaker was heard to remark that "Clark must have got his wrist starched for his wedding night."

The government also had trouble communicating. On the possible privatization of Petrocan, then a Crown corporation, Treasury Board president Sinclair Stevens said, "I am supportive of Prime Minister Clark's position on Petrocan, which will be clarified in due course. Clark is always clear and I rest my case there."

Standing beside Clark throughout his rise and fall was Nova Scotian Lowell Murray. The former chief of staff to Stanfield had once shared an apartment with Clark. Clark persuaded Murray to stay in Ottawa to help him govern by appointing him to the Senate, which comes with a life annuity. The Tory party supplemented Murray's Senate wages with a stipend of $60,000. The party also helped furnish his Ottawa condominium.

Often derided as a wimp, Clark was determined to be tough: "If we don't live up to our promises, we're dead." However, he backtracked on a number of campaign promises, with good reason. None was more significant than relocating the Canadian embassy in Israel to Jerusalem, a decision based more on politics than principle.

Ron Atkey had run for the party in the Toronto riding of St. Paul's in 1972 and 1974 and had come up short by a little more than 1,000 votes each time. The Jewish contingent of the riding was sufficient to make the difference between winning and losing. Atkey had the ear of Maureen McTeer, and she set the wheels in motion on an Israeli-friendly policy of moving the Canadian embassy from Tel Aviv to Jerusalem. Clark announced his embassy policy in the run-up to the election on April 25, 1979, just minutes before he met with the Canada-Israel committee. For Atkey, the embassy policy worked like a charm. He was elected MP for St. Paul's in 1979 by a margin of 1,212 votes.

Within days of taking office, Clark signalled he was serious about moving swiftly on the embassy move. He then faced an outraged Arab community that stigmatized the policy shift as "an act of aggression." In addition to the obvious political implications, there was almost $1 billion in merchandise trade with Arab nations at stake and a half billion dollars in consulting services. Canadian companies—such as Bell, Air Canada, and Westinghouse Canada—were at risk of losing huge contracts. The Arabs threatened an oil boycott against Canada and the Arab Monetary Fund announced it would not deposit funds in Canadian banks. Ron Atkey dismissed the threat, claiming, "The Arab bark is worse than their bite." Palestinian leader Yasser Arafat was incensed: "Our Arab nation must teach the Canadian scoundrels lessons that would ensure the protection of our dignity."

Flora McDonald, minister of external affairs, tried to have it both ways: "We are prepared to make accommodations with Arab states over this move and we will be discussing with them how best we can carry out our stated intentions." But she said privately to Canadian Jewish leaders, "The embassy will be moved. There should be no doubt about that."

We could expect Israel's ambassador to Canada was thrilled to have steadfast support from Canada's prime minister. But he told the press Canada's support for the Israeli people was unquestioned and the embassy move was not requested. So why inflame the Arabs? The answer might simply have been to elect Ron Atkey in St. Paul's.

Clark encountered resistance even within his caucus. On August 8, 1979, eight days before his death, Diefenbaker spoke out: "That young fellow (Clark) has only ever asked me for advice on one occasion. He phoned me, during the campaign, to say he was thinking of promising to move our [Israel] embassy to Jerusalem. The course I recommended was that he forget it. It could only cause trouble, I said. And the next day—the very next day—that young man went out and did the very opposite to the course I had recommended to him. That's the history of our relationship."

Clark discreetly tried to extract himself from the mess and asked Bob Stanfield to be his "special representative" to work out a solution. After meetings with representatives of the Arab countries, Stanfield advised Clark to back down. "The transfer of the Canadian Embassy in Israel from Tel Aviv to Jerusalem would be viewed by the Arabs as . . . pre-judging the outcome of negotiations which have not yet taken place." On October 29, Joe Clark stood in the House of Commons and said, "We do not intend to move the embassy from Tel Aviv to Jerusalem."

Closer to home, Clark had to deal with pent-up expectations among Tory stalwarts who expected to be rewarded for their patience and loyalty over the thirteen years the Liberals had controlled patronage appointments. Senior Québec Cabinet minister Roch LaSalle said, "I don't intend to pass up our opportunity." Clark, amusingly, agreed. "Certainly we are going to ensure, in a reasonable way, a way that maintains propriety, the activities undertaken by the Conservative government do not benefit the Liberal party . . . The problem in the past has been that in certain cases it is not enough for a Conservative to be competent. It has been necessary for him to be a Liberal. I naturally am not going to exclude from consideration Canadians who happen to share my confidence and my political affiliation."

Clark instructed his ministers not to fill any positions that had been vacant for six months or more. The government wanted to reduce the size of the public service by 60,000 jobs, so it had implemented a hiring freeze. However, Clark was prepared to use procurement to effect patronage, particularly in Québec. "Roch LaSalle is responsible for purchasing policy," Clark told supporters in Québec. "Roch, you know, is also a political manager here, and that too, is important."

Publicly, Clark took a pragmatic approach to federalism, but he discreetly asked a Conservative senator to tour provinces behind the scenes to develop a set of proposals to reform the Constitution, in preparation for the pending referendum in Québec.

On November 1, 1979, the government in Québec released the text of the referendum question on "sovereignty association." Clark declared that it was unacceptable to the Government of Canada. "We won't negotiate Canada's breakup . . . there is no legal means by which self-determination can be realized." This sounded very much like the policies Reform MP Stephen Harper would initiate in the mid 1990s, which were later adopted by the Liberal government in the drafting of the Clarity Act. But Clark, who had started by talking tough on Québec, backed down in the face of criticism. "Obviously, if there were a massive political determination, one would have to consider changing the law."

Clark said that he would not campaign in the referendum, arguing he did not want to interfere with the vote. Pressed to enter the fray, Clark declared: "I am not a resident of Québec." Indeed, the separatists were pleased that Clark, rather than Trudeau, was the lead federal representative. But Clark could easily have gone to Québec and repeated what he had been saying about Canada all along. Clark's vision was vaguely described as a "community of communities." This contrasted with the centralizing big government concept of the Liberal party. Clark's vision certainly squared with the view of Québec nationalists more than Trudeau's did.

On provincial relations, Clark chose a different path from Trudeau's. Rather than confrontation and inflexibility, Clark chose consultation and conciliation and took action in support of provincial autonomy. He gave jurisdiction of lotteries to the provinces. In September 1979, Clark granted Newfoundland and Nova Scotia control over their offshore mineral rights.

Granting provinces offshore rights required constitutional change and might take three or four years to implement. Another tantalizing reason, figured Clark, for Atlantic Canadians to keep him in power.

The speech from the throne on October 9 made no mention of the upcoming referendum in Québec on sovereignty association. The new government set a path towards federal-provincial cooperation, energy self-sufficiency, lower taxes, greater reward for initiative, and a mortgage-interest tax credit.

Listening intently to the speech in the far corner of the chamber were the Tories' political cousins, the remaining rump of the Social Credit caucus, now known as Créditiste. With only six members, they had only half the number required to gain official party status. The threshold of 12 members allows a party to ask more questions in the House and access funds from the parliamentary budget to conduct research. In 1974, Social Credit had been granted official party status with only 11 members, so a precedent existed to bend the rules. Some Tories hoped that by denying the Créditiste party status they would cross the floor, giving Clark a majority government.

Short of bringing the Créditistes into the Tory fold, Clark could have made another deal: Créditiste votes in exchange for official party status. Granting official status could have sustained a Conservative administration over many years.

In the third week of September, Créditiste MP Richard Janelle, a unilingual Francophone, crossed the floor and joined the government. Since Clark had reappointed Liberal James Jerome Speaker of the House, the government was now only three votes short of majority. Roch LaSalle tried to bring more Québec MPs onside from both Liberal and Créditiste ranks. There were accusations that Tories were offering up Cabinet posts for those who switched sides, and the Créditiste leader asked the RCMP to investigate possible illegal offers.

After official party status was formally denied, Créditiste MPs protested in the House. They rose in their seats to ask questions, but were not recognized by the speaker: "We'll keep on doing it until they realize that we have rights here," said leader Fabian Roy. Government House leader Walter Baker urged the Speaker to relent, but this made little impression on the five remaining Créditistes.

Finance minister John Crosbie, determined to follow a responsible course in a "face the facts" budget to eliminate the deficit, delivered the Tory's first budget in the House of Commons on December 11, 1979. It was memorable mostly for a provision to increase the excise tax on gasoline by

18 cents per gallon (about 4 cents per litre), a measure designed to reduce the projected $13 billion deficit and reduce Canada's consumption of energy. Not quite a "green shift" carbon tax, but a step in that direction.

The following day, the buzz at the Liberal caucus Christmas party was that the Tories had blundered on the budget. MP and former Cabinet member Marc Lalonde concluded, "People will never accept that 18 cent excise tax." Liberals, he threatened, were prepared to defeat the government on this measure alone. It was not an idle threat. "We got those two guys in hospital, but one is coming up tonight, I think, and the other is coming tomorrow night for sure. We'll have all our members there." Lalonde and the Liberals had reason to be confident. The most recent Gallup Poll had the Tories at 28 percent support, 19 percentage points behind the Grits. The Tories, meanwhile, had limited insight on their standing, having conducted only one poll since the election on their political fortunes.

The Créditistes also opposed the 18 cent hike in gasoline tax because they said it would disproportionately affect the poor and vowed to abstain from any vote if it wasn't eliminated from the budget.

Clark had survived no-confidence votes before, including a key vote on the government's policies on Petro Canada, with the support of the Créditistes. But Petro Canada was not an issue that had the potential to excite Canadians, not like an 18-cent-a-gallon tax hike. The retiring Trudeau told his colleagues to vote their consciences on the budget: then added that if the government was defeated he would not lead the party in the election. The warning had no impact on warhorse Allan McEachern, who jumped to his feet in the Liberal caucus saying the Liberals had to take down the Tory government.

The Liberals and the NDP collaborated to draft the non-confidence motion, which was introduced by Bob Rae, who was then on the NDP front bench as finance critic: "This house unreservedly condemns the government for its outright betrayal of its election promises to lower interest rates, to cut taxes and to stimulate the growth of the Canadian economy without a mandate from the Canadian people for such a reversal."

While the plotting among opposition parties was in full swing, the Prime Minister's Office went about its business blissfully unaware. At a breakfast meeting on December 13, Nancy Jamieson, the prime minister's legislative assistant, reported at the end of the daily morning briefing to anyone who would listen that the government would be defeated that evening in the House of Commons. She was met with disbelief. Conservative whip Bill Kempling reported that six Conservative MPs would be unavailable to vote. If, as looked likely, the Créditistes abstained, the government simply did not have the votes. Clark's Chief of Staff, Bill Neville, dismissed the warning. Despite being far behind in the polls, Lowell Murray offered that the Tories would surely win a snap election. But even an elementary analysis of the political dynamic that December ought to have made it clear to the Tory brain trust that the Liberals would not hesitate to bring down the government.

The Clark government had momentum, but it was all downward. Since it had lost the popular vote in 1979, polling numbers had dropped. By November, the Tories were at 20 percent compared with 47 percent for the Liberals. The embassy issue had hurt Clark, inflation had worsened, and the privatization of Petrocan was going badly. Clark had cooked up a plan to give half of the government's shares in Petro Canada to Canadians, sell 20 percent, and keep 30 percent in the hands of government. The plan, made up on the fly, confused Canadians. But the most important issue was Québec. English Canadians had no confidence in Clark's ability to lead during the referendum. Four times as many Canadians thought Trudeau would be a better prime minister than Clark.

Even leaderless, the Liberals were not going to squander an opportunity to go to the people with a 20-point lead in the polls.

All efforts were made to bring the six MPs back to the house for the vote. Flora MacDonald, minister of external affairs, was in Brussels. The night before the vote she received a cable from the PMO, "Despite bold talk we believe diplomatic flu will hit the Liberal benches." Before leaving for Brussels she had inquired of the whip's office about pairing with a Liberal member and was told not to worry. A second MP was in the South Pacific. Two MPs—upset with Clark—were temporarily AWOL. The fifth, a defence lawyer, was in the middle of a trial in Calgary. The sixth was undergoing kidney treatment.

The government sought the opinion of the Privy Council Office on its options in the event it was defeated in the House. The memo from the clerk said: "Although any defeat during the budget debate would be regarded generally as a major defeat for the government, technically at least dissolution is not your only option."

There was one precedent worth noting: Lester Pearson had lost a confidence vote in 1968, just prior to his retirement and in advance of the scheduled Liberal leadership convention. Bob Stanfield let the government off the hook after being persuaded an election might damage confidence in the Canadian dollar.

A more practical and sensible option for Clark would have been to postpone the budget vote. The government's parliamentary House leader simply could have changed the order of debate to delay the non-confidence motion. Although this would have been met with howls of outrage and charges of foul play by the Opposition, who outside the parliamentary precinct would have understood or cared? A delay would have given the government time to marshal its forces and bring the Créditistes on side. It was that simple.

But Clark unwisely chose this occasion to make a defiant stand. Prime minister for only 28 weeks, he thought he could nimbly outflank the Liberals, who had been in power the whole of the previous sixteen years.

In a speech to the Burlington Chamber of Commerce on December 13, the day of the budget vote, Clark defended his government, saying it saw a lower deficit "as absolutely essential to achieving our far more important goals of lower inflation and lower unemployment. . . . there is not gain without pain." But selling pain and macroeconomics is rarely a winning political strategy.

Not all Liberals were keen to have an election. Leadership aspirant Jean Chrétien suggested to NDP leader Ed Broadbent on the evening of the vote that each party hold back two MPs to allow the government to survive. But Broadbent was intent on seeing the Clark government defeated.

The vote was scheduled for 9:45 p.m. In the late afternoon, a meeting was arranged between Tory emissaries and Créditiste leader Fabien Roy. He said his caucus would support the government if all the revenues from the 18 cent tax increase would go to Québec, a preposterous proposal that was immediately rejected.

By 6 p.m. the PMO was preparing a contingency plan in the event the vote was lost, and alerted the governor general's office of the need for a meeting the following morning.

Some 15 minutes before the confidence vote, the Créditistes made another offer. They would support the government if a tax credit was given to the poor to help offset the increase in the gas tax. It meant a tax expenditure of $1 billion, a huge blow to the government's effort to reduce the deficit. But it was a serious offer that was worth considering. Ray Hnatyshyn, the energy minister, recommended to Clark that he accept. But Clark was in no mood to back down. Fabien Roy claimed Clark was too proud for his own good. Clark denied a legitimate offer had been made, adding, "They certainly didn't make it to me because they knew I wouldn't have taken it seriously."

When it came time for the vote, and after much scrambling and cajoling, three Conservative MPs were absent. Only one Liberal member, Serge Joyal, was not in his seat. The Liberals and NDP combined to vote yea: 139 in all. The 133 Conservatives in the House voted nay. The two Créditistes abstained.

Clark immediately rose to his feet. "I rise on a point of order. The government has lost the vote on a matter which we have no alternative but to regard as a question of confidence. I simply want to advise the House that I will be seeing his Excellency the Governor General tomorrow morning."

John Crosbie claimed the nine-month government was "long enough to conceive, just not long enough to deliver." In a media scrum in the foyer of the House of Commons immediately after the no-confidence vote, Crosbie vented his outrage: "There is going to be revulsion at the avidity for power, at the lust for power, displayed by the Liberal opposition. Disgusting. When they don't even have a leader themselves . . . The people of Canada are going to rise up against this and put an end to the years of Liberal arrogance and dominance in this country."

The election date was set for February 18, 1980.

Trudeau announced a special Liberal caucus meeting for the morning after the non-confidence vote. He told his caucus that he would fight the campaign as leader but, in typical arrogant Trudeau style, he said, "The sovereign would have to ask me three times." The gist of his message was that the call to return would have to be overwhelming, if not unanimous. For the Liberals, many issues came into play: the upcoming referendum on sovereignty in Québec, the ambitions of leadership hopefuls, the constitution of the Liberal party, and the practicalities of holding a convention in the middle of an election. Then there were political considerations. Could Trudeau win? What would be the impact on his legacy if he lost? Would the Liberal party end up being nothing more than a home base for Québec politicians?

Defeating the government while they themselves had no leader was an astonishing display of bravado for the Liberal caucus. Of course the polls were influential, but they also believed that Clark was in over his head and that his 1979 win was a fluke.

Trudeau did not receive the unanimous support he had outlined as a condition to his return. The following Monday evening he told his advisers he was going for a walk and would announce his decision at a news conference the following morning. At 8:30 a.m. on Tuesday, he told his personal secretary he was stepping down. Later that morning he addressed the media: "I have accepted the strong appeal of the national Liberal caucus and the national Liberal executive and I will lead our party in the current election campaign. . . . My duty is to accept the draft of my party—that duty was stronger even than my desire to continue with my plan to re-enter private life."

No one in the Liberal caucus challenged this questionable version of events, and no one disputed Trudeau's right to rescind his resignation.

WHAT CANADIANS KNEW of the Clark government was mostly negative— specifically, bungling the embassy in Israel and the 18-cent-per-gallon tax increase. They knew little of Clark's proposals to increase transparency and accountability in government. These included better use of parliamentary committees; immigration files disclosed to the Human Rights Commissioner; immigration eligibility rules made public; a central registry of lobbyists; restrictions on crown privilege related to access of information requests; and less party discipline in the House of Commons. These reforms were important, but not likely to resonate during an election.

Clark refused to make any appointments after the writ was dropped, saying they would be illegitimate and unethical. Clark's appointments chief, Jean Pigott, had amassed multiple binders listing appointments intended for Tory hopefuls. But Clark never took the list to Cabinet.

As much as Tories hoped the campaign would be about Liberal arrogance and the past failures of Trudeau administrations, the real issue was the leadership of Joe Clark. The Liberal campaign motto neatly summed up the problem: "A leader must be a leader." Clark highlighted Liberal arrogance as the main campaign issue: "The opposition parties have decided to disrupt the nation's business. That was not our choice; we wanted to get on with governing the country . . . Unfortunately from the first day, the opposition party showed no interest in making Parliament work. . . . Now they have brought it to a complete halt."

If you are returned with either a minority or majority government, reporters asked him, will you reintroduce the 18-cent-per-gallon tax increase? Clark responded with a firm "yes." Clark should have noticed that Ontario PC Premier Bill Davis had spoken out against the gas tax increase over fears it would harm the Ontario economy. But Clark could hardly repudiate the budget measure that had precipitated the election.

With a big lead in the polls the Liberal strategy was to keep Pierre Trudeau under wraps and out of sight. So invisible was Trudeau that 29 journalists signed a petition in week five of the campaign demanding he hold a press conference. The Liberals even declined to put Trudeau in a leader's debate against Clark.

Clark went on the offensive against the AWOL Liberal leader. "[Trudeau] is the only political leader in the history of this country . . . whose slogan has been 'elect me and I will quit'. Of course, you have to remember, he is the fellow who said in 1974 'elect me and I will never introduce wage and price controls' . . . the Liberals have a 'peek-a-boo' campaign . . . and the whole theme of their campaign is to have [Trudeau] sneak in and out of town before anyone can notice."

This campaign was about leadership all right, but it was Clark's leadership, not Trudeau's. The Tories had to bring Trudeau down by reminding Canadians of his free-spending socialist policies. While Clark held that Canada was a "community of communities," Trudeau claimed the Tory leader was nothing more than a head waiter to the provinces. Clark, who campaigned under the slogan "Real change deserves a fair chance," did his best to contrast his style of leadership with Trudeau's: ". . . leadership is not just a matter of appearing on camera. . . . Leadership is also a matter of being able to establish priorities and manage people . . . Things that went wrong during the Trudeau years went wrong precisely because there had been a failure at the center to be able to bring people together and point them in the direction where they could take the country. And I think we have been much more successful, not only in attracting good people but in keeping them and in getting them working together. That . . . is my definition of what leadership should be."

The only good news in the Tory campaign came on January 27, 1980, when American diplomats stationed in Iran were led to safety using Canadian passports. In this instance Clark demonstrated he could handle both a crisis and international affairs. The Liberals wisely pulled television ads slamming Clark off the air for a few days while the Iran caper played itself out.

Election Day was like a funeral for the Tory party. The Liberals increased their popular support by 4.2 percentage points over the 1979 election, while the Tories' fell by 3.4 points. It was enough to give Trudeau a commanding majority government. The Clark government had lasted eight months and twenty-seven days.

The Tory caucus was reduced to 103 seats from the 136 it had won only months earlier. Losses came in every province except Alberta, where the Tories won every seat in both campaigns. The major damage was done in Ontario, where the Tories lost 18 seats to the Liberals and one to the NDP. It was also a bad day for the Créditistes, who were rewarded for their role in defeating the government by losing all their seats. After that, the party ceased to exist as a political force.

All this could easily have been avoided had Clark not bungled the vote on his government's budget on December 13. What was at stake was enormous. With the levers of power back in the hands of Pierre Trudeau the government implemented the National Energy Program (causing economic dislocation and a rapid rise if western alienation), the Foreign Investment Review Agency (undermining the confidence of international and domestic investors) and constitutional reform that proceeded without the agreement of the government of Québec (giving ammunition to Québec's separatist movement). It was a costly mistake for Clark to make for his party and the country.

DESPITE LONG ODDS, Clark chose to hang onto the leadership to fight another day. At a 1981 party convention in Ottawa, he survived a vote on his leadership with a weak approval rating of 66 percent.

Clark's most notable accomplishment during his second term as Opposition leader was standing up to Pierre Trudeau's constitutional proposals. The amending formula advocated by Trudeau was so rigid and narrow it would have weakened the clout of western provinces. Facing stiff opposition from Clark, Trudeau referred his proposal to the Supreme Court and on September 28, 1981 the court upheld Trudeau's plan as constitutional, but raised concerns about the legitimacy of Trudeau's approach because of a lack of provincial support. This led to another round of negotiations that ultimately produced an agreement between the federal government and every province except Québec.

Trudeau was undaunted and ignored Québec's traditional veto over constitutional change. In effect, he ignored the advice of Sir John A. Macdonald that a prime minister ought not to meddle with the Constitution until it is evident that people are suffering from its effects. The new Constitution was signed in the presence of the Queen on April 17, 1982, a day of self-declared mourning for nationalists in Québec. When Trudeau was about to affix his signature to the document, Liberal senator Jean Marchand whispered into the ear of Maureen McTeer calling Trudeau a "Traitre."

Clark's next test of leadership came at the party's convention in Winnipeg in January 1983. Clark used the resources of his office and party headquarters to shore up his support. But he could not persuade many caucus members who believed the party would never win under his leadership.

On December 6, 1982, Clark lined up an endorsement from Brian Mulroney at a press conference at Montréal's Ritz-Carlton Hotel. Mulroney said, "Mr. Clark's reconfirmation as leader is an important part of (changing the government). His subsequent re-election as Prime Minister will be good for Canada." When asked privately by Clark what he thought was required in Winnipeg to sustain his leadership, Mulroney replied: "Well, Joseph, if 66 percent was good enough in 1981, it goddamn will be good enough today." The following morning, on CBC Radio, Mulroney expanded on the reasons he was backing his leader: "Joe Clark won [one] and lost one (election) . . . this is an old baseball town and we don't put .500 hitters on waivers . . . I'm going to vote for Mr. Clark."

Many of Mulroney's supporters were furious at his entente with Clark. Despite it, however, a team fronted by former Newfoundland premier Frank Moores led a stealth campaign against Clark and for a leadership review. "The thing was to work hard without anyone knowing about it," said Moores. Elmer McKay, a Nova Scotia MP, was the key link in caucus. He had gathered a petition signed by Tory MPs asking Clark to step down.

A senior Clark aide confidently predicted that his leader would eclipse the psychologically important 70 percent mark at the Winnipeg convention on January 28. A pre-convention CTV news poll predicted 76 percent would support Clark as leader. Technically, all Clark required was a vote of 50 percent to avoid a full-scale leadership contest. But after the ballots were counted, he was taken into a private room and was told he had received only 66 percent support.

Senator Lowell Murray told Clark 66 percent "was not enough." Finlay Macdonald cautioned Clark to wait thirty-six hours before making a decision. "You go and tell them thanks for the support, it wasn't quite what I was looking for and I'll announce my decision to the national executive on Sunday." Clark remembered some placards carried by delegates on the floor with the bold phrase "Go, Joe, Go . . . Please!" More important, over half the Tory caucus had voted for a leadership review. Although the PC party was at 49 percent in the public opinion polls, sporting a 20 percentage point lead over the Grits, the caucus thought Clark would find a way to lose the election.

After taking time to collect his thoughts, Clark decided he could not lead with that level of dissension. According to Maureen McTeer, "The back-stabbing and endless undermining of his leadership and personal integrity had to stop. If he won, he would have the authority to move forward with confidence to lead the party in Parliament and into the next election, expected within the year. . . . If he lost, well . . . we did not think about losing."

After the result of the vote was announced Clark addressed delegates and a national television audience. He was going to put his leadership to the ultimate test, much the same way he had put his government to the test in December 1979. "I asked tonight for a clear mandate to carry the party to victory. I received the support of a clear majority of the delegates voting here . . . but that mandate is not clear enough. . . . It is not clear enough to enforce the kind of discipline and achieve the kind of unity that this party requires . . . my friends, we know that the greatest enemy this party faces is uncertainty about our unity . . . I have been struggling to hold this party together for the last two years. But until we have silenced all the serious critics in our ranks we will not prove our capacity to form a government to the people of his country. Consequently, I will be recommending to the national executive of the party that they call a convention at the earliest possible time. I want to take this occasion to announce . . . I will be a candidate for that leadership."

Mulroney was flabbergasted, but Elmer MacKay was not surprised. "Sure, he could've hung on. But it would have been the bloodiest fight the party had ever seen. The people who were opposing him were pretty strong-minded guys."

Clark had been forced to listen to a storm of abuse from his critics: that he was weak, timid, and incompetent. He was determined to prove them wrong, or go down in flames trying.

Surrendering the leader's chair nullified his agreement with Mulroney. Those in caucus who supported Clark out of deference to their leader were liberated to speak their minds and support others. The party divided into two camps: pro-Clark and anybody but Clark.

Clark's judgment in resigning as leader after receiving two-thirds support from party delegates was enough to convince party members that he wasn't up to the job. His next official position would be as minister for external affairs in the government of Brian Mulroney.

SECTION VII

CHOOSING TO WIN:
MARTIN BRIAN MULRONEY

CHAPTER 23

FIRST QUÉBECER TO LEAD

*Let us accept Macdonald's invitation and let us recreate that grand
alliance, and in the process, together we shall build a new Conservative Party and
we shall build a brand new Canada.*

AFTER SIR JOHN A. MACDONALD, the next greatest Canadian
Conservative coalition builder is Brian Mulroney. He did what most
Canadians thought impossible: he won two successive Conservative
majority governments and 81 percent of the seats in Québec. When it came
to governing, Mulroney was a free spender of political capital. He pushed
through fundamental—often unpopular—changes. He restructured the
Canadian economy and built a new foundation that would deliver prosperity
for decades to come. These fundamental but contentious reforms have stood
the test of time; his record in economic, environmental and international relations stands above most prime ministers in any party. He irritated many, and
when he left office he took with him the lowest approval ratings of any prime
minister. To this day he remains a fixture in the consciousness of Canadians,
drawing both praise and scorn in large doses.

Martin Brian Mulroney was born on March 20, 1939, the third of six
children for Ben Mulroney and Mary Irene O'Shea. Ben Mulroney was an
electrician who moved to the company town of Baie Comeau on the north
shore of the St. Lawrence to work in the pulp and paper mill. The town was
established in the 1930s by Robert McCormick to produce the pulp to make

newsprint for American newspapers, of which owned many.

Young Brian thrived in Baie Comeau. He moved effortlessly between the French and English elements in the town and was known to be a connector and mediator between the two communities. Not a gifted academic, he had a natural curiosity about history and politics. He and his dictionary were never far apart, and he had a passion for singing. When he was seven or eight years old he was asked by Colonel McCormick to sing an old standard, "Dearie," for which he was given a crisp $50 bill. But it was his ability in public speaking that proved more important to his ultimate career choice. Mulroney won every public speaking contest he entered.

Mulroney attended St. Thomas College in New Brunswick then enrolled at St. Francis Xavier University in Antigonish, Nova Scotia in 1955. At St. FX, where he was nicknamed "bones" on account of his physique, he was active in student politics and was elected leader of the campus PC club. He met many lifelong friends in the club, notably Sam Wakim, Fred Doucet, and Pat McAdam. Lowell Murray was also part of their clique. Mulroney would venture off campus to work on political campaigns when he could. In 1956, he attended the national Conservative leadership convention and was a vice-chairman of Youth for Diefenbaker. In the model Parliament at St. FX, Mulroney, eighteen, was prime minister. In his senior year at university he was elected vice president of the national PC Student Federation.

He graduated in 1959, and entered law school at Laval University, where he established a new gang of friends, including Lucien Bouchard, Peter White, and Michael Meighen. In Québec City he befriended Daniel Johnson, then leader of the Union Nationale and leader of the opposition in the Québec legislature. Another friend was future Liberal Cabinet minister, Pierre de Bané. "Brian was the only guy in the class everybody liked," said de Bané. "He was very popular with all the guys, left–right, federalist–indépendantiste, English or French. He crossed all those lines."

At Laval he was also a leading organizer of the "Congres des Affaires Canadiennes" held in 1961. It was through this event and his academic studies that Mulroney developed his sense of Québec's place in the Canadian political dynamic. He even corresponded with Pierre Trudeau on the matter.

Mulroney's heart and mind were never far away from federal politics. He regularly spoke or corresponded with Prime Minister Diefenbaker and in 1962 took a summer job working in the office of Alvin Hamilton, minister of agriculture. After his fellow students belittled Mulroney's claim that he had political connections, he brought Prime Minister Diefenbaker to a law school class.

Mulroney was hired by the prestigious Montréal law firm of Howard, Cate, Ogilvy. There was a hiccup in launching his legal career: Mulroney flunked the bar exam on procedure.

Mulroney's skills as a mediator and negotiator made him a natural for labour law. It was a contentious time for labour-management relations, particularly on the Montréal waterfront where strikes were common and often turned violent. Mulroney was always on the management side of the table.

His abilities came to the attention of Paul Desmarais, who was anxious to end a work stoppage at his newspaper, *La Presse*. A typical Mulroney tactic was employed: hunker down with the parties in a high-price hotel; give them lavish amounts of food and booze; and work around-the-clock until a deal was done.

While practising law, Mulroney remained active within the PC party as an organizer and fundraiser. There were few like him in Québec at the time— in fact there were few PCs in Québec at all. Mulroney's political connections occasionally resulted in business opportunities. In 1969, he was offered the Lotto Québec franchise for the West Island of Montréal. "I said no," Mulroney told biographer L. Ian MacDonald. "I felt it was improper for someone who had been involved in politics to gain from it. And I turned it down . . . I knew that one day I would be actively involved, not in the back rooms, and I never wanted it said of me that I ever, ever, made a nickel in politics." Ironically, some 15 years after his retirement, the former prime minister would be hounded by accusations of unethical conduct related to lobbying activity for which he was paid in cash.

As the key Québec organizer for Tory leader Bob Stanfield in the early 1970s, Mulroney was instrumental in persuading former Cabinet minister and judge Claude Wagner to run for the party. A $300,000 trust fund formed part of the bargain. It may not have been so untoward for Wagner to seek financial security before agreeing to a very risky venture; however, Wagner turned it into a major story when he denied such a fund existed.

Mulroney was thus well-known inside Tory party circles but had little, if any, public persona. That changed when Québec premier Robert Bourassa tagged Mulroney to serve as one of three panelists on a commission examining the violence and corruption in Québec's construction industry. The work of the commission, which featured almost daily titillating detail of scandalous behaviour, put Mulroney in the newspapers and on television. Mulroney recruited his friend Lucien Bouchard to serve as the commission's associate counsel.

In 1973, Mulroney married Mila Pivnicki, a university student he had met poolside at the Mount Royal Tennis Club the year before. The Mulroneys had four children, Caroline, Ben, Mark, and Nicolas, the youngest born on the first anniversary of Mulroney's 1984 election win.

BY THE TIME ROBERT STANFIELD stepped down as leader in 1976, many in the party had identified Mulroney as a potential leader. From his days in the YPC, to his organizing in Québec, Mulroney had at his disposal a deep and wide network of influential contacts across the country. With strong financial backing he declared his candidacy on November 13, 1975. "It doesn't take a doctorate from the Université de Montréal to know that it is out of the question for the Conservative party to form a government without substantial support from Québec." Despite his well-formed ideas on Québec's place in Confederation, he was perceived as vague on matters of policy. Columnist Alan Fotheringham dubbed Mulroney "the candidate from whimsy."

Mulroney had never before placed his name on a ballot, and the 1976 convention did not go well. In the preamble to the convention, John Diefenbaker admonished any candidate who sought to lead without the benefit of parliamentary experience. Mulroney murmured to himself, "I'm going to get hammered badly. The great gang bang is on."

The thirty-six-year-old candidate placed second on the first ballot, behind Claude Wagner. He was also 80 votes ahead of the eventual winner, Joe Clark, who had started out in third place with 12 percent support. And while Mulroney's support grew on the second ballot, he was overtaken by Clark, who gobbled up the delegates from lesser-ranked candidates unimpressed with either Mulroney or Wagner. Other than being a Québecer, Mulroney was knocked for being too slick, too close to the powerful. He had never held elected office, was too imperial, and perhaps perceived too successful to relate to the rank-and-file of the party. Mulroney was devastated. After the defeat, Pierre Trudeau thought enough of Mulroney to offer him a seat in the Liberal Cabinet. "I'm a Conservative," was the reply.

His legal and business acumen, as well as his political connections, made Mulroney attractive to the private sector. Not long after the leadership defeat, he was comfortably ensconced as the president of the Iron Ore Company of Canada Ltd. He was sufficiently comfortable in the role of business tycoon that when Joe Clark's leadership faced the inevitable rough patches after the 1980 election, Mulroney never became personally engaged in the campaign for a leadership review, and in 1982 he appeared with Joe Clark at the Ritz-Carlton Hotel to offer his support. Such support was not forthcoming from many of Mulroney's friends, many of who had actively organized against Clark, including Guy Charbonneau, Frank Moores, Peter White, Sam Wakim, Elmer McKay, and Michel Cogger. These men would become key players on Mulroney's 1983 leadership campaign team.

Before and at the 1983 PC Winnipeg convention that voted on Clark's leadership, Mulroney kept his distance. "I didn't want anyone organizing in my name and I counselled (my friends) not to organize at all." Former Newfoundland premier, Frank Moores, who led a discreet campaign for a leadership review at the convention, described his dilemma: "It's been a hectic two years. The thing was to work hard without anyone knowing about it."

With the American steel industry facing severe cutbacks, the Iron Ore Company mine in Schefferville, Québec was slated for closure. Putting hundreds of Québec workers on the unemployment lines would likely doom any entry into elected politics for Mulroney. But Mulroney handled the closure with compassion, sensitivity, and generosity to the laid-off workers. In the process, he earned the respect and admiration of the people of Schefferville and of Québec's opinion leaders, and escaped a potential landmine without being damaged.

In 1983, the Conservative party came to accept Mulroney's fundamental argument that it was time a Québecer took the helm. Only once in its history had the party tried a Québecer as party leader—anglophone John Abbott, who held the post for eighteen months at the end of the previous century. Abbott was not a defender of the French fact in Canada, however. If anything, he was motivated to protect English minority rights in Québec.

Mulroney said he was as surprised as anyone when Joe Clark decided that the support of 66 percent of the delegates was not enough for him to lead the party into the next election. But from the day Clark declared the party would hold a leadership convention, Mulroney was a contender.

Mulroney waited until provincial premiers Bill Davis from Ontario and Peter Lougheed from Alberta decided they would not contest the leadership contest before he made his decision to run. On March 21, 1983, the first day of spring, he announced his candidacy at the National Press Theatre in Ottawa, and made the outrageous pledge that he would become prime minister by winning seats for the Tories in Québec. Mulroney's oft-repeated refrain went something like this: "There are 102 seats with the Francophone component of more than 10 percent (in Québec, New Brunswick and Ontario). In 1980, the Tory party won two. In Québec we lost our deposits in 56 seats, we finished third in 41 seats, were behind the NDP in 39 seats, and behind the Rhinoceros party in two." The data were a less-than-subtle dig at Clark, who won only two of Québec's 75 seats in 1979, and only one as prime minister in 1980.

Mulroney's entry into the race coincided with that of John Crosbie, Clark's former minister of finance. Thinking he might need support from Crosbie down the line, Mulroney called him to apologize if the timing was an inconvenience. Mulroney wanted warm relations with every candidate, with the possible exception of Joe Clark. "It was clear to me that the mood between candidates was going to be important, and that because of a number of matters it would not be favourable to Clark."

Although Clark had resigned as leader, he carried many of the advantages of incumbency. His team controlled party headquarters, where pressure was exerted to hold delegate selection meetings as early as possible before other candidates could get organized. The brevity of preparation for Mulroney's team necessitated creative measures in recruiting party members, such as tapping the residents from the "Old Brewery Mission." Party rules allowed for delegates from accredited educational institutions, and leadership candidates left no "driving Academy, flying school or beauty college" unrepresented at the convention. Clark was not beyond aggressive tactics of his own, noting, "Democracy isn't a tea party."

Unlike 1976, this time Mulroney had support from the Tory caucus. Before he announced his decision to run, Mulroney went to Ottawa to meet caucus members. George Hees, the MP from the Ontario riding of Northumberland, got right to the point: "Brian. Let's cut the bullshit. You have my support." Hees later explained why he was not supporting Clark. "Well, I'll tell you something, Brian. Joe Clark is a fine man and all that, but when he walks into a room, I don't know whether to stand up and salute, or send him for a fresh pack of Sweet Caps [cigarettes]."

In the course of the leadership campaign Clark made inroads in Québec by recruiting soft nationalists to his team. Mulroney accused him of "playing footsies with the Parti Québecois." Clark even received the endorsement of well-known Québec separatist Pierre Bourgault. Conrad Black believed separatists aligned with Clark because they thought he was a "pushover." In the end, Clark and Mulroney had recruited roughly the same number of delegates in Québec, a huge victory for Clark against a native son.

Clark also ruffled feathers in Ontario when he alluded to Bill Davis, then Ontario premier and rumoured to be entering the contest, as a "regional candidate." It was enough to swing Davis loyalists into the ABC, "Anybody but Clark," camp.

Heading into the convention, most of the momentum was with John Crosbie. But the colourful Newfoundlander undermined his chances with short-tempered remarks interpreted by some as anti-French. Being unilingual, argued Crosbie, did not mean he could not communicate with the French. "I cannot talk to the Chinese people in their language either." It was a typical Crosbie quip, but Québecers were unimpressed. Initially, Crosbie was unapologetic. "There are 18 to 19 million unilingual Canadians and I don't think they should be disenfranchised . . . It is better to be honest and sincere in one language than a twister, a trickster, and a twit in two." Mulroney took the opening that was offered: "We expect a finance minister to know something about economics . . . and we expect our Prime Minister to know something about Québec."

Mulroney had to address the perceptions, based largely on his performance in the 1976 leadership campaign, that he lacked vision, was too slick, was beholden to the powerful and wealthy, and was disconnected from the grassroots of the party. This time around, he ran a low-lustre, lowbrow, alcohol-free, and Main Street campaign. He toned down the charm and bluster and presented himself in a more serious light. His credentials: he was the only leading candidate with private sector experience—and he would win Québec. Mulroney shored up his policy flank by releasing a 103-page paperback book titled "Where I Stand," and distributed it free to all 3,000 delegates. The book was neither deep nor provocative, but it did address the charge that he was weak on policy. Of the multi-nation theory of Canada that had been debated by the party at the 1967 convention, he wrote, "In any discussion of constitutional reform, I start from the premise of an indivisible Canada . . . I do not believe in the theory of two nations, five nations, or 10 nations . . . Nor do I believe in the concept that would give any one province an advantage over the other." He also reminded readers why Conservatives had such a long losing record: "A condition precedent to electoral success must be tangible proof to the Canadian people the Progressive Conservative party is genuinely united."

Mulroney attempted to neutralize the impact of a perception that he was generally weak on policy by saying, "All of the candidates have good policies, but all of these policies aren't worth the powder to blow them across the street if we don't get elected." His overarching message was "elect me and we will form government."

He tantalized party faithful with the power of patronage. "Look around this room," he said in a meeting of delegates. "I see half a dozen senators, maybe one or two judges. . . . Oh, there'll be jobs for Liberals and NDPers too, but only after I've been Prime Minister for 15 years and I can't find a single living, breathing Tory to appoint."

Mulroney sought support among the right-wing delegates by saying he would give civil servants "a pink slip and a pair of running shoes." But John Crosbie was the darling of the right. "What would be the point of having a Conservative party," declared Crosbie, "if it is not to the right? We might as well be Liberals or socialists. I am to the right."

Crosbie, whose campaign team was led by one of Canada's leading political professionals, John Laschinger, was gaining ground as everyone's "second choice," an enviable place given the strong sentiment to oust Clark. Crosbie explained why he wanted the top job. "If you are in business you want to become president of the company, if you're in politics you want to become leader." Crosbie had the capacity to entertain and was full of one-liners. When the Liberals changed the country to the metric system, Crosbie quipped, "Nothing could be sweeter than to fool you with the litre." On the Crown Corporation, Canadair, he said, ". . . it should be called how can they dare!"

But Crosbie was no "slash and burn" politician. "The Canadian people are moving to the right . . . and I'm to the right in my business and finance positions. I try to emphasize that but, no, I wouldn't cut a dollar from any social program." Crosbie went out on a limb during the campaign and boldly advocated a free trade agreement or common market arrangement with the United States. "I'm not afraid to have this issue discussed, to put it before the Canadian people and I believe that any further steps taken along the road of so-called Canadian economic nationalism will doom the people of this country to a dubious and diminishing economic future. This is not a pro-American approach, it is pro-Canadian."

Referring to Mulroney's lack of parliamentary experience, Crosbie noted, "Unless you've been in the trenches, unless you've been 'over-the-top' as a corporal, or a sergeant or Captain . . . you should not expect to become the commanding general. I have a seat in Parliament. If I'm elected leader, I only have to move over two places."

But it was an exasperated Crosbie's impertinent remarks about the French language that defined and would doom his campaign: "I'm not some kind of criminal. I'm just an ordinary Canadian who has been in politics for a long time and has a lot to offer. Just because I'm not fluent in French language doesn't mean that disaster is going to occur. There are 20 million of us who are unilingual English or French . . . I don't think that the 3.7 million who are bilingual should suddenly think themselves some kind of aristocracy and only leaders can come from their small group."

Crosbie later apologized. In his convention speech, he tried speaking French, fractured as it was, to mollify his critics. But the damage was done.

Michael Wilson was another key figure in the leadership race. Elected

to Parliament in 1974 from the Toronto-area riding of Etobicoke, thoughtful and serious, though often described as wooden, Wilson had the austere
posture of a finance minister. While he was a man to be respected, he was
not a serious contender. What Wilson did have was the potential to be kingmaker. He had been unfailingly loyal to Clark right up until the leadership
race was thrown wide open in Winnipeg. In deciding to run against Clark,
Wilson remarked, "Frankly, I got tired of having to defend him." Wilson
positioned himself as a unity candidate, someone who could draw the party
together. But he needed a strong first-ballot result, something greater than
the 12 percent support Clark had received at the 1976 convention. Wilson
thought he had a chance.

Rounding out the leadership contestants were former Toronto Mayor
David Crombie, lawyer John Gamble, public servant Neil Fraser, and high-
flying Alberta entrepreneur and owner of the Edmonton Oilers Peter
Pocklington. In his book on the art of political campaigning, *Lesser Mortals*,
John Laschinger recounted the trials of Pocklington's inexperience. Trying
to drum up support in PEI, he came face to face with some tough questions.
Pocklington replied:

"That was a very good question. What's your name?"

"My name is Jim Lee," came the response.

"And what do you do in Prince Edward Island, Jim?"

"I'm the Premier."

Mulroney addressed the convention on June 10, 1983, the day before the
vote. His speech dealt not with innovative policy initiatives or a national
vision, but with a political strategy based on a grand coalition that would
bring Conservatives, at long last, out of the wilderness and into power. "Our
major purpose . . . in being here is to drive the Liberals from office and bring
about a majority Progressive Conservative government." Mulroney called
party unity a pre-condition to victory, and pledged to follow an eleventh
commandment: "Thou Shall Never Speak Ill of Another Conservative."
Recognizing the breadth of Conservatives represented in the party, Mulroney
said, "There shall be no incivility because of divergent views . . . there shall be
no ideological tests of purity, absolutely none."

Mulroney boldly challenged the delegates to face up to a historical reality: "Why is it that when we put on our hats as federal Conservatives . . .
everyone says we are a bunch of losers? . . . [O]ur area of weakness in French
Canada, time after time, decade after decade, election after election, has
staggered this Party and debilitated the nation."

Invoking the memory of the Old Chieftain, Mulroney continued: "Let us accept Macdonald's invitation and let us recreate that grand alliance, English and French, East and West, new Canadians and old, and in the process, together we shall build a new Conservative Party and we shall build a brand new Canada."

In other words, elect me as leader and I will deliver seats from Québec. Given Liberal hegemony in Québec, few believed this was possible. But Mulroney had deep connections in Québec and a political machine the Tories had not had at their disposal since 1958 when Diefenbaker had the support of Québec premier Maurice Duplessis. Mulroney's appeal to soft Québec nationalists was unspoken, but real and legitimate. The party could also verify Mulroney's Québec bona fides by the large number of Québec delegates he brought with him to the convention.

Clark came into the convention with the most pledged delegates, but was far from a majority. To win, most pundits thought he needed to have at least 40 percent of the vote on the first ballot or the "ABC movement" would overwhelm him. The next big convention test was between Mulroney and Crosbie for who would face Clark on the final ballot. Pundits thought Crosbie needed to be within 150 votes of Mulroney on the first ballot to have a chance.

The first ballot put Clark in the lead with 1,091 votes or 36.5 percent support. If he could bring on board about 400 delegates supporting other candidates, about one in five, the leadership was his. But he was doomed from the outset.

After the vote, Peter Pocklington called Michael Wilson. He was going to Mulroney and wanted Wilson with him. Pocklington had told Crosbie the night before that he would support the Newfoundlander if he was within 200 votes of Mulroney. The actual difference was 235 votes (874 to 639). Mulroney, who was eager for Pocklington's 102 delegates, was willing to consider Pocklington's idea for a royal commission on taxation. Pocklington and Wilson initially walked in the direction of Crosbie, causing a near panic in the Mulroney box. They quickly reversed direction, however, and landed in Mulroney's section.

Three of Clark's key supporters—Bill McKnight, Don Mazankowski, and Jake Epp—were disheartened by the first ballot and had concluded their man would lose to Mulroney on the final ballot. They told John Laschinger that unless Clark gained support on the second ballot they would move to Crosbie on the third, to prevent a Mulroney victory. David Crombie, who stayed on after the first ballot despite receiving a paltry 67 votes, had made this fairly complicated scenario possible. If Crombie had pulled out, Crosbie would have been in last place, and out after the second ballot. With Crombie staying in, Crosbie had a chance to reshape the convention dynamic.

Mulroney's organizers knew they would win a final ballot against Clark, but were equally sure that they would lose to Crosbie if Clark's forces drifted to Crosbie on the third ballot. When some Clark youth delegates came to Mulroney's box after the first ballot they were told by organizer Bill Pristanski to stay put until the final ballot. To thwart Crosbie, Mulroney did not want to precipitate Clark's early demise.

On the second ballot, Clark lost six votes. Crombie was low man and went to Crosbie. Clark was stunned. "I had no idea desire for change was so great." Mulroney increased his total by 147 and Crosbie gained 142, leaving the gap between Mulroney and Crosbie at 240 votes. Crosbie's team knew Clark's day was done. John Laschinger told Lowell Murray, "Our people prefer Mulroney two to one over Clark . . . You can lose to us or lose to Mulroney."

In her autobiography, Maureen McTeer described the scene in which Newfoundland Premier Brian Peckford asked her husband to withdraw before the third ballot and support Crosbie: "The number-three person on the ballot was asking the number-one candidate and current leader to fold up his tent and join his camp against the number-two contender. It might have made sense to the Crosbie team, but it made no sense to us at all . . . I turned to Doug Bassett . . . and said, 'Get this stupid bastard out of here.'"

A proud man, Clark could not swallow what was being asked of him and he couldn't fathom ganging-up on Mulroney, which would have caused further splits for the party in Québec.

The third ballot showed further decline in Clark's number, to 35.8 percent, but he remained in first place. Crosbie placed third, setting up a final ballot between Clark and Mulroney. All the suspense was gone. Mulroney's victory was assured. As predicted, Crosbie's vote went to Mulroney by a margin of slightly more than two to one. Mulroney won with 54.5 percent of the final ballot votes.

Mulroney immediately reached out to the other seven leadership contestants, all of whom represented different Conservative constituencies. In his convention acceptance speech, he publicly indicated his desire to work with friend and foe alike. Erik Nielsen, the party's interim leader, was at the podium after Mulroney had been declared victorious. Nielsen reminded the delegates that Mulroney had not been *his* first choice. Without missing a beat, Mulroney announced that Nielsen was *his* first choice as deputy leader. In that instant, Mulroney showed the discipline, wisdom, and grace that inspired loyalty and drew the Conservative family together. Mulroney also graciously embraced Mazankowski, McKnight and Epp into his inner circle despite them conspiring against him on the convention floor. "That's just leadership politics," Mulroney explained.

To reinvigorate the failed leadership candidates, Mulroney ensured that their campaign debts were paid off, principally by helping out with fundraisers. It's a lesson former Liberal leader Stéphane Dion ignored. In 2008, nearly two years after the Liberal leadership contest was decided, he sat idly by while his front bench filled the obligatory repayment plans with Elections Canada on how they proposed to address a collective debt of close to $2 million. This did not help Liberal party unity or endear Dion's rivals to their new boss, though his tenure was short lived.

Mulroney then turned his attention to party finances. "He didn't want to go to the people of Canada to elect his party and him as prime minister if we didn't have our own books balanced and if we didn't have a frugal mindset," said Mulroney team member David Angus. "We had to be able to present a responsible financial position, which we did." It is ironic that, having placed such a premium on getting his party's financial house in order, Mulroney would come to be so heavily criticized when it came to dealing with the government deficit.

Mulroney recognized that his coalition had four distinct blocs. He would deliver Québec, but he needed support from deep conservative Atlantic roots, the western free enterprise crowd, and Ontario's "big blue machine." David Angus recalls that Mulroney counted on the provincial party machines to deliver the vote in the regions of the country in which he was least known: "But Québec was the key to this thing. The Créditistes were no longer active, and Brian had a tremendous network in Québec with an organization on the ground. We had organizers from the Québec Liberal Party and the Parti Québécois. Brian seemed to know everybody."

Mulroney was anxious to confront Trudeau in the House of Commons. Elmer MacKay resigned his Central Nova seat in Nova Scotia in favour of his leader, and schooled Mulroney in the art of small-town politics. The Liberals contested the by-election, but the Mulroney charm and his addiction to hard work produced a landslide victory on August 29, 1983. His overarching message was "elect me and we will form government."

At the time, the national polls placed the Tories on top with 62 percent support, compared with Trudeau's 23 percent.

Before Parliament reconvened from the summer break, Mulroney met with his caucus. "The real prize," he told them, "is over there at 24 Sussex

Drive, but we can't get there without discipline." The first test of discipline arose on September 13, Mulroney's second day in the House, when the Liberals set a trap that they were sure would divide Tory ranks. Liberal MP Robert Bockstael introduced a motion in support of French language education rights in Manitoba. This issue had led to the defeat of a previous Tory government and caused much grief for Stanfield and every Tory leader back to Macdonald. Mulroney, whose leadership was being tested in caucus and by his opponents, was up to the task. He challenged caucus not to be duped by Liberal tactics. "(The resolution) is based on the assumption that each and every one of you is stupid enough not to recognize what is going on, and that some of you will vote against this, thereby splitting the party and holding us up to the accusation that if we can't govern ourselves, we can't govern Canada."

When it was reported to Mulroney that he did not have unanimous caucus support, he replied, "That's too bad because that would break the unanimity we require at this time and on this issue, and might keep us from taking office. To ensure this will happen, I will personally *expel* from caucus any of my members who propose to vote against the resolution."

This was a defining moment for the Tory party. After decades of failure Mulroney had challenged them to do whatever was necessary to win nationally. Failure was no longer an option. This time, the party listened. Mulroney's knowledge of and appreciation for the lessons of history allowed him to respond instinctively to the challenges from the Liberals. "Here I am not 24 hours in the place, I don't know my way to the can, and the Liberals play their trump." But to Trudeau's dismay, Mulroney united his caucus. As one Liberal Cabinet minister admitted, "Trap? Some fucking trap."

Not everything went so well in the House. Heckled on his second day by an overweight Liberal Monique Bégin, who yelled "Accouchez," the equivalent of "giving birth" to urge Mulroney to ask his question he retorted, "I'm getting there, Monique. And speaking of giving birth, when's it due?"

AFTER AN EVENING STROLL in the snow, Pierre Trudeau announced his resignation on February 29, 1984. Later that spring, Liberals chose John Turner as leader, a man unsullied by Trudeau's abysmal record on the economy. In fact, Turner had parted company with Trudeau in 1975 after serving as his minister of finance. Turner now brought the Liberals solidly back into first place in the polls, with a ten-point gap on the Tories.

During the Liberal leadership campaign, Mulroney embarked on an extensive cross-country tour with his family. Mulroney dubbed this his "boonies tour." It was unusual for party members to have a leader in their hometown except during an election. "I am leaving a series of pearls in all these communities across Canada. The moment that the new PM calls an election, the pearls will be strung together. Then just watch us!" In caucus, MP Patrick Nowlan claimed Mulroney's visits were hurting the party. But before Mulroney could rise to defend himself, MP Steve Paproski admonished Nowlan, "Pat, I joined this caucus in 1968. You were an asshole then and you are an asshole today." The remark demonstrated that Mulroney had both the respect and loyalty of caucus.

An overconfident Turner called for an election for September 4, going to the people before facing the House of Commons or healing the unavoidable wounds that follow a leadership campaign. While Mulroney entered the contest as an underdog, the timing of the election delighted him. He bid farewell to his constituents in Central Nova and registered for the ballot in the riding of Manicouagan, home to his birthplace, Baie Comeau, Québec.

Mulroney assembled a new coalition of Conservatives, adding a vibrant Québec contingent to the already strong Tory presence in the West. He was a great campaigner, and delivered a knockout punch during the national leaders' debates with Prime Minister John Turner on the issue of patronage. When he took over the leadership, Turner had accepted terms from Pierre Trudeau that compelled him to appoint 200 or so Liberals to various patronage positions. In the televised debate, Mulroney confronted the meek and beleaguered Turner, who claimed, "I had no option" over the appointments. Mulroney forcefully responded with his most famous and devastating line: "You had an option, sir. You could have said, 'I am not going to do it. This is wrong for Canada and I am not going to ask Canadians to pay the price.' You had an option, sir, to say no. And you chose to say yes to the old attitudes and the old stories of the Liberal party. That sir, if I may say respectfully, that is not good enough for Canadians."

When Turner again replied, "I had no option," Mulroney went in for the kill. "That is an avowal of failure. That is confession of non-leadership and this country needs leadership. You had an option, sir. You could have done better."

To ensure a massive victory in Québec, Mulroney delivered a speech, written in part by his friend Lucien Bouchard, at Sept-Isles on August 6 that laid the groundwork for future constitutional negotiations: "Not one person in Québec authorized the federal Liberals to take advantage of the confusion that prevailed in Québec following the referendum in order to ostracize the province constitutionally. My party takes no pleasure in the politically weak position in which these deplorable events have placed Québec. If Québec is strong, then Canada is strong. There is room in Canada for all identities to be affirmed, for all aspirations to be respected, and for all ideals to be pursued ... (The objective) is to convince the Québec national assembly to give its consent to the new Canadian constitution with honor and enthusiasm."

Mulroney drew support from every quarter of Québec. In some regions, he tapped into the Parti Québécois network for help; in other areas, provincial Liberals took the lead. It was a remarkable and unstoppable coalition which came to be known as Mulroney's "Blue Thunder." Mulroney held the federal Liberals accountable for imposing a new constitution on the country without the support of the Québec government, bypassing its traditional veto over such action. Confronted with Liberal accusations that separatists supported the Tories, Mulroney replied, "They're all federalists now."

During a swing through eastern Québec in August, Mulroney was advised by Jacques Blanchard, a regional organizer, that the party would win 21 of 22 seats in his district. All that was needed for a clean sweep, said Blanchard, was a visit by Mulroney to the lone questionable riding. Mulroney turned to his assistant, Bill Pristanski, and said, "Make it happen." On election night, all 22 ridings went Bleu.

Charley McMillan, a policy advisor to Mulroney, was frequently quoted as saying, "You know Brian, he's about as ideological as that coffee pot." It was a knock that resonated with some in the far right-wing of the party. However, Mulroney's record of transformative change easily marks him as Canada's most ideologically conservative prime minister. Asked before the campaign what he wanted to be remembered for should he be given the responsibility of office, he listed four items: a constitutional agreement with Québec, a restructured and modernized Canadian economy, a consolidation of a role for middle powers in international relations, and improving the social and economic condition of Canada's Native communities. Mulroney knew even then the place he wanted in the history books, but he needed the office to make his mark. His friend Lucien Bouchard once said, "Brian just doesn't want to be Prime Minister. He wants to live in history." All the while, Mulroney had the end-game in mind. "One thing I've learned and that's how to keep my eye in the ball. It's going to take me all the way to 24 Sussex Drive."

Results from the 1984 election were better than even the most optimistic Conservatives could have imagined. Mulroney earned a popular vote of just over 50 percent; the first time a true majority in popular vote had been recorded in a Canadian election since the Diefenbaker sweep of 1958.

By comparison, Trudeau's share of the popular vote in the 1968 "Trudeaumania" election was 45.5 percent. Mulroney won 58 of 75 seats from Québec and 86 of the 102 ridings with a francophone population of 10 percent or more. In the previous twenty years, Conservatives had never won more than eight Québec seats. Mulroney had a majority of members from every province, and his 211-member caucus dwarfed the 40 Liberal and 30 NDP members in the House of Commons.

It was anyone's guess how long the Mulroney coalition would last. Building a coalition from the opposition benches was one thing. Keeping it together while in government was quite another. Diefenbaker himself had failed to keep control of an inordinately large caucus. It was time for Mulroney to heed the words of Sir John A.: "A government with a big surplus, a big majority, and a weak opposition could debauch a committee of archangels." Well, Mulroney certainly didn't assume government in a surplus position. Far from it.

CHAPTER 24

POWER AND DISCIPLINE

There is a general consensus that we must seek to secure and improve our trade
with the United States. To shrink from this challenge and opportunity would
be an act of timidity unworthy of Canada.

FROM HIS YOUTH, Mulroney had wanted to be prime minister. He had only observed one role model to follow and that was John Diefenbaker. But Mulroney was not a populist like the Chief and he always told himself that he would govern with one fundamental objective in mind: what was right for Canada over the long term.

There were no shortages of problems facing the Mulroney government when it was sworn into office on September 17, 1984. The economy was in a shambles, wracked by low productivity, inflation, and high unemployment. Internationally, Canada's voice was irrelevant and ignored. Relations with the Americans, the country's largest trading partner, were strained. National unity and federal-provincial relations had suffered enormously under Trudeau. Most pressing of all, the country faced an unprecedented annual deficit. Mulroney confronted each of these fundamental challenges over his first term with the most comprehensive and conservative program of reform in the country's history.

On economic management, the government moved quickly to eradicate the Liberal party's National Energy Program and repealed the petroleum and gas revenue tax, both of which were despised in the West. It replaced

the restrictive Foreign Investment Review Agency (FIRA) with Investment
Canada, giving it a mandate to promote, rather than repel, foreign direct
investment. It took steps to reduce government subsidies and identified
Crown corporations for privatization. On tax reform, an innovative
$500,000 capital gains exemption was implemented to encourage risk-taking
and change the investment climate in the country.

Mulroney steadily improved relations with Canada's allies, particularly
the United States. His cordial and respectful relations with presidents
Ronald Reagan and George H.W. Bush provided a platform for continent-
wide investments and regulations that countered the ravages to the
environment by acid rain. As he told the press prior to his first visit to the
White House, "A healthy, strong relationship with the United States of
America in no way presupposes any degree of subservience on our part."

The federal deficit was a supertanker, not easily turned, the result of
runaway spending, a weak economy, and Liberal neglect. The Mulroney government faced a projected $42 billion deficit and a burgeoning level of
public debt. It was the government's number one priority.

On November 8, 1984, Finance Minister Michael Wilson reported, "For
too long, the government has . . . allowed the fiscal situation to deteriorate
and the debt to increase. . . . we must put our fiscal house in order so that we
can limit, and ultimately reverse, the massive build-up in public debt and the
damaging impact this has on confidence and growth." Measures were
announced in a November 1984 economic statement that reduced government spending by about $4 billion in the short term.

The following May, the government ran into trouble when it proposed
the partial de-indexation of various tax items and social payments. Faced
with a public outcry, the government reversed the more controversial and
objectionable elements of its fiscal plan. The reversal can be traced back to
a pledge Mulroney made during the 1984 election to treat government
social programs as a "sacred trust." The pledge had quelled fears that a
prospective Conservative government had a hidden agenda, and would
"slash and burn" government spending on the altar of the deficit. Disinclined
to validate the maxim that "Tory times are tough times," Mulroney had comforted voters before the election by assuring them that savings would be
found elsewhere in the system to reduce the deficit.

But the event that galvanized public opinion against Mulroney was an
unplanned confrontation he had with a sixty-three-year-old woman, Solange
Denis, an active Liberal who had been protesting outside Mulroney's
Langevin Block offices because of pension de-indexing. The prime minister

was caught totally off guard when Denis declared, "You made promises that you wouldn't touch anything . . . you lied to us. I was made to vote for you and then it's Goodbye Charlie Brown." The government backed down. Its opponents took that as evidence that it was not committed to balancing the books.

The Conservative plan to reduce the deficit had three elements: first, a growing economy would produce higher revenues; second, program spending would be limited to increases at or below the rate of inflation; third, selected spending cuts would be made in low-priority areas. Together, these three elements would slowly strengthen government finances without causing any great shock to the economy. Progress would be steady and incremental.

Holding spending increases to the rate of inflation might not seem particularly ambitious now, but in the post-Trudeau era it was considered an astounding achievement. During the Trudeau years, the average increase in program spending was 13.1 percent per year. In the early to mid-1970s, the average increase was over 17 percent per year. The record year was 1974–75, when Trudeau's minority Liberal government was being propped up by the NDP. Program spending increased by a whopping 27.9 percent. Out of control spending and persistent deficits had taken their toll on government finances: Canada's national debt under Trudeau (1968–1984) had increased ten fold, from $19.2 to $194.4 billion.

In Wilson's first year as finance minister, program spending decreased by $800 million, one full percentage point. Clearly, the brakes on spending had been applied. Over the first four years of Conservative administration, program spending increased on average 3.8 percent, one-third of the previous administration's level of increase. Program spending in Mulroney's first term declined from 18.5 percent of GDP to 15.7 percent. Had government spending maintained the same share of the economy during Mulroney's first term, the size of the deficit would have been at least $17 billion higher than the one ultimately recorded. In a symbolic gesture, Mulroney took a 15 percent pay cut and his ministers took a 10 percent cut.

Leaving the debt and interest costs aside, the Mulroney government went from an operating deficit of $12.2 in 1984–85 to an operating surplus of $7.5 billion at the end of its first term, a turnaround of $19.7 billion. But because of the burden of compounding debt and rising interest rates, the bottom-line deficit number barely budged. The deficit had shrunk by almost half, from 8.3 percent of GDP to 4.6 percent. But the bottom-line deficit number was distressing, particularly to small-c Conservatives who thought Mulroney had a mandate to balance the books. Nowhere was the distress more apparent than in Western Canada.

Preston Manning, son of former Alberta Social Credit premier Ernest Manning, meanwhile, was looking for an opening to enter the national political arena. On October 31, 1986, the Mulroney government announced that a maintenance contract for Canada's CF-18 fighter jets was, contrary to the recommendation made by a panel assembled to evaluate competitive bids, being awarded to Canadair in Montréal. The panel had decided that Bristol Aerospace Ltd. of Manitoba submitted the superior technical and financial bid.

Mulroney was mindful of the large number of companies that had fled Québec in 1976, when the sovereignist Parti Québécois was elected. He wanted to reverse that trend. The controversial Canadair decision was, Mulroney argued, in the national interest because the technology embedded in the CF-18 contract would be used by Canadair to create manufacturing jobs in Canada. He believed young francophones in Montréal needed opportunities for high-paying jobs in growth sectors of the worldwide economy. In his memoirs, however, Mulroney would admit he erred in his handling of the CF-18 decision.

Preston Manning used the CF-18 decision to catapult the launch of the Reform party, a new western-based political party whose mantra, "The West Wants In," put a more positive spin on western alienation.

Mulroney's government took the lead on a number of international fronts, including the establishment of La Francophonie, a conference comprising 55 nations whose common language was French. Canada was singled out for its role in the release of Nelson Mandela from his South African prison and in ending apartheid. In the process, Mulroney opposed a determined and forceful Conservative British prime minister, Margaret Thatcher, who rejected the trade sanctions and other measures designed to spur reform. At successive Commonwealth meetings, Mulroney built a coalition of like-minded countries—Canada, India, Australia, Bahamas, Tanzania—to take on British opposition.

To acknowledge Mulroney's efforts, Mandela chose Canada as the destination for his first international trip as a free man, and addressed the House of Commons, paying special tribute to Mulroney "who acted against apartheid because he knew that no person of conscience could stand aside as a crime against humanity was being committed. Mr. Prime Minister, our people and organization respect you and admire you as a friend."

The Mulroney government had the courage to review and expose long-standing and shameful Canadian actions in harbouring Nazi war criminals. And on behalf of all Canadians, in September 1988, it issued a formal apology

to Japanese Canadians interned in camps and stripped of their property during World War II. A compensation package of $300 million was paid to fulfill
a promise Mulroney made while leader of the Opposition. Mulroney had
urged all-party support on a resolution to acknowledge and apologize for
the treatment of Japanese Canadians during the war. Trudeau had refused;
Mulroney delivered.

In September 1985, the report by the Royal Commission on the
Economic Union and development prospects for Canada, chaired by former
Liberal finance minister Donald Macdonald, called on Canada to make a
"leap of faith" and pursue a free trade agreement with the United States.
Lowering trade barriers had been discussed at the "Shamrock Summit"
between Mulroney and U.S. President Ronald Reagan on March 17 of that
year, but free trade was a much higher leap. Later that month, Cabinet
endorsed the commission's report. Mulroney confirmed the decision in a
phone call with Reagan, and then addressed the issue in the House of
Commons:

> There is a general consensus that we must seek to secure and improve
> our trade with the United States. To shrink from this challenge and
> opportunity would be an act of timidity unworthy of Canada. It would
> be contrary to our national interest. Our political sovereignty, our sys-
> tem of social programs, our commitment to fight regional disparities,
> our unique cultural identity, our special linguistic character—these
> are the essence of Canada. They are not at issue in these negotiations.
> They will be stronger at all times in a Canada made more confident
> and prosperous from a secure and dynamic trading relationship with
> our biggest customer, our close friend and with all the world.

Producing a free trade agreement required the direct involvement of
Mulroney and Reagan, as well as constant intervention by senior Cabinet
officials on both sides. The main sticking point was a dispute settlement
mechanism to ensure that challenges to the provisions of the agreement
would be resolved impartially and independent of political influence by
elected officials seized by the need to protect jobs in their home constituencies. This issue was resolved only when the deadline for reaching a
fast-tracked agreement, October 3, 1987, was imminent. In the hours leading up to the deadline, when hope of an agreement seemed lost, Mulroney
called Reagan: "Ron, how come the Americans can do a nuclear arms limitation deal with their worst enemies, the USSR, but can't do a trade deal

with their best friends, the Canadians?" The Americans took the leap of faith and accepted a dispute settlement panel.

To strengthen provincial finances and autonomy, the government, through the 1985 Atlantic Accord, entitled the Maritime provinces to establish and collect revenues from offshore resources as if the resources were on land. A major step towards economic self-sufficiency for Newfoundland, the accord gave the province hope that its young people would not have to move off "The Rock" to find a job.

HAVING BEEN OUT OF POWER for close to a generation, some members of Cabinet, and sometimes the prime minister, did not always maintain the appropriate boundaries required by the governing party. John Fraser, Sinclair Stevens, André Bissonnette, and Bob Coates were either dismissed or resigned from Cabinet over relatively minor issues to which the prime minister overreacted. This appearance of repetitive scandals in Mulroney's first term as prime minister created the impression among Canadians that the government lacked integrity.

Long respectful of the Constitution, the Tories pledged to respect the separation of powers between the federal and provincial governments. Needless and unproductive conflict with the provinces was replaced with dialogue and compromise. Arguably, the defining act of Mulroney's term as prime minister was the Meech Lake Accord, designed to end Québec's constitutional isolation after the province had refused to accept Pierre Trudeau's constitutional package in 1982. Ironically, Trudeau's version of the Constitution made subsequent reform considerably more difficult to achieve because it required unanimity among the federal government and all provinces to insert the provisions sought by Québec as a condition of signing the Constitution.

Leaving Québec isolated in 1982 was a stain on Canada, one readily identified by former Tory leader Bob Stanfield: "No premier of Québec within living memory would have agreed to the Constitution of 1982. . . . I believed and I still believe that the exercise of 1982 endangers Canada as a country. We gave the separatists a stick to beat us with . . . Ottawa had betrayed the French-speaking Québecers who had voted for constitution renewal (in the referendum)."

Even Liberals felt some shame over what Trudeau had done. At the signing ceremony in 1982, the Liberal Speaker of the House of Commons, Jeanne Sauvé, turned to her husband and said, "My God, what have we done?"

Mulroney had been nursing the constitutional file in the early years of his administration. The opportunity to act came in December 1985, when Robert Bourassa, a Liberal, was elected premier of Québec. He won election on a platform that included constitutional reconciliation with Canada under certain conditions, similar in tone to what Mulroney had proposed in the 1984 federal campaign. When the prime minister and provincial premiers met in August 1986, it was unanimously agreed that a constitutional agreement would be pursued on the basis of addressing Québec's conditions.

The prime minister and the premiers met at Meech Lake in April 1987 without the meddlesome intrusions of officials and bureaucrats. The Constitution was to be amended, with Québec's signature, under provisions that recognized Québec as a "distinct society within Canada." In addition, the federal government would select senators from lists submitted by the provinces, and federal spending power would be limited in areas of exclusive provincial jurisdiction.

Pierre Trudeau had proposed virtually every element in the Meech Lake Accord at one time or another in his career, but he vehemently opposed this agreement. He called Mulroney "a weakling" for rendering the Canadian state "totally impotent" and destined to "be governed by eunuchs." This from the man who enabled the provinces to override his Charter of Rights and Freedoms through a "notwithstanding clause." Trudeau's words were so strong that, according to Bob Rae, "Trudeau made anti-French bigotry respectable."

In a marathon meeting in Ottawa on June 3, 1987, Mulroney and the provincial premiers tweaked the Meech Lake Accord. The agreement passed in the House of Commons by a vote of 200 to seven. From that moment the clock began to count down towards a three-year deadline for ratification by the federal and all provincial legislative assemblies. In Mulroney's second term, the ratification process would be taken to the brink.

THE TORIES HAD INSTITUTED profound and meaningful reforms in virtually every area of government. It made mistakes along the way, certainly, and Mulroney's charm, though always a tremendous asset in caucus and on the world stage, began to grate on Canadians. Support in the polls and the prime minister's approval rating were both in decline. With his eye on maintaining government, Mulroney sought to strengthen the party's position in Québec by recruiting his long-time friend Lucien Bouchard, Canada's ambassador to France, into Cabinet. Following a difficult and uncertain by-election, Bouchard became a member of the Tory caucus on June 20, 1988.

Buoyed by a resurgent economy, a deficit cut in half, the Meech Lake Accord, and a free trade agreement with the United States, Brian Mulroney went to the polls on November 21, 1988. As much as the government wanted to run on its record of strong economic management and job creation, the election was dominated by a contentious debate over the Free Trade Agreement. The floundering Liberal leader, John Turner, declared opposition to the FTA the supreme cause of his political life. Like Borden in 1911, the charisma-challenged Turner was behind in the public opinion polls, and desperately needed an issue to define his campaign.

Mulroney fully expected the election would be about leadership, and he happily contrasted his performance as prime minister against the stunningly unimpressive record of the hapless and unsteady Turner. But underestimating Turner would prove to be a mistake.

Having been skewered in the 1984 debate, Turner had his revenge in 1988. The nationally televised debate was generally going well for Mulroney, when Turner suddenly upped the ante on free trade near the end of the broadcast. "We built a country east and west and north. We built it on an infrastructure that deliberately resisted the continental pressure of the United States. For 120 years we've done it. With one signature of a pen, you've reversed that, thrown us into the north-south influence of the United States and will reduce us, I am sure, to a colony of the United States, because when the economic levers go the political independence is sure to follow."

Mulroney was incredulous: "With a commercial document that is cancellable on six months' notice."

Turner quickly retorted, "Commercial document? That document relates to . . . every facet of our life!"

"Please be serious," said Mulroney.

Turner turned his steely blue eyes on the prime minister and replied, "Well, I am serious. And I've never been more serious in my life."

Suddenly, Turner caught momentum and the polls swung solidly in his favour. Across the country, voters were talking about free trade and genuinely feared the potential loss of political independence.

According to Mulroney's autobiography, Tory campaign chair Norman Atkins advised Derek Burney, the prime minister's chief of staff, that the party should pull free trade from the platform and promise a referendum on the FTA. Campaign insiders suggest this was simply an option to consider. According to Deputy Prime Minister Don Mazankowski, "That was when Mulroney turned on the jets and put the campaign in overdrive." Campaign strategist Harry Near said, "After the debate the prime minister literally

carried the campaign on his back for four of five days." If Turner had defined
the quintessential ballot question, Mulroney was determined to answer it.
To that end, Mulroney was aligned with the business community, who desperately wanted the FTA ratified.

The Tories launched an all-out attack on John Turner and the Liberals'
credibility, motives, and leadership. "The only job Turner wants to protect,"
lambasted Tory ads, "is his own." Mulroney turned the tide and shifted the
debate away from sovereignty and patriotism and towards increased opportunity and job creation.

On November 21, 1988 Canadians rewarded Mulroney with a second
majority government. Excluding Borden's coalition win as a Union government in 1917, it was the first back-to-back Conservative majority since
Macdonald. Mulroney found himself in the rarefied company he had sought
for so long. True, thirty-four fewer Tories were elected than in 1984, but
Mulroney had earned a comfortable majority, with 169 MPs to the Liberals'
83 and the NDP's 43. The key for the Tories had been winning 63 of
Québec's 75 seats. Never in the party's history, not even in Macdonald's day,
had Conservatives sustained such a stronghold in French Canada. Mulroney
had delivered what he had promised at the leadership convention in 1983:
"Elect me and I will deliver Québec." Not once, but twice.

With a renewed majority, a strengthening economy, and constitutional
calm, Mulroney approached his second term with confidence and purpose.
But dangers lurked. First, the Meech Lake Accord was not a done deal.
Second, Preston Manning was fomenting western alienation. Although the
Tories had won seven of 14 seats in Manitoba despite the CF-18 decision, it
was politically unwise to ignore the Reform party. Third, phase one of a tax
reform package that lowered personal income tax rates, had been popularly
delivered in Mulroney's first mandate. Phase two of tax reform, slated for
introduction in Mulroney's second term, featured the introduction of the
Goods and Services Tax (GST). It would take all of Mulroney's political capital, and then some, in an attempt to carry these three issues.

CHAPTER 25

A TEST OF NATIONAL UNITY

Obviously, I didn't always succeed but I always tried to do what I thought would be right for Canada in the long term, not what could be politically popular in the short term.

I N HIS SECOND TERM as prime minister, Brian Mulroney had some notable successes—in particular, the landmark agreements with the United States on free trade and acid rain. But the second term was marked by difficult issues and a string of failures—the rejection of the Meech Lake Accord and its successor, the Charlottetown Accord; the challenge of coping with a worldwide recession; high interest rates that stifled economic growth; and the replacement of a destructive manufacturers' sales tax with the wildly unpopular Goods and Services Tax. On the political front, the coalition that Mulroney had assembled in 1984 and sustained through 1988 crumbled. Two regionally-based political parties emerged and made Mulroney's second term unmanageable. In his memoirs Mulroney used a single word to describe the mood in Canada in 1988: "*sour.*"

An omen of serious western discontent appeared just a few months after the 1988 campaign. John Dahmer, despite having to campaign from his deathbed, won his Beaver River, Alberta seat for the Tories in the general election. His passing resulted in a by-election on March 13, 1989. The Reform party candidate, Deborah Grey, who had been an afterthought in the 1988 general election, won decisively in the by-election. She received nearly as many votes as her PC, Liberal, and NDP opponents combined.

Mulroney confided to author Peter C. Newman that he had no clear idea what Reform even represented. "The Reform party is anti-*everything*. There is a a deep-seated racism there. I still don't know what to make of Reform. I know that for the moment it's growing. But these are one-trick ponies. They are not standing on a whole lot of sound ground. It's all negative."

The Reform party received just over 2 percent of the votes in the general election, and 8.5 percent of the votes cast in the 72 ridings where it fielded a candidate. In Alberta, however, where the Tories won 25 of 26 ridings, Reform managed 15.3 percent of the vote, with support from both urban and rural ridings. Though the Free Trade Agreement was secure, Alberta had cast a meaningful protest vote, a warning that Mulroney and his western ministers should have heeded. Reform had shown that it was far from being on the fringe.

Mulroney believed he had delivered for the West and was puzzled about what Preston Manning was after. Mulroney saw the Reform party as nothing but the old Social Credit party dressed up under a new name. Just when the centre-right was gaining strength, Conservative forces were beginning to divide.

Mulroney's western lieutenant, Don Mazankowski, wanted to make peace with Reform, but "I said let's not fight them; let's hug them to death to try and bring them back into the fold." But Preston Manning wasn't interested in Tory affection and had a different agenda. Manning wanted to make his mark on the national stage and test the political realignment theory that had been in his head for much of the previous twenty years. He would not have joined the PC ranks even if the party had addressed his issues his way.

Reform hammered away at the government's record on the debt and deficit. Despite sustained efforts to contain it, the deficit rose for most of Mulroney's second term, ending up at $38.5 billion for the year ended March 31, 2003. The final two years of the Mulroney administration produced the two highest nominal deficits in the country's history. The operating surplus had shrunk from a peak of $12.1 billion for 1988–89 to just $1.5 billion in 1993–94. No longer could the finger be pointed at the previous Liberal government for this financial mess.

Kim Campbell, a rookie MP from British Columbia, was frustrated by her government's unwillingness—or inability—to tackle the deficit problem. "Much was expected of the first budget of a new mandate [after the 1988 election]. The response from many conservatives was disappointment. When the B.C. Ministers held a conference call to discuss the budget with members of the party executive in the province, we heard almost uniform criticism that it didn't go far enough to restrain expenditures."

In Mulroney's first term the debt grew, but so did the economy. In the second term, however, all key economic indicators headed south. Government revenues, which had grown by an average of 10.1 percent per year over Mulroney's first term, limped along at an anemic 2.4 percent in his second term. Revenues actually decreased by an average of 2.8 percent for the last two years. It was no comfort to Canadians that the recession was worldwide, a fact voters rarely take into account when assessing blame. Adding insult to injury, interest rates remained stubbornly high, which hurt both government finances and consumer confidence. The Bank of Canada's doctrinaire governor, John Crow, set an unrealistic and unhealthy inflation target of zero, which may well have exacerbated the severity of the recession. With the attendant rise in unemployment, the recession triggered automatic increases in public spending on Employment Insurance and other social programs, placing an even greater strain on the nation's finances. The belief that Conservatives were better managers of the economy was being tested.

Undeterred by the weak economy, the Mulroney government then bravely tackled the hidden, yet profoundly destructive Manufacturers' Sales Tax (MST). Charged at the rate of 13.5 percent on manufactured goods, the MST made exports more expensive while imposing a tax that favoured importers over domestic manufacturers. Every government for the previous thirty years had studied the MST and been challenged by economists and business leaders to replace it. Only Mulroney had the courage to take the political heat and reform the system. While there were hints of sales tax reform in the Tories' 1988 election platform, it was not until early into their second mandate that the government proposed replacing the MST with a value-added tax called the Goods and Services Tax (GST). Mulroney knew he would spend considerable political capital pushing sales tax reform, but it was an initiative his able finance minister had requested, and anyone who had ever studied the damaging effects of the MST knew it was the right thing to do.

But the GST turned out to be a public relations nightmare. Rather than the 30,000 manufacturers that came under the MST, the GST required over a million businesses and not-for-profit organizations to register and then manage the system. Most of the small businesses that were drawn into the new system were ill-equipped to administer a value-added tax.

Mulroney had backed off on a budget measure once before when he reversed course on a plan to de-index old age pensions. But he displayed fortitude in the face of the huge public outcry over the GST. Two caucus members, Alex Kindy and David Kilgour, were expelled for voting against the GST in the House of Commons. To get the GST through the Senate, Mulroney invoked little-known Section 26 of the Constitution (the deadlock clause) allowing him to appoint eight "emergency" senators to break a Liberal filibuster.

Still, the grief over the GST paled in comparison to the anguish over the Meech Lake Accord. Easily passed by Parliament, the Accord required ratification by all provincial legislatures within the prescribed three-year time frame. Every provincial premier had signed the original Accord in 1987, but ensuing provincial elections had brought a different slate of premiers to the table, with varying enthusiasm towards Meech Lake. When Tory Premier Richard Hatfield of New Brunswick was defeated by Liberal Frank McKenna, the first premier to oppose Meech Lake took his seat at the first ministers' table.

Passage of the Accord was further impeded when the Québec government used the notwithstanding clause in the Constitution to override a decision of the Supreme Court of Canada on its law restricting the use of English on signs. In the aftermath, a number of provinces reconsidered their support for Meech Lake.

Realizing that some provinces might scuttle the Accord unless their specific concerns were addressed, Mulroney took their criticisms of Meech to heart. To help end the impasse, he asked Québec Tory MP Jean Charest to chair a committee to look at a "companion resolution" to Meech Lake. Like Sir John A., and not unlike the Fathers of Confederation in their discussions at Charlottetown and Québec City, Mulroney was prepared to compromise to reach an honourable deal. In his journal on May 19, 1990, he wrote: "I believe the case for Canadian unity is so vital that I am inclined to take any reasonable initiative to ensure its durability." The companion resolution, though critical, would not change so much as a comma or period of Meech Lake, but it did clarify its intent and meaning.

Meech Lake was still alive, but barely. Frank McKenna's objections were subsequently, if not painfully, addressed. But this opened the door for more dissent. Manitoba and Newfoundland were the most troublesome. Premier Clyde Wells of Newfoundland and Manitoba Opposition leader Sharon Carstairs of Manitoba were both staunch loyalists of former prime minister Pierre Trudeau with strong connections to Liberal leader Jean Chrétien.

Preston Manning also had a role to play. His opposition to Meech Lake placed him in the unlikely company of Pierre Trudeau and Jean Chrétien.

This common ground gave Manning excellent cover. Without Trudeau's opposition, Manning might well have been perceived as anti-French, but with Trudeau and Chrétien on his side, such a charge was not possible.

Lowell Murray, minister of state for federal-provincial relations, and his deputy, Norman Spector, devised a communication strategy aimed at opinion makers and the elite, bypassing ordinary Canadians. They argued the public need not be engaged, leaving Trudeau and Manning a wide berth from which to stir up angst among the masses.

The next blow came from within. With the deadline for ratification looming, Mulroney's friend and Québec lieutenant, Lucien Bouchard, betrayed his prime minister in an attempt to scuttle the Accord. From Europe, Bouchard sent a telegram to delegates at a meeting of the sovereignist Parti Québécois. The telegram paid tribute to those who supported the YES side in the 1980 referendum on sovereignty–association and honoured the memory of René Lévesque, "the one," claimed Bouchard, "who led Québécois to realize they had the inalienable right to decide their own destiny." Bouchard, it turned out, had been planning the creation of a new Québec-based political party to represent the sovereignty movement in the federal House of Commons. Mulroney asked for, and received, Bouchard's resignation.

The Bouchard-led Bloc Québécois was established on June 15, 1991, and drew support largely from the ranks of the PC party, which had dominated Québec in the previous two elections. With the emergence of the Bloc, Mulroney's national coalition suffered a punishing blow. With western alienation on the rise, fuelled by the Reform party, the coalition was irreparably fractured.

Clyde Wells's finance minister, Hubert Kitchen, once remarked "Québec got us by the short hairs on Upper Churchill. We've got them in the same place on Meech." Wells played his hand coldly, without compromise or fear. He led a province with less than two percent of the nation's population, whose income was largely dependent on transfers from the federal government, but Wells was prepared to risk everything. His vision for Canada, not unlike Sir John A. Macdonald's, was of a state where the federal government played a dominant role. But unlike Macdonald, Wells did not understand that for the sake of Canadian unity, compromise was required. Without Macdonald's understanding and respect for the cultural differences that existed among the provinces, Canada could never have been created.

Mulroney implored Wells. The separatists' hand would be profoundly strengthened by the failure of Meech, he cautioned, and the outcome of a second referendum on Québec sovereignty might well hang in the balance.

Provincial premiers reminded Wells that he had not won government in Newfoundland by drawing a line in the sand on Meech Lake. Wells responded: "My position is that the nation comes first, Newfoundland second. I am dedicated to the preservation of Canada as a federal state and to the fundamental principles of federalism."

The first ministers met in a marathon session to reach agreement on a companion resolution to Meech, which was informed by the parliamentary committee headed by Charest. All governments were onside except Newfoundland. "I regret that I cannot sign the document as it is," said Wells. "I will honour the commitment to take the proposal back to Newfoundland to place it before the Cabinet and to ask for legislative approval in a free vote, or to put it to a referendum . . . I'll invite every one of you to appear before the legislature to make the wonderful arguments you have made in this room. . . . I will not campaign against this agreement."

The day before the scheduled vote, Mulroney did travel to Newfoundland and made the case for Meech and for the importance of Québec signing the nation's Constitution to the provincial House of Assembly. The next day, Clyde Wells reneged on his promise and cancelled the vote. Meech was dead.

A few days later, at the Liberal leadership convention, Wells was seen on national television being hugged by Pierre Trudeau and Jean Chrétien. When reporters pressed Wells about whether he had told Mulroney while the prime minister was in Newfoundland that he was going to cancel the vote, perhaps the most significant decision of his political career, he replied, "Honestly, I just don't remember."

Mulroney described the end of Meech "like a death in the family." His Québec Cabinet ministers openly wept. On the evening of its demise, Mulroney spoke to the nation, saying, "I would rather have failed trying to advance the cause of Canada's unity than to simply have played it safe, done nothing or criticized from the sidelines."

Mulroney then initiated a second round of constitutional talks that led to a national referendum and another great disaster, this one of a different sort. Its beginning was anything but confident. As Mulroney noted in his journal on January 30, 1991, "I am no longer sure that Canada can be saved, her unity maintained. Nor am I sure that I'm the leader to bring that about." But as prime minister he had to try.

Even the federalists in Québec were talking about a referendum on the province's continuing role in Confederation. This second round of constitutional negotiations, however, covered far more than Québec.

Mulroney put Joe Clark in charge as lead negotiator for Canada. The result was the Charlottetown Accord, a tribute to process but a failure in content. Charlottetown was born of desperation, designed to give something to everyone, a mish-mash of provisions with no clear vision or coherence. Despite all-party support among federalist politicians and unanimity among provincial premiers and Native leaders, the agreement was a confusing mess that fatigued Canadians.

Joe Clark produced the Charlottetown Accord, but Mulroney was blamed for its demise. As prime minister, certainly, he was accountable. However, Mulroney was dismayed by many of the provisions and was at odds with Joe Clark over how the accord was struck. Clark was determined to reach an agreement "at all costs." Mulroney thought if the negotiations failed he could pass a resolution in the House of Commons, then place the matter before the people in a national referendum. But Clark blazed ahead, ultimately telling the prime minister, "You and I have different instincts and I was not prepared to defer to yours." After he met with the premiers to assess the prospects for Charlottetown's success, Mulroney jotted in his personal journal, "What in God's name possessed Joe Clark to proclaim this disaster the greatest constitutional agreement since 1867?" Charlottetown was defeated in a national referendum on October 26, 1992, by a margin of almost ten percentage points. Only Newfoundland, PEI, New Brunswick and Ontario voted yes. Strong support in Newfoundland, the second highest in the country, supports the view that Clyde Wells overstated the case when he claimed his province would never have accepted the Meech Lake Accord.

Where Mulroney felt most comfortable in his second term as prime minister was on the international stage. He had become an elder statesman at international conferences, such as the G8, and enjoyed the clear respect and attention of the world's most powerful leaders.

While Mulroney played a major leadership role in the Commonwealth, the Francophonie, the Organization of American States, and APEC, his international clout was largely achieved at the G7. In his first term he played mediator between presidents Reagan and François Mitterrand of France. In addition to his skills as a negotiator, he was able to speak to each in his mother tongue. He also developed a personal relationship with Vice President George H.W. Bush. When Bush became president, he turned to Mulroney for help to assemble a coalition of nations to support a United Nations resolution authorizing the use of force to expel the Iraqi army after it invaded Kuwait in 1991. Canada's military enforced a trade blockade against Iraq, provided air support, attacked ground targets, and manned a field hospital. More generally, Mulroney was anxious to increase the military budget to put Canada's investment in security more in line with our major trading partners, but was constrained by the weak economy and large deficits.

Besides national unity and the economy, the government's next most important initiative was the green plan: an outline for a new approach to environmental sustainability. A new Cabinet committee was formed to give priority to environmental issues, consulting with provinces, industry, and non-governmental organizations. Its green plan was comprehensive and included measures to protect wildlife, forests, soil, water, and land. More important, the plan was funded to the tune of $3 billion over five years. At the Earth Summit in Rio de Janeiro, the Sierra Club of Canada's Elizabeth May was effusive about Mulroney's influence. "Let's face it," said May, "Canada saved the biodiversity treaty. Let's not be modest just because we are Canadians. Brian Mulroney accomplished something really significant by being willing, within hours of Bush saying he wasn't going to sign it, by saying Canada was."

Mulroney's popularity was highest during the 1984 and 1988 elections, precisely when it was most beneficial. By 1992, however, the Mulroney mystique had been damaged beyond his ability to repair it. His approval ratings over his second term set record lows. With the failures of the Meech Lake and Charlottetown Accords, the introduction of the GST, high interest rates to battle inflation, and the economy in recession, fully 85 percent of Canadians disapproved of the job Mulroney was doing. The best election strategy for the PCS was to look for new leadership.

In response to questions about his low approval ratings, Mulroney said, "Every time you make tough decisions you lose friends. . . . Whether one agrees with our solutions or not, none will accuse us, I think, of having chosen to evade our responsibilities by side stepping the most controversial questions of our time. From free trade, NAFTA, tax reform, the GST, privatizations, deficit reduction, fighting inflation, and lowering interest rates, we have made the decisions that are now strengthening Canada's competitive position."

Saying that he had only ever intended to serve two terms, and facing the statutory end of his term as prime minister, Mulroney resigned on February 24, 1993.

NOT MANY YEARS after Mulroney left office, his contribution to Canada began to be appreciated. Though his initiatives—free trade and the GST—

were the subject of enduring criticism, his successors left them untouched. When Mulroney retired, then deputy minister of finance—and future Governor of the Bank of Canada—David Dodge wrote to him, using language unprecedented for a bureaucrat: "When the history books are written a decade from now, I know they will indicate that your economic reforms were unparalleled by any Canadian government in the twentieth century. My only regret is that the real fruits of your efforts will only become fully evident after you leave office."

Mulroney's record was one of transformative change. He is arguably one of the most conservative prime ministers the country has ever seen.

In a comprehensive study of prime ministers over the previous fifty years, sponsored by the Institute for Research on Public Policy, Mulroney was ranked second, behind Pearson, but ahead of Trudeau, St. Laurent, Chrétien, and Diefenbaker, in that order. Two distinguished McGill professors judged Mulroney's the best economic record of the previous fifty years. In 2006 a panel of leading environmentalists determined that Mulroney had been Canada's "Greenest Prime Minister" of all time.

Mulroney left politics quietly and did not return to Parliament Hill until November 19, 2002, for the unveiling of his official portrait. At the ceremony, Speaker Peter Milliken recalled a description of Mulroney that had appeared in the *Edmonton Journal* some twenty years before. "The eyes are Paul Newman blue. His hair has the swoop of the Robert Redford style and the voice and resonance of a Lorne Greene school of broadcasting. The jaw is by Gibraltar."

Outside the political arena, Mulroney established himself as a leading advisor in the world of international business. He sat on boards, received awards, and delivered keynote addresses on important matters of international public policy.

He was not totally divorced from domestic Canadian politics. In 2003, he made a rare but vintage appearance at the PC party leadership convention. While acknowledging his personal unpopularity, Mulroney reminded delegates of his accomplishments. In detail, Mulroney outlined the specific measures he had undertaken as prime minister to respond to regional frustration from the West. After setting the record straight, and with a strong rebuke aimed at Preston Manning, Mulroney then told delegates it was time to "turn the page." He meant that it was time to reunite the conservative coalition and cooperate with Stephen Harper to put an end to Liberal rule in Canada. With unity, Conservatives had purpose and a path to power.

Mulroney entered the private sector in 1993 as an elite member of the

"A" team on international business and geo-political consultants. Given this success, and his early statements as a young lawyer in Québec about not mixing politics and personal finances, his cash business dealings with lobby-ist Karlheinz Schreiber are all the more surprising. For those who dislike and distrust Mulroney, his association with Schreiber validates their suspicions. But, just as the Pacific Scandal does not define the legacy and contribution made to Canada by Sir John A. Macdonald, and Shawinigate does not define Jean Chrétien, so too the Schreiber affair, which happened while Mulroney was out of office, should not define the man or his legacy.

Despite his failings, the universal loyalty and affection Mulroney enjoyed from those who served with him in caucus and cabinet was sustained even decades after having he left office. Having inspired those with whom he served through encouragement, attentiveness, decency and respect, Mulroney is revered by his former colleagues. His approach stands in contrast to Stephen Harper's, whose inclinations were to motivate through intimida-tion, fear and raw intellectual power. Unlike Mulroney, it is doubtful that Harper will be defended by his colleagues as vigorously as those who defend Mulroney in times of difficulty, particularly after he leaves office.

As Tory leader his only real comparison is with Sir John A. Macdonald. They both built coalitions, East and West, French and English. They fash-ioned their message as needed to ensure they sat on the government side of the House of Commons. They both governed with a vision for transforma-tive change. Macdonald built a railroad and a nation that reached across the continent; Mulroney restructured the economy and nearly brought consti-tutional peace and unity to Canada. Both were flawed. But when it counted most, Mulroney's belief in a grand national coalition, like Macdonald's before him, turned Conservatives from losers to winners.

SECTION VIII

DECADE OF DARKNESS

CHAPTER 26

KIM CAMPBELL: DEFEAT PERSONIFIED

*The issues are much too complex to try and generate some kind of a
blueprint in the forty-seven days that's available in an election
campaign. . . . This is not the time, I don't think, to get involved in a
debate on very, very serious issues.*

KIM CAMPBELL WAS NEW. And different. So much so that many
Conservatives didn't know what to make of her. At the leadership
convention that brought Campbell to power, one anonymous Nova
Scotia delegate said, "I knew we were in trouble when I got to the Tory
convention and saw the men wearing pink and drinking bottled water."
Intelligent, articulate, and persuasive, Campbell was branded a potential
leader as soon as she arrived on Parliament Hill. But Campbell was no
leader. By her own admission, she was overpowered by her election team,
and was unable to assert herself sufficiently to follow the path she thought
was right for the country, her party, and herself. Aside from her claim that
she "wanted to do politics differently," Campbell had no vision or set of
clear policies to take to the electorate. Consequently, and despite all of
Campbell's obvious strengths, her one and only election campaign as PC
party leader and prime minister of Canada will go down on record as the
worst Canadian political performance of all time.

Avril Phaedra Campbell—the Avril an oddball reminder of the
expected month of birth, and Phaedra, from a Greek myth about a woman

who fell in love and hanged herself, when rebuffed—was born prematurely in Port Alberni, British Columbia on March 10, 1947. Names were fluid in her family. Her mother, Lissa, did not like her husband's given name of George and persuaded him to change it to Paul. In search of a new identity, the adolescent Avril changed her name to Kim.

A gifted child with a passion for music and study, Kim could not escape the misery of her parents' bad marriage. After Kim and her sister Alix were sent to boarding school, Lissa Campbell abruptly left the family home and disappeared from Kim's life for ten years.

Kim was attentive to her studies and declared to her childhood friends that one day she would become prime minister. The first female to be elected president of her high school student council, she completed her graduating year as class valedictorian and was a member of her school's "Reach for the Top" academic team (a distinction shared by Stephen Harper).

Campbell continued in student politics at the University of British Columbia and joined the university's Gilbert and Sullivan Society. Here she met her future husband, math professor Nathan Divinsky, a father of three, an ardent conservative and libertarian who followed the teachings of Ayn Rand. The intellectual attraction was sufficient to overcome a twenty-two-year age gap. Campbell married Divinsky in 1972. The marriage lasted a decade.

In student government, Campbell went reverse counter-culture and adopted a conservative perspective. She saw nothing inconsistent about a university being "a hotbed of revolutionary activity in the bastion of conservatism." Campbell studied at the master's level at the London School of Economics but did not obtain a degree. Later she did course work towards a doctorate degree but did not complete a thesis.

At age thirty-two, Campbell changed course and enrolled in law school at the University of British Columbia, graduating in 1983. While a university student, she was elected trustee at the Vancouver School Board, a position once held by her husband. She brought a strident conservative perspective to council deliberations. Some called her a bully; others said she was unpredictable. Whichever, she made herself heard, so much so that she earned the position of board chair. In setting the board's budget she was more supportive of gifted programs than of educational programs targeted to the needy, which gave her an elitist reputation. She did not mince words. When teachers threatened to strike, Campbell replied, "I hope they get kicked in the ass."

In 1984 she ran for the conservative-minded Social Credit party in the British Columbia provincial election and came in a distant third. However, Premier Bill Bennett was sufficiently impressed that he offered her a research position on his staff. The independent Campbell declared her maturity and loyalty. "I'm not going to shoot my mouth off like I did with the school board job. I'm working for somebody else now." She also remarried, this time to Harvard-educated lawyer and academic Howard Eddy, a divorced father of three.

When Premier Bennett resigned, he tipped the race towards his former principal secretary, Bud Smith, Campbell's former supervisor. Campbell believed she was better qualified for the job. It was audacious for a low-level political assistant to seek the premier's chair. She was unprepared, inexperienced and under-funded. But there was nothing deferential about Campbell, telling reporters of the eventual winner, Bill Vander Zalm: "I only wish I knew him before his lobotomy . . . (and) charisma without substance is a dangerous thing." But Campbell had difficulty connecting with ordinary citizens and rank-and-file delegates. She once quipped, "I suppose they would find me as boring as I would find them."

At the convention, she came in dead last with an embarrassing 14 votes.

However, she stuck with politics and won a seat in the legislature in 1986. Apparently, Premier Vander Zalm did not recover from his "lobotomy" and did not invite Campbell into Cabinet. She fell further out of favour when she refused to toe the party line on withholding provincial funding for abortions that were not otherwise approved by a hospital's therapeutic abortion committee.

In disfavour, Campbell jumped at the chance to represent the federal riding of Vancouver Center in 1988. She became the Progressive Conservative candidate two weeks into the election campaign after the incumbent, Pat Carney, declined to run due to ill health. Campbell captured nationwide attention during an acrimonious debate over free trade when she shrieked on camera, "What are you afraid of?" She won the election by 269 votes.

IN 1989, PRIME MINISTER MULRONEY made Campbell minister of state for Indian and northern affairs. After demonstrating solid support for the government's agenda, including the sensitive issue of advancing legislation to make abortion a matter between a woman and her doctor, Campbell was rewarded with the position of minister of justice in 1990, the first woman to hold the portfolio. This appointment brought Campbell into the inner circle of Cabinet. The demands of the office also contributed to the end of her second marriage, in 1991.

Campbell had an inner need to prove herself correct and intelligent, occasionally focusing on details that had little relevance to Canadians. There was nothing to be gained by maintaining that "The Star Spangled Banner" was musically superior to "O Canada," for example, or that the lyric "all thy sons command" should be changed to "all thy children's command."

If Canadians were looking for something different in a politician, then Campbell was happy to oblige. She certainly appeared different when she posed bare-shouldered behind a screen holding her legal robes in a manner that suggested she was naked. The photo was splashed across the front page of Canadian newspapers nationwide. When reporters asked her if this was her Madonna pose, Campbell replied: "Seriously, the notion that the bare shoulders of a forty-three-year-old woman are the source of prurient comment or titillation, I mean, I suppose I should be complimented."

That photo helped launch Campbell into the consciousness of Canadians as someone dramatically different from Brian Mulroney and, perhaps, sufficiently independent of mind to be considered as a future leader. Campbell's irreverence reminded some of Pierre Trudeau.

Brian Mulroney again boosted Campbell's leadership stock by promoting her to minister of national defence and minister for veterans' affairs on January 3, 1993. This broadened her experience and gave her two ministerial staff complements, which helped her to organize a leadership campaign. The key issue in her portfolio was the replacement of aging helicopters with the $4.4 billion EH-101 state-of-the-art search and rescue aircraft.

Campbell entered the leadership race as the clear front-runner to replace Brian Mulroney. Polls favoured her for prime minister over Liberal leader Jean Chrétien by a margin of two to one. That was all that most of the other prospective candidates needed to hear before they dropped out of the race. Some who had been cultivating contacts and raising money for years declined to run, which included: Michael Wilson, Perrin Beatty, Bernard Valcourt, Barbara McDougall. Had Brian Mulroney not intervened to put in place the necessary supports for Jean Charest to enter the race, Campbell might not have had any meaningful opposition.

Campbell had come a long way in seven years. In the excitement, reporters understandably began to ask the question: who is Kim Campbell?

Campbell's inexperience and lack of leadership skills were evident throughout her run for the leadership, but the Tories were so anxious for change that they failed to heed the warning signs. From the outset, Campbell had an almost insurmountable lead in public, political, and financial support. But when Jean Charest started to build momentum, Campbell told her campaign team, "Jean Charest has a strategy, and I want a strategy."

Short on policy and long on catchphrases, Campbell claimed that as prime minister she would "do politics differently." She would be more inclusive and consultative. As to specifics, well, that would follow. Her campaign manager, fellow MP Ross Reid, commented, "People don't want to focus on that kind of minutiae. Canadians don't expect all of the options from politicians." But as reporters began to dig deeper into Campbell's makeup, Jean Charest continued to chip away at her lead, and Joe Clark and Hugh Segal mused about being late entries into the race, reinforcing a concern that Campbell was not yet ready for prime time. In a profile piece by Peter C. Newman, Campbell let her guard down: "The thing that infuriates me is apathy. People who boast about how they've never been involved in a political party . . . who do they think is working to keep the society intact so they can have the luxury of sitting back and being such condescending SOBs? To hell with them."

The portrait being painted was of an elite intellectual who was disconnected from the lives of ordinary Canadians.

Polls nearer the convention showed that Jean Charest was best equipped to take on the Liberals. A stream of endorsements, including one from former leader Joe Clark, came at a time when momentum mattered most. After the convention speeches, Brian Mulroney wrote in his personal journal what a lot of the country was thinking: "Jean Charest gave a barnburner and Kim Campbell sounded like an accountant before the Rotary. He clearly has the momentum and now could win today on the first ballot, and definitely if a second ballot is required. What a sea change."

But the organization established by Campbell early in the campaign was strong and her early lead could not be overcome. On the first ballot, she came within 71 votes of winning the leadership. Third-place finisher Jim Edwards backed away from a deal with Charest because he thought Campbell couldn't possibly lose and he wanted a guaranteed place in her Cabinet. Campbell won on the second ballot with 1817 votes to 1630 for Charest. Kim Campbell was the new leader of the Progressive Conservative party and the first female prime minister of Canada.

Campbell had previously demonstrated her capacity to do what she thought was right, often boldly standing up to authority to make a point. Burdened by leadership, however, she became deferential to her advisors, many of whom had been put in place by Mulroney and did not know her well. As minister of national defence, Campbell had ably held the file to replace Canada's aging fleet of helicopters. Yet, as prime minister, when her national campaign team advised her to relent and scale back on the unpopular purchase, she was powerless to resist. Told what to do by her campaign team, she dutifully backed down, later saying, "There was no time to argue the issue; the speech was set. Against my better judgment, I put the best face on it I could. It was a disaster. . . ."

Despite weak leadership and various stumbles, however, once she was in office Campbell's personality and new approach to policy won her remarkable support. She recorded among the highest approval ratings for any prime minister since the early 1960s.

Campbell thought she could win the coming election and so did many Canadians. Conservative polls showed Conservatives six points ahead, 35 to 29 percent, among decided voters. Newspaper polls had the Tories and Liberals in a dead heat. Few people would say that Mulroney had bequeathed a winning hand to his successor, but it was far from a sure loss. By Labour Day, an election was hers to win or lose.

Campbell had the right to reconvene Parliament, present a throne speech and budget to the House of Commons, define a modern vision for the country, then call an election. She could have attended the G-7 summit to give her profile on the world stage. She could have taken advantage of the office of prime minister. Instead, on September 8, Campbell visited the governor general at Rideau Hall and requested the dissolution of Parliament for a general election to be held on October 25, 1993. Stumbling out of the gate, Campbell told reporters waiting outside Rideau Hall, that Canadians might have to wait until the turn of the century before meaningful and sustained progress would be made on unemployment. Politicians—especially when stumping—are supposed to inspire hope, not deliver grim doses of reality. Even though her statement would turn out to be accurate, the media jumped all over the "gaffe," an early indication that the press was intent on giving the prime minister a rough ride for the duration of the campaign.

From the outset, the PC strategy was to ignore Preston Manning's Reform party. From a base level of 2 percent in the 1988 election, Reform support crested in the early 1990s at nearly 16 percent. At its peak, Reform could claim a higher standing in the polls than the governing PC party in areas outside Québec. However, by the time the general election was called in 1993, national Reform support was closer to 10 percent—still significant, but lacking momentum. It was concentrated in areas where the PC party was naturally strong, but it was not high enough to threaten the insurmountable lead that the PCs had enjoyed in the West for a generation or more. A sudden rise in Reform support at the outset of the campaign should have caught the attention of the Tory strategists, but it didn't. They continued to underestimate Preston Manning until it was too late to make a difference.

Earlier in the year, the Reform party had published its platform, which included a "zero-in-three" plan to eliminate the deficit. On September 23, the *Globe and Mail* editorial scrutinized the Reform plan under the headline, "The only deficit plan we've seen." Reform could no longer be castigated as extreme and scary. The editorial underscored the public's widespread view that the Tories had a dismal record on financial management and no plan to fix the problem: "Reform is the only party that has yet shown a credible commitment to getting control of the national debt: a commitment made credible by its detailed 'zero-in-three' plan to halt the growth of public debt. Ms. Campbell is at pains to display how emotionally committed she is to the task, but can't tell us how she would go about it."

Those words from the *Globe* editorial shook Tory campaign headquarters badly.

The PC election team had put all its eggs into one basket. Not the Conservative record over the past nine years, not a plan for the future, and not a comparative analysis of the weakness of the opposition—the basket was Kim Campbell. The team was selling her style, her gender, and her new consultative way of doing politics.

Despite Campbell's early gaffes, in the first few weeks of the campaign the Tories were still running neck and neck with the Liberals. Polls were telling PC strategists that unemployment was the most important issue over the deficit by a factor of five to one. Then, on the same day the *Globe and Mail* ran its editorial praising Preston Manning's zero-in-three deficit plan, Campbell made one of the most astonishing and puzzling statements ever uttered by a national leader. Pressed by reporters about a so-called hidden agenda on social programs, the prime minister said, "The first budget of the new government will be in February of 1994, and Parliament will come back this fall. I think there is ample opportunity to engage Canadians in a serious dialogue and to work with provinces to find the best way to deliver those services."

This response struck reporters as odd. Did she not think that the best time for dialogue with Canadians on these issues was during an election? She disagreed: "I think that's the worst possible time to have that kind of dialogue . . . the issues are much too complex to try and generate some kind of a blueprint in the forty-seven days that's available in an election campaign. . . . This is not the time . . . to get involved in a debate on very, very serious issues."

The egg in the basket had cracked! The Tories were left with nothing—no platform, no vision to fall back on and, now, no credible candidate. They became desperate as their poll numbers plummeted. At the same time,

Reform numbers began to climb. Campaign manager John Tory wanted Campbell to meet the *Globe*'s editorial board to undo the damage, to demonstrate that a Campbell government would be serious about the deficit and had a comprehensive plan to balance the budget. An appropriate response, perhaps. Problem was, she had no such plan. Campbell couldn't get her facts straight or answer the *Globe*'s questions. The *Globe* concluded that only Preston Manning had command of the issue.

With only twenty days left in the election campaign, the *Globe and Mail* reported the results of a stunning poll: because of the strength of Reform, the PC party could be reduced to only 35 seats. Worse news followed. A Tory television ad began to air nationally near the end of the campaign. Campbell had been briefed about the ad, but had not seen it beforehand. In an attempt to ridicule Liberal leader Jean Chrétien, the ad mocked his facial disability. The ad backfired disastrously. And it offered up a golden opportunity for Chrétien who, speaking in Lunenberg, Nova Scotia, said, "It's true that I have a physical defect, God gave it to me. When I was a kid people were laughing at me. But I accepted that God gave me other qualities and I'm grateful." For Campbell and the Tories, the game was now truly over.

The Tories went from being badly defeated to being nearly annihilated. Reform exceeded even its own pre-writ predictions, winning 52 seats in the House of Commons, just two behind the Bloc Québécois, which now became Her Majesty's Loyal Opposition. Reform beat the PCs in popular vote by a small margin, 18.7 percent to 16 percent. The Tories ended up with a humiliating two seats: Jean Charest in Québec and Elsie Wayne in New Brunswick.

There is every reason to believe that the Reform party was successful in 1993 because Campbell failed during the campaign. Had Mulroney stayed on as prime minister, holding together the weakened strands of his coalition, or had Jean Charest won the leadership and performed as he was capable, Manning and his team might have been held to a handful of seats. One study of voting defection in the western provinces between the 1988 and 1993 campaigns isolated the source of Reform's support. Compared to the 1988 campaign, the PC party lost 55 percent of its vote to Reform, double the rate of Liberal defections to Reform, and six times the rate of loss from the NDP. In other words, Kim Campbell's loss was Preston Manning's gain.

Jean Chrétien won the election by default. David McLaughlin, author of a book on Campbell's demise, summed up the Tory loss and the Liberal win this way: "Tories refused to put ideas on the table for Canadians to consider because they either had none or did not want to tell what they actually intended to do. . . . The overriding lesson from the election is simple: ideas do count. Standing for something does matter."

Party veterans like Don Mazankowski placed much of the blame on Kim Campbell's performance. "We felt it was time to turn the page and present a new image. Had we known what was going to happen many of us would have stuck around to fight the good fight. We may not have won the election but we sure would have come back with more than two seats."

Canadians would have not been surprised if Progressive Conservatives succumbed to the humiliation and folded the party's tent. Under a mountain of debt, they did not even have enough seats to be recognized as an official political party in the House of Commons. Perhaps it would have been better for the nation if they had closed shop and let Reform have a clear run at government. But Tory party roots run deep. Also, little was known about Reform or its leader Preston Manning and old Tories were wary enough to keep fighting. Yet the question was legitimate: could and should the Progressive Conservative Party of Canada be given up for dead?

The man who couldn't stop smiling was Jean Chrétien. He had had an awkward run as Opposition leader and had come into the election campaign the clear underdog. Few expected a majority Liberal government and few expected Chrétien, often dubbed "yesterday's man," would out-campaign Kim Campbell. His party now held 177 seats in a 295-seat legislature. Chrétien took power all in stride. "Politics is about wanting power, exercising it, and keeping it . . . Politics is a sport in which the desire for victory is everything." In defeat, Kim Campbell was left unemployed; that is, until Chrétien appointed her to be Canada's Consul General in Los Angeles, a long way from 24 Sussex Drive.

CHAPTER 27

MANNING VERSUS CHAREST: FUTILITY PERSONIFIED

I wondered whether the Conservatives had been born under an unlucky star, with a
congenital inability to govern themselves, let alone the country.—Preston Manning

The separatists are going to ask you to turn in your passport!
What do you think about that? —Jean Charest

CONSERVATIVES WOULD RATHER FORGET the 1993 election and
the decade that followed. A time of profound division, conservative
forces and factions fought one another for survival and supremacy,
and in turn they gave three successive Liberal majorities to Jean Chrétien,
who never had to break a sweat. There was no effective opposition to the
government in the House of Commons and no government in waiting. What
transpired inside conservative ranks was pointless and futile. And Canada
suffered the consequences.

Between 1993 and 2003, conservatism was represented by two political
parties. The Reform party and its successor, the Canadian Alliance, were largely
western-based conservative populists. The Progressive Conservative party, with
support that was a mile wide and an inch deep, represented the remaining
strands of the once great Tory party. Leading the two Conservative flanks were
Jean Charest and Joe Clark for the PCs; and Preston Manning and Stockwell
Day for Reform/Alliance. Former Mulroney Cabinet minister Lucien
Bouchard could be thought of as part of the mix because he represented the

Québec Conservative contingent, but his political creation, the Bloc Québecois, was effectively divorced from conservative thought. Its exclusive mission was Québec sovereignty, while its economic leanings drifted to the left.

Preston Manning came to national politics with all the credibility and sophistication that we would expect of the son of one of Canada's right-wing political icons. Ernest Manning not only directed Canada's National Bible Hour, a radio broadcast syndicated to over ninety outlets, he was also, for 25 years, the Social Credit premier of Alberta.

Born June 10, 1942, Preston was raised in the evangelical Christian tradition and with a strong sense of civic duty. This is not something he picked up casually at the dinner table. He had a small side office in the Alberta Legislature, immediately beside his father's. While other kids played in the streets after school, Preston did his homework in the office next to the premier—until his dad was ready to drive him home. The accomplishments of the senior Manning helped to instill in Preston a strong sense of destiny, a high dose of ego, and a legitimate legacy on which to build.

Parents of five children, Preston Manning and his wife Sandra have struggled with how best to integrate their faith with a life of politics. In his first autobiography, Manning devoted an entire chapter to the subject of faith under the title "The Spiritual Dimension." However, on matters of morality and conscience, Manning is a fervent democrat and believes that citizens, not politicians, should determine public policy on such issues.

Manning was raised to be suspicious of the intentions and deeds of all the mainstream political parties, and was deeply rooted in the populist political traditions of Western Canada. His father, at the age of twenty-six, was one of 56 Socred candidates thrust into power in the Alberta provincial election of August 22, 1935, a scant five months after the party was founded. When Preston Manning talks of a spark that can ignite a prairie firestorm, he only has to think of the rapid and overwhelming ascent of Social Credit in Alberta in 1935.

Although conservative by nature, Manning was never an advocate or supporter of the Progressive Conservative Party. He ran for Parliament as a Socred in 1962 at the age of twenty, the election when Diefenbaker went from a record-breaking majority to a thin-minority government. While there is nothing in the Social Credit name that implies conservatism, most historians would agree that it was a conservative party through and through; it just had a different name. Manning thought very little of the PC party and wondered "whether the Conservatives had been born under an unlucky star, with a congenital inability to govern themselves, let alone the country."

Manning was more influenced by populism than by the world's great conservative leaders of that era. His heroes were more likely to be Canadians
who countered established norms and order: Louis Riel, Joseph Howe of
Nova Scotia, and the visionaries and builders of Québec's Quiet Revolution.

With his father out of office, Preston decided to lie low. Rather than
enter the fray and join the only conservative option available in Alberta,
Preston bided his time. He believed that in every generation, an opportunity
arises that invites fundamental reform of political parties and institutions.
This sense of destiny was imparted to Preston by his father and was articulated in a book that they researched and wrote together in 1967. The central
thesis of Ernest Manning's book on political realignment was that meaningful political choice did not exist in Canada because the federal Progressive
Conservative party and the federal Liberal party were ideologically indis-
tinguishable. What was needed, argued the elder Manning, was a social
conservative movement.

Manning could not implement his plan while the Liberals were in power
because most western Canadians had pinned their hopes for reforming the
national government on the Progressive Conservative party. Western
Canada was a political wasteland for the Liberals after their introduction of
the destructive National Energy Program (NEP) in 1980. The NEP increased
Canadian control and ownership of the energy industry while shielding the
country, and the East in particular, from the impact of rising oil prices. Many
companies operating in the oil patch responded by leaving the province,
leaving many Albertans jobless.

We can conclude from Manning's writing and conduct that he never
wanted Brian Mulroney's PC government to succeed. On October 17,
1986, Manning made the case to some senior oil industry executives "for a
new federal political movement dedicated to reforms that would make the
West an equal partner in Confederation." It was a speech Manning had been
delivering in his mind and in public for 20 years. Manning expressed his
view that the West was going to produce something new, provided it had
the leadership and funds to do the job.

The October 31, 1986 decision by the Mulroney government to award
a maintenance contract for Canada's CF-18 fighter jets to Canadair, from
Montréal, was the spark Manning needed to start his prairie brushfire. Said
Manning: "The West felt the Liberals always bent over backwards to accom-
modate Quebec and didn't even hear what the West was saying. Here were
the new guys ... who were going to do it different, doing exactly the same
thing." Manning knew that westerners were hungry for a legitimate and

credible voice that could articulate their resentment, and remarked "The time for 'waiting for something to happen' was over. Something was happening. It was time to act."

The Western Assembly on Canada's Economic and Political Future was held in Vancouver on May 29–31, 1987. Under the banner "The West Wants In," about 300 delegates, including Stephen Harper, coalesced around issues such as regional fairness, balanced budgets, Senate reform, and free trade. The convention that established the Reform Party of Canada took place in Winnipeg from October 30 to November 1, 1987.

Preston Manning believed that the Reform party crossed all political lines and appealed to the masses of Canadians disillusioned with the traditional political parties. By this measure, Manning's Reform party would, in theory, draw support from the mainstream parties in roughly the same proportions as these individuals would otherwise have voted. He did not want to accept that Reform was really another Conservative party because he did not want to debate an inherent and obvious strategic flaw: that the Reform party was splitting votes with the Tories and thereby electing Liberals and NDP members of Parliament. Ted Byfield, a Reform party founder and creator of *Alberta Report*, did not believe Manning was a populist, and suggested that his interest was more about control and power: "It always seems to me that [Manning] is always advocating something [populism] that is incompatible with his own instincts.... And I think that will likely get him into trouble before he's finished, too, because it isn't his [first] instinct. [Preston] is the authoritarian of the first order, [just] as his father was...."

Manning brought his vision of a "New Canada" to Québec. He rejected the notion that Canada is a product of two founding peoples, English and French, arguing instead for a single nation of equal provinces. Manning opposed the 1987 Meech Lake Accord largely because he thought it unlikely that Québec would agree to accept a formula that gave equality to every other province in a reformed Senate. His message fell flat with both federalists and sovereignists in Québec, which includes almost everyone. Jean Chrétien observed in his memoirs that, "Manning knew he could never become Prime Minister of Canada because of Québec and, consequently, that he wouldn't have been terribly sorry to see it leave the federation."

The 1988 election was problematic for Reform because it was on the same side as Mulroney on free trade. It was too risky for many western conservatives to register a protest vote with Reform, fearing they would place in jeopardy something the West had wanted for a century. The major distinguishing issue that Reform brought to the electorate was financial mismanagement, which stood in contrast to the inability of Mulroney's government to balance the books. On the award of the CF-18 maintenance contract, Reformers told Manitobans, "Don't Get Mad, Get Even."

For a first attempt in a strategically difficult election, Reform performed remarkably well. It received slightly more than 2 percent of votes cast nationally and 8.5 percent of votes cast in the 72 ridings in which it fielded a candidate. The Tories won 25 of 26 Alberta ridings, but Reform captured 15.3 percent of the vote, with support in both urban and rural ridings. Preston Manning placed second in Yellowhead, reducing Joe Clark's popular vote from 74 percent in 1984 to 45 percent in 1988. While the Free Trade Agreement was secure, Alberta had still managed to cast a meaningful protest vote, something that Progressive Conservatives should have heeded as a warning. Reform had shown itself to be more than a fringe element.

AFTER THE 1988 CAMPAIGN, Manning was determined to run candidates across the country. While there was some indication in the early 1990s that Reform could elect members from the West, few commentators gave it even a remote chance of translating western resentment and alienation into a platform it could take across the country. However, the Reform party gained national attention, as well as valuable political and organizational experience, when it opposed the Charlottetown Constitutional Accord.

Between the 1988 and 1993 elections, Manning affixed himself to the national political scene. The Reform party won an election in Alberta that nominated a senator to Parliament's Red Chamber. In 1989, Reform candidate Deborah Grey won a by-election to the House of Commons. At times, the Reform party ranked ahead of the PC party in the polls outside Québec. And, giving breadth and meaning to Reform, Manning released a lengthy autobiography under the bold title *The New Canada*.

Manning struggled for attention going into the 1993 campaign, but as Kim Campbell disintegrated, he and his party were given a closer look. When the PCs failed to offer hope and vision, they lost the mantle of conservatism. In the vacuum, the deficit-fighting platform assembled by Reform's Stephen Harper was the only conservative meat on the table. By focusing on his platform, Manning sidestepped the many accusations that he led a party of red-neck extremists.

Manning came within two seats of becoming leader of the Opposition. Although it ran 207 candidates, Reform won only one seat east of the

Manitoba border, so did not meet the test of a national party. A concentrated vote enabled Reform to win 25 times the number of seats as the PC party with only 2.6 percentage points between them in the popular vote.

In the House of Commons, Manning would face a Liberal majority government, the Bloc Québecois as official Opposition, and two lonely MPs from the PC party: Elsie Wayne from New Brunswick and Jean Charest from Québec.

WITH REFORM DWARFING the Progressive Conservative caucus, Manning might easily have taken the lead in forming a partnership with the Tories to take on the Liberal government. But ignoring reality, Manning did not see Charest and the Tories as political cousins. In the end, neither of these men would see their political dreams realized.

John James Charest was born on St. Jean Baptiste day, June 24, 1958. Or so the birth certificate claims. In fact, his father named him *Jean*, he thought of himself as *Jean*, and his friends in the French school he attended called him *Jean*. Blame sloppy record keeping by the parish priest.

In his youth, the bilingual Charest was known to mediate between the English- and French-speaking gangs. Like Brian Mulroney, he reprised this role throughout much of his life. He did not excel academically, but displays of leadership, such as serving as council president in his high school, were conspicuous. While ad-libbing during a speech for his first elected school office Charest's natural ability to communicate and connect with his fellow students became evident to his teachers and fellow students, and more important, to himself.

In his mid-teens, Michelle Dionne, daughter of surgeon Philippe Dionne and his wife Lisette Plourde, caught Charest's eye. Jean and Michelle complemented each other well. She was the organizer while he was the dreamer and front-man.

Growing up, Jean Charest's household was filled with politics. His father, named *Red*, was in fact true *blue*. The younger Charest was keenly attuned to current events and political developments. In 1976, he voted for the sovereignist Parti Québecois in the provincial election, largely because his favoured Union Nationale party was a non-factor and he wanted the Liberals removed from office.

He had barely reached voting age when he predicted that one day he would become leader of the Union Nationale and premier of Québec. When it was pointed out that the Union Nationale was passé, he suggested becoming leader of the Progressive Conservative party and prime minister of Canada.

Charest pursued law as a career because he "liked the idea of giving people a hand." His Sherbrooke University law professors remarked that Charest didn't so much ask questions in class, as give speeches. Surprisingly, the politically motivated Charest was not involved in the 1980 Québec referendum on sovereignty. At the time, he was working at a summer job as an assistant mechanic on a Great Lakes freighter and did not even vote.

After passing his bar exams, Charest was itching for courtroom experience and—over his first three years practising law—he argued eight cases before a jury. Politics, however, was never far from his mind. He enthusiastically joined Joe Clark's team in 1983 to help win delegates to sustain the embattled leader's job. The quid pro quo from the Clark camp was the party's nomination for Sherbrooke in the next election. Charest helped to deliver Clark delegates, but after Mulroney won the leadership, his deal for the Tory nomination was worthless. Mulroney's team gave the nod to Claude Métras, but Charest was prepared to fight. At the nomination meeting on May 15, 1984, Charest reached out for support from English and French, federalist and sovereignist, friends and family. Red Charest alone sold 700 memberships. Charest beat Métras 908 to 804.

The twenty-six-year-old had no practical political experience, but immediately established his presence in local debates. His Liberal opponent, Irénée Pelletier, had won the riding in four consecutive elections, including the 1980 campaign by over 23,000 votes. On September 4, 1984 Charest was the victor by a margin of 7,625 votes.

Charest arrived in Ottawa with a bang. He appeared at national campaign headquarters the day after the election to offer his personal thanks to party workers. He invited members of the Québec Tory caucus to his apartment for a get-together before the first session of Parliament. The Charest campaign team sent a videotape of his riding debate performance to the Prime Minister's Office, hoping it would help get him a position of responsibility in Mulroney's first administration. He ended up as the lowly assistant deputy speaker.

On June 30, 1986, Charest, twenty-eight, was sworn in as minister of state for youth. He remains the youngest MP ever to be appointed to Cabinet. He initiated programs such as "Stay in School" and was not beyond creative, sometimes nefarious, methods to advance his agenda. Though happy to be at the large Cabinet table, Charest hungered for more responsibility. Being called a "mini minister" by Liberal members rankled and he was strongly motivated to rise through the ranks.

In 1988 he was appointed to the newly created post of minister for fitness and amateur sport, a portfolio that did not match his lifestyle or physique. But he embraced the responsibility and won the enthusiastic support of the sports community. He held the position during the Olympic Games in Seoul, when Canada's Ben Johnson was disqualified for using a banned substance. Without consultation and due process, Charest announced in the House of Commons, "The consequence is a life suspension for Ben Johnson from Sport Canada funding and participation on national teams." The decision may have come too quickly, but it put minister Charest on the national stage.

Charest was confident going into the 1988 election, but he left nothing to chance. To cover his bases he chose as his chief organizer a well-known sovereignist. This time he won with a margin of 22,224 votes.

CHAREST'S POLITICAL LIFE is marked by a fateful telephone call he made from New Zealand on January 23, 1990 to Mr. Justice Yvan Macerola of the Québec Superior Court. Charest contends that he was asked to make the call to clear up an issue related to the status of track and field coach Daniel Saint-Hilaire, whose case was being considered before Macerola's court. The justice immediately alerted Charest to the impropriety of the call. Charest made a mistake that a lawyer ought not to have made. The prime minister asked for, and received, his minister's resignation. Mulroney did have the good grace to call Red Charest to tell him his son had a bright future in politics and it would not be too long before Jean was back at the Cabinet table.

As the Meech Lake Accord unravelled, Mulroney and his Québec lieutenant, Lucien Bouchard, tagged Charest to chair an all-party special committee to resolve a deadlock caused by dissenting provinces; notably Newfoundland, Manitoba, and New Brunswick. The two-month mandate involved cross-country hearings. Charest and his committee delivered a unanimous report. Addressing the House of Commons, Charest said, "In the committee's opinion, a companion resolution which adds clauses to the Meech Lake Accord, without eliminating anything whatever, is probably the best way to resolve the constitutional dilemma." But Bouchard took exception to any companion resolution that might alter the meaning of the original constitutional deal. In other words, he set Charest up to take responsibility for a task that was impossible to achieve. "This report should not have existed. I am against it," said Bouchard. "And I find that I will have to leave the government with pain and sadness." In the process, Meech Lake died.

Brian Mulroney kept his promise to Red Charest. On April 21, 1991, Jean Charest was appointed minister of the environment and a member of the Cabinet's priorities and planning committee. Charest had lurched from a low-ranking portfolio to backbench MP to the inner circle. He represented the government at the Earth Summit at Rio de Janeiro in 1992 and received acclaim for his leadership and inspiration. It was the springboard to the 1993 race for the leadership of the Progressive Conservative party and the job of prime minister.

Then the untested and unknown Kim Campbell came flying out of the blocks and scared almost every high-ranking leadership contender out of the race. Charest might easily have been another dropout, if not for the critical intervention and pledges of support from Brian Mulroney. While an initial goal may have been to avoid humiliation, as the party got to know both Campbell and Charest, the race became heated and the gap started to close.

Charest was thirty-four when he entered the leadership race and he made it a contest between the tortoise and the hare. "In Ottawa they seem to have decided everything. But that's not the way you choose a prime minister, without discussing a single idea. Democratic debate is first and foremost a debate of ideas, which can't be replaced by a contest between organizations." When told the party needed a leader from outside Québec, Charest said, "Nominating only one party leader from Québec in 125 years isn't exactly an abuse of the rule of alternation." Like most leadership contests it was a rough-and-tumble affair. At one delegate selection meeting, a party member explained to a reporter why he was supporting Charest: "Because, as a Haitian like us, he can help us get out of the crisis."

As the convention neared, the national opinion polls suggested Charest had a better chance of beating the Liberals than Campbell did. At the convention, he gave a rousing speech, but he came up short. Had 94 of Campbell's delegates on the final ballot sided with Charest he would have become prime minister of Canada. All Campbell could say was, "Jean, you're one hell of a tortoise!"

Charest served as deputy prime minister and minister of industry and science in the short-lived Campbell government. While her once-mighty party was reduced to two seats, Charest's victory in Sherbrooke by 8,181 votes remains the stuff of legend.

After the mess Campbell had made, there was only one person who could put the broken pieces of the PC party back together. Jean Charest was given the leadership unopposed and promptly went to work rebuilding the party. It was on Charest's shoulders that the PC party would live or die. He was the franchise and the last great hope.

The challenge Charest faced in Parliament could not have been tougher.

The Liberals played hardball and were so small-minded that they initially refused to let Charest sit beside the other Tory MP, Elsie Wayne, in the House of Commons. His party had not only lost the levers of government, for the first time since Confederation it was not recognized in the House of Commons as an official party. There would be few opportunities to ask questions in the House, and virtually no parliamentary budget to support the leader or research the issues. On top of that, the party was $10 million in debt, so there was no money available to hire staff or conduct much of a leader's tour. What Charest did have at his disposal, however, thanks to nine years of Tory rule, was a majority in the Senate. Charest persuaded the senators to surrender their budgets to the leader's discretion in a single pool of funds.

A critical thrust of the PC rebuilding process was reforms designed to give more influence to rank and file members, largely by placing a "national council" between the members and the executive. The council would comprise one representative from each of the 295 federal ridings. Other initiatives included a national membership program, greater influence for party members through a "bottom-up" policy review process, and increased transparency and accountability on party finances.

A bottom-up grass roots policy development process had its flaws. Charest, who wanted to offer "conservatism with a human face," clashed with Tory youth who wanted a doctrinaire program of right-wing policies. By slashing taxes and spending, the youth wanted to win back hardline western conservatives who had defected to the Reform Party. They also wanted to emulate the success of the Conservatives in Ontario, led by Mike Harris. Charest, who was prepared to accept some right-wing policies, knew his history and believed that moderate inclusive policies and approaches were generally required to win government. This policy split within the party caused conservative commentator David Frum to remark, "The federal PCs are now two parties. The first block is the Harris Tories, who are some of the most conservative people in Canada. And then there is the Charest party, which is, with the possible exception of the NDP, the least conservative party in Canada. And there's a big gap between them."

Somewhat independent of the political parties, about seventy right-leaning thinkers, activists, and academics convened in Calgary in May 1996 to find a way to unite conservative political forces in advance of the next election. Organized by conservative writers and activists David Frum and Ezra Levant, the closed-door meeting labelled "Winds of Change" was designed to connect the divided yet like-minded forces in the Canadian conservative movement. Practically, conference organizers had set their sights on something less than a full-scale merger. Though that may have been their ultimate goal, the proposition presented at the conference was for electoral cooperation between Reform and the PCs as the best strategy for ending Liberal hegemony. Some referred to this cooperation as "sisterhood." But party leaders and strategists almost immediately dismissed the idea. It seemed illogical to National Citizen's Coalition president Stephen Harper for the PC and Reform parties to be battling over second place. "I can't understand the [PC] political strategy," said Harper. "To the extent they have one, it seems to be everybody's second choice, and in this political system, that's absolutely suicidal."

It was Charest's good political fortune that Québec became immersed in a referendum on sovereignty in 1995. In the early days of the campaign, the federalist forces, led by the provincial Liberal leader Daniel Johnson, had a comfortable lead in the polls. But the tide turned overnight when Québec premier Jacques Parizeau announced Lucien Bouchard as his chief negotiator. Charest, who had been crisscrossing the province making speeches for the federalist side, was acknowledged as the "no" team's most persuasive platform speaker. Charest asked Québecers the tough questions. "The separatists are going to ask you to turn in your passport! What do you think about that?" Charest appealed to the hearts and minds of Québec voters, and made a clear difference in the outcome. But when it came time to hear from Charest on the evening of the razor-thin federalist victory, Jean Chrétien deliberately preempted his appearance on national television. It was a lesson for Charest: Liberals play the political game for keeps.

OVER CHRÉTIEN'S FIRST TERM as prime minister the Liberal party had been hovering comfortably in the polls between 40 and 50 percent support. The Reform and PC parties each languished around 10 percent and posed no threat to win government heading into the 1997 election. Even combined, the Tory and Reform vote was way behind the Liberals.

These were not good times for conservatives of any stripe and Chrétien knew it. In his political memoirs, he wrote that he liked his odds in 1997: "The opposition was divided and in disarray. Reform and the Tories were still a long way from merging and neither party was in a credible position to criticize us for not cutting the deficit. . . . There might never be a better moment for the Liberals to win a second majority." And it was not just the split of the conservative vote in English Canada that worked in Chrétien's favour. The presence of the sovereignist Bloc Québecois in Québec was also in his party's interests. Chrétien wrote, "In normal circumstances, as long as the

Bloc exists, it will split the anti-Liberal vote with the Tories and let us take more seats in the province."

Despite long odds Charest was hopeful going into the 1997 election. First, the PCs were slightly ahead of Reform. Second, an April 1997 Ekos poll showed that the Tories were the most popular "second choice" for both Liberal and Reform supporters by a significant margin. In fact, Liberal party supporters were three times more likely to switch to the Tories than to Reform. Third, Jean Charest rated higher than Preston Manning on the issue of trust (27 to 21 percent). All this meant that the Tories had more potential to increase their level of support than Reform did. In 1997, the PC party had a stronger leader and a more focused campaign. They had misunderstood and underestimated Reform last time out, but were better prepared this time.

It was clear that the Reform and PC parties would battle one another for the conservative vote. But given the split, the election outcome was never in doubt: Chrétien had a second successive majority in the bag. The only question the election might settle was which of the two conservative-minded parties would survive.

Reform wanted to finish off the PC party, but its strategy was unclear. After 1993, two logical paths were open to Manning. He could have sought a respectful accommodation and brought his western base into a national coalition that included the PC MPs. Or, he could have declared war on the PC party with the explicit aim of wiping it off the political map, giving him a clear run in the 1997 election. But he chose neither of these strategies, which, to Jean Chrétien, was Politics 101. "I would have moved heaven and earth to take over the Progressive Conservative party as quickly as possible. The Tories were down and out, with virtually nothing left but their history, so it would have been easy for Reform to take control from the inside by buying up memberships, riding by riding...I don't know why Manning didn't do that. Perhaps he had come to hate the Tories too much for what he saw as their betrayals of true conservatism. Perhaps he thought that his right-wing Western supporters would never accept the kinds of compromise that Brian Mulroney had made with the Ontario Red Tories for the sake of power."

Instead, Manning largely ignored the PC party, pretending it was not his competition. He believed his populist approach to governance and policy-making was sufficient to appeal to voters across a wide political spectrum. His strategy, however, papered over a fatal flaw: how could a populist party rooted in Alberta be anything but conservative? Indeed, Reform was no garden-variety conservative party. By its own survey, Reform party members placed themselves on the far-right wing of the political spectrum.

The campaign theme for Reform was called "Fresh Start." Wanting to look more like a winning politician, Manning had gone to great pains to look "fresh" by undergoing a personal makeover. He had laser surgery on his eyes, shed his nerdy glasses, his teeth were capped, his hair coiffed. He had a colour chart done, his wardrobe was updated, and a voice coach was added to the Reform team. Both reporters and political opponents alike would ridicule this makeover, remarking that while Manning came to Ottawa to change government, it looked like Manning was the one undergoing the change. Always strong on content, he now had a new look. The one thing he was still missing was passion, which was not something he could fake or manufacture. In the leaders' debates, Manning's lack of passion was in stark contrast to the more youthful, energetic, and emotional Jean Charest. After the debates, Manning acknowledged to his team that Charest had overwhelmed him and that he had let his troops down.

As the campaign progressed, Reform became desperate. Midway, the polls showed that the Tories had rebounded and were now expected to replace Reform as the official Opposition. While the Liberals were still comfortably ahead in a *Globe and Mail*/Environics poll at 40 percent, the Tories, at 25 percent, were substantially ahead of Reform who had 18 percent. The *Globe and Mail* also endorsed the Tories as the preferred choice for the nation's official Opposition, a dramatic contrast to the 1993 campaign when the *Globe and Mail* had legitimized Reform, endorsing its "zero-in-three" deficit elimination plan.

In a desperate move to "torque up" Reform's campaign, Manning began to tap into the base anger and resentment many western Canadians felt about the special treatment they believed had been reserved for Québec. This included a highly controversial Reform election ad suggesting Canada had had enough of national leaders from Québec. The ad featured Québec politicians, including Chrétien and Charest, with a red circle and bar emblazoned across their faces, similar to hazardous warning labels. The ads gave both Chrétien and Charest an opening to undermine Manning on the national stage, describing him as a "divisive" and "bigoted" leader who was attempting to appeal to extreme and destructive forces in certain parts of Canada. But the hard-hitting Reform ads seemed to work, as polls showed Tory numbers starting to fall and Reform numbers starting to climb. Manning had given up on attacking Liberals and had set his sights on holding his base in western Canada.

Post-campaign, Brian Mulroney commented on the controversial Reform Party ads, reminding Canadians that a leader is someone who builds unity, not division, in the country. He also warned about the intolerance of Reform: "[I] would [n]ever have countenanced an advertisement which drew big slashes of disapproval through the faces of leaders who happened to be French Canadians from Québec. The message could not have been clearer or more odious."

In referring to Manning's prospects of ever being able to "unite the right," Mulroney would later remark, "While it was a natural extension of what he was saying, the guy who authorized those ads in 1997 was no nation builder. He could never be Prime Minister. Never. Nor was he ever going to get his hands on the Conservative franchise and its 135 years of history."

Manning confirmed that he had no interest in coalition building when he mused about a minority government near the end of the 1997 campaign: "In the West, a minority government was not seen as a problem to be concerned about but a result to be welcomed . . . And if a Conservative rump, mainly Red Tories, joined the Liberals to prop them up, so much the better. That's where Red Tories belonged anyway." Manning was prepared to lose centrist Conservatives to the Liberals, abandoning his populist dream while accepting the reality that the Reform party was simply a party of conservatives of a different name and colour.

On paper, the Reform party could claim a substantial victory in the 1997 federal election. Its seat total increased by 15 percent over the 1993 campaign, climbing from 52 to 60 seats. It ran candidates in 227 of 301 ridings, including some in Québec. More important, it rose from being the third party in the House of Commons to the official Opposition, replacing the Bloc Québécois. The symbolism of removing a separatist party from official Opposition status and assuming the "government in waiting" tag was powerful. However, the 1997 election result was a deep disappointment for Reform. Despite the increase in seats, the popular vote for Reform, at 19.4 percent, increased less than one point over 1993. And, short of winning government, Reform's next most significant objective had been to gain a meaningful breakthrough east of the Manitoba border and drive a solid nail into the Tory coffin. But east of Manitoba, Reform was shut out.

In the end, the Liberals received another majority government even though they secured only 38.5 percent of the popular vote. With a strong showing from the NDP and Tories, as well as the modest pick-up by Reform, Chrétien's majority was reduced to 155 seats out of a 301-seat legislature. But he was still the prime minister, despite electing no members from Nova

Scotia, only one member from Saskatchewan, two from Alberta, and six from British Columbia: nine out of a possible 71 seats. Ontario was the Liberals' saviour, where they won 101 of 103 seats.

Worse for Reform than a Liberal win was the showing of the Tories. Far from dead, under Jean Charest's leadership the popular vote for the Tories increased from the 1993 election by a larger proportion than it did for Reform. At 18.8 percent, the Tories were only six-tenths of one percentage point behind Reform. The Tory seat total rose from two to 20, with a particularly strong showing in Atlantic Canada and Québec.

Charest had performed a minor miracle and resuscitated his party from intensive care, if not the last rites. Along with Elsie Wayne, the only other Tory MP elected in 1993, and with the support of many PC senators, the PC party was kept alive at the grassroots level. The Tories may not have been able to compete with Reform for seats in the West, but they still managed to poll close to 15 percent of the vote in Alberta.

While Reform pretended to be a national party, it had no roots in Atlantic Canada and did not have a message or platform that could generate much support outside its western base. As a result, the Tories outpolled Reform by a factor of 14.7 to one in Newfoundland, 25.3 to one in Prince Edward Island, 3.2 to one in Nova Scotia, 2.7 to one in New Brunswick, and 74 to one in Québec.

Charest discovered over the course of the campaign that his most likely wins would come from Québec and Atlantic Canada, where the vote was not being split with Reform. Adapting to his new audience, and sweeping his platform aside, Charest attacked the Liberals for their cutbacks to unemployment insurance and regional development programs to demonstrate empathy to his newfound eastern friends. It worked. With the ongoing existence of the Progressive Conservative Party very much on his shoulders, Jean Charest was able to tap into the Tory party legacy, particularly in Atlantic Canada where Conservative support is passed from one generation to the next.

Despite breathing life back into the Tory party, there was a tinge of disappointment on election night in Sherbrooke, Québec. Early campaign momentum had stalled in the final weeks, especially in Québec. Despite the setback there, however, there was more joy than sorrow for the PCs on election night. The party had just taken its first serious step in the rebuilding process. "We retained one critical aspect in 1997. We remained a national political party," said Geoff Norquay. "We secured votes in all parts of Canada. Because we were a mile wide and an inch deep we didn't win many seats, but it was a foundation on which we could build."

CHAPTER 28

CLARK VERSUS DAY: FUTILITY CONFIRMED

The good news is that I am widely trusted and popular. The bad news is that we cannot translate those qualities into votes for the party. —Joe Clark

Under a Canadian Alliance government, we will see a new birth of freedom in this land. —Stockwell Day

SOON AFTER THE 1997 ELECTION, Jean Charest declared war. "Preston Manning and the Reform party have misrepresented who and what they are to Canadians. We need to make our case to people who have voted Reform that they have been victims of this misrepresentation." Refuting any suggestion that a merger between the PCs and Reform was in the works, Charest quipped, "Hell hasn't frozen over yet." Charest was preparing himself for battle. However, the day after he made those remarks, Daniel Johnson, the leader of the Québec Liberal party, resigned. The entire country, except for Québec sovereignists, wanted Charest to take his place. Rarely in the history of Canadian politics has there been such a strong and resounding movement to draft a "saviour" into a position of leadership. Charest took over the Québec Liberal party on April 30, 1998.

Many conservatives viewed the open Tory leadership as an opportunity to unite PC and Reform forces. Some PC caucus members invited Stephen Harper to contest the leadership then spearhead a merger. Peter MacKay, however, was leery, fearing it would be a disguised attempt by Reformers to "completely take over our party." MacKay went on to say that whoever replaced Charest would have to be someone determined not to merge with the Reform party. Harper declined the offers, largely because he did not want to face Preston Manning and his former Reform colleagues directly in battle.

With Charest's abrupt departure the race to become Tory leader was a wide open affair with some unexpected entrants.

David Orchard was a fourth generation organic farmer and economic nationalist. He had grown up just a few kilometres from the John Diefenbaker's homestead. Why David Orchard wanted to be leader of the PC party is an intriguing question. He had campaigned against the Free Trade Agreement in 1988 through an organization he co-founded called Citizens Concerned about Free Trade. And he wrote a book in 1993, *The Fight for Canada: Four Centuries of Resistance to American Expansionism*, which included strong opposition to many of Mulroney's policies. Orchard used the relatively weak PC party as a vehicle for his strident views, responding to the criticism from long-standing Tories who felt he didn't belong by saying he was the one most faithful to the party's roots in opposing free trade. Of course, he had to go back to the days of Diefenbaker, and perhaps Borden, to make such a claim. Joe Clark dismissed Orchard as a "tourist" in the party.

Joe Clark was an equally surprising entrant to the race. Those who knew Clark best tried to talk him out of seeking the leadership, including his wife, his former political advisors, and former staff members who had served him when he was party leader and minister of external affairs. But Clark was convinced he could win both his party and the country and was undeterred by those who told him his time had passed. Clark enjoyed significant support from the Tory caucus, though not from Peter MacKay, whose candidate of choice was Hugh Segal, who had briefly served as Brian Mulroney's chief of staff.

The first ballot was held on October 24, 1998. Clark received 48.5 percent support; Segal was second with 18.9 percent; and Orchard was a respectable third with 16.3 percent. Orchard stubbornly stayed on for a second ballot, a move he claims gave the party much needed public attention.

Restored as leader, Clark was determined to reclaim past PC glory. He had no appetite for electoral cooperation with the Reform party. Clark backed up his tough talk by leading the passage of an amendment to the PC party constitution that required the party to field candidates in every riding. This prevented local riding associations from cooperating with

Reform party riding associations that may have wanted to field a single or joint candidate.

Preston Manning made several direct appeals to Joe Clark for cooperation. However, what Clark wanted was for Reform to withdraw from the political arena and join the PCs, with himself as leader. Since neither the Reform nor the PC party wanted to dissolve, and because neither wanted to become a junior partner, other options were required. Manning had some experience creating political parties and energizing discontented troops. His idea should have come as no surprise: to form a new and more broadly supported political party. He wanted to build a broader coalition, and bring disaffected PC party members who were unhappy with Joe Clark to his side.

The founding convention for the Canadian Conservative Reform Alliance was held in Ottawa on January 29, 2000. Were it not for the need to hold a leadership contest, all the party would have had to do was rename itself, because the Canadian Alliance was little more than the Reform party under another name. Manning would attempt what Joe Clark had in 1983: win a leadership after resigning a leadership. It didn't work out for Clark. Manning would fare no better.

One man in Canada who did not want to see Preston Manning continue in national politics was Brian Mulroney. In a rare appearance at a partisan event, Mulroney addressed the Tory faithful on June 9, 2000, and offered his bluntest assessment of Manning and Reform to date. Not inclined to reconcile then, Mulroney cautioned PC supporters against being drawn into Manning's new United Alternative approach, ". . . Now our daring revolutionary—realizing that Reform is a spent force with no prospect of ever forming a national government and doing little except ensure power for the Liberals—has changed course. 'Forget the negative things I've said about you for years', Mr. Manning says to the Conservatives, 'Hey, I love you now. True, I've demonized your leaders, denigrated your policies and ridiculed your candidates in my implacable campaign to destroy your party, your reputation and your legacy. But now, I've changed, I think you're great. Let me welcome you into my new party.'"

MANNING'S PRINCIPAL OPPONENT for the Alliance leadership was Albertan treasurer, *Stockwell Day*. Born in Barrie, Ontario on August 16, 1950, Day had lived in several places throughout the country in his youth. He considered himself a "retail brat" since his father, an executive with Zellers, was frequently transferred, landing in Ontario, Québec, and Atlantic Canada. In school, Day was active in sports and in persuasion.

Frustrated that his high school was not supporting his soccer team, he arranged to address a school assembly on the matter. At the next game he had cheerleaders on the sidelines.

He had a keen memory and was quick to invoke a poem when appropriate. This skill was most impressively displayed when, as Alberta treasurer, he delivered an entire budget speech without notes. Day was a troublemaker as a teen, but also achieved academic excellence when motivated, winning an award for all-around excellence in his junior year at the demanding and exclusive Ashbury College.

Politics was the main topic of conversation in the Day household. Stockwell's father ran for Parliament for the Social Credit party, facing NDP giant Tommy Douglas. Day's deposit was not returned. The Day family provided a temporary home to Robert Thompson, just after the Social Credit leader defected to the Tories. If there was frustration about politics in the house, it was that Conservatives were not conservative enough.

Day was not afraid of hard work and had entrepreneurial instincts, beginning in his teens scalping Montréal Canadiens tickets. His schemes were not all so glamorous; one such venture involved raising chickens in the back of his car.

Day's early career path suggested an ending other than leader of the official Opposition. He worked odd jobs throughout his twenties. For a time he drove a hearse, worked construction, and otherwise led a nomadic life. In 1971, he married dog groomer Valorie Martin. Beyond inspiring a more serious and settled life—they eventually had three children—Valorie inspired Stockwell to reflect on the meaning of God and faith.

An auction business literally went up in flames when a fire destroyed the assets of the enterprise. If this was a test of faith it did not affect Stockwell and Valorie, who then volunteered to counsel evangelical youth groups. There were short stints working construction in the Far North, followed by a job installing drapery tracks in Edmonton, including a project at the provincial legislature.

After completing studies at Northwest Bible College, Stockwell Day became the assistant pastor at the Bentley Christian Training Centre. The Alberta government didn't know how to deal with Christian schools and independent education, so Day stepped in and helped form the Alberta Association of Independent Schools, which lobbied for funding and regulatory reform on behalf of all Christian schools. This effort inspired Day to think that there might be a place for his skills in electoral politics.

Politics and faith are a potent and risky combination, but less so in

Alberta than in the rest of the country. For the most part, Day's evangelical Christian background and social conservative beliefs were a boost to his early political career. He was elected to the Alberta legislature as a Progressive Conservative member for Red Deer North in 1986 and made it into Ralph Klein's Cabinet as minister of labour in 1992. He subsequently took the portfolios of government house leader and social services, and in March 1997 he became treasurer.

Being treasurer at a time when the Alberta economy was booming was an enviable position and a tough job for Day to leave. With good luck and good management, Day looked like a politician on the move, possibly the next premier of Alberta. In the meantime, the leadership of the Canadian Alliance had been thrown open by Preston Manning. A broadly based "draft Day" movement came to him equipped with polls that indicated he could win the Alliance leadership, as well as pledges of financial support to ensure a campaign would not end up in debt. Day recalls that the campaign to beat Preston Manning was simply, "just sell more memberships." His team knew that Manning had much of the existing membership behind him and that they would need to bring in a substantial number of new members to win. The strategy was to attract large groups of conservative-minded Canadians. Later, much was made of how Day recruited throngs of evangelical Christians to his side, but he also spent as much time in secular colleges, beer halls, and dance halls as he did in places of worship. Day describes his campaign as energetic, youthful, and broadly based. In most cases he won over supporters because of his approach to fiscal issues, and by not being Preston Manning. Day emphasized this point in the leadership campaign: "Be assured if I lead the Canadian Alliance our ads won't say that we need a prime minister from somewhere other than Québec."

There is no question that Day was attractive to evangelical Christians, who were filling charismatic churches, especially in western Canada. Preston Manning held similar Christian views but he also believed that free votes and voter-initiated referenda should rule supreme. Day's supporters thought their candidate would be more likely to govern with regard to his faith. Throughout his political career, Day had been an outspoken, if not controversial, supporter of family values.

The leadership selection process was "one member, one vote" with a true majority required to win. The first ballot was held June 24, 2000. Stockwell Day held the lead with 44 percent support, followed by Preston Manning at 36 percent. Ontario-based candidate Tom Long, with the support of Stephen Harper, carried 18 percent support and was taken off the second ballot. But Day swept up nearly all Tom Long's vote and was confirmed leader on July 8.

THE BY-ELECTIONS that brought Stockwell Day and Joe Clark into the House of Commons were held on September 11, 2000. Day ran unopposed by Liberals and the Tories. Clark faced an Alliance opponent who finished a distant third. It was not an entirely pleasant victory party for Clark, however. The by-election coincided with the defection of two of his Québec caucus members to the Liberals, David Price and Diane St-Jacques.

It was clear from the outset of Day's ascendance to Opposition leader that the press was in no mood to give him a honeymoon. The day after his by-election victory, Day held a press conference on the shores of Okanagan Lake, arriving on a jet ski and dressed in a wetsuit. The media ridiculed this demonstration of vigour and change, saying the stunt made him look frivolous and clown-like. Yet when Trudeau orchestrated photos of himself doing a flip off a diving board or when Chrétien invited a Canadian Press photographer to capture him water skiing at the outset of the 1993 election campaign, the media covered their exploits as signs of youth and vitality.

The press hounded Day over his inclination to combine religion and politics. Day's refusal to work on Sunday was seen as an indication that he would not be a prime minister who identified with Canadian diversity. Day spoke not of religion but of values: "Personal responsibility, community, faith and family . . . Yes Canada is a free country. But it is not as free as it should be. Under a Canadian Alliance government, we will see a new birth of freedom in this land." To the press, and many voters, this sounded less like the Canadian mantra of peace, order and good government, and more like an American-style Declaration of Independence.

Stockwell Day took his seat across from Prime Minister Jean Chrétien as Opposition leader in the House of Commons on September 19, 2000. He had been leader for little more than two months, he had no experience in the House, and it was not much more than three years since the last election. Yet, unwisely, Day challenged the prime minister to call an election. Chrétien, who relished the opportunity to take on a divided opposition, had been looking for an excuse to call an early election. While he said he had never intended to run for a third term, the machinations of his ambitious finance minister, Paul Martin, made him mad. "I was damned if I was going to let myself be shown to the door by a gang of self-serving goons. By trying to force me to go, they aroused my competitive instinct, ignited my anger, and inadvertently gave me the blessing I needed from (my wife) to fight for a third term."

Chrétien's advisors counselled against an election, fearing it would be perceived as opportunistic. They reminded him of the recent Ontario provincial election when Liberal leader David Peterson was defeated for going to the polls before the end of his mandate. To avoid a similar situation, Chrétien needed an opening to call an election. Day gave it to him gift-wrapped. "Stockwell Day got up to ask an innocent question about taxes and concluded by demanding an election. I almost crossed the floor to kiss him," wrote Chrétien. Even communist Cuban dictator Fidel Castro gave Chrétien advice at the time, saying, "If I were you, I'd call an election." Both Chrétien and Castro knew that as long as the Canadian Alliance and the Tories were splitting the conservative vote, a Liberal victory was assured.

The election call was delayed because of the death of Pierre Trudeau on September 28, and came on October 22 for a vote on November 27, 2000. The polls in 2000 were clearly favourable to the Liberals. They went into the campaign with 48 percent support, compared with the Alliance at 21 percent, the Bloc and NDP at 10 percent each, and the Tories pulling up the rear with 8 percent support respectively. Rarely had the Tory numbers been so low. While prospects for the Alliance were substantially higher than anything the Reform party had previously experienced, pollsters were warning they had peaked.

No one expected the government to be defeated. But with the Tories so far behind, Day might have seen his chance to kill the PC party and end vote-splitting once and for all. Tory leader Joe Clark bravely decided to run in Calgary. A defeat in his home province would surely mean the end of his term as party leader. Even if there was no chance that the Liberals would be defeated, the survival of the PC party was still very much as stake in the 2000 election. The risk of a terminal defeat was much higher in 2000 than it had been when Jean Charest led the party into the 1997 campaign. In his first election as leader of the Tories since the defeat of his government in 1980, Joe Clark failed to generate much excitement. However, the lone bright moment was in the televised leaders' debates when he accused Prime Minister Chrétien of taking the country into an election because of his ego and his desire to keep leadership rival Paul Martin away from the top job. Otherwise, the PC party was widely ignored during the campaign. The party had no money, and many provincial teams that could otherwise be counted on for support were either sitting on their hands or helping Stockwell Day and the Alliance.

For a time in the campaign, the Alliance had momentum and was within striking distance of the Liberal party in the polls. But Liberal fearmongering

over Day's social conservative views, reinforced by Day's refusal to campaign on Sundays, as well as a weak performance in the debates, turned the
campaign against the Alliance.

The outcome of the election, much like the previous two Liberal majority victories, was never in doubt. Chrétien was an easy and predictable
winner. The Liberals took 172 seats, a gain of 17 from the 1997 campaign.
The Canadian Alliance maintained Opposition status with 66 seats, a gain of
six. The NDP seat total plummeted from 21 to 13, enough to stay alive at the
margins, a place where they are most familiar.

The Progressive Conservatives stayed alive, but barely. From the 1997
campaign, the Tories went from 20 seats to 12; from 18.8 percent of the
vote to just over 12 percent. But if this was the best shot the Alliance would
have to wipe the Tories off the map, it failed. Joe Clark even managed to win
his PC seat in Alberta by a comfortable 4,304 votes, in a province where the
Alliance won 23 of 26 seats. There was solid evidence that Liberals had voted
for Joe Clark to help keep the family feud among conservatives alive. Had
Clark lost, or the Tories been reduced below 12 seats, the threshold for official party status, the party might well have died. What saved the Tories once
again was the thin blue line of Tory support in Atlantic Canada, which delivered nine of the party's 12 seats.

Conservatives, once again, were left to ponder the results. What if there
had been one main opposition party fighting the Liberals, rather than two?
Analysts were quick to superimpose the results of the 2000 campaign onto
a combined Tory–Alliance scenario that assumed total retention of votes
under the single party. While a more forceful opposition would result,
Liberals would still have claimed the top prize. And the Liberals would still
have won the popular vote (40.8 to 37.7), which was a wider gap than from
the 1997 campaign. The Liberals would also have had more seats: 142 to
118. While this would have placed the Liberal government in a minority
position, it was cold comfort to conservatives, who thought all they had to
do to beat the Liberals was to join forces. These results showed that, to win,
the conservative movement had to do much more than merely combine the
parties.

With an ineffective opposition and no "government in waiting," elections had become meaningless. In short, democracy existed in name only.
Canada deserved better.

Stockwell Day could claim victories on the battleground, but not in the
outcome of the war. The Alliance vote, at 25.5 percent, was more than double the Tory result. In the 1997 campaign, the Reform Party and PCs had

been less than one percentage point apart, with neither party reaching 20 percent of the popular vote. In the 2000 campaign, the Alliance was over 13 percentage points ahead. Yet, this result would not be enough for the Alliance Party to let Stockwell Day keep his job as leader. His caucus imploded and Day had little choice but to open up the leadership, the same thing Joe Clark had done in 1983 and Preston Manning in 2000.

Joe Clark, too, was also unable to sustain his leadership. Announcing his resignation on August 6, 2002, he said: "The good news is that I am widely trusted and popular. The bad news is that we cannot translate those qualities into votes for the party." Clark confirmed to the national media what was already painfully obvious to anyone reading the polls: "For the party itself, the bad news is that [Progressive Conservatives] have not yet built a critical mass of Canadians who treat us as their first choice in an election." Clark had to face facts. Though he had kept the party from dying in 2000, it had lost about one-third of its seats under his leadership and had won in only 12 of 301 ridings. Clark's decision to resign precluded a party convention vote on his leadership, thereby avoiding the embarrassment of being officially and publicly rejected by party members.

SECTION IX

FULL CIRCLE

CHAPTER 29

MACKAY AND HARPER: NEW LEADERSHIP BRINGS RESULTS

I could hardly sleep last night. It is like Christmas morning. Our swords will henceforth be pointed at the Liberals, not at each other. —Stephen Harper

I put the country first. —Peter MacKay

STEPHEN JOSEPH HARPER was born in Toronto on April 30, 1959, the son of Joseph and Margaret Harper, and the older brother of Grant and Robert. His parents met at their local church. Stephen grew up in the Toronto area, in Leaside and Etobicoke, within a loving, supportive, and happy family. He has family roots in Atlantic Canada, where he spent many of his childhood summers with his grandparents in New Brunswick. He was a quiet, thoughtful, and brilliant child, yet, despite an A+ average, he was said to be a difficult student to teach. Given his academic success, we can imagine that Harper's intelligence and impatience posed a challenge to his teachers.

Harper won the gold medal for top high school marks when he graduated from Richview Collegiate Institute. Though he excelled at academics, he suffered from asthma, which limited his ability to compete in sports. Nonetheless, Stephen joined his school's cross-country running team.

His first taste of politics was in Liberal circles. His friend Paul Watson claims Harper's involvement was superficial: "[He was] definitely not a Liberal. I roped him in because I needed the numbers (for an event)." Harper's flirtation with the Liberal party would not last. While he had a certain admiration for Trudeau's intellect, his intrinsic beliefs and character were conservative.

Harper enrolled at the University of Toronto to study business. Shockingly, he dropped out of university after only two months saying he didn't know what he wanted to do. Harper landed an administrative job at Imperial Oil in Edmonton, in 1978, the company his father had worked for. After a few years in the workforce, he returned to university, pursuing a bachelor's degree in economics at the University of Calgary. In speeches, Harper has self-deprecatingly commented on his career choice, saying that, "I didn't have the personality to become an accountant, so I became an economist." His degree was in economics, but his passion had become politics.

Academically he was aligned with the conservative leaders of the present and conservative intellectuals of the past. But it took Pierre Trudeau and the National Energy Program to convert Stephen Harper from academic conservative into a lifelong partisan activist. The NEP's intrusion into areas of provincial jurisdiction also inspired Harper to study the Constitution and the separation of powers between the federal and provincial governments.

Harper got his first taste of street politics as a volunteer in the 1984 campaign of Calgary West Progressive Conservative candidate Jim Hawkes. Not that the incumbent MP needed the help, but even in a sea of volunteers Hawkes noticed Harper. So much so that when Harper graduated from university the following year, Hawkes brought him to Ottawa to work as his legislative assistant. While this meant that Harper would be returning East, it would hardly feel as if he were going home. Although raised in Ontario, he had evolved into a western Canadian, a transformation that was made complete by the NEP. Harper was coming to Ottawa, not with cowboy boots and a ten-gallon hat, but as an intellect with a can-do western attitude.

While passionate about issues, Harper lacked the social skills to be thought of as someone who would run for office. He was not a gregarious man and did not overwhelm anyone with his warmth or charm. Politics was a place where he could express his ideas, indulge his curiosities, and engage in social banter most would refer to as debate.

Ottawa in 1985 did not impress the young Stephen Harper. It was relatively early in the Mulroney administration, and Harper had begun his year-long sojourn with high hopes for a fundamental conservative transformation in government. He had hoped to find Parliament bubbling with new and exciting ideas, integrity, debate, and intellectual stimulation. What he discovered instead was an exceedingly dull environment filled with trivial and meaningless chatter and policies too mainstream for his liking. Harper had no interest in playing the Ottawa game of glad-handing and networking. While most politicians and party aspirants frequented hip power-broker restaurants and bars, he went to the Parliamentary library to study. As a keen conservative, Harper had set his sights on reforms to the unemployment insurance program.

Harper was disillusioned by what he saw as a failure of Conservative leadership that meekly compromised in the name of a broader coalition. Fed up and lonely, he returned to the University of Calgary to pursue postgraduate studies. He was more interested in ideas than money, an intellectual who might easily have pursued a comfortable life as a professor at a Canadian or American university.

But given Harper's trial run in Ottawa, it is not surprising that he would become much more than an academic contributing thoughtful essays in refereed journals. He was still very much a partisan and wondered how he and others could persuade Mulroney and the PC party to shift to the right and follow a purer form of conservatism, the kind being pursued by Ronald Reagan and Margaret Thatcher. Harper felt there was not much cause for optimism in this mission because the Red Tories—those to the middle and perhaps the left of the political spectrum—were, in his opinion, in charge of the PC party. He felt that the PC party's leadership lacked political will. Nonetheless, his first instinct was to work within the PC party to try and move it to the right of centre by building a "Blue Tory" network.

"The 'Blue Tory' network was basically two guys: Stephen, and me," recalled John Weissenberger, a colleague of Harper's at the University of Calgary. "The idea behind the Blue Tory network," said Weissenberger, "was to find a home for philosophical conservatives, who did not exist at the time within the PC party."

Weissenberger and Harper developed terms of reference for their network and identified a number of caucus members who they thought might support it. It is clear that Harper and Weissenberger wanted to remain politically active and their first choice was to work within the structure of the existing system: that is, the PC Party of Canada. "But the whole Blue Tory network thing got short circuited," said Weissenberger. That's when Robert Mansell, the head of the economics department at the University of Calgary, introduced Stephen Harper and John Weissenberger to Preston Manning. This was no chance introduction: Manning had asked Mansell for his best and brightest student, and Mansell thought of Harper. He was, recalled

Mansell, ". . . a reluctant politician—an ideal politician in my sense." The Manning option was the path of least resistance to Harper: "Had we carried on with the Blue Tory network, we would have been going against the party establishment. We would have been going against the flow," said Weissenberger.

Harper gave Manning and an upstart political movement intellectual content and credibility. According to Manning, Harper ". . . shattered all the stereotypes (reactionary, backward looking, narrow, simplistic, extreme) that are often applied to a new political party struggling for legitimacy from a western base." In a speech that led to the founding of the Reform party, Harper demonstrated the extent to which the West gave far more than it received within Confederation. Whether it was transfer payments, regional economic development, unemployment insurance, government employment, or tariff protection, the West was consistently on the short end of the stick. Power, Harper suggested, was concentrated in the hands of eastern elites who sought to perpetuate the welfare state and seek appeasement from Québec. Those agitated by the awarding of the CF-18 maintenance contract that favoured Québec over Manitoba now had a cogent and articulate framework in which to situate their angst. No longer, Harper argued, should the country, ". . . be built on the economic exploitation and political disenfranchisement of western Canada."

As the party's first chief policy officer, Harper had been instrumental in crafting Reform's 1988 election platform. He also ran under the Reform banner in 1988 against his old boss Jim Hawkes. Harper finished a respectable second in the election with 16.6 percent of the vote, compared with 58.5 percent for Hawkes. Harper took Hawkes on again in 1993, and won 52 percent of the popular vote to only 27 percent for his Tory rival.

IT WAS EVIDENT EARLY ON that Preston Manning and Stephen Harper did not agree on some fundamental questions of political philosophy and political strategy. Harper was a conservative; Manning a populist. Harper saw issues from a political spectrum of right and left; Manning saw life from East and West. Harper wanted to build a principled conservative party; Manning wanted to appeal to disaffected Canadians across all political spectrums. Harper could identify with the view of libertarians; Manning was most comfortable with Christian values. Harper was inclined to leadership and serious debate; Manning was more comfortable in grassroots policy development. Harper was deeply thoughtful and analytical; Manning more intuitive and political. Harper was distrustful of political elites; Manning was prepared to bring professional political strategists into the party. That these differences would result in a rift was inevitable.

Harper was also out of step with many rank and file Reformers on a number of controversial issues. He supported bilingualism in key national institutions, although he opposed Trudeau's vision of a bilingual Canada in favour of a predominantly unilingual French Québec with English dominating in the rest of Canada. Harper thought that provinces should have primary, if not exclusive, authority over matters of language and culture. He also opposed controls on immigration based on country of origin, arguing that economic interest should be the sole criterion for admittance. And though he was opposed to both government intervention in economic matters and a welfare state, he was not a zealot for the emasculation of government.

However, Harper and Manning both agreed on one thing: they both viewed the Tory party as a visionless creature born of central Canadian elites. Neither trusted the political elite, particularly those that sought special status for Québec as a strategy for winning electoral support.

William Johnson, in his 2005 biography of Stephen Harper, *Stephen Harper and the Future of Canada*, suggests that it was Harper who pushed Reform into chastising the government for failing to develop a Plan B in the event of victory by the sovereignty forces in the 1995 Québec referendum. Countering the view that Québec had a unilateral right to self-determination, Harper argued that the rule of law should supersede any romantic notion of a province becoming a nation. An important point here is that the Canadian Constitution did not contemplate the dismemberment of the country or any part thereof and thus does not authorize the federal government to negotiate any other arrangement with Québec. Consequently, the government of Canada had no authority on the matter, and separation was illegal.

According to Harper, Québec's argument that it never signed the 1982 Constitution was specious and had no bearing on the need to apply the rule of law. For a province to leave Confederation, the Constitution would have to be amended, specifying how such an outcome would be achieved. This constitutional amendment would require the approval of the federal and all provincial governments, and would likely include specific terms and conditions that some provinces might not like. Accepting a Plan B approach was a hard sell to those who were more comfortable speaking eloquently and emotionally about a Canada that included Québec. Harper was pitching stone cold reality. The terms and conditions of separation were the subjects of a private member's bill introduced by Harper in 1993. But, like most private members' bills, Harper's proposed legislation went nowhere. However, his judgment on the need for such legislation was vindicated five years after the referendum when the Chrétien government drafted the Clarity Act.

Manning's autobiography makes frequent references to disagreements and frustrations he had with Stephen Harper. According to Manning, they shared Conservative values but Harper "had serious reservations about Reform's . . . belief in the value of grassroots consultation and participation in key decisions." Manning also complained about Harper's ego, noting that he "had difficulty accepting that there might be a few other people (not many, perhaps, but a few) who were as smart as he was with respect to policy and strategy. And Stephen . . . was not prepared to be a team player and team builder." Manning did concede, however, that Harper was the party's best mind regarding policy and strategy.

On January 14, 1997, before his first term as an MP was over, Harper stunned the Reform Party and the National Press Gallery when he resigned his seat to become vice president of the National Citizen's Coalition (NCC), a right-wing lobby group. According to Manning, Harper left Parliament and "gloomily concluded that (Reform) was going nowhere and would likely lose badly in the next election." Harper told reporters that he resigned because he did not want to be bound by party discipline and wanted to be free to speak his mind.

Other than sitting out the 1997 election, another event took place that year that is worth noting: Harper married graphic artist Laureen Teskey. Laureen first spotted her future husband at a Reform party convention when he delivered one of his many keynote addresses. Previously married, Laureen was introduced to Stephen by one of his former girlfriends, Cynthia Williams. Two children would soon follow: Ben and Rachel.

AFTER LEAVING PARLIAMENT, Harper looked like someone who never again wanted to be a politician. Freed from the constraints of electoral politics and party discipline, he began his new career with the National Citizens Coalition, an environment much closer to the freethinking academic life he had intended to pursue after leaving Ottawa in 1987.

While Harper was sympathetic to the need for a single, principled Conservative political party, he initially argued for some form of cooperation among conservative factions, "sisters" he called them, as a method to win power. "If co-operation (as opposed to a merger) is ever to work, the fragments of Canadian conservatism must recognize that each represents an authentic aspect of a larger conservative philosophy. Reformers will have to realize that there is something genuinely conservative in the Tory penchant for compromise and incrementalism. Tories will have to admit that compromise, to be honourable, must be guided by underlying principles, and that Reformers are not extremists for openly advocating smaller government, free markets, traditional values, and equality before law. And both will have to recognize that Québec nationalism, while not in itself a conservative movement, appeals to the kind of voters who in other provinces support conservative parties."

Harper mused about the possibility of sustaining two, three or even more conservative parties. Each would be regionally based (West, Ontario, Québec, and East), but they would come together to form a coalition government. It was hard for conservatives to understand how such an arrangement could work or be good for the country. The messiness of such a triad coordinating their efforts during a national election, through a coalition government, including the thorny issue of selecting a leader and forming a Cabinet, was probably enough of a headache to cause conservatives across the country to seek a simpler arrangement than what Harper was suggesting: a merger, for example.

Harper next took on the issue of Western alienation. In a commentary he co-wrote with Tom Flanagan for the *Calgary Herald*, Harper suggested that Reform had only been successful in the West because it was the West that had to bear the greatest share of the cost of regional transfers to keep Québec and the Maritimes "happy."

Harper hardly looked like a prospective candidate for the leadership of a national political party when he penned an article for the *National Post* in December of 2000. Looking more like a provincial premier than a future prime minister, Harper lamented the future of the nation in words that would later be used against him: "Canada appears content to become a second-tier socialistic country, boasting ever more loudly about its economy and social services to mask its second-rate status, led by a second-world strongman (Chrétien) appropriately suited for the task. . . . It is time to take the bricks and begin building another home; a stronger and much more autonomous Alberta. It is time to look at Québec and to learn. What Albertans should take from this example is to become 'maîtres chez nous.'"

About a month later, Harper followed up his maîtres-chez-nous article with an open letter to Alberta premier Ralph Klein, which quickly became known as the "firewall" letter. Principally, Harper was trying to inoculate Alberta from a virus often delivered to provinces by the federal government. Harper and his six fellow signatories began the letter by suggesting that "the Chrétien government undertook a series of attacks not merely designed to defeat its partisan opponents, but to marginalize Alberta and Albertans within Canada's political system."They then proposed that "...Albertans... take greater charge of our own future. This means resuming control of the powers that we possess under the Constitution of Canada but that we have allowed the federal government to exercise."They concluded with a plea to Premier Klein "to build firewalls around Alberta, to limit the extent to which an aggressive and hostile federal government can encroach upon legitimate provincial jurisdiction."

NOT LONG AFTER THE NOVEMBER 2000 CAMPAIGN, the knives came out in the Alliance Party. Following the disappointing election results, and a steady stream of self-inflicted wounds, Stockwell Day had lost the confidence of some key MPs and they wanted him out. A group of dissident Alliance MPs aligned themselves with Progressive Conservatives under the banner, Progressive Conservative-Democratic-Representative Coalition. Stockwell Day called for a leadership contest.

Harper had been spared much of the internal wrangling and discord in the Reform and Canadian Alliance parties. He had to answer one question for himself in 2001: was the Alliance party worth saving? He concluded, "If this party didn't exist, we'd need to create it. The party must not be allowed to implode. And if keeping the party alive requires me to run for the leadership, that's what I'll do because the party must survive."

Perhaps the most persuasive argument was Harper's fear that Joe Clark would end up as the voice of conservatism in Canada. At the outset of the campaign Harper was critical of both the Manning-created Reform party and the lacklustre PC party: "What we've got to do is turn this party into an institution. It's too often been viewed as a popular protest movement or a regional fragment or a leader-centric vehicle or a coalition thrown together for a single election. I think the way to address that is to show people that we are prepared to build a permanent professional political institution, one that they can dedicate their loyalty to on an ongoing basis."

Harper won the one-member, one-vote contest with the support of 55 percent of the 88,228 votes cast. Day finished second with a respectable 37.5 percent of the votes. The other leadership candidates, Diane Ablonczy and Grant Hill, were both pro-merger with the Tories, but, combined, only received 7.5 percent of the votes cast. Harper inherited a party almost $3 million in debt and support in the polls at around 10 percent.

Under Harper's leadership, the Alliance party emerged from its populist roots of disgruntled westerners advocating economic and social policies that were out of touch with mainstream Canadians, and became a more focused, thoughtful, and intelligent conservative party. Harper brought recalcitrant Alliance MPs back into the fold, then reached out to Joe Clark to seek a merger of the parties or some other form of agreement that would end vote splitting. Some close to the discussion between Clark and Harper saw ambition as a stumbling block to progress, suggesting Harper was prepared to put his leadership on the line but Clark wasn't.

When Harper took over the Alliance leadership, he brought with him more than the usual assortment of baggage, including the perception he was a right-wing ideologue without a sense of the nation. On an East Coast swing in May 2002, Harper said, "I think in Atlantic Canada, because of what happened in the decades following Confederation, there is a culture of defeat that we have to overcome. . . . Atlantic Canada's culture of defeat will be hard to overcome as long as Atlantic Canada is actually fiscally trailing the rest of the country." For a leader who needed to build support and coalitions across the country, belittling the electorate is rarely a successful strategy. The Nova Scotia legislature, in a unanimous resolution, encouraged Harper to, among other things, reflect on the reality of achievement and optimism in the Atlantic region with his party's persistent string of defeats in most provinces.

By the end of 2002, Harper had led his party for about nine months, yet the Alliance party had not moved in the polls. Prime Minister Paul Martin was poised to receive one of the most dominant election results in Canadian history.

THE OTHER PART OF the Canadian conservative family facing Harper was led by Peter MacKay. First elected to office at the age of thirty-two in 1997, the fresh-faced, homespun and dynamic MacKay belonged to a new generation of technologically-savvy politicians.

For the record, Peter Gordon MacKay, born on September 27, 1965, on Temperance Street, in New Glasgow, Nova Scotia, was the second of Elmer and Macha MacKay's four children. Reflecting on his youth, Peter points out that he was lucky enough to have two additional sets of parents. Indeed, McKay is as likely to tell stories about his grandparents as about his mom and dad.

Life changed for Peter at the age of six. His dad, a popular and respected community lawyer, was recruited to be the Progressive Conservative candidate in a federal by-election in Central Nova in 1971. This was a seat the Liberals were supposed to win. But the residents of Central Nova proudly shunned the Liberal government's promise of goodies and sent Elmer MacKay to Ottawa with a healthy surplus of votes. Elmer's absence was hard on Peter, and hard on the MacKay marriage. Under the stress of politics, it only lasted two more years.

Whereas Peter's father was a well-known Conservative, his mother was a socialist. She rebuilt her life post-marriage by earning a master's degree in psychology and pursued her passion for international justice and women's health issues.

Peter was always involved in sports; he was passionate about hockey, football, baseball, and rugby. Not known for raw talent or finesse, he was skillful as a mucker and grinder, someone who would tough it out in the corners fighting for an edge against opponents.

Despite having a father in the federal Cabinet and a community-minded activist mother, Peter was adamant in his youth that he was not going to be a politician. He knew from experience that achieving the life-work-family balance would be next to impossible. Elmer MacKay describes his young son as the quintessential Canadian lad. "He was kind, hard-working, conscientious, and never complained. He always wanted to do what was right." Although his family had means, Peter was not spoiled with material goods.

Peter was a steady student who accomplished the trilogy of a strong academic average, an active social life, and a daily dose of sports. His passion for competitive team sports eclipsed any interest in politics that one might expect in a politician's kid. Peter's first meaningful exposure to politics came when he was seventeen in the 1983 by-election in Central Nova when Peter's father resigned his seat so that Brian Mulroney, the newly elected leader of the PC Party, could enter the House of Commons. Peter's main job was as Mila Mulroney's driver. While he enjoyed the glamour of driving the powerful and the beautiful past the local ball fields where his friends were playing, what he remembers most about the by-election was hockey legend Bobby Orr coming to the riding to help Mulroney.

MacKay graduated from Acadia University in Wolfville, Nova Scotia in 1987 with a bachelor of arts, majoring in history and politics. He had declared in his high school yearbook that he wanted to be a trial lawyer. It was a good choice for a competitive rugby player. However, he thought he would become defence counsel, not a prosecutor: "That was probably my mother's altruistic influence; that it was a noble thing to do." He studied law at Dalhousie University and soon thereafter followed his father's footsteps and set up a private practice in New Glasgow. His law office was above the local pizzeria, not more than a few blocks from where his father had set up his own law practice. "I had some clients who were the sons of the people my father defended: for him it was bootlegging, in my generation it was drugs."

MacKay took per diem legal work for the Crown prosecutor's office, which eventually became a full-time job. As a Crown prosecutor, MacKay handled everything from shoplifting to first-degree murder cases.

MacKay had not thought of running for office before the fall of 1996. That was when he first met PC leader Jean Charest. Charest asked MacKay about running as a candidate at the same time as MacKay's frustration level with the criminal justice system was at its peak. While MacKay could nominally rely on his father's good name and political network, neither of these factors could guarantee him a nomination win. The riding boundaries had changed substantially since his father had been a member and now included the county of Antigonish. As much as Elmer MacKay wanted to help his son, he understood that it would have been diminishing for Peter to be seen standing in his father's shadow. Over 5,000 residents had bought party membership: an incredible number for a party that had been left for dead four years before and reduced to only two seats in the House of Commons. The 800 or so party members that MacKay's team signed up were new to the political process, mostly people that MacKay had worked with in the criminal justice system. The nomination meeting took a full day and the maximum three ballots in a noisy hockey arena to settle the contest.

Beyond his own hard work, personal network, and solid reputation as a Crown prosecutor, there were three main reasons why Mackay won the 1997 election: Jean Charest, Jean Chrétien, and the "thin blue line."

MacKay defines the "thin blue line" this way: "There were people in Atlantic Canada who simply would not let the PC Party die.... Call it a 'goal line stand' or the 'last sentinels,' but they were committed to the history and traditions of the PC Party. There was also no way they would let Reform take hold in Nova Scotia."

Charest was personally attractive to Nova Scotia voters. He was young, articulate, and forward-looking. Jean Chrétien was another matter. He and Paul Martin had dispensed some tough financial medicine to the country. This included measures that were particularly unpopular in Nova Scotia, namely, cutting transfer payments to the provinces and reforms to the Employment Insurance system. Though Chrétien won all 11 seats in Nova Scotia in 1993, he lost every one of them in 1997. MacKay's voters cared little that the platform being offered by the Tories in 1997 offered an even stronger dose of right-wing economics. They wanted to punish the Liberals.

MacKay won handily in Pictou-Antigonish-Guysborough with almost 50 percent of the vote.

Charest offered MacKay the job as House leader. Always the team player, MacKay readily accepted, even though he knew little of what the job entailed. It turned out to be a terrific assignment for the rookie MP because he was forced to become an expert on rules and procedures. His experience as a prosecutor was put to good use, particularly when the collective opposition was building a case against Prime Minister Chrétien for linkages between his private holding in a golf course in Shawinigan, Québec, and his involvement in government loans and grants that affected the value of his property.

MacKay's prosecutorial and oratorical skills in the House of Commons won him instant praise in the media. In his early days as a parliamentarian, he was given "star" treatment by the press. When Charest resigned as federal PC leader in 1998 to lead the federalist forces in Québec, a number of Tories urged MacKay to go after the top job. MacKay still thought of himself as "wet behind the ears." The candidates trying to replace Charest spent a lot of time and energy vying for MacKay's support. "I didn't know Joe Clark very well. And I felt we needed a new face to expand the base of the party. I am a competitor and I wanted someone who I thought could win the country." Having met the two main contenders, MacKay chose to support Hugh Segal.

Following Clark's victory, MacKay kept his position as house leader despite having supported Segal. MacKay returned Clark's confidence with steadfast loyalty. "I have an abiding respect for Joe Clark," said MacKay. "He has an incredible work ethic and was always well prepared for whatever task he set his mind to." When Clark canvassed his caucus to determine who would be willing to resign so he could enter the House of Commons in a by-election, MacKay unhesitatingly offered his seat, though Clark ultimately decided to run in a different Nova Scotia riding. By the 2000 election, MacKay had earned—after just three years on the job—a solid reputation as an effective parliamentarian. He had emerged from his father's shadow to become a political force in his own right.

WHEN CLARK ANNOUNCED his resignation as leader in 2003, the media pundits handicapping the Tory leadership race made Peter MacKay the early favourite. MacKay had earned his way to front-runner status by virtue of his performance in Parliament and his ability to build strong and meaningful relationships with Tories in all parts of the country. Besides MacKay, the only other opponent from caucus was Scott Brison. Joe Clark favoured Scott Brison; in fact, they had a partnership in which the duo were dubbed the Batman and

Robin of the PC party. Calgary lawyer and Native land claims specialist Jim Prentice was the only Albertan in the race. Prentice was the elected treasurer of the party during the final years of the Mulroney government and had the unenviable task of dealing with bankers and donors immediately after the party's massive defeat in 1993. He was also one of the few Albertans who stayed loyal to the Tories during the rise of Preston Manning's Reform party. Anti–free trade activist David Orchard picked up where he left off in 1998. Orchard entered the race knowing he had no chance of winning, but happy to advance his anti–free trade nationalist causes.

Going into the convention, the published tally of elected delegates put MacKay out front with 42 percent support. Orchard was comfortably in second place with 25 percent, followed by Prentice at 15 percent, and Brison in last place with 10 percent. Since no candidate had a majority of delegates going into the convention, it was inevitable that deal-making would occur. While MacKay needed the support of only one of his opponents to win, technically the other candidates required absolute unity to overcome MacKay's commanding lead. To MacKay's campaign manager, John Laschinger, it was elementary convention politics: "When you need second ballot support to win you can't make a deal with the frontrunner. It was everybody against Peter."

As expected, MacKay lead the first ballot with 41 percent support, David Orchard followed with 24.3 percent, Jim Prentice was third at 18.2 percent, and Scott Brison was last with 13.4 percent. The key revelation from the first ballot was that Brison and Prentice had more support from the ex-officio or automatic delegates than expected.

The math at this point was simple. MacKay needed to attract 235 more delegates. Conversely, 234 delegates were all the other candidates could lose from their pool of 1,549 votes, or MacKay would win. The numbers disappointed MacKay. To win without making a deal with another candidate, MacKay strategists thought they needed 45 percent on the first ballot. When they fell short of that mark, their attention turned to the other candidates.

On the second ballot, MacKay retained a commanding but reduced lead with 39.7 percent of the delegates. David Orchard and Jim Prentice also lost votes, but their ranking did not change. The only candidate with momentum on the second ballot was Scott Brison. He picked up thirty-two votes and finished only three votes behind Jim Prentice. Nonetheless, Brison was still in last place and was dropped from the ballot. Going into the convention, Brison and Prentice had to strike a deal to have any chance of winning. The only issue was whether the survivor could persuade Orchard to join in their deal-making. Horrified that David Orchard might become the kingmaker of the convention, Joe Clark beseeched Brison to go to MacKay. But Brison rejected Clark's advice to support a fellow Nova Scotian. "I was not surprised," said MacKay. "He had been churlish and small throughout the campaign, attacking me personally while cozying up to Prentice at every opportunity."

After the second ballot, Orchard's cell phone was the most popular one at the convention, and his bleachers the most active. With third-ballot voting underway, MacKay knew he would not gain enough freethinking Brison delegates to win. In a face-to-face meeting, MacKay and Orchard signed a deal that stipulated there would be no merger with the Alliance, plus a review panel would be struck to review the Free Trade Agreement. MacKay's choice was to sign the deal and win, or refuse and let Prentice win with Orchard, explaining later, "I signed that deal thinking there was no way between now and the next election that we were going to bring these parties together. Now, in retrospect, anybody could see that it had to happen. But that wasn't the atmosphere leading up to and in the aftermath of the leadership convention."

Just after MacKay signed the agreement, his campaign chair, Bill Pristanski, called Brian Mulroney to bring him up to date. Mulroney replied, "Don't worry. A deal between MacKay and Orchard to review the NAFTA was hardly going to jeopardize the trade in goods and services across North America." Mulroney reassured Pristanski that MacKay had done the right thing. "I think the point of going to a convention was to win."

The results of the final ballot were a foregone conclusion: MacKay ended up with 64.8 percent of the votes. The media had expected a MacKay victory. It was *how* he did it that was the big news. Screaming newspaper headlines vilifying MacKay appeared across the country. Mulroney biographer and Montréal *Gazette* columnist L. Ian Macdonald was scandalized: "A dumb, stupid deal: Peter MacKay's signed pact with David Orchard is reason to question the new Tory leader's integrity and judgment." Outrage over the MacKay–Orchard deal reached such dizzying proportions that some editors and columnists began describing its essence in epic, even folkloric terms. "A Faustian Bargain," thundered one. MacKay bristled at the "pact with the Devil" reference, saying he had made a practical decision based on the reality he faced: it was either make the deal or lose.

The MacKay–Orchard deal *was* unexpected; perhaps it may have been a tad unseemly, but the media's nuclear strike response to it was highly disproportionate. In 1993, Jean Chrétien told the voters he was going to scrap the GST and repeal the Free Trade Agreement; in 1974, Pierre Trudeau ridiculed Robert Stanfield for his position on wage and price controls. Both elections turned on these issues; in *both* cases the Liberals reversed their position *after* winning. Chrétien and Trudeau's cynical about-face on critical issues cost Canadians billions of dollars, not to mention the broken trust with voters. Yet what Trudeau and Chrétien did was considered to be within the cut and thrust of politics. Why, wondered MacKay, was he being held to such a ridiculously high standard?

Instead of basking in the exhilarating glow of victory, in the aftermath of the vote MacKay realized he had squandered considerable political capital and faced even more of an uphill battle than he had anticipated.

Paul Martin and the Liberal party could not have been happier. Not only did the convention agreement guarantee that the vote splitting on the right would continue, but MacKay entered the House as PC leader in a weakened state. Just as Jean Chrétien had been blessed by the arrival of Preston Manning, Paul Martin had David Orchard to thank for keeping the conservative movement in disarray.

Or so he thought.

Despite the full-court bad press over the Orchard agreement, polling data told a more encouraging story for MacKay. Post-convention, the Tories were slightly ahead of the Harper-led Alliance (16.7 percent to 11.2 percent) although both parties were dwarfed by the whopping 54 percent Liberal support. Most encouraging to PCs was the fact that they were the "second choice" of most voters, indicating a growth opportunity.

Two weeks after being elected leader, Peter MacKay attended the annual Press Gallery Dinner. The dinner is an unrepentantly humorous evening where speeches are judged by the quality of their self-deprecation. MacKay began his remarks by saying, "I am sorry if I have to leave early. I told David Orchard I would be in by eleven." The crowd erupted in laughter. He carried on. "I've been called treacherous, stupid, venal, lazy . . . and that's only by the Tories." It looked like MacKay had found his stride.

SINCE TAKING OVER the Alliance leadership, Stephen Harper had become convinced that a deal with the Tories was not only desirable, but essential. One event just a few weeks before the Tory leadership convention sealed his conviction. By then, Harper had been leader of the Alliance for more than a year and had invested much of his time trying to build support in seat-rich Ontario. An important test of his progress was a by-election in Perth-Middlesex on May 12, 2003. The results were Harper's worst nightmare. Not only did Alliance lose; the rival Tories won. Far from showing any momentum, the Alliance received 4,385 fewer votes than they had garnered in the 2000 general election. More than any poll or optimistic forecast, the Perth-Middlesex by-election left a deep scar on the Alliance psyche. "Stephen made the decision he had to merge with the Tories after the Perth-Middlesex by-election," said Tom Jarmyn, a political advisor from Harper's staff. There was only one answer to Ontario: an Alliance-PC merger.

MacKay gave every indication in the days after the convention that he would defend his agreement with Orchard and not deal with the Alliance. Reminding reporters that he had never been an advocate of an institutional merger, Mackay said, "In the next federal election, the Progressive Conservative party will present 301 candidates." Despite the rhetoric, there were faint but unmistakable indications from the two leaders that a merger was still possible before the next election.

In a speech to party supporters at a luncheon meeting in Ottawa of the Confederation Club in mid June, MacKay offered an "open hand" to Harper. "I said the door is open for discussions. I'm not only open; I'm enthusiastic about having discussions with Mr. Harper," said MacKay. Harper quickly responded. "I am encouraged by Peter's remarks today and his openness to discussing a common cause."

The first face-to-face encounter between Harper and MacKay occurred in late June. MacKay approached Harper in the lobby of the House of Commons. In plain view of other members, he told Harper that he had just instructed PC party legal counsel to drop a lawsuit against the Alliance that Clark had launched in May of 2000. MacKay said to Harper, "You and I have to talk." Harper was taken aback—pleasantly—and immediately accepted the offer.

Magna International CEO Belinda Stronach organized the venue for the Harper and MacKay meeting, held north of Toronto on June 26, 2003. On the table was a discussion about a cooperation agreement. Both leaders agreed to appoint emissaries to initiate "talks" between the parties. The emissaries met over the course of the summer and reported back to their leaders on what they thought could be achieved over the short term.

At the outset, both Harper and MacKay were hoping the talks would lead to greater cooperation in the House of Commons and, possibly, a strategy to deal with vote splitting in the next election. They both thought the emissary process was an important first step in what would become a multi-year process.

The PC emissaries were Bill Davis, former premier of Ontario, Loyola Hearn, an MP from Newfoundland, and Don Mazankowski, the revered former deputy prime minister in Mulroney's administration. On the Alliance side were former Reform MP Ray Speaker, sitting MP Scott Reid, and Alliance Senator Gerry St. Germain.

Mazankowski might not have accepted the role but for a chance encounter with Senator Gerry St. Germain in the Winnipeg airport in early August. St. Germain remembers a conversation that went something like this:

St. Germain:	Maz. I hear they've asked you to negotiate this thing. Are you going to do it?
Mazankowski:	I don't think so.
St. G:	I can't believe you're not. Do you know that they're prepared to call it the Conservative Party of Canada?
M:	Oh, they'll never do that.
St. G:	Believe me. I know what they're thinking and this is a given.
M:	Oh, they can't do that.

Mazankowski recalls the thought process he went through before becoming an emissary. "I wasn't thinking merger until I heard the Alliance was ready to name it the Conservative Party of Canada. If it had been the Conservative Alliance or the Conservative Reform Party, I don't think I would have been there."

The emissaries met over the summer and quickly agreed to pursue a full-scale merger of the parties. Progressive Conservative emissaries were stunned that Alliance emissaries agreed to adopt the aims and principles that were embedded in the constitution of the Progressive Conservative party. In fact, the founding principles of the new Conservative Party were lifted virtually verbatim from the PC party constitution—the same words, in the same order. If the PC emissaries were surprised at how well the negotiations were going, however, it was because they had limited insight into what the Alliance team really wanted. Short of a merger, Stephen Harper had few firm conditions. Because the PCs had a constitution that reflected conservative values, Harper saw little point in debating the issue. "We didn't give them anything that we didn't already believe in," said Harper staff member Tom Jarmyn.

Ultimately there was only one thorny issue in the merger negotiations— leadership selection. Harper wanted a one-member, one-vote system. Under this system, the leader would be chosen by a majority of votes cast. MacKay wanted a leadership selection system that gave equal weight to each constituency in Canada. Under this system, each constituency would get the same number of votes to elect the leader, whether the constituency had 10,000 members or 100. While that might seem unfair and disproportionate, MacKay argued that it was fundamental to building a truly national party and entirely consistent with how governments are elected in Canada. Under MacKay's "equal weight" system, leadership candidates would be forced to establish networks and members in every region and riding in Canada. The emissaries tried and failed to reach an agreement on the leadership selection process. Ultimately, it was up to the leaders to negotiate face-to-face.

Just before Thanksgiving weekend, Harper spoke with MacKay and offered to accept the equality of ridings, but with a formula that would be determined only at the party's founding policy convention. Again MacKay said no. Both leaders decided to take the long weekend to reflect. In his admiring and well-researched biography of Stephen Harper, William Johnson gushes praise onto Harper for being principled, inflexible, and clear-headed. Yet when it came to the governance of the new Conservative party, Johnson wrote that Harper demonstrated a different persona: "Harper may have the image of an inflexible, ideologically driven politician; he was proving to be the opposite in these negotiations where he, rather than the Tories, made all the compromises."

MacKay did not feel pressured to compromise. He was comfortable driving a hard bargain. The pressure came only when it looked as if Harper was ready to let him have everything he had asked for.

> Since the convention, my life was made miserable from all sides. My own loyalists were furious with me for having done this Shakespearean tragedy...Then as things progressed, and the quiet discussions with the Alliance leaked out, the old Red Tory element, some of whom were with me, were incensed that I would even entertain talks of doing this. Then you had the Orchard faction that was screaming blue bloody murder for any thought of talking with Alliance....There was the pure of heart: the PCS that said, 'Never surrender—Damn it all we are the true bloods. Our DNA goes back to John A: not those Alliance guys. They are the ones that have caused the problem.' And I understood that. I had a lot of that myself with animosity, although it was emotionally based ...The emotional response wasn't clear thinking or strategic political thinking. As much as I think of myself as a Progressive Conservative I am also a practical conservative, a pragmatic conservative. This civil war, that then turned into the cold war among conservatives, has got to end.

The fateful telephone call from Harper came in the early morning of Tuesday, October 14, with both men in their constituency offices, Harper in a Calgary strip mall and MacKay in a New Glasgow strip mall. As they arrived at the section of the document that dealt with leadership selection, Harper paused. "I have been thinking a lot about this. We have made a lot of progress," said Harper. "This is a very historic decision," was MacKay's reply. Signalling that he was accepting all of MacKay's conditions, Harper said, "We should do this."

Stephen Harper was downright gleeful when he announced the merger of the parties to the press on October 16. The painfully reserved and often emotionless Harper declared: "I could hardly sleep last night. It is like Christmas morning. Our swords will henceforth be pointed at the Liberals, not at each other." Sensing that many members of his party would receive the news with mixed feelings, the usually jocular and energetic MacKay was more reserved: "This is something that, when I began in June to pursue, quite frankly I didn't think it would go this far, this fast." It was a tough decision but he had signed "not only an agreement in principle, [but] a principled agreement." MacKay then asked party members to join him and Harper in the historic initiative.

Brian Mulroney offered immediate support for the agreement and suggested it was something the Liberals should fear. Speaking from Berlin, Mulroney said that "the greatest democratic deficit has come from the divided opposition . . . I think in the interests of democracy, this is an important turning point."

WITH THE AGREEMENT DONE, the next deadline was December 12, 2003: the date when party members had to ratify the agreement.

The tight timeline for ratification was dictated by the upcoming election, almost certain to be called for spring 2004. There was little doubt that the Alliance party membership would endorse the merger. However, taking into account the predictable opposition by the David Orchard faction, not to mention Joe Clark and his friend Senator Lowell Murray, ratification by two-thirds in the PC party was anything but certain. MacKay would have only eight of twelve PC members squarely on his side—including himself. MacKay also had to deal with the furious David Orchard, who had called the merger agreement "a complete and utter betrayal of our agreement; but more importantly . . . a betrayal of the PC Party of Canada, its constitution and its history. . . . This new creature, this so-called Conservative Party of Canada, if it goes forward, will be an illegitimate creation conceived in deception and born in betrayal." MacKay countered that he had a responsibility that extended beyond David Orchard: "My main responsibility as leader of the PC Party is to promote the aims and principles of the party. These principles are at the heart of the recommendations contained in the agreement. This question can't be decided unilaterally by Mr. Orchard, by me, or by Mr. Harper. It must be decided and will be decided in a democratic process that involves every member of our party."

The result of the Alliance mail-in vote was announced on December 4. Stephen Harper buoyantly reported that 95.9 percent of the mail-in ballots were in favour of the merger. Harper called the merger agreement "the beginning of a new era in Canadian politics."

The Tory vote was held the following day. The final tally was 2,234 delegates in favour and 247 opposed; slightly more than 90 percent support, a much better result than MacKay had anticipated. It is worth noting that the votes were cast by delegates who had been elected as representatives from their ridings. Under such a system, a full slate of delegates could be elected in a riding either for or against the merger by a vote of 51 percent of party members. In other words, the 90 percent ratification vote does not necessarily mean that 90 percent of PC party members supported the merger. In fact, there was no tally of votes at the riding level in favour and opposed to the merger.

MacKay was ecstatic. "With this overwhelming vote, we have just become Paul Martin's worst nightmare." Later, a reporter pressed MacKay on the particulars of the deal. "Why bother to win a leadership only to give it away a few months later?"

"Because I put the country first," said MacKay.

Jubilant party members might have thought that joining forces would give them a fighting chance in the next election, but the polls indicated otherwise. The bad news was spelled out in a headline in the *Globe and Mail* on December 5: "Layton's NDP inching past Conservatives." The Liberals had a commanding lead of 43 percent. NDP support was at 15 percent. The Progressive Conservatives and the Canadian Alliance rounded out the bottom of the list at 14 percent and 10 percent respectively. A perfect combination of Conservative support would yield no better than a measly 25 percent of the popular vote. The parties had travelled a great distance, but they were still far from their goal.

CHAPTER 30

HARPER'S WILL TO WIN

Québec's place isn't in the bleachers. Québec's place is on the ice.

T HE NEW CONSERVATIVE PARTY OF CANADA had legal form, but to
Canadians it was an unknown political animal. The two warring factions had joined forces, but the new party had no policies; more
important, it needed a leader.

In a 2003 year-end interview from his Parliament Hill office, Peter
MacKay mused about the prospects of entering the race to lead the new party.
He spoke of the fatigue from the year-long struggle to win the PC leadership,
then negotiating an agreement with the Alliance, and finally the ratification
from party members. "I think the toll has been more on my political capital as
opposed to my own constitution. I'm not physically tired . . . but I feel it. This
has been an incredibly intense, condensed and forced period in my life."

In naming Stephen Harper his 2003 "politician of the year," political
columnist Don Martin handicapped MacKay's prospects for the leadership
this way: "There is, one could argue, legitimate competition for top honours from MacKay, who sacrificed more and had to push harder to make
the deal a reality as the lesser of the two party leaders. But the selling of his
soul in the Orchard deal and the almost instantaneous U-turn on the anti-
merger terms precludes him from consideration." So, despite his heroics in
bringing the two parties together, Don Martin agreed with MacKay that he
would be "damaged goods."

When Stephen Harper announced his candidacy for leader on January 12, 2004, he said he was ready to welcome support from all conservative factions. It was clear, however, that he was most comfortable with the Reform–Alliance side of the House. He didn't, at least initially, want to be called a Tory. "It's actually not a label I love," said Harper. "I am more comfortable with a more populist tradition of conservatism. Toryism has the historical context of hierarchy and elitism and is a different kind of political philosophy. It's not my favourite term, but we're probably stuck with it." Nonetheless, Harper attracted a number of PC party stalwarts to his side, such as 1998 leadership candidate and Québecer Michael Fortier.

Stephen Harper began the campaign with a huge advantage over his prospective opponents. First, he had recently and decisively won the Alliance leadership. Second, he was well-known and widely supported by the Alliance rank and file, which enjoyed a two-to-one margin in party membership over the PCs. Third, he was unlikely to face any Alliance opponents. Fourth, he had a sophisticated fundraising and direct mail system that would be a huge advantage in a short campaign. Fifth, he had universal respect among conservative activists based on his writings and speeches over the previous decade. Finally, the size and demographics of the combined party memberships made it difficult for any single special interest group to dominate and take over the party.

But as a candidate Harper was not without liabilities and significant weaknesses. He had virtually no organization in Québec, which would account for roughly 25 percent of the vote. Second, his past statements about a "culture of defeat" made him unpopular in Atlantic Canada. Third, his image as an inflexible right-wing ideologue would cost him support outside of western Canada.

Setting low expectations and staking out his ground as the underdog, Harper said, "I warn you that I am no Paul Martin. I have not been packaged by an empire of pollsters and media managers. I have not been groomed by the experts and the influential." Reinforcing what he saw as another key advantage, Harper added, "I don't stand for patronage because I don't owe anybody anything."

Former Ontario health minister Tony Clement jumped into the race on January 15. Clement's strategy was to capture much of his home province while also presenting a safe alternative to those who thought the new party needed a leader not burdened by past PC-Reform-Alliance battles. A seasoned provincial politician, Clement offered something none of his opponents could: practical experience with the levers of government, and even a solid international track record thanks to his leadership during the SARS crisis. Nevertheless, his candidacy would not generate much passion or enthusiasm.

Speculation began to build in the fall of 2003 that Belinda Stronach would be a candidate to lead the party she helped to found. On January 20, Stronach stepped before the national media to announce she was running for the Conservative leadership to help Canada build a "bigger economic pie." Hostile commentators would use this clumsy metaphor to ridicule her lack of policy depth and political experience. Beyond personal wealth, where Stronach did distinguish herself from her peers was in the area of social policy. A moderate, she staked out ground on progressive-leaning social policies that would put her at odds with the more socially conservative views that were commonplace in the Alliance, including support for same-sex marriage. And to ensure there was no confusion, her campaign hastened to add she was pro-choice.

But there was a flaw in Stronach's strategy: there weren't enough PC or moderate votes in the new party to give her a win. Even if Stronach swept the PC vote, she would end up finishing no better than a distant second place. To win, Stronach needed to broaden her base and bring tens of thousands of new members into the party. Her personal wealth and access to the Magna International supplier list gave her campaign an overwhelming advantage in campaign funding. With such a huge financial disparity, Stronach was able to outmaneuver her opponents on several fronts. She hired seasoned political strategists and field organizers. She used sophisticated phone banks to recruit members. Nowhere was money more influential to the outcome than in Québec where a derelict riding association with only a handful of members was every bit as important as an Alberta riding association with 5,000 members. Stronach was a natural for Québec Conservatives. She had glamour, money, sex appeal, and the liberal social views that Québecers love. There was only one problem: she could barely speak a word of French.

John Laschinger, who went from managing MacKay's campaign to Stronach's, had a lot of ground to cover to have his candidate taken seriously by a skeptical media that saw Stronach as without depth, vision, or experience. But what Stronach lacked in experience she compensated for with enthusiasm, money, energy, and hard work. Senator David Angus initially thought Stronach could overcome her weaknesses but as the campaign evolved, he came to a different view. "I believed she was bilingual, which she obviously wasn't. She was not properly prepared. She wasn't ready."

But Canadians were fascinated by the upstart Stronach. A February poll of the general public showed that Stronach had slightly more appeal than Stephen Harper among voters. But this was not a general election; party members were voting for a new Conservative leader.

Meanwhile, Stephen Harper was busy fashioning a Québec strategy of his own. Although bilingual, Harper had the dubious misfortune of being as misunderstood in French as he often was in English. At best, Québecers knew him as an opponent of the Meech Lake Accord. At worst, Harper did not believe that Québec was a distinct and sovereign society. A few remembered him as one of the founding architects of the Clarity Act. However, soft Québec nationalists who dug deeper into Harper's writings found common ground in his approach to provincial rights. Harper needed a powerful local ally who could rewrite the headlines that had unfairly and misleadingly portrayed him as anti-Québec. He found that man in Mario Dumont, leader of the Action démocratique du Québec. Dumont's powerful political network offered indispensable support to Harper's recruiting efforts in many rural Québec ridings.

Harper had another surprising supporter from Québec, Brian Mulroney, whose discreet but pivotal relationship with Harper stretched back many years. While leading the Alliance, Harper went out of his way to praise Mulroney, telling Jean Chrétien in the House of Commons, "When it comes to United States-Canada relations, the government has much to learn from former prime minister Brian Mulroney." Mulroney had been a merger advocate for a number of years and believed that Harper was the natural choice to lead the newly merged party.

THE VOTING PROCEEDED on March 20, 2004. Deep bank accounts, progressive social policies, and media hype had helped Stronach overcome linguistic limitations: she won 61 percent of the Québec vote. But she needed closer to 90 percent if she was to have any hope of derailing Harper. With the help of the Action démocratique du Québec, Harper captured a surprising 33 percent of Québec's vote. As expected, Stronach won a majority in Atlantic Canada, but not by much. In a region where Stronach needed to dominate, Harper attracted 35 percent of the vote. Harper won handily in the West. In the end, it all boiled down to Ontario. Stronach and Clement, both from Ontario, had expected to fare well. But Harper shocked them both by winning Ontario decisively. Combined, Stronach and Clement captured 43 percent while Harper steamrolled to victory with an astounding 57 percent. Columnist and future Stronach biographer Don Martin quipped, "In the end, it could not be bought." In the three-way race, Harper dominated: Harper 55.5 percent, Stronach 35.5 percent, and Clement 9.5 percent.

AT HIS FIRST CAUCUS MEETING AS LEADER, Harper began by speaking of the need to draw together the various strands of a broad Conservative coalition. He pointed out that both Preston Manning and Brian Mulroney were an essential part of the party's rich and varied heritage. Summoning up heroes of the past, Harper declared proudly that he was leading the party of Sir John A. Macdonald and Sir Georges-Étienne Cartier. The lesson was not lost on his audience: the party's lineage dated all the way back to the earliest days of Confederation, *not* to December 7, 2003, when it was technically registered with the Chief Electoral Officer of Canada. Harper's emphasis was on the continuity of the Conservative tradition, not on party innovation.

Harper the intellectual showed himself to be an able leader and even an inspiring politician. Demonstrating an unexpected sensitivity to different points of view, he even charmed caucus members who had been hesitant about the merger.

Harper's efforts to unite the party, however, were not universally successful. Joe Clark used his last day as a parliamentarian to burn his remaining bridges with his former party. With an election call imminent, Clark ruminated on CTV's *Question Period* that "The issue is going to be which leader is better, which leader is worse, and I think the question is a very tough one. . . . I would be extremely worried about Mr. Harper. I personally would prefer to go with the devil we know. I'm that concerned about the imprint of Stephen Harper." While Clark would encourage voters to base their voting choice on the strength of local candidates, equating Harper with the devil was a terminal act that would prevent him from ever having influence or any involvement with the new Tory party.

Harper did not have long to draw the party together. The next election was looming, and that gave him very little time to demonstrate that he was leading a moderate, inclusive national party that was sensitive to all conservative factions and all regions of the country. It also gave him precious little time to build a campaign team. As it turned out, Harper only had about two months following his leadership victory before Paul Martin asked that the writ be dropped, on May 24, for an election on June 28.

This 2004 election would be the first time the Liberals faced a unified Conservative party since they had lost to Brian Mulroney in the free trade vote of 1988. In the previous three elections, Liberals had had to do little more than show up to win successive majorities. Lacking competition, they had become lazy and arrogant. The only real battles Paul Martin and Jean Chrétien had faced were within the Liberal party.

There was harshness to the 2004 Conservative election campaign, something the party desperately needed to avoid if they hoped to portray Harper as an agent of moderate and safe change. The 46-page election platform came with the ornery title "Demanding Better." Reminiscent of the old saw "we're mad as hell and we aren't going to take it anymore," the platform preface declared that "Canadians have had enough." It was time to demand better accountability, stronger economic performance, improved heath care, safer communities, and meaningful national security.

The platform included a reduction in the tax rate on middle-income Canadians by more than 25 percent, and a $2,000 per child deduction for all dependent children under the age of 16. There was also a pledge to hold a free vote in the House of Commons on the issue of same-sex marriage. Far from a slash-and-burn tax-fighter mentality, the platform included increases in both spending and revenue over the projections of the current Liberal administration. But the platform was just as interesting for what it did not contain. There was nothing in the document tailored specifically to the needs and interest of Québecers. There was nothing about regional economic development, other than to say that regional considerations would not be a factor in determining how funds would be allocated by federal granting councils. There was nothing about "hot button" issues near and dear to the former Alliance side, such as abortion or capital punishment. And though there was a pledge to increase the size of Canada's armed forces to 80,000 troops, there was no mention of Canada joining the war in Iraq, which Harper had vocally supported in the past.

When the writ was dropped in late May, the Liberals were enjoying a comfortable 8 to 10 percentage point lead in the polls. By the end of the first week in June, however, the Tories were showing a slight lead. That was enough to ratchet up public and media scrutiny on Stephen Harper and his band of candidates. Despite Harper's calm and measured public persona throughout the campaign, the media pounced on any gaffe or misstep that might reveal him as a wolf in sheep's clothing. The media were only too happy to scour the country and look for statements, current and past, from any of the 308 Tory candidates that made the point that Harper's Tories were intolerant social conservatives. MP Scott Reid spoke out against Canada's official bilingual policy early in the campaign, costing him his job as the critic for official languages. Cheryl Gallant got into hot water for comparing abortion to the beheading of an American in Iraq. And Rob Merrifield's recommendation for third-party counselling before a woman could terminate her pregnancy, challenged the accepted position of most Canadians, and the Supreme Court.

In an effort to limit damage from incompetent remarks, Harper imposed restrictions on his candidates. Candidates were required to sign a pledge that they agreed "not to publicly criticize any other colleague or the Leader or the Party." But the need for restrictions only fuelled suspicion about the "extreme" views of Harper's team. Attempts to "muzzle" candidates drew disapproving headlines like "Tory candidates sign gag order, document shows."

Harper's pledge of free votes in Parliament on social issues, coupled with media amplification of every extreme and supposed "intolerant" statement by one of his candidates, made it easy for Paul Martin to stick the "hidden agenda" label on him. The Liberals could find nothing substantive in the Conservative platform that was scary or extreme but, thanks to outspoken and undisciplined Tory candidates, they were able to cobble together a number of television ads that portrayed Harper as a leader who was more comfortable in George Bush's America than in Canada.

Coming into the final week of the campaign, just as some pollsters were hinting at a Conservative victory, more controversy hit. Randy White, longtime Reform and Alliance MP and co-chair of the Conservative's election-readiness committee, gave an interview for an as-yet-unreleased documentary, and said, "If the Charter of Rights and Freedoms is going to be used as a crutch to carry forward what social libertarians want, then there's got to be for us conservatives out there a way to put checks and balances in there. So the notwithstanding clause . . . should be used, and I would think not just for the definition of marriage." Martin sounded the alarm. He claimed the Tories' social agenda was more important to them that the Charter of Rights and Freedoms. It was fearmongering, but nonetheless effective, and being so close to Election Day, Harper had little time to respond.

Meanwhile, Harper began to make public statements about transitioning into the role of prime minister. It was enough to cause Canadian voters to do precisely what was suggested in Liberal attack ads: "Think twice." When Harper chose to spend the final days of the campaign in the West, and boasted about how Alberta was about to take its rightful place in the halls of power, Ontario contracted a bad case of cold feet. Returning to right-wing Alberta was not only damaging, it was pointless: Harper had already won the province. He should have been in Ontario where Conservative momentum was sliding.

At the outset of the campaign, Conservatives would have been ecstatic at the prospect of limiting the Martin Liberals to a minority government. However, after leading in the polls the week before the vote, coming in second place was a deep disappointment.

With 36.7 percent of the popular vote the Liberals won the election, taking 135 seats, a loss of 37 members. The Conservatives won 99 seats, an increase of 21 from the combined PC and Canadian Alliance total. The Bloc Québécois won 54, up 16 from 2000, mainly because Québecers were punishing the Liberals over the sponsorship scandal. The NDP maintained official party status with 19 seats, an increase of six over 2000.

If the theory of a united Conservative party was to end vote splitting—particularly in Ontario—then the merger had proved a raging success. Having won only two Alliance seats in 2000, Harper's new Conservatives came in with a whopping 24 of Ontario's seats. But this was still less than 25 percent of Ontario's 106 seats. The net gain of 22 there was offset by a net decrease of three seats in the rest of the country. The party was down in four provinces—Nova Scotia, New Brunswick, Québec, and British Columbia—with only modest gains in Alberta and Saskatchewan. Whereas the Conservatives held the clear majority of seats in the West, they could win only seven of 32 seats in Atlantic Canada and were shut out in all 75 ridings in Québec. The Conservatives had won 31 out of a possible 213 seats east of the Manitoba border. Hardly an unfamiliar ending.

The 29.6 percent popular vote for the Tories was a far cry from the combined PC and Alliance total of 37.7 percent in the 2000 campaign. The Alliance party on its own had polled 25.5 percent in 2000. Assuming that most of the Alliance voters from 2000 would have stayed with the Conservative party under Stephen Harper, we might conclude that a majority of the PC supporters went to other parties in 2004. Anchoring the relatively poor popular vote was the 8.8 percent vote in Québec, well below the combined 11.8 percent of the PC-Alliance vote in 2000.

Conservatives needed to remind themselves how far they had come. Conservative strategist and CPAC panelist Bill Pristanski made the point. "Harper did a remarkable job as leader. Six months earlier the pundits had been musing that Martin would win the largest majority in Canadian history. We now had time to re-group and learn from our mistakes."

After the dust had settled on the campaign, the Conservative party assessed its overall progress. It failed to generate support across all regions of Canada; in fact, in Québec it was a non-factor. The party had not managed to articulate a message that could translate into a broad national coalition. There was nothing extreme or inflammatory in the official party platform, but the intemperate outspokenness of the more radical candidates had been a huge problem. The attention they drew worked against efforts to popularize Harper's more moderate and mainstream message. Harper's leadership had been forceful and decisive most of the time, but near the end of the campaign it may have appeared as if he had lost the reins, and looked more like a regional leader than a national one.

But one area where Harper and the party scored well was party unity. The core group of Canadians who called themselves Conservatives was relatively small, but with a national campaign now behind them they were firmly behind their party and its leader. They had transformed what many thought would be a Liberal landslide into a minority government. Harper and the Conservative Party of Canada would live to fight another day.

When Harper considered his options after the 2004 election defeat, including resignation, Mulroney encouraged him to continue to lead the Conservative charge. Mulroney also advised Harper on what it took to win. The question Mulroney put to Harper was whether he wanted to be leader of the Opposition or prime minister of Canada. Mulroney had set an example for Harper to follow: build a national coalition of Conservatives that was moderate in policy and tone, ditch any far-right policies, and avoid any "hot button" social issues. The other key to success was Québec. Though conventional thinking was that Conservatives could not win in Québec, Mulroney thought otherwise, and encouraged Harper to build bridges there.

Harper took Mulroney's advice; Tories would make a serious investment in Québec. After the 2004 election, Josée Verner became one of Harper's most important Québec operatives. She was Harper's most successful Québec candidate in 2004, finishing ahead of the Liberal candidate, and second to the BQ victor by only 3,281 votes in her Québec City riding of Louis-Saint-Laurent. Harper named the unelected Verner to his shadow Cabinet and invited her to attend caucus meetings. He also appointed her chair of the Québec Conservative caucus.

A COMMON REFRAIN from Liberal spin-doctors in the 2004 election was that Stephen Harper had a hidden and scary agenda for Canada. Liberal attack ads had guns being pointed at Canadians and women fretting about losing the right to choose to have an abortion if Stephen Harper became prime minister. The Liberals pointed to the fact that, in its haste to unite, the Conservative party had yet to hold its first policy conference. Without clear direction from party members, Liberals argued, Stephen Harper had carte blanche to implement whatever scary idea came into his head. Those who understand party politics would recognize this as a ridiculous proposition, but it may well have helped to persuade voters that the Conservatives were not ready to govern.

Because the Tories had been shut out in Québec in the 2004 election, Montréal was chosen as the host city for its March 17–19, 2005 convention. It is ironic that Québec gave nothing to the Tories but got the royal treatment. Regional dimensions aside, delegates and the press came to the convention for serious business. They wanted to know if Harper's Conservative party had gone mainstream, or if the more socially conservative views from the Alliance would prevail in the merged party. The litmus test was the issue of abortion. As expected, delegates made motions in the workshops on abortion that went against Harper's stated views. Harper had consistently maintained that the party should not adopt policy on issues of conscience. Rather, members of Parliament should have a free vote on such questions. The delegates supported Harper's position, although by only a narrow margins: 55 percent to 45 percent. Had that vote gone the other way, the Conservatives would have carried a millstone around their necks that would almost certainly have defeated them in the next election. While social conservatives were disappointed with the result, they were nonetheless prepared to stay with the party.

Party unity and moderate social policies were critical to a successful convention. So was clear and strong leadership. Despite having fumbled a lead towards the end of the 2004 election, Harper received an impressive 84 percent support from the delegates for his leadership. There was no question that the party was prepared to support Harper into another election.

Harper encouraged dialogue among those with diverging social views in his caucus. In the fall of 2003, Harper had been asked how he would reconcile the openly gay PC Scott Brison with Alliance MP Larry Spence, who said he would not be opposed to laws making homosexuality a crime. Harper had replied that he would make them seatmates in the House of Commons. That's precisely what he did with the evangelical Stockwell Day and the progressively-minded Belinda Stronach. Harper was determined to build a broad, inclusive Conservative party.

Intent on demonstrating his commitment to the policy positions adopted in Montréal, Harper affirmed his newfound moderation before the Fraser Institute, an organization committed to market solutions for public policy problems. He began his April 2005 luncheon speech with, "Today, I will say some things some of you in the Fraser Institute may not want to hear." Maintaining that he was open to new ideas from the Fraser Institute, Harper responded to recent suggestions by former Ontario premier Mike Harris and Reform Party founder Preston Manning to reform the Canada

Health Act as "non-starters." Leaving behind his economist past, Harper stated, directly and somewhat confrontationally, "If this represents a departure from the market norms that guide much of the public policy thinking of this Institute, then so be it . . .The ability to pay cannot control access to necessary medical services for ordinary Canadians and it will not in a national Conservative government."

The late spring of 2005 was beginning to look like the dream scenario for Conservatives. Not only had they mustered enough votes in the House of Commons to defeat the Martin government, but support for Conservatives in the polls had also reached record levels. These changing fortunes were largely attributed to the release of shocking testimony at the Gomery inquiry about systemic abuses of the public treasury by the Liberal party, as well as illegal and fraudulent activity by some advertising executives and Liberal party insiders in what became known as "the sponsorship scandal." Canadians believed Martin should be held accountable for the mess by a margin of two to one. Just as the opposition parties were about to defeat the government on a vote of non-confidence in mid-May, however, a political bomb went off in Ottawa. Belinda Stronach crossed the floor to the Liberal benches.

Beyond forestalling the defeat of the Liberal government, and the pure drama of the moment, the defection of Belinda Stronach from Conservative opposition trade critic to Liberal minister of human resources and parliamentary reform was an important test for Stephen Harper and the Conservative coalition he was trying to build. Whatever bona fides Stronach had gained in the Conservative party, they did not come from her merger support or her premature run for the leadership bid in the spring of 2004. But after toughing it out and winning a seat in Parliament, she was warmly welcomed into the Conservative caucus, assigned a good seat in the House of Commons, and placed in the shadow Cabinet.

In early January of 2005, news reports began to circulate of a romance between the twice-divorced Stronach and Peter MacKay. MacKay seemed more willing to speak of the romance than Stronach: "Suffice it to say, I'm very happy and quite smitten," beamed MacKay. "Belinda is just a terrific person and we're getting along famously." If Stronach was getting along with MacKay, the same did not hold true of her relationship with the leader. Harper did not appreciate being undermined by the freewheeling Stronach, and as an ambitious Harper contrarian, Stronach did not like being disciplined.

One of Stronach's key confidantes in her run for the leadership and the period thereafter had been Conservative Senator David Angus. Stronach confided to Angus that she was unhappy with how Harper was treating her. Angus agreed to speak with Harper on her behalf. Angus began the meeting with, "This will only take five minutes." "David," came the reply, "take whatever time you need." Angus said he was there to talk about Belinda. With that one sentence the conversation came to an abrupt end. "David, she is not there for us." Angus asked, "What do you mean? She was great at the Montréal convention and she represents a dimension to the Party that is badly needed in Québec." Harper was not moved. "That's your view, David, but she is just not there for us and she is not on my radar screen." Angus ultimately concluded, "Harper's judgment on Belinda was better than mine."

By chance, on May 12, Stronach ran into former Liberal premier of Ontario David Peterson at an event honouring former Ontario PC premier William Davis. Stronach told Peterson of her unhappiness over a range of issues. Peterson brought Tim Murphy, Martin's chief of staff, into the loop. Murphy then briefed the prime minister. Following a weekend of discussion and negotiations, Peterson travelled to Ottawa the following Monday. At 4:00 p.m., he met Stronach and Murphy at the Château Laurier, where the deal was finalized. Stronach would cross the floor and enter Cabinet.

At the announcement, Paul Martin remarked, "She and I have agreed that she fits more comfortably, can serve more appropriately and can contribute more substantially as a member of the government caucus." Martin concluded his remarks by calling Stronach "gutsy" and declaring that he was "proud to have Belinda Stronach as part of my team."

Stronach's statement was designed to portray her decision as one based on deep principle and concern for the welfare of the nation with Harper as a potential prime minister. "I've been uncomfortable for some time with the direction the leader of the Conservative Party has been taking. . . . I do not believe the party leader is truly sensitive to the needs of each part of the country and how big and complicated Canada really is." Perhaps she was thinking of Peter MacKay when she said, "There are many good and talented folks that I have a great deal of respect for in the Conservative Party." That was cold comfort to MacKay.

Stronach claimed to be switching parties because the Conservatives were aligning themselves with the Bloc Québécois to defeat the government. "The result," she warned, "will be to stack the deck in favour of separatism and the possibility of a Conservative government beholden to the separatists. After agonizing soul-searching, I just cannot support such a large risk with my country."

Harper took his own shot at Stronach, saying he was not surprised by the defection, which he attributed to Stronach's unsatisfied leadership ambitions that "weren't in the cards" in the Conservative party. When a reporter asked him about the complex reasons Stronach had offered for her decision, Harper replied, "I've never noticed complexity to be Belinda's strong point."

MacKay also wanted to demonstrate that the reasons for Stronach's defection were misguided and misplaced: "We are not aligning ourselves with the Bloc...that's nonsense...The problem in Québec is directly attributed to the actions of the Liberal Party who have been corrupt...who have through criminal means tried to buy people and simultaneously reward their own party for political gain. This is what has given rise to separatism. Nothing that the Conservative Party under Stephen Harper has done. It is perverse to suggest otherwise."

With Stronach's defection, the confidence vote held on May 19, 2005, ended in a tie. In accordance with convention for such cases, Speaker Peter Milliken cast the deciding vote for the government. Belinda Stronach had changed the course of political history, allowing Paul Martin's government to live another day.

The polls showed a dip in Tory support just following Stronach's defection, but the damage to Harper and the party would prove short-lived. Most in caucus thought it was better that Stronach had left outside an election period. Also, because it shored up the Liberals on another vote, the defection gave Harper and his party more time to prepare for the next election.

HARPER HAD SPENT THE SUMMER OF 2005 on a cross-country "barbecue" tour that had yet to yield any positive results. The tour had been Harper's attempt to get closer to voters and soften his image as a stiff intellectual who lacked emotion and warmth, a chance to listen more than talk. The press had ridiculed the effort. One photo from the tour ended up across the front pages of virtually every newspaper in the country. It showed a very ill-at-ease Harper at the Calgary Stampede dressed in a cowboy hat, string tie, and leather vest. One headline proclaimed, "More Gobsmacked than Gunsmoke." Harper responded by poking fun at himself. "My dad would have said, 'To me, you look like a cowboy, but I'm not sure to a cowboy you look like a cowboy.'"

In the fall of 2005, Harper put himself and his party in election ready mode. The brutal 2004 election post-mortem had resulted in bold new strategies and tactics designed to prevent Martin and the media from casting Harper as "scary" or a man with a "hidden agenda." A key element of the new strategy was to control the agenda by getting the media and voters talking about Conservative issues and policies of the day. That meant speaking less of Liberal failures and more about Conservative ideas. It meant releasing a new promise virtually every day of the campaign to give the media something of substance to report about Harper. Campaign events would be held early in the morning to get a lead in media coverage and put Martin in a defensive and reactive position. The tour would also stay out of Alberta and would not visit the same riding more than once, no matter what. Most important, the platform would be so detailed, so specific and comprehensive that no one could possibly fear something was being hidden. In fact, many of the promises did not speak of change, but of maintaining many of the programs and policies that the Liberal government had recently implemented.

Harper decided to build a *national* coalition, just as Mulroney had done to win in 1984. He set aside his economist instincts about policy in favour of what—within the bounds of centre-right conservative thinking—would make him prime minister. In other words, Harper had acquired the will to win. According to his colleague and friend of two decades John Weissenberger, Harper had concluded that, "half a loaf is better than no loaf."

But Harper needed a push to get the campaign started. On November 1, Mr. Justice John Gomery issued his first report on the sponsorship scandal, titled *Who is Responsible?* In his preface, Judge Gomery stated: "The report that follows chronicles a depressing story of multiple failures to plan a government program appropriately and to control waste—a story of greed, venality and misconduct both in government and advertising and communications agencies, all of which contributed to the loss and misuse of huge amounts of money at the expense of Canadian taxpayers. They are outraged and have valid reasons for their anger."

Gomery's language was concise and his conclusions were clear. His report offered numerous statements that Conservatives could lift as campaign themes and slogans. Many of the major findings stuck directly to the Liberal government of Jean Chrétien and to the Liberal party. Harper's political instincts told him that with this damning report an election had to be called sooner rather than later. With allegations of criminal misconduct by persons close to the Liberal party, Harper asserted that the government has lost its moral authority to govern.

Harper introduced, and Jack Layton seconded, the fatal motion on November 24: "That this House has lost confidence in the government." Four days later, it passed by a vote of 171 to 133. The following day, Martin visited the governor general and the election date was set for January 23, 2006. The eight-week campaign would be the longest one in twenty-one years.

The most compelling evidence of Harper's commitment to win in 2006 was his platform. The specifics of the 2006 platform contrasted sharply with the much harsher and more narrowly cast platform of 2004. Even the title, "Stand up for Canada," was more positive and inspiring than "Demanding Better." To ensure there was no confusion about what Harper did and did not stand for, the crisp 46-page document featured over 400 bulleted policy positions.

The 2004 platform said nothing about regional economic development. Now "Standing up for Canada" spoke of maintaining current funding levels for regional development agencies. It also pledged to develop a "northern vision" that would guide economic, social, and environmental progress in the region. Rather than stick with exclusively federal areas of jurisdiction, Harper's Conservatives would maintain funding for a new deal for cities, and maintain existing infrastructure agreements between the federal government, the provinces, and municipalities. This included a promise of $591 million to support the Pacific Gateway Initiative. This gave greater freedom to B.C. and the other partners, in effect, allowing the regions to get federal money without the political interference they had come to expect from Liberals. And in a move that left Reform party founders shaking their heads, Harper pledged to, "ensure that the CBC and Radio-Canada continue to perform their vital role as national public service broadcasters," while preserving "the role of the National Film Board, the Canada Council, and other federal arts and culture agencies."

The 2004 platform had been virtually silent on Québec issues or the French language. In 2006, Harper committed to establish a francophone secretariat within the department of Canadian heritage, invite the Government of Québec to play a role at UNESCO, and to support the Official Languages Act. Even more significant to Québec was a commitment that a Conservative government would work with the provinces to achieve a long-term agreement that would permanently address the issue of fiscal imbalance.

Beyond the platform document, Harper spoke of an "open federalism" in a December 19 stop in Québec City. Leading Québec journalists like André Pratte admired not only the speech, but also the timing, which gave Québecers time to reflect about what Harper was saying over the festive season. Many Conservatives, as well as members of the media, thought Harper was wasting his time in Québec. Even those inside the campaign thought that, best-case scenario, there were only two seats to be had in the province. But Harper believed otherwise. So did Mulroney. More important, so did Québec premier Jean Charest, who told reporters he had taken note of what Harper was saying. The endorsement of Harper by influential Québec newspapers *La Presse*, *Le Droit*, and *Le Soleil* was more than Harper could have imagined. Harper reminded Québecers that his party could be far more useful to them than the perpetual outsiders: the Bloc Québécois. Using easily understood language, Harper said, "Québec's place isn't in the bleachers. Québec's place is on the ice."

On top of the significant policy shifts to bring the regions and Québec into his coalition were the five priorities: cleaning up government by passing the Federal Accountability Act; tax relief by cutting the GST; making streets and communities safer by cracking down on crime; helping parents with the cost of raising their children; and working with the provinces to establish a Patient Wait Times Guarantee. The five priorities were useful for giving perspective to the 400-plus promises in the platform, and also for contrasting Paul Martin's image as a dithering and indecisive politician, a label first given to him by the *Economist*. Under the title, "Mr. Dithers and his Distracting Fiscal Cafeteria," its February 17, 2005 editorial contrasted Martin the decisive deficit fighter with Martin the man not big enough to be an effective prime minister.

The promise to offer $100 per month for each child under six became significant only when Martin's communications chief scoffed on national television that parents might well use the money to buy "beer and popcorn." No Conservative could have articulated the differing philosophies of the two leading parties more effectively. Harper would declare at every partisan rally that his plan was based on his party's consultation with the real childcare experts in the country—parents.

The promise to reduce the GST immediately from 7 to 6, and later to 5 percent before the end of the first mandate was perhaps the most telling indicator that Harper was prepared to do whatever it took to win. How could an economist propose reducing the GST, a tax that discourages consumption, rather than cutting income taxes, which discourage work and productivity? This policy would violate every economist inclination Harper had ever held. It was also a bold stroke of political brilliance. He not only distinguished himself from Mulroney, but painted Martin into a corner. What could Martin do: defend the hated GST, the tax the Liberals pledged to kill in 1993? It was also good street politics for Harper. Unlike income tax, which is taken from Canadians without much of a fight, the GST is visible, mostly unavoidable, and paid by every Canadian. Even children and the poorest of the poor pay the GST.

Harper's brain trust also developed a marketing campaign targeted at what it called a "conservative universe." Inspired by strategists Tom Flanagan and Patrick Muttart, and informed by recent successful conservative campaigns worldwide, the 2006 strategy was based on knowing where votes could be won while ignoring the remainder. The campaign assigned fictitious names to describe the archetypal Canadian voter, some in the "universe" and some not. "Dougie" was a hypothetical tradesman, single, who liked to hunt. He was in the universe but would vote only if motivated. "Zoe," on the other hand, was an urbane, single, cat-loving condo owner with a stud in her nose and drank a $7 latté every morning. She was never going to warm up to Harper. It was a far more sophisticated approach than the one Conservatives had cobbled together in 2004. Said war-room veteran Yaroslav Baran, "Last time we went on assumptions about who would vote for us. This time it was based on science."

Beyond targeting subsets of votes, there was one broad category of voters Harper pursued in 2006. Harper, the intellectual economist, was going mainstream. He would not be the leader of the cold-hearted, government-hating party of the far right. His language was plain and his sentences crisp. Harper would look and talk more like Don Cherry than Adam Smith. "He was appealing to the lunch bucket crowd that read *Sun* newspapers rather than the *Globe and Mail*," said Baran.

It is worth remembering that when Stephen Harper forced the election, his party was 8 percentage points behind in the polls. He took a big risk. In Québec, Conservatives were in single digits whereas the Liberals were at about 30 percent support. Polls showed that 65 percent of Canadians thought Martin would return as prime minister. Only 18 percent gave Harper a chance of winning. Despite Liberal scandal and Martin's dithering, Harper still trailed Martin as the best leader for Canada by a significant margin. Harper proved himself courageous by taking the government down on November 28, 2005.

When Conservatives fell behind by as many as 15 percentage points early in the campaign, Harper did not panic or change course. Capitalizing on a series of Liberal blunders, including allegations of leaks from the November Economic Statement that led to an RCMP investigation, Harper followed the strategy he had laid out at the start.

The 2006 vote was historic for any number of reasons, but the most significant was that after more than twelve years of Liberal rule, Canadians elected a Conservative government. Stephen Harper, who just two years previously had been leader of the Canadian Alliance, was now the Conservative prime minister of Canada. Peter MacKay, who had surrendered his newly-won position as leader of the Progressive Conservative Party of Canada, would represent the country internationally as Canada's minister for foreign affairs and later as minister of defence.

Harper's Conservatives won 124 of 308 seats, 31 seats short of a majority. Though the Liberals retained a strong position in the House of Common with 103 seats, it was not enough for Martin to retain his leadership. The BQ fell to 51 seats, and the NDP was pleased it had increased its members by a third, tallying 29 seats.

The Conservatives increased their popular vote by 6.7 percentage points over their 2004 results. They had won with only 36.3 percent of the voting public, slightly less than the 36.7 percent Martin received in 2004. In many respects, the results of the 2006 election were largely a reversal of 2004 Conservative and Liberal fortunes.

One of the most impressive things about the Conservative win was the fact that for the first time since 1988, a Canadian government had strong representation from every region of Canada. Unlike Liberal governments over the previous four elections, which had heavily depended on Ontario voters to win power, Conservatives had reasonable representation in every province but one. Prince Edward Island was the only province that did not return a Conservative to Ottawa (it was not for lack of trying, however. Harper visited the island province late in the campaign). Conservatives held 9 seats in Atlantic Canada, a gain of two. They elected 16 new members from Ontario, to hold 40 of 106 seats. As expected, they steamrolled the Prairies and won 48 of 56 seats. British Columbia was the only sore spot: they lost five seats to the NDP, but with 17 of 36 seats, retained a significant BC caucus.

And most impressive of all was that Québec, a traditional Tory wasteland, gave the Conservatives 10 of 75 seats. The Conservative share of the Québec popular vote increased by 15.8 percentage points from 2004, and they cut heavily into the BQ vote. While BQ leader Gilles Duceppe predicted his party would eclipse the 50 percent vote threshold, the theoretical level his party sought to win a sovereignty referendum, he ended up with 42.1 percent, a 6.7 percent drop from 2004. Belinda Stronach's worries had been misplaced: defeating the Liberals was not bad for federalist forces. Some would call Tory success in Québec a miracle, just as they had when Brian Mulroney swept the province in 1984. Had those 10 Québec seats gone Liberal, the national result would have been 114 for the Tories to 113 for the

Grits.

Harper's caucus was national, but it was also largely rural. Conservatives were once again shut out in Toronto, just as they had been since 1988. They had equally unimpressive results in Canada's two next largest cities, Montréal and Vancouver, where they lost every seat.

Paul Martin exited centre stage gracefully, concluding it was time for the Liberal party to reinvent itself after being held accountable for the sponsorship scandal. Meanwhile, Stephen Harper was rewarded for taking a big risk, plunging the country into an election when the polls indicated he would lose. He became one of only seven Tories to win a federal election.

SECTION X

LOOKING BACK—LOOKING AHEAD

CHAPTER 31

PRIME MINISTER
STEPHEN HARPER

Election Night January 23, 2006—Minority governments are never easy
Election Night October 14, 2008—Regardless of how you voted, know that we will
form an inclusive and responsive government that protects the interests of all
Canadians in all communities of this country.

SINCE CONFEDERATION only five Tory leaders have delivered successive victories, but unlike other multiple winners, Stephen Harper has
not earned a majority government.

In 2008 Harper enjoyed some of the most favourable election conditions faced by a Tory leader since Brian Mulroney. Tory opposition was
fractured into four parties; Liberal leader Stéphane Dion was ridiculed from
within his own party and had proposed a complicated and seriously flawed
platform; the prospects for a Tory breakthrough in Québec were palpable;
and Harper had led the nation through robust economic times. Despite a
superior ranking in the polls as the strongest of the party leaders, Harper
could only sustain a minority government.

After three general elections as leader, including two victories, Harper
had not earned a place alongside the big four: Macdonald, Borden,
Diefenbaker, and Mulroney. But the lessons from those who have won successive elections and majority governments were available to Harper, and to
any future Conservative leader, as history tells us that Canada's most successful Tory leaders have been, to varying degrees:

1. Nation builders; relevant in all parts of Canada
2. Visionaries
3. A force of unity in their party
4. Coalition builders
5. Tough, but not authoritarian
6. Able to divide and conquer their opponents
7. Completely committed to winning

And what of Stephen Harper? How has he fared in these seven areas up to the beginning of 2009 when compared with his most successful predecessors?

1. To win and sustain office, and then succeed as prime minister, the top Tory must have strength and relevance in all regions of Canada; even better a nation-builder. Given Tory history, the leader needs to pay particular attention to Québec.

HARPER SOUGHT THE CONSERVATIVE PARTY leadership in 2004 from a strong base in Western Canada and with healthy respect in rural Ontario; but he was weak in Québec, Atlantic Canada, and large urban centres.

In a one-member one-vote contest, Harper's strength in the West would have overcome his deficiencies in the rest of the country. However, he was forced to become a national politician after Peter MacKay insisted in the PC-Alliance merger that each riding be given the same weight in a leadership vote.

To win the leadership in 2004, Harper had to establish political connections in those areas where he was weak. His new network included Québec, where ADQ leader Mario Dumont found in Harper a man who respected the constitutional division of powers and opposed a large central government. Harper also established an organization in Atlantic Canada, not easy after his outburst in 2002 against Atlantic dependency on federal largesse. By demonstrating sensitivity to regional issues and acting like a national leader, he earned respectable support from party members in all parts of Canada: not less than 33 percent in any region.

Between winning the leadership and preparing for the 2004 general election, however, there was little time for Harper to develop targeted policies that would appeal to Québecers and Atlantic Canadians. Running against Paul Martin's Liberals, the Tories gained a substantial number of seats overall in 2004, but won only seven of the 107 seats east of the Ontario border.

During the next campaign, in 2006, Harper faced up to his "culture of defeat" remarks and apologized to Atlantic Canadians, something he had stubbornly refused to do two years earlier. The Tories picked up only two additional seats in Atlantic Canada in 2006, but Harper had taken an important and crucial first step in the quest to re-establish Tory roots in the Atlantic region.

Conciliation did not come easy to Harper. He was naturally confrontational, which, during his first term as prime minister, resulted in pointless and acrimonious altercations with some Atlantic premiers over offshore royalties and federal transfers. While a prime minister must always assert the national interest, Harper belatedly softened his stance on transfers. The dispute lingered, particularly in Newfoundland. On the other hand, Harper had become a surprising advocate for regional development programs, a mainstay in Atlantic Canada. His commitment to invest in the Canadian military, an important economic driver in the East, also played well in the region. Harper understood that being sensitive to regional imbalances was good politics.

By 2008, Harper's most vocal Atlantic adversary did not come from the opposing parties, but from Newfoundland's *Progressive Conservative* Premier Danny Williams. The pugnacious premier went so far as to register with Elections Canada the "ABC—Anything but Conservative" entity that enabled him to advertise during the federal election period. Williams pulled no punches: "Trust should be a fundamental quality in any prime minister and unfortunately we do not have that in Stephen Harper. His government has proven repeatedly that promises are meaningless, and that they are not a party of principle or integrity."

Williams was accused of overplaying his hand, particularly since Liberal tax policy was unfavourable to the energy sector that was responsible for Newfoundland's economic turnaround, but he had an impact. The Tories were shut out of Newfoundland in 2008, losing two seats to the Liberals and one to the NDP. Elsewhere in Atlantic Canada the Tories picked up seats: they earned their first seat in PEI since the 1984 election; held their ground in Nova Scotia; and doubled their seat count in New Brunswick from three to six.

On the whole, then, Harper made slow but steady progress in Atlantic Canada over three federal elections, which indicated these voters were prepared to forgive and forget. After having delivered his message, Danny Williams also said he was prepared to put the past behind him and would work constructively with Stephen Harper in the best interests of the citizens of Newfoundland.

Harper's next area of weakness was urban Canada. This he shared with his predecessors, who had not won a seat in Montréal, Toronto, and

Vancouver in every federal election after 1988. Conservative values such as personal responsibility, individual freedom, small government, as well as a pledge to terminate a wasteful long-gun registry are intrinsically appealing in *rural* Canada. With the possible exception of a tax credit for riders of public transit, however, there was little in Harper's strategy book over his first term as prime minister to address inherent Tory weakness in *urban* Canada, and more specifically in MTV (Montréal, Toronto, Vancouver).

Tory strategists were, apparently, prepared to forgo seats in large urban centres in favour of building a reliable following in rural and suburban Canada. Although the Conservatives won 46 percent of the seats nationwide in 2008, their losing streak in Montreal and Toronto continued. In the greater Montreal area Tories went zero for thirty-three. In the city of Toronto Harper was zero for twenty-two. And they didn't just lose these seats, they lost them badly. Harper's Ontario-based finance minister didn't help the Tory cause in his home province in the spring of 2008 when he said, "If you're going to make a new business investment in Canada, and you're concerned about taxes, the last place you will go is the province of Ontario."

Without urban seats the Tories had to win 61 percent of the seats in the rest of the country to earn a majority government. Tories believed that increasing the total seats in the rest of Canada, including seats in ethnically diverse suburban ridings, was easier than turning around huge blocks of urban voters in Canada's three largest cities. Indeed, there were sufficient rural seats that Harper did not win in 2008 that would have bridged the gap between minority to majority, but he fell short.

Atlantic Canada and major urban centres aside, Harper pinned his hopes for a majority in 2008 on Québec. After losing the 2004 election, Harper had turned for advice to the man who swept French Canada for the Tories in 1984 and 1988. Brian Mulroney told Harper he could win seats in Québec if he invested time and money in the province. Over the protest of Tory strategists who thought campaigning in Québec was futile, Harper took Mulroney's advice and directed precious campaign resources into Québec. He expanded his Québec connections to include its premier, Jean Charest. He invited defeated 2004 Québec candidate Josée Verner into his caucus, and recruited business leader Michael Fortier to build organizational strength. Harper endorsed Québec-friendly initiatives that a decade earlier he would have thought objectionable. The payoff in 2006 was ten new Québec seats. Without a Québec front and these ten seats, Stephen Harper would not have become prime minister.

Building on this success, Harper's most daring and controversial act of nation-building involved Québec. In November 2006, amidst the turmoil of a Liberal leadership campaign, a sure-footed Prime Minister Harper introduced a resolution in Parliament that read, "This House recognizes that the Québécois form a nation within a united Canada." While Harper thought that the most serious objections to this bold move would come from within his own party, he suffered only one minor casualty when Intergovernmental Affairs Minister Michael Chong resigned from Cabinet.

What made the move a political masterpiece was its impact on Harper's opponents.

Harper's resolution did not come out of the Tory platform and was not developed through interprovincial dialogue. Indeed, Harper had Bloc Québecois leader Gilles Duceppe to thank for this opportunity. Duceppe had announced his intention to bring a "nation" resolution to the floor of the House of Commons on one of the opposition days. Not wanting to risk the ire of Québec nationalists by voting against the Bloc resolution, Harper preempted Duceppe by proposing a resolution of his own. Duceppe was so stunned he didn't know whether to claim victory or lament another humiliation for Québec. His hesitation made him appear weak and unsure.

Harper had secured Liberal-leadership combatant Stéphane Dion's approval of the resolution in advance, the man who had been Chrétien's point-man on Québec issues. With Dion on side, there would be no cohesive Liberal attack to the resolution. There was the added bonus of exploiting divisions in the Liberal party over the issue of Québec, since leadership candidates Ken Dryden and Joe Volpe were among the sixteen MPs in the House of Commons to oppose the resolution.

The media were astonished and fascinated. *Ottawa Citizen* columnist Susan Riley, who rarely found anything positive to say about a Tory, was flummoxed:

> So has Harper, the ardent critic of the Meech Lake Accord (which only recognized Québec as a 'distinct society') evolved, or has he ditched some unfashionable principles—and risked western support—to make gains in Québec? Or was Harper showing the boldness and flexibility required of a national leader? That 'flexibility' will take getting used to: It hasn't been an element of Harper's style to date.

In one bold act, Harper disrupted the Liberal leadership race, discomfited the sovereignist Bloc Québécois, bewildered and impressed the national media, and strengthened his hand as a champion of Québec nationalism.

Lost in the din was the sound of John Diefenbaker rolling over in his grave as his "One Canada" vision vanished into the mist. But Sir John A. Macdonald would have saluted Harper as a brilliant tactician and a man of grand vision. Of Québecers, Macdonald had notably said, "Respect their nationality. Treat them as a nation and they will act as a free people generally do—generously. Call them a faction and they become factious." Placing Canada's pre-eminent nation builder and Stephen Harper on the same political page is a well-deserved accolade.

Harper continued on this theme by cementing the bond between Québec nationalists and the Tory party. At a *Fête nationale du Québec* celebration Harper proclaimed, "True nationalists don't want to demolish, they want to build. We are the true nationalists." He chided the Bloc as permanent outsiders to decision-making in Ottawa. "They haven't done anything because they can't do anything." Elect Conservatives, he argued, and Canada will be strong, united and free, "with a Québec [that is] autonomous and proud." He even quoted Québec's controversial former premier Maurice Duplessis, who liked to say, "Two parties is enough. A good one and a bad one."

By recognizing the distinctiveness of the Québecois at the federal level, Harper took a stick out of separatist hands. Harper accomplished this turnaround with a simple non-binding resolution in the House of Commons that passed by a vote of 266 to 16. Making friends with Québec nationalists was in Harper's short-term political interests, but it came at considerable risk. Harper was proven correct as support for sovereignty within Québec waned after the resolution was passed. Harper, who has come to terms with his youthful distaste for Québec politics, explained his thinking this way:

> In politics you take risks—that's what we did—but national unity, national reconciliation are more important than any one party or than any one individual . . . Canadians across the country said 'yes' to Québec, 'yes' to Québecers, and Québecers said 'yes' to Canada . . . People in Québec are always going to have a deep pride and identity with the things that make them, you know, a unique culture, a unique language, a unique society. But we have to, at the same time, marry that with strong support for the Canadian federation and for Québec's historic role within that federation.

Come 2008, Harper was poised to convert his kinship with Québec nationalists into a majority government. Riding high in the polls, the Tories were favoured to win much of rural Québec, plus the ridings in and around

Québec City. At the outset of the campaign Bloc Québecois leader Gilles Duceppe had lost his bearings. All but abandoning political sovereignty for Québec, his party's *raison d'etre*, Duceppe told Québecers that he was the only one who could stop a Harper majority. He argued that Harper was out of touch with Québec values. But where was Duceppe's evidence? As prime minister Harper supported Québec's social, economic, and cultural aspirations. The best Duceppe could do was to rehash ancient history: to wit, the Kyoto environmental accord was a "socialist plot" and Canada should have sent troops to Iraq. Without fresh material, Duceppe's warnings sounded hollow and desperate. Meanwhile, under the weak leadership of Stéphane Dion, Québec Liberals outside of the island of Montreal were in freefall. It looked like Québec was going to be a two-horse race with the Tories owning the federalist and soft-nationalist vote.

Tories were dreaming of the sort of momentum in Québec that Brian Mulroney built when he took the Tories from one seat to 58 in 1984. Of course Mulroney did not have to contend with the Bloc. Still, Harper had a realistic chance of doubling or tripling the ten seats he unexpectedly took in 2006. Given their nearly flawless campaign in 2006, few expected that the Tories would stumble.

To solidify and motivate the social conservative base in the rest of Canada, Harper launched a salvo against what he called the "cultural elite," claiming that taxpayers should not be footing the bill for "rich galas." Harper then turned his sights on juveniles, pledging that those who commit serious violent crime would be harshly sentenced and would have their identities revealed. This was all the proof Duceppe needed to prove his point: Harper was an ideologue who did not understand Québec. More tolerant and culturally protective than the rest of Canada, Québecers immediately and dramatically turned away from Harper. Québec artist Michel Rivard led the charge, posting a brilliant and widely viewed satire on YouTube that spoofed a Québec musician being ridiculed by a panel of uptight, bigoted Anglophones.

The Tory blunder was all the more astonishing given that little or nothing was needed to motivate social conservatives, and that the amounts of money involved in the culture cuts represented a mere rounding error in the national fiscal framework. The $65 million proposed in cuts to cultural spending, with an estimated one-third going to Québec, was a fraction of the $110 million the federal government pumped into the projects related to the 400th anniversary of the founding of Québec City.

The Tory drop in Québec showed up in the polls overnight, and Harper went into damage control. On September 19, he announced $25 million in new funding over five years in support of tv5, Québec's commercial-free arts and culture channel. Ten days later, Harper promised a tax credit of up to $500 against fees paid for children under sixteen who participated in eligible arts activities. A desperate Harper implored Québecers: "Today's announcement shows once again, *as I've been saying*, that this government, in fact, does support culture and arts." These new programs would, according to the Tories, cost $435 million over four years and $155 million for every year thereafter. But none of this mattered. Harper was out of touch. He did not understand Québec's values and could not be trusted to protect its interests: exactly what Duceppe had proclaimed at the outset of the campaign.

While Québecers were feeling disconnected with their prime minister, senior Québec Minister Michael Fortier, standing on a mobile billboard, told Québecers that they had wasted their votes over the previous five elections by sending Bloc members to Ottawa. Rather than looking ahead, the *unelected* Senator Fortier chose to insult Québecers, calling them, in effect, stupid for wasting their votes in every election since 1993. The people he was insulting were precisely the voters Harper needed to attract to win over to gain more seats in the province.

On election night Harper could only imagine what might have been in Québec. While his seat total remained the same, his share of the popular vote declined from 24.6 percent to 21.7 percent. He went from second place in the province to third.

Harper's instincts had told him that his target voter would applaud cuts to ritzy galas, but he had a tin ear when it came to Québec. Unlike almost every previous anglophone prime minister, Harper had no Québec lieutenant that was powerful enough to steer him straight on this issue. Four years of cultivating support in Québec, two and a half as prime minister, went down the drain. His triumph in recognizing the Québecois as a nation was quickly forgotten.

It is perhaps too much to ask that any prime minister know all of Canada; that any anglophone would understand Québec. That's why, in a nation so culturally diverse, a leader needs to share power with strong people from every corner of the country. There were few such regional leaders in Cabinet, or in the prime minister's office, who could stop Harper in his tracks when he was about to make a mistake. Despite the errors, the government Harper earned in 2008 had meaningful representation in every province but one. Although there was a dearth of Tory seats in the large city centres, he broadened his rural base in 2008 to include seats from adjacent suburbs. After the 2008 election Harper held the most regionally diverse caucus since Mulroney's in 1988. The Liberals held a majority of seats in only two provinces: Newfoundland and PEI. Québec remained a weak spot.

Given that a seemingly minor decision on culture in the 2008 election cost him a majority, we would have expected hyper-sensitivity on Harper's part on anything to do with Québec. Yet, when his government faced defeat in the House of Commons weeks after the 2008 election from a coalition of parties that included support from the *sovereignist* Bloc Québecois, Harper lashed out against the deal because separatists were involved. He abandoned the respectful treatment he had given to Québec "nationalists" and derisively labeled anyone who supported the Bloc an "enemy." Powerful rhetoric, yes; appealing to those outside Québec, yes; the easiest hot button Harper could find in a moment of desperation, yes. But there were other equally effective ways of undermining the coalition without inflaming resentment towards a large segment of the population of Québec, many of whom Harper may look to for support if he were to run in a subsequent election.

Harper could have focused his attack on the weakest link of the coalition, which was not the Bloc, but Stéphane Dion. The disgraced Liberal leader had desperately grasped at the offer to join with the NDP in the Bloc in order to save face following the worst election showing for his party at any time since Confederation. In fact, Dion's attempt to become prime minister through a coalition only hastened his demise and accentuated his disgrace.

Other than national security, a prime minister's most important duty is to protect and enhance the unity of the country. By choosing to undermine the coalition only because it was beholden to the "separatists" Harper distanced his national government from a great many Québecers. The first instincts of Macdonald and Mulroney were always to be inclusive and respectful of Québecers. They would have reached out to federalist and nationalist Québecers, Liberals and otherwise, in language that would have stirred a more positive attachment to Canada.

So, as a nation-builder Harper has earned a mixed review. At times he engaged in pointless acrimony with provinces; then, when pressed, he became conciliatory. He boldly triumphed in Québec by recognizing nation status, but then squandered the gains he thought were secure by proposing policies that a majority of Québecers opposed.

Harper can be faulted for not surrounding himself with powerful advisers, in cabinet and elsewhere, to give him the pulse of the nation and to ensure he is mindful of the national interest. Harper's autocratic tendencies do not align with Canada's greatest nation-builder, Sir John A., who made supporters of those who opposed his vision. Macdonald never demeaned those whom he thought he might later seek to court—Joseph Howe, for example, who advocated Nova Scotia's separation from Canada—and never burned bridges he might later need to cross.

2. *"Where there is no vision, the people perish."That quote from the Book of Proverbs is inscribed on the Peace Tower on Parliament Hill. A leader needs to inspire the nation with a vision that offers hope. The most successful visions are often embodied in a single slogan. They are not ideological and they are never extreme.*

MACDONALD HAD A NATIONAL VISION. Borden pledged total fidelity to Canadian soldiers fighting overseas and envisioned an international identity for Canada. Diefenbaker had a northern vision. And Mulroney offered a vision of national reconciliation and economic renewal. These broad strokes were simple and powerful.

Harper has never been an advocate of strong or sweeping visions. When he lead the Alliance he told supporters, "There isn't going to be any visionary statement. You can deduce the vision when you see us in action, but we're not going to talk in these grand abstractions."

The cornerstone of Harper's vision for the 2006 election was appropriate, if modest. He stood for *accountability*. That word underscored the failings of the previous Liberal government in waste, mismanagement, and the ethical lapses associated with the sponsorship scandal. Some might say that Harper's five priorities in the 2006 election constituted a vision. But really, they were part of a strategy to distinguish the Tories from a Liberal leader who believed every issue was *very, very, very* important.

Aside from punishing the Liberals for bad conduct, what Canadians really bought in 2006 was a prime minister who would take responsibility, and be transparent and ethical in his conduct. Accordingly, the first piece of legislation Harper introduced was the Accountability Act. To curtail the effects of money in the political process, this Act completely banned corporate, union, and large personal political donations; imposed detailed monitoring on lobbying; provided additional protection for whistleblowers; and enhanced the powers of the Auditor General. In addition, the government enacted legislation to set a fixed election date, provided the government was not defeated on a vote of confidence in the House of Commons.

Offsetting these measures were some stunning decisions Harper took when he announced his cabinet, undercutting his accountability agenda and abruptly ceding the customary honeymoon period enjoyed by a new prime minister. First, he appointed Michael Fortier, a key political organizer for him in Québec, to the Senate and then to cabinet. Fortier did not help matters with the smug remark, "I didn't want to," when asked why he had not run to be an MP if he wanted a place in cabinet.

More shocking was Harper's invitation to Liberal MP David Emerson to join the Conservative cabinet. Emerson had served as Paul Martin's minister of industry and was elected in 2006 in Vancouver Kingsway as a member of the Liberal party. Harper's move showed toughness, that he was prepared to take a hit to increase the strength of his cabinet. However, it also showed that he was opportunistic, with a variable commitment to democratic principles. Harper's former mentor, Preston Manning, criticized the move, saying that a by-election should be called to let Emerson's constituents have their say. Harper could not satisfactorily explain to the voters of Vancouver Kingsway why the man they elected as a Liberal was now sitting on the Tory front bench. Across the nation, Canadians wondered if this was the sort of accountability vision Harper had in mind in the campaign.

Most commentators believed that David Emerson was a closet Tory anyway, that it was not much of a stretch for him to agree with Harper on the issues. Harper was confident that Emerson's conversion to the Tory cause was sincere. However, Harper and Emerson underestimated the clamour this action would cause, and in 2008 Emerson did not seek re-election. A wise move: the Tory candidate in Vancouver Kingsway ran third in 2008.

Harper treaded more cautiously before he welcomed Liberal MP Wajid Khan into the Tory tent. In August 2006, Harper appointed Khan, who had left the Liberal caucus, his special adviser on the Middle East and Afghanistan, a full five months before Khan officially joined the Tory caucus on January 5, 2007. In 2008 Khan was defeated and his seat reverted to Liberal hands. Another questionable move was calling the election in 2008.

In so doing Harper violated the spirit of the law his government had passed setting fixed election dates. Before that law was passed, Harper boasted that "Fixed election dates stop leaders from trying to manipulate the calendar simply for partisan political advantage." He added, "So unless we're defeated or prevented from governing, we want to keep moving forward to make this minority parliament work over the next three and a half years." So the election should have fallen in October 2009. In 2007 and 2008 Harper's government had made a confidence vote out of several non-budgetary issues, hoping to force the opposition parties into bringing down the government. Instead, Stéphane Dion whipped his MPs to abstain from voting to avoid an election. As a consequence Dion's poll numbers fell further, and so the Tories desired an election all the more.

Harper pulled the plug on his government one year early because, as he claimed, the Parliament that reconvened in the fall of 2008 would have been dysfunctional. More likely, however, he did it for reasons of political opportunism; that and to prevent the opposition parties from controlling the destiny of his government by defeating it at a time of their choosing.

As Tory strategist and former Harper chief-of-staff Tom Flanagan observed of Harper, "He doesn't like being at the mercy of others. He likes to be in control of what he's doing." In September 2008 the conditions to expand his minority, perhaps to achieve a majority, were favourable. The polls were strong, Harper rated highly on leadership and competence, the left was deeply fractured, and last rites had already been administered to Liberal leader Stéphane Dion by his own party. The vision of accountability had clearly taken second place to Harper's broader political calculations, which, given their history of losing elections, was a response Tories could admire.

So, if not accountability, what is Harper's vision for Canada? Throughout Harper's first term, Canadians remained apprehensive and uncertain about their new prime minister. Pollster Nik Nanos looked at his numbers early in 2008 and concluded that, "Canadians really haven't seen the Stephen Harper big picture on what he'd like Canada to be." Tom Flanagan suggested that the appropriate place for Tories was slightly to the right of the Liberals, enough to make a difference, but not far enough to appear extreme. In a minority government, Tories had become the party of incremental change, advancing conservative thought and ideals ever so slowly. In terms of incrementalism, Harper aligned with Liberals like Mackenzie King, Lester Pearson, and Jean Chrétien, though Harper was more decisive.

As prime minister Harper had not been forced to make many difficult or unpopular decisions. His controversial cuts to the GST hardly compare with Mulroney's decision to introduce the tax during tough economic times. Indeed, Harper assumed office in an era of relative prosperity with high employment, low inflation, and declining debt. Other than Sir John A., he was the first Tory to form a government during favourable economic times. He was able to deliver on promised tax cuts without risking a deficit or the need to spend on programs. Aside from his decision to abandon a campaign promise on the taxation of income trusts, Harper hoarded his political capital.

It was thus hard to get a sense from what Harper has done with the levers of power to predict where he wanted to take the country.

As Harper's government coasted into its third year, it flirted with a vision for a more robust role for the Canadian military. Its "Canada First" military strategy was thinly sketched out in speeches by Harper and Defence Minister Peter MacKay. The commitment to boost military spending and increase the number of armed forces was long overdue. For Harper, it gave Canada a more legitimate voice on the world stage: "If you want to be taken seriously in the world, you need the capacity to act—it's that simple. The Canada First Defence Strategy will strengthen our sovereignty and security at home and bolster our ability to defend our values and interests abroad." This military strategy included a pledge to develop related technology and increase the presence of the military in the far north, where Canada's claims to territorial sovereignty have been frequently tested. But a stronger and more independent military and foreign policy was hardly a compelling vision to stir the nation.

During the 2008 campaign, the Tories harkened back to a failed slogan from 1972, Pierre Trudeau's claim that *The Land is Strong*. Borrowing a lyric from our national anthem, Harper's slogan was: *Canada: The True North, Strong and Free*. But what did that mean, precisely?

It meant that under Harper's prudent leadership jobs were created, taxes were lowered, and the national debt was reduced. Harper claimed that "People who work hard, pay their taxes, and play by the rules are getting ahead." To Harper *strong and free* meant being tough on crime. It meant a more united Canada, a more confident and purposeful Canada on the world stage. And the *true north* recognized various measures designed to defend Canadian sovereignty in the Arctic.

Modest and *realistic* were how Tories described their approach to governing, hardly the stuff of inspiration. But the Québecois nation aside, this was how Canadians had come to think of their prime minister. Harper campaigned in 2008 on more of the same: steady as she goes. There was not one bold idea in the Tory plan.

The election, according to the Tory platform, was a ". . . choice between the Harper Conservatives' credible and affordable plan, and risky tax-and-spend experiments that will drive up the cost of everything from groceries to gas and throw Canada back into a deficit." In other words, the Tory vision was not the Liberal vision.

While it may have frustrated conservative ideologues, Harper had good reason not to offer bold policy changes. First, lingering concerns in the minds of voters over a Harper "hidden agenda" kept him in a reassuring mode: there was nothing to fear from a Tory government. Second, Harper knew Tory history and that their penchant for dramatic reform had kept them from being elected or re-elected. Over Canada's history, the masters of moderation have been Liberals, not Conservatives. In 2008, the tables were turned. It was the Liberals talking about transformative change, while the Tories safely hugged the political centre

To establish a political dynasty, Harper pursued a "conservative light" agenda. Against the urgings of many party members and right-wing think tanks, he advanced only those conservative ideas and principles that he believed mainstream Canada was prepared to support. That strategy left him with this simple vision for Canada: *a country where ordinary hard-working, law-abiding Canadians get ahead.*

Consistent with this vision, Harper shed the image of the Tory party as the home of heartless bankers, economists, and big business. He understood that the wealthy and powerful were less in need of a prime minister than average Canadian families struggling to make ends meet.

Identifying with ordinary Canadians over political or economic ideology put Harper in the company of Macdonald and Diefenbaker. John Diefenbaker in particular reached out to those who felt marginalized from the political process and excelled at taking on the powerful and wealthy for the sake of ordinary Canadians.

Harper reinforced his connection with ordinary Canadians by rejecting the trappings of power. He did not have a personal entourage and was not trying to impress anyone on the world stage. Like Trudeau, he had the ability to impress by quoting philosophers and ancient leaders, but he didn't do it. He frequently attended hockey games with his son and was working on a book about hockey history as his hobby. Harper shunned the jargon and pretensions of most economists and had rarely, if ever, spoken about ideology as a driving force behind his decision making.

Stephen Harper governed where the Liberal party was for much of the previous hundred years: in the political middle. He quieted the boisterous right-wing revolutionaries and social conservatives in his party. The GST cut was felt directly by every Canadian consumer. The Fitness Tax Credit connected the government with soccer and hockey parents across the nation. The tax credit for apprentices demonstrated the government was more concerned with the needs of front-line workers than business executives. Likewise the tax credit for transit passes. Too bad that none of these policies achieved their stated objective. The fitness tax credit, for example, was supposed to get the sedentary into sports, but the credit went mostly to families who already had their children enrolled in these programs. However, these credits fulfilled a more important needs for Tories—they returned money to Canadian families and won votes.

Harper was not a strict laissez-faire capitalist. He was a regulator when it came to product safety. In his words, "Canadians shouldn't have to worry about the toys they're putting under the tree, they shouldn't have to worry about the food they eat, and they shouldn't have to worry about drugs that may do more harm than good." What Canadian family would disagree with that? As a largely precautionary measure, Canada was the first nation to ban plastic bottles containing bisphenol A (BPA).

HARPER TOOK PEOPLE-GRABBING INITIATIVES to a highly targeted level. The special provision in the 2007 budget to enhance the deductibility of meals for truckers was a brazen play for votes. Giving seniors the ability to split taxable incomes, while helping to offset the reversal on income trusts, shored up support among a traditionally Tory-loving demographic. Any segment of society that did not or would not vote Tory was out of luck in getting a tax credit of their own.

While committed small-c conservatives were not impressed by these policies, they were prepared to be tolerant in the hopes of a bigger payoff. Noted economist and academic William Watson observed in his syndicated column, "If $160 million for kids' fitness eases the way for multi-billion dollar purchases of hard-power hardware [conservative policies], then, sure, let's subsidize spelling bees and teen-engineering contests and solar-powered kindergartens. But only if they're a means to a greater policy end. If they're solely the means to longer-lasting power, the Tories will have become Liberals."

By appealing to hard-working, law-abiding Canadians, Harper's government was both family-oriented and voter-centric. Rather than lament the "big government" Liberal approach to child care, Harper gave tax dollars to the real experts in taking care of children: parents. Rather than cozy up to corporate Canada, the finance minister took pot shots at the banking community over excessive user fees.

In response to new user fees on incoming cellphone text messages, industry minister Jim Prentice summoned business executives to Ottawa for a dressing down. *Ottawa Citizen* columnist Mark Sutcliffe observed that Conservatives were showing a surprising tendency to intervene in the marketplace over meaningless issues and called Jim Prentice the "Minister of Immaterial and Irrelevant Intervention." And rather than rubber-stamp the American takeover of a strategically important Canadian company—the space technology division of Vancouver-based MacDonald, Dettwiler and Associates—Harper's government boldly rejected the deal. "Not in the national interest" was the response. *Maclean's* national editor Andrew Coyne, known for espousing conservative principles, called this a Tory flip-flop of the highest order. Harper's decision to reject the takeover aligned him with the Canadian Auto Workers' union, not a traditional bastion of Tory supporters.

In Harper's Main Street government, the barons of Bay Street had no real clout. If Harper left himself open to criticism, especially from members of his own party, it was that he was too mainstream, too moderate, and too political.

Strategist Tom Flanagan suggested that the trend of change was most important, that as long as the country was moving *towards* a conservative perspective he was thankful for the progress. However, looking at the GST cut instead of income tax reductions, at a larger government with more regulations, and at direct interference in commercial activity, conservatives were hard-pressed to see progress.

Perhaps because he was accused of harbouring a hidden agenda, Harper took his mainstream, moderate approach to extremes. Such overreaction is not uncommon among politicians. People thought Brian Mulroney was insensitive to the environment when he was first elected, but in 2006 he earned the accolade "Canada's Greenest Prime Minister."

In the 2008 leaders' debates, Harper's opponents cast him as a "laissez-faire and I-don't-care" prime minister. However, they couldn't point to any particular policy that substantiated this allegation. In fact, Harper was at pains to point out the many instances where his government had intervened in economic matters by making strategic investments in the manufacturing and forestry sectors. Far from claiming that capitalism would sort out all that was wrong with the economy, Harper amplified the actions he had taken to support ailing industries, thus demonstrating that he was committed to using the levers of government in response to an economic downturn.

Given all that Harper had done to connect with ordinary Canadians, his timid response to the anxieties Canadians experienced during the financial and stock market meltdown in the penultimate week of the 2008 election campaign was perplexing. Harper could have taken on the reckless American credit practices and corporate greed as the sources of the problem. Instead, he went into reassuring mode and tried to convince Canadians nothing was wrong. At a time when Canadians had lost hundreds of billions of dollars of savings, Harper should have taken charge. When his decisiveness was most needed, he hesitated, fearing perhaps that a harsh response would counter the softer image he had donned at the outset of the campaign. Instead, he spoke like an optimistic stock broker, urging people to pick up bargains in a depressed market.

Harper insisted he had a financial plan, but no one believed it was designed to cope with an economic tsunami that had engulfed the world and that few had predicted. The opposition parties scored points on Harper, not because of his ideology, but because he lacked understanding of and compassion for the anxieties of much of the nation. Coming into the home stretch of the campaign, not only did his coveted majority appear to be in doubt, but the country seemed to be thinking of defeating the Tory government. Harper had failed to live up to the vision that he had advanced over much of the previous three years: that he was on the side of ordinary Canadians.

Harper's attempt to transform from his perceived agenda, that of a right-wing ideologue, to pragmatic main street Conservative was largely successful. He overcame the fear mongering of his opponents by carving out a moderate and uninspiring centrist vision that appealed to a wide swath of voters. He earned a stronger minority government without a sweeping vision because Canadians accepted that he was competent and decisive, or at least more so than his opponents. He was fortunate however, that none of his opponents, weak as they were, were able to offer a compelling vision of their own.

While Stephen Harper did not perish without an inspiring vision, as the carving on Parliament Hill predicted he did not win a majority government either. With the opportunity and circumstances he faced in 2008, to many Tories the election was a loss.

3. Sir John A. Macdonald once said, "We can't slay the bear unless we work together . . . I don't need caucus when I succeed; I need them when I fail."

MACDONALD AND MULRONEY invested heavily in the needs and egos of caucus members to earn their affection. Both sent personalized notes to their members of Parliament. Mulroney faithfully attended weekly caucus meetings, keeping members informed and entranced with entertaining inside stories, and routinely called distressed MPs to offer encouragement. Diefenbaker suffered because he did not have command of his caucus, Bennett paid little attention to his, and Meighen had strained relations with his Québec members. Borden was known to confuse his MPs with the page boys in the House of Commons. Until Stanfield got tough with his caucus and quelled destructive outbursts, he was a weakened leader.

Some leaders promote unity by tolerating dissent. American president Lyndon B. Johnson used to say it was probably better to have FBI Director J. Edgar Hoover "inside the tent pissing out, then outside pissing in." Harper would probably disagree. He seems to believe in cutting out "bad weeds" so they can't foment trouble from within.

Every time a Tory caucus member was ousted or disciplined, a chilling message was sent through the ranks: free wheel at your peril. Harper's commanding and confident presence, combined with the threat of expulsion, kept Tory MPs from speaking out, either about his leadership or on issues. Harper once issued an edict to his caucus that anyone who criticized budget cuts ". . . would have a very short political career."

Just days after the 2006 election, Halton MP Garth Turner publicly opposed accepting David Emerson into the Tory caucus. Turner continued to irritate the prime minister with postings on his blog that violated the principle of caucus confidentiality. Turner was expelled from caucus in October 2006 and later joined Liberal ranks where he continued to annoy until defeated by Tory Lisa Raitt in 2008.

Bill Casey, the amiable member for Cumberland-Colchester-Musquodoboit Valley in Nova Scotia, had run for the Tories in every election since 1988, earning handsome victories in five of six contests. But Casey had a spat with Harper over the terms of the Atlantic Accord. At issue was the exclusion of offshore resource revenues from the equalization formula used to redistribute wealth among the provinces. Casey voted against his government's budget because it did not, in his opinion, honour the prime minister's 2006 election promise. He was immediately expelled from caucus. Indeed, no prime minister could have tolerated such dissent. When two of Mulroney's caucus members voted against the legislation establishing the GST, they were similarly dismissed. But Harper took the punishment much further. To reinforce the importance of party discipline, he dictated that there was no room for an apology, for forgiveness or reconciliation:

> Mr. Casey is not welcome into our caucus. And just so as I can be as clear as I can be on it, when there is the next federal election there will be a Conservative candidate in Mr. Casey's riding, and it will not be Mr. Casey.

Harper's decision put him at odds with the local and provincial Tory associations, both of which stood behind Casey. After this incident, *National*

Post columnist Don Martin labeled Harper "a control freak with a mean streak." Casey became a folk hero in Nova Scotia and was re-elected in his riding in 2008 as an Independent with an astonishing 69 percent of the popular vote. His Tory opponent received 8.9 percent of the vote. Harper would have done better to suspend rather than permanently banish Casey.

Successful Tory leaders have built bridges with provincial parties, mostly with provincial parties of the same name. But over time, federal Conservatives have informally linked with Social Credit, Union Nationale, the ADQ, and even the Liberal party in British Columbia and Québec. Here the only provincial government with which Harper enjoyed warm and politically useful relations was Québec's Liberal government led by Jean Charest, although in 2008 the relationship suffered.

While Harper has attended provincial Progressive Conservative conferences, he was better known for his nasty disputes with Atlantic Canadian leaders over equalization payments and offshore royalties. In an angry outburst in April 2007, Newfoundland Progressive Conservative premier Danny Williams said, "The quicker this [Harper] government could be out of office would [*sic*] make me very happy . . . I don't like what Mr. Harper represents, I don't like what Conservatives are representing right now in this country." Harper relented and compromised to get fiscal agreements with some maritime provinces. Better that he had worked cooperatively in the first place, particularly with those of Progressive Conservative persuasion, and avoided the acrimony.

Brian Mulroney was criticized for being loyal to a fault. Mulroney did, in fact, make some questionable and unpopular patronage appointments because he supported the people that stood with him during his political career. Stephen Harper holds the opposite view. "I don't stand for patronage," Harper boasted during the 2004 election, "because I don't owe anybody anything." That included, apparently, Brian Mulroney. Harper's response to a Mulroney crisis reveals an important facet of his character.

In 2007, to avoid extradition to Germany where he was wanted on numerous criminal charges, Karlheinz Schreiber was busy rehashing and inventing allegations of scandal and misconduct against Mulroney. An authority no less than the Supreme Court of Canada confirmed Schreiber's extradition order. The Schreiber story went back to 2001 when *National Post* reporter William Mathias discovered evidence that Schreiber paid Mulroney cash for consulting services. Lacking grounds of relevance Mathias was unable to get his story published. Mathias later took his story to William Kaplan, author of *Presumed Guilty: Brian Mulroney, the Airbus Affair, and the*

Government of Canada. Kaplan recounted Mathias's discovery in a November 10, 2003, *Globe and Mail* article entitled, "Schreiber hired Mulroney." Thereafter, reporters and commentators would occasionally refer to the peculiarity and unseemliness of the transaction, but not until 2007, when he was headed for Germany to stand trial, did Schreiber conspire with journalists and Liberal officials to hint that more damning evidence was available against Mulroney.

Working for cash was stupid and the former prime minister had to avail himself of Canada Revenue Agency's Voluntary Disclosure program in which criminal prosecutions and civil penalties can be waived when a taxpayer volunteers to report unclaimed income. While Mulroney correctly and legally cleared up the matter with the authorities, he was left to explain his lack of judgment. The lapse is particularly stark given that the risk to Mulroney's reputation was over an amount of money he could easily earn delivering four twenty-minute speeches at international conventions.

After the CBC's *the fifth estate* aired an inflammatory exposé of the affair in the fall of 2007 the opposition parties called for a public inquiry. Harper was initially dismissive: "Do they really want to say that I, as prime minister, should have a free hand to launch inquiries against my predecessors?" Musing about inquiries into Chrétien's dealings with a Shawinigan golf course and hotel, or Paul Martin's involvement with the Canada Steamship Lines while prime minister, Harper said, "I don't think that if the Liberal party thought twice about it, it is a power they would want to give me."

However, Harper quickly changed his mind after the imprisoned Schreiber alleged in an affidavit that Mulroney had told him earlier that year that he would bring correspondence supportive of Schreiber's plight to Harper at Harrington Lake, the prime minister's retreat, in the summer of 2007. This despite the fact that Mulroney had not spoken with Schreiber over the previous seven years. The allegation was false, but for the first time Harper's name was raised in the scandal, and he responded vigorously. "Mister Mulroney never talked to me about Mr. Schreiber and he never gave me any documents." Claiming he did not know how best to respond, and stopping short of a full public inquiry, Harper said he would appoint an independent person, "to give us a recommendation on how to proceed, what the most appropriate venue and most appropriate process is to proceed after reviewing all the documents."

Mulroney went on the offensive and asked for the public inquiry himself, provided it fully covered the Airbus transaction from its inception, so that he could once again clear his name. He didn't want a narrowly focused inquiry, but neither did he want to be seen as fearing one.

Harper was not about to take any heat over Mulroney's conduct, however, and set him adrift. He forbade cabinet ministers and party workers from having anything to do with Mulroney. Many Canadians may have appreciated Harper's tough stand, but Mulroney loyalists were upset with Harper for abandoning a former leader who had helped the Tories regain power. Mulroney, they contended, deserved better than to be targeted by a multi-million-dollar public inquiry into allegations that essentially covered his conduct while no longer prime minister.

Harper has suffered the consequences of his decision. First, he lost Mulroney and his wide network of operatives, which was significant in Québec in the 2008 election where the Tories blundered and failed to pick up seats. Second, no matter how hard he tries in the future to distance himself from a predecessor, conspiracy theorists will taint Harper with guilt by association. As Mulroney and Paul Martin both learned while in office, a public inquiry never helps a sitting government.

What cabinet ministers learned from Harper's aggressive response was that should they ever fall out of line he would not be there to defend them. There is a place for loyalty in politics, although it appears to be in short supply with Harper at the helm.

On the whole, Harper's discipline and tough love seems to have worked. Mulroney loyalists and a provincial premier aside, Harper's leadership was not seriously questioned. He had command of his cabinet, caucus, and the rank and file of party membership. Harper united the party and filled its coffers. The enthusiasm was evident at campaign stops in 2008 where boisterous supporters filled the halls, while his opponents often appeared before captive audiences in a school or at a chamber of commerce luncheon.

Over their history, Tories have rarely achieved such discipline. Too many Tory leaders have suffered from disunity, giving Liberals the opportunity to ask, "If they can't unite their party how can they be expected them to run the country." However, having motivated by fear and intimidation, what he risked with his strict approach to discipline was this: If things turn against him, loyalty from his cabinet or caucus colleagues might be in short supply, and many will not willingly go down with Harper should he be the commander of a sinking ship.

4. There aren't enough self-identified ideological conservatives outside of Alberta to elect a chief dogcatcher. Without forgoing broad appeal, the successful Tory leader must keep the core conservative vote intact and quell any fringe parties that might appeal to extreme conservative elements.

THE VARIANTS OF CONSERVATISM in Canada run deep and wide, offering any number of inherent conflicts, contradictions, and inconsistencies. The successful Conservative leader is judged not by an ability to carry the flag for a particular faction, but by an ability to draw the wide range of conservative factions together into common cause. Internal battles are inevitable among like-minded people in a broadly-based political party, just as a single faction of a party will naturally want to prevail. In a big political tent, however, not all can get their way. An effective leader of a broad, inclusive party tolerates and manages dissent to keep the coalition united against its opponents. Successful leadership is not about letting one side of the movement dominate, but about fostering unity among a very broad and multifaceted coalition. Collective success comes from accepting and embracing the movement in its widest possible form. In Canada, that also means drawing together English and French Conservatives.

But as all Tory leaders over the past hundred years came to realize, there aren't enough self-identified conservatives in Canada for the Conservative party to win government. After he united the parties, Harper had to keep core conservatives on side while making the Conservative party attractive to independent voters. How could Harper offer a range of conservative-minded policies in a country that doesn't think in ideological terms and also attract non-aligned or centrist voters to his side? Harper's answer was to embrace a mainstream and pragmatic form of conservatism.

Certainly, nothing of Harper's *actions* as prime minister during his first term suggested he was anything but moderate and mainstream, which is where most of the voters are. Nonetheless, over three elections with Harper at the helm, Liberals have claimed that Harper is a sham; a wolf in sheep's clothing. Give him a majority, they warned, and then we will see the *real* Stephen.

Keeping the social conservative faction of his coalition onside was Harper's riskiest challenge. He succeeded in his first term as prime minister by offering six important policy shifts that appealed to social conservatives, yet did not offend mainstream Canadian sensibilities.

First, his government gave money to parents to help them with the cost of raising children, in contrast to the Liberal approach of institutionalized childcare. Policies that support individuals rather than institutions are rooted in conservative ideology, but this particular policy also had widespread appeal among those who claim no political ties. Second, Harper respectfully honoured a commitment to social conservatives for a free vote in the House of Commons on same-sex marriage, even though he knew it would be defeated. He thus managed to keep a promise without risking an outcome that was opposed by a majority of Canadians. Third, Harper's government eliminated the Court Challenges Program, a target of social conservatives because it funded cases and causes that often went against family values. Few Canadians, other than social conservatives, knew or cared about the program. Fourth, the government reversed a long-standing policy of seeking to commute death sentences imposed on Canadian nationals in foreign countries. Social conservatives might like to have the death penalty restored, but that was unlikely to happen. Fifth, the Tory government gave law enforcement authorities a voice in the appointment of judges. Social conservatives are inclined to be tough on crime and support the police. Finally, Harper's government proposed a ministerial veto over the funding of Canadian films with content "contrary to public policy." Few politicians want to be front and centre defending taxpayer support for a movie, however critically acclaimed, provocatively entitled *Young People Fucking*.

Social conservatives did not get from Harper what they really wanted— restricted access to abortions and an outright ban on gay marriages. But they took comfort in the knowledge that none of the modest social conservative measures that Harper pursued would have been introduced by a Liberal government.

While Harper cleverly navigated most social conservative issues as prime minister, over the course of the 2008 campaign he learned to his dismay that many Canadians, and especially Québecers, remained uncomfortable with some of the views embraced in other parts of Canada. Harper's misstep on support for public spending on culture and on young offenders were prime examples of modest social conservative instincts going against the grain of mainstream Québec. To stem the slide in support in Québec in the final week of the campaign, the Tory platform slipped in a pledge that a re-elected Conservative government "will not reintroduce the Bill c-10 … and will take into account the serious concerns that have been expressed by film creators and investors." It was, however, too little and too late. There was nothing that contributed more to his failure to win a majority than his fundamental policy miscalculation on culture, which points to the inherent danger in any policy that smacks of social conservatism.

BRIAN MULRONEY WAS THE ONLY TORY LEADER ever elected with even a hint of a right-wing economic agenda in Canada. Comparatively, Harper's budgets were markedly tame by conservative standards. Although he achieved modest debt and tax reductions, he did not transform or liberate the economy. There was not much in the Tory economic plan over its first three years in office that inspired a new generation of entrepreneurs.

Harper's claims to economic fame on taxes included reducing the GST from 7 percent to 5 percent, lowering some business taxes, and introducing a modest $5,000 Tax Free Savings account that began in 2009. Most economic conservatives would have preferred deeper income tax cuts over the politically popular GST cut that helped win the 2006 election. The collection of tax credits the government introduced in its first mandate (for public transportation, children's fitness, and apprentice tools) have limited appeal to fiscal conservatives, and involve complex policy contortions that only tinker with the system. They came with huge compliance costs and provided minimal tax relief.

Fiscal conservatives were also distressed when Harper shut down the income trust sector on October 31, 2006. Their preference would have been a wholesale reduction in tax rates, if not the elimination of corporate income tax.

But what bothered fiscal conservatives most was that under the Harper government spending hit an all-time high. To fiscal conservatives small government is better government. In their ideal world, Harper would simultaneously slash spending and taxes. Yet in the 2008 campaign Harper promised more spending, albeit at levels far below those of his opponents. Over four years, Tory promises added $8.7 billion to the already record level of federal expenditures. There was not one important measure in the Tory platform that economic conservatives could take to the bank as making Canada more competitive. This idea reinforced Tom Flanagan's point that to sustain their core vote, Conservatives need only be slightly to the right of the Liberal party.

As long as fiscal conservatives had nowhere else to go, no Reform party, for example, the Tory coalition would remain intact. Given Harper's roots in the West, he calculated that another Reform party was not likely to surface.

As a coalition builder Harper did not talk in terms of ideology, right-wing or otherwise, and he redefined the political centre as a place of moderation that represents the values of law-abiding, hard-working Canadian families. At a Tory policy convention the month after the 2008 election, in his keynote speech, Harper proclaimed: "Conservatives scored a victory that firmly established us as the biggest, the broadest, and the most national of Canada's political parties. Because the Conservative party is Canada's party!"

Hardened conservatives were disappointed with the slow pace of change and unhappy with some decisions that could just as easily have been proposed by the NDP. Nonetheless, Harper successfully sustained the unity of social and fiscal conservatives and obviated the creation of new political entities on the right. Fiscal conservatives were patient and stayed with Harper in the belief that a strong economic agenda was incompatible with a minority Parliament. But questionable efforts to motivate his social conservative base clashed with sensibilities in Québec, which cost him a majority government.

5. Nice guys finish last. Just think of Bob Stanfield. Voters want tough, determined leaders who vigorously defend the national interests. But they don't want authoritarian leaders who pick fights for no good reason.

VOTERS DISTRUSTED ARTHUR MEIGHEN. He was mean-spirited during the Winnipeg strike, tilted the 1917 election through flagrant rule changes, and was heavy-handed to those who were drafted during the war. They admired Diefenbaker for sticking up for ordinary Canadians after he refused the Newfoundland government's request to send in the RCMP to quell labour unrest. But Diefenbaker was no softie and was respected for his ability to pillory his opponents. While Diefenbaker pounced on the Liberals when they were down and out, winning the largest majority in Canadian history, Bob Stanfield let them off the hook after having defeated the Liberal government in the House of Commons in the midst of their leadership race.

Being tough, even dark, appears to be Harper's natural emotional predisposition. But if there is a fine line between tough and mean, Harper is on its edge. While he impressed his caucus each week with his wit and tactical cunning, Harper was also a strict disciplinarian. Minority governments usually require sensitivity to keep wayward MPs on side, but Harper showed he was not afraid of losing members who did not fall into line. It was not so much that he imposed caucus discipline, but that he seemed to enjoy doing it.

Harper was at least as tough on his cabinet ministers as he was on backbench MPs. One senior bureaucratic official who observed Harper in action at the cabinet table offered this assessment: "There's a menacing undertone sometimes. He can go very cold and cut ministers to the quick. He uses an icy, cold voice....When he gets mad, he speaks softly but he gets very red in the face and goes to that mean, partisan place. He's very capable of making a piercing comment that's part of the intimidation." Adding to this portrait, columnist Lawrence Martin reported that Harper had once told his cabinet colleagues, "When I'm hiring someone, I want to see fear in their eyes."

Politics, according to Tom Flanagan, is not the place for Boy Scouts. But how far can a party bend or break the rules to suit itself? In his book, *Harper's Team*, Flanagan referred to the 2004 election and noted, "Even though there is a cap on national campaign spending, it is easy and legal to *exceed* it by transferring expenditures to local campaigns that are not able to spend up to their legal limits." The "in and out" scheme not only artificially messed with the spending cap, it added taxpayer-funded subsidies to local campaigns where a rebate of 60 percent on total spending was available. In 2006, Canada's Chief Elections Officer refused to pay the election subsidy on such transfers. Then Elections Canada accused the Tories of violating elections law by exceeding the allowable spending limit. The marginal benefit of additional advertising was certainly not worth the negative publicity that ensued from the clash with Elections Canada and it was an unwise move for a prime minister who liked to boast he was running a "clean and accountable" government.

Another troubling incident involved Surrey North, BC, MP Chuck Cadman. The maverick MP had won three consecutive elections: with the Reform party in 1997, then under the Canadian Alliance in 1997, and finally, after failing to win the Conservative nomination in 2004, as an Independent. Cadman's biographer alleged that Tory campaign officials, later named as Doug Finley and Tom Flanagan, attempted to influence Cadman's vote in the House of Commons to defeat Paul Martin's minority Liberal government in May 2005. Cadman was terminally ill and did not want to risk losing the million-dollar life insurance policy given to members of Parliament through an election defeat. The Tories allegedly offered to make good on the death benefit out of their own kitty if Cadman died while not in office. In effect, they freed Cadman to vote for what he thought was best for Canada, not for what sustained his life insurance policy. Cadman went on record denying that any such offer had been made, which meant he avoided the accusation that his vote was influenced by personal financial considerations. Those allegedly involved in the caper went silent. And even though Cadman's wife, Donna, backed Harper and won a seat as a Tory in 2008, the allegation, along with a tape recorded interview in which Harper discussed the matter, hurt the Tories.

Over Harper's first two years on the job, the national media wondered if he was capable of seeing a belt without hitting below it. Les MacPherson of the Saskatoon *Star Phoenix* wrote that Harper is "good at almost everything except making friends." While members of the press gallery admired Harper's intellect and strategic smarts, few were seduced by his charms. The Prime Minister's Office sustained a long-running feud with the National Press Gallery that began when the national media refused to bend to PMO directives on when and how questions were to be asked of the prime minister. Every political party spins the media and leaks stories to favoured journalists, but they need to be clever about it or they'll look stupid. When Tory party strategists attempted secretly to brief a select group of journalists about the party's position on alleged election financing violations, "uninvited journalists" attempted to crash the meeting. The scene turned into a farce as Tory officials used the fire exit to avoid a throng of reporters. The ensuing news coverage focused on the clumsiness of the event and the fact that Tory backroom officials were trying to control media reporting. *Maclean's* magazine pointed out that "Underhandedness foiled by incompetence is always a crowd-pleaser." The incident spoke to poor judgment in Harper's senior team, fueled in part by a misplaced sense of invincibility that made them think they didn't have to play by the rules.

Just prior to the 2008 election Harper accepted that he couldn't win a fight with the press. Sandra Buckler, who had held a firm grip on government communications, was replaced by Kory Teneycke, a former executive director of the Canadian Renewable Fuels Association who had links to the Reform party and the Mike Harris Tory government in Ontario. The affable Teneycke gave the media a more friendly point of entry and greater access to the prime minister and his cabinet. This change was a sign that Harper was softening his rough edges.

The symbol of this softer and gentler Harper was the "blue sweater" that he wore in the Tory election ads that ran before the election was called. A folksy Harper, speaking from the prime minister's residence at Harrington Lake, spoke from the heart about the importance of being a father, how immigrants built this country, the gratitude the nation felt towards its veterans, and how Canada would come through some tough economic times better and stronger. His opponents—those who had been on the receiving end of many of Harper's attacks in the House of Commons, and especially Stéphane Dion who sustained a full frontal assault on his leadership through extensive media advertising—predictably doubted Harper's sincerity and ridiculed this newfound niceness.

The Harper makeover was a necessary evil. His inner circle had determined that to win a majority the Tory universe had to be expanded to include more women, who had not yet warmed up to the prime minister. But was Harper's transformation believable? Harper himself was a reluctant convert to the strategy saying, "[My staff] feel that voters don't yet know me the way they know me, the way my caucus knows me. And we should probably go out of our way to highlight the non-podium parts of the job."

These ads were not the first time Canada had seen the emotional side of Stephen Harper. When he lead the Canadian delegation at the rededication of the Vimy Memorial in France to mark the 90th anniversary of the battle, Prime Minister Harper was visibly moved. There was also a tender moment on a related trip to a cemetery near Vimy Ridge when Harper comforted his tearful wife Laureen as she knelt beside the gravesite of her great-uncle, Private James Teskey, who died in the Battle of Arras. Perhaps the prime minister's most visible emotional moment was in the House of Commons in June 2008 when he rose to offer an apology on behalf of the people of Canada to those who had suffered abuse in native residential schools. His voice cracked when he said, "We now recognize that, in separating children from their families, we undermined the ability of many to adequately parent their own children and sowed the seeds for generations to follow." In that moment Canadians got a sense of how important fatherhood is to Stephen Harper.

But these moments of tenderness were few and far between, and the polls told Tory strategists they needed to show women the more compassionate and likeable side of Stephen Harper.

In the spring of 2008 a Harris/Decima poll reported that 55 percent of respondents agreed with the statement, "There is something about Stephen Harper that I just don't like." Going into the election campaign that fall, the party needed to remake Harper's image into a thoughtful, balanced, folksy, sensitive, and caring man who just happened to wear a blue sweater. Party strategists determined that Harper would present himself in the 2008 campaign to be not only prime-ministerial, but less partisan and less combative. It was one thing to remake one man's image, but it was quite another to tone down the entire Tory team, which had been in attack mode every day since the last election.

The first glitch involved the Tory campaign website, which featured a hapless looking Dion being defecated upon by a flying puffin. Harper apologized, calling the ad "tasteless and inappropriate." The footage was a juvenile prank, but it became a regular feature in the round-the-clock news cycle and it took Harper off his message.

Far more serious was a call made by Tory campaign worker Ryan Sparrow to Jenna Fyfe of CTV News pointing out that Jim Davis, who had criticized Stephen Harper's decision to set a firm date of 2011 to withdraw Canadian troops out of Afghanistan, was in fact a Liberal supporter. Jim Davis was the father of a soldier who died in Afghanistan. Even if the grief-stricken father had been a Liberal candidate or on the Liberal party payroll, it would have been offensive to diminish him in this way. Harper accepted

Sparrow's resignation from the campaign. Another campaign aide, Darlene Lannigan, who worked for Transport Minister Lawrence Cannon, found herself in the news cycle after responding condescendingly to native leader Norman Matchewan when he requested a meeting with her minister: "If you behave and you're sober and there's no problems and if you don't do a sit down and whatever, I don't care."

Then there was Agriculture Minister Gerry Ritz. In a pre-campaign conference call about the listeriosis outbreak—the bacterial infection traced to contaminated meat products that had already killed seventeen people in Canada and prompted a nationwide recall of meat products from Maple Leaf Foods—Ritz used the occasion to demonstrate his sense of humour. The disease "is like a death by a thousand cuts. Or should I say cold cuts," he quipped. When informed of a new listeriosis death in Prince Edward Island, Ritz responded, "Please tell me it's [Liberal Agriculture critic] Wayne Easter." The opposition leaders demanded Ritz's immediate resignation. Ritz delivered an awkward public apology, claiming he was under a great deal of stress at the time of his inappropriate remarks.

While these five incidents were distracting to the Tory campaign and obscured their daily policy announcements, Harper was not directly implicated. He did not excuse the conduct and his responses were appropriate to the severity of the infractions. If this were a football game, Team Harper warranted five unsportsmanlike penalties, but remained comfortably ahead on the scoreboard.

Harper was determined to make nice. At a campaign stop at a Winnipeg produce warehouse, the prime minister was asked this goofy question, "If you were a vegetable, what type of vegetable would you be and why?" Harper was momentarily stumped: "Um, I, um, you know, I really don't know how to answer that one. I've never been asked that question before and I have a feeling that I can't win by answering that question." But then he connected the dots: "Let me say this: I would choose, if I had to, instead to be a fruit. Just what I am, sweet and colourful." The press didn't know whether to laugh or groan.

Harper was clearly sticking with his new image because it was working. His personal leadership numbers remained high and progress was made in appealing to women voters. Pollster Donna Dasko of Environics Research Group was perplexed by numbers at the outset of the campaign that showed the Tories leading among women by a margin of 35 to 28 over the Liberals. "I find this an interesting development. I can't quite figure out why it is. There certainly has been a traditional advantage for the Liberals to win women's votes." Perhaps the Liberal carbon tax was less appealing than the $100 per month for every child under six that Harper had delivered as prime minister.

In the final week of the campaign a much-hyped book by Julie Couillard was released that chronicled her relationship with Maxime Bernier while he was Harper's Foreign Affairs minister. Bernier was dismissed from cabinet after it was revealed he had asked Couillard to throw confidential documents related to national security out with the weekly garbage. On the advice of her lawyer, Couillard returned the documents to Foreign Affairs. Couillard had a colourful past, including relationships with members of the Hells Angels biker gang. In the book she recounted the affair with Bernier and described Bernier's alleged impressions of Harper and his staff. Damaging excerpts from the book appeared in the newspapers, including Couillard's claim that Harper's staff were controlling to the point of dictating with whom the most senior ministers of the crown could have lunch. This claim reinforced an April 2008 report from Tory MPs that they were required to carry a wallet-sized, laminated card entitled "When a Reporter Calls," which instructed members to seek permission from the Prime Minister's Office before speaking with a journalist.

Still, the Tories held a lead in the polls. They had been knocked off stride in Québec over their blunder on cultural funding and young offenders, but election predictions were still for either a Tory minority or majority.
That changed, and the Tories almost lost the election, after a meek response to an economic crisis that exploded in the final days of the campaign. Over a two-week period concluding on the Friday before Election Day, the stock market lost nearly 30 percent of its value. Millions of Canadians saving for their retirement through RRSPs were particularly hard hit. The prime minister's handling of the economic meltdown revealed the full extent of his inability to relate to the emotional distress of other people. This was a moment when he needed to shift gears, away from the warm "all is well" persona he had adopted at the outset of the campaign, into a decisive, take-charge, action-oriented leader who understood and was empathetic to the anxiety the nation was experiencing.

Harper had signaled a personal weakness early in the campaign in an interview with *Maclean's* magazine. "I guess I come from a background—I admit to being, culturally, very British or English—where you tend to be distrustful of people who talk about themselves too much or make it about themselves. Obviously, we're more reticent about expressing ourselves and our emotions. But, you know, I'm working with it and getting my own comfort level with it."

As the economic crisis deepened Harper's emotional struggles exacerbated the situation. He did not respond with the action that was needed and he failed to show Canadians he cared. He appeared aloof, lacking empathy, and failed to acknowledge the carnage that was taking place. Worse, he dispensed investment advice, suggesting there were good buying opportunities in the stock market. Montreal *Gazette* columnist L. Ian Macdonald pointed out the obvious: "The prime minister never comments on the stock market, any more than he does the dollar. It's a cardinal rule." The man known for strategic brilliance was undisciplined, carelessly freelancing in an area where there was no upside.

Given the pressing need to calm the markets, and sensing a steady decline in the polls, Finance Minister Jim Flaherty left the campaign trail to announce measures that added liquidity to the financial system. Then the prime minister drew his ultimate emotional weapon: his mother. "We're getting this criticism that I somehow don't understand the stock market or I don't understand what people are feeling about the stock market. I use my mother as an obvious example because, you know, she's the person closest to me who's most worried about the stock market these days. And believe me, I get quicker updates from her on the stock market than I do from the Department of Finance." The evocation of Margaret Harper, action by his finance minister, the fear of those four words (*Prime Minister Stéphane Dion*), and finally a raging Election Day rally on the stock market—these were the four elixirs that helped regain the Tory campaign momentum.

DURING HIS VICTORY SPEECH on election night Harper was uncharacteristically humble and indicated he would tone down his partisanship. But, while delivering an economic update six weeks after the election, Harper's finance minister launched a missile into the camp of every opposition party. Besides measures to remove the right to strike in the public service and an amendment to pay equity provisions, the government proposed eliminating taxpayer subsidies for political parties. The subsidy scheme had been worked out during the Chrétien administration and had imposed restrictions on corporate and union donations, while placing limits on individual contributions. The *quid pro quo* was that political parties were to receive an annual subsidy that was calculated with reference to the number of votes received at the most recent election. Harper's finance minister argued that during difficult economic times the $30 million per year in subsidies were a luxury the nation could do without. Besides, they argued, as the party that received the most number of votes in the last election the change in policy would hurt Tories the most. In truth the policy did not hurt Tories anywhere near as much as the other parties. The Tories had developed sophisticated fundraising machinery that made them considerably less reliant than other parties on the subsidy. In fact, the Liberal finances and fundraising were in such decrepit state that the loss of the subsidy would have made them insolvent. The Bloc Québecois would have lost 86 percent of their annual political budget.

To say the opposition was outraged was an understatement. "It's a very cynical ploy on Mr. Harper's part obviously geared toward bankrupting the Liberal party more than helping out the Canadian taxpayer," quipped Green Leader Elizabeth May. But even more than the Liberals, the Greens were dependent on taxpayer funds, having received 6.8 percent of the popular vote and no seats in the House of Commons.

Harper miscalculated when he thought the opposition parties would vote for a measure that could leave them bankrupt simply because they were unprepared for an election. They developed another plan: defeat the government and join in a coalition to take over the government without the inconvenience of an election. Even though Stéphane Dion had suffered the lowest popular vote of any Liberal leader, he had unbelievably crafted a credible path to replace Stephen Harper as prime minister.

Harper panicked, retreated, and then abandoned all controversial measures attached to the economic statement. While the matter should have ended there, the coalition forces unwisely persisted, allowing Harper to regain the upper hand.

No one in cabinet or the PMO was sacrificed or claimed responsibility for the blunder, which likely meant it was all Harper's doing. Privately, the prime minister's chief of staff and many cabinet ministers said they tried to talk Harper out of poking his opponents in the eye with a sharp stick, but his bully instincts prevailed.

So Harper was never going to win a congeniality award. Neither would have Robert Borden, R.B. Bennett, or Pierre Trudeau for that matter. Stephen Harper was not the person Canadians wanted to invite for dinner. But likeability has never been an essential ingredient in a politician. We admire intelligence and toughness in our leaders, not emotional dribble.

When Harper made a conscious effort to soften his voice he came across as insincere and awkward. Harper was at his best when he was tough on his opponents; but his tendency to pathological partisanship left the impression that he was mean-spirited and vindictive. Being a tough, optimistic, and visionary leader, rather than a gruff loner and bully, was the path followed by Canada's most successful Tory leaders.

6. Successful Tory leaders divide and conquer their opponents.

MACDONALD WAS A MASTER at provoking division among Liberals. And he knew when to disengage and let the divisions fester to his advantage. Pierre Trudeau tried to do it with Brian Mulroney. Trudeau didn't care that bringing the explosive issue of provincial minority language rights to the federal House of Commons might harm national unity, so long as it exposed a division on bilingualism in the Tory caucus and made its new leader appear powerless. Mulroney recognized the assault for what it was, however, and marshalled his forces for a disciplined counterattack. Few other Tory leaders could have responded so effectively to Trudeau's cunning.

Harper knows how to throw his own hand grenades. He lobbed one over Québec nationhood, and another over Canada's participation in Afghanistan. It may have seemed peculiar that a man known to be controlling and decisive put the issue of Canada's role in Afghanistan, a deployment near and dear to his heart, into the hands of a panel led by former *Liberal* Cabinet minister John Manley. However, it was clear from the outset that Manley and the other panelists could be counted upon to deliver a recommendation that fit neatly with Harper's view of the mission. The political mission was tactical, designed to unsettle Liberal ranks. And Manley delivered in spades, implying that Canada's role in Afghanistan was right and also consistent with the tradition of peacekeeping left by Liberal prime minister Lester B. Pearson:

> We're a rich country, we've got to do some of this stuff . . . The world isn't a pretty place but I happen to believe that the people who came before me in the Liberal party believed in a strong role for Canada on the international stage and would say there are times when we have to be counted, times when it matters.

Even with the Manley report in hand, Harper let the ultimate fate of the mission would be determined by Parliament. Since Harper's Tories were solidly behind the mission, it would take the Liberal opposition to bring it to an end. To do so, they would have to explain why a Liberal government had put Canada in Afghanistan in the first place, only to abandon the mission before the job was done. Harper looked statesmanlike and conciliatory as he called for consensus around troop deployment.

> I would wait to see some degree of consensus around [extending the mission in Afghanistan]. I don't want to send people into a mission if

the opposition is going to, at home, undercut the dangerous work that they are doing in the field. My own sense, listening to the comments of some leaders of the opposition, of the Liberal leader, the Bloc leader is that I don't think they are suggesting, based on recent comments, that we would simply abandon Afghanistan in 2009. So I hope that sometime in the next few months, we will be able to get a meeting of the minds on what the appropriate next steps are.

Harper's political strategy accomplished two objectives. It exposed and exacerbated a split in Liberal ranks, and it achieved the policy outcome he sought.

Harper had no difficulty going for the jugular. His direct, unrelenting, and somewhat brutish attacks on Liberal leader Stéphane Dion accomplished what many thought impossible. While Dion used his bona fides on the environment to win the Liberal leadership, the Tories accused Dion of environmental indifference and ineffectiveness. The Tory party flexed its political and financial muscle by purchasing radio and television commercials outside of an election period to lambaste Dion as weak and indecisive. They turned an apparent strength into weakness. Public perception of Dion changed from self-proclaimed international leader on the environment to the status of a poser.

Well before the 2008 election loss Liberals were openly expressing doubt about Dion's ability to win. Even before the election was called Michael Ignatieff felt compelled to make declarations in support of his leader: "Let's take the labels off our necks here. There are no more Ignatieff people, Dion people, Dryden people, Brison people. They're Liberals."

Sounding much like Sir John A., Ignatieff reminded Liberals of the political maxim: "We have to fight and win as a team. We need discipline. We need unity. United parties win, and divided parties lose." But the fact that Ignatieff was forced to talk openly about party unity meant Liberals were not spending their energy attacking Stephen Harper.

Dion started so slowly in the 2008 campaign that one of his aides angrily asked one reporter, "Why bother covering the campaign if you think it's over?" In fact, Harper had taken a considerable risk. By eviscerating Dion so completely, expectations were set so low that Dion only had to show up to exceed them. Indeed, some polls suggested he won the French and English leader's debates largely because viewers expected incoherence and hesitation. He was much better than that and for the week after the debates he had momentum. When the Liberals looked as if they had an outside chance at winning, however, three times during the same press conference Harper asked reporters a variation of this basic question: "Do Canadians really want to be led by prime minister Stéphane Dion?" That question drove home the importance of the year-long string of Tory attack ads.

While Harper was tough on Dion, he rarely confronted the NDP or the Green Party, because neither threatened to govern. Indeed, both parties were much more likely to draw off Liberal than Tory votes. In a first-past-the-post electoral system, it is far easier for Tories to win ridings against three or more opponents than against a lone Liberal candidate.

In the 2008 campaign the Tories initially refused their consent to permit Green Party leader Elizabeth May, a former environmental activist, from participating in the leaders debates. Allowing a wild card like May into the forum was a risk the front-runner didn't want to take. May and Dion were buddies, and the pair could be counted upon to launch a coordinated attack against the prime minister. Plus, if leaders received equal time it would be four against one with May rather than three against one. The NDP had an even stronger reason to keep the Greens out of the debate since they traditionally counted on the votes from enthusiastic environmentalists. Despite these risks, however, there were good reasons for Harper to agree to include May.

First, the initial refusal was newsworthy and made the Tories appear anti-democratic and possibly misogynistic. Second, a strong performance by May would not damage Harper's vote; it would simply dilute the opposition. Harper knew this. He simply didn't want to take the risk that May would unsettle the dynamic of the debates. In the end both the Tories and NDP relented, creating something of a folk hero out of May. Allowing each opposing party some strength, while sustaining their divisions, was to Harper's advantage.

But Harper could not resist pummeling his opponents when they were down and out. When he proposed terminating political party subsidies in the 2008 economic update he gave his opponents unity and purpose. He was forced to retreat and renege on a series of economic measures to forestall a possible coalition, even merger, of some of his opponents. This incident, combined with a flawed 2008 election campaign, seriously eroded Harper's standing as a master strategist.

Harper effortlessly dissected his opponents in the House of Commons. His skills were amplified by a weak Liberal leader and his 2008 election win was made easier by the rise of the Green party under the charismatic Elizabeth May. However, his weakness was not knowing when to restrain himself from pillorying his opponents when the opportunities were presented. On this score, he has much to learn from Macdonald, who gave this

good advice: "The great reason why I have always been able to beat the opposition is that I have been able to look a little ahead, while (they) could on no
occasion forgo the temptation of a temporary triumph. Politics is a game
requiring great coolness and an utter abnegation of prejudice and personal
feeling."

*7. Politics is not a debating society. When the prize is government, winning is
everything.*

ARTHUR MEIGHEN ONCE OBSERVED that "there are times when no prime
minister can be true to his trust to the nation he has sworn to serve, save at
the temporary sacrifice of the party he is appointed to lead." Indeed,
Conservative leaders seem to abandon party interests once they achieve
power in a rush to accomplish what they believe is right for the nation, party
be damned. That's why Tories have perennially occupied the opposition
benches. Historically they have publicly fought each other over the right
thing to do even before they have won office. As Bob Stanfield once
observed, some Conservatives would rather fight each other than win.

Macdonald is the only Tory leader who thought and acted in terms of
dynasty. All the rest overspent their political capital and allowed their political
organization to wallow. Macdonald never did. Acutely aware of political mine-
fields, he rarely went further than his political antennae told him he could.

Developing the will to win is where Harper demonstrated great skills
as a leader. It took quite a transformation. As an MP's assistant in 1986, he
was a right-wing ideologue who lacked empathy for Québec's nationalist
aspirations or for the plight of disadvantaged regions. He left Ottawa disillusioned by Mulroney's brokerage politics. He was drawn to the Reform
party, but before his first term as a Reform MP was up, he came to understand its fatal flaw.

After witnessing Jean Chrétien win three straight majorities, Harper set
out to build a broad centrist conservative coalition by turning the Alliance
party "into a permanent professional political institution that [voters] can
dedicate their loyalty to on an ongoing basis." Then he agreed to any and all
merger terms put on the table by Progressive Conservative leader Peter
MacKay. His goal was one united conservative party, because he recognized
that there was no other way to defeat the Liberals. After combining the many
strands of Canadian conservatism, Harper then compromised on a platform
to expand the party's appeal, adopting the sorts of policies that he had railed
against in the 1980s when Brian Mulroney originally proposed them.

There is no great secret to Liberal success over the past one hundred years or Tory success in the nineteenth century. The parties that focused on winning elections above all else formed government. The parties that stubbornly clung to ideology over people, principles over common sense, and dogma over an inspirational vision earned their place on the opposition benches.

Stephen Harper wanted to win. To sustain his government after the election in 2006, he warmed to climate change and the environment. He overcame his distaste of regional development programs. He neutralized the issue of Canadian participation in the war in Afghanistan by letting Parliament decide its fate. When the 2008 campaign turned on the culture issue, Harper responded by spending millions on funding for a Québec television station and tax credit to offset the cost of art instruction for children.

In his first three years as prime minister, Harper was in perpetual campaign mode and travelled the nation extensively, often taking the time to visit small or remote communities. His party raised money at double or more the pace of its opponents and flexed this financial muscle by advertising outside of a writ period. The Tory campaign team was in a perpetual state of readiness, with a fully operational campaign office and war room.

Every policy, budget, and speech was examined through a political lens, because Harper concluded that half a loaf—even a single slice—was better than no loaf at all. Most observers expected Harper to be more ideological than political, but he was just the opposite. Harper enacted policies he didn't believe in to secure a political payoff. Cutting the GST rather than income taxes and policies on climate change are cases in point. Some criticized him for opportunism, but he simply stole a page from the Liberal playbook: win at all costs. Harper's determination to win is as strong as anything the Tories have ever seen.

OVERALL ON THESE SEVEN ELEMENTS of success, Harper earned a mixed grade. His intelligence and strategic sense rivaled Macdonald's, but his tendency to take meaningless jabs at the provinces and his opponents indicated that he did not possess the Old Chieftain's sense of nation-building. Like Borden, Harper asserted an independent Canadian foreign policy. Like Diefenbaker, Harper had some libertarian tendencies, especially a disdain for the powerful and for the elite. Harper shared Diefenbaker's ability to pillory opponents.

He was as intimidating as Diefenbaker was on the floor of the House of Commons, but he lacked the charisma, the oratory, and the penchant for drama that made Dief the Chief so captivating. Harper had nothing in common with Bob Stanfield or Joe Clark, including their misplaced sense of civility. Like Mulroney, Harper understood Canada's political history. They both believed that Tory success hinged on making breakthroughs in Québec, although, as a native son, Mulroney executed brilliantly where Harper has faltered.

Harper was in league with Macdonald, Diefenbaker, and Mulroney in his desire to win. He understood that it was more important to win than to have the textbook answer to policy issues. Harper reduced the GST instead of cutting income tax against the recommendation of virtually every university economist in the country. Whether genuine or not, his conversion on climate change, his embracing of Québec nationalism, and his newfound love of regional development programs all demonstrated that he was serious about holding power.

His pragmatic, centrist, and cleverly hidden agenda was no more than to win election after election. He was willing to look at all issues through a political lens to hold government. But the compromises he made to do so will likely occasion his biggest disappointment; that he was unable to implement the policies he believed in and obtain a majority.

Most remarkable about Harper was the degree to which he evolved since he first came to Ottawa in 1986. He was an ideologue then, uncompromising and unsympathetic to any accommodation or special status for Québec, with a taste for dogmatic right-wing conservative solutions to every problem under the sun. Then he learned to compromise. He developed a sense of nationhood and its component parts. He found the will to win, he took risks, and he became Canada's twenty-second prime minister.

CHAPTER 32

EVOLUTION

Our aim should be to enlarge the bounds of our party so as to embrace
every person desirous of being counted as a progressive conservative, and
who will join in a series of measures to put an end to the corruption which has
ruined the present government and debauched all of its followers
—Sir John A.Macdonald (1854)

FOR 141 YEARS, the Conservative party and its leaders have made far-reaching and fundamental contributions that have helped to define the nation.

Conservatives fashioned Confederation to strengthen the bond amongst British colonies to the mother country and to create a nation capable of withstanding the relentless pull into the political realm of the United States. Confederation gave us a robust central government while affording provinces sufficient power to sustain local practices and cultures that would end, it was hoped, the dissension between French and English in Canada East and Canada West.

Under Macdonald, the only Tory leader to have been favourably reviewed by historians and academics, Tories recognized the French and English as the founding races of Canada and built the coalitions required to govern the nation over most of the nineteenth century. The party successfully pursued the vision of a nation that stretched across the continent. Using nationalist trade policies, Macdonald put Canada on the path towards economic independence. By developing institutions of good governance, Canada advanced its political independence.

Much has been made in the history books of Macdonald's drinking. He did not win six of seven elections, build an improbable nation, and manage the nation's affairs for close to nineteen years, however, without having a steady command of his faculties. It is popularly believed that the Tory government was eager to see Louis Riel hanged. However, Macdonald's instincts were to "deal liberally with him and make him a good subject again."That was before Riel led his followers into battle against the Canadian government, after which a trial by jury, not Cabinet, found Riel guilty of treason.

After Macdonald's death, the party floundered under four successive leaders over a ten-year period until a determined Robert Borden revived Tory spirits, although it took him three elections to win government. Opposition to the Liberal program of free trade with the Americans provided his decisive issue.

World War 1 gave Borden's Tories a new policy plank: conscription. This was the inevitable consequence of Canada's allegiance to Great Britain. In the face of Québec's widespread opposition to compulsory service, Borden stood firm in support of the Empire. More important to Borden, however, was the bond he believed the nation held with Canadian soldiers. While popular in most of Canada, conscription placed Tory party fortunes in the ash heap in Québec. The Québec Tory caucus was reduced from 26 to three in the 1917 election, then to zero in 1921. The number of seats won by Conservatives in Québec over nine of the ten elections between 1917 and 1953 can be counted on one hand.

For an entire generation Conservatives were not a national political party. The tragedy of the Tory demise was that conscription had only a symbolic impact on the outcome of the war. While spontaneous protests were breaking out in Québec, the United States entered the war, marginalizing our incremental contribution from conscription. Borden's policy gave comfort to our soldiers overseas, but it undermined national unity. More than the hanging of Louis Riel, conscription doomed the Tory party to opposition status. Macdonald would not have initiated or allowed such divisions. Borden's intent was noble, but the price the party paid was high. To his credit, Borden built the widest coalition possible in support of his policies, and welcomed many Liberals into a coalition government of common cause. But he effectively excluded Québec, a founding partner of Canada, from that coalition. Such an exclusion was at least as damaging to national unity as Trudeau's patriation of the constitution was in 1982 without the signature of Québec's government.

Through three elections in the 1920s, the Tories under Arthur Meighen could not break free of their conscription legacy. The party was non-existent in Québec and too rigid and authoritarian to appeal to mainstream Canada. Meighen nearly held a winning hand in 1925 but was outmaneuvered by a clever Liberal leader who cast Tories as more committed to Great Britain than to an independent Canada.

Winning the 1930 election was a mixed blessing. Governing during the Depression gave the Liberal opposition the chance to coin the phrase "Tory times are hard times." But it was also an opportunity for the party to implement dramatic reforms, many of which redefined government and the nation. In response to unprecedented economic challenges, the government of R.B. Bennett established transformative institutions—the Bank of Canada, farm marketing boards, credit agencies, and the CBC—all of which have stood the test of time and remain cornerstones of Canadian life. Despite such valiant and far-reaching reforms, however, it would have taken a miracle to re-elect his depression-era government. It did not help that Conservative forces had split just prior to the 1935 election, with Henry Herbert Stevens and his Reconstruction party taking 8.8 percent of the national vote. Though Bennett held government for only a single term, his legacy is not to be diminished.

For the twenty-year period surrounding World War II, the Tories struggled with issues of identity and relevance. Was the party modern, inclusive, and compassionate? Or was it hard-hitting, anti-communist, pro-business? The hangover from Borden's conscription policies meant that the party remained a non-factor in Québec during the war. Despite their best efforts, neither Bracken nor Drew could overcome Québecers' distrust of the Tory brand or present the sorts of social policy reforms that voters there wanted. Against a nation eager to modernize, the Tories looked like stodgy bankers trying to take the fun out of Canada.

In the late 1950s, a populist, libertarian, charismatic leader redefined the party in bold and inspiring strokes. Not since Sir John A. Macdonald had the party connected so well with Main Street Canada. Diefenbaker's northern vision had grandeur and was in the same mould as Macdonald's national vision. Diefenbaker was probably the most captivating campaigner the Tories have ever known, but he could not unite his Cabinet or caucus. His distrust of authority generally, and President John F. Kennedy specifically, made him a better agitator than prime minister. Dreaming of great things for Canada and standing up to authority, however, does not make him the madman as he is so often portrayed in historical accounts. He is a prime architect of Canadian freedoms and was a trailblazer for tolerance, equality, inclusiveness, and diversity.

The Conservative party took on a softer and more progressive tone in the decades after Diefenbaker. It became the champion of the provinces, developed greater sensitivity to Québec, and established policies to deliver sustainable economic growth. But under Stanfield and Clark the party did not have the toughness or determination to win office. Stanfield was better suited to governing than campaigning, an unfortunate attribute in an Opposition leader. Clark was simply inept.

Fortunes rose dramatically in 1983 when, for the first time in its history, the party elected a Quebécer as leader. Like Macdonald in 1867, Mulroney built a grand national coalition and led a disciplined party. He offered a vision of economic renewal and constitutional reconciliation. And he wanted to win an election more than he wanted to win a debate over policy. Incredibly, he did both.

In office, Mulroney rewrote our foreign and domestic policies and gave Canada one of its most conservative administrations ever. He thus rewrote the Tory playbook and took a diametrically different position from his predecessors, notably Macdonald, on the United States. This friendly and more cooperative relationship led to a Free Trade Agreement and a treaty on acid rain. Mulroney believed Canada had come of age and no longer needed protectionist trade policies. It has since been proven that our political independence and robust national institutions were sufficient to overcome any need to keep our distance from our closest neighbour and most important business partner.

Despite such groundbreaking initiatives, however, Mulroney's coalition imploded in its second term. The Reform party hived off the western faction, while the Bloc Québecois took hold in *la belle province*. Kim Campbell's incompetence and lack of vision sealed the Tory fate in 1993 and a decade of futility ensued.

Not until 2003 did the Conservatives muster the dedication necessary to win. Under the bold leadership of Peter MacKay and Stephen Harper, the party broke through its divisions. A united party under Harper offered Canada a moderate, inclusive, and national alternative that was worthy of support from one end of the country to the other. It extended the hand of open federalism to Québecers. The party also benefitted from a sloppy, arrogant, and unfocused Liberal government under Paul Martin. He was supposed to win the largest majority in Canadian history, but his government was reduced to a minority during phase one of the Tory rebuilding process.

In 2006 Stephen Harper led a mainstream Conservative Party of Canada to power. His first minority government proved to be the most productive and long-lasting in Canadian history. Harper was rewarded with another opportunity to govern on October 14, 2008, although he fell short of a majority.

FEW CONSERVATIVE LEADERS have mastered the art of coalition building. Fewer still have enviable election records. Against his predecessors Harper ranks high, with one defeat and two minority victories. But if Conservatives are to match electoral standings with Liberals, they need to figure out what has worked for them in the past and what has caused their repeated failures. Out of power, a political party lacks relevance and purpose, which has been the Tory plight for much of the past century.

In fact Tory governments have largely been interregnums between Liberal administrations. Conservatives would have to hold the office of prime minister from 2009 until 2035 to match the Liberals.

If the Tories need a hidden agenda it is this: *Win*. Not just the next election but many elections to come. History shows that the party wins when it is pragmatic, not ideological. It wins when it is in touch with the hearts and minds of ordinary Canadians.

Successful Tory leaders advanced conservative-minded policies to the extent only that they resonated with Main Street Canada. They have never talked in terms of ideology, right-wing or otherwise. They redefined the political centre, not in terms of socialist and capitalist extremes, but as a place of moderation that represents the wider values of Canadian society. The successful Tory leaders are not attached to right-wing think tanks, the elite, the wealthy or the powerful, but to ordinary Canadians.

Too often the Tory party has lacked unity and has divided into regional factions that can't win elections. While vote splitting has often worked against the Tories, in 2008 a centrist conservative movement faced four opposing parties huddled on the left of the political spectrum. So long as the left divides and the Tories govern from the centre, they have a shot at delivering a dynasty. Such a prospect is not something Canadians need fear since a competent Tory ministry will implement only those conservative ideas the nation can embrace.

A Conservative dynasty may appear improbable in a country where the

Liberal party has earned the moniker of Canada's natural governing party. Of course Macdonald gave his party a rousing start, winning six of Canada's first seven elections. He achieved such victories because he was a nation builder who respected the French fact in Canada. He assembled coalitions, united his party, and divided his opponents. Macdonald was respected and admired because he governed with a moderate hand, but he was as tough as he needed to be to win.

Macdonald has no equal. Most Tory prime ministers overspent their political capital and returned their party for long periods to the opposition benches. Borden's conscription policy doomed his party in Québec for ten elections. Diefenbaker was thrown a lifeline by Québec's premier Maurice Duplessis, but his *One Canada* vision failed to recognize Québec's cultural distinctiveness. Only Mulroney came close to Macdonald in achieving party unity while building the coalitions required to lead the nation. But Macdonald and Mulroney had a common failing: succession.

For 141 years Sir John A. Macdonald has been the inspiration for every success that Conservatives have enjoyed. He is as relevant to the Tories in the twenty-first century as he was in the nineteenth.

LEADERSHIP AND ELECTION DATA

Every American statesman covets Canada. The greed for its acquisition is still on the increase,
and God knows where it will all end....We must face the fight at our next election, and
it is only the conviction that the battle will be better fought under my guidance than under
another that makes me undertake the task, handicapped as I am, with the infirmities of old age
—Sir John A. Macdonald (1891)

Not counting interim leaders, seventeen men and one woman have led the Conservative party in its various forms.

Leaders of the Conservative Party of Canada

Conservative Party of Canada	
Macdonald, John Alexander	1867.07.01—1891.06.06
Abbott, John Joseph Caldwell	1891.06.16—1892.11.24
Thompson, John Sparrow David	1892.12.05—1894.12.12
Bowell, Mackenzie	1894.12.21—1896.04.27
Tupper, Charles	1896.05.01—1901.02.05
Borden, Robert Laird	1901.02.06—1920.07.09
Meighen, Arthur	1920.07.10—1926.09.24
Bennett, Richard Bedford	1927.10.12—1938.07.06
Manion, Robert James	1938.07.07—1940.05.13
Meighen, Arthur	1941.11.12—1942.12.09
Bracken, John	1942.12.11—1948.07.20
Drew, George Alexander	1948.10.02—1956.11.29
Diefenbaker, John George	1956.12.14—1967.09.08
Stanfield, Robert	1967.09.09—1976.02.21
Clark, Charles Joseph (Joe)	1976.02.22—1983.02.18
Mulroney, Martin Brian	1983.06.11—1993.06.12
Campbell, A. Kim	1993.06.13—1993.12.13
Charest, Jean J.	1993.12.14—1998.04.02
Clark, Charles Joseph (Joe)	1998.11.14—2003.05.30
MacKay, Peter Gordon	2003.05.31—2004.02.01
Harper, Stephen Joseph	2004.03.20—

Conservative Party of Canada—Interim leaders

Guthrie, Hugh	1926.10.11—1927.10.11
Hanson, Richard Burpee	1940.05.14—1941.11.11
Nielsen, Erik	1983.02.19—1983.06.10
Wayne, Elsie Eleanore	1998.04.02—1998.11.13
Lynch-Staunton, John	2003.12.08—2004.03.19

The Reform party and its successor, the Canadian Conservative Reform Alliance merged with the Progressive Conservative Party in 2003.

Reform Party

Manning, Ernest Preston	1987.11.01—2000.03.26

Canadian Reform Conservative Alliance

Day, Stockwell Burt	2000.07.08—2001.12.11
Harper, Stephen Joseph	2002.03.20—2004.01.21

Canadian Reform Conservative Alliance—Interim leaders

Grey, Deborah C.	2000.03.27—2000.07.07
Reynolds, John Douglas	2001.12.12—2002.03.19

Macdonald and his four immediate successors were chosen to lead the party by the governor general. Borden and Meighen were caucus selections. Thereafter, the choice of leader was determined by delegates to national conventions.

Conservative Leadership Conventions

October 12, 1927

(Winnipeg, Manitoba)	Ballot 1		Ballot 2	
Bennett, Richard Bedford	594	38.0%	780	50.2%
Guthrie, Hugh	345	22.1%	320	20.6%
Cahan, Charles Hazlitt	310	19.8%	266	17.1%
Manion, Robert James	170	10.9%	148	9.5%
Rogers, Robert	114	7.3%	37	2.4%
Drayton, Henry Lumley	31	2.0%	3	0.2%
TOTAL	1564	100.0%	1554	100.0%

July 7, 1938

(Ottawa, Ontario)	Ballot 1		Ballot 2	
Manion, Robert James	726	46.4%	830	53.0%
MacPherson, Murdoch Alexander	475	30.4%	648	41.4%
Harris, Joseph Henry	131	8.4%	49	3.1%
Massey, Denton	128	8.2%	39	2.5%
Lawson, James Earl	105	6.7%		
TOTAL	1565	100.0%	1566	100.0%

December 11, 1942

(Winnipeg, Manitoba)	Ballot 1		Ballot 2	
Bracken, John	420	48.3%	538	61.7%
MacPherson, Murdoch Alexander	222	25.5%	255	29.2%
Diefenbaker, John George	120	13.8%	79	9.1%
Green, Howard Charles	88	10.1%		
Stevens, Henry Herbert	20	2.3%		
TOTAL	870	100.0%	872	100.0%

October 2, 1948

(Ottawa, Ontario)	Ballot 1	
Drew, George Alexander	827	66.6%
Diefenbaker, John George	311	25.0%
Fleming, Donald Methuen	104	8.4%
TOTAL	1242	100.0%

December 14, 1956

(Ottawa, Ontario)	Ballot 1	
Diefenbaker, John George	774	60.3%
Fleming, Donald Methuen	393	30.6%
Fulton, Edmund Davie	117	9.1%
TOTAL	1284	100.0%

September 9, 1967

(Toronto, Ontario)	Ballot 1		Ballot 2		Ballot 3		Ballot 4		Ballot 5	
Stanfield, Robert Lorne	519	23.3%	613	27.7%	717	32.7%	865	40.0%	1150	54.3%
Roblin, Dufferin (Duff)	347	15.6%	430	19.4%	541	24.7%	771	35.7%	969	45.7%
Fulton, Edmund Davie	343	15.4%	346	15.6%	361	16.5%	357	16.5%		
Hees, George Harris	295	13.2%	299	13.5%	277	12.6%				
Diefenbaker, John George	271	12.1%	172	7.8%	114	5.2%				
McCutcheon, Malcolm Wallace	137	6.1%	76	3.4%						
Hamilton, Francis Alvin George	136	6.1%	127	5.7%	106	4.8%	167	7.7%		
Fleming, Donald Methuen	126	5.6%	115	5.2%	76	3.5%				
Starr, Michael	45	2.0%	34	1.5%						
MacLean, John	10	0.4%								
Walker-Sawka, Mary	2	0.1%								
TOTAL	2231	100.0%	2212	100.0%	2192	100.0%	2160	100.0%	2119	100.0%

February 22, 1976

(Ottawa, Ontario)	Ballot 1		Ballot 2		Ballot 3		Ballot 4	
Wagner, Claude	531	22.5%	667	28.5%	1003	42.8%	1122	48.6%
Mulroney, Martin Brian	357	15.1%	419	17.9%	369	15.8%		
Clark, Charles Joseph (Joe)	277	11.7%	532	22.8%	969	41.4%	1187	51.4%
Horner, John (Jack) Henry	235	10.0%	286	12.2%				
Hellyer, Paul Theodore	231	9.8%	118	5.0%				
MacDonald, Flora Isabel	214	9.1%	239	10.2%				
Stevens, Sinclair McKnight	182	7.7%						
Fraser, John	127	5.4%	34	1.5%				
Gillies, James McPhail	87	3.7%		0.0%				
Nowlan, John Patrick (Pat)	86	3.6%	42	1.8%				
Grafftey, William Heward	33	1.4%						
TOTAL	2360	100.0%	2337	100.0%	2341	100.0%	2309	100.0%

June 11, 1983

(Ottawa, Ontario)	Ballot 1		Ballot 2		Ballot 3		Ballot 4	
Clark, Charles Joseph (Joe)	1091	36.5%	1085	36.7%	1058	35.8%	1325	45.5%
Mulroney, Martin Brian	874	29.3%	1021	34.6%	1036	35.1%	1584	54.5%
Crosbie, John Carnell	639	21.4%	781	26.4%	858	29.1%		
Wilson, Michael Holcombe	144	4.8%						
Crombie, David Edward	116	3.9%	67	2.3%				
Pocklington, Peter	102	3.4%						
Gamble, John Albert	17	0.6%						
Fraser, Neil	5	0.2%						
TOTAL	2988	100.0%	2954	100.0%	2952	100.0%	2909	100.0%

June 13, 1993

(Ottawa, Ontario)	Ballot 1		Ballot 2	
Campbell, A. Kim	1664	48.0%	1817	52.7%
Charest, Jean J.	1369	39.5%	1630	47.3%
Edwards, James (Jim) Stewart	307	8.8%		
Turner, Garth	76	2.2%		
Boyer, Patrick	53	1.5%		
TOTAL	3469	100.0%	3447	100.0%

April 29, 1995 (Hull, Québec)   Ballot 1

	Ballot 1	
Charest, Jean J.	1187	100%
TOTAL	1187	100%

October 24 and Nov. 14, 1998   Ballot 1

	Ballot 1		Ballot 2	
Clark, Charles Joseph (Joe)	14592	48.5%	23321	77.5%
Segal, Hugh	5689	18.9%		
Orchard, David	4916	16.3%	6779	22.5%
Palliser, Brian	3676	12.2%		
Fortier, Michael	1227	4.1%		
TOTAL	30100	100.0%	30100	100.0%

May 31, 2003 (Toronto, Ontario)	Ballot 1		Ballot 2		Ballot 3		Ballot 4	
MacKay, Peter Gordon	1080	41.1%	1018	39.7%	1128	45.0%	1538	64.8%
Orchard, David	640	24.3%	619	24.1%	617	24.6%		
Prentice, Jim	478	18.2%	466	18.2%	761	30.4%	836	35.2%
Brison, Scott	431	16.4%	463	18.0%				
Chandler, Craig	0	0.0%						
TOTAL	2629	100.0%	2566	100.0%	2506	100.0%	2374	100.0%

March 20, 2004

(Toronto, Ontario)	Ballot 1	
Harper, Stephen Joseph	16149	55.5%
Stronach, Belinda	10196	35.0%
Clement, Tony	2755	9.5%
TOTAL	29100	100.0%

Canadian Reform Conservative Alliance

July 8, 2000

(Toronto, Ontario)	Ballot No. 1		Ballot No. 2	
Day, Stockwell Burt	53249	44.2%	72349	63.3%
Manning, Ernest Preston	43527	36.1%	41869	36.7%
Long, Tom	21894	18.2%		
Martin, Keith P.	1676	1.4%		
Stachow, John	211	0.2%		
TOTAL	120557	100.0%	114218	100.0%

March 20, 2002

(Calgary, Canada)	Ballot No. 1	
Harper, Stephen Joseph	48561	55.0%
Day, Stockwell Burt	33074	37.5%
Ablonczy, Diane	3370	3.8%
Hill, Grant	3223	3.7%
TOTAL	88228	100.0%

The record of these leaders in winning government is such that Liberals are known as Canada's Natural Governing Party.

Time in office by party—As of October 14, 2008

Liberal Party of Canada	30,340 Days (83 years, 24 days)
Conservative Party	20,842 days (57 years, 19 days)

From Election Day 2008, it would take 26 years of continuous Tory rule, for the Tories to equal the Liberal hold on power. The longest serving prime minister of all time, William Lyon Mackenzie King, served for 21 years, five months and two days. Harper has a big challenge ahead if he wants to even the score.

The record of accomplishment most political leaders aspire to hold is duration as prime minister. Among Conservatives, Macdonald is in a league of his own. Mulroney and Borden remain the only other leaders to win successive majority governments.

Longest Duration as Prime Minister

Sir John A. Macdonald	18 years 11 months and 24 days
Brian Mulroney	8 years 9 months and 8 days
Robert Borden	8 years 8 months and 30 days
John Diefenbaker	5 years 10 months and 1 day
Richard Bennett	5 years 2 months and 27 days

Ignoring those who left office on account of illness or death, the Tory leaders who have held the office of prime minister for the shortest period offer lessons on how not to govern and campaign. Bowell faced mutiny by his caucus, then handed Tupper a hopeless cause. Kim Campbell and Arthur Meighen never won an election and were unable to translate the prime minister's chair to any particular advantage. Joe Clark stands alone as the only leader to win an election only to squander power with ineptness.

Shortest Duration as Prime Minister

Charles Tupper	2 months and 7 days
Kim Campbell	4 months and 10 days
Joe Clark	8 months and 27 days
Mackenzie Bowell	1 year 4 months and 15 days
Arthur Meighen	1 year 8 months and 16 days

The record of won/loss and majority/minority government reveals only Brian Mulroney with a perfect election record, though others—notably Sir John A. Macdonald, John Diefenbaker, and Robert Borden—were tested more.

ELECTIONS

	WON		LOST		TOTAL
	Majority	Minority	Majority	Minority	
Sir John A. Macdonald	6		1		7
John G. Diefenbaker	1	2		2	5
Robert Borden	2		2		4
Arthur Meighen			1	2	3
Joe Clark		1	2		3
Bob Stanfield			2	1	3
Stephen Harper		2		1	3
Brian Mulroney	2				2
Richard B. Bennett	1		1		2
Sir Charles Tupper			2		2
George Drew			2		2
Jean Charest			1		1
Kim Campbell			1		1
Robert Manion			1		1
John Bracken			1		1
Mackenzie Bowell					0
John Thomson					0
John Abbott					0
Peter MacKay					0

The longest-serving leaders tend to have the best election records. The exceptions are Joe Clark, who lasted 11 years, and Brian Mulroney, who does not make it into the top five (he served as leader for 10 years and a day).

Longest Term as Leader	
John A Macdonald	23 years 11 months 5 days
Robert Borden	19 years 5 months 3 days
Joe Clark	11 years 6 months 22 days
John Diefenbaker	10 years 8 months 24 days
Richard Bennett	10 years 8 months 24 days

Three of the five shortest-serving leaders never faced the electorate. Notably, Peter MacKay's brief stint covered the period just before Conservative forces united into a single party. Abbott resigned due to ill health and Campbell resigned after the decimation of the party in 1993.

Shortest Term as Leader	
Kim Campbell	6 months 0 days
Peter Mackay	9 months 1 day
Mackenzie Bowell	1 year 4 months 6 days
John Abbott	1 year 5 months 8 days
Robert Manion	1 year 10 months 6 days

The following table provides data for each general election since Confederation. It reveals that over 40 elections Tories have won 40.7 percent of the popular vote compared with 42.5 percent for the Liberals. The seat total also favours the Liberals: 47.1 percent to 41.8 percent.

ELECTION # AND DATE			SEATS WON BY PARTY AFFILIATION				
No. Year	Date	Liberal	Tory	Reform/Alliance	SOCRED	Progressive
1 1867	Sep-20	80	101			
2 1872	Oct-12	97	103			
3 1874	Jan-22	133	73			
4 1878	Sep-17	69	137			
5 1882	Jun-20	71	139			
6 1887	Feb-22	92	123			
7 1891	Mar-05	92	123			
8 1896	Jun-23	118	88			
9 1900	Nov-07	132	81			
10 1904	Nov-03	139	75			
11 1908	Oct-26	133	85			
12 1911	Sep-21	86	133			
13 1917	Dec-17	82	153			
14 1921	Dec-06	116	50			58
15 1925	Oct-29	99	116			22
16 1926	Sep-14	116	91			11
17 1930	Jul-28	91	137			3
18 1935	Oct-14	171	39		17	
19 1940	Mar-26	178	39		10	
20 1945	Jun-11	125	67		13	
21 1949	Jun-27	190	41		10	
22 1953	Aug-10	171	51		15	
23 1957	Jun-10	105	112		19	
24 1958	Mar-31	49	208			
25 1962	Jun-18	99	116		30	
26 1963	Apr-08	129	95		24	
27 1965	Nov-08	131	97		14	
28 1968	Jun-25	155	72		14	
29 1972	Oct-30	109	107		15	
30 1974	Jul-08	141	95		11	
31 1979	May-22	114	136		6	
32 1980	Feb-18	147	103			
33 1984	Sep-04	40	211			
34 1988	Nov-21	83	169			
35 1993	Oct-25	177	2	52		
36 1997	June 2	155	20	60		
37 2000	Nov-27	172	12	66		
38 2004	Jun-28	135	99			
39 2006	Jan-23	103	124			
40 2008	Oct-14	76	143			

Bloc Que.	NDP/CCF	Other	Total	POPULAR VOTE		% OF SEATS	
				Tory	Liberal	Tory	Liberal
			181	50%	49%	56%	44%
			200	49%	49%	52%	49%
			206	45%	53%	35%	65%
			206	53%	45%	67%	33%
			210	53%	46%	66%	34%
			215	50%	48%	57%	43%
			215	52%	46%	57%	43%
		7	213	46%	45%	41%	55%
			213	47%	52%	38%	62%
			214	46%	52%	35%	65%
		3	221	47%	50%	38%	60%
		2	221	51%	47%	60%	39%
			235	57%	40%	65%	35%
		11	235	30%	40%	21%	49%
		8	245	46%	40%	47%	40%
		27	245	46%	43%	37%	47%
		14	245	49%	43%	56%	37%
	7	11	245	29%	44%	16%	70%
	8	10	245	30%	54%	16%	73%
	28	12	245	27%	41%	27%	51%
	13	8	262	29%	50%	16%	73%
	23	5	265	31%	50%	19%	65%
	25	4	265	39%	42%	42%	40%
	8		265	53%	33%	78%	18%
	19	1	265	37%	37%	44%	37%
	17		265	32%	41%	36%	49%
	21	2	265	32%	39%	37%	49%
	22	1	264	31%	45%	27%	59%
	31	2	264	35%	38%	41%	41%
	16	1	264	35%	43%	36%	53%
	26		282	35%	40%	48%	40%
	32		282	32%	44%	37%	52%
	30	1	282	50%	28%	75%	14%
	43		295	43%	31%	57%	28%
54	9	1	295	34%	41%	18%	60%
44	21	1	301	37%	38%	27%	51%
38	13		301	37%	40%	26%	57%
54	19	1	308	29%	36%	32%	44%
51	29	1	308	36%	30%	40%	33%
50	37	2	308	38%	26%	46%	25%
			Averages	40.7%	42.5%	41.8%	47.1%

Critical to winning government is performance in Québec. Brian Mulroney, the first native Québecer to lead the Tory party, has the party's best record in French Canada by a landslide. Macdonald is the only other leader with a winning record. Joe Clark and Bob Stanfield made valiant efforts to build support in Québec, but came up largely empty-handed. In each of the 2006 and 2008 elections Stephen Harper took ten seats, or 13.3 percent of Québec's 75 seats.

Percent of Available Seats won in Québec

Brian Mulroney	80.7%
John A. Macdonald	56.3%
John Diefenbaker	23.5%
Richard Bennett	22.3%
Robert Borden	20.4%
Charles Tupper	18.5%
Stephen Harper	08.9%
Jean Charest	06.7%
Bob Stanfield	04.1%
Arthur Meighen	04.1%
George Drew	04.0%
Joe Clark	01.8%
John Bracken	01.5%
Kim Campbell	01.3%
Robert Manion	00.0%

Among the generally negative election data, it is worth noting that 13 of Canada's 22 prime ministers were Conservative. However, of the 13, six did not win an election. And, of Canadian elections won with more than 50 percent of the popular vote, the tally is nine for the Conservatives to seven for the Liberals.

SUCCESS AND FAILURE

These subjective evaluations highlight the best and worst of Tory leadership performance. Since he continues to serve as party leader Prime Minister Harper is excluded from this evaluation.

NATION-BUILDING AND NATIONAL UNITY—MACDONALD

Sir John ranks head and shoulders above any leader of party on nation-building. His triumph of Confederation, expansion of territory and provinces across the continent, building of the national railroad, and the growth and diversity of Canada through expansionist immigration policies have made Macdonald our most accomplished nation-builder.

The only other Tory who made a substantive attempt at nation-building was Brian Mulroney. His effort to get Québec's signature on the Canadian constitution warrants an honourable mention.

Arthur Meighen and Robert Borden rank poorly in this category. They both took a law-and-order approach to regional dissent and created antipathy towards the Tory party in Québec with the conscription policy.

ECONOMIC DEVELOPMENT AND PROSPERITY—MULRONEY

During Brian Mulroney's tenure, Crown corporations were privatized, interest rates were brought under control, operational spending of government was reduced, and a fundamentally flawed sales tax system was fixed. Mulroney's crowning policy jewel was free trade with the United States. Increased government debt, caused largely by a worldwide recession and high interest rates, was the only negative to Mulroney's economic record.

Macdonald deserves mention for the investments he made in infrastructure and for opening up Canada to immigrants to build an economy that could sustain the country from coast to coast.

Diefenbaker governed during tough economic times, but was more attentive to the short-term plight of individual Canadians than to the reforms that would have strengthened the economy as a whole. His ill-advised attempts to divert trade away from the United States, and his inability to maintain confidence in the Canadian dollar and the underlying economy gives Diefenbaker a low ranking on economic management.

INTERNATIONAL RELATIONS—BORDEN

Canada gained its independence on the world stage through the sacrifices of its young soldiers on the battlefields of Europe during World War 1. Robert Borden demanded that Canadian sacrifices be recognized by claiming an independent voice for Canada in world affairs. He stood up first to Great Britain and then to the United States.

Brian Mulroney and John Diefenbaker deserve honourable mentions for their principled stance in opposition to apartheid. However, these men differed on Canada's relationship with the United States. Mulroney built strong personal relations with American presidents which he used to secure trade and environmental agreements in Canada's interests. John Diefenbaker was loath to play second fiddle to anyone, in particular President John F. Kennedy. Diefenbaker's hesitation during the Cuban missile crisis and his threat to use a confidential presidential briefing memo were low points in Canadian–American relations. However, Diefenbaker earns accolades for standing up to Russian President Nikita Khrushchev on the floor of the United Nations when he bellowed, "How many human beings have been liberated by the USSR?"

Joe Clark's promise to move the Canadian embassy in Israel from Tel Aviv to Jerusalem explains in part why he lost the confidence of the Canadian people. Surprisingly, Clark's position had not been sought by the Israeli government, which believed Canada had adequately demonstrated its friendship. The move outraged Arab nations in the region and Clark ultimately abandoned his proposal.

BIGGEST BLUNDER—CLARK

Joe Clark could easily have avoided losing government, but he was afraid of being perceived as weak. Rather than demonstrate his skills and insight as a politician. Joe Clark lost government quickly, stupidly, and needlessly. Only Kim Campbell's performance in the 1993 campaign can be mentioned in the same breath as Clark's 1979 calamity.

ENVIRONMENT—MULRONEY

Brian Mulroney used his political capital, both domestically and internationally, to advance the cause of environmental sustainability. For his accomplishments (notably the Acid Rain Treaty and the Environmental Assessment Act), a distinguished panel awarded him the title of Canada's Greenest Prime Minister.

Diefenbaker was a great believer in national parks and preserving wilderness. However, he also led a government that was determined to build an economy by extracting natural resources from the Far North. These policies caused environmentalists to cringe.

THE MILITARY AND NATIONAL SECURITY—BORDEN

The only Conservative to have governed at a time of world war was Robert Borden. His commitment to military success, and his unwavering support for the troops in the field, makes him the leader most likely to be saluted by Canadian troops.

Macdonald suffers from the ill-advised actions of various military parties seeking to quell uprisings in the West. It was not under his orders or direction that Louis Riel and his followers were engaged in battle, but it was under his watch.

SELFLESS LEADERSHIP—MACKAY

There are few politicians who set aside ambition for the sake of their party. Peter MacKay's surrender of the leadership of the Progressive Conservative Party of Canada in 2003 stands tall among personal sacrifices made by a Tory leader for the good of Canada. He could easily have taken the PC party into a national election campaign, but his noble act removed the key obstacle that had kept Conservative forces divided for a decade. After Jean Chrétien was given three majority governments, MacKay's bold and unexpected move helped to restore democracy to Canada and set the stage for Stephen Harper to become prime minister.

BEST CAMPAIGNER—MULRONEY

There are three leaders that deserve to be mentioned in this category: Macdonald, Diefenbaker, and Mulroney. Each one brought a unique set of skills and attributes to the cause. When it comes to raw and electrifying performance at the podium, and for his ability to campaign from behind and exceed expectations, Diefenbaker has no equal. Macdonald's strengths were strategy and coalition building, but not so much as a stump speaker or crowd rouser. He was a charmer, a story-teller and witty. Mulroney, the only leader with a perfect election record, knew how to win and never took his eye off the prize. When it looked like his government might be defeated in 1988, Mulroney single-handedly turned the momentum around with a remarkable display of campaigning. He had Irish charm and French-Canadian passion.

WORST CAMPAIGNER—CAMPBELL

Kim Campbell took the Progressive Conservative party from a majority government and a lead in the polls down to a lowly two seats in the legislature. She showed much promise while campaigning for the leadership and in her early days as prime minister, but delivered the worst election performance of all time in a campaign riddled with mind-numbing errors that left her even her ardent supporters scratching their heads.

MOST HUMBLE LEADER—STANFIELD

Bob Stanfield was a gentleman of the highest order. If Canada had had the wisdom to elect him prime minister, he surely would have held the job as long as his health allowed. However, Stanfield's virtue was often exploited by Liberals.

WORST TIMING—MANION

Robert J. Manion, a Catholic Ontarian who married a French Canadian, brought progressive social policies and a Québec connection to the 1940 general election. Despite howls of protest within his party, Manion opposed conscription and struck a deal with

Québec premier Maurice Duplessis that could have delivered enough seats to restore the Tories to power. However, war came and Liberal fearmongering had voters believing that Tories would bring in conscription. This helped to defeat and neutralize Tory support in Québec. Though Manion correctly prepared his party for victory, he was denied by the onset of the war and a cagey opponent.

Bennett had the bad fortune to gain power at the outset of the Depression. While the reforms he initiated have stood the test of time, he governed during times when re-election was nearly impossible.

MOST AUTHORITARIAN—MEIGHEN

Some lead by inspiration, some by intimidation. Some resist antagonizing unrest while others have a zeal for law-and-order. Tough-minded authoritarian types might do well in a crisis, but they never govern for long.

Macdonald's instinct was to make peace with forces of strife. Diefenbaker refused to allow the RCMP to intervene after a labour dispute in Newfoundland turned violent. Both Diefenbaker and Stanfield were among the few voices that warned of the inherent danger in giving government the powers vested under the War Measures Act. Mulroney demonstrated remarkable patience after Native protestors occupied disputed lands near Oka, Québec. That is not to say that these leaders did not believe in the rule of law. But they were careful how they used the most powerful tools available to the state in dealing with its own citizens.

Authoritarian leaders believe the ends justify the means. Meighen, Bennett, and Borden were this sort of leader. To them, the deaths that resulted after the military intervened to quell civilian protest were simply a consequence of lawlessness. The inappropriateness of the response to the Winnipeg strike should have been obvious to Borden and Meighen after soldiers returning from battlefields of Europe joined in the protests. Meighen in particular stands out for his lack of empathy for those who opposed government policies. He made inflammatory statements that haunted the Tory party in Québec for a generation.

THE GREATEST OF ALL—MACDONALD

Winner of six majority governments, longest serving leader, loved by English and French, and the true Father of Confederation, Macdonald stands head and shoulders above all other Conservative leaders. He has no equal.

SELECTED BIBLIOGRAPHY

Bliss, Michael. Right Honorable Men: The Descent of Canadian Politics from Macdonald to Mulroney. Toronto: Harper Collins, 1994.

Black, Conrad. Render Unto Caesar: The Life and Legacy Of Maurice Duplessis. Toronto: Key Porter Books Ltd, 2002.

Brimelow, Peter. The Patriot Game: National Dreams and Political Realities. Toronto: Key Porter Books, 1986.

Brown, Robert Craig. Robert Laird Borden: A Biography, Volume II, 1914–1937. Toronto: Macmillan of Canada, 1980.

Camp, Dalton. Gentlemen, Players and Politicians. Ottawa: Deneau & Greenberg, 1970.

Charest, Jean. My Road to Québec. Saint-Laurent: Éditions Pierre Tisseyre, 1998.

Cohen, Andrew. A Deal Undone: The Making and the Breaking of the Meech Lake Accord. Vancouver: Douglas and McIntyre. 1990.

Cook, Ramsay, and Real Belanger. Canada's Prime Ministers: Macdonald to Trudeau. Toronto: University of Toronto Press, 2007.

Courtney, John C. The Selection of National Party Leaders in Canada. Toronto: Macmillan Company of Canada, 1973.

Coyne, Andrew. "Anatomy of a Red Tory," National Post, May 15, 2000, A17.

Chrétien, Jean. My Years as Prime Minister. A Ron Graham book. Toronto: Alfred A. Knopf Canada, 2007.

Creighton, Donald. John A. Macdonald: The Old Chieftain. Toronto: Macmillan Company of Canada Ltd., 1955.

Creighton, Donald. John A. Macdonald: The Young Politician. Toronto: Macmillan Company of Canada Ltd., 1952.

Crosbie, John. No Holds Barred: My Life in Politics. McClelland & Stewart, 1997

Dean, John W. Conservatives Without Conscience. New York: Viking, 2006.

English, John. Borden: His Life and World. Toronto: McGraw-Hill Ryerson Limited, 1977.

English, John. The Decline of Politics: the Conservatives and the Party System, 1901–1920. Toronto: University of Toronto Press, 1993.

Flanagan, Tom. Harper's Team: Behind the Scenes in the Conservative Rise to Power. Kingston: McGill-Queen's University Press, 2007.

Flanagan, Tom. Waiting for the Wave: The Reform Party and Preston Manning. Toronto: Stoddart Publishing, 1995.

Fleming, Donald. So Very Near: The Political Memoirs of the Honourable Donald M. Fleming. Toronto: McClelland & Stewart, 1985.

Frum, David. What's Right: The New Conservatism and What It Means for Canada. Toronto: Random House of Canada, 1989.

Fyfe, Robert. Kim Campbell: The Making of a Politician. Toronto: Harper Collins, 1993.

Glassford, Larry A. Reaction & Reform: The Politics of the Conservative Party under R.B. Bennett, 1927–1938. Toronto: University of Toronto Press, 1992.

Granatstein, J.L. The Politics of Survival: The Conservative Party of Canada, 1939–1945. Toronto: University of Toronto Press, 1967.

Granatstein, J.L., and Norman Hillmer. Prime Ministers: Ranking Canada's Leaders. Toronto: Harper Collins, 1999.

Gwyn, Richard. John A. The Man Who Made Us: The Life and Times of Sir John A. Macdonald. Volume One: 1815–1867. Toronto: Random House Canada, 2007.

Harrison, Trevor. Requiem for a Lightweight: Stockwell Day and Image Politics. Black Rose Books, 2002.

Hogan, George. The Conservative in Canada. Toronto: McClelland & Stewart, 1963.

Hopkins, J. Castell. Life and Work of The Rt. Hon. Sir John Thompson, Prime Minister of Canada. Toronto: United Publishing Houses, 1895.

Humphreys, David L. Joe Clark: A Portrait. Deneau & and Greenberg, 1978.

Johnson, William. Stephen Harper and the Future of Canada. Toronto: McClelland & Stewart Ltd., 2005.

Kendle, John. John Bracken: A Political Biography. Toronto: University of Toronto Press, 1979.

Kheiriddin, Tasha and Adam Daifallah. Rescuing Canada's Right: Blueprint for a Conservative Revolution. Mississauga: John Wiley and Sons Canada, Ltd., 2005.

Macdonald, L. Ian. Mulroney: The Making of the Prime Minister. Toronto: McClelland & Stewart, 1984.

Macdonald, Donald C. The Happy Warrior. Toronto: Dundurn Press, 1998.

Macquarie, Heath. Red Tory Blues: A Political Memoir. Toronto: University of Toronto Press, 1992.

Manthorpe, Jonathan. The Power and the Tories. Toronto: Macmillan, 1974.

Martin, Lawrence. Pledge of Allegiance: The Americanization of Canada in the Mulroney Years. Toronto: McClelland & Stewart, 1993.

McTeer, Maureen. In My Own Name: A Memoir. Toronto: Random House, 2003.

Mulroney, Brian. Memoirs: 1939–1993. Toronto: McClelland & Stewart, Douglas Gibson Book, 2007.

Newman, Peter C. The Secret Mulroney Tapes: Unguarded Confessions of a Prime Minister. Toronto: Random House, 2005.

Newman, Peter C. Renegade in Power: The Diefenbaker Years. Toronto/Montréal: McClelland & Stewart, 1963.

O'Leary, Grattan. Recollections of People, Press and Politics. Toronto: Macmillan, 1977.

Perlin, George C. The Tory Syndrome: Leadership Politics in the Progressive Conservative Party. Montréal: McGill-Queen's University Press, 1980.

Phenix, Patricia. Private Demons: The Tragic Personal Life of Sir John A. Macdonald. Toronto: McClelland & Stewart Ltd., 2006.

Pickersgill, J. W. My Years with Louis St. Laurent. Toronto: University of Toronto Press, 1975.

Plamondon, Bob. Full Circle: Death and Resurrection in Canadian Conservative Politics. Toronto: Key Porter, 2006.

Pratte, André. Charest: His Life and Politics. Toronto: Stoddart Publishing Co. Ltd., 1998.

Regenstreif, Peter. The Diefenbaker Interlude. Toronto: Longmans, 1965.

Reid, E.M. Canadian Political Parties (Contributions to Canadian Economics, Vol. vi, 1933).

Saunders, Kathleen. The Canadians: Robert Borden. Toronto: Fitzhenry and Whiteside Limited, 1978.

Saunders, Robert. The Canadians: R.B. Bennett. Toronto: Fitzhenry and Whiteside Limited, 1979.

Segal, Hugh. The Long Road Back: The Conservative Journey, 1993–2006. Toronto: Harper Collins Canada, 2006.

Segal, Hugh. Beyond Greed: A Traditional Conservative Confronts Neoconservative Excess. Toronto: Stoddart, 1997.

Siggins, Maggie. Bassett: A Biography. Toronto: James Lorimer, 1979.

Simpson, Jeffrey. Discipline of Power: The Conservative Interlude and the Liberal Restoration. Toronto: University of Toronto Press, 1980.

Smith, Denis. Rogue Tory: The Life and Legend of John G. Diefenbaker. Toronto: Macfarlane, Walter & Ross, 1995.

Stevens, Geoffrey. Stanfield. Toronto: McClelland & Stewart, 1976.

Stursberg, Peter. Diefenbaker 1952–1957. Toronto: University of Toronto Press, 1975.

Taylor, Charles. Radical Tories: The Conservative Tradition in Canada. Toronto: House of Anansi Press, 1982.

Thorburn, Hugh G. Party Politics in Canada, Second Edition. Scarborough: Prentice-Hall of Canada, 1967.

Troyer, Warner. 200 Days: Joe Clark and Power: The Anatomy of the Rise and Fall of the 21st Government. Toronto: Personal Library Publishers, 1980.

Waite, Peter B. The Man from Halifax: Sir John Thompson. Toronto: University of Toronto Press, 1985.

Wells, Paul. Right Side Up: The Fall of Paul Martin and the Rise of Stephen Harper's New Conservatism. Toronto: Douglas Gibson Books, 2006.

Williams, John L. The Conservative Party in Canada: 1920–1949. Durham, NC: Duke University Press, 1956.

INDEX

Business War Profits Tax, 116
Byfield, Ted, 365
Byng, Lord, 145

Cadman, Chuck, 456
Cahan, Charles H., 153–54, 175
Camp, Dalton, 207–9, 220–21, 224,
    251, 253, 255–57, 259–62, 270, 275,
    278, 280
Campbell, Alix, 354
Campbell, "George". *See* Campbell, Paul
Campbell, Kim, 16, 341–42, 353–61,
    370, 472
Campbell, Lissa, 354
Campbell, Paul, 354
Canada Central Railway, 78
Canada First Defence Strategy, 413
Canadian Criminal Code, 84
Canadian National Railway, 40, 44, 50,
    56, 66–67, 79, 127, 157
Canadian Pacific Railway, 50–54, 61–64,
    68, 78–79, 94
Canadian Radio Broadcasting Commis-
    sion, 162–63, 423
Canadair, 332, 334, 364
Cartier, Georges-Étienne, 30, 33, 35–36,
    41, 49, 52–53
Cardin, Lucien, 239, 259
Carstairs, Sharon, 343
Casey, Bill, 448–49
Castro, Fidel, 383
Celtic Society, 24
CF-18, 334, 339, 364, 366, 392
Charbonneau, Guy, 319
Charest, Jean, 343, 345, 356–57, 360,
    362, 367–78, 399–400, 424
Charest, Red, 369–70
Charlottetown Accord, 340, 346–47, 366
Charlottetown Conference, 35, 38, 45–
    46, 95, 343
Chong, Michael, 435
Chrétien, Jean, 305, 343–45, 356, 365,
    374, 395–96, 399, 412, 466; charac-
    ter/leadership, 360–62, 372–73, 375–
    76, 382–84; national views/policies,

285, 403; scandals, 349, 400, 42, 450
Churchill, Gordon, 249
Churchill, Winston, 176, 186, 227
Civil War (U.S.), 33–34
Clarity Act, 412
Clark, Champ, 108
Clark, Charles, Jr., 292
Clark, Charles, Sr., 292
Clark, Joe, 33, 263, 276, 346, 357, 382,
    396, 400–401, 407: character/leader-
    ship, 292–96, 298–99, 301–5, 303–11,
    318–20, 323, 383–85, 397, 400, 413;
    national views/policies, 297, 299–300
Clark, Isabella. *See* Macdonald, Isabella
Clark, Michael, 112
Clement, Tony, 410–12
Clergy Reserves Bill, 28
Coates, Bob, 282, 336
Cogger, Michel, 319
Colonial Office. *See* British Colonial Office
Confederation, 31, 33–41, 44–47, 69,
    94–96
conscription, 15, 120–23, 125, 127, 141,
    151, 179–80, 184–89, 198, 200
Couillard, Julie, 460
Cowan, W. D., 164
Coyne, Andrew, 446
Coyne, James, 234, 242–45
Creighton, Donald, 257
Crerar, Thomas, 125, 142–43
Crombie, David, 323–25
Crosbie, John, 302–3, 306, 320–22,
    324–25
Cross, James, 284
Crow, John, 342
Currie, Sir Arthur, 127

Dahmer, John, 340
Dasko, Donna, 459–60
Davis, Bill, 307, 319–20, 405, 420
Davis, Jim, 458
Day, Stockwell, 362, 379–85, 396, 418
de Bané, Pierre, 316
Denning, Charles, 156
Denis, Solange, 332–33

PHOTO CREDITS

Key to photo credits:
LAC: Library and Archives Canada
CP: Canadian Press

Cover photos (left to right and top to bottom):
Macdonald (LAC C-006513)
Borden (LAC PA-028128)
Meighen (LAC PA-026987)
MacKay (CP 3864770)
Diefenbaker (LAC C-006779)
Mulroney (CP 788953)
Drew (LAC PA-053853)
Clark (LAC PA-116450)
Bennett (LAC C-000687)
Tupper (LAC PA-027743)
Stanfield (CP 791030)
Bracken (LAC C-042407)
Harper (CP 730414)

Interior photos:
p. 23, Macdonald (LAC C-006513)
p. 77, Abbott (LAC C-000697)
p. 82, Thompson (LAC C-068645)
p. 87, Bowell (LAC PA-027159)
p. 93, Tupper (LAC PA-027743)
p. 103, Borden (LAC PA-028128)
p. 139, Meighen (LAC PA-026987)
p. 148, Bennett (LAC C-000687)
p. 177, Manion (LAC C-007774)
p. 193, Bracken (LAC C-042407)
p. 202, Drew (LAC PA-053853)
p. 213, Diefenbaker (LAC C-006779)
p. 267, Stanfield (CP 791030)
p. 292, Clark (LAC PA-116450)
p. 315, Mulroney (CP 788953)
p. 353, Campbell (LAC PA-197391)
p. 362, Manning (CP 872585) and Charest (CP 3997113)
p. 377, Clark (LAC PA-116450) and Day (CP 5313916)
p. 389, MacKay (CP 3864770) and Harper (CP 730414)
p. 409, Harper (CP 730414)